E.C. Adams

Practical & Decorative Woodworking Joints

Practical & Decorative Woodworking Joints

John E. N. Bairstow

 Sterling Publishing Co. Inc. New York

Copyright © 1984 by John E.N. Bairstow
Published in 1985 by Sterling Publishing Co., Inc.
Two Park Avenue, New York, N.Y. 10016
First published in Great Britain in 1984
by B.T. Batsford Ltd.
Distributed in Canada by Oak Tree Press Ltd.
c/o Canadian Manda Group, P.O. Box 920, Station U,
Toronto, Ontario, Canada M8Z 5P9
All rights reserved
Library of Congress Catalog Card No.: 84-51838
Sterling ISBN 0-8069-5544-9 Trade
                    0-8069-7948-8 Paper

Printed in Great Britain

Contents

Acknowledgement

The author would also like to thank the following for permission to photograph items in their collections: Miss J.N. Muncey (colour plates 1 and 3); Mr and Mrs L. Ellis (colour plate 7).

My grateful thanks are due first to the Winston Churchill Memorial Trust for assisting me to undertake valuable research in the U.S.A.; to Mr W.A.W. Elloway for continued support in the development of my work; to John Harlow Ott and June Sprigg of Hancock Shaker Village, Brother Theodore Johnson and family of Sabbathday Lake, Mr Randell L. Makinson, Mr Robert H. Ellsworth, Wendell Castle and Stephen Proctor for various parts of my research. Finally to Miss Gillian Bairstow, Mr Brian Mee and Mr Robert Cox for assistance in completing the book.

Introduction

Ever since the earliest days of timber being used as a constructional material, some method of connecting the components has been sought. Many types of joint have been developed, varying greatly in their complexity, and it is to the woodworker's advantage to have a firm grasp of the principles behind their creation.

The development of the functional aspect of the joint has been extensive, with various forms of the dovetail and mortise and tenon being the mainstay of wooden construction for centuries. However, although it has always been the tendency to apply decoration to a piece of furniture – such as carving, inlay or marquetry – the decorative potential of the joint has remained relatively undeveloped. Examples of standard and decorative joinery are illustrated in this book in an attempt to show the many variations available to anyone working in wood.

Although a limited number of exposed joints have always been used, they became increasingly less popular with the introduction of machinery into furniture manufacture which made it cheaper to produce simple, 'secret' joinery. An additional problem is that most standard types of joint, such as the dovetail, rarely relate to the form of a piece of furniture because they concentrate all the interest along the corners. This is fine if it is being closely inspected but, when viewed from more than a few feet away, the beauty of detail is lost and the most striking thing is the overall form.

In selecting timbers for constructing a decorative joint, two points must be considered if it is to be successful. The development of modern adhesives allows far more enterprising configurations to be made where the glue line is often stronger than the timber. However, this must not conflict with the nature of wood, or weakness could ensue. In addition, contrasting timbers should have similar qualities to prevent undue contrasts in rates of expansion and contraction.

Wooden structures are usually built in either the frame or the carcase, each having its own types of joint. Both areas are studied, with various decorative possibilities being discussed and illustrated. The splicing joint, while no longer an essential form of construction due to modern adhesives, is important because it shows what can be achieved when new forms are considered, and will be of interest to the woodworker because of its complexity.

The process of cutting any joint is variable and depends on the maker's preferences. All the following joints, other than my own designs, are a personal interpretation which have been found to work effectively in their chosen situation.

1 Preparation and Working Methods

If any joint is to be made to a high standard, then each component must be prepared accurately to length, width and thickness. After checking the timber carefully for defects, initial cutting should allow an additional 1.2cm (½in.) in the length and 6mm (¼in.) on the width of finished sizes. Depending on the size of timber being used, an allowance of 3mm (⅛in.) is usually allowed for planing to thickness. Large boards may require more than this if sticking or cutting to thickness has been badly executed.

Initially, the face side is planed flat using the jack plane and working with the grain to prevent tearing (*diagram 1*). When working with wide boards, planing diagonally or across the grain, particularly if it is interlocking, will yield better results. The surface should be checked continually with a straight edge for flatness and with winding strips for twist. If the board is twisted the winding strips will help to show it (*diagram 2*), and efforts should be made to correct it

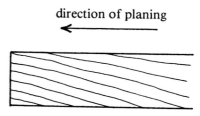

direction of planing

Diagram 1 *Planing should follow the same direction as the grain to prevent the tearing of timber fibres*

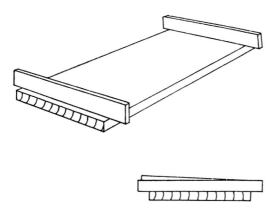

by removing timber at the high points until flatness is achieved (*diagram 3*). Any roughness or rippling is removed by taking fine shavings, initially with the try-plane and finishing with the smoothing plane, to give a good clean

Diagram 2 *Winding strips help to show if a board is twisted.*

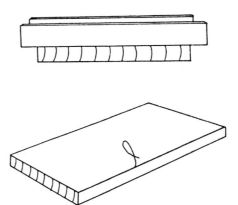

Diagram 3 *Parallel winding strips indicate that twist has been removed.*

Diagram 4 *A simple, looped pencil line indicates the face side.*

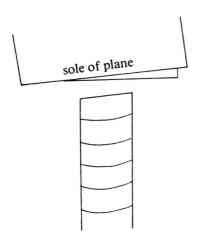

sole of plane

Diagram 5 *Lateral adjustment of the plane blade helps correct a bevelled edge.*

Diagram 6 *The face edge is marked as indicated when it is straight and perpendicular to the face side.*

surface. This can then be marked as the face side (*diagram 4*).

The face edge, which is straight in its length and square to the face side, is planed true with the try-plane. Although achieving a straight edge is relatively simple, difficulty may be experienced when attempting to make it square with the face side, the usual result being a bevel. This should be corrected by adjusting the blade laterally to compensate for the angle (*diagram 5*), removing more timber at the high point. The ability to tilt the sole of the plane to correct the bevel requires experience in tool use and should not be attempted by beginners. When this edge is correct it can be marked as the face edge (*diagram 6*). The importance of an accurate face side and face edge cannot be over-stressed if marking out of the joint is to be accurate, as all lines stem from these surfaces.

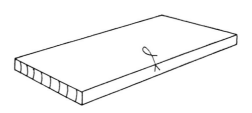

The required thickness is determined by gauging around the edges with a marking gauge and planing down to these lines with a try-plane (*diagram 7*). There is usually a tendency to remove waste at the edges more quickly than at the middle of the board and this should be avoided by continual checking with a straight edge.

The finished width of the board is scribed from the face

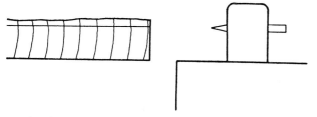

Diagram 7 *The marking gauge scribes in the board thickness.*

edge on both surfaces using the marking gauge (*diagram 8*). The waste is removed with the try-plane to give a parallel edged board.

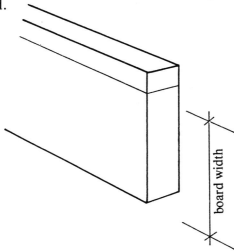

board width

Diagram 8 *The board width is scribed with the marking gauge from the face edge.*

The length of the timber is determined by squaring round each end with the knife and try-square. In most exposed joinery the length is usually increased by adding 1.5mm (¹⁄₁₆in.) at each end for planing back to the surface after construction. If the timber is small enough to allow easy handling, a shooting board is used to remove the waste (*diagram 9*). Alternatively, the timber is placed in the vice,

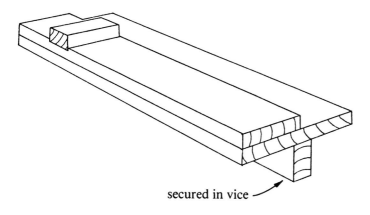

secured in vice

Diagram 9 *The shooting board, used to plane square the end grain of a component.*

Diagram 10 *The waste at one corner should be removed before attempting to plane across the full width of a board.*

and waste removed by working in both directions with the try-plane (*diagram 10*). This will prevent the timber splitting, which would occur if an attempt were made to remove waste from one direction only (*diagram 11*). The

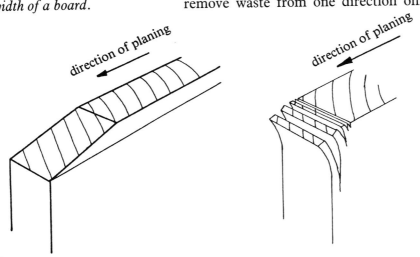

Diagram 11 *The end grain will split if an attempt is made to plane beyond it.*

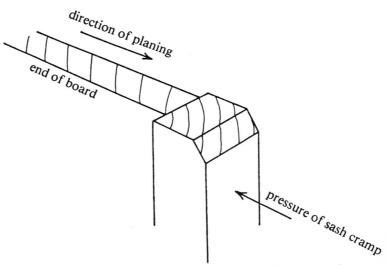

Diagram 12 *Waste material supports the timber to prevent splitting.*

timber can be worked in one direction if a piece of waste material is cramped to the end (*diagram 12*).

If this procedure is followed, the timber will be ready for jointing. It should, however, be stacked between stickers (*diagram 13*) when not in use to help prevent any sort of movement, such as twisting or cupping.

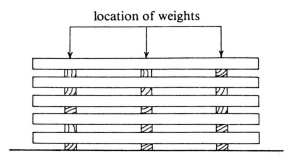

location of weights

Diagram 13 *Stacking timber between stickers allows air to circulate, thus preventing undue drying out as well as minimizing any tendency to warp or cup.*

MARKING OUT

Precise, distinct marking out lines will greatly assist in the accurate cutting of any joint. Generally, all lines in a joint that run across the grain or are trimmed with a chisel (such as at the inside shoulder) should be marked with a knife, usually with the aid of a try-square or sliding bevel. Using a single-bevelled knife, press the try-square into position,

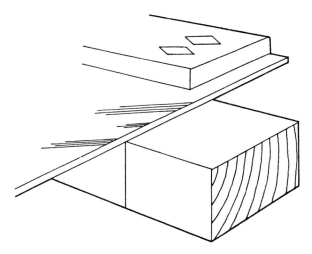

Diagram 14 *Always place the try-square blade on the timber that will be retained.*

resting on the part of the timber that will be retained (*diagram 14*) and cut in the line. On the side nearest the square the line will be clean and sharp, while the other side will be slightly bevelled (*diagram 15*). Although this may seem a minor point, every effort should be made to produce a well-fitting joint. If opposite joints have the same inside shoulder, the two components can be cramped together and marked, giving identical lengths.

All lines that run parallel to the face side or face edge, such as the outline of a tenon, are scribed with the marking gauge or mortise gauge. There are, of course, exceptions to this,

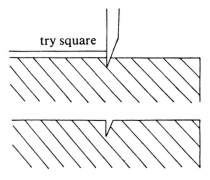

try square

Diagram 15 *The knife cut will be square at one side and slightly bevelled on the other.*

such as marking in the finger joint which is treated like the dovetail joint. This should always be carried out with a sharp H pencil to give a positive, easy-to-read line. For such accurate work, never use a soft lead as this gives an inaccurate reading, or a hard lead, which may not show up significantly.

The mitre is an important feature in many of the joints to be discussed and has to be set out accurately for it to be efficient. The commercially available mitre square is rarely set at precisely 45° and, although it is usually only slightly out of true, will cause considerable error if used on all four corners of a carcase, which will multiply the inaccuracy four times.

To achieve the precise angle use the sliding bevel which is infinitely variable and therefore easily set. To set it, first test a try-square for 90° by holding its stock against a straight edge and drawing in the right angle. Reverse the square and re-align the blade with the pencil line. This should be the same if the square is a true right angle (*diagram 16*). Plane a

Diagram 16 *Parallel lines indicate a true right angle while any deviation shows the try-square to be at fault.*

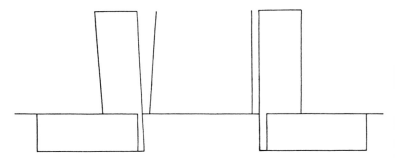

square corner on a piece of plywood and test it for accuracy with the try-square. When this is true, set the sliding bevel to about 45°, press the stock against one edge of the corner and draw in the angle using a sharp pencil. Set the stock on the adjacent edge and line up the blade with the pencil line. Only when the two readings give the same line will the angle on the sliding bevel be at exactly 45°.

CUTTING

This is usually done with a tenon or dovetail saw, depending on the size of the joint to be cut. To start the cut off accurately, use a few teeth at the front of the saw on the corner of the timber with the blade held at 45° (*diagram 17*). As the cut gets deeper, gradually use more of the blade and bring it into the horizontal position. The cut is then made in this position down to the shoulder line.

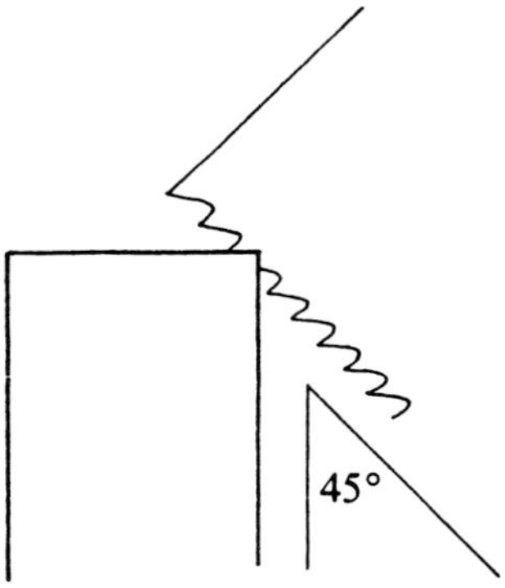

Diagram 17 *Start a sawcut by using the front few teeth of a blade held at 45°.*

45°

FITTING

Invariably, there will be the occasion when a joint is cut that is too tight a fit and requires further removal of waste. If this is done at the wrong point then a gap in the finished joint may result, and so some knowledge of where to trim the timber is essential. To test for fit, the joint will have been lightly tapped together, but tightness in certain areas will prevent its assembly. Take the joint apart and look at the meeting faces of the joint for any areas that shine when held up to the light. Over-tightness of the joint will cause compression of the fibres which will show as a reflective surface. Such areas should be lightly trimmed before attempting to put the joint together again.

GLUING

When gluing a joint together with either C-cramp or sash cramp, some form of block will be needed between the metal and the timber to prevent any sort of bruising occuring while applying pressure where it is needed. The dovetail or finger joint requires specially prepared blocks to exert pressure on

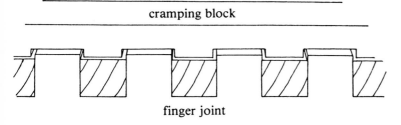

cramping block

finger joint

Diagram 18 *Cramping blocks are shaped to provide pressure only where it is needed.*

the tail or finger while spanning the protrusions of the adjoining panel (*diagram 18*). The block can be slightly curved so that, when the cramps are tightened on the outsides, initial pressure is exerted in the centre (*diagram 19*).

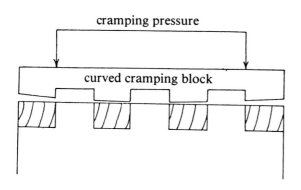

cramping pressure

curved cramping block

Diagram 19 *Curved cramping blocks provide pressure at the centre when cramped on the outsides.*

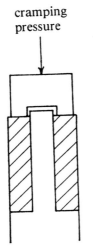

cramping
pressure

Diagram 20 *The cramping block used on the through mortise and tenon is shaped to span the protrusion.*

Other through joints, such as the mortise and tenon, are treated in a similar way, the blocks being shaped to span any protrusion (*diagram 20*).

Conventional methods of gluing together a mitred frame or carcase are usually difficult because of the number of cramps needed to run across all corners. This can be overcome by gluing a triangular block on to the timber so that one of its sides is parallel to the face of the mitre (*diagram 21*). Adjacent panels are then glued together by exerting pressure with C-cramps across the blocks (*diagram 22*). This method allows fine adjustment of each mitre without upsetting any other corner, which is what usually happens when using the sash-cramp. The blocks are easily removed by sawing and planing once the joint is secure.

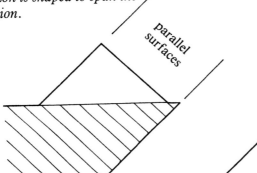

parallel surfaces

Diagram 21 *A triangular block glued to the board should have one face parallel to the mitre.*

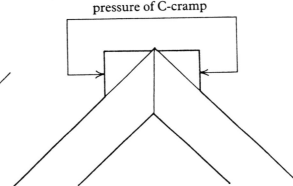

pressure of C-cramp

Diagram 22 *Adjacent boards are joined by applying pressure on the triangular blocks with C-cramps.*

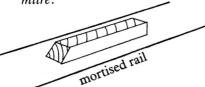

mortised rail

Diagram 23 *The end grain of any protrusion is prevented from splitting by removing the inside corner with a chisel and planing towards it.*

Diagram 24 *The front of the plane is pressed on the adjacent panel or rail while cuts are made to remove the waste.*

Finishing

When a joint has been glued together, there should be some protrusion of waste timber that has to be removed in order to finish off the construction and this is done by planing across the end grain. In order to prevent this splitting, remove the inside corners of the waste and plane towards this (*diagram 23*). Press the front of the plane on the adjacent panel or rail (*diagram 24*) and make cuts until the sole is gradually worked into the horizontal position.

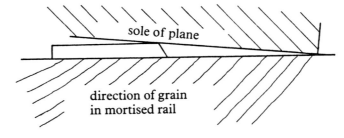

sole of plane

direction of grain
in mortised rail

16

2 Framing Joints

MORTISE AND TENON

The basis for many joints used in framework is the mortise and tenon and it is an essential starting point in the development of wooden construction. It forms the foundation of many of the decorative and practical joints under discussion in this chapter.

Basic mortise and tenon

The variations of mortise and tenon are used to connect two pieces of timber most commonly at a right angle. In its basic form, the joint is used to connect a rail to a leg using a stopped mortise and stub tenon (*diagram 25*).

Initial marking out of the leg gives the mortise a length that is approximately 6mm (¼in.) shorter than the width of the connecting rail. Set the mortise gauge to approximately one-third of the rail thickness, in fact to the nearest available mortise chisel. The parallel lines are then scribed between the extremities of the mortise (*diagram 26*). Its depth is about three-quarters the thickness of the leg.

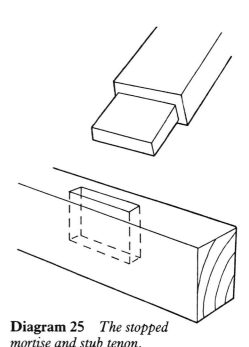

Diagram 25 *The stopped mortise and stub tenon.*

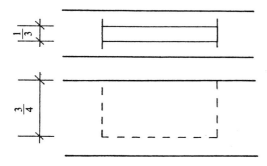

Diagram 26 *The outline of the mortise.*

The length of the tenon is slightly shorter than the depth of the mortise, measured from the end of the rail and marked in with the aid of a knife and try-square. A small gap at the

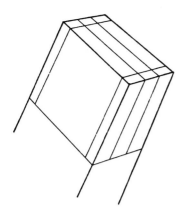

Diagram 27 *The outline of the tenon, marked with the mortise and marking gauges.*

Diagram 28 *Waste is removed with a brace and bit. The bit should be slightly smaller than the mortise width.*

bottom of the mortise will be produced, because of the difference in length, which will take up any excess glue and so alleviate unnecessary pressure. The mortise gauge is used at the same setting to mark in the thickness of the tenon and a marking gauge set at 3mm (⅛in.) scribes the shoulder from each edge (*diagram 27*). The dimension of the tenon should be the same as the mortise.

The mortise is cut first. If it is located near the end of the timber it is advisable to apply a C-cramp to prevent splitting. Secure the leg to the bench and remove as much of the waste as possible with a brace and bit. The bit should be slightly smaller than the width of the mortise (*diagram 28*). When doing this, view the bit from the end of the component as this will help keep the cut parallel to the face side (*diagram 29*). The remaining waste is then taken out with the mortise chisel, starting at the centre and gradually working outwards, with the final cuts being made on the marked lines. Take care when making these last cuts not to lever out the waste as this will round over the corners of the mortise and may in some instances be visible in the final construction. Masking tape wrapped around the drill bit and mortise chisel is used to denote the depth of cut (*diagram 30*).

masking tape

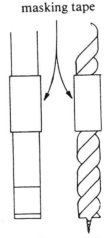

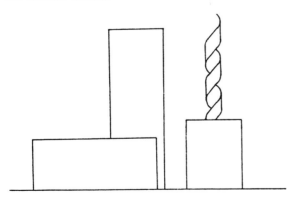

Diagram 29 *When removing the mortise waste, view the bit from the end of the timber to ensure a cut that is parallel to the face side.*

Diagram 30 *Masking tape wrapped around the mortise chisel and drill bit denotes the depth of cut.*

To cut the tenon, secure the rail in the vice at an angle of about 45° and away from the saw (*diagram 31*). With the blade working on the waste side of the line, start the cut on the corner and saw horizontally down to the shoulder,

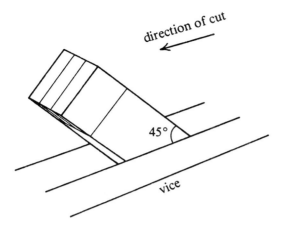

direction of cut

45°

vice

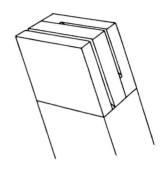

Diagram 31 *The rail is held in the vice at an angle of 45°, and away from the saw.*

checking continually to ensure that the blade keeps to its path (*diagram 32*). Move the rail into the vertical position, and complete the cut using the existing saw kerf as a guide. Vertical cuts have also to be made at the shoulder line (*diagram 33*). Care should be taken when approaching the shoulder as any cut beyond it will result in a permanent flaw. The waste is then removed by making cuts on all four sides, leaving about 1mm (¹⁄₁₆in.) of waste. This is then removed by placing a paring chisel in the knifeline of the shoulder and chopping down to the tenon, making sure to keep the blade square to the face side. This method gives a clean, crisp shoulder superior to alternative types.

With all cutting operations complete, the joint should go together with slight pressure, its entry being assisted by chamfering the end of the tenon (*diagram 34*). An efficient joint will result if accuracy is maintained; a loose joint will provide little strength, while a tight fit may split the mortise.

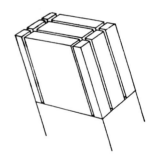

Diagram 32 *Diagonal sawcuts are made on the waste side of the line from the outside corner to the opposite inside shoulder.*

Diagram 33 *All sawcuts are made down to the shoulder line.*

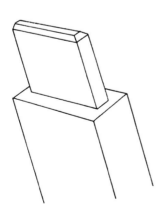

Diagram 34 *The tenon's entry is assisted by chamfering its end.*

19

Diagram 35 *Faults in constructing the mortise and tenon joint: 1. Undercut shoulders caused by cutting the tenon's shoulder incorrectly. 2. Overtight tenon causes the mortise to split. 3. Sawcuts taken beyond the shoulder lines of the tenon. 4. Shoulders of the tenon are uneven.*

A number of faults may cause the joint to be inefficient (*diagram 35*).

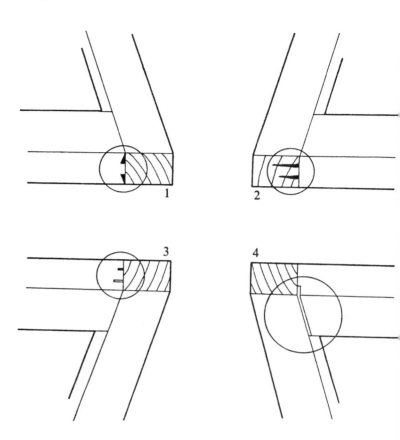

The method of draw-boring can be applied to the joint and is used to pull its shoulders together as well as to lock it. A dowel passes through the joint, the holes being slightly offset so that a compressive force is created. When the joint has been fitted, bore a hole through the mortice using waste material to prevent timber break out. Cramp the joint together and press the drill bit into the hole so that a centre mark is made on the tenon. Remove the tenon, and bore a hole through it slightly nearer the shoulder than the mark (*diagram 36*). A dowel with a heavily tapered end will allow easy access to the staggered holes and considerably tighten the joint when driven in (*diagram 37*).

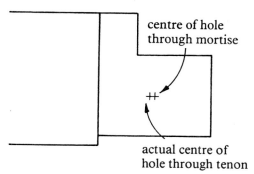

centre of hole
through mortise

actual centre of
hole through tenon

Diagram 36 *The hole in the tenon is drilled slightly nearer the shoulder than that through the mortise.*

Through mortise with securing wedges

A much improved type of mortise and tenon joint uses a through mortise with securing wedges to give additional mechanical strength (*diagram 38* and *figure 1*). The general procedure for marking out is repeated with the exception of the mortise, the lines being taken to both edges.

Cutting of the mortise is done from both sides rather than attempting to cut all the way through from one side, as this may result in timber breakout. The mortise has to be tapered from the outside to allow the tenon to spread when the

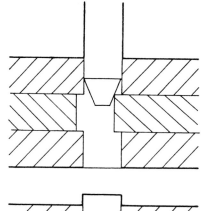

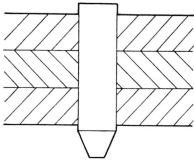

Diagram 37 *A heavily tapered dowel driven through the staggered holes will pull the joint together.*

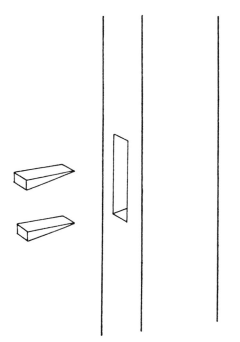

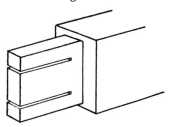

Diagram 38 *The through mortise and tenon with securing wedges.*

Figure 1 *Through mortise and tenon with securing wedges.*

wedges are driven in. This should start about 6mm (¼in.) from the inside edge and lengthen the mortise by 6mm (¼in.), although measurements will vary depending on the size of joint (*diagram 39*).

Diagram 39 *Section through the rail showing how the mortise is shaped to accept the wedges.*

Diagram 40 *Sawcuts made in the tenon to accept both wedges.*

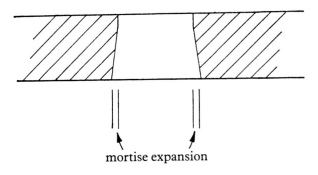

mortise expansion

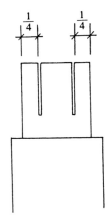

The tenon is made slightly longer than the mortise depth to allow for trimming after construction. The sawcuts that receive the wedges should be set in from the outer edge by one-quarter of the tenon width and terminate 6mm (¼in.) from the shoulder (*diagram 40*). The wedges can be made in a contrasting timber, but care should be taken to ensure that they are the same size and driven in an equal amount (*diagram 41*).

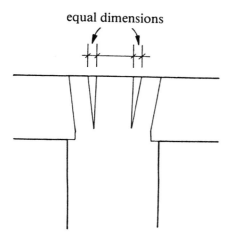

equal dimensions

Diagram 41 *Both wedges should have the same thickness on the outside after construction.*

Fox-wedged mortise and tenon

A similar joint that uses a stopped rather than a through mortice is called the fox-wedged mortise and tenon (*diagram 42*) and is used when the strength of wedging is required but a through mortice is undesirable. Great care must be taken in its construction if it is to perform at its best.

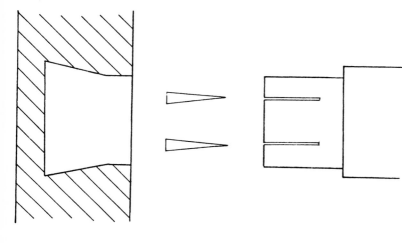

Diagram 42 *Fox-wedged mortise and tenon.*

Diagram 43 *The wedges should spread the tenon to fill the mortise as the shoulder meets the rail edge.*

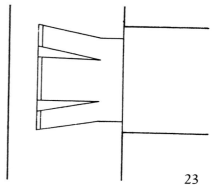

The process of cutting a standard mortise and tenon (*diagram 25, p. 17*) is carried out initially. The mortise is adjusted by undercutting its ends, starting about 6mm (¼in.) in from the edge, spreading the length by a further 6mm (¼in.) (*diagram 43*). When the wedges are inserted into the sawcuts, the tenon has to spread out to fill the mortise as the shoulder butts up to the edge. Faults obviously occur if either the wedges are so thin that the mortise is not filled or they are too thick and the mortise is filled before the shoulder closes up (*diagram 44*).

Diagram 44   *If the wedges are too thick, the mortise will be filled before the joint is together. Alternatively, if the wedges are too thin, the tenon will not fill the mortise.*

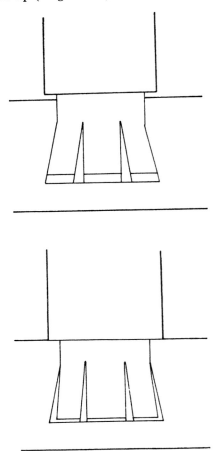

Diagram 45   *Short grain results if a rail is curved.*

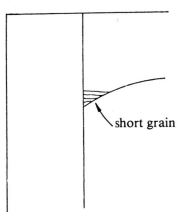

short grain

Gunstock mortise and tenon

Adaptations of the tenon shoulder are needed, for example when the rail is curved (*diagram 45*). If the square shoulder is used, short grain will occur at the end of the curve making it particularly weak. To compensate for this, the mitred shoulder is used with the joint being called a gunstock mortise and tenon (*diagram 46*). Two variations of the shoulder can be used.

The standard haunched mortise and tenon is made, allowing an additional 6mm (¼in.) on the tenon's shoulder to accept the mitre. This is marked in with a sliding bevel and knife (*diagram 47*). The joint is pushed together to mark the

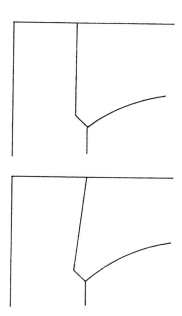

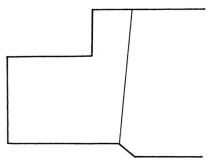

Diagram 47 *The shoulder of the tenoned component is marked in with a knife and sliding bevel.*

Diagram 46 *Two versions of the gunstock mortise and tenon.*

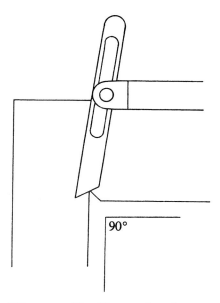

angle on the mortised component and so its internal corner should be a right angle (*diagram 48*). The shoulder can then be cut and the joint fitted.

Diagram 48 *Ensure that the internal angle of the leg and rail is at 90° when marking the shoulder of the mortise.*

GROOVES AND REBATES

It often occurs when constructing a frame that a panel of some sort has to be included which requires the cutting of a groove or rebate. This is made easier by adjusting the joint to allow a through, rather than a stopped, rebate or groove.

When using a groove, its dimensions should ideally be the same as the square haunch so that they can be cut together (*diagram 49*). It can be made smaller than the haunch but anything larger will mean removing timber that should be retained.

A rebate requires much more adjustment of the joint to allow easy cutting. If it is cut in a standard mortise and tenoned frame, the shoulder of one side of the mortise will be removed (*diagram 50*). This has to be filled by adjusting the

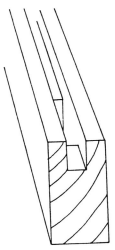

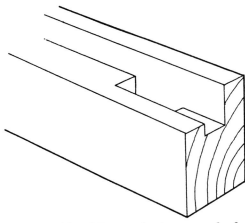

Diagram 50   *One side of the mortise is removed when a rebate is*

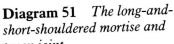

Diagram 49   *Ideally, the groove should be the same width as the mortise.*

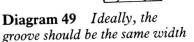

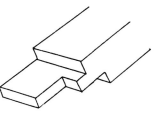

Diagram 51   *The long-and-short-shouldered mortise and tenon joint.*

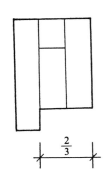

$$\frac{2}{3}$$

Diagram 52   *The rebate should be two-thirds the rail thickness and flush with the tenon's face.*

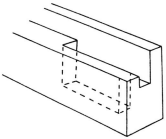

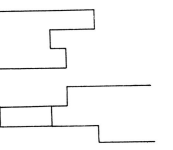

Diagram 53   *The back shoulder is extended by the rebate width.*

shoulder of the tenoned component, the resulting adaptation being called a long-and-short-shouldered mortise and tenon (*diagram 51*).

The rebate should be two-thirds the thickness of the rail and line up with the face of the tenon (*diagram 52*). Having made the mortise, use a rebate or plough plane to cut the through rebate, making sure that its fence is always pressed tightly against the timber as any deviation may result in a step forming in the corner. Any final trimming that may be necessary can be done with a shoulder plane.

Adjustment of the tenon is achieved by extending the back shoulder by the width of the rebate (*diagram 53*). The initial shoulder line is only marked in lightly as a temporary measure. The long shoulder is then found by cramping the faces of the two adjoining components together and marking it from the inside of the rebate (*diagram 54*). The width of the tenon is determined by the depth of the rebate, and should not be so deep that the strength of the joint is affected (*diagram 55*).

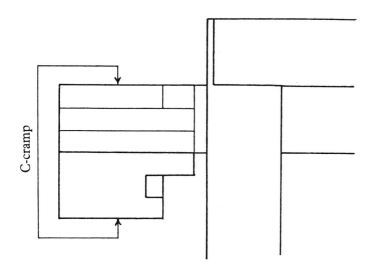

C-cramp

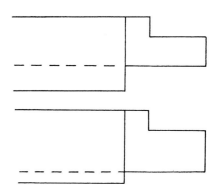

Diagram 54 *Cramp two adjoining rails together to mark in the length of the shoulder extension.*

Diagram 55 *Too wide a rebate will reduce the strength of the tenon. The lower diagram shows appropriate proportions.*

DRY JOINTING

In Eastern societies, the joint was a very important part of the total design in both furniture and architecture. The use of dry joinery (glue was not used) was the mainstay of their constructions, with locking components predominating. These required the design of intricate configurations that had a high strength factor. The craftsmen maintained total accuracy and a range of joints was achieved which were unsurpassed in their technical excellence.

It is clear from extant examples of Chinese furniture that the two types of construction most widely used were the panelled frame and the joint used to attach the leg to a table top. A typical frame (*diagram 56*) illustrates the basic elements of Chinese joinery and is a good example of a mitred, mortise and tenon frame with dovetailed transverse brace and tongue and grooved floating panels. This method of framing was used extensively for cabinet construction in doors, tops, sides and backs, varying in degrees of refinement according to the object's intended environment.

Diagram 56 *The typical type of frame used in Chinese furniture.*

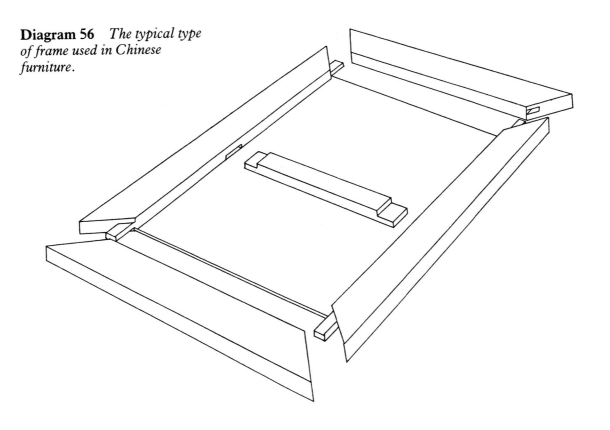

Chinese mortise and tenon

The corner joint used in this type of frame, though a simple form of mortise and tenon, is important because of its frequent use in Chinese furniture. It is also a good platform on which to base one's knowledge of how the Eastern style of joinery was constructed (*diagram 57, figure 2*).

Having prepared all the components, the mitres are marked on each end, working from the face side and face edge (*diagram 58*). The through mortise can then be marked in, the inside shoulder line being the same as the mitres and its width being one-third the thickness of the rail. Set the mortise gauge so that its points are symmetrical, and scribe lines on both edges. Its length is one-third the width of the rail (*diagram 59*).

The tenon is marked out in virtually the same way, the gauge being used at the same setting to scribe its thickness on the inside edge and end of the rail. Its width is measured from

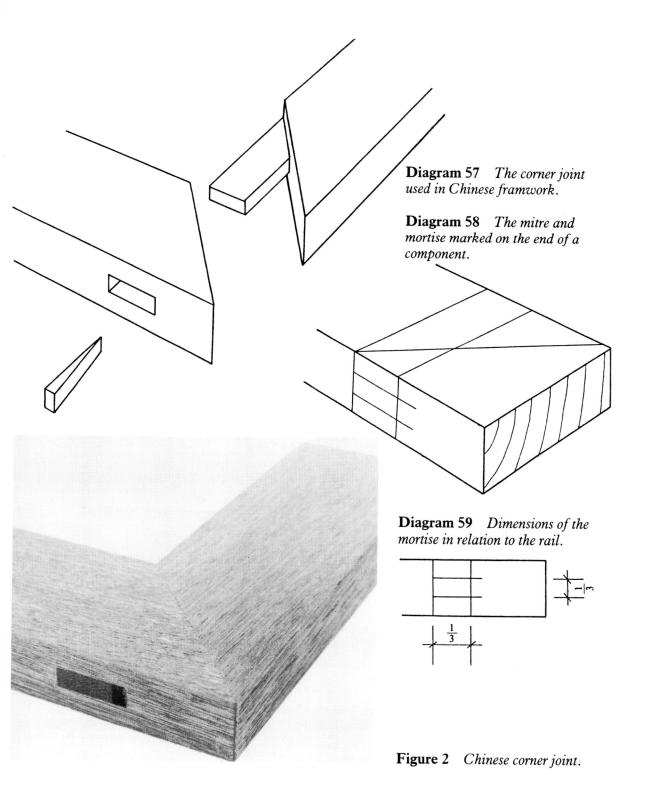

Diagram 57 *The corner joint used in Chinese framwork.*

Diagram 58 *The mitre and mortise marked on the end of a component.*

Diagram 59 *Dimensions of the mortise in relation to the rail.*

$\frac{1}{3}$

$\frac{1}{3}$

Figure 2 *Chinese corner joint.*

29

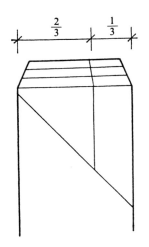

$\frac{2}{3}$ $\frac{1}{3}$

the mortise and scribed with a marking gauge from the edge (*diagram 60*).

To avoid removing the outline of the joint, cut the mortise before the mitre. This should be done from both sides, as described when cutting the through mortise and tenon with securing wedges (*diagram 38, p. 21*). The mortise should only be enlarged on the outside end to allow access for the wedge (*diagram 61*). The final operation on this part of the joint is to

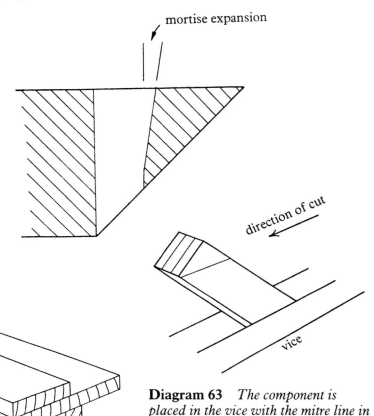

Diagram 60   *The tenon width is one-third that of the rail and scribed from the inside edge.*

Diagram 61   *The mortise should only be enlarged on the outside end to accept the wedge.*

Diagram 62   *Mitre shooting board.*

mortise expansion

direction of cut

vice

Diagram 63   *The component is placed in the vice with the mitre line in a horizontal position.*

cut the mitre. Most of the waste can be sawn away, leaving a slight amount for trimming. The ideal method of planing back to the shoulder is to use a mitre shooting board (*diagram 62*).

When forming the tenon, all sawcuts should be made before removing any waste as this process may eliminate the gauge lines. As there are only two surfaces to work from, the rail is placed in the vice with the mitre line in an horizontal position (*diagram 63*) and cuts are made to the shoulder.

Then move the rail into the vertical position and make the cut that gives the tenon width. Waste is then removed by cutting around the mitre. This can be trimmed back with a paring chisel, keeping it square to the face side.

Both mitres should be checked across the width for flatness as any projection in the middle will prevent the joint fitting on the outside. This will occur if the chisel is not held square when removing the waste (*diagram 64*).

If all the cutting has been carried out accurately then the joint should go together with light pressure. If there are any particularly tight areas, further removal of waste is needed. When the joint fits comfortably, pull the mitre together and drive in the wedge. Any protrusion of the tenon can then be planed flush to the outer edge.

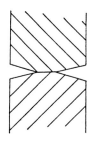

Diagram 64 *Enlarged sectional view of the mitre showing a protrusion at the centre, preventing the joint meeting on the outside.*

Three-way mitre

The joint described above was the foundation of many Chinese furniture designs, and there were, inevitably, variations on the basic theme. By introducing another rail, a three-way mitre can be made, giving a clean and simple outer appearance, that is joined by a system of mortise and tenons on the inside (*diagram 65*). The three rails have to be square so that all outer angles are 45°.

The construction of the horizontal frame is similar to the previous example, with a difference in size and placement of the tenon being the only major change. Its thickness is now one-quarter of the rail thickness and is placed above the centre line (*diagram 66*). This change is essential in order to avoid the mitre that will be cut to accept the vertical component.

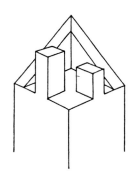

Diagram 65 *Vertical component showing the mortise configuration of a three-way mitre.*

Diagram 66 *The dimensions of the tenon which is placed above the centre line.*

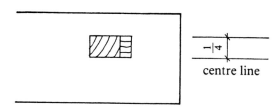

centre line

When marking out the joint that connects the vertical member to the horizontal frame, care must be taken to ensure that the mortise does not run out into the mitre. To achieve this, the end grain should be scribed into five equal divisions with the mortise gauge (*diagram 67*).

Two other variations show a simple oval leg tenoned into the framed top (*diagram 68*), and an elaborate construction

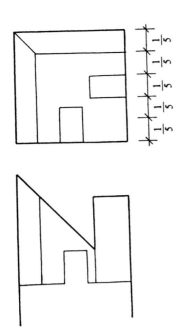

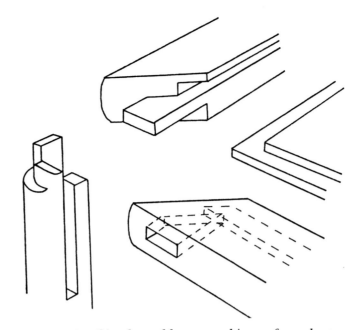

Diagram 67 *The end grain of the vertical component is divided into five equal parts when marking in the joint.*

Diagram 68 *Simple oval leg tenoned into a framed top.*

Diagram 69 *The elaborate form of leg joint used in a table of distinctive Chinese style.*

where the addition of a rail and complex shaping creates the distinctive style established by the Chinese craftsman (*diagram 69*).

Chinese and Japanese craftsmen developed a vast repertoire of joinery for any situation that might arise, the common feature being some form of mechanical locking device. Inevitably the dovetail-shaped tenon played a major role in many of these joints.

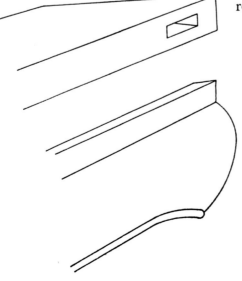

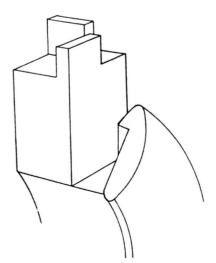

Slide-lock mortise and tenon

Having built the panelled frame, the craftsman had to find some method of joining the pieces together to create a carcase. The wedge-shaped, slide-lock mortise and tenon (*diagram 70*) was devised for such an occasion, usually for large pieces of furniture meant to be readily disassembled for easy transportation.

The locking component (*diagram 71*) is cut independently of both adjoining panels, and is then permanently tenoned into one, while slide locking into the other. This should be made first and all subsequent dimensions taken from it. Its dimensions depend on the size of panels being joined, but are generally found as follows: length equals three-quarters the width of rail in panel one, plus three-quarters the thickness of rail in panel two; width is dependent on panel size, but is half the length of the mortise; and thickness equals one-third the thickness of panel one (*diagram 72*). When the timber is cut to these dimensions, the only shaping to be done is to remove a small wedge from each side to create the locking

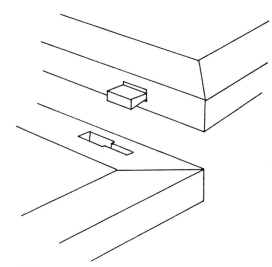

Diagram 70   *The wedge-shaped, slide-lock mortise and tenon.*

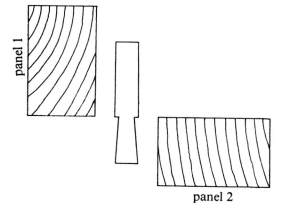

panel 1

panel 2

Diagram 72   *Proportions of the locking component in relation to adjacent rails.*

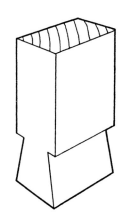

Diagram 71   *The locking component.*

mechanism. Its length should be equal to three-quarters the thickness of panel two, measured from the end (*diagram 73*). The dimensions of each mortise can be taken from the locking component and scribed on to the panel rails; note that the vertical panel is stepped in by 3mm (⅛in.) from the edge of the horizontal panel.

The locking component should be first glued into the mortise of the vertical panel. The mortise on the horizontal panel is cut so that the wedge-shaped half terminates at the

Diagram 73   *Shaded areas denote waste timber that has to be removed.*

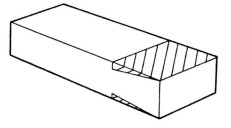

same distance from the edge of the panel as does the tenon (*diagram 74*). This ensures that the carcase will be flush at the

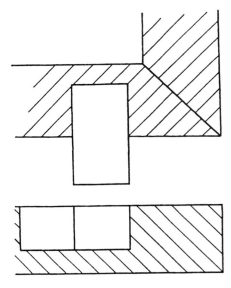

Diagram 74 *Section through each rail showing the locking component in position and its adjacent mortise.*

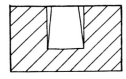

Diagram 75 *Section of the mortised rail.*

front when put together. The mortise is cut twice as long as the tenon width, one half being square and the other half being narrower at the surface but fully square on the inside (*diagram 75*). This allows the tenons to drop into one half and slide into the V-shaped section, locking the tenon in position.

Japanese *Sage kama*

The development of Japanese architectural style followed a similar pattern in its use of dry-jointing methods. To resist lateral forces, rails were used rather than the diagonal bracing associated with Western architecture. Rails and tie-beams served the normal function of horizontal bracing, giving rigidity to a framework and strengthening posts under compressive loads. These rails were subject to stress and so required joints that not only remained strong under tension but could be made without the excessive removal of timber which would reduce efficiency. The *Sage kama* (wedged through half dovetail; *diagram 76* and *figure 3*) fills these requirements. The half dovetail of the rail effectively hangs on the mortise, providing a very tight joint as the wedge is driven in which cannot slip or be pulled out.

Rails used in Japanese constructions were generally 25 x 150mm (1 x 6in.) or 50 x 250mm (2 x 10in.), which meant that a small amount of cutting to create a joint would quickly

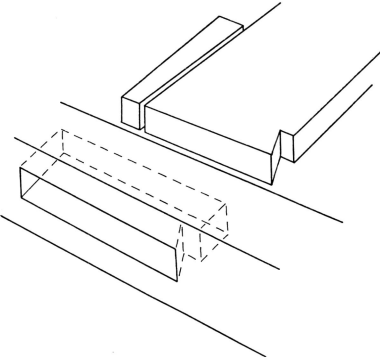

Diagram 76 Saga-kama
(*wedged through half dovetail
joint*).

Figure 3 Sage-kama (*wedged
through half dovetail*)

cause weakness. *Sage kama* was probably designed to be the least destructive method of joining rail to post and, therefore, the most effective way of maintaining stability. The compression of the joint created by the introduction of the wedge makes it better adapted to resist tension stress than other forms of connection. The same principles apply on much lighter structures, which makes the *Sage kama* the ideal joint to use on stretchers in knock down chairs and tables.

Generally the *Sage kama* uses a post that is three times the thickness of the rail. The rail should be cut to the same thickness as a suitable mortise chisel because the mortise will be barefaced. This is initially cut to the same dimension as the rail and then shaped at each end to allow access for the wedge and dovetail (*diagram 77*). The upper end is cut at an

Diagram 77   *Section of the mortised rail showing necessary adjustments to accept the rail and wedge.*

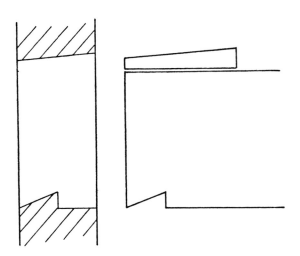

angle of 10°, reducing the mortise length towards the outside. The lower end has the same shoulderline on the outside surfaces, but is cut to accept the dovetail. The inner half is cut square while the outer half is tapered at the same angle as the dovetail (about 1:6). The rail merely requires the removal of a wedge-shaped section to match the shaping of the mortise. The joint can then be pushed together and a wedge cut and fitted to secure it.

Ari-otoshi (housed dovetail joint)
A similar joint, *Ari-otoshi* (housed dovetail joint; *diagram 78*), was used on a much wider rail with the full dovetail fitted to a blind mortise. The first step in constructing the joint should

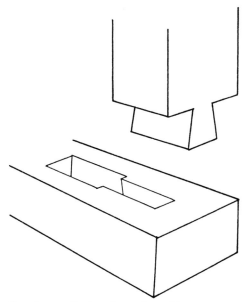

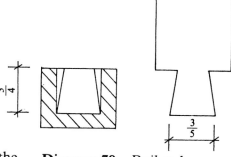

Diagram 78 Ari-otoshi (*housed dovetail joint*).

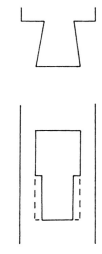

Diagram 79 *Rail and sectioned post showing the relative proportions of the joint.*

be to cut the dovetailed rail so that all measurements for the mortise can be taken from it. A sliding bevel is set at an angle of 1:6 and used to mark the dovetail from the square-ended rail. The shoulder is set in from the end by three-quarters of the post's thickness. The tail width is three-fifths of the rail (*diagram 79*).

The upper half of the mortise must be the same dimension as the end of the tail and should be square, while the lower half is cut to the shape of the tail (*diagram 80*). Both parts of the mortise are initially cut square with the lower half then being cut back at an angle of 1:6. By making this part of the mortise slightly shorter than the thickness of the rail, compressive pressure is exerted when the securing wedge is driven in.

Diagram 80 *One-half of the mortise is shaped to the same angle as the dovetailed rail.*

Kamasen-uchi (gooseneck mortise and tenon)
The next logical step in the development of a locking joint is to produce a construction that gives the effect of a rail protruding from both sides of the post. This was achieved by using the *kamasen-uchi* (gooseneck mortise and tenon; *diagram 81*) which uses a spliced rail set in a through mortise.

Cramp the two rails together and mark in the shoulderline which should be less than the thickness of the post by 6mm (¼in.). Set the mortise gauge to one-quarter of the rail width and scribe the neck of the joint centrally from shoulder to end. At the point where these lines meet the end, using a sliding bevel set at 1:5, scribe in the tapered end; this should

37

Diagram 81 Kamasen-uchi *(gooseneck mortise and tenon joint).*

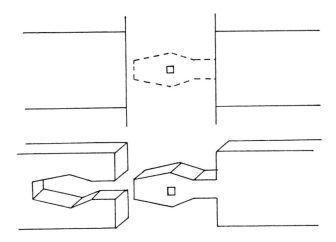

be one-half the rail width at its widest point. The outline is completed by taking this point back to the neck at an angle of 1:3 (*diagram 82*). This part of the joint can then be cut, making sure that the edges always remain square.

Using the gooseneck as a template, place it on top of the adjoining rail, with its end on the shoulderline, and scribe in the joint (*diagram 83*). To remove the waste, use a drill of suitable size to cut the head and then saw down the neck to connect the end with it. The internal faces can then be trimmed back and the two rails fitted.

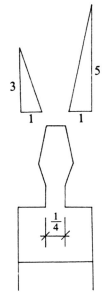

Diagram 82 *Outline of the gooseneck with relative angles.*

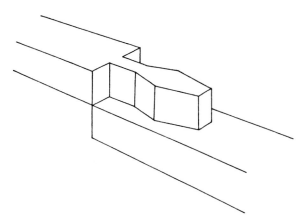

Diagram 83 *The gooseneck is used as a template to scribe the adjoining rail.*

Prior to cutting the through mortise, a round or square hole should be made to accept the securing peg; this

38

operation is made easier if carried out at this stage. The mortise is then cut to accept the rail and, as it is barefaced, care should be taken to ensure that all corners remain square.

The joint is constructed by pushing the female member through the mortise so that its shoulder extends beyond the post, inserting the male component and pulling back the joint into the mortise. The hole is then extended through the rail and the peg driven in to lock the joint in position.

GLUED JOINTS

The common variations on the mortise and tenon have been discussed with the first hints of decoration seen in the use of contrasting wedges and dowels to help strengthen them. But what of the more visually interesting construction that can be used to replace these standard, usually secret joints? By introducing a combination of contrasting splines, dowels or pegs, a major decorative feature can be used that still has all the necessary strength expected from a joint. One of the most advanced ranges of joinery using this principle was designed by Charles and Henry Greene, who practised as architects in Pasadena, California, in the early part of this century. They made a conscious effort to create a visually expressive style that used the basic principles of construction, and this became one of the key characteristics of their architecture and furniture. The joinery varied considerably from the simple to the complex and the more complex it became, the further the principle developed.

Butt mitre with contrasting spline and dowels

One of the simplest joints uses a butt mitre in combination with a contrasting spline and dowels (*diagram 84* and *figure 4*). It is similar to a mitred bridle, the difference being that the spline is a separate, contrasting insert.

Mitres should be marked on the end of each rail, using the knife and sliding bevel, which are then cut and finished with the aid of a mitre shooting board (*diagram 62 on p. 30*). The spline should be approximately one-third the thickness of the rail but set to the nearest mortise chisel. If the exact size is not available, make the spline slightly thicker in order to improve the visual appearance of the joint.

The mortise is scribed centrally on the edge of the rail, extending beyond the inside shoulder by one-fifth the rail

Diagram 84 *The butt mitre in combination with contrasting spline and dowels.*

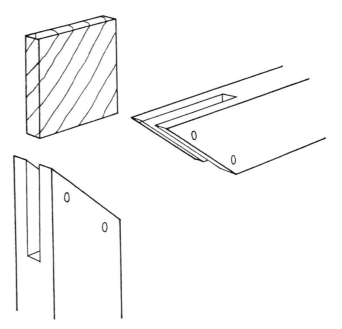

Figure 4 *Mitre in combination with contrasting spline and dowels.*

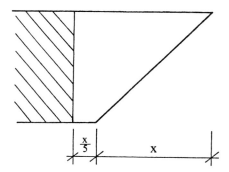

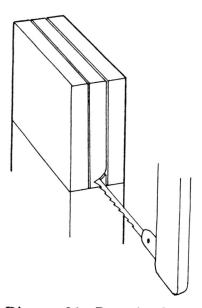

Diagram 85 *The inside shoulder of the mortise is extended beyond the inside shoulder of the mitre by one-fifth of the rail width.*

width (*diagram 85*). This extension increases the size of slip giving more material in which to locate the dowels.

The cutting of the joint is similar to that of a tenon but, as the central portion is to be removed, sawing is done on the inside of the gauge lines. The waste can be removed either with a coping saw or by drilling with a brace and bit, working from both sides (*diagram 86*). The shoulder is then trimmed with the mortise chisel. When both ends have been cut, a contrasting spline should be planed to the same thickness as the mortise with its grain running perpendicular to the mitre (*diagram 87*).

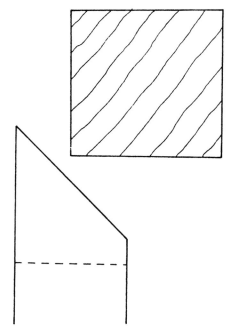

Diagram 86 *Removing the waste with a coping saw.*

Diagram 87 *The grain of the contrasting slip is perpendicular to the mitre line.*

Two holes are bored through the mortise, positioned within 1.2cm (½in.) of the edge, though the exact position

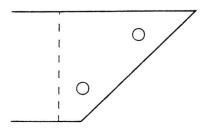

Diagram 88 *Position of holes to be bored through the mortise.*

depends on the size of joint (*diagram 88*). To avoid splitting the timber when drilling, a temporary filling is placed in the mortise and a waste piece cramped to the back.

When fitting the spline, cramp it up to the shoulder in one mortise and drill the holes, using those already cut, as a guide. This part of the joint can then be secured temporarily with dowels.

The fitting of the adjacent rail requires particularly accurate work because the mitre must meet at the same time as the spline butts up to the inside shoulder of the mortise. Place it on top of the protruding spline, holding the mitre together, and mark on the inside shoulder (*diagram 89*). This point is then squared round the spline and used as a guide to plane down to. Continually check the fit of the joint when planing to the line until it is located accurately.

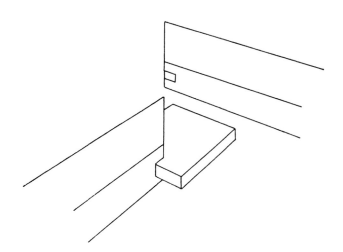

Diagram 89 *The adjacent rail is placed on top of the protruding spline to mark in the inside shoulder.*

When all necessary fitting is complete, it should be decided how to finish the spline and dowels; they can be either raised or planed flush to the rail. Visually, greater emphasis is placed on the joint if they are raised by about 3mm (⅛in.) with all sharp corners rounded prior to gluing. If a flush joint is required, any protrusions can be planed down after construction. The joint is visually improved by shaping the components as they approach the corner *figure 5*).

Square butt with dovetail-shaped spline
A joint that is both technically complex and more visually appealing uses the same basic principle of construction but

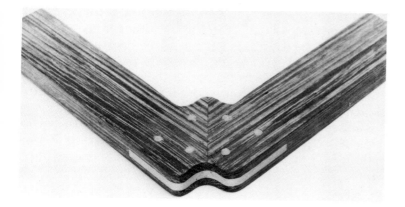

Figure 5 *Shaped components create further visual interest.*

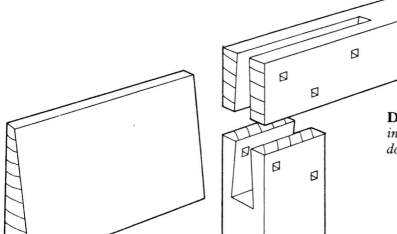

Diagram 90 *The square butt in conjunction with a contrasting dovetail spline and pegs.*

has a dovetail-shaped spline with a square butt replacing the mitre (*diagram 90*).

The contrasting spline is made first; this should be twice the width of the horizontal component and twice as long as the vertical component. The dovetail angle depends on the size of joints, but is generally one-half the rail thickness at its widest, tapering down to one-quarter. To allow for cleaning up after construction, the spline should be made about 6mm (¼in.) longer and wider.

The socket in the vertical member is cut first. The inside shoulder is set in from the end and the spline used as a template to scribe its outline in a central position (*diagram 91*). Place the component in the vice with the scribed lines in

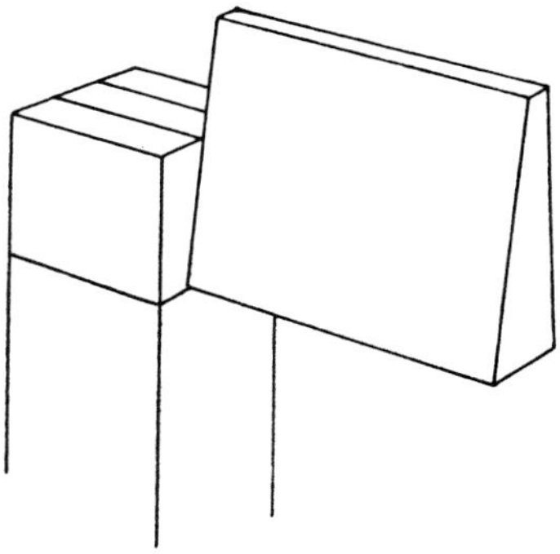

Diagram 91 *Use the dovetail spline as a template to mark the socket outline on the vertical component.*

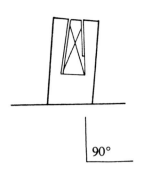

Diagram 92 *Place the component in the vice so that the sawcut is made vertically.*

Diagram 93 *A rounded shoulder prevents the spline fitting on the outside edges.*

a vertical position and cut down to the shoulder, working on the waste side, taking care not to deviate from the lines (*diagram 92*). The waste is then removed and any necessary trimming done with a paring chisel.

When the spline is in the socket the position of the pegs should be decided, with no more than three being used, to prevent the joint being weakened. The holes can then be drilled, placing waste timber in and behind the socket to prevent breakout. The square peg is visually superior in this joint and will require additional cutting. The spline is pulled tightly against the shoulder by using the draw-boring method to locate the pegs (*see diagram 37 on p. 21*). The spline is marked at the point where it emerges from the end of the socket and removed with this part complete.

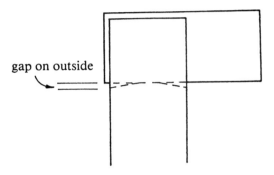

gap on outside

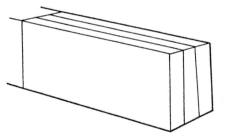

Diagram 94 *Having marked in the outline of the socket on the end grain, scribe parallel lines back to the shoulder line using a mortise gauge.*

Again, using the spline as a template, scribe in the socket on the end of the horizontal component. Locate the inside shoulder and use a mortise gauge to extend the outline of the joint from it to the end (*diagram 94*). Repeat the cutting of the shoulder and the peg holes.

If the spline is to be left proud, cut it to within 3mm (⅛in.) of the inside and outside edges and round all sharp corners. The end of the horizontal component should be planed flush with the outer edge when the joint is together. The construction can be improved visually by shaping the components as they approach the joint.

The use of the contrasting spline is probably one of the most successful methods of creating a joint that is decorative and still has the necessary strength required to lock two components. The following examples show variations on this theme, using the spline to connect rails that meet with a butt or mitre. Methods of extending the decoration from joint to joint in a frame can also be introduced.

Splined mitre with contrasting inserts

The splined mitre (*diagram 95* and *figure 6*) can use any number of contrasting inserts, depending on the rail width, to create visual appeal, and is one of the simpler joints to construct. Before introducing the spline, the frame is constructed using simple, butt-mitred corners. In this example two splines are used with a thickness slightly less than one-fifth the rail width.

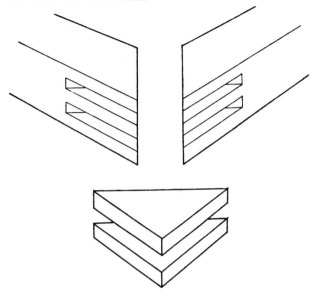

Diagram 95 *Splined mitre with two inserts.*

Figure 6 *Splined mitre.*

Diagram 96 *Socket depth is two-thirds of the mitre length.*

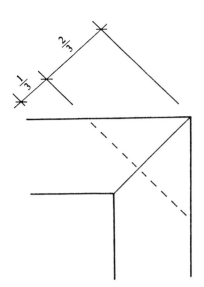

Diagram 97 *The mortise gauge is used to mark in the socket working from both edges.*

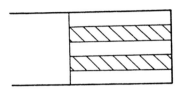

Diagram 98 *Place the frame in the vice with the shoulder line in the horizontal position.*

The shoulder of each socket is set in by two-thirds of the mitre length and at right angles to it (*diagram 96*). The sockets are scribed in, with the mortise gauge working from both edges to give a symmetrical joint (*diagram 97*).

The cutting of the sockets is made easier by placing the frame in the vice with the shoulder placed horizontally (*diagram 98*). Most of the waste is taken out with the coping saw and trimmed back with a mortise chisel, working from

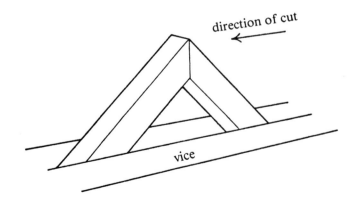

both sides. Because the joint has a long internal shoulder, its cutting may result in a slightly raised surface which will prevent the spline bedding down properly on the outside (*diagram 99*). Further removal of timber is necessary and, if

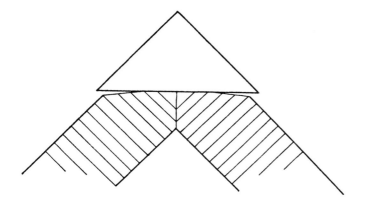

true flatness is difficult to achieve, it is preferable to have it slightly hollow (*diagram 100*).

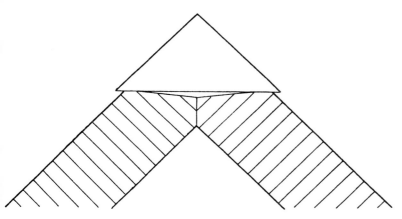

Splines are made to fit the socket with a push fit and can be planed flush after gluing. Alternatively they can be left proud, in which case a protrusion of about 3mm (⅛in.) is left with all corners rounded.

The construction of the joint can be further reflected and visually extended around the frame, by gluing strips of timber with the same thickness as the splines to both sides of each rail prior to construction (*diagram 101* and *figure 7*).

Diagram 101 *A contrasting strip of timber glued on to each edge improves visual quality.*

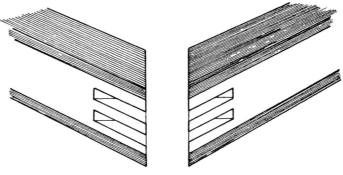

Figure 7 *Variation of splined mitre*

Square butt with contrasting inserts

A similar type of joint using the same method of construction replaces the mitre with a square butt and is built in the same manner as the standard bridle joint (*diagram 102* and *figure 8*).

Diagram 102 *Contrasting splines used in conjunction with a square butt.*

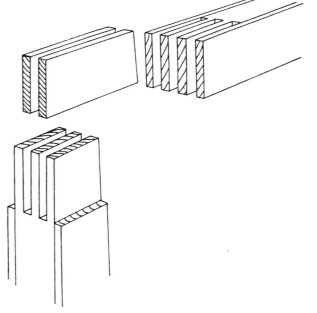

The tenons are made in a contrasting timber and built into a rail. These should be twice as long as the rail width and should be set in by one-half of it (*diagram 103*). The sockets that accept them are identical for adjacent rails and should be marked together (*diagram 104*). The splines should be set into the sockets of one rail, and left protruding on both edges, to be planed flush after gluing. The two components should now go together.

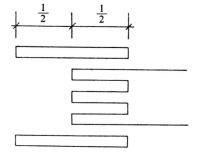

Diagram 103 *The spline is twice as long as the mortise.*

Diagram 104 *The inside shoulders of adjacent components can be marked together.*

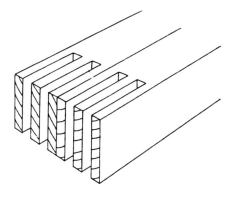

49

The two previous examples can be varied further by using a number of staggered inserts (*diagram 105* and *figure 9*). Joints of this type create great visual interest using a simple construction that is particularly strong due to the large gluing area.

Diagram 105 *Variation in spline length creates further interest.*

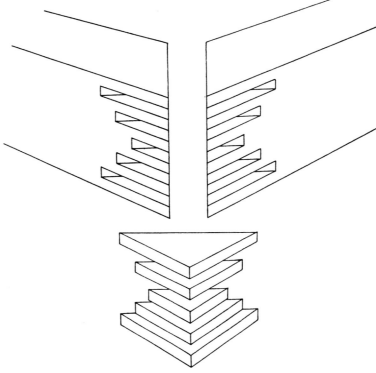

Figure 9 *Mitre and staggered inserts.*

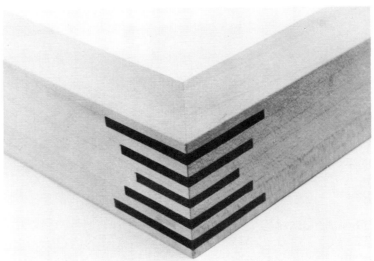

3 Carcase Joinery

DECORATIVE DOVETAIL JOINTS

The traditional joint used in the construction of a carcase is the dovetail, primarily because it provides the strongest method of connecting two boards. Of the three main types of dovetail – through, lapped and secret – the through method provides the greatest visual interest because of the contrast between end and side grain emphasized in the proportions of pin to tail (*diagram 106* and *figure 10*). The strongest joint has

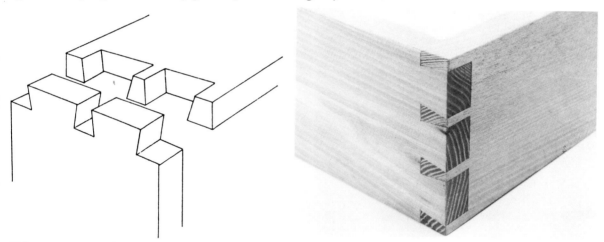

Diagram 106 *Standard through dovetail joint.*

Figure 10 *Through dovetail joint.*

both pins and tails of equal dimension, although a compromise is usually reached between strength and proportion by making the tails about twice the width of the pins at the shoulder (*diagram 107*).

Through dovetail

The pins are cut first, which will allow the tails to be marked easily; the sockets for the pins are usually too small to allow

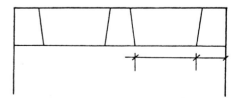

Diagram 107 *The pins and half pins are half the width of the tails at the inside shoulder.*

51

access for a pencil. The first step is to scribe the inside shoulder, which is measured in from the end of the board. This dimension should be the thickness of the board plus 1.5mm (1/16in.), which allows for any necessary planing down after construction. This is done lightly either with a knife and try-square working from the face side and face edge, or using a cutting gauge against the square end of the board. The depth of the lines can be increased in the waste areas after marking out the pins.

The width of pin and half pin are equal at the widest point, with the tail twice this width at its narrowest. Having decided the number of pins to use, divide the shoulder line up on the face side, which should be the inside of the carcase (*diagram 108*). These divisions are then drawn in from the inside shoulder to the end using a pencil and try-square.

The angle of the tail will depend on the type of work being undertaken and the timber being used for it. The usual practice is to have a steeper angle of about 1:5 in softer materials and for work where appearance is not important and an angle of about 1:8 for finer jointing (*diagram 109*). It is up to the individual to select the correct angle for a particular job, but he should be aware that a sharp angle will result in weak, short grain at the extremity of the tail, while a shallow angle will reduce mechanical efficiency. When the

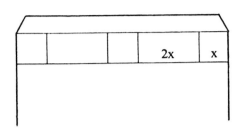

Diagram 108 *The joint is divided up on the face side*

Diagram 109 *The angle of the dovetail can vary between 1:5 and 1:8 depending on use and material.*

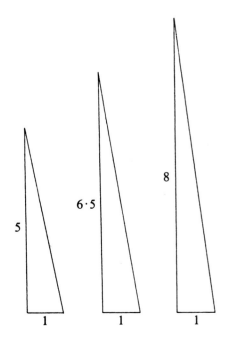

angle is established, set it on a sliding bevel and pencil in the lines of the end grain (*diagram 110*). The marking of the tail is then completed by taking the lines from the end to the inside shoulder and shading all the waste area to denote its removal. An alternative method of marking the joint is to make a number of dovetail templates at varying angles and select one for a specific purpose.

Place the board vertically in the vice and, using a fine dovetail saw, make cuts on the waste side of the lines down to the shoulder. Make sure the saw blade is kept in the vertical position, only cutting into the waste, as any deviation may be visible in the finished joint. A coping saw is used to remove most of the waste; work its blade down the vertical sawcut and gradually bring it into the horizontal position close to the shoulder line, leaving about 1mm (¹⁄₃₂in.) of waste (*diagram 111*). The advantage of distinct knife lines is illustrated at

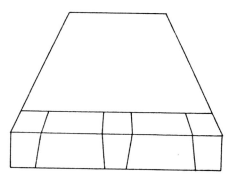

Diagram 110 *The sliding bevel and pencil are used to mark the angle on the end grain.*

Diagram 111 *Most of the waste is removed with the coping saw.*

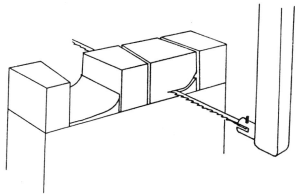

this point, the location of the paring chisel being made easy when removing the waste (*diagram 112*). The chisel should be kept at right angles to the board, cutting from both sides

Diagram 112 *The paring chisel is used to cut back to the shoulder.*

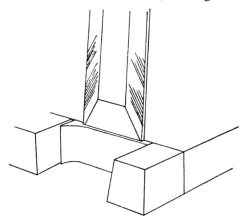

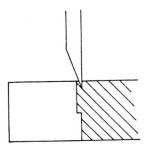

Diagram 113 *Waste is removed from both sides.*

to prevent timber break-out (*diagram 113*). Any remaining waste on the tails should also be taken back to the lines with a paring chisel.

When complete, the pins are used as a template to mark out the tails on the adjacent panel. The boards are held at right angles, with the inside of the pins resting on the shoulder line and each face edge being flush (*diagram 114*). If the boards are large, some method of holding them steady should be found, such as cramping them lightly to the bench. The tails can then be marked in with pencil (*diagram 115*).

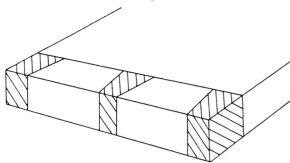

Diagram 115 *Shaded areas denote waste.*

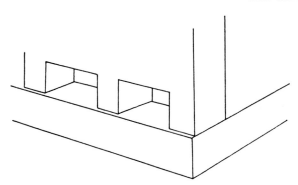

Diagram 114 *Use the pins as a template to mark in the tails.*

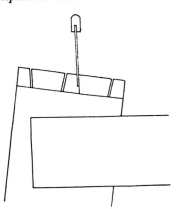

The cutting of the tails follows the same process as the pins, but to assist accurate cutting, place the outline of the tail in a vertical position when securing it in the vice (*diagram 116*). When cutting back to the shoulder, select a chisel that is slightly narrower than the width of the socket, and work from both sides. If the joint has been cut accurately it should go together with a few taps of the hammer (use scrap material to prevent bruising of the panels). Problems may occur if the shoulders have not been cut accurately, a common fault being to leave a protrusion at the centre of the shoulder which obviously prevents the joint going together on the outside (*diagram 117*). It may be preferable to have a slight hollow on

Diagram 116 *The panel is placed in the vice so that sawcuts are made vertically.*

Diagram 117 *Any protrusion will prevent joint assembly.*

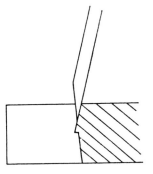

54

the shoulder which should be made when the waste is removed. This is done by paring down vertically for one-quarter of the thickness and then tilting the chisel forward slightly and cutting to the middle. The panel is then reversed and the operation repeated (*diagram 118*). Another fault is to leave waste material in the corners of the sockets, which again prevents the joint going together, and this should be removed.

Dovetail joint with intermediate pins

Variations of the dovetail joint often create further visual interest. By introducing intermediate pins into the main tails the decorative quality of the joint is considerably increased and this has the added advantage of providing additional strength where it is needed, i.e. at the centre of a wide tail (*diagram 119* and *figure 11*). As visual quality is of great importance, marking out must be accurate, with neat cutting of both pins and tails, and so the use of this method on thin boards is inadvisable.

Preparation of the boards is virtually the same as for the through dovetail up to the marking out stage, but should

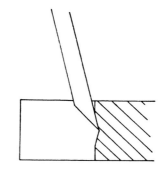

Diagram 118   *The hollow shoulder can be used.*

Diagram 119   *Decorative dovetail joint.*

Figure 11   *Decorative dovetail joint.*

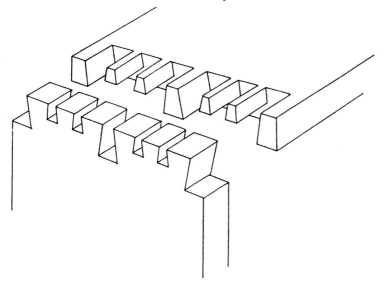

55

include the inside shoulder of the small pins which is one-half the board thickness measured from the main shoulder line (*diagram 120*). Because of the introduction of small pins, a wider tail must be used in order to accommodate them. Their

Diagram 120   *The shoulders of the small pins have to be marked.*

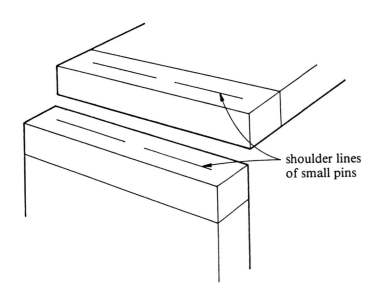

shoulder lines of small pins

centres are found by dividing the tail into three equal parts at its widest (*diagram 121*).

Waste areas are again shaded and vertical sawcuts made on the waste side of the lines. The inside half of waste must be removed completely and this should be done by chopping from the top end while the board is secured to a solid worktop (*diagram 122*). The remaining waste can mostly be taken out with a coping saw and trimmed back to the shoulder. A waste

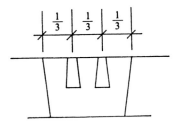

Diagram 121   *Small pins are set symmetrically through the tail.*

Diagram 122   *The inside half of the waste is initially removed.*

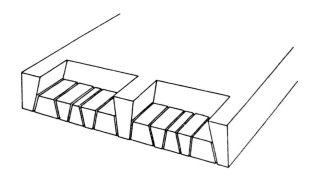

block equal to one-half the board thickness should be inserted to prevent the timber splitting (*diagram 123*).

Sawing the tails follows the same procedure as a standard dovetail, setting the board in the vice with the marked lines in a vertical position. To assist location of the joint, the internal corners of the tails can be slightly relieved (*diagram 124*).

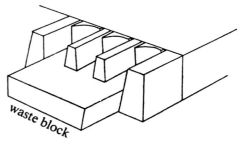

Diagram 123 *A waste block prevents the timber splitting.*

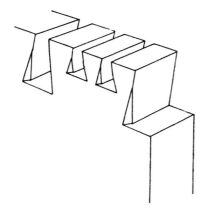

Diagram 124 *Inside corners can be removed to assist assembly.*

Dovetail joint with contrasting tails

The problem with the previously mentioned dovetail joints is that they are visually confined to the corner in the carcase. A variation that overcomes this uses the insertion of contrasting components to create the tails of the joint (*diagram 125* and

Diagram 125 *Contrasting inserts create the tails.*

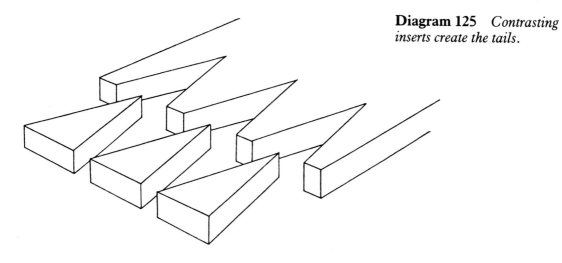

Figure 12 *V-shaped inserts create the tail in the joint.*

figure 12). These are made approximately 3mm (⅛in.) thicker than the boards they are to be set into and have an internal angle of 30°. Their ends can either be rounded to any convenient diameter or left pointed, although the latter may cause difficulty when cutting the internal angle of the socket.

The number of inserts will depend on the width of the panel, and should be shaped with all square edges, as any deviation will result in a badly fitting joint. The panels they are to be set into should be prepared with square ends and a length equal to the internal dimension of the finished carcase.

To mark out the sockets, use each insert as a template set onto the board and spaced at regular intervals (*diagram 126*).

Diagram 126 *Each insert is used as a template to mark the outline of each socket.*

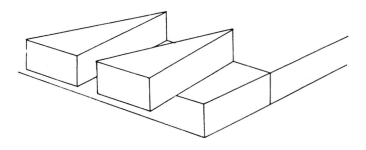

If a rounded end is preferred, drill holes through the board and set the inserts on top of them. A knife is then used to mark in the sockets. To assist their location, draw in centre lines to correspond to those on the panel (*diagram 127*).

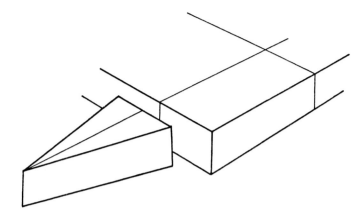

Diagram 127 *Centre lines help locate the insert on the board.*

The type of saw that is used to remove the waste will depend on the length of cut. Since dovetail and tenon saws are restricted, a panel saw or even a Japanese Ryoba saw should be employed. Cutting on the waste side of the line, saw down to the internal corner or pre-cut hole on both sides to create the socket. Any deviation of the blade into the waste can be trimmed with a chisel, but if the cut goes beyond the socket line then a blemish in the final joint will result.

Fit and glue the inserts into their corresponding sockets, each one slightly protruding on both sides of the panel. These can then be planed flush to the panel when the glue is set (*diagram 128*).

The tailed panel is used to mark the adjoining pins in a

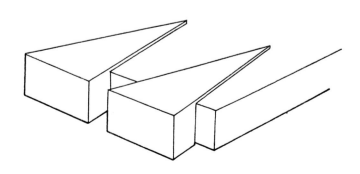

Diagram 128 *Any protrusion of the insert is planed flush after the glue has set.*

similar manner to the standard dovetails, the process being reversed on this occasion.

Variations on this theme can be achieved in a number of ways. Inlaid strips can be used to link up the tails on opposite corners (*diagram 129* and *figure 13*) or the adjoining panel can be made of the same type of timber as the inserts.

Diagram 129   *Inlayed strips of veneer visually extend the joint from corner to corner.*

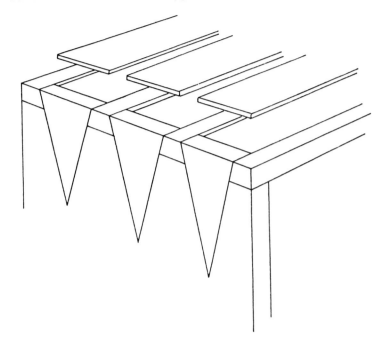

Figure 13   *Inlayed strips link up opposite corners.*

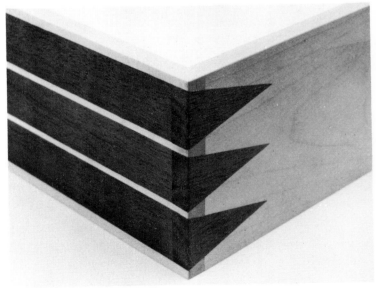

Alternatively, the length of each insert can vary, which will in turn vary the width of tails. If each insert lengthens towards the centre of the panel, the tails are narrowest at the outer edge, thus giving additional strength where it is most needed (*diagram 130* and *figure 14*).

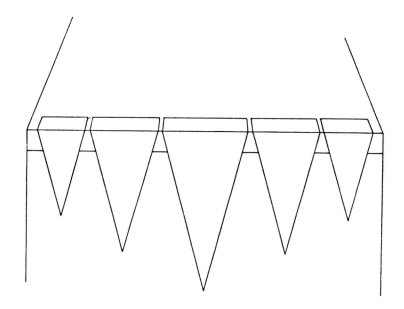

Diagram 130 *Variation in tail length creates further interest.*

Figure 14 *Variation of tail width.*

Butt mitre with dovetail key

The basic principle of locking two panels together by the use of a dovetail can be used to great visual effect when employing a shaped key in conjunction with the mitre (*diagram 131* and *figure 15*). The carcase must be constructed

Diagram 131 *The butt mitre used in conjunction with a dovetail.*

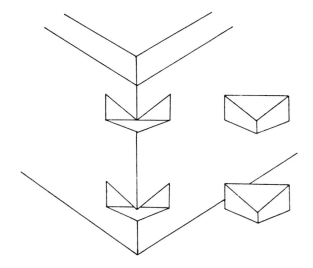

Figure 15 *Mitre and dovetail key.*

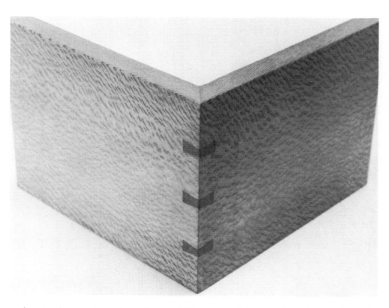

prior to inserting the dovetail keys and is made with a simple butt mitre cut on the donkey's ear (*diagram 132*). This can be virtually finished prior to cutting the sockets, but care must be taken as it may not withstand rough handling.

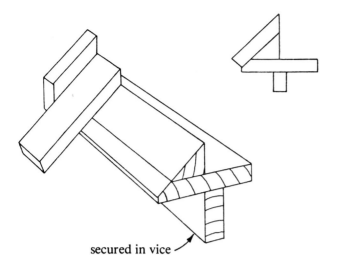

secured in vice

Diagram 132 *The donkey's ear.*

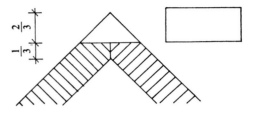

Diagram 133 *The shoulder is set in by two-thirds of the mitre length.*

To mark out the sockets, set a sliding bevel at an angle of 1:8 and pencil in the outline on both surfaces. At its narrowest part it should not exceed 3mm (⅛in.) and be finer if possible. The inside shoulder of the socket is set in by two-thirds of the mitre width and square to it (*diagram 133*).

Difficulty may be experienced when removing the waste in trying to keep the sawcut exactly to the line on both surfaces. Continual checking of the cut as the operation progresses is essential because subsequent trimming with a chisel is extremely difficult due to the narrow access available. Most of the waste is removed with a coping saw, and is trimmed back to the shoulder with a fine paring chisel to give a flat shoulder. Care should be taken to avoid any protrusions which may prevent the dovetail key slipping in easily. Entry is made easier by having a slightly hollow shoulder (*diagram 134*).

The keys are made by planing a long strip of timber to the correct angle and cutting it to the required lengths. To assist the shaping, two simple jigs are made in which to rest the timber (*diagram 135*). Each key is individually fitted until all

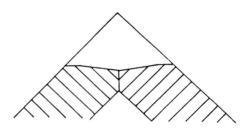

Diagram 134 *A hollow shoulder assists spline entry.*

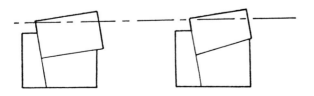

Diagram 135 *Two jigs are used to assist planing of the dovetail keys.*

Diagram 136 *Chamfering each key will assist its entry.*

Diagram 137 *Excess timber is removed by planing with the grain of the key.*

are a hand-push fit, and they are then glued into position, one end being chamfered to assist entry (*diagram 136*). When the glue is set, excess timber is removed by planing with the grain of the keys (*diagram 137*).

direction of planing

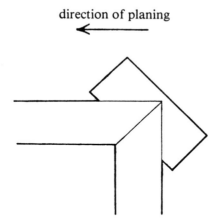

DECORATIVE FINGER (CORNER-LOCK) JOINTS

By replacing the dovetail with the finger (corner-lock) joint in a carcase construction, many more variations are possible. This usually provides additional strength as well as introducing contrasting members to highlight the structure.

Probably one of the most successful methods of increasing visual and structural quality was again a product of the Greene brothers, who enjoyed considerable success with its use. The strength of the finger joint is considerably increased by the introduction of contrasting pegs which lock the construction in both planes (*diagram 138* and *figure 16*).

Diagram 138 *The finger joint used in conjunction with contrasting dowels.*

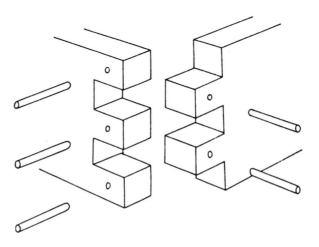

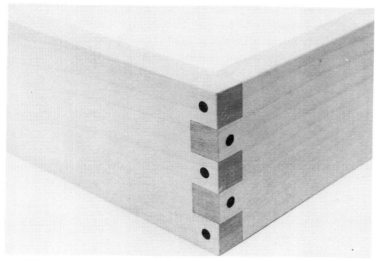

Figure 16 *Finger joint and contrasting pegs.*

With all timber prepared, opposite boards can be cramped together and the fingers marked by dividing their width up into an odd number of parts with equal dimensions (*diagram 139*). Separate the boards and take the lines from the end to the shoulder using a pencil and try-square (*diagram 140*).

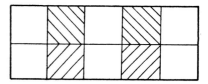

Diagram 139 *Opposite boards are marked together.*

Diagram 140 *Use a pencil and try-square to take the lines from the end to the shoulder.*

Diagram 141 *Waste areas should be shaded.*

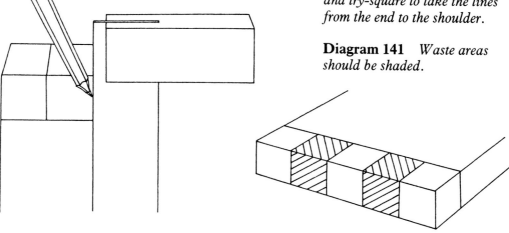

Shade all the waste areas and emphasize the shoulder line to assist location of the chisel (*diagram 141*).

Place the board in the vice with the fingers held vertically, and use a dovetail saw to make the cuts on the waste side of

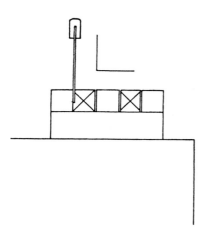

the line down to the shoulder (*diagram 142*). The process of removing the waste is the same as for the dovetail joint but made easier because of the square shoulders (*diagram 143*).

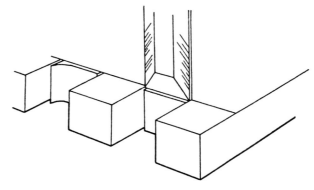

Diagram 142 *All sawcuts are made vertically.*

Diagram 143 *Waste is removed by a paring chisel.*

The finished fingers are used as a template to mark those on the adjoining board (*diagram 144*), and the cutting process is repeated. If the operations are carried out accurately, the joint will go together with a gentle tap of the hammer, using a piece of waste material on the panel to prevent bruising. To

Diagram 144 *The finished fingers of one panel are used as a template to mark those on the adjoining panel.*

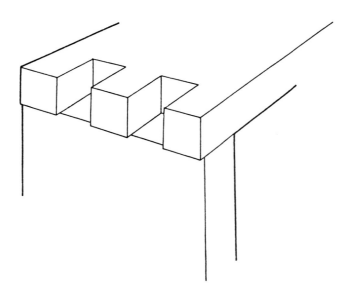

help it go together either remove the internal corners, or slightly chamfer the waste at the end of the fingers (*diagram 145*). The carcase is glued together with the aid of cramping blocks that give pressure only where needed, pushing each

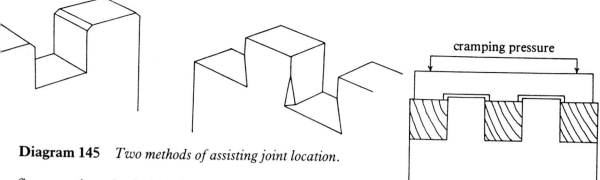

Diagram 145   *Two methods of assisting joint location.*

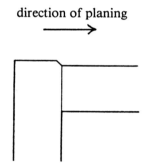

Diagram 146   *A cramping block made to give pressure where needed.*

finger against the inside shoulder (*diagram 146*). After the glue has set, the protruding waste can be planed away leaving a flush joint. To prevent the end grain splitting, the corner of each finger is removed on the inside (*diagram 147*).

The joint is now ready to accept the pegs. Each hole is drilled at the centre of the finger using a brad-point drill which will give a positive location and clean cut (*diagram 148*). If a square hole is needed, the round hole is squared off

direction of planing

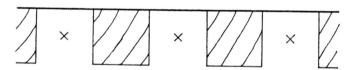

Diagram 148   *The centres of the holes are marked in a symmetrical position.*

Diagram 147   *The removal of the internal corner prevents the timber splitting.*

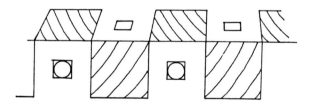

Diagram 149   *Round holes are squared off to receive a square peg.*

Diagram 150   *A space between the bottom of the hole and the end of the peg takes up excess glue.*

to accept the corresponding peg (*diagram 149*). When gluing in the peg, allow a small airspace at the bottom of the hole to take up any excess glue which will otherwise have nowhere to escape and may cause the timber to split (*diagram 150*). Many variations of this joint are possible and the Greenes incorporated many examples in their work. The width of the

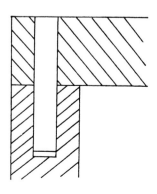

67

finger can be varied with the corresponding number of pegs in it increased (*diagram 151, figure 17*).

Ideally, the perfect decorative joint should extend beyond the confines of the corner and become a major visual element in a design that continually draws the eye back to the method of construction. This is successfully achieved by building up the panels from strips of contrasting timber. This method will also give a perfectly fitting joint if the process is carried out accurately prior to laminating the strips.

Diagram 151 *Variation of finger width and number of dowels.*

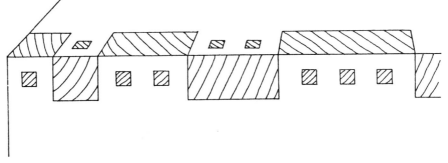

Figure 17 *Variation in finger width and corresponding number of pegs.*

Finger joints with contrasting panels

The first example in this range introduces a contrasting veneer between each strip (*diagram 152, figure 18*). To make it, begin by veneering both sides of a wide board to produce the strip in the panel. The thickness of this board, including the veneer combination, will be the width of the laminated fingers in the joint and is therefore an important dimension. If the joint is to be used on a large structure, it may be advisable to purchase panels that have been accurately

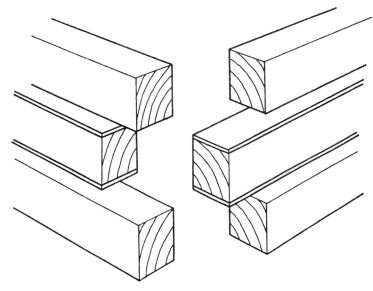

Diagram 152 *A contrasting veneer provides decoration.*

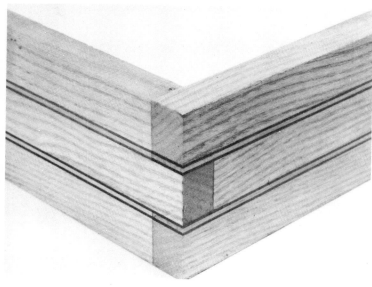

Figure 18 *Contrasting veneer used in the finger joint.*

planed by machine. This, and an unveneered board, is cut into strips, their width being slightly larger than the thickness of the finished panels. Their ends are planed square at alternate lengths; the shorter ones determine the inside dimension of each side of the finished carcase and the long ones are slightly greater than the outside dimension.

When all the strips have been prepared, a simple jig is required to glue up the panel which will locate the inside shoulder of the joint (*diagram 153*). Two through housings

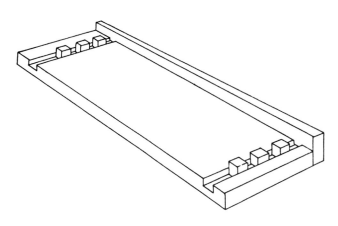

Diagram 153   *The jig used to locate the strips in the panel.*

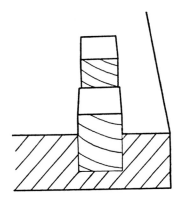

Diagram 154   *Inserted stops used to locate inside shoulders.*

are cut on a flat board (plywood, chipboard, etc.) into which are pressed pieces of timber to form the stops (*diagram 154*).

Difficulty may be experienced when cramping the strips together if movement occurs, as this could result in a bowed panel. This is overcome by placing blocks of timber across the panel's width, which are then cramped to the jig (*diagram 155*). These blocks and the jig should be pre-waxed to prevent their adhesion to the panel. When the glue is set, take the panels out of the jig and lightly plane both sides prior to constructing the carcase. If the original boards were accurately planed, the joint should fit perfectly.

Diagram 155   *Blocks of timber prevent cupping of the panel.*

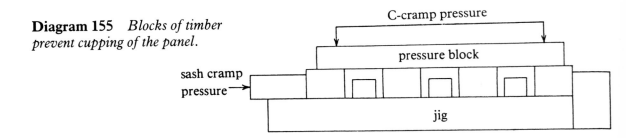

This method of construction offers great scope for a wide variety of decorative joinery. The strips can be made of contrasting timber to form another simple decorative effect (*diagram 156, figure 19*), or developed further by varying their width, increasing in size towards the centre of the panel (*diagram 157, figure 20*). Each of these joints can be formed

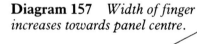

Diagram 156   *Strips can be made in contrasting timber.*

Figure 19   *Finger joint using contrasting strips of timber.*

Figure 20   *A joint using varying finger widths.*

Diagram 157   *Width of finger increases towards panel centre.*

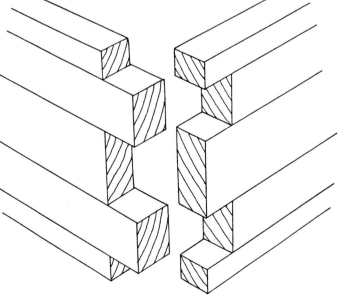

Figure 21 *Three-way corner using a finger joint.*

into a three-way corner by using a mitre to join two surfaces (*figure 21*).

Finger-joint with V-shaped inserts

A further example of a decorative finger joint has panels that are constructed in a completely different manner to previous examples (*diagram 158, figure 22*). Cut the timber to the required length, width and thickness. The length will form the inside dimension of the carcase, the width is twice that of the finger in the joint (*diagram 159*), and the thickness should be slightly greater than the finished panel size.

The mitred corners require great accuracy if the joint is to function efficiently and should be cut using either a guillotine or a mitre shooting board (*see diagram 62, p. 30*). The contrasting fingers should also be cut in this way.

Each panel is glued together with the aid of a jig similar to that in diagram 154, leaving out the two components that form the front and back edges. This allows a through groove to be cut on the end of each panel that will accept the plywood spline (*diagram 160*). This is cut with a plough plane and the panel then finished by gluing on the remaining components. The groove is extended into these components by removing the waste with a mortise chisel of equal dimension. A similar

1 Jewellery casket in French walnut and sycamore

2 Jewellery casket open

3 Triangular box in yew and walnut with cedar lining

4 Low tables in rosewood/yew and black bean/sycamore

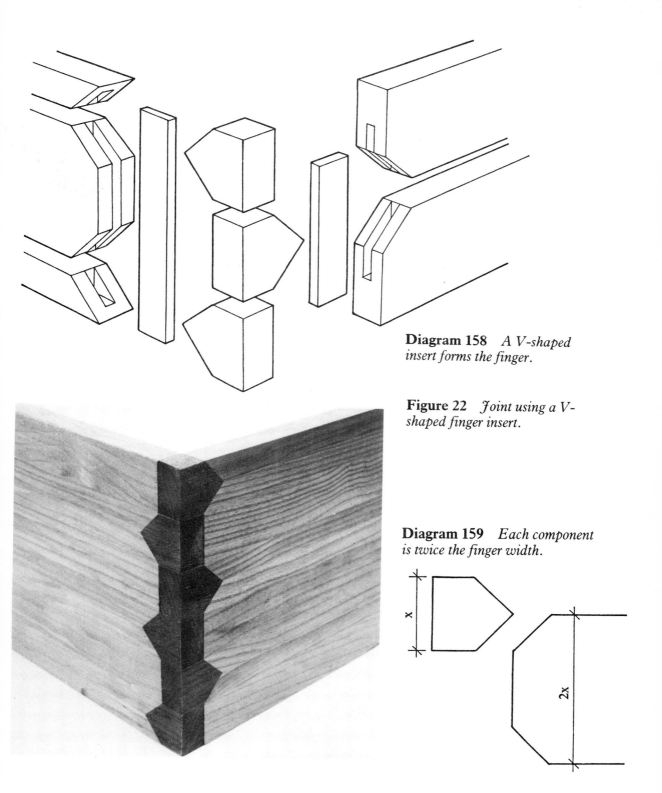

Diagram 158 *A V-shaped insert forms the finger.*

Figure 22 *Joint using a V-shaped finger insert.*

Diagram 159 *Each component is twice the finger width.*

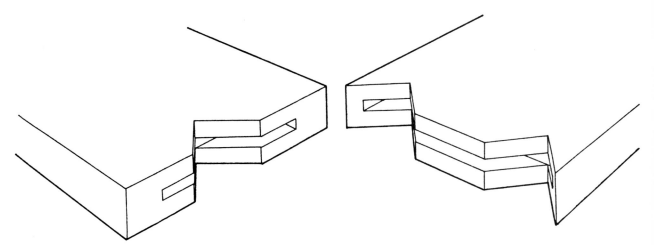

Diagram 160 *A groove in the end grain accepts the plywood spline.*

groove is cut into the end of each finger insert. The panels are then completed by gluing each finger into its respective recess in the panel. Finally, lightly plane each side of the panel to remove any discrepancy, and glue the carcase together.

In an effort to extend the joint visually around the carcase, strips of veneer can be applied to the edge of each component prior to removing the corners. This will result in a series of fine lines connecting the points of the contrasting finger inserts (*diagram 161, figure 23*).

Figure 23 *Variation on figure 22.*

Diagram 161 *Additional interest is created by veneering the edge of each component.*

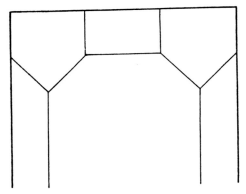

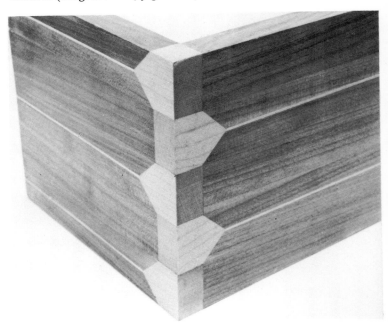

DECORATIVE MITRE JOINTS

The use of the butt mitre together with a strengthening insert has been illustrated when discussing the dovetail joint (*see diagram 131, p. 62*). The mitre, although not usually thought strong enough to be the sole method of corner fastening, offers the foundation for many visually interesting joints when used with other contrasting components.

Mitre joint with contrasting strips

The insertion of thin strips of timber running from corner to corner shows one simple method of adding strength while leading the eye around the carcase to the decorative corners (*diagram 162* and *figure 24*).

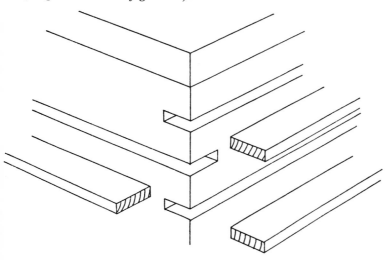

Diagram 162   *Thin strips of timber set into a mitre create additional strength.*

Figure 24   *Mitre and strip inserts.*

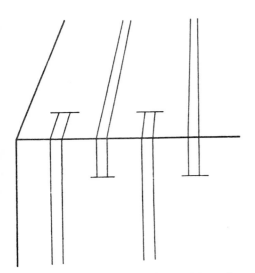

Starting with a mitred carcase, determine the number and position of strips to be used. Select a plough plane blade of appropriate width and set the points of a mortice gauge to it. Adjusting the fence of the gauge when necessary, scribe in the position of each strip, working from both edges of the panel (*diagram 163*). The depth of each slot is marked in with a cutting gauge, with the parallel lines scribed up to it. Prior to cutting the grooves, waste should be removed at the corners to prevent timber splitting as the blade runs through the end (*diagram 164*).

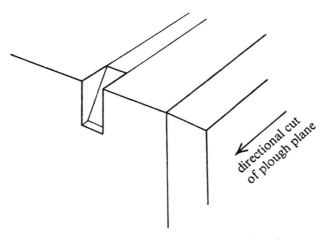

directional cut of plough plane

Diagram 163   *The position of each slot is scribed with the marking gauge.*

Diagram 164   *Waste is removed at one end to prevent break-out as the plane blade emerges.*

With all the slots cut to the correct depth, contrasting strips of timber are planed to the same dimension. Working on opposite panels in each operation, apply glue to the slots and insert the strips, exerting pressure at the corners to ensure that they bed down accurately (*diagram 165*). When the glue is set, the strips are planed flush to the panel and the operation repeated on the two remaining surfaces.

Diagram 165   *Cramping blocks are used to bed down each strip accurately.*

cramping pressure

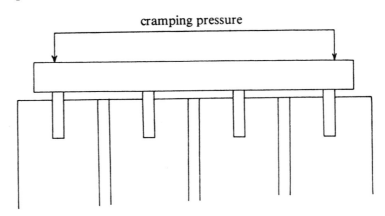

An alternative method of using these strips would be to terminate them a short way into the carcase in which case the stopped grooves would have to be chopped out with a mortise chisel (*diagram 166* and *figure 25*). Further visual

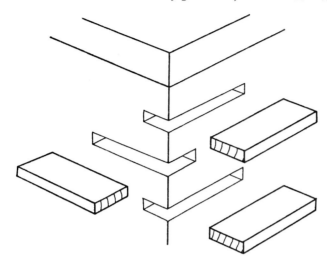

Diagram 166 *Short strips of timber can also be used.*

Figure 25 *Mitre and stopped-strip inserts.*

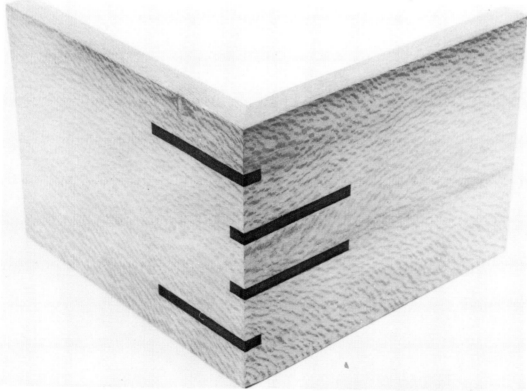

improvement of this example is achieved by joining the ends of the strips across the grain (*diagram 167* and *figure 26*).

Occasionally, certain parts of different joints can be combined to create new decorative constructions. A combination of the strips used in the previous example and

Diagram 167   *Visual quality is improved by joining up the ends of the strips with a veneer inlay.*

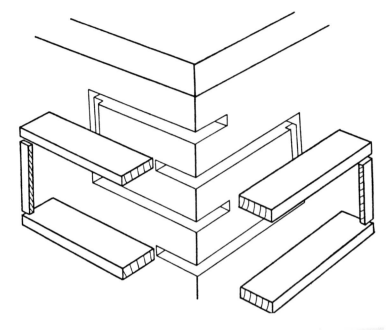

Figure 26   *Mitre and stopped-strip inserts with ends joined by inlays.*

the varying finger width seen in diagram 157 (*see p. 71*) is a good example of this. The number of inserted strips in a finger corresponds to its increase in width, creating a visually complex joint with exceptional strength due to high gluing area (*diagram 168* and *figure 27*).

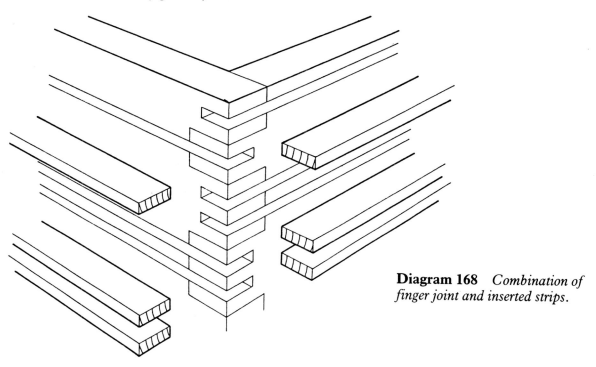

Diagram 168 *Combination of finger joint and inserted strips.*

Figure 27 *Combination of finger joint and strip inserts.*

Mitre joint with dowel

The use of an inserted dowel is another simple yet effective method of introducing decoration to a mitred corner. By introducing it in a diagonal plane along the mitre (*diagram 169*) a very strong joint is produced which provides interest in the elliptical end grain. Drilling the holes must be

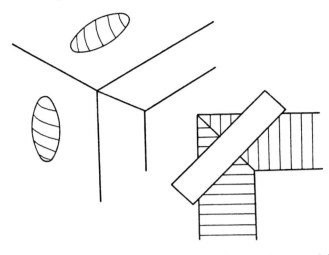

Diagram 169   *The dowel runs perpendicular to the mitre line.*

extremely accurate for the dowels to be positioned symmetrically to each other and the corner. To achieve this, a simple jig is made to cramp on the corner which will guide the drill bit accurately (*diagram 170*). In addition to this, some form of support is needed to prevent the timber from splitting as the bit emerges from the carcase. This is most effectively done by gluing a strip of waste timber to the carcase which can be planed away easily after completing the drilling operation.

The dowels are made to be a hand-push fit into the holes; if they are tight and need to be driven in, the glue line of the mitre may break. Prior to gluing the dowels in position, one end should be chamfered to assist location (*diagram 171*).

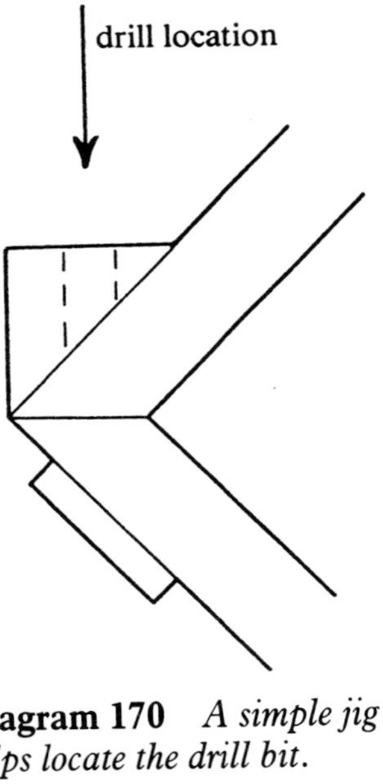

drill location

Diagram 170   *A simple jig helps locate the drill bit.*

Diagram 171   *Dowel location is assisted by chamfering one end.*

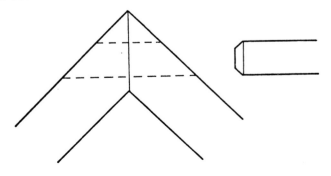

When they have been glued in, the excess is planed away, working into the carcase all the time (*diagram 172*).

By replacing the finger joint with a butt mitre in figure 16 (*see p. 65*), further use of the dowel and mitre combination is found (*diagram 173* and *figure 28*). The placement of the dowels can form any configuration and is really left up to the

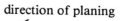

direction of planing

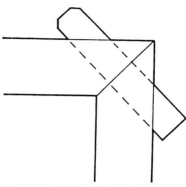

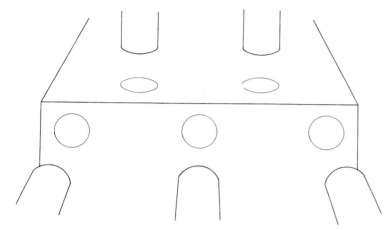

Diagram 172   *Plane into the carcase to remove dowel waste.*

Diagram 173   *Dowel and mitre combination.*

Figure 28   *Mitre with dowel combination.*

maker's choice, although they should be used on both surfaces to lock the joint securely. Cutting the holes accurately, preferably with a brad point drill bit, is essential if a neat, symmetrical joint is to be made.

One further variation of mitre/dowel combination that provides for greater interest, uses the same method of construction as diagram 173, but moves the centre of the hole nearer the edge so that part of the dowel protrudes above the surface of the carcase (*diagram 174* and *figure 29*). More than

Diagram 174 *Dowel protrudes through the surface of each panel.*

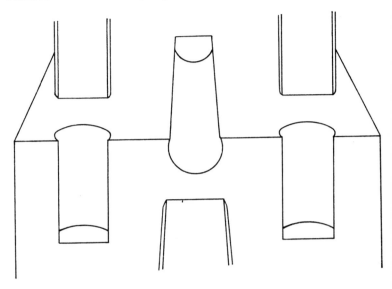

Figure 29 *Mitre with dowel protruding above the surface.*

one half of the dowel should be retained so that it acts as a locking device.

To provide a clean-cut hole on the outside surface, use a forstner bit that will give neat, parallel edges and a flat bottom. When the dowels have been inserted, the exposed part can either be left proud or made flush to the carcase. The dowels can be linked up across the ends by inlaying a strip of timber across the grain to give a further variation (*diagram 175* and *figure 30*).

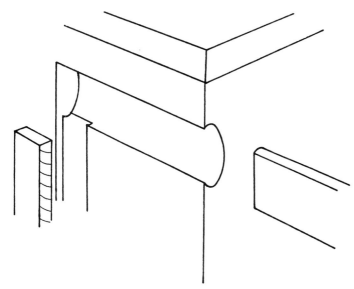

Diagram 175 *The ends of the dowels can be joined by a veneer inlay.*

Figure 30 *Mitre with dowel ends joined by inlays.*

4 Splicing Joints

Before the introduction of adhesives and metal reinforcements, the difficulty in obtaining the long lengths of timber required for some architectural structures led to the development of a splicing or scarf joint that could be used to connect shorter timbers. This became an important feature in both Eastern and Western societies; the great revolution in Japanese joinery being in the Yayoi period (200 B.C.-A.D. 250), while in England it lasted from the twelfth to the sixteenth century. It was a style of jointing that hadn't been seen before and was left entirely to the woodworker's imagination. Increasingly intricate forms were created in an attempt to achieve the maximum strength. Many woodworkers will find the intricacies of splicing quite fascinating and, although their use is not essential because of modern adhesives, will no doubt want to experience the complexities of cutting such joinery.

ENGLISH SCARF JOINTS
Splayed scarf joints
At the start of the twelfth century in England, the predominating scarf joint was the splayed type with some variations being the strongest examples of spliced joints ever produced. The stop-splayed scarf, using the under-squinted and sallied butt with four face pegs and one face key which is twice edge-pegged (*diagram 176*), is a good example of the concept behind this type of construction.

Both halves of the joint are identical, therefore marking out can be done at the same time for each component. Since the angle of splay will depend on the length and width of joint, all examples in this section will be discussed with a length of two-and-a-half times the width of timber. Sections of timber will be 4cm (1½in.) square with a joint length of 10cm (3¾in.), any variation in size always being to this proportion.

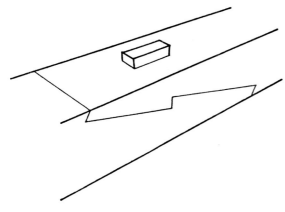

Diagram 176 *Stop-splayed scarf, using under-squinted and sallied butt, with four face pegs and one face key which is twice edge-pegged.*

The extremities of the joint are set in by 5mm (³⁄₁₆in.) from the upper and lower surface, and the two points connected to give the angle of splay. The butted ends are then taken to the outside at an angle of 60° (*diagram 177*). The outline of the joint is completed by squaring across from the outer edge. All lines should be made with a knife and sliding bevel.

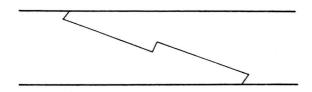

Diagram 177 *Outline of the joint on the edge of the timber.*

Sawcuts are made as close to the lines as possible, which should remove most of the waste, the remainder being cut away with a chisel or shoulder plane (*diagram 178*). The

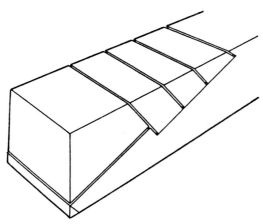

Diagram 178 *Sawcuts are made to assist waste removal.*

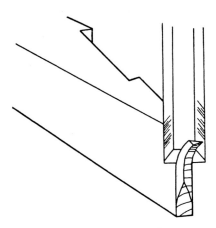

under-squinted square butt is formed by carefully trimming with the paring chisel (*diagram 179*).

To mark out the mortise for the key, the joint should be temporarily pushed together. A section of 2 x 1cm (¾ x ⅜in.) is drawn in a symmetrical position on the top surface and taken round the sides to the bottom at an angle of 15° (*diagram 180*). The lines on the side can be off-set by 1mm

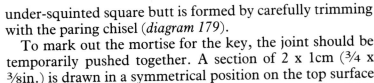

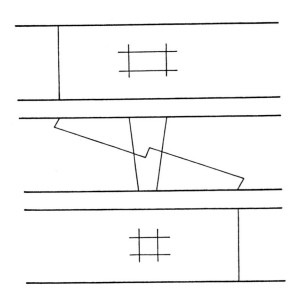

Diagram 179   *The under-squinted square butt is trimmed with a paring chisel.*

Diagram 180   *Marking out the mortise to accept the face key.*

(¹⁄₃₂in.) so that a compressive force is created when the key is driven into the mortise (*diagram 181*). When the joint is

Diagram 181   *Off-set mortise helps create a compressive force when the key is driven in.*

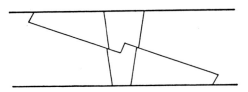

taken apart, the lines on each side are squared across the splay and the width of the mortise marked in with the mortise gauge (*diagram 182*).

To cut the mortise, remove most of the waste with the brace and bit, and trim back to the lines using the mortise and paring chisels. A key is then shaped to correspond to the angle of the mortise and driven in when the joint is together

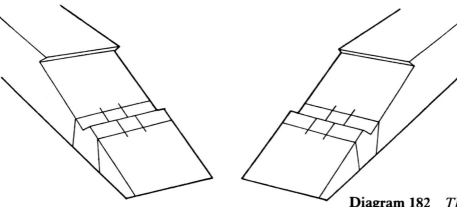

Diagram 182 *The outline of*
the mortise should be scribed
across each splay.

(*diagram 183*). The pegs that secure the key are set in a
central position on each half of the joint with a diameter of
4mm (⁵⁄₃₂in.). The pegs on the top surface, also with a 4mm
(⁵⁄₃₂in.) diameter, are set in by 1cm (²⁄₅in.) from the edge
and 2cm (⁴⁄₅in.) from the end (*diagram 184*). They should be
square to the upper surface.

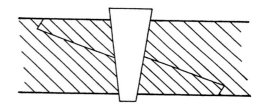

Diagram 183 *Section through
the joint showing the face key in
position.*

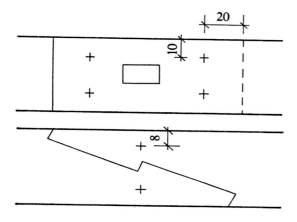

Diagram 184 *Location of face
pegs.*

A development from this last example into what is
probably the strongest type of splayed scarf joint uses under-
squinted square butts with transverse key and four face pegs
(*diagram 185* and *figure 31*). Its basic principles can be found
in Roman ship construction, English and Japanese
architecture and Chinese furniture. The insertion of the key
forces the joint together, closing the butts and creating
compression at the splay, giving great mechanical efficiency.
The addition of four dowels perpendicular to the splay
prevents any lateral movement.

Diagram 185 *Splayed scarf using under-squinted butts with transverse key and four face pegs.*

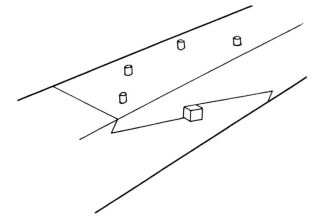

Figure 31 *Splayed scarf with under-squinted square butts, transverse key and four face pegs.*

Again, the two halves of the joint are identical and can be marked together. The end of the square butt is set in by 5mm (³⁄₁₆in.) and then taken back to the outside at an angle of 60°. Parallel lines should then be drawn in, connecting the inner point to the opposite outer edge (*diagram 186*). At the centre

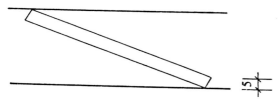

Diagram 186 *Profile of the joint on the timber's edge.*

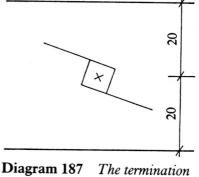

Diagram 187 *The termination of each splay forms the mortise to accept the transverse key.*

of these lines, a square should be marked in to signify the mortise for the key and the termination of the tabled splay (*diagram 187*).

The removal of the waste is similar to cutting parts of a bridle joint. Having squared round all marking-out lines, saw cuts are made, terminating at the lower splay (*diagram 188*) with extra cuts made in between to assist timber removal. The waste should be pared away, initially taking off the corners from both sides and gradually working to a flat plane (*diagram 189*). The upper splay of the joint can then be

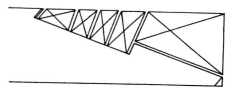

Diagram 188 *Sawcuts assist waste removal.*

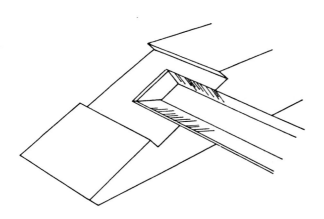

Diagram 189 *The splay is flattened with a paring chisel.*

finished, first removing most of the waste with the saw and then planing back to the line to give a flat surface. The under-squinting is then trimmed back and the square ends planed to the corresponding angle of 60°. The joint should now go together.

Prepare a key to fit into the mortise so that the joint tightens when it is driven in. Holes of 4mm (⁵⁄₃₂in.) diameter can then be drilled perpendicular to the splay and the dowels inserted. Connect the diagonals of each splay and set in the centre of the holes by 1.5cm (⅝in.) from the corner (*diagram 190*).

Diagram 190   *Location of dowel centres on the splay.*

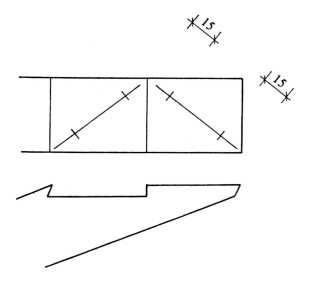

Edge-halved scarf

The inevitable development in this style of jointing saw a transition from the splayed type to the edge-halving with the stop-splayed scarf. This has vertical bridled butts and incorporates four face pegs and two edge pegs (*diagram 191* and *figure 32*) combining both elements.

Figure 32   *Stop-splayed scarf with vertical bridled butts, four face pegs and two edge pegs.*

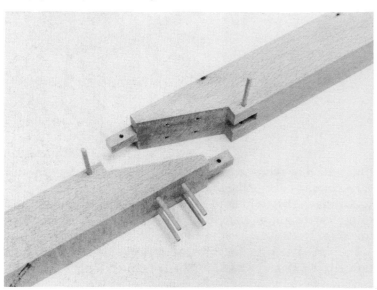

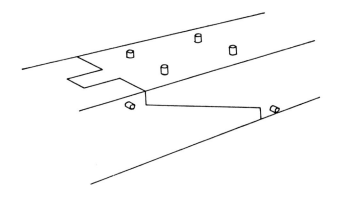

Diagram 191 *Edge-halved, stop-splayed scarf with vertical bridled butts, incorporating four face pegs and two edge pegs.*

The length and depth of the bridled end is 2cm (¾in.) and 8mm (⁵⁄₁₆in.) respectively and should be marked on the side of each piece of timber. The angle of splay is ascertained by connecting the two internal corners. The width of the bridle is 1cm (³⁄₈in.) and should be marked symmetrically on both top and bottom surfaces (*diagram 192*).

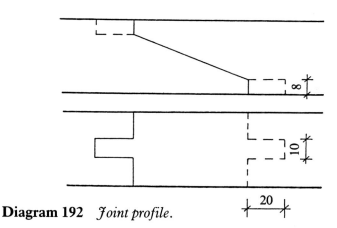

Diagram 192 *Joint profile.*

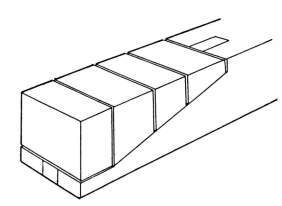

Diagram 193 *Sawcuts assist waste removal.*

Sawcuts should be made to remove most of the waste around the bridle and at intermediate points along the length to assist removal of waste from the splay (*diagram 193*). All waste should then be removed, trimming back to the lines with the aid of a paring chisel and shoulder plane (*diagram 194*). To remove the waste of the mortise, make diagonal sawcuts connecting the two inner points (*diagram 195*). Timber can then be chopped out with a suitable sized mortise chisel, with any necessary trimming of the sides done with

Diagram 194 *Either a paring chisel or a shoulder plane can be used to trim the splay.*

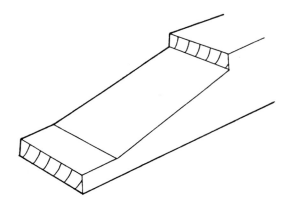

Diagram 195 *Diagonal sawcuts help to remove mortise waste.*

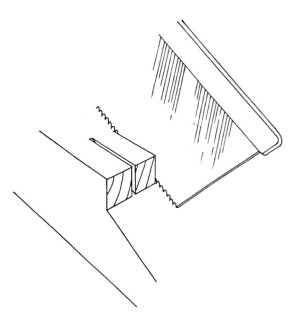

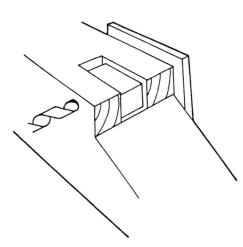

Diagram 196 *Waste prevents timber breakout when drilling the hole for the edge peg.*

the paring chisel. Care should be taken to ensure that the mortise is flat-bottomed.

A symmetrically positioned hole of 3mm (⅛in.) diameter is drilled from the side through the mortise, with waste timber being used to prevent breakout as the bit emerges (*diagram 196*). The joint can then be pushed together and the centre for the hole in the tenon found by using that through the mortise as a guide. The centre can be slightly offset, which will help draw the joint together when the dowel is driven in.

When the joint is together, the four holes on the face can be drilled to accept dowels of 3mm (⅛in.) diameter. These should be set in by 1cm (⅜in.) from the edge and 2cm (¾in.) from the termination of the splay (*diagram 197*).

A similar type of joint shows the full use of the edge-halved scarf at the expense of the splay and is cut in a similar manner (*diagram 198*).

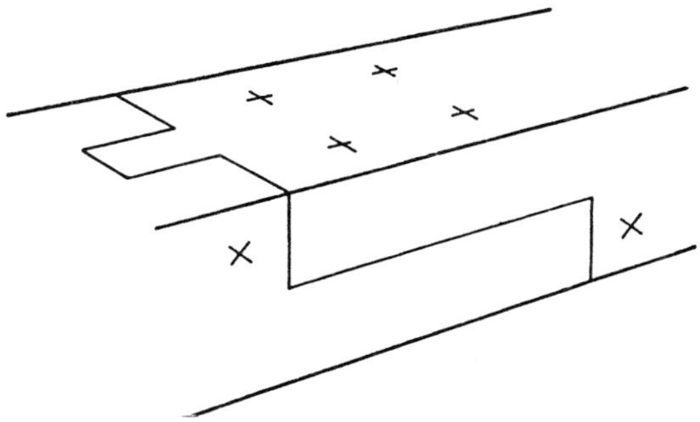

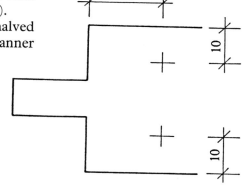

Diagram 197 *Location of face pegs.*

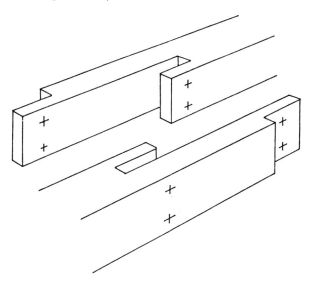

Diagram 198 *Full edge-halved scarf similar to diagram 191.*

Face-halved and bladed scarf
The third significant style of scarf joint developed in the British Isles was the bladed type, the face-halved and bladed scarf with thick central peg and four edge pegs being a typical example (*diagram 199*).

Diagram 199 *Face-halved and bladed scarf with thick central peg and four face pegs.*

A mortise gauge is set to approximately 1cm (⅜in.) between points (to the nearest mortise chisel), and from point to fence so that when working from both edges the outer point scribes the same line (*diagram 200*). The

Diagram 200 *Profile of joint on each component.*

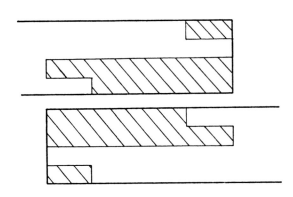

Diagram 201 *Sawcuts are made to remove most of the waste.*

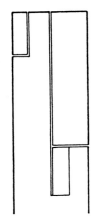

Diagram 202 *The final cut is made on the inside face of the mortise.*

shoulders of the two outer quarters should be set in by 2.5cm (1in.) from the end.

The outer part of the tenon is formed by making two simple sawcuts close to the marked lines which will remove most of the waste, with any necessary trimming done with the paring chisel and shoulder plane. A long saw cut has to be made on the waste side of the centre line which may be too long for a standard tenon saw, in which case a panel saw or preferably a Japanese Ryoba saw should be used (*diagram 201*). A sawcut across the end of the outside tenon will remove more of the waste, which leaves one final cut to be made on the inside face of the mortise (*diagram 202*). The final piece of waste is removed with a coping saw and any necessary trimming done on all surfaces.

The process of drilling the holes should be repeated, as in the previous example, so that the joint is tightened when the dowels (3mm diameter, [⅛in.]) are driven in. Their centres are located 1.25cm (½in.) from the end of the tenon and 1cm (⅜in.) from the upper and lower face (*diagram 203*). The

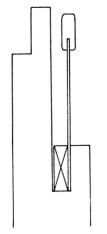

Diagram 203 *Dowel location on the edge of the joint.*

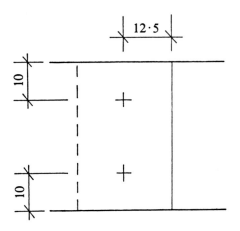

joint is then put together, a central hole of 5mm (³⁄₁₆in.) diameter drilled and a matching dowel fitted.

By the eighteenth century, the introduction of iron plates and bolts as strengtheners virtually ended the use of the purely wooden scarf joint.

Edge-halved scarf with under-squinted butts

One other significant example of a scarf joint used in Western societies was designed by the Greene brothers and used on the interiors of their buildings, particularly in the Gamble house. As the brothers were strongly influenced by the Japanese style, obvious links can be seen in the construction, the edge-halved scarf with under-squinted butts with securing peg (*diagram 204*) being typical. To emphasize the joint, all corners were slightly rounded.

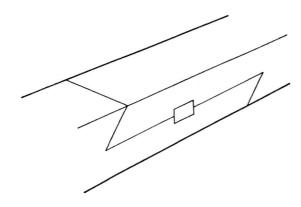

Diagram 204 *Edge-halved scarf with under-squinted butts and securing peg.*

Using a marking gauge set at 2cm (³⁄₄in.) scribe in the halving on both edges of each component. The angle of the under-squint is taken from the centre to the outside at an angle of 60° using a sliding bevel and knife (*diagram 205*).

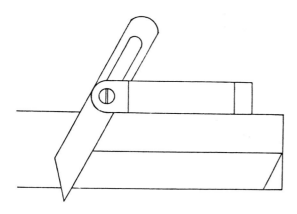

Diagram 205 *The angle of the under-squint is marked with a knife and sliding bevel.*

The lines are then squared across the top and bottom face to complete the outline of the joint.

The majority of waste can be removed with the tenon saw, making cuts on the waste side of the lines. The halving and under-squinted shoulder can be trimmed back with the paring chisel and shoulder plane if necessary, with the end being planed to the correct angle (*diagram 206*).

Diagram 206   *Profile of the scarf cut on the end of one component.*

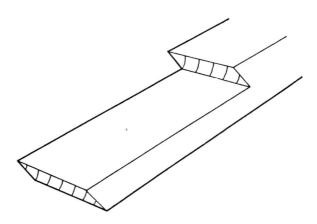

The next step is to cut a housing on each halving, which will create a mortise to accept the key when the joint is put together. This should be set in from the end by 4cm with a dimension of 2cm x 5mm (¾ x ³⁄₁₆in.) (*diagram 207*). If the

Diagram 207   *Positioning of mortise.*

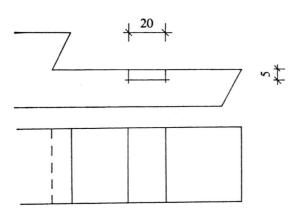

Diagram 208   *Off-set mortise will create a compressive force when the peg is driven in.*

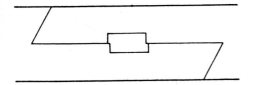

two halvings are slightly off-set when put together, the joint will be tightened as the key is driven in (*diagram 208*). When making the key, ensure that pressure is not exerted at the bottom of each housing as this will tend to push the joint apart.

5 Mantel clock in
black bean and
sycamore

6 Chest of drawers in black bean and English oak

7 Dining table in wenge and Japanese oak

EASTERN SCARF JOINTS

Japanese architecture has undoubtedly been one of the most influential styles of wooden construction. With the introduction of iron tools in the Yayoi period (200 B.C.- A.D. 250), their style advanced to the post and lintel system which allowed a greater architectural freedom. Differences obviously occur in their approach which had considerable effect on style, the most significant being the use of the saw and plane. They cut on the pull rather than the push which gives them a greater accuracy but a loss of cutting power.

Kanawa-tsugi (mortised, rebated, oblique scarf)

The Japanese style of construction, a simple post-beam framework without any braces or struts, required the use of strong, accurately executed joinery. The splicing joint has many different configurations with the more complex being particularly interesting. *Kanawa-tsugi* (mortised, rebated, oblique scarf joint; *diagram 209* and *figure 33*) is, without

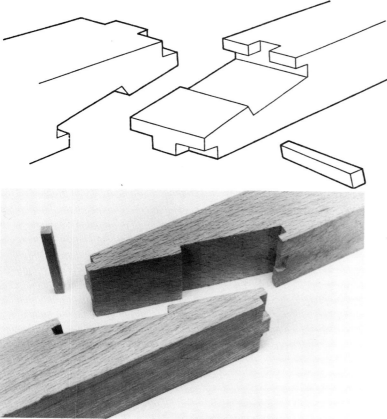

Diagram 209 Kanawa-tsugi (*mortised, rebated, oblique scarf joint*).

Figure 33 Kanawa-tsugi (*mortised, rebated, oblique scarf joint*).

97

doubt, the most fascinating, and probably the strongest type of dry joint produced by the Japanese. The stub tenons cut into the mortised ends prevent any lateral movement, but an adjustment to the internal faces is necessary to get the joint together in this way. This is achieved by reducing their total length by that of the stub tenons, taking an equal amount off each face. The key to fit in the resulting mortise forces the joint together in a similar way to the strong English type (*see diagram 185*). The stub tenon makes it slightly stronger than the under-squinted version.

Using 4cm (1½in.) square, sectioned timber with a 10cm (3¾in.) long splice, the joint is marked out as illustrated (*diagram 210*). The angle of the splay is found by connecting

Diagram 210   *Profile of the splicing joint.*

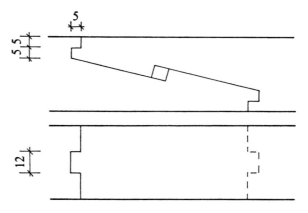

the two points of the inner mortise with the corners of the stub tenon, with the key being located centrally between the two lines. The stub mortise and tenon should be marked centrally at a width of 1cm on the top and bottom face.

The stub tenons should be formed initially so that the waste timber of the splay can be used as a support (*diagram 212*). Two simple sawcuts will remove the main bulk of waste

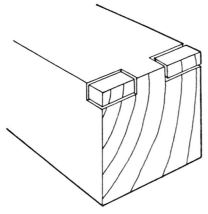

Diagram 211   *The diagonal sawcuts help form the stub tenons.*

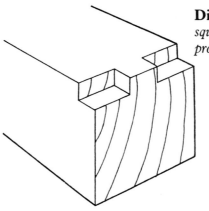

Diagram 212   *A clean, square corner should be produced.*

at the splay, with the upper half being planed flat (*diagram 213*). The lower level of the two-tiered splay is created by paring away the waste in the same way as a halving is cut (*diagram 214*). The next step is to cut the mortise that accepts

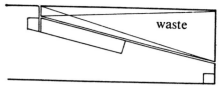

Diagram 213 *Sawcuts remove most of the waste.*

Diagram 214 *The lower splay is pared away.*

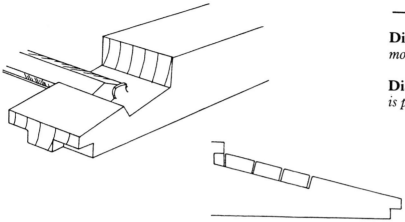

the stub tenon, initially chopping down from the top face so that timber breakout is prevented by the remaining waste (*diagram 215*).

Diagram 215 *Cutting the mortise that accepts the stub tenon.*

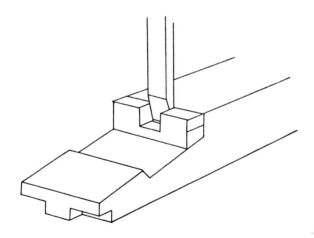

When all corners have been thoroughly cleaned out, the joint should go together. A key is then made to fit the mortise which is driven in to secure the joint.

Having developed such a strong joint in comparison to earlier examples, it was inevitable that variations would be used. *Okkake-daisen-tsugi* (rebated oblique scarf joint) is a similar joint, but lacks the securing key, which is replaced by

Diagram 216 Okkake-daisen-tsugi (*rebated, oblique scarf joint*).

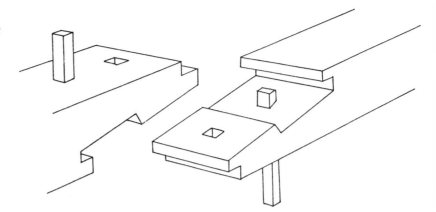

a pair of pegs running through the splay (*diagram 216*). The joint can be tightened by off-setting the mortise on each component to draw it together as the pegs are driven in (*diagram 217*).

Diagram 217 *Off-set mortises will draw the joint together.*

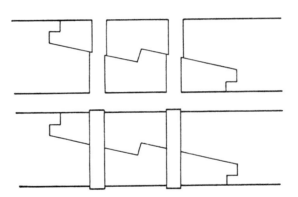

Chinese scarf joint

A similar joint to the *Kanawa-tsugi* was used in the construction of the traditional style of Chinese chair back (*diagram 218*). It was the craftsman's practice to create the curve by using three or, most commonly, five pieces of timber joined end to end in this way, with final finishing done by hand. The process of cutting the joint is the same as *Kanawa-tsugi*, but an additional difficulty is experienced because of the curved sides. Accuracy must be maintained on the inner surfaces as they may be exposed when the final shaping is complete. Further variations were used, but

100

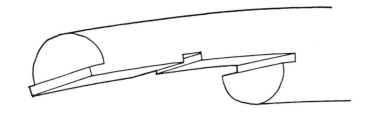

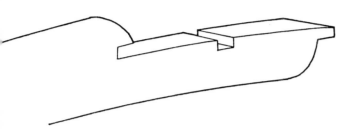

Diagram 218 *Chinese joint used on the traditional chair back.*

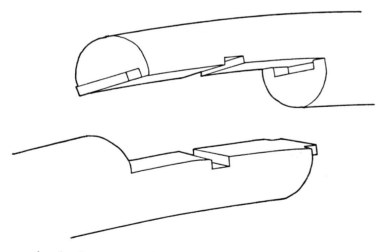

Diagram 219 *Variation of Chinese splicing joint.*

remained the personal choice of individual craftsmen (*diagram 219*).

SPECIALIZED SCARF JOINTS
Many scarf joints were designed for specific situations, such as the *Sao-tsugi* (lapped rod mortise and tenon), used when it was only possible to drop the male member on to the female

member (*diagram 220, figure 34*). Many variations on the neck length can be used, but the joint's strength does not increase significantly by making it longer, although, at first sight, this may seem to be the case.

Diagram 220 Sao-tsugi (*lapped rod mortise and tenon*).

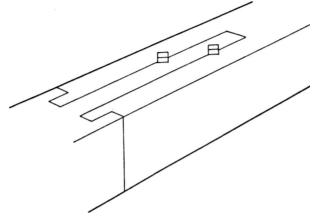

Figure 34 Sao-tsugi (*lapped rod mortise and tenon joint*).

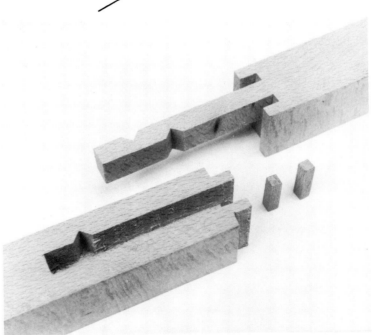

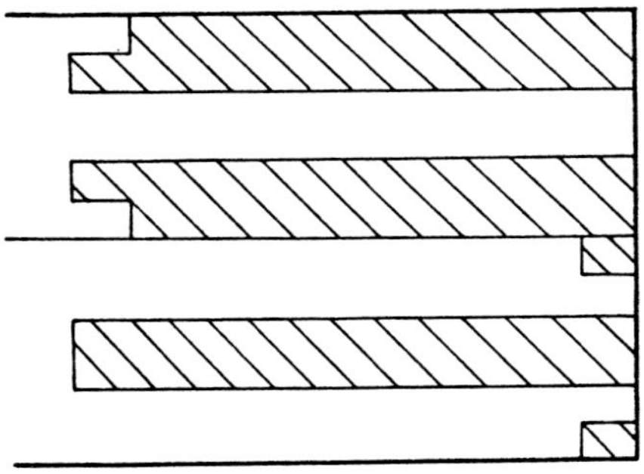

Diagram 221 *Profile of the joint on each face of the components.*

Marking out on the top surface should be done with both pieces of timber fastened together (*diagram 221*). The stub tenon is 1cm x 7mm (³⁄₈ x ¼in.) with the rod tenon scribed centrally at a width of 1.2cm (½in.). The depth of the rod tenon is set in from the top face by 2cm (¾in.). The male component is made first, most of the waste being removed by four sawcuts (*diagram 222*). The mortise that accepts the stub

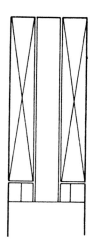

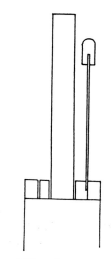

Diagram 222 *Waste removal by sawcuts.*

tenon is then cut using a chisel of appropriate width (*diagram 223*). To complete this part of the joint, the rod tenon has to be reduced in width by 2cm (³⁄₄in.), leaving a haunch of 5 mm (³⁄₁₆in.) at the shoulder (*diagram 224*).

Diagram 223 *Removal of waste left in the mortise.*

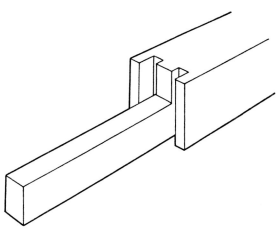

Diagram 224 *The underface of the joint shows the rod tenon reduced by one-half leaving a haunch of 5mm (¹⁄₁₆in.).*

The female component requires a long stopped mortise to be cut, and is made initially by removing the bulk of the waste with a flat-bottomed drill bit and then trimming back to the lines with a mortise chisel of appropriate size. The outer corners of the shoulder should be removed to create the stub tenons, and a mortise cut to accept the haunch of the male member.

With all corners thoroughly cleaned out, the joint can be pushed together and the position of the two keys located.

Diagram 225 *Off-set mortises will help draw the joint together.*

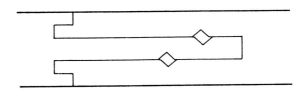

These should be set in from the end by 2cm (¾in.) and 4cm (1½in.) respectively, and set at an angle of 45° to the edge. By slightly off-setting the position of each half of the key, the joint can be pulled together when constructed (*diagram 225*).

Other examples of English (*diagrams 226-228*) and Japanese (*diagrams 229-231*) splicing joints illustrate further variations developed to create a sound construction when used in a particular situation.

Diagram 226 *Stop-splayed scarf with under-squinted and sallied butt, four face pegs and one face key.*

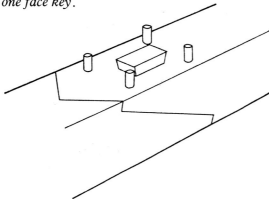

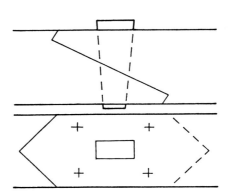

Diagram 227 *Fished scarf with face-housed fish piece and four edge pegs.*

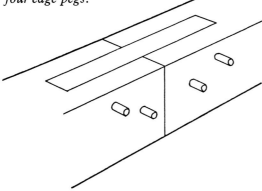

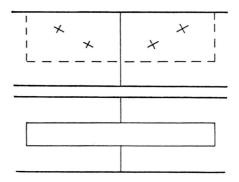

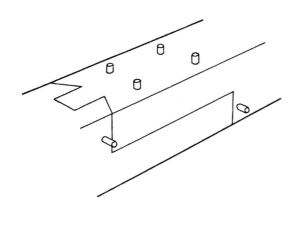

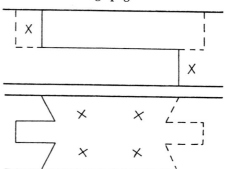

Diagram 228 *Edge-halved scarf with bird's-mouthed bridled butts, four face pegs and two edge pegs.*

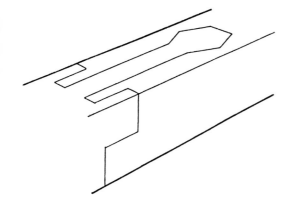

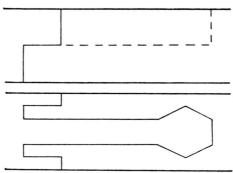

Diagram 229 Mechigai-koshikake-kama-tsugi *(lapped, gooseneck mortise and tenon joint with stub tenon).*

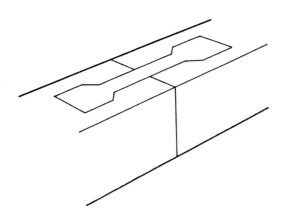

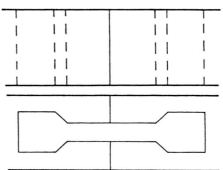

Diagram 230 Chigiri-tsugi *(inserted tenon joint).*

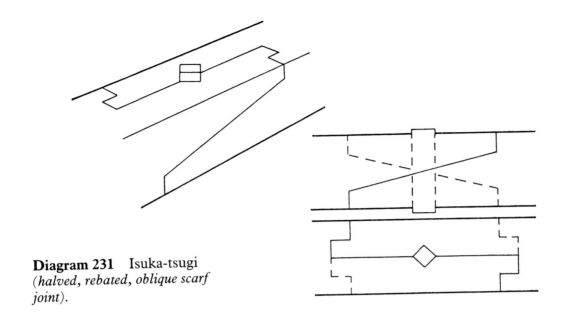

Diagram 231 Isuka-tsugi
(*halved, rebated, oblique scarf
joint*).

106

5 Miscellaneous Joints

Inevitably there are joints that do not come under any of the previous chapter headings, usually because they have been designed for specific, specialized situations.

JOINTS ALLOWING FOR EXPANSION AND CONTRACTION

Tenoned and mitred clamp

The problem of preventing warpage while allowing for expansion and contraction in a solid table top is usually overcome by using a tenoned and mitred clamp (*diagram 232*). This may not be ideal in every case because the mitre

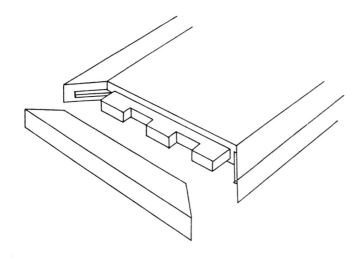

Diagram 232 *Tenoned and mitred clamp.*

will tend to open. The Greene brothers devised a method of overcoming this problem, using their familiar type of contrasting insert to create visual interest (*diagram 233* and *figure 35*).

When boards have been edge-jointed to make up the top, each end is planed square and a wide tenon formed. This

Diagram 233 *Alternative edge clamp devised by the Greene brothers.*

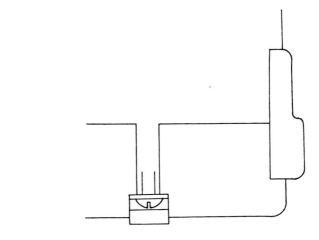

Figure 35 *Tenoned clamp with contrasting plugs.*

should be one-third the thickness of the boards with a length dependent on the size of top. A corresponding groove is cut into the clamp and placed in position (*diagram 234*).

On the outside edge of the clamp, a series of mortises are cut at regular intervals, depending on the width of board, to accept the round-headed screw and washer. This should

Diagram 234 *The wide tenon at the end of the board and the corresponding groove in the clamp.*

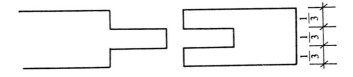

allow expansion and contraction to take place. The width of the through mortise is one-quarter of the clamp thickness, with the stopped mortise being as big again and symmetrical to it (*diagram 235*).

The clamp is left slightly longer than the width of the board, and a contrasting peg set into a mortise is used to cover the edge (*diagram 236*). This peg is glued into the main board but left dry on the clamp to allow for any necessary movement. Each mortise is plugged with the same type of contrasting material.

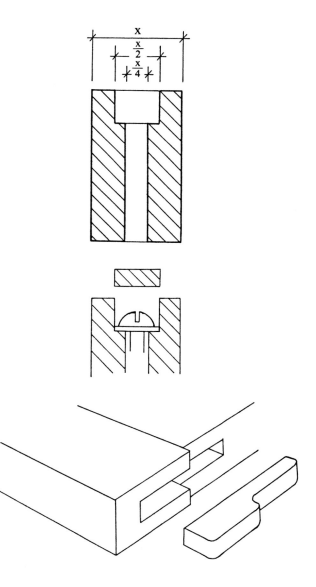

Diagram 235 *Sectional profile of the through and stopped mortises.*

Diagram 236 *Contrasting inserts are cut in the edge and end of the clamp.*

Mirror frame decorative joint

A similar type of joint used by the Greene brothers can be seen in a mirror frame and is more decorative than structural (*diagram 237* and *figure 36*). It is used in addition to a butt mortise and tenon, resisting any tendency to twist in the rail.

Diagram 237 *The decorative joint used in a mirror frame by the Greene brothers.*

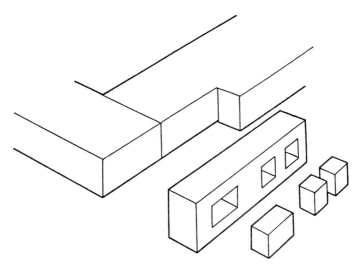

Figure 36 *Decorative joint used in a mirror frame.*

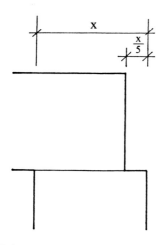

Diagram 238 *Proportions of adjacent rails.*

The frame is made in the same manner as a standard mortise and tenon frame, except that the length of tenon should be one-fifth the rail width. The overlapping rail is shorter than the outside dimension of the frame by two-fifths of its width (*diagram 238*). After gluing the frame together, extend the recess that accepts the contrasting slip into the adjoining rail (*diagram 239*).

To allow for expansion and contraction, the contrasting

110

slip should be glued and screwed to the side grain of one rail and slot screwed into the end grain of the other (*diagram 240*). All dimensions of the slip are made slightly larger than the recess and all protruding corners heavily rounded. The plugs that cover the screwheads can also be raised and rounded, if desired.

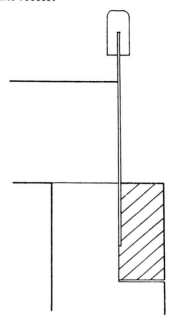

Diagram 239   *Sawcuts extend the recess.*

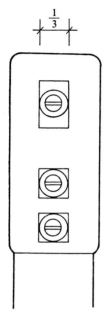

Diagram 240   *Position of each mortise that accepts the round-headed screw and washer.*

EDGE-JOINTING
Double dovetail (butterfly key) joint

If boards had to be edge jointed, the double dovetail or butterfly key was often used as a mechanical fastening to hold them together (*diagram 241* and *figure 37*). It is one of the oldest methods of construction, first developed for use in Egyptian boat-building.

Figure 37   *Double dovetail or butterfly key used when edge-jointing*

Diagram 241   *The double dovetail or butterfly key.*

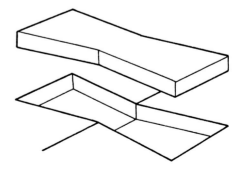

111

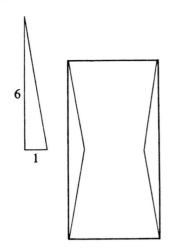

Diagram 242 *Profile of the key.*

A butterfly insert is cut with its grain running perpendicular to the boards, the length and width varying according to the size of boards being joined, and the maker's personal preference. Starting with a rectangular piece of timber approximately one-third the board's thickness, mark in the angles of the dovetail from the square end using a knife and sliding bevel (*diagram 242*). The waste is easily removed by sawing and trimming back to the lines with a paring chisel.

When the insert is complete, it is used as a template to mark out the recess with the internal 'V' lining up with the edge of the board (*diagram 243*). Sawcuts are made near the outline and across the width of waste which will assist timber removal (*diagram 244*). The recess is completed by removing the waste with the paring chisel and hand router.

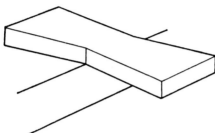

Diagram 243 *Using the key as a template.*

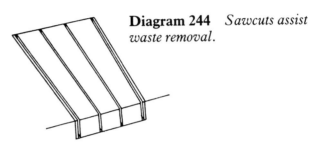

Diagram 244 *Sawcuts assist waste removal.*

When each key has been fitted into its respective recess, the boards can be assembled by applying glue to the edge and recess and cramping them together. Any protrusions should be planed flush after the glue has set.

Edge-jointing using contrasting dowel
An alternative method of employing a mechanical fastening when edge jointing boards uses a contrasting dowel to create visual interest (*diagram 245* and *figure 38*).

Diagram 245 *Edge joint using contrasting dowels and insert.*

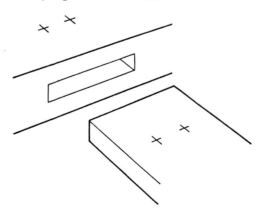

Figure 38 *Contrasting dowels used in the edge joint.*

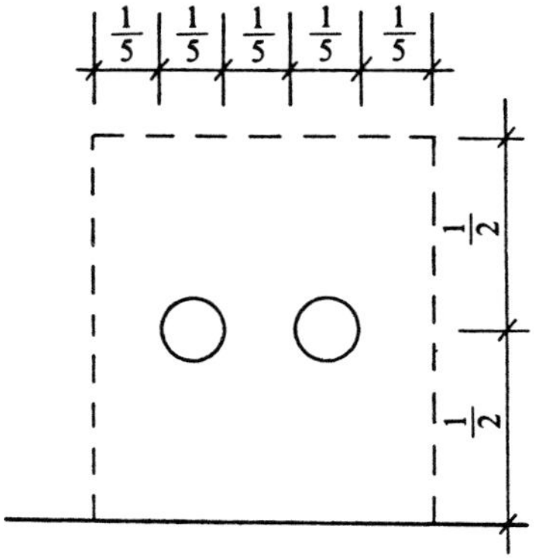

A series of mortises are cut on the edge of the boards, their size and number depending on the maker's preference. A spline is cut that gives a hand-push fit with a length that is slightly shorter than the combined depth of matching mortises. The space that this creates at the bottom of each mortise will take up any excess glue.

The dowels are positioned symmetrically across the width of the mortise (*diagram 246*) with waste timber being used to prevent timber break-out as the holes are cut. One end of the slip can then be pushed into the mortise and holes drilled in it, using those in the board as a guide. The dowels can then be driven in temporarily while the boards are pushed together to locate the remaining centres on the tenon. These should be slightly offset so as to draw the boards together when constructed (*diagram 247*).

Alternatively, a gap can be left between the boards to create further interest (*diagram 248* and *figure 39*). The

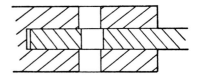

Diagram 246 *Position of dowels in relation to the insert.*

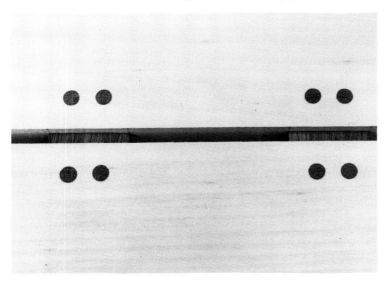

Diagram 247 *A staggered hole will draw the joint together as the dowel is driven in.*

Figure 39 *Contrasting dowels and spline with a gap between the boards.*

113

Diagram 248 *An alternative edge joint to diagram 245 creates a gap between the boards.*

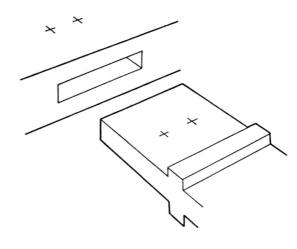

Diagram 249 *Proportions of contrasting insert.*

process of cutting is repeated with a shoulder being formed on the slip (*diagram 249*).

Shaker furniture

The search for perfection achieved in the simplistic forms of Shaker furniture is illustrated in the construction of the traditional oval box (*diagram 250* and *figure 40*). Visual interest centres around the joint which often varied in size depending on the box, but always used the same construction method.

Diagram 250 *The finger joint used in the traditional oval box produced by the Shakers.*

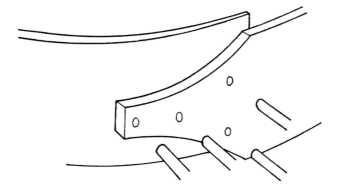

A broad band of timber (maple, cherry, etc.) usually about 3mm (⅛in.) thick was shaped at one end to form the fingers of the joint (*diagram 251*). A cardboard template should be made and used to mark in the outline on the timber. A coping saw is then used to remove most of the waste with trimming and chamfering done with the paring chisel. The opposite end of the timber is planed to a taper to prevent excessive thickness at the joint (*diagram 252*).

With all cutting done, the timber is steam bent around a pre-cut elliptical template. If more complex equipment is not available, simply hold the timber over the spout of a boiling kettle until the required flexibility is achieved. The projecting fingers can then be secured with copper rivets.

When the oval shape is set in position, discs of pine are fitted to create the top and bottom.

Figure 40 *Traditional oval box produced by the Shakers.*

Diagram 251 *Profile of the fingers.*

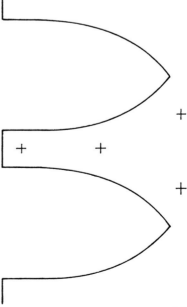

Diagram 252 *The opposite end of the strip of timber should be tapered to prevent thickness at the joint.*

115

Glossary

Bevel (sliding)   For measuring or marking any required angle

Boring   The process of cutting a cylindrical hole

Brace   A crank-shaped tool for holding and turning auger bits

Butt joint   Made by fastening together the ends or edges of two pieces of timber; the butt mitre uses two ends, each cut at 45°

C- or G-cramp   A fastening device shaped like the letter

Centre lines   Vertical or horizontal lines representing the centre of a symmetrical object

Chamfer   Bevelled edge or corner

Coping saw   A steel bow frame holding a narrow saw-blade

Groove   Channel or groove running with the grain

Housing   Channel or groove running across the grain

Jack plane   A general utility plane

Jig   A special device used for holding or guiding a tool

Kerf   The cut made by a saw

Laminate   To glue wood in layers; usually stronger than the original wood

Mortise   Usually a rectangular shaped hole cut into a piece of timber to accept another

Rebate or rabbet   Step-shaped reduction cut along timber's edge

Ryoba saw   Japanese-style saw that cuts on the pull

Sallying   To point or go forth

Smoothing plane   A short-soled plane used for final finishing

Splay   Divergent surface making oblique angle with another

Squinting   Oblique opening

Stickers   Thin strips of timber placed between boards to allow air to circulate

Taper   Narrowing gradually to one end

Template   A pattern or guide

Tenon   A projection cut on the end of a piece of timber which then fits into a mortise

Try-plane   Long-soled plane used for planing long square edges; a short version is called a fore-plane while the longer type is a jointer

Try-square   Used to check or mark a right angle

Veneer   Thin layer of timber

Vice   Used to secure timber while it is being worked

Index

Keys to Economic Prosperity

These keys to the economic prosperity of a nation are highlighted throughout the text.

1. **Human Ingenuity.** Economic goods are the result of human ingenuity and action; thus, the size of the economic pie is variable, not fixed. [Economics Chapter 2; Macroeconomics Chapter 2; Microeconomics Chapter 2]

2. **Private Ownership.** Private ownership provides people with a strong incentive to take care of things and develop resources in ways that are highly valued by others. [Economics Chapter 2; Macroeconomics Chapter 2; Microeconomics Chapter 2]

3. **Gains from Trade.** Trade makes it possible for individuals to generate more output through specialization and division of labor, large-scale production processes, and the dissemination of improved products and production methods. [Economics Chapter 2; Macroeconomics Chapter 2; Microeconomics Chapter 2]

4. **Invisible Hand Principle.** Market prices coordinate the actions of self-interested individuals and direct them toward activities that promote the general welfare. [Economics Chapter 3; Macroeconomics Chapter 3; Microeconomics Chapter 3]

5. **Profits and Losses.** Profits direct producers toward activities that increase the value of resources; losses impose a penalty on those who reduce the value of resources. [Economics Chapter 3; Macroeconomics Chapter 3; Microeconomics Chapter 3]

6. **Competition.** Competition motivates businesses to produce efficiently, cater to the views of consumers, and search for innovative improvements. [Economics Chapter 22; Microeconomics Chapter 9]

7. **Entrepreneurship.** The entrepreneurial discovery and development of improved products and production processes is a central element of economic progress. [Economics Chapter 23; Microeconomics Chapter 10]

8. **Productivity and Earnings.** In a market economy, productivity and earnings are closely linked. In order to earn a large income, one must provide large benefits to others. [Economics Chapter 26; Microeconomics Chapter 13]

9. **Innovation and the Capital Market.** If the potential gains from innovative ideas and human ingenuity are going to be fully realized, it must be relatively easy for individuals to try their innovative and potentially ingenious ideas, but difficult to continue if the idea is a bad one. [Economics Chapter 27; Microeconomics Chapter 14]

10. **Price Stability.** Maintenance of price stability is the essence of sound monetary policy; price stability provides the foundation for both economic stability and the efficient operation of markets. [Economics Chapter 15; Macroeconomics Chapter 15]

11. **International Trade.** When people are permitted to engage freely in international trade, they are able to achieve higher income levels and living standards than would otherwise be possible. [Economics Chapter 18; Macroeconomics Chapter 18; Microeconomics Chapter 16]

12. **Role of Government.** Governments promote economic progress when they protect individuals and their property, enforce contracts impartially, provide access to money of stable value, avoid high taxes and excessive regulation, and foster competitive markets and free international trade. [Economics Chapter 16; Macroeconomics Chapter 16]

MICROECONOMICS

PRIVATE AND PUBLIC CHOICE

FOURTEENTH EDITION

SOUTH-WESTERN
CENGAGE Learning

Australia • Brazil • Japan • Korea • Mexico • Singapore • Spain • United Kingdom • United States

MICROECONOMICS

PRIVATE AND PUBLIC CHOICE

FOURTEENTH EDITION

JAMES D. GWARTNEY
Florida State University

RICHARD L. STROUP
Montana State University

RUSSELL S. SOBEL
West Virginia University

DAVID A. MACPHERSON
Trinity University, San Antonio TX

SOUTH-WESTERN
CENGAGE Learning

Australia • Brazil • Japan • Korea • Mexico • Singapore • Spain • United Kingdom • United States

iStockphoto.com/sorendls

SOUTH-WESTERN
CENGAGE Learning

Microeconomics: Private and Public Choice,
Fourteenth Edition
James D. Gwartney
Richard L. Stroup
Russell S. Sobel
David A. Macpherson

Vice President of Editorial, Business:
Jack W. Calhoun

Editor-in-Chief: Joe Sabatino

Executive Editor: Michael Worls

Senior Acquisitions Editor: Steve Scoble

Senior Development Editor: Susanna C. Smart

Editorial Assistant: Allyn Bissmeyer

Senior Marketing Communications Manager:
Sarah Greber

Senior Marketing Manager: John Carey

Associate Marketing Manager: Betty Jung

Marketing Coordinator: Suellen Ruttkay

Director, Education Production: Barbara Fuller
Jacobsen

Content Project Manager: Emily Nesheim

Media Editor: Sharon Morgan

Manufacturing Planner: Kevin Kluck

Production Service: MPS, a Macmillan Company

Senior Art Director: Michelle Kunkler

Cover and Internal Designer: Stratton Design

Cover Images: iStockphoto.com/sorendls;
iStockphoto.com/nicoolay

Rights Acquisition Director: Audrey Pettengill

Senior Rights Acquisition Specialist (images):
Deanna Ettinger

Rights Acquisition Specialist (text):
Sam Marshall

For product information and technology assistance, contact us at
Cengage Learning Customer & Sales Support, 1-800-354-9706

For permission to use material from this text or product,
submit all requests online at **www.cengage.com/permissions**
Further permissions questions can be emailed to
permissionrequest@cengage.com

Exam*View*® is a registered trademark of eInstruction Corp. Windows is a registered trademark of the Microsoft Corporation used herein under license. Macintosh and Power Macintosh are registered trademarks of Apple Computer, Inc. used herein under license.
© 2013 Cengage Learning. All Rights Reserved.

Library of Congress Control Number: 2011943654

ISBN-13: 978-1-111-97061-1
ISBN-10: 1-111-97061-0

South-Western
5191 Natorp Boulevard
Mason, OH 45040
USA

Cengage Learning products are represented in Canada by Nelson Education, Ltd.

For your course and learning solutions, visit **www.cengage.com**

Purchase any of our products at your local college store or at our preferred online store **www.cengagebrain.com**

Printed in the United States of America
1 2 3 4 5 6 7 15 14 13 12 11

Brief Contents

Contents

RELATIONSHIP BETWEEN MAIN EDITION AND THE MACRO/MICRO EDITIONS

CHAPTERS

MACRO	MICRO	FULL LENGTH BOOK MACRO— FIRST VERSION	FULL LENGTH BOOK MICRO— FIRST VERSION	
1	1	1	1	The Economic Approach
2	2	2	2	Some Tools of the Economist
3	3	3	3	Supply, Demand, and the Market Process
4	4	4	4	Supply and Demand: Applications and Extensions
5	5	5	5	Difficult Cases for the Market, and the Role of Government
6	6	6	6	The Economics of Collective Decision-Making
7		7	17	Taking the Nation's Economic Pulse
8		8	18	Economic Fluctuations, Unemployment, and Inflation
9		9	19	An Introduction to Basic Macroeconomic Markets
10		10	20	Dynamic Change, Economic Fluctuations, and the AD–AS Model
11		11	21	Fiscal Policy: The Keynesian View and Historical Perspective
12		12	22	Fiscal Policy, Incentives, and Secondary Effects
13		13	23	Money and the Banking System
14		14	24	Modern Macroeconomics and Monetary Policy
15		15	25	Stabilization Policy, Output, and Employment
16		16	26	Creating an Environment for Growth and Prosperity
17		17	27	Institutions, Policies, and Cross-Country Differences in Income and Growth
18	16	18	16	Gaining from International Trade
19		19	28	International Finance and the Foreign Exchange Market
	7	20	7	Consumer Choice and Elasticity
	8	21	8	Costs and the Supply of Goods
	9	22	9	Price Takers and the Competitive Process
	10	23	10	Price-Searcher Markets with Low Entry Barriers
	11	24	11	Price-Searcher Markets with High Entry Barriers
	12	25	12	The Supply of and Demand for Productive Resources
	13	26	13	Earnings, Productivity, and the Job Market
	14	27	14	Investment, the Capital Market, and the Wealth of Nations
	15	28	15	Income Inequality and Poverty

SPECIAL TOPICS

Core Topic	Topic Title	Macro Topic	Micro Topic
1	Government Spending and Taxation	1	1
2	The Economics of Social Security	2	2
3	The Stock Market: Its Function, Performance, and Potential as an Investment Opportunity	3	3
4	Great Debates in Economics: Keynes versus Hayek	4	4
5	The Crisis of 2008: Causes and Lessons for the Future	5	5
6	Lessons from the Great Depression	6	6
7	Lessons from Japan and Canada	7	
8	The Federal Budget and the National Debt	8	
9	The Economics of Health Care		7
10	Educations: Problems and Performance		8
11	Earnings Differences Between Men and Women		9
12	Do Labor Unions Increase the Wages of Workers?		10
13	The Question of Resource Exhaustion		11
14	Difficult Environmental Cases and the Role of Government		12

Preface

The lives of most of us have been affected by the recent troubles of the U.S. economy. What led to these difficulties? Has the political response saved us from economic catastrophe, or has it made matters worse? What can we learn from other countries that have experienced similar conditions in the past? These are vitally important questions that are on the minds of our students. This text addresses all of them and provides both economic analysis and empirical evidence that will enhance the understanding of these critical issues.

Throughout the life of this text, our goal has been to use the tools of economics to explain how the real world works and to do so in a clear and understandable manner. Perhaps more than ever before, students are seeking to understand the world in which they live and the critical issues we confront. Indeed, this is a teachable moment for economics instructors. This thought was constantly on our minds as we revised this edition.

ORGANIZATION OF THE TEXT AND INSTRUCTOR FLEXIBILITY

The organization of *Economics: Private and Public Choice* is designed to provide instructors with maximum flexibility. Those using the full-length text for a two-semester course can cover either microeconomics or macroeconomics first. As in recent editions, the text is divided into core chapters and a concluding special topics section. The 28 core chapters cover all of the material taught in most principles courses, and they are presented in the usual manner. Examples and data from the real world are used to reinforce the analysis. In addition, Beyond the Basics includes 14 relatively short special topic applications on high-profile topics such as Social Security, the Crisis of 2008, the budget deficits and growth of government debt, and the economics of health care. Also included in this section are Applications that address questions such as, "Is discrimination responsible for the earnings differences between men and women?" and "Are we running out of resources?" These features are sure to grab the interest of students and are short enough for coverage during a single class period. Our own teaching experience indicates that these applications will enrich an economics course. They will also make it easier for instructors to "pick and choose" and thereby tailor the text readings to fit their own preferences and objectives.

Instructors integrating public choice throughout their course will probably want to cover Chapters 5 and 6 before moving to the core micro or macro material. Others teaching a microeconomics course will want to jump from Chapter 4 directly to the core micro chapters. Correspondingly, some macroeconomics instructors will want to move directly from Chapter 3 or 4 to the core macro material. The chapters have been written so there will be no problem with any of these options.

The text is accompanied by a robust set of online learning tools designed to support your classroom work and an Aplia component that includes real-time, interactive tutorials, online experiments, and automatically graded problem sets. Likewise, the book's dynamic PowerPoint presentation—considered by many to be the best in the principles market—has been further enhanced with multimedia to facilitate your teaching.

CHANGES IN THIS EDITION

Substantial changes in both conditions and policies have occurred in recent years. These changes are reflected fully in this edition. Macroeconomic issues have been front-page news during the past several years, and the debate on the impact of fiscal and monetary policy, growth of government debt, and what can be done to speed recovery from recession is sure to continue in the years immediately ahead. The core macroeconomic material is organized in a manner that will make it easier to understand current issues and controversies.

Economists are not of one mind with regard to fiscal policy, and the core macroeconomic chapters reflect this view. Chapter 11 presents the Keynesian view of fiscal policy and considers its historical development and evolutionary change during recent decades. Chapter 12 presents alternative perspectives that highlight the importance of incentives and secondary effects. Chapter 12 also addresses the "great debates" about the effectiveness of fiscal stimulus and the potential dangers accompanying the growth of government debt. Taken together, these two fiscal policy chapters bring today's news alive and provide a balanced comprehensive analysis of the modern debate about the potential and limitations of fiscal policy.

Chapter 13 on money and banking has been updated to reflect both the recent changes in how the Federal Reserve controls the money supply and the response of the Fed to the financial crisis and severe recession of 2008–2009. Chapter 14 analyzes the impact of monetary policy and its potential and limitations as a stabilization tool. A new feature on the Austrian view of the business cycle is also integrated into this chapter.

Chapter 15 on stabilization policy highlights both points of agreement and areas of continuing debate regarding the impact of macroeconomic policy. This chapter also contains a new section comparing the two most severe recessions of the post–World War II era: the current one and the 1982 recession. Both the policy response and the strength of the recoveries from these two severe recessions are analyzed.

The last two chapters of the core macro focus on economic growth. They highlight the importance of trade, entrepreneurship and innovation, and investment as sources of growth. Building on the work of Douglass North, Joseph Schumpeter, William Baumol, and Daron Acemoglu, these chapters focus on the institutional foundations of growth and prosperity.

Several changes were made in the Beyond the Basics special topics that will help you make economics come alive for your students. We have added a new Special Topic 4, Great Debates in Economics: Keynes versus Hayek. This special topic, developed around the highly popular video raps on the Keynes–Hayek debates, is designed to highlight the alternative views of economists on major issues and to show that the study of economics can be fun. Special Topic 1 on government spending and taxation has a new section that provides data on recent trends in the share of the population receiving benefits and paying taxes and examines their implications for the future of democracy. Special Topic 5 focuses on the policies and choices underlying the financial crisis of 2008. Special Topic 6 on the Great Depression analyzes the economics of this catastrophic era in a manner that is seldom presented in American history classes. Special Topic 7 on lessons from Japan and Canada considers the experiences of these two countries during the 1990s and their different responses to conditions similar to those currently confronted by the United States. Special Topic 8 on federal deficits and the national debt has a new section on the interaction between political incentives and the growth of government debt that examines what will happen if the federal debt continues to grow. This package of applications provides instructors with powerful materials with which to address the current economic difficulties and their future implications.

If you have not integrated the special topic materials into your course, please consider doing so. They will help your students better understand the political economy debates that dominate the daily news of our world.

We worked hard to reduce the length of this edition. The word count is approximately 10 percent less than the 13th edition. We deleted a number of the addendums that were included last time. However, they have been updated in the format of this edition and are available on the open access student Web site. These include the following: Understanding Graphs (addendum to Chapter 1); Incentives and Economic Organization: Who Produces, Who Pays, and Why It Matters (addendum to Chapter 6); the Keynesian Aggregate Expenditure Model (addendum to Chapter 11); and Consumer Choice and Indifference Curves (addendum to Chapter 20). These materials are freely available to students on the open access Web site for the text. Thus, instructors can freely assign them if they would like to do so.

ADDITIONAL TEXT FEATURES

Economics: Private and Public Choice retains several features that make the presentation of economics both more interesting and understandable.

- Keys to Economic Prosperity. Students often fail to appreciate the organizational and institutional factors that are the foundation for economic progress. To help remedy this situation, we have incorporated a "Keys to Economic Prosperity" feature that highlights the importance of factors like gains from trade, secure property rights, competition, and free trade as sources of economic prosperity. In all, 12 key factors that underlie modern economic prosperity are highlighted at appropriate places throughout the text and are also listed inside of the front cover.
- Applications in Economics. "Applications in Economics" boxes apply economic theory to real-world issues and controversies. These features illustrate the importance and power of the principles covered in the text.
- Measures of Economic Activity. The "Measures of Economic Activity" boxes explain how important economic indicators such as the unemployment rate and the index of leading indicators are assembled and what they mean.
- Outstanding Economists. Boxes throughout the text highlight the lives of major economists and focus on how their work has contributed to the development of economics.
- Myths of Economics. These boxed articles dispel commonly held fallacies of economic reasoning. Because they are tomorrow's leaders, we believe that all students should be aware of common economic misperceptions that tend to hamper a nation's economic progress.
- Chapter Focus Questions and Closing Key Point Summaries. Each chapter begins with four or five questions that summarize the focus of the chapter. At the end of each chapter, the Key Points section provides the student with a concise statement of the material covered in the chapter (the chapter learning objectives). These two features help students better integrate the material into the broader economic picture.
- Critical Analysis Questions. Each chapter concludes with a set of discussion questions and problems designed to test the student's ability to analyze economic issues and to apply economic theory to real-world events. Appendix B at the end of the text contains suggested answers for approximately half of these questions.

SUPPLEMENTARY MATERIALS

FOR THE STUDENT

Coursebooks The Coursebooks for this edition were prepared by our co-author Russell Sobel and are now available in three versions covering all three courses: economics, microeconomics, and macroeconomics. The Coursebooks are more than study guides. Each includes numerous multiple-choice, true–false, and discussion questions to help students self-test their knowledge of each chapter. Answers and short explanations for most questions are provided in the back of the Coursebooks. Each chapter also contains problem and project exercises designed to improve the student's knowledge of the mechanics. Like the textbook, the Coursebooks are designed to help students develop the economic way of thinking.

Product Support Web Site (www.cengagebrain.com) Valuable resources can be found on the text's Internet support site. Students will find an interactive study center as well as online practice quizzes.

Economic News Videos News video segments from the BBC deliver the "real world" right to students' desktops, giving students a context for how economic topics affect world and national events as well as their own daily lives and helping them learn material by applying it to current events.

Tomlinson Learning Path Videos The Tomlinson videos are an online multimedia video lecture series that provides students with instructional assistance 24/7. Students can watch these segments over and over as they prepare for class, review topics, and study for exams. Lecture notes and quizzes for each segment are also available. Professors may require students to view the videos before class to leave the class time free for activities or further explanation.

FOR THE INSTRUCTOR

We feel sure that many of the features incorporated with this textbook will help you become a better teacher and make your classes more interesting to students. Personally, we have incorporated the Keys to Economic Prosperity series, economics video clips, homework assignments, and online quiz questions into our own classes with great success. The full set of supplements that can accompany the book include the following.

Aplia Aplia™ is an online interactive learning solution that improves comprehension and outcomes by increasing student effort and engagement. Founded by a professor to enhance his own courses, Aplia provides automatically graded assignments that were written to make the most of the Web medium and contain detailed, immediate explanations on every question. Aplia is available in more than 15 disciplines and has been used by more than 2 million students at more than 1800 institutions. Visit www.cengage.com/coursemaster for more details.

Economics CourseMate: Engaging, Trackable, Affordable Economics CourseMate brings course concepts to life with interactive learning, study, and exam preparation tools that support the printed textbook. Watch student comprehension soar as your class works with the printed textbook and the text-specific Web site, Economics CourseMate goes beyond the book to deliver what you need!

Engagement Tracker How do you know your students have read the material or viewed the resources you've assigned? How can you tell if your students are struggling with a concept? Engagement Tracker assesses student preparation and engagement. Use the tracking tools to see progress for the class as a whole or for individual students. Identify students at risk early in the course. Uncover which concepts are most difficult for your class. Monitor time on task. Keep your students engaged.

Interactive Teaching and Learning Tools Economics CourseMate includes interactive teaching and learning tools:

- Quizzes
- Flashcards
- Videos
- Graphing tutorials
- News, debates, and data

Interactive eBook In addition to interactive teaching and learning tools, Economics CourseMate includes an interactive eBook. Students can take notes, highlight, search and interact with embedded media specific to their book. Use it as a supplement to the printed text, or as a substitute—the choice is up to your students with CourseMate. Go to **login .cengage.com** to access these resources within CourseMate.

CengageNOW Ensure that your students have the understanding they need of procedures and concepts they need to know with CengageNOW. This integrated, online course management and learning system combines the best of current technology to save to time in planning and managing your course and assignments. You can reinforce comprehension with customized student learning paths and efficiently test and automatically grade assignments with reports that correspond to AACSB standards. For your convenience, CengageNOW is also compatible with WebCT® and Blackboard®. For more information, visit **cengage.com/cengagenow**.

WebTutor™ ToolBox for WebCT, Blackboard, and eCollege WebTutor will allow you to jumpstart your course whether you want to simply Web enable your class or put an entire course online. Using a WebTutor cartridge, it's easy to add, edit, reorganize, or delete content customized for *Economics: Private and Public Choice*. The content includes media assets, quizzing, Web links, discussion topics, interactive games and exercises, and more. To find out more about WebTutor, contact your local South-Western representative. (Other platform choices are available on request.)

Test Banks The test banks for the 14th edition were prepared by the author team with the assistance of Joe Calhoun. The authors have worked hard to update and improve the test banks for this edition. The two test banks contain approximately 7,000 questions—multiple-choice and short answer. Within each chapter, the questions correspond to the major subheadings of the text. The first 10 questions of each chapter are suitable for use as a comprehensive quiz covering the material of the chapter. The multiple-choice questions from the Coursebook and online practice quizzes are also included in special sections of the test bank. Instructors who would like to motivate their students to study the Coursebook and online practice quizzes can easily use these questions and incorporate them into their quizzes and exams.

Computerized Test Banks (ExamView®) The computerized test banks for this edition have been enhanced significantly. ExamView contains all of the questions in the printed test bank so you create and customize tests in minutes. You can easily edit and import your own questions and graphics and edit and maneuver existing questions. You can also use ExamView to test and grade online.

PowerPoint We believe our PowerPoint presentation, prepared by Charles Skipton of the University of Tampa, is the best you will find in the principles market. The presentation includes chapter-by-chapter lecture notes with fully animated, hyperlinked slides of the textbook's exhibits. Its dynamic graphs and accompanying captions make it easy for instructors to present (and students to follow) sequential changes. The graphs are also used to highlight various relationships among economic variables. To facilitate classroom discussion and interaction, questions are strategically interspersed throughout the PowerPoint slides to help students develop the economic way of thinking. Instructions explaining how professors can easily add, delete, and modify slides in order to tailor make the presentation to their liking are included. If instructors want to make the PowerPoint presentation available to students, they can place it on their Web site (or the site for their course).

Instructor's Manual and Instructor's Resource CD The *Instructor's Manual* was prepared by co-author David Macpherson. It contains special sections for Advanced Placement instructors prepared by James Chasey and Francis McMann, two of the nation's leading AP instructors. Information on how to use and modify the PowerPoint material is contained in the front of the instructor's manual. Also included at the front of the manual is information about Examview, the computerized testing software that accompanies the book. The manual is divided by chapters, and each chapter is divided into three parts. The first part consists of a detailed chapter outline in lecture-note form. It is designed to help instructors organize their notes to match the 14th edition of the book. Instructors can easily prepare detailed, personalized notes by revising the computerized version of the lecture notes on the *Instructor's Resource CD*. The second part of each chapter contains teaching tips, sources of supplementary materials, and other helpful information. Part 3 of each chapter consists of in-class economic games and experiments. Contributed in part by Professor Charles Stull of Kalamazoo College, the games are highly popular with many instructors. We hope you will try them.

The *Instructor's Resource CD* contains the key supplements designed to aid instructors, including the content from the instructor's manual, test banks, and PowerPoint lecture and exhibit slides for overhead use.

Support Web site for Instructors (www.cengage.com/economics/gwartney) This password-protected Web site includes some of the same essential resources that can be found on the *Instructor's Resource CD*, including instructor's manuals and test banks in Microsoft Word, and the PowerPoint lecture and exhibit slides. To access the site to download these supplements, register online at **www.cengage.com/economics/gwartney**.

A NOTE TO INSTRUCTORS

As we try to improve the book from one edition to the next, we rely heavily on our experiences as teachers. But our experience using the book is minuscule compared with that of the hundreds of instructors who use it nationwide. If you encounter problems or have suggestions for improving the book, we urge you to let us know by writing to us in care of Cengage South-Western, 5191 Natorp Blvd., Mason, OH 45040.

A NOTE TO STUDENTS

This textbook contains several features we think will help you *maximize* (a good economic term) the returns of your study efforts. Here are some of the things that will help you and a few tips for making the most of them.

- Each chapter begins with a series of focus questions that communicate the central issues of the chapter. Before you read the chapter, briefly think about the focus questions, why they are important, and how they relate to the material in prior chapters.
- The textbook is organized in the form of an outline. The headings within the text (in green) are the major points of the outline. Minor headings are subpoints under the major headings. In addition, important subpoints within sections are often set off and numbered. **Bold italicized** type is used to highlight material that is particularly important. Sometimes "thumbnail sketches" are included to recap material and help the reader keep the important points mentally organized. Careful use of the headings, highlighted material, and the thumbnail sketches will help you master the material.
- A "Key Points" summary appears at the end of each chapter. Use the summary as a checklist to determine whether you understand the major points of the chapter.
- A review of the exhibits and illustrative pictures will also provide you with a summary of the key points of each chapter. The accompanying captions briefly describe the economic phenomena illustrated by the exhibits.
- The key terms introduced in each chapter are defined in the margins. As you study the chapter, go over the marginal definition of each key term as it is introduced. Later, you may also find it useful to review the marginal definitions. If you have forgotten the meaning of a term introduced earlier, consult the glossary at the end of the book.
- The boxed features go into more depth on various topics without disrupting the flow of the text. In general, the topics of the boxed features have been chosen because they are a good application of the theory described in the book or because students tend to be interested in them. The boxed features will supplement the text and enhance your understanding of important economic concepts.
- The critical analysis questions at the end of each chapter are intended to test your understanding of the economic way of thinking. Solving these questions and problems will greatly enhance your knowledge of the material. Answers to approximately half of these questions are provided in Appendix B.

If you need more practice, be sure to obtain a Coursebook and solve the questions and problems for each chapter. The Coursebook also contains the answers to the multiple-choice questions and a brief explanation of why an answer is correct (and other choices incorrect). In most cases, if you master the concepts of the test items in the Coursebook, you will do well on the quizzes and examinations of your instructor. For extra help, in addition to the Coursebook, visit the book's student support Web site **www.cengagebrain.com** for online quizzes and other tutorials.

ACKNOWLEDGMENTS

A project of this type is a team effort. Through the years, numerous people have assisted us in various ways. We are also very much indebted to the excellent team of professionals at South-Western, including Steve Scoble, senior acquisitions editor, for his help and support of our efforts; Susan Smart, senior developmental editor, for her commitment to the development of the project and keeping it on schedule; Emily Nesheim, content project manager, for orchestrating the copyediting, proofreading, and indexing; Deanna Ettinger, senior rights editor, who helped us locate and obtain permissions for the many photos; and John Carey, marketing manager, who worked hard to inform the marketplace about the advantages of the book.

As with previous editions, the contributions of Amy Gwartney were invaluable. She edited several chapters prior to their submission to the publisher and proofed every page of the text. Joab Corey, Joe Connors, Joe Calhoun, and Tawni Ferrarini provided us with valuable suggestions for improvement of the text and assistance with supplementary materials. Daniel Bennett of Florida State University provided us with research assistance. James Chasey and Francis McMann provided valuable suggestions and handled the parts of the Instructor's Manual designed for those teaching the Advance Placement macroeconomics and microeconomics courses. Robert Lawson of Southern Methodist University assisted us with the preparation of several exhibits. The text still bears an imprint of the contributions of Woody Studenmund of Occidental College and Gary Galles of Pepperdine University, who assisted us in numerous ways with past editions.

Many instructors made important contributions to the 14th edition by providing us with insightful critical reviews. The following reviewers helped us improve this edition immensely, and we thank them for their comments:

Barbara Moore, University of Central Florida; Thomas McCaleb, Florida State University; Seth Gershenson, Michigan State University: Gerry Simons, Grand Valley State University; Aaron Lowen, Grand Valley State University; Pete Calcagno, College of Charleston; Joseph Calhoun, Florida State University; Cathy Carey, Bowling Green University; Lee Coppock, University of Virginia; Tawni Ferrerini, Northern Michigan University; Burton Folsom, Hillsdale College; Robert Higgs, Independent Institute; Randall Holcombe, Florida State University; and Ivan Pongracic, Hillsdale College.

We have often revised material in light of suggestions made by reviewers, users, friends, and even a few competitors. In this regard, we would like to express our appreciation to the following people for their reviews and helpful suggestions for recent editions:

Steve Abid, Grand Rapids Community College; Douglas Agbetsiafa, Indiana University, South Bend; James C. W. Ahiakpor, California State University, Hayward; Ali T. Akarca, University of Illinois at Chicago; Ryan C. Amacher, University of Texas at Arlington; Stephen A. Baker, Capital University; Bharati Basu, Central Michigan University; Don Bellante, University of South Florida; Alana Bhatia, University of Colorado at Boulder; Charles A. Booth, University of Alabama at Birmingham; Donald Boudreaux, George Mason University; George Bowling, St. Charles Community College; Robert Brittingham, Christian Brothers University; Byron Brown, Michigan State University; Ford J. Brown, University of Minnesota—Morris; Dennis Brennen, Harper College; James Bryan, Manhattanville College; Darcy R. Carr, Coastal Carolina University; Kathy Clark, Edison College; Jim Cobbe, Florida State University; Mike Cohick, Collin County Community College; David S. Collins, Virginia Highlands Community College; Jim F. Couch, University of North Alabama; Steven R. Cunningham, University of Connecticut; Dusan Curcic, University of Virginia; George W. Dollar, Clearwater Christian College; Jeff Edwards, Collin County Community College; Ann Eike, University of Kentucky; Christina Esquivel, Navarro College; Robert C. Eyler, Sonoma State University; James R. Fain, Oklahoma State University; Kathryn Finn, Western Washington University; Andrew W. Foshee, McNeese State University; Mark Funk, University of Arkansas; Gary Galles, Pepperdine

University; Marsha Goldfarb, University of Maryland Baltimore County; Richard Gosselin, Houston Community College; Darrin Gulla, University of Kentucky; David Harris, Northwood University; Barry Haworth, University of Louisville; Ronald Helgens, Golden Gate University; Robert E. Herman, Nassau Community College/SUNY; William D. Hermann, Golden Gate University, San Francisco; Rey Hernandez, Metropolitan State College of Denver; Brad Hobbs, Florida Gulf Coast University; Randall Holcombe, Florida State University; Jim Hubert, Seattle Central Community College; Katherine Huger, Charleston Southern University; Woodrow W. Hughes, Jr., Converse College; Jeffrey Rogers Hummel, San Jose State University; Tom Jeitschko, Michigan State University, East Lansing; Rob H. Kamery, Christian Brothers University; Derek Kellenberg, University of Montana; Robert Kling, Colorado State University; Frederic R. Kolb, University of Wisconsin, Eau Claire; Barbara Kouskoulas, Lawrence Technological University; David W. Kreutzer, James Madison University; Cory Krupp, Duke University; Jean Kujawa, Lourdes College; George Kuljurgis, Oakland University; Randy W. LaHote, Washtenaw Community College; TsungHui Lai, Liberty University; John Larrivee, Mount St. Mary's University; Robert Lawson, Southern Methodist University; Don R. Leet, California State University, Fresno; George P. Lephardt, Milwaukee School of Engineering; Joe LeVesque, Northwood University; Andrew Light, Liberty University; Stephen Lile, Western Kentucky University; Felix Ling (formerly San Jose State University); Edward J. López, San Jose State University; Dale Matcheck, Northwood University; G. Dirk Mateer, Penn State University; John McArthur, Wofford College; Ed Mills, Kendell College; David M. Mitchell, Oklahoma State University; Hadley Mitchell, Taylor University; Glen A. Moots, Northwood University; Debasri Mukherjee, Western Michigan University; Todd Myers, Grossmont College; John R. Neal, Lake Sumter Community College; Jennifer Offenberg, Loyola Marymount University; Lloyd Orr, Indiana University, Bloomington; Judd W. Patton, Bellevue College; James Payne, Florida State University; Robert Pennington, UCF–Orlando; Claudiney Pereira, Tulane University; Jennifer Platania, Elon University; Robert Reinke, University of South Dakota; Robert C. Rencher, Jr., Liberty University; Dan Rickman, Oklahoma State University; Karin L. Russell, Keiser College; Allen Sanderson, University of Chicago; Lewis F. Schlossinger, Community College of Aurora; Thomas W. Secrest, USC Coastal Carolina; Tim Shaugnessey, Louisiana State University–Shreveport; Ben S. Shippen, Jr., Mercer University; Gerald Simons, Grand Valley State University; Charles D. Skipton, University of Tampa; John Solow, University of Iowa; Ken Somppi, Southern Union State Community College; John Sophocleus, Auburn; William A. Steiden, Jefferson Community College; Edward Stringham, San Jose State University; Marcia Snyder, College of Charleston; David Switzer, St. Cloud State University; Richard D.C. Trainer, Warsaw School of Economics; Bich Tran, San Jacinto College; Scott Ward, East Texas Baptist University; Tom Lee Waterston, Northwood University; Christopher Westley, Jacksonville State University; David Wharton, Washington College; Jim Wharton, Northwood University; Mark Wheeler, Western Michigan University; Janice Yee, Wartburg College; Edward Wolpert, University of Central Florida; and Anthony Zambelli, Cuyamaca College.

About the Authors

James D. Gwartney holds the Gus A. Stavros Eminent Scholar Chair at Florida State University, where he directs the Stavros Center for the Advancement of Free Enterprise and Economic Education. His writings have been widely published in both professional journals and popular media. He is the co-author of *Common Sense Economics: What Everyone Should Know About Wealth and Prosperity* (St. Martin's Press, 2010), a primer on economics and personal finance. His current research focuses on the measurement and determination of factors that influence cross-country differences in income levels and growth rates. In this regard he is the co-author (with Robert Lawson) of the annual report, *Economic Freedom of the World*, which provides information on the institutions and policies of 141 countries. This data set, published by a worldwide network of institutes in 79 countries, is widely used by scholars investigating topics ranging from economic growth to peaceful relations among nations. He served as Chief Economist of the Joint Economic Committee of the U.S. Congress during 1999–2000. Gwartney was invited by the incoming Putin Administration in March 2000 to make presentations and have discussions with leading Russian economists concerning the future of the Russian economy. In 2004, he was the recipient of the Adam Smith Award of the Association of Private Enterprise Education for his contribution to the advancement of free market ideals. He is a past President of the Southern Economic Association and the Association for Private Enterprise Education. His PhD in economics is from the University of Washington.

Richard L. Stroup is Professor of Economics Emeritus at Montana State University, as well as a Senior Fellow at the Property and Environment Research Center (PERC) and a Visiting Professor in Economics at North Carolina State University. For the three years before his retirement from Montana State University, he served as head of its Department of Agricultural Economics & Economics. Professor Stroup, who has a PhD in economics from the University of Washington, was one of the originators of the New Resource Economics, the academic approach popularly known as free market environmentalism. He also served as director of the Office of Policy Analysis in the U.S. Department of the Interior and has been published widely in professional journals and popular publications. He is author or contributing editor of numerous books on the economics of resources and the environment and the author of *Economics: What Everyone Should Know about Economics and the Environment* (Cato Institute). Most recently, he co-authored *Common Sense Economics: What Everyone Should Know about Wealth and Prosperity* (St. Martin's Press, 2005) with James Gwartney and Dwight Lee. Stroup has lectured throughout the United States and abroad to professional and general audiences. He also is an adjunct scholar with the Cato Institute.

Russell S. Sobel is Professor of Economics and holder of the James Clark Coffman Distinguished Chair in Entrepreneurial Studies at West Virginia University. He received his PhD in economics from Florida State University in 1994. He has published over 150 books and articles, and has received national recognition for his works on Entrepreneurship and FEMA reform. Sobel was the founding Director of the West Virginia University Entrepreneurship Center, and he serves on the advisory boards of four major professional and academic organizations. He has received numerous awards for both his teaching and research. He regularly teaches courses in both principles of economics and public economics, and gives lectures at economic education outreach programs.

David A. Macpherson is the E.M. Stevens Professor of Economics at Trinity University. Previously, he was Director of the Pepper Institute on Aging and Public Policy and the Rod and Hope Brim Eminent Scholar of Economics at Florida State University, where he has received two university-wide awards for teaching excellence. Professor Macpherson is the author of many articles in leading labor economics and industrial relations journals, including the *Journal of Labor Economics, Journal of Human Resources,* and *Industrial and Labor Relations Review.* He is also co-author of *Contemporary Labor Economics,* 9th edition, as well as the annual *Union Membership and Earnings Data Book: Compilations from the Current Population Survey.* His specialty is applied labor economics. His current research interests include pensions, discrimination, labor unions, and the minimum wage. He received his undergraduate degree and PhD from the Pennsylvania State University.

The Economic Way of Thinking

Economics is about how people choose. The choices we make influence our lives and those of others. Your future will be influenced by the choices you make with regard to education, job opportunities, savings, and investment. Furthermore, changes in technology, demographics, communications, and transportation are constantly altering the attractiveness of various options and the opportunities available to us. The economic way of thinking is all about how incentives alter the choices people make. It can help you make better choices and enhance your understanding of our dynamic world.

PART

1

Life is a series of choices

The Economic Approach

CHAPTER FOCUS

- What is scarcity, and why is it important even in relatively wealthy economies?
- How does scarcity differ from poverty? Why does scarcity necessitate rationing and cause competition?
- What is the economic way of thinking? What is different about the way economists look at choices and human decision-making?
- What is the difference between positive and normative economics?

iStockphoto.com/sorendls

Economist, n.–A scoundrel whose faulty vision sees things as they really are, not as they ought to be.

—Daniel K. Benjamin, after Ambrose Bierce

Welcome to the world of economics. Lately there has been a lot about the economy in the news. The recent recession and high rates of unemployment have affected us all. The lives of many Americans were turned upside down by the boom and bust in housing prices and the soaring foreclosure rates that followed. Unrest in the Middle East; soaring prices of commodities like corn, wheat, and gasoline; and the rising cost of higher education: Economics will enhance your understanding of all of these topics and many more. You will soon see that economics is about much more than just financial markets and economic policy. In fact, a field trip to the fruits and vegetables section at your local grocery store could well be filled with more economics lessons than a trip to the New York Stock Exchange.

In a nutshell, economics is the study of human behavior, with a particular focus on human decision-making. It will introduce you to a new and powerful way of thinking that will both help you make better decisions and enhance your understanding of how the world works.

You may have heard some of the following statements: The federal government's debt is growing rapidly, and we need to get it under control. Without additional government stimulus, recovery from the recession will be slow. Gas prices are so high that the government should regulate them. Americans would be better off if we did not buy so many things from foreigners. A higher minimum wage will help the poor. Health care should be freely available to everyone. Are these statements true? This course will provide you with knowledge that will enhance your understanding of issues like these and numerous others. It may even alter the way you think about them.

The origins of economics date back to Adam Smith, a Scottish moral philosopher, who expressed the first economic ideas in his breakthrough book, *An Inquiry into the Nature and Causes of the Wealth of Nations,* published in 1776. As the title of his book suggests, Smith sought to explain why people in some nations were wealthier than those in others. This very question is still a central issue in economics. It is so important that throughout this book we will use a special "Keys to Economic Prosperity" symbol ⚷ in the margin to highlight sections that focus on this topic. A listing of the major keys to prosperity is presented inside the front cover of the book. These keys and accompanying discussions will help you understand what factors enable economies, and their citizens, to grow wealthier and prosper.

iStockphoto.com/nicoolay, Key: iStockphoto.com/Scott Dunlap

OUTSTANDING ECONOMIST

The Importance of Adam Smith, the Father of Economic Science

Economics is a relatively young science. The foundation of economics was laid in 1776, when Adam Smith (1723–1790) published *An Inquiry into the Nature and Causes of the Wealth of Nations.*

Smith was a lecturer at the University of Glasgow, in his native Scotland. Before economics, morals and ethics were actually his concern. His first book was *The Theory of Moral Sentiments.* For Smith, self-interest and sympathy for others were complementary. However, he did not believe that charity alone would provide the essentials for a good life.

Smith stressed that free exchange and competitive markets would harness self-interest as a creative force. He believed that individuals *pursuing their own interests* would be directed by the "invisible hand" of market prices toward the production of those goods that were most advantageous to society. He argued that the wealth of a nation does not lie in gold and silver, but rather in the goods and services produced and consumed by people. According to Smith, competitive markets would lead to coordination, order, and efficiency without the direction of a central authority.

These were revolutionary ideas at the time, but they had consequences. Smith's ideas greatly influenced not only Europeans but also those who developed the political economy structure of the United States. Further, Smith's notion of the "invisible hand" of the market continues to enhance our understanding of why some nations prosper while others stagnate.[1]

[1]For an excellent biographical sketch of Adam Smith, see David Henderson, ed., *The Fortune Encyclopedia of Economics* (New York: Warner Books, 1993), 836–38. The entire text of this useful encyclopedia is now available online, free of charge, at http://www.econlib.org.

© Bettmann/CORBIS

iStockphoto.com/sorendls

WHAT IS ECONOMICS ABOUT?

Economics is about scarcity and the choices we have to make because our desire for goods and services is far greater than their availability from nature. Would you like some new clothes, a nicer car, and a larger apartment? How about better grades and more time to watch television, go skiing, and travel? Do you dream of driving your brand-new Porsche into the driveway of your oceanfront house? As individuals, we have a desire for goods that is virtually unlimited. We may want all of these things. Unfortunately, both as individuals and as a society we face a constraint called scarcity that prevents us from being able to completely fulfill our desires.

Scarcity
Fundamental concept of economics that indicates that there is less of a good freely available from nature than people would like.

Scarcity is present whenever there is less of a good or resource freely available from nature than people would like. There are some things that are not scarce—seawater comes to mind; nature has provided as much of it as people want. But almost everything else you can think of—even your time—is scarce. In economics, the word *scarce* has a very specific meaning that differs slightly from the way it is commonly used. Even if large amounts of a good have been produced, it is still scarce as long as there is not as much of it *freely available from nature* as we would all like. For example, even though goods like apples and automobiles are relatively abundant in the United States, they are still scarce because we would like to have more of them than nature has freely provided. In economics, we generally wish to determine only if a good is scarce or not, and refrain from using the term to refer to the relative availability or abundance of a good or resource.

Choice
The act of selecting among alternatives.

Because of scarcity, we have to make choices. Should I spend the next hour studying or watching TV? Should I spend my last $20 on a new CD or on a shirt? Should this factory be used to produce clothing or furniture? Choice, the act of selecting among alternatives, is the logical consequence of scarcity. When we make choices, we constantly face trade-offs between meeting one desire or another. To meet one need, we must let another go unmet. The basic ideas of *scarcity* and *choice*, along with the *trade-offs* we face, provide the foundation for economic analysis.

Resource
An input used to produce economic goods. Land, labor, skills, natural resources, and human-made tools and equipment provide examples. Throughout history, people have struggled to transform available, but limited, resources into things they would like to have—economic goods.

Resources are the ingredients, or inputs, that people use to produce goods and services. Our ability to produce goods and services is limited precisely because of the limited nature of our resources.

Exhibit 1 lists a number of scarce goods and the limited resources that might be used to produce them. There are three general categories of resources. First, there are *human resources*—the productive knowledge, skill, and strength of human beings. Second, there are *physical resources*—things like tools, machines, and buildings that enhance our ability to produce goods. Economists often use the term capital when referring to these human-made resources. Third, there are *natural resources*—things like land, mineral deposits,

Capital
Human-made resources (such as tools, equipment, and structures) used to produce other goods and services. They enhance our ability to produce in the future.

Exhibit 1		
	SCARCE GOODS	**LIMITED RESOURCES**
A General Listing of Scarce Goods and Limited Resources History is a record of our struggle to transform available, but limited, resources into goods that we would like to have.	Food (bread, milk, meat, eggs, vegetables, coffee, etc.) Clothing (shirts, pants, blouses, shoes, socks, coats, sweaters, etc.) Household goods (tables, chairs, rugs, beds, dressers, television sets, etc.) Education National defense Leisure time Entertainment Clean air Pleasant environment (trees, lakes, rivers, open spaces, etc.) Pleasant working conditions	Land (various degrees of fertility) Natural resources (rivers, trees, minerals, oceans, etc.) Machines and other human-made physical resources Nonhuman animal resources Technology (physical and scientific "recipes" of history) Human resources (the knowledge, skill, and talent of individual human beings)

oceans, and rivers. The ingenuity of humans is often required to make these natural resources useful in production. For example, until recently, the yew tree was considered a "trash tree," having no economic value. Then, scientists discovered that the tree produces taxol, a substance that could be used to fight cancer. Human knowledge and ingenuity made yew trees a valuable resource. As you can see, natural resources are important, but knowing how to use them productively is just as important.

As economist Thomas Sowell points out, cavemen had the same natural resources at their disposal that we do today. The huge difference between their standard of living and ours reflects the difference in the knowledge they could bring to bear on those resources versus what we can.[1] Over time, human ingenuity, discovery, improved knowledge, and better technology have enabled us to produce more goods and services from the available resources. Nonetheless, our desire for goods and services is still far greater than our ability to produce them. Thus, scarcity is a fact of life today, and in the foreseeable future. As a result, we confront trade-offs and have to make choices. This is what economics is about.

SCARCITY AND POVERTY ARE NOT THE SAME

Think for a moment about what life was like in 1750. People all over the world struggled 50, 60, and 70 hours a week to obtain the basic necessities of life—food, clothing, and shelter. Manual labor was the major source of income. Animals provided the means of transportation. Tools and machines were primitive by today's standards. As the English philosopher Thomas Hobbes stated in the seventeenth century, life was "solitary, poor, nasty, brutish, and short."[2]

Throughout much of South America, Africa, and Asia, economic conditions today continue to make life difficult. In North America, Western Europe, Oceania, and some parts of Asia, however, economic progress has substantially reduced physical hardship and human drudgery. In these regions, the typical family is more likely to worry about financing its summer vacation than about obtaining food and shelter. As anyone who has watched the TV reality show *Survivor* knows, we take for granted many of the items that modern technological advances have allowed us to produce at unbelievably low prices. Contestants on *Survivor* struggle with even basic things like starting a fire, finding shelter, and catching

Bill Inoshita/CBS Photo Archive/Getty Images

The degree to which modern technology and knowledge allow us to fulfill our desires and ease the grip of scarcity is often taken for granted—as the castaways on the CBS reality series Survivor *quickly find out when they have to struggle to meet even basic needs, such as food, shelter, and cleaning their bodies and clothes.*

---

[1]Thomas Sowell, *Knowledge and Decisions* (New York: Basic Books, 1980), 47.
[2]Thomas Hobbes, *Leviathan* (1651), Part I, Chapter 13.

fish. They are thrilled when they win ordinary items like shampoo, rice, and toilet paper. During one episode, a contestant eagerly paid over $125 for a small chocolate bar and spoonful of peanut butter at an auction—and she considered it a great bargain!

It is important to note that scarcity and poverty are not the same thing. Scarcity is an **objective** concept that describes a factual situation in which the limited nature of our resources keeps us from being able to completely fulfill our desires for goods and services. In contrast, poverty is a **subjective** concept that refers to a personal opinion of whether someone meets an arbitrarily defined level of income. This distinction is made even clearer when you realize that different people have vastly different ideas of what it means to be poor. The average family in the United States that meets the federal government's definition of being "in poverty" would be considered wealthy in most any country in Africa. A family in the United States in the 1950s would have been considered fairly wealthy if it had air conditioning, an automatic dishwasher or clothes dryer, or a television set. Today, the majority of U.S. families officially classified as poor have many items that would have been viewed as symbols of great wealth just 60 years ago.

People always want more and better goods for themselves and others about whom they care. Scarcity is the constraint that prevents us from having as much of *all* goods as we would like, but it is not the same as poverty. Even if every individual were rich, scarcity would still be present.

SCARCITY NECESSITATES RATIONING

Scarcity makes **rationing** a necessity. When a good or resource is scarce, some criterion must be used to determine who will receive it and who will go without. The choice of which method is used will, however, have an influence on human behavior. When rationing is done through the government sector, a person's political status and ability to manipulate the political process are the key factors. Powerful interest groups and those in good favor with influential politicians will be the ones who obtain goods and resources. When this method of rationing is used, people will devote time and resources to lobbying and favor seeking with those who have political power, rather than to productive activities.

When the criterion is first-come, first-served, goods are allocated to those who are fastest at getting in line or willing to spend the longest time waiting in line. Many colleges use this method to ration tickets to sporting events, and the result is students waiting in long lines. Sometimes, as at Duke University during basketball season, they even camp out for multiple nights to get good tickets! Imagine how the behavior of students would change if tickets were instead given out to the students with the highest grade point average.

In a market economy, price is generally used to ration goods and resources only to those who are willing and able to pay the prevailing market price. Because only those goods that are scarce require rationing, in a market economy, one easy way to determine whether a good or resource is scarce is to ask if it sells for a price. If you have to pay for something, it is scarce.

THE METHOD OF RATIONING INFLUENCES THE NATURE OF COMPETITION

Competition is a natural outgrowth of scarcity and the desire of human beings to improve their conditions. Competition exists in every economy and every society. But the criteria used to ration scarce goods and resources will influence the competitive techniques employed. When the rationing criterion is price, individuals will engage in income-generating activities that enhance their ability to pay the price needed to buy the goods and services they want. Thus, one benefit of using price as a rationing mechanism is that it encourages individuals to engage in the production of goods and services to generate income. In contrast, rationing on the basis of first-come, first-served encourages individuals to waste a substantial amount of time waiting in line, while rationing through the political process encourages individuals to waste time and other resources in competing with others to influence the political process.

Objective
A fact based on observable phenomena that is not influenced by differences in personal opinion.

Subjective
An opinion based on personal preferences and value judgments.

Rationing
Allocating a limited supply of a good or resource among people who would like to have more of it. When price performs the rationing function, the good or resource is allocated to those willing to give up the most "other things" in order to get it.

Within a market setting, the competition that results from scarcity is an important ingredient in economic progress. Competition among business firms for customers results in newer, better, and less expensive goods and services. Competition between employers for workers results in higher wages, benefits, and better working conditions. Further, competition encourages discovery and innovation, two important sources of growth and higher living standards.

THE ECONOMIC WAY OF THINKING

One does not have to spend much time around economists to recognize that there is an "economic way of thinking." Admittedly, economists, like others, differ widely in their ideological views. A news commentator once remarked that "any half-dozen economists will normally come up with about six different policy prescriptions." Yet, in spite of their philosophical differences, the approaches of economists reflect common ground.

That common ground is **economic theory**, developed from basic principles of human behavior. Economic researchers are constantly involved in testing and seeking to verify their theories. When the evidence from the testing is consistent with a theory, eventually that theory will become widely accepted among economists. Economic theory, like a road map or a guidebook, establishes reference points indicating what to look for and how economic issues are interrelated. To a large degree, the basic economic principles are merely common sense. When applied consistently, however, these commonsense concepts can provide powerful and sometimes surprising insights.

It [economics] is a method rather than a doctrine, an apparatus of the mind, a technique of thinking which helps its possessor to draw correct conclusions.

—*John Maynard Keynes*[3]

Economic theory
A set of definitions, postulates, and principles assembled in a manner that makes clear the "cause-and-effect" relationships.

EIGHT GUIDEPOSTS TO ECONOMIC THINKING

The economic way of thinking requires incorporating certain guidelines—some would say the building blocks of basic economic theory—into your own thought process. Once you incorporate these guidelines, economics can be a relatively easy subject to master. Students who have difficulty with economics have almost always failed to assimilate one or more of these principles. The following are eight principles that characterize the economic way of thinking. We will discuss each of these principles in more depth throughout the book so that you will be sure to understand how and when to apply them.

1. The use of scarce resources is costly, so decision-makers must make trade-offs. Economists sometimes refer to this as the "there is no such thing as a free lunch" principle. Because resources are scarce, the use of resources to produce one good diverts those resources from the production of other goods. A parcel of undeveloped land could be used for a new hospital or a parking lot, or it could simply be left undeveloped. No option is free of cost—there is always a trade-off. A decision to pursue any one of these options means that the decision-maker must sacrifice the others. The highest valued alternative that is sacrificed is the **opportunity cost** of the option chosen. For example, if you use one hour of your scarce time to study economics, you will have one hour less time to watch television, read magazines, sleep, work at a job, or study other subjects. Whichever one of these options you would have chosen had you *not* spent the hour studying economics is your highest valued option forgone. If you would have slept, then the opportunity cost of this hour spent studying economics is a forgone hour of sleep. In economics, the opportunity cost of an action is the highest valued option given up when a choice is made.

It is important to recognize that the use of scarce resources to produce a good is always costly, regardless of who pays for the good or service produced. In many countries, various kinds of schooling are provided free of charge *to students*. However, provision

Opportunity cost
The highest valued alternative that must be sacrificed as a result of choosing an option.

When a scarce resource is used to meet one need, other competing needs must be sacrificed. The forgone shoe store is an example of the opportunity cost of building the new drugstore.

of the schooling is not free *to the community as a whole*. The scarce resources used to produce the schooling—to construct the building, hire teachers, buy equipment, and so on—could have been used instead to produce more recreation, entertainment, housing, medical care, or other goods. The opportunity cost of the schooling is the highest valued option that must now be given up because the required resources were used to produce the schooling.

By now, the central point should be obvious. As we make choices, we always face trade-offs. Using resources to do one thing leaves fewer resources to do another.

Consider one final example. Mandatory air bags in automobiles save an estimated 400 lives each year. Economic thinking, however, forces us to ask ourselves if the $50 billion spent on air bags could have been used in a better way—perhaps say, for cancer research that could have saved *more* than 400 lives per year. Most people don't like to think of air bags and cancer research as an "either/or" proposition. It's more convenient to ignore these trade-offs. But if we want to get the most out of our resources, we have to consider all of our alternatives. In this case, the appropriate analysis is not simply the lives saved with air bags versus dollars spent on them, but also the number of lives that could have been saved (or other things that could have been accomplished) if the $50 billion had been used differently. A candid consideration of hard trade-offs like this is essential to using our resources wisely.

2. Individuals choose purposefully—they try to get the most from their limited resources. People try not to squander their valuable resources deliberately. Instead, they try to choose the options that best advance their personal desires and goals at the least possible cost. This is called **economizing behavior**. Economizing behavior is the result of purposeful, or rational, decision-making. When choosing among things of equal benefit, an economizer will select the cheapest option. For example, if a pizza, a lobster dinner, and a sirloin steak are expected to yield identical benefits for Mary (including the enjoyment of eating them), economizing behavior implies that Mary will select the cheapest of the three alternatives, probably the pizza. Similarly, when choosing among alternatives of equal cost, economizing decision-makers will select the option that yields the greatest benefit. If the prices of several dinner specials are equal, for example, economizers will choose the one they like the best. Because of economizing behavior, the desires or preferences of individuals are revealed by the choices they make.

Economizing behavior
Choosing the option that offers the greatest benefit at the least possible cost.

Purposeful choosing implies that decision-makers have some basis for their evaluation of alternatives. Economists refer to this evaluation as **utility**—the benefit or satisfaction that an individual expects from the choice of a specific alternative. Utility is highly subjective, often differing widely from person to person. The steak dinner that delights one person may be repulsive to another (a vegetarian, for example).

Utility
The subjective benefit or satisfaction a person expects from a choice or course of action.

The idea that people behave rationally to get the greatest benefit at the least possible cost is a powerful tool. It can help us understand their choices. However, we need to realize that a rational choice is not the same thing as a "right" choice. If we want to understand people's choices, we need to understand their own subjective evaluations of their options *as they see them*. As we have said, different people have different preferences. If Joan prefers $50 worth of chocolate to $50 worth of vegetables, buying the chocolate would be the rational choice for her, even though some outside observer might say that Joan is making a "bad" decision. Similarly, some motorcycle riders choose to ride without a helmet because they believe the enjoyment they get from riding without one is greater than the cost (the risk of injury). When people weigh the benefits they receive from an activity against its cost, they are making a rational choice—even though it might not be the choice you or I would make in the same situation.

3. Incentives matter—changes in incentives influence human choices in a predictable way. Both monetary and nonmonetary incentives matter. If the personal cost of an option increases, people will be less likely to choose it. Correspondingly, when an option becomes more attractive, people will be more likely to choose it. This vitally important guidepost, sometimes called the basic postulate of economics, is a powerful tool because it applies to almost everything that we do.

Think about the implications of this proposition. When late for an appointment, a person will be less likely to take time to stop and visit with a friend. Fewer people will go picnicking on a cold and rainy day. Higher prices will reduce the number of units sold. Attendance in college classes will be below normal the day before spring break. In each case, the explanation is the same: As the option becomes more costly, less is chosen.

Similarly, when the payoff derived from a choice increases, people will be more likely to choose it. A person will be more likely to bend over and pick up a quarter than a penny. Students will attend and pay more attention in class when the material is covered extensively on exams. Customers will buy more from stores that offer low prices, high-quality service, and a convenient location. Senior voters will be more likely to support candidates who favor higher Social Security benefits. All of these outcomes are highly predictable, and they merely reflect the "incentives matter" postulate of economics.

Noneconomists sometimes argue that people respond to incentives only because they are selfish and greedy. This view is false. People are motivated by a variety of goals, some humanitarian and some selfish, and incentives matter equally in both. Even an unselfish individual would be more likely to attempt to rescue a drowning child from a three-foot swimming pool than the rapid currents approaching Niagara Falls. Similarly, people are more likely to give a needy person their hand-me-downs rather than their favorite new clothes.

Just how far can we push the idea that incentives matter? If asked what would happen to the number of funerals performed in your town if the price of funerals rose, how would you respond? The "incentives matter" postulate predicts that the higher cost would reduce the number of funerals. While the same number of people will still die each year, the number of funerals performed will still fall as more people choose to be cremated or buried in cemeteries in other towns. Substitutes are everywhere—even for funerals. Individuals also respond to incentives when committing crimes—precisely the reason why people put signs in their yard saying "This house protected by XYZ security."

4. Individuals make decisions at the margin. When making a choice between two alternatives, individuals generally focus on the *difference* in the costs and benefits between alternatives. Economists describe this process as **marginal** decision-making, or "thinking at the margin." The last time you went to eat fast food, you probably faced a decision that highlights this type of thinking. Will you get the $1.50 cheeseburger and the $1.00 medium drink, or instead get the $3.00 value meal that has the cheeseburger and drink and also comes with a medium order of fries? Naturally, individual decision-making focuses on the difference between the alternatives. The value meal costs 50 cents more (its marginal cost) but will give you one extra food item—the fries (its marginal benefit). Your marginal decision is whether it is worth the extra 50 cents to have the fries. If you pay attention, you'll notice yourself frequently thinking at the margin. Next time you find yourself asking a salesclerk, "How much *more* is this one?" when you are choosing between two items, you are doing a marginal analysis.

Marginal choices always involve the effects of net additions to or subtractions from current conditions. In fact, the word *additional* is often used as a substitute for *marginal*.

albanova/Shutterstock.com

Because consumers respond to incentives, store owners know they can sell off excess inventory by reducing prices.

Marginal
Term used to describe the effects of a change in the current situation. For example, a producer's marginal cost is the cost of producing an additional unit of a product, given the producer's current facility and production rate.

For example, a business decision-maker might ask, "What is the additional (or marginal) cost of producing one more unit?" Marginal decisions may involve large or small changes. The "one more unit" could be a new factory or a new stapler. It is marginal because it involves additional costs and additional benefits. Given the current situation, what marginal benefits (additional sales revenues, for example) can be expected from the new factory, and what will be the marginal cost of constructing it? What is the marginal benefit versus marginal cost of purchasing a new stapler? The answers to these questions will determine whether building the new factory or buying the new stapler is a good decision.

It is important to distinguish between *average* and *marginal*. A manufacturer's average cost of producing automobiles (which would be the total cost of production divided by the total number of cars the manufacturer produces) may be $25,000, but the marginal cost of producing an additional automobile (or an additional 1,000 automobiles) might be much lower, say, $10,000 per car. Costs associated with research, testing, design, molds, heavy equipment, and similar factors of production must be incurred whether the manufacturer is going to produce 1,000 units, 10,000 units, or 100,000 units. Such costs will clearly contribute to the average cost of an automobile, but they will change very little as additional units are produced. Thus, the marginal cost of additional units may be substantially less than the average cost. Should production be expanded or reduced? That choice should be based on marginal costs, which indicate the *change* in total cost due to the decision.

People commonly ignore the implications of marginal thinking in their comments, but seldom in their actions. Thus, the concept is far better at explaining how people act than what they say. Students are often overheard telling other students that they shouldn't skip class because they have paid to enroll in it. Of course, the tuition is not a factor relevant at the margin—it will be the same whether or not the student attends class on that particular day. The only real marginal considerations are what the student will miss that day (a quiz, information for the exam, etc.) versus what he or she could do with the extra time by skipping class. This explains why even students who tell others they paid too much for the class to skip it will ignore the tuition costs when they themselves decide to skip class.

Decisions are made at the margin. That means that they almost always involve additions to, or subtractions from, current conditions. If we are going to get the most out of our resources, activities that generate more benefits than costs should be undertaken, while those that are more costly than they are worth should not be undertaken. This principle of sound decision-making applies to individuals, businesses, governments, and for society as a whole.

5. Although information can help us make better choices, its acquisition is costly. Information that helps us make better choices is valuable. However, the time needed to gather it is scarce, making information costly to acquire. As a result, people economize on their search for information just like they do anything else. For example, when you purchase a pair of jeans, you might evaluate the quality and prices of jeans at several different stores. At some point, though, you will decide that additional comparison-shopping is simply not worth the trouble. You will make a choice based on the limited information you already have.

The process is similar when individuals search for a restaurant, a new car, or a roommate. They will seek to acquire some information, but at some point, they will decide that the expected benefit derived from gathering still more information is simply not worth the cost. When differences among the alternatives are important to decision-makers, they will spend more time and effort gathering information. People are much more likely to read a consumer ratings magazine before purchasing a new automobile than they are before purchasing a new can opener. Because information is costly for people to acquire, limited knowledge and uncertainty about the outcome generally characterize the decision-making process.

6. Beware of the secondary effects: economic actions often generate indirect as well as direct effects. In addition to direct effects that are quickly visible, people's decisions often generate indirect, or "secondary," effects that may be observable only with time. Failure to consider secondary effects is one of the most common economic errors because these effects are often quite different from initial, or direct, effects. Frédéric Bastiat, a nineteenth-century French economist, stated that the difference between a good and a bad economist is that the bad economist considers only the immediate, visible effects, whereas the good economist is also aware of the secondary effects. The true cause of these secondary effects might not be seen, even later, except by those using the logic of good economics.

Perhaps a few simple examples that involve both immediate (direct) and secondary (indirect) effects will help illustrate the point. The immediate effect of an aspirin is a bitter taste in one's mouth. The secondary effect, which is not immediately observable, is relief from a headache. The short-term direct effect of drinking twelve cans of beer might be a warm, jolly feeling. In contrast, the secondary effect is likely to be a sluggish feeling the next morning, and perhaps a pounding headache.

Sometimes, as in the case of the aspirin, the secondary effect— headache relief—is actually an intended consequence of the action. In other cases, however, the secondary effects are unintended. Changes in government policy often alter incentives, indirectly affecting how much people work, earn, invest, consume, and conserve for the future. When a change alters incentives, *unintended consequences* that are quite different from the intended consequences may occur.

Let's consider a couple of examples that illustrate the potential importance of unintended consequences. In an effort to reduce gasoline consumption, the federal government mandates that automobiles be more fuel efficient. Is this regulation a sound policy? It may be, but when evaluating the policy's overall impact, one should not overlook its secondary effects. To achieve the higher fuel efficiency, auto manufacturers reduced the size and weight of vehicles. As a result, there are more highway deaths—about 2,500 more per year—than would otherwise occur because these lighter cars do not offer as much protection for occupants. Furthermore, because the higher mileage standards for cars and light trucks make driving cheaper, people tend to drive more than they otherwise would. This increases congestion and results in a smaller reduction in gasoline consumption than was intended by the regulation. Once you consider the secondary effects, the fuel efficiency regulations are much less beneficial than they might first appear.

Trade restrictions between nations have important secondary effects as well. The proponents of tariffs and quotas on foreign goods almost always ignore the secondary effects of their policies. Import quotas restricting the sale of foreign-produced sugar in the U.S. market, for example, have resulted in domestic sugar prices that have often been two or three times the price in the rest of the world. The proponents of this policy—primarily sugar producers—argue that the quotas "save jobs" and increase employment. No doubt, the employment of sugar growers in the United States is higher than it otherwise would be. But what about the secondary effects? The higher sugar prices mean it's more expensive for U.S. firms to produce candy and other products that use a lot of sugar. As a result, many candy producers, including the makers of Life Savers, Jaw Breakers, Red Hots, and Fannie May and Fanny Farmer chocolates, have moved to countries like Canada and Mexico, where sugar can be purchased at its true market price. Thus, employment among sugar-using firms in the United States is reduced. Further, because foreigners sell less sugar in the United States, they have less purchasing power with which to buy products we export to them. This, too, reduces U.S. employment.

Once the secondary effects of trade restrictions like the sugar quota program are taken into consideration, we have no reason to expect that U.S. employment will increase as a result. There may be more jobs in favored industries, but there will be less employment in others. Trade restrictions reshuffle employment rather than increase it. But those who unwittingly fail to consider the secondary effects will miss this point. Clearly, consideration of the secondary effects is an important ingredient of the economic way of thinking.

THE FAMILY CIRCUS®   By Bil Keane

3-25
Copyright 1988
Cowles Syndicate, Inc

Bil Keane, Inc King Features Syndicate

"Everybody wants to be sick. I'm using M&M's for pills."

Sometimes actions change the incentives people face and they respond accordingly, creating secondary effects that were not intended.

Secondary effects
The indirect impact of an event or policy that may not be easily and immediately observable. In the area of policy, these effects are often both unintended and overlooked.

7. The value of a good or service is subjective. Preferences differ, sometimes dramatically, between individuals. How much is a ticket to see a performance of the Bolshoi Ballet worth? Some people would be willing to pay a very high price, while others might prefer to stay home, even if tickets were free! Circumstances can change from day to day, even for a given individual. Alice, a ballet fan who usually would value the ticket at more than its price of $100, is invited to a party and suddenly becomes uninterested in attending the ballet. Now what is the ticket worth? If she knows a friend who would give her $40 for the ticket, it is worth at least that much. If she advertises the ticket on eBay and gets $60 for it, a higher value is created. But if someone who doesn't know of the ticket would have been willing to pay even more, then a potential trade creating even more value is missed. If that particular performance is sold out, perhaps someone in town would be willing to pay $120. One thing is certain: The value of the ticket depends on several things, including who uses it and under what circumstances.

Economics recognizes that people can and do value goods differently. Mike may prefer to have a grass field rather than a parking lot next to his workplace and be willing to bear the cost of walking farther from his car each day. Kim, on the other hand, may prefer the parking lot and the shorter walk. As a science, economics does not place any inherent moral judgment or value on one person's preferences over another's—in economics, all individuals' preferences are counted equally. Because the subjective preferences of individuals differ, it is difficult for one person to know how much another will value an item.

Think about how hard it is to know what would make a good gift for even a close friend or family member. Thus, arranging trades, or otherwise moving items to higher valued users and uses, is not a simple task. The entrepreneurial individual, who knows how to locate the right buyers and arranges for goods to flow to their highest valued use, can sometimes create huge increases in value from existing resources. In fact, moving goods toward those who value them most and combining resources into goods that individuals value more highly are primary sources of economic progress.

Scientific thinking
Developing a theory from basic principles and testing it against events in the real world. Good theories are consistent with and help explain real-world events. Theories that are inconsistent with the real world are invalid and must be rejected.

8. The test of a theory is its ability to predict. Economic thinking is **scientific thinking**. The proof of the pudding is in the eating. How useful an economic theory is depends on how well it predicts the future consequences of economic action. Economists develop economic theories using scientific thinking based on basic principles. The idea is to predict how incentives will affect decision makers and compare the predictions against real-world events. If the events in the real world are consistent with a theory, we say that the theory has *predictive value* and is therefore valid.

If it is impossible to test the theoretical relationships of a discipline, the discipline does not qualify as a science. Because economics deals with human beings who can think and respond in a variety of ways, can economic theories really be tested? The answer to this question is yes, if, on average, human beings respond in predictable and consistent ways to changes in economic conditions. The economist believes that this is the case, even though not all individuals will respond in the specified manner. Economists usually do not try to predict the behavior of a specific individual; instead, they focus on the general behavior of a large number of individuals.

In the 1950s, economists began to do laboratory experiments to test economic theories. Individuals were brought into laboratories to see how they would act in buying and selling situations, under differing rules. For example, cash rewards were given to individuals who, when an auction was conducted, were able to sell at high prices and buy at low prices, thus approximating real-world market incentives. These experiments have verified many of the important propositions of economic theory.

Laboratory experiments, however, cannot duplicate all real economic interactions. How can we test economic theory when controlled experiments are not feasible? This is a problem, but economics is no different from astronomy in this respect. Astronomers can use theories tested in physics laboratories, but they must also deal with the world as it is. They cannot change the course of the stars or planets to see what impact the change would have on the gravitational pull of Earth. Similarly, economists cannot arbitrarily change the prices of cars or unskilled-labor services in real markets just to observe the effects on quantities purchased or levels of employment. However, economic conditions (for example, prices, production costs, technology, and transportation costs), like the location of the planets, do change from time to time. As actual conditions change, an economic theory can be tested by comparing its predictions with real-world outcomes. Just as the universe is the main laboratory of the astronomer, the real-world economy is the primary laboratory of the economist.

POSITIVE AND NORMATIVE ECONOMICS

As a social science, economics is concerned with predicting or determining the impact of changes in economic variables on the actions of human beings. Scientific economics, commonly referred to as positive economics, attempts to determine "what is." Positive economic statements involve potentially verifiable or refutable propositions. For example, "If the price of gasoline rises, people will buy less gasoline." We can statistically investigate (and estimate) the relationship between gasoline prices and gallons sold. We can analyze the facts to determine the correctness of a positive economic statement. Remember, a positive economic statement need not be correct; it simply must be testable.

Positive economics
The scientific study of "what is" among economic relationships.

In contrast, normative economics is about "what ought to be," given the preferences and philosophical views of the advocate. Value judgments often result in disagreement about normative economic matters. Two people may differ on a policy matter because one is from one political party and the other is from another, or because one wants cheaper food while the other favors organic farming (which is more expensive), and so on. They may even agree about the expected outcome of altering an economic variable (that is, the positive economics of an issue), but disagree as to whether that outcome is desirable.

Normative economics
Judgments about "what ought to be" in economic matters. Normative economic views cannot be proven false because they are based on value judgments.

Unlike positive economic statements, normative economic statements can neither be confirmed nor proven false by scientific testing. "Business firms should not be concerned with profits." "We should have fewer parking lots and more green space on campus." "The price of gasoline is too high." These normative statements cannot be scientifically tested because their validity rests on value judgments.

Normative economic views can sometimes influence our attitude toward positive economic analysis, however. When we agree with the objectives of a policy, it's easy to overlook the warnings of positive economics. Although positive economics does not tell us which policy is best, it can provide evidence about the likely effects of a policy. Sometimes proponents unknowingly support policies that are actually in conflict with their own goals and objectives. Positive economics, based on sound economic logic, can help overcome this potential problem.

Economics can expand our knowledge of how the real world operates, in both the private and the public (government) sectors. However, it is not always easy to isolate the impact of economic changes. Let's now consider some pitfalls to avoid in economic thinking.

PITFALLS TO AVOID IN ECONOMIC THINKING

VIOLATION OF THE *CETERIS PARIBUS* CONDITION CAN LEAD ONE TO DRAW THE WRONG CONCLUSION

Economists often qualify their statements with the words *ceteris paribus*. *Ceteris paribus* is a Latin term meaning "other things constant." An example of a *ceteris paribus* statement would be the following: "*Ceteris paribus*, an increase in the price of housing will cause buyers to reduce their purchases of housing." Unfortunately, we live in a dynamic world, so things seldom remain constant. For example, as the price of housing rises, the income of consumers might also increase for unrelated reasons. Each of these factors—higher housing prices and increasing consumer income—will have an impact on housing purchases. In fact, we would generally expect them to have opposite effects: Higher prices are likely to reduce housing purchases, whereas higher consumer incomes are likely to increase them.

Ceteris paribus
A Latin term meaning "other things constant" that is used when the effect of one change is being described, recognizing that if other things changed, they also could affect the result. Economists often describe the effects of one change, knowing that in the real world, other things might change and also exert an effect.

We point out this pitfall because sometimes statistical data (or casual observations) do not support economic theories. In most of these cases, other factors have also changed. The effects observed simply reflect the combined effect of these changes.

The task of sorting out the effects of two or more variables that change at the same time is difficult. However, with a strong grip on economic theory, some ingenuity, and enough data, it can usually be done. This is, in fact, precisely the day-to-day work of many professional economists.

GOOD INTENTIONS DO NOT GUARANTEE DESIRABLE OUTCOMES

There is a tendency to believe that if the proponents of a policy have good intentions, their proposals must be sound. This is not necessarily the case. Proponents may be unaware of some of the adverse secondary effects of their proposals, particularly when they are indirect and observable only over time. Even if their policies would be largely ineffective, politicians may still find it advantageous to call attention to the severity of a problem and propose a program to deal with it. In other cases, proponents of a policy may actually be seeking a goal other than the one they espouse. They may tie their arguments to objectives that are widely supported by the general populace. Thus, the fact that an advocate says a program will help the economy, expand employment, help the poor, increase wages, improve health care, or achieve some other highly desirable objective does not necessarily make it so.

Let's begin with a couple of straightforward examples. Federal legislation has been introduced that would require all children, including those under age two, to be fastened in a child safety seat when traveling by air. Proponents argue the legislation will increase the survival rate of children in the case of an airline crash and thereby save lives. Certainly, saving lives is a highly desirable objective, but will this really be the case? *Some* lives will probably be saved. But what about the secondary effects? The legislation would mean that a parent traveling with a small child would have to purchase an additional ticket, which will make it more expensive to fly. As a result, many families will choose to travel by auto rather than air. Because the likelihood of a serious accident per mile traveled in an automobile is several times higher than for air travel, more automobile travel will result in more injuries and fatalities. In fact, studies indicate that the increase in injuries and fatalities from additional auto travel will exceed the number of lives saved by airline safety seats.[4] Thus, even though the intentions of the proponents may well be lofty, there is reason to believe that the net impact of their proposal will be more fatalities and injuries than would be the case in the absence of the legislation.

The stated objective of the Endangered Species Act is to protect various species that are on the verge of extinction. Certainly, this is an admirable objective, but there is nonetheless reason to question the effectiveness of the act itself. The Endangered Species Act allows the government to regulate the use of individual private property if an endangered species is found present on *or* near an individual's land. To avoid losing control of their property, many landowners have taken steps to make their land less attractive as a natural habitat for these endangered species. For example, the endangered red-cockaded woodpecker nests primarily in old trees within southern pine ecosystems. Landowners have responded by cutting down trees the woodpeckers like to nest in to avoid having one nest on their land, which would result in the owner losing control of this part of their property. The end result is that the habitat for these birds has actually been disappearing more rapidly.

As you can see, good intentions are not enough. An unsound proposal will lead to undesirable outcomes, even if it is supported by proponents with good intentions. In fact, many economists believe that the recent financial crisis is a secondary effect of well-intended government regulations and policies that lowered mortgage lending standards in order to expand homeownership. Sound economic reasoning can help us better anticipate the secondary effects of policy changes and avoid the pitfall of thinking that good intentions are enough.

---

[4]For a detailed analysis of this subject, see Thomas B. Newman, Brian D. Johnston, and David C. Grossman, "Effects and Costs of Requiring Child-Restraint Systems for Young Children Traveling on Commercial Airplanes," *Archives of Pediatrics and Adolescent Medicine* 157 (October 2003): 969–74.

ASSOCIATION IS NOT CAUSATION

In economics, identifying cause-and-effect relationships is very important. But statistical association alone cannot establish this causation. Perhaps an extreme example will illustrate the point. Suppose that each November, a witch doctor performs a voodoo dance designed to summon the gods of winter, and that soon after the dance is performed, the weather in fact begins to turn cold. The witch doctor's dance is associated with the arrival of winter, meaning that the two events appear to have happened in conjunction with one another. But is this really evidence that the witch doctor's dance actually caused the arrival of winter? Most of us would answer no, even though the two events seemed to happen in conjunction with one another.

Those who argue that a causal relationship exists simply because of the presence of statistical association are committing a logical fallacy known as the *post hoc propter ergo hoc* fallacy. Sound economics warns against this potential source of error.

THE FALLACY OF COMPOSITION: WHAT'S TRUE FOR ONE MIGHT NOT BE TRUE FOR ALL

What is true for the individual (or subcomponent) may not be true for the group (or the whole). If you stand up for an exciting play during a football game, you will be better able to see. But what happens if everyone stands up at the same time? Will everyone be better able to see? The answer is, of course, no. Thus, what is true for a single individual does not necessarily apply to the group as a whole. When everyone stands up, the view for individual spectators fails to improve; in fact, it may even become worse.

People who mistakenly argue that what is true for the part is also true for the whole are said to be committing the **fallacy of composition**. What is true for the individual can be misleading and is often fallacious when applied to the entire economy. The fallacy of composition highlights the importance of considering both a micro view and a macro view in the study of economics. **Microeconomics** focuses on the decision-making of consumers, producers, and resource suppliers operating in a narrowly defined market, such as that for a specific good or resource. Because individual decision-makers are the moving force behind all economic action, the foundations of economics are clearly rooted in a micro view.

As we have seen, however, what is true for a small unit may not be true in the aggregate. **Macroeconomics** focuses on how the aggregation of individual micro-units affects our analysis. Like microeconomics, it is concerned with incentives, prices, and output. Macroeconomics, however, aggregates markets, lumping together all 115 million households in this country. Macroeconomics involves topics like total consumption spending, saving, and employment, in the economy as a whole. Similarly, the nation's 25 million business firms are lumped together in "the business sector." What factors determine the level of aggregate output, the rate of inflation, the amount of unemployment, and interest rates? These are macroeconomic questions. In short, macroeconomics examines the forest rather than the individual trees. As we move from the microcomponents to a macro view of the whole, it is important that we beware of the fallacy of composition.

Fallacy of composition
Erroneous view that what is true for the individual (or the part) will also be true for the group (or the whole).

Microeconomics
The branch of economics that focuses on how human behavior affects the conduct of affairs within narrowly defined units, such as individual households or business firms.

Macroeconomics
The branch of economics that focuses on how human behavior affects outcomes in highly aggregated markets, such as the markets for labor or consumer products.

Looking Ahead

The primary purpose of this book is to encourage you to develop the economic way of thinking so that you can separate sound reasoning from economic nonsense. Once you have developed the economic way of thinking, economics will be relatively easy. Using the economic way of thinking can also be fun. Moreover, it will help you become a better citizen. It will give you a different and fascinating perspective on what motivates people, why they act the way they do, and why their actions sometimes go against the best interest of the community or nation. It will also give you valuable insight into how people's actions can be rechanneled for the benefit of the community at large.

iStockphoto.com/gaspr13

KEY POINTS

- Scarcity and choice are the two essential ingredients of economic analysis. A good is scarce when the human desire for it exceeds the amount freely available from nature. Scarcity requires us to choose among available alternatives. Every choice entails a trade-off.

- Every society will have to devise some method of rationing scarce resources among competing uses. Markets generally use price as the rationing device. Competition is a natural outgrowth of the need to ration scarce goods.

- Scarcity and poverty are not the same thing. Absence of poverty implies that some basic level of need has been met. An absence of scarcity implies that our desires for goods are fully satisfied. We may someday eliminate poverty, but scarcity will always be with us.

- Economics is a way of thinking that emphasizes eight points:
  1. The use of scarce resources to produce a good always has an opportunity cost.
  2. Individuals make decisions purposefully, always seeking to choose the option they expect to be most consistent with their personal goals.
  3. Incentives matter. The likelihood of people choosing an option increases as personal benefits rise and personal costs decline.
  4. Economic reasoning focuses on the impact of marginal changes because it is the marginal benefits and marginal costs that influence choices.
  5. Because information is scarce, uncertainty is a fact of life.
  6. In addition to their direct impact, economic changes often generate secondary effects.
  7. The value of a good or service is subjective and varies with individual preferences and circumstances.
  8. The test of an economic theory is its ability to predict and explain events in the real world.

- Economic science is positive; it attempts to explain the actual consequences of economic actions or "what is." Normative economics goes further, applying value judgments to make suggestions about what "ought to be."

- Microeconomics focuses on narrowly defined units, while macroeconomics is concerned with highly aggregated units. When shifting focus from micro to macro, one must beware of the fallacy of composition: What's good for the individual may not be good for the group as a whole.

- The origin of economics as a science dates to the publication of *An Inquiry into the Nature and Causes of the Wealth of Nations* by Adam Smith in 1776. Smith believed a market economy would generally bring individual self-interest and the public interest into harmony.

CRITICAL ANALYSIS QUESTIONS

1. Indicate how each of the following changes would influence the incentive of a decision-maker to undertake the action described.
   a. A reduction in the temperature from 80° to 50° on one's decision to go swimming
   b. A change in the meeting time of the introductory economics course from 11:00 A.M. to 7:30 A.M. on one's decision to attend the lectures
   c. A reduction in the number of exam questions that relate directly to the text on the student's decision to read the text
   d. An increase in the price of beef on one's decision to buy steak
   e. An increase in the rental rates of apartments on one's decision to build additional rental housing units

2. *"The government should provide such goods as health care, education, and highways because it can provide them for free." Is this statement true or false? Explain your answer.

3. a. What method is used to ration goods in a market economy? How does this rationing method influence the incentive of individuals to supply goods, services, and resources to others?
   b. How are grades rationed in your economics class? How does this rationing method influence student behavior? Suppose the highest grades were rationed to those whom the teacher liked best. How would this method of rationing influence student behavior?

4. *In recent years, both the personal exemption and child tax credit have been increased in the United States. According to the basic principles of economics, how will the birthrate be affected by policies that reduce the taxes imposed on those with children?

5. *"The economic way of thinking stresses that good intentions lead to sound policy." Is this statement true or false? Explain your answer.

6. Self-interest is a powerful motivator. Does this necessarily imply that people are selfish and greedy? Do self-interest and selfishness mean the same thing?

7. A restaurant offers an "all you can eat" lunch buffet for $10. Shawn has already eaten three servings, and is trying to decide whether to go back for a fourth. Describe how Shawn can use marginal analysis to make his decision.

8. *"Individuals who economize are missing the point of life. Money is not so important that it should rule the way we live." Evaluate this statement.

9. *"Positive economics cannot tell us which agricultural policy is better, so it is useless to policy makers." Evaluate this statement.

10. *"I examined the statistics for our basketball team's wins last year and found that, when the third team played more, the winning margin increased. If the coach played the third team more, we would win by a bigger margin." Evaluate this statement.

11. *Which of the following are positive economic statements and which are normative?

    a. The speed limit should be lowered to 55 miles per hour on interstate highways.

    b. Higher gasoline prices cause the quantity of gasoline that consumers buy to decrease.

    c. A comparison of costs and benefits should not be used to assess environmental regulations.

    d. Higher taxes on alcohol result in less drinking and driving.

12. Why can't we consume as much of each good or service as we would like? If we become richer in the future, do you think we will eventually be able to consume as much of everything as we would like? Why or why not?

13. Suppose that in an effort to help low-skill workers the government raises the permissible minimum wage to $10 per hour. Can you think of any unintended secondary effects that will result from this action? Will all low-skill workers be helped by the minimum wage law?

14. *Should the United States attempt to reduce air and water pollution to zero? Why or why not?

*Asterisk denotes questions for which answers are given in Appendix B.

CHAPTER

2

Some Tools of the Economist

The key insight of Adam Smith's Wealth of Nations *is misleadingly simple: if an exchange between two parties is voluntary, it will not take place unless both believe they will benefit from it. Most economic fallacies derive from the neglect of this simple insight, from the tendency to assume that there is a fixed pie, that one party can gain only at the expense of another.*

—*Milton and Rose Friedman*[1]

---

[1]Milton Friedman and Rose Friedman, *Free to Choose* (Harcourt Brace, 1990), 13.

In the preceding chapter, you were introduced to the economic way of thinking. We will now begin to apply that approach. This chapter focuses on five topics: opportunity cost, trade, property rights, the potential output level of an economy, and the creation of wealth. These seemingly diverse topics are in fact highly inter-related. For example, the opportunity cost of goods determines which ones an individual or a nation should produce and which should be acquired through trade. In turn, the ways in which trade and property rights are structured influence the amount of output and wealth an economy can create. These tools of economics are important for answering the basic economic questions: what to produce, how to produce it, and for whom it will be produced. We will begin by first explaining in more detail what opportunity cost is.

WHAT SHALL WE GIVE UP?

Because of scarcity, we can't have everything we want. As a result, we constantly face choices that involve trade-offs between our competing desires. Most of us would like to have more time for leisure, recreation, vacations, hobbies, education, and skill development. We would also like to have more wealth, a larger savings account, and more consumable goods. However, all these things are scarce, in the sense that they are limited. Our efforts to get more of one will conflict with our efforts to get more of others.

OPPORTUNITY COST

The choice to do one thing is, at the same time, a choice *not* to do something else. Your choice to spend time reading this book is a choice not to spend the time playing video games, listening to a math lecture, or going to a party. These things must be given up because you decided to read this book instead. As we indicated in Chapter 1, the highest valued alternative sacrificed in order to choose an option is called the *opportunity cost* of that choice.

Opportunity costs are subjective because they depend on how the decision-maker values his or her options. They are also based on the expectations of the decision-maker—what he or she expects the value of the forgone alternatives will be. Because of this, opportunity cost can never be directly measured by someone other than the decision-maker. Only the person choosing can know the value of what is given up.[2] This makes it difficult for someone other than the decision-maker—including experts and elected officials—to make choices on that person's behalf. Moreover, not only do people differ in the trade-offs they prefer to make, but their preferences also change with time and circumstances. Thus, the decision-maker is the only person who can properly evaluate the options and decide which is the best, given his or her preferences and current circumstances.

Monetary costs reflect opportunities foregone, and they can be measured objectively in terms of dollars and cents. If you spend $20 on a new CD, you must now forgo the other items you could have purchased with the $20—a new shirt, for example. However, it is important to recognize that monetary costs do not represent the total opportunity cost of an option. The total cost of attending a football game, for example, is the highest valued opportunity lost as a result of both the time you spend at the game and the amount of money you pay for your ticket. In cases like the online purchase of a music album, for which there is minimal outlay of time, effort, and other resources to make the purchase, the monetary cost will approximate the total cost. Contrast this with a decision to sit on your sofa and listen to your new music, which involves little or no monetary cost, but has a clear opportunity cost of your time. In this second case, the monetary cost is a poor measure of the total cost.

---

[2]See James M. Buchanan, *Cost and Choice* (Chicago: Markham, 1969), for a classic work on the relationship between cost and choice.

OPPORTUNITY COST AND THE REAL WORLD

Is real-world decision making influenced by opportunity costs? Consider your own decision to attend college. Your opportunity cost of going to college is the value of the next best alternative, which could be measured as the salary you would earn if you had chosen to go directly into full-time work instead. Every year you stay in college, you give up what you could have earned by working that year. Typically, students incur opportunity costs of $80,000 or more in forgone income during their stay in college.

But what if the opportunity cost of attending college changes? How will it affect your decision? Suppose, for example, that you received a job offer today for $250,000 per year as an athlete or an entertainer, but the job would require so much travel that school would be impossible. Would this change in the opportunity cost of going to college affect your choice as to whether to continue in school? It likely would. Going to college would mean you would have to say good-bye to the huge salary you've been offered. (See the accompanying illustration on LeBron James for a good example.) You can clearly tell from this example that the monetary cost of college (tuition, books, and so forth) isn't the only factor influencing your decision. Your opportunity cost plays a part, too.

Even when their parents pay all the monetary expenses of their college education, some students are surprised to learn that they are actually incurring more of the total cost of going to college than their parents are. For example, the average monetary cost (tuition, room and board, books, and so forth) for a student attending college is about $10,000 per year ($40,000 over four years). Even if the student's next best alternative were working at a job that paid only $15,000 per year, over four years, that would amount to $60,000 in forgone earnings, So, the total cost of the student's education would be $100,000 ($40,000 in monetary costs paid by the parents and $60,000 in opportunity costs incurred by the student).[3]

Now consider another decision made by college students—whether to attend a particular class meeting. The monetary cost of attending class (bus fare, parking, gasoline costs, and so on) remains fairly constant from day to day. Why then do students choose to attend class on some days and not on others? Even though the monetary cost of attending class is fairly constant, a student's opportunity cost can change dramatically from day to day. Some days, the next best alternative to attending class may be sleeping in or watching TV. Other days, the opportunity cost may be substantially larger, perhaps the value of attending a big football game, getting an early start on spring break, or having additional study time for a crucial exam in another class. As options like these increase the cost of attending class, more students will decide not to attend.

Failure to consider opportunity cost often leads to unwise decision-making. Suppose that your community builds a beautiful new civic center. The mayor, speaking at the dedication ceremony, tells the world that the center will improve the quality of life in your community. People who understand the concept of opportunity cost may question this view. If the center had not been built, the resources might have funded construction of a new hospital, improvements to the educational system, or housing for low-income families.

LeBron James understands opportunity cost. As a high school player, James was already one of the best basketball players in the nation. He had received numerous scholarship offers and was considering attending college at Ohio State, the University of North Carolina, Michigan State, or the University of California. However, after high school graduation, LeBron decided to go directly into the NBA because the opportunity cost of college was simply too high. He was selected as the first pick in the 2003 NBA draft, signing a three-year contract worth almost $13 million, with an option for a fourth year at $5.8 million. Had he decided to go to college instead, James would have incurred an opportunity cost of at least $19 million in forgone income to earn a four-year college degree! Would you have skipped college if your opportunity cost had been that high?

Garrett Ellwood/NBAE via Getty Images

---

[3]From the standpoint of the family's total economic cost of sending a child to college, some of the monetary costs, such as room and board, are not costs of choosing to go to college. The cost of living does have to be covered, but it would be incurred whether or not the student went to college.

OUTSTANDING ECONOMIST

Thomas Sowell (1930–)

Thomas Sowell, a senior fellow at the Hoover Institution, recognizes the critical importance of the institutions—the "rules of the game"—that shape human interactions. His book *Knowledge and Decisions* stresses the role of knowledge in the economy and how different institutional arrangements compare at using scarce information. Sowell is the author of many books and journal articles and writes a nationally syndicated column that appears in more than 150 newspapers. His writings address subjects ranging from race preferences and cultural differences to the origins and ideology of political conflict.

iStockphoto.com/sorendls

Will the civic center contribute more to the well-being of people in your community than would these other facilities? If so, it was a wise investment. If not, your community will be worse off than it would have been if decision makers had chosen a higher valued project.

TRADE CREATES VALUE

Why do individuals trade with each other, and what is the significance of this exchange? We have learned that value is subjective. It is wrong to assume that a particular good or service has a fixed objective value just because it exists.[4] The value of goods and services generally depends on who uses them, and on circumstances, such as when and where they are used, as well as on the physical characteristics. Some people love onions, whereas others dislike them very much. Thus, when we speak of the "value of an onion," this makes sense only within the context of its value to a specific person. Similarly, to most people an umbrella is more valuable on a rainy day than on a sunny one.

Consider the case of Janet, who loves tomatoes but hates onions, and Brad, who loves onions but hates tomatoes. They go out to dinner together and the waiter brings their salads. Brad turns to Janet and says, "I'll trade you the tomatoes on my salad for the onions on yours." Janet gladly agrees to the exchange. This simple example will help us illustrate two important aspects of voluntary exchange.

1. When individuals engage in a voluntary exchange, both parties are made better off. In the previous example, Janet has the option of accepting or declining Brad's offer of a trade. If she accepts his offer, she does so *voluntarily*. Janet would agree to this exchange only if she expects to be better off as a result. Because she likes tomatoes better than onions, Janet's enjoyment of her salad will be greater with this trade than without it. On the other side, Brad has voluntarily made this offer of an exchange to Janet because Brad believes he will also be better off as a result of the exchange.

People tend to think of making, building, and creating things as productive activities. Agriculture and manufacturing are like this. On the one hand, they create something genuinely new, something that was not there before. On the other hand, trade—the mere exchange of one thing for another—does not create new material items. It is tempting to think that if nothing new is created, the action cannot generate gain. But this is a fallacy, and the motivation for trade illustrates why. An exchange will not occur unless both parties agree to it and they will not do so unless the exchange makes them better off. As the chapter-opening quotation of Milton and Rose Friedman illustrates, many errors in economic reasoning happen when we forget that voluntary trades, like the one between Janet and Brad, make both parties better off.

[4]An illuminating discussion of this subject, termed the "physical fallacy," is found in Thomas Sowell, *Knowledge and Decisions* (New York: Basic Books, 1980), 67–72.

2. By channeling goods and resources to those who value them most, trade creates value and increases the wealth created by a society's resources. Because preferences differ among individuals, the value of an item can vary greatly from one person to another. Therefore, trade can create value by moving goods from those who value them less to those who value them more. The simple exchange between Janet and Brad also illustrates this point. Imagine for a moment that Brad and Janet had never met and instead were both eating their salads alone. Without the ability to engage in this exchange, both would have eaten their salads but would not have had as much enjoyment from them. When goods are moved to individuals who value them more, the total value created by a society's limited resources is increased. The same two salads create more value when the trade occurs than when it doesn't.

It is easy to think of material things as wealth, but material things are not wealth until they are in the hands of someone who values them. A highly technical book on electronics that is of no value to an art collector may be worth several hundred dollars to an engineer. Similarly, a painting that is unappreciated by an engineer may be of great value to an art collector. Therefore, a voluntary exchange that moves the electronics book to the engineer and the painting to the art collector will increase the value of both goods. By channeling goods and resources toward those who value them most, trade creates wealth for both the trading partners and for the nation.

TRANSACTION COSTS—A BARRIER TO TRADE

How many times have you been sitting home late at night, hungry, wishing you had a meal from your favorite fast-food restaurant? You would gladly pay the $4 price for the value meal you have in mind, but you feel it is just not worth the time and effort to get dressed and make that drive. The costs of the time, effort, and other resources necessary to search out, negotiate, and conclude an exchange are called **transaction costs**. High transaction costs can be a barrier to potentially productive exchange.

Because of transaction costs, we should not expect all potentially valuable trades to take place, any more than we expect all useful knowledge to be learned, all safety measures to be taken, or all potential "A" grades to be earned. Students often discover that finding someone willing to pay an attractive price for a used book at the end of a semester or an unused ticket to a football game is not worth the cost. The cost of information, transportation, and other elements of transaction costs will some times be so great that potential gains from trade will go unrealized.

Reductions in transaction costs will increase the gains from trade. The Internet has significantly lowered transaction costs. The auction Web site eBay helps sellers to reach millions of potential buyers with little effort and few costs. Buyers can easily search eBay for items they want to buy, even if the items are located halfway around the world. Other Web sites, such as Bizrate and PriceGrabber, scour online shopping sites for the lowest prices so buyers don't have to. Consumers can also readily find detailed information about products on any number of sites. Amazon.com posts prices, product information provided by manufacturers, and reviews from other buyers. By reducing transaction costs, the Internet creates value and wealth. It expands the number of trades that are made, and makes it faster and easier to make them.

THE MIDDLEMAN AS A COST REDUCER

Because it is costly for buyers and sellers to find each other and to negotiate the exchange, an entrepreneurial opportunity exists for people to become **middlemen**. Middlemen provide buyers and sellers information at a lower cost and arrange trades between them. Many people think middlemen just add to the buyer's expense without performing a useful function. However, because of transaction costs, without middlemen, many trades would never happen (nor would the gains from them be realized). An auto dealer, for example, is a middleman. An auto dealer helps both the manufacturer and the buyer. The dealer helps buyers by maintaining an inventory of vehicles for them to choose from. Knowledgeable salespeople hired by the dealer help car shoppers quickly learn about the vehicles they're interested in and the pros and cons of each. Car buyers also like to know that a local dealer

Transaction costs
The time, effort, and other resources needed to search out, negotiate, and complete an exchange.

Middlemen
People who buy and sell goods or services or arrange trades. A middleman reduces transaction costs.

will honor the manufacturer's warranty and provide parts and service for the car. The dealer helps manufacturers by handling tasks like these so they can concentrate on designing and making better cars.

Grocers are also middlemen. Each of us could deal with farmers directly to buy our food—probably at a lower monetary cost. But that would have a high opportunity cost. Finding and dealing with different farmers for every product we wanted to buy would take a lot of time. Alternatively, we could form consumer cooperatives, banding together to eliminate the middleman, using our own warehouses and our own volunteer labor to order, receive, display, distribute, and collect payment for the food. In fact, some cooperatives like this do exist. But most people prefer instead to pay a grocer to provide all of the goods they want rather than trying to trade with different farmers.

Stockbrokers, realtors, publishers, and merchants of all sorts are other kinds of middlemen. For a fee, they reduce transaction costs for both buyers and sellers. By making exchanges cheaper and more convenient, middlemen cause more efficient trades to happen. In so doing, they themselves create value.

THE IMPORTANCE OF PROPERTY RIGHTS

The buyer of an apple, a CD, a television set, or an automobile generally takes the item home. The buyer of a steamship or an office building, though, may never touch it. When exchange occurs, it's really the **property rights** of the item that change hands.

Private-property rights involve three things:

1. the right to exclusive use of the property (that is, the owner has sole possession, control, and use of the property, including the right to exclude others);
2. legal protection against invasion from other individuals who would seek to use or abuse the property without the owner's permission; and
3. the right to transfer, sell, exchange, or mortgage the property.

Private owners can do anything they want with their property as long as they do not use it in a manner that invades or infringes on the rights of another. For example, I cannot throw the hammer that I own through the television set that you own. If I did, I would be violating your property right to your television. The same is true if I operate a factory spewing out pollution harming you or your land.[5] Because an owner has the right to control the use of property, the owner also must accept responsibility for the outcomes of that control.

In contrast to private ownership, common-property ownership occurs when multiple people simultaneously have or claim ownership rights to a good or resource. If the resource is open to all, none of the common owners can prevent the others from using or damaging the property. Most beaches, rivers, and roads are examples of commonly owned property. The distinction between private- and common-property ownership is important because common ownership does not create the same powerful incentives for conservation and efficient use as private ownership. Economists are fond of saying that when everybody owns something, nobody owns it.

Property rights
The rights to use, control, and obtain the benefits from a good or resource.

Private-property rights
Property rights that are exclusively held by an owner and protected against invasion by others. Private property can be transferred, sold, or mortgaged at the owner's discretion.

Private Ownership
Private ownership provides people with a strong incentive to take care of things and develop resources in ways that are highly valued by others.

keys to economic prosperity

iStockphoto.com/Scott Dunlap

---

[5]For a detailed explanation of how property rights protect the environment, with several real-world examples, see Roger E. Meiners and Bruce Yandle, *The Common Law: How It Protects the Environment* (Bozeman, MT: PERC, 1998), available online at http://www.perc.org.

Clearly defined and enforced private-property rights are a key to economic progress because of the powerful incentive effects that private ownership generates. The following four incentives are particularly important:

1. Private owners can gain by employing their resources in ways that are beneficial to others, and they bear the opportunity cost of ignoring the wishes of others. Realtors often advise homeowners to use neutral colors for countertops and walls in their house because they will improve the resale value of the home. As a private owner, you could install bright green fixtures and paint your walls deep purple, but you will bear the cost (in terms of a lower selling price) of ignoring the wishes of others who might want to buy your house later. Conversely, by fixing up a house and doing things to it that others find beneficial, you can reap the benefit of a higher selling price. Similarly, you could spray paint orange designs all over the outside of your brand-new car, but private ownership gives you an incentive not to do so because the resale value of the car depends on the value that *others* place on it.

Consider a parcel of undeveloped, privately owned land near a university. The private owner of the land can do many things with it. For example, she could leave it undeveloped, turn it into a metered parking lot, erect a restaurant, or build rental housing. Will the wishes and desires of the nearby students be reflected in her choice, even though they are not the owners of the property? Yes. Whichever use is more highly valued by potential customers will earn her the highest investment return. If housing is relatively hard to find but there are plenty of other restaurants, the profitability of using her land for housing will be higher than the profitability of using it for a restaurant. Private ownership gives her a strong incentive to use her property in a way that will also fulfill the wishes of others. If she decides to leave the property undeveloped instead of erecting housing that would benefit the students, she will bear the opportunity cost of forgone rental income from the property.

Consider a second example: the incentive structure confronted by the owner of an apartment complex near your campus. The owner may not care much for swimming pools, workout facilities, study desks, washers and dryers, or green areas. Nonetheless, private ownership provides the owner with a strong incentive to provide these items if students and other potential customers value them more than the costs of their provision. Why? Because tenants will be willing to pay higher rents to live in a complex with amenities that they value. The owners of rental property can profit by providing an additional amenity that tenants value as long as the tenants are willing to pay enough additional rent to cover their cost.

2. Private owners have a strong incentive to care for and properly manage what they own. Will Ed regularly change the oil in his car? Will he see to it that the seats don't get torn? Probably so, because being careless about these things would reduce the car's value, both to him and to any future owner. The car and its value—the sale price if he sells it—belong just to Ed, so he would bear the burden of a decline in the car's value if the oil ran low and ruined the engine, or if the seats were torn. Similarly, he would capture the value of an expenditure that improved the car, like a new paint job. As the owner, Ed has both the authority and the incentive to protect the car against harm

"Their house looks so nice. They must be getting ready to sell it."

A private owner has a strong incentive to do things with his or her property that increase its value to others.

When apartments and other investment properties are owned privately, the owner has a strong incentive to provide amenities that others value highly relative to their cost.

or neglect and even to enhance its value. Private-property rights give owners a strong incentive for good stewardship.

Do you take equally good care not to damage an apartment you rent as you would your own house? If you share an apartment with several roommates, are the common areas of the apartment (such as the kitchen and living room) as neatly kept as the bedrooms? Based on economic theory, we guess that the answer to both of these questions is probably "No."

A few years ago, the student government association at Berry College in Georgia purchased 20 bicycles to be placed around campus for everyone's use.[6] These $200 Schwinn Cruiser bicycles were painted red and were marked with a plate reading "Berry Bike." The bikes were available on a first-come, first-served basis, and students were encouraged to take them whenever they needed them and leave them anywhere on campus for others to use when they were finished. What do you think happened to these bikes? Within two months, most of these high-quality bikes were severely damaged or lost. The campus newspaper reported on the "mangled corpses of twisted red metal that lie about campus." Over the summer break, the student government replaced or fixed the bikes, but despite its pleas to "treat the bikes as if they were your own property," the same thing happened the following fall precisely because the bikes weren't the students' own property. It wasn't that the students at Berry College were inherently destructive; after all, there were no problems on campus with privately owned bikes being lost or abused during this time. It was a matter of the different incentives they faced. The student government association eventually abandoned the program and began leasing the remaining bikes to individual students instead. As you can see, there is no denying the strong incentive that private ownership creates for owners to care for their property (or the lack of the incentive to do so when private ownership is absent.)

3. Private owners have an incentive to conserve for the future—particularly if the property is expected to increase in value. People have a much stronger incentive to conserve privately owned property than they do commonly owned property. For example, when Steven was in college, the general rule among his roommates was that any food or drink in the house was common property—open game for the hungry or thirsty mouth of anyone who stumbled across it. There was never a reason for Steven to conserve food or drinks in the house because it would be quickly consumed by a roommate coming in later that night. When Steven first started living alone, he noticed a dramatic change in his behav-

Without clearly defined private-property rights, there is less of an incentive to take proper care of things—as the student government administration at Berry College found out when it provided common-property bikes to be used around campus.

ior. When he ordered a pizza, he would save some for the next day's lunch rather than eating it all that night. Steven began counting his drinks before he had one to make sure there were enough left for the next day. When Steven was the sole owner, he began delaying his current consumption to conserve for the future because he was the one, not his roommates, who reaped the benefit from his conservation.

Similarly, when more than one individual has the right to drill oil from an underground pool of oil, each has an incentive to extract as much as possible, as quickly as possible. Any oil conserved for the future will probably be taken by someone else. In contrast, when only one owner has the right to drill, the oil will be extracted more slowly. The same applies to the common-property problems involved in overfishing of the sea compared with fisheries that use privately owned ponds.

Courtesy of Berry College, Mount Berry, GA

---

[6]Daniel L. Alban and E. Frank Stephenson, "The 'Berry Bikes': A Lesson in Private Property," *Ideas on Liberty* 49, no. 10 (October 1999): 8–9.

Someone who owns land, a house, or a factory has a strong incentive to bear costs now, if necessary, to preserve the asset's value for the future. The owner's wealth is tied up in the value of the property, which reflects nothing more than the net benefits that will be available to a future owner. Thus, the wealth of private owners is dependent upon their willingness and ability to look ahead, maintain, and conserve those things that will be more highly valued in the future. This is why private ownership is particularly important for the optimal conservation of natural resources.

4. Private owners have an incentive to lower the chance that their property will cause damage to the property of others. Private ownership links responsibility with the right of control. Private owners can be held accountable for damage done to others through the misuse of their property. A car owner has a right to drive his car, but will be held accountable if the brakes aren't maintained and the car damages someone else's property. Similarly, a chemical company has control over its products, but, exactly for that reason, it is legally liable for damages if it mishandles the chemicals. Courts of law recognize and enforce the authority granted by ownership, but they also enforce the responsibility that goes with that authority. Because private-property owners can be held accountable for damages they cause, they have an incentive to use their property responsibly and take steps to reduce the likelihood of harm to others. A property owner, for example, has an incentive to cut down a dying tree before it falls into a neighbor's house and to leash or restrain his or her dog if it's likely to bite others.

PRIVATE OWNERSHIP AND MARKETS

Private ownership and competitive markets provide the foundation for cooperative behavior among individuals. When private-property rights are protected and enforced, the permission of the owner must be sought before anyone else can use the property. Put another way, if you want to use a good or resource, you must either buy or lease it from the owner. This means that each of us must face the cost of using scarce resources. Furthermore, market prices give private owners a strong incentive to consider the desires of others and use their resources in ways others value.

Friedrich Hayek, the winner of the 1974 Nobel Prize in economics, used the expression "the extended order" to refer to the tendency for markets to lead perfect strangers from different backgrounds around the world to cooperate with one another. Let's go back to the example of the property owner who has the choice of leaving her land idle or building housing to benefit students. The landowner might not know any students in her town nor particularly care about providing them housing. However, because she is motivated by market prices, she might build an apartment complex and eventually do business with a lot of students she never intended to get to know. In the process, she will purchase materials, goods, and services produced by other strangers.

Things are different in countries that don't recognize private-ownership rights or enforce them. In these countries, whoever has the political power or authority can simply seize property from whomever might have it without compensating them. In his book *The Mystery of Capital*, economist Hernando de Soto argues that the lack of well-defined and enforced property rights explains why some underdeveloped countries (despite being market based) have made little economic progress. He points out that in many of these nations, generations of people have squatted on the land without any legal deed giving them formal ownership. The problem is these squatters cannot borrow against the land or the homes they built on it to generate capital because they don't have a deed to it, nor can they prevent someone else from arbitrarily taking the land away from them.

Private ownership and markets can also play an important role in environmental protection and natural-resource conservation. Ocean fishing rights, tradable rights to pollute, and private ownership of endangered species are just some examples. The accompanying Applications in Economics feature, "Protecting Endangered Species with Private-Property Rights," explores some of these issues.

APPLICATIONS IN ECONOMICS

Protecting Endangered Species with Private-Property Rights

Tom Brakefield/Getty Images

Have you ever wondered why the wild tiger is endangered in much of the world but most cats are thriving? Or why spotted owls are threatened in the Pacific Northwest but chickens are not? Why have elephant and rhinoceros populations declined in number but not cattle or hogs? The incentives accompanying private ownership provide the answer.

To understand why many wild animals are scarce, consider what happens with animals that provide food, most of which are privately owned. Suppose that people decided to eat less beef. Beef prices would fall, and the incentive for individuals to dedicate land and other resources to raise cattle would decline. The result would be fewer cows. The market demand for beef *creates* the incentive for suppliers to maintain herds of cattle and to protect them under a system of private ownership.

In some ways, the rhinoceros is similar to a cow. A rhino, like a large bull in a cattle herd, may charge if disturbed. At 3,000 pounds, a charging rhino can be very dangerous to humans. Also like cattle, rhinos can be valuable to people—a single horn from a black rhino, used for artistic carvings and medicines, can sell for up to $30,000. But when hunting rhinos and selling their horns is illegal, rhinos become a favorite target of poachers—people who hunt illegally. Poachers are sometimes even assisted by local people eager to see fewer rhinos present because rhinos make life risky for humans and they also compete for food and water.

However, rhinos are very different from cattle in one important respect: In most of Africa where they naturally range, private ownership of the rhino is prohibited. Since 1977, many nations have outlawed rhino hunting and forbidden the sale of rhino parts. But this approach has only made things worse for the rhino: between 1970 and 1994, the number of black rhinos declined by 95%.[1] According to South African economist Michael 't Sas-Rolfes, the trade ban "has not had a discernible effect on rhino numbers and does not seem to have stopped the trade in rhino horn. If anything, the . . . listings led to a sharp increase in the black market price of rhino horn, which simply fuelled further poaching and encouraged speculative stockpiling of horn."

But what if the powerful incentives created by private ownership were instead brought to bear on the rhino? That actually happened for a while in Zimbabwe. Landowners were allowed to fence and manage game animals on their property. Because they could profit from protecting the big animals, some ranchers shifted their operations from producing cattle to wildlife protection, ecotourism, and hunting, often in cooperation with neighboring landowners. Under these rules, the black rhino population climbed dramatically. And because ranchers were allowed to cooperate and combine operations, they could reduce fencing between ranches and manage the larger preserves as a unit, better helping not only rhinos but other valued wildlife as well.

Indeed, several parts of southern Africa have a tradition, extending back to the 1960s, of allowing ownership of wildlife. Namibia, for example, gave those rights to private landholders in the 1960s and extended them to communal lands in the mid-1990s. "These institutional reforms led to wildlife becoming an economically valued land use at the local level," says wildlife specialist Fred Nelson. "For example, in 2003, Namibia's local communal landholders earned over US $1 million from wildlife-based enterprises such as tourism and hunting."[2] Landholders had invested in conservation measures to speed up the recovery that made these revenues possible.

Nelson reports that wildlife on private lands in Namibia increased by an estimated 80% from 1972 to 1992 as a result of the new policies. Where similar policy changes have occurred, wildlife has increased, says Nelson. "In South Africa, Namibia, Botswana, and Zimbabwe (prior to its sociopolitical collapse, 2000–present), the proportion of large herbivore species that are increasing or stable substantially exceeds the number that are declining." Clearly, property rights to ownership or use are one key to conservation.

[1]See Michael De Alessi, *Private Conservation and Black Rhinos in Zimbabwe: The Savé Valley and Bubiana Conservancies,* available online at http://www.cei.org/gencon/025,01687.cfm.

[2]Fred Nelson, "Are Large Mammal Declines in Africa Inevitable?" *African Journal of Ecology* 46 (2007): 3–4.

PRODUCTION POSSIBILITIES CURVE

Production possibilities curve
A curve that outlines all possible combinations of total output that could be produced, assuming (1) a fixed amount of productive resources, (2) a given amount of technical knowledge, and (3) full and efficient use of those resources. The slope of the curve indicates the amount of one product that must be given up to produce more of the other.

People try to get the most from their limited resources by making purposeful choices and engaging in economizing behavior. This can be illustrated using a conceptual tool called the **production possibilities curve**. The production possibilities curve shows the maximum amount of any two products that can be produced from a fixed set of resources, and the possible trade-offs in production between them. The real economy obviously produces more than just two products, but this concept can help us understand a number of important economic ideas.

Exhibit 1 illustrates the production possibilities curve for Susan, an intelligent economics major. This curve indicates the combinations of English and economics grades that she thinks she can earn if she spends a total of ten hours per week studying for the two subjects. Currently, she is choosing to study the material in each course that she expects will help her grade the most for the time spent, and she is allocating five hours of study time to each course. She expects that this amount of time, carefully spent on each course, will allow her to earn a B grade in both, indicated at point *T*. But if she were to take some time away from studying one of the two subjects and spend it studying the other, she could raise her grade in the course receiving more study time. However, it would come at the cost of a lower grade in the course she spends less time studying for. If she were to move to point *S* by spending more hours on economics and fewer on English, for example, her expected economics grade would rise, while her expected English grade would fall. This illustrates an important point: the idea of trade-offs in the use of scarce resources. Whenever more of one thing is produced, there is an opportunity cost in terms of something else that now must be forgone.

You might notice that Susan's production possibilities curve indicates that the additional study time required to raise her economics grade by one letter, from a B to an A (moving from point *T* to point *S*), would require giving up two letter grades in her English class, not just one, reducing her English grade from a B to a D. If, alternatively, Susan were to move from point *T* to point *U*, the opposite would be true—she would improve her English grade by one letter at the expense of two letter grades in economics. You can understand this by thinking about your own studying behavior. When you have only a limited amount of time to study a subject, you begin by studying the most important (grade-increasing) material first. As you spend additional time on that subject, you begin studying topics that are of decreasing importance for your grade. Thus, adding an hour of study time to the subject Susan studies least will have a larger impact on her grade than will taking away an hour from the subject on which she currently spends more time.

This idea of increasing opportunity cost is reflected in the slope of the production possibilities curve. The curve is flatter to the left of point *T*, and steeper to the right, showing

---

Exhibit 1

Production Possibilities Curve for Susan's Grades in English and Economics

The production possibilities for Susan, in terms of grades, are illustrated for ten hours of total study time. If Susan studied ten hours per week in these two classes, she could attain a D in English and an A in economics (point *S*), a B in English and a B in economics (point *T*), or a D in economics and an A in English (point *U*).

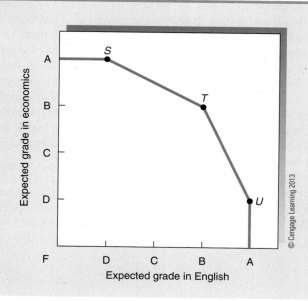

© Cengage Learning 2013

that, as Susan takes more and more of her resources (time, in this case) from one course and puts it into the other, she must give up greater and greater amounts of productivity in the course getting fewer resources.

Of course, Susan could study more economics *without* giving up her English study time, if she gave up some leisure, or study time for other courses, or her part-time job in the campus bookstore. If she gave up leisure or her job and added those hours to the ten hours of study time for economics and English, the entire curve in Exhibit 1 would shift outward. She could get better grades in both classes by having more time to study.

Can the production possibilities concept be applied to the entire economy? Yes. We can grow more soybeans if we grow less corn, because both can be grown on the same land. Beefing up the nation's military would mean we would have to produce fewer nonmilitary goods than we could otherwise. When scarce resources are being used efficiently, getting more of one requires that we sacrifice others.

Exhibit 2 shows a hypothetical production possibilities curve for an economy with a limited amount of resources that produces only two goods: food and clothing. The points along the curve represent all possible combinations of food and clothing that could be produced with the current level of resources and technology of the economy (assuming the resources are being used efficiently). A point outside the production possibilities curve (such as point *E*) would be considered unattainable at the present time. A point inside the production possibilities curve (such as point *D*) is attainable, but producing that amount would mean that the economy is not making maximum use of its resources (some resources are being underutilized). Thus, point *D* is considered inefficient.

More specifically, the production possibilities curve shows all of the maximum combinations of two goods that an economy will be able to produce: (1) given a fixed quantity of resources, (2) holding the level of technology constant, and (3) assuming that all resources are used efficiently.

When these three conditions are met, the economy will be at the edge of its production possibilities frontier (where points *A*, *B*, and *C* lie), and producing more of one good will necessitate producing less of others. If condition 3 above is not met, and resources are being used inefficiently, an economy would be operating inside its production possibilities curve. If the level of resources and technology change (conditions 1 and 2), it will result in an outward shift in the production possibilities curve. We will return to these factors that can shift the production possibilities curve in a moment.

Notice that the production possibilities curve is concave (or bowed out) to the origin, just as Susan's was in Exhibit 1 because of the concept of increasing opportunity cost. Here, the curved shape reflects the fact that an economy's resources are not equally well suited

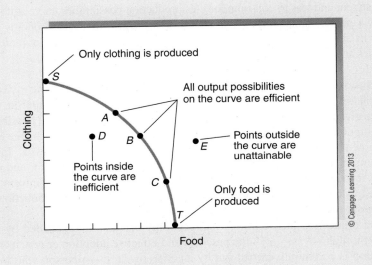

Exhibit 2

Concept of Production Possibilities Curve for an Economy

When an economy is using its limited resources efficiently, production of more clothing requires that the economy give up some other goods—such as food in this example. In time, improved technology, more resources, or improvement in its economic organization could make it possible to produce more of both goods by shifting the production possibilities curve outward.

to produce food and clothing. If an economy were using all its resources to produce clothing (point *S*), transferring those resources least suited for producing clothing toward food production would reduce clothing output a little but increase food output a lot. Because the resources transferred would be those better suited for producing food and less suited for producing clothing, the opportunity cost of producing additional food (in terms of clothing forgone) is low—near point *S*. However, as more and more resources are devoted to food production and successively larger amounts of food are produced (moving the economy from *S* to *A* to *B* and so on), the opportunity cost of food will rise. This is because, as more and more food is produced, additional food output can be achieved only by using resources that are less and less suitable for the production of food relative to clothing. Thus, as food output is expanded, successively larger amounts of clothing must be forgone per unit of additional food. This is similar to what happened to Susan when she diverted study hours from one course to another. Only this time, we are talking about an entire economy.

SHIFTING THE PRODUCTION POSSIBILITIES CURVE OUTWARD

What restricts an economy—once its resources are fully utilized—from producing more of everything? Why can't we get more of something produced without having to give up the production of something else? The same constraint that kept Susan from simultaneously making a higher grade in both English and economics: a lack of resources. As long as all current resources are being used efficiently, the only way to get more of one good is to sacrifice some of the other. Over time, however, it is possible for a country's production possibilities curve to shift outward, making it possible for more of all goods to be produced. There are four factors that could potentially shift the production possibilities curve outward.

1. An increase in the economy's resource base would expand our ability to produce goods and services. If we had more or better resources, we could produce a greater amount of all goods. Resources such as machinery, buildings, tools, and education are human-made, and thus we can expand our resource base by devoting some of our efforts to producing them. This **investment** would provide us with better tools and skills and increase our ability to produce goods and services in the future. However, like with the production of other goods, devoting effort and resources toward producing these long-lasting physical assets means fewer resources are available to produce other things, in this case goods for current consumption. Thus, the choice between using resources to produce goods for current consumption and using them to produce investment goods for the future can also be illustrated within the production possibilities framework. The two economies illustrated in **Exhibit 3** begin with identical production possibilities curves (*RS*). Notice that Economy A dedicates more of its output to investment (shown by I_A) than does Economy B (shown by I_B). Economy B, on the other hand, consumes more than Economy A. Because Economy A allocates more of its resources to investment and less to consumption, A's production possibilities curve shifts outward over time by a greater amount than B's. In other words, the growth rate of Economy A—the expansion of its ability to produce goods—is enhanced by this investment. But more investment in machines and human skills requires a reduction in current consumption.

2. Advancements in technology can expand the economy's production possibilities. **Technology** determines the maximum amount of output an economy can produce given the resources it has. New and better technology makes it possible for us to get more output from our resources. An important form of technological change is **invention**—the use of science and engineering to create new products or processes. In recent years, for example, inventions have allowed us to develop photographs faster and more cheaply, process data more rapidly, get more oil from existing fields, and send information instantly and cheaply by satellite. Such technological advances increase our production possibilities, shifting our economy's entire production possibilities curve outward.

The production possibilities of an economy can also be expanded by technological change through **innovation**—the practical and effective adoption of new techniques. Such innovation is commonly carried out by an **entrepreneur**—a person who introduces new products or improved techniques to satisfy consumers at a lower cost. Take, for example,

Investment
The purchase, construction, or development of resources, including physical assets, such as plants and machinery, and human assets, such as better education. Investment expands an economy's resources. The process of investment is sometimes called capital formation.

Technology
The technological knowledge available in an economy at any given time. The level of technology determines the amount of output we can generate with our limited resources.

Invention
The creation of a new product or process, often facilitated by the knowledge of engineering and science.

Innovation
The successful introduction and adoption of a new product or process; the economic application of inventions and marketing techniques.

Entrepreneur
A person who introduces new products or improved technologies and decides which projects to undertake. A successful entrepreneur's actions will increase the value of resources and expand the size of the economic pie.

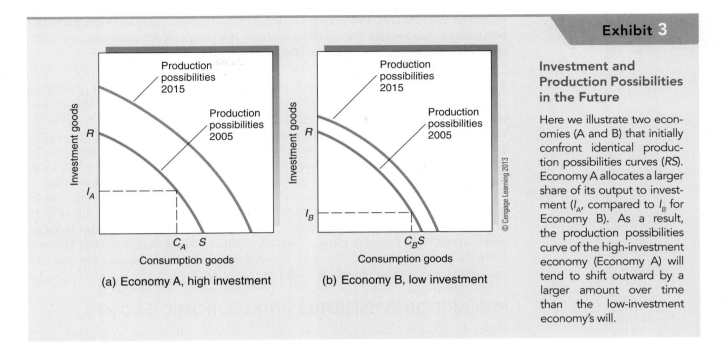

Exhibit 3

Investment and Production Possibilities in the Future

Here we illustrate two economies (A and B) that initially confront identical production possibilities curves (*RS*). Economy A allocates a larger share of its output to investment (I_A, compared to I_B for Economy B). As a result, the production possibilities curve of the high-investment economy (Economy A) will tend to shift outward by a larger amount over time than the low-investment economy's will.

(a) Economy A, high investment

(b) Economy B, low investment

Henry Ford, an entrepreneur who changed how cars were made by pioneering the assembly line. With the same amount of labor and materials, Ford made more cars more cheaply. Another entrepreneur, the late Ray Kroc, purchased a hamburger restaurant from Richard and Maurice McDonald and built it into the world's largest fast-food chain. Kroc revolutionized fast food by offering attractive food at economical prices. He also developed a franchising system that resulted in uniform quality across the many different McDonald's restaurants worldwide. More recently, entrepreneurs like Steven Jobs (Apple Computer) and Bill Gates (Microsoft) helped develop the personal computer and software programs that dramatically increased their usefulness to businesses and households.

Through entrepreneurial discovery and innovation, new products and methods of production are continuously replacing old ones. The great Harvard economist, Joseph Schumpeter, called this process **creative destruction**. The compact disc, for example, rendered vinyl records obsolete, while the automobile caused the demise of the horse and buggy industry. Although this process destroys some businesses or industries, it creates new and arguably better ones in their place. Creative destruction is a powerful force leading to economic growth and prosperity.

3. An improvement in the rules under which the economy functions can also increase output. The legal system of a country influences the ability of people to cooperate with one another and produce goods. Changes in legal institutions that promote social cooperation and motivate people to produce what others want will also push the production possibilities curve outward. However, poor institutions can reduce both the level of resources used (shifting the curve inward) and how efficiently they are used (causing the economy to operate inside its production possibilities curve).

Historically, legal innovations have been an important source of economic progress. During the eighteenth century, a system of patents was established in Europe and North America, giving inventors private-property rights to their ideas. At about the same time, laws were passed allowing businesses to establish themselves legally as corporations, reducing the cost of forming large firms that were often required for the mass production of manufactured goods. Both of these legal changes allowed improved forms of economic organization and accelerated the growth of output by shifting the production possibilities curve outward more rapidly.

Sometimes governments, perhaps because of ignorance or prejudice, adopt legal institutions that reduce production possibilities. Laws that restrict or prohibit trade are one example. For almost a hundred years following the American Civil War, the laws of several southern states

Creative destruction
The replacement of old products and production methods by innovative new ones that consumers judge to be superior. The process generates economic growth and higher living standards.

prohibited hiring African Americans for certain jobs and restricted other economic exchanges between blacks and whites. The legislation not only was harmful to African Americans; it also retarded economic progress and reduced the production possibilities of these states.

4. By working harder and giving up current leisure, we could increase our production of goods and services. Hypothetically, the production possibilities curve would shift outward if everyone worked more hours and took less leisure time. Strictly speaking, however, leisure is also a good, so we would simply be giving up leisure to have more of other things. If we were to construct a production possibilities curve for leisure versus other goods, this would be shown as simply a movement along the curve. However, if we restrict our model to only material goods and services, a change in the amount we work would be shown as a shift in the curve.

How much people work depends not only on their personal preferences but also on public policy. For example, high tax rates on personal income may cause people to work less. This is because high tax rates reduce the payoff from working. When this happens, people spend more time doing other, untaxed activities—like leisure activities. This will move the production possibilities curve for material goods inward because the economy can't produce as much when people work less.

PRODUCTION POSSIBILITIES AND ECONOMIC GROWTH

Within the production possibilities framework, economic growth is simply an outward shift in the curve through time. The more rapidly the curve shifts outward, the more rapid is economic growth. There are other economic models that are used to analyze economic growth; however, they all share the production possibilities curve as a foundation. Economic growth is one of the most important topics in modern economics for good reason. On the one hand, an economic growth rate of 3 percent per year will result in living standards doubling approximately every 23 years. On the other hand, in a country experiencing an economic growth rate of only 1 percent, it will take approximately seventy years for living standards to double.

TRADE, OUTPUT, AND LIVING STANDARDS

keys to economic prosperity

iStockphoto.com/Scott Dunlap

Gains from Trade

Trade makes it possible for people to generate more output through specialization and division of labor, large-scale production processes, and the dissemination of improved products and production methods.

Division of labor
A method that breaks down the production of a product into a series of specific tasks, each performed by a different worker.

As we previously discussed, trade creates value by moving goods from people who value them less to people who value them more. However, this is only part of the story. Trade also makes it possible for people to expand their output through specialization and **division of labor**, large-scale production, and the dissemination of better products and production methods.

GAINS FROM SPECIALIZATION AND DIVISION OF LABOR

Businesses can achieve higher output levels and greater productivity from their workers through specialization and division of labor. More than 230 years ago, Adam Smith noted the importance of this factor. Observing the operation of a pin manufacturer, Smith noted that when each worker specialized in a separate function needed to make pins, 10 workers together were able to produce 48,000 pins per day, or 4,800 pins per worker. Smith doubted an individual worker could produce even 20 pins per day working alone from start to finish on each pin.[7]

---

[7]See Adam Smith, *An Inquiry into the Nature and Causes of the Wealth of Nations* (1776; Cannan's ed., Chicago: University of Chicago Press, 1976), 7–16, for additional detail on the importance of the division of labor.

The division of labor separates production tasks into a series of related operations. Each worker performs one or a few of perhaps hundreds of tasks necessary to produce something. This process makes it possible to assign different tasks to those individuals who are able to accomplish them most efficiently (that is, at the lowest cost). Furthermore, a worker who specializes in just one narrow area becomes more experienced and more skilled in that task over time.

Trading partners can also benefit from specialization and the division of labor. The **law of comparative advantage**, developed in the early 1800s by the great English economist David Ricardo, explains why this is true. ***The law of comparative advantage states that the total output of a group of individuals, an entire economy, or a group of nations will be greatest when the output of each good is produced by the person (or firm) with the lowest opportunity cost for that good.***

Comparative advantage applies to trade among individuals, business firms, regions, and even nations. When trading partners are able to use more of their time and resources to produce the things each is best at, they will be able to produce more together than would otherwise have been possible. In turn, the mutual gains they get from trading will result in higher levels of income for each. It's a win-win situation for both.

If a good or service can be obtained more economically through trade, it makes sense to get it that way rather than producing it for yourself. When you think about it, the law of comparative advantage is common sense. If someone else is willing to supply you with a good at a lower cost than you can produce it yourself, doesn't it make sense to trade for it and use your time and resources to produce more of the things you can produce most efficiently? Consider the situation of Andrea, an attorney who earns $100 per hour providing legal services. She has several documents that need to be typed, and she is thinking about hiring a typist earning $15 per hour to do it. Andrea is an excellent typist, much faster than the prospective employee. She could do the job in 20 hours, whereas the typist would take 40 hours.

Because of her greater typing speed, some might think Andrea should handle the job herself. This is not the case. If she types the documents, the job will cost her $2,000—the opportunity cost of 20 hours of practicing law at $100 per hour. Alternatively, the cost of having the documents typed by the typist is only $600 (40 hours at $15 per hour). Andrea's comparative advantage lies in practicing law. By hiring the typist, she will increase her own productivity for clients and will make more money.

The implications of the law of comparative advantage are universal. Any group will be able to produce more output from its available resources when each good or service is produced by the person with the lowest opportunity cost. This insight is particularly important in understanding the way a market economy works. Buyers will try to get the most for their money. They will not knowingly choose a high-cost option when a lower-cost alternative of the same value is available. This places low-cost suppliers at a competitive advantage. Thus, low-cost producers will generally survive and prosper in a market economy. As a result, the production of goods and resources will naturally tend to be allocated according to comparative advantage.

Most people recognize that Americans benefit from trade among the nation's 50 states. For example, the residents of Nebraska and Florida are able to produce a larger joint output and achieve higher income levels when Nebraskans specialize in producing corn and other grain products and Floridians specialize in producing oranges and other citrus products. The same is true for trade among nations. Like Nebraskans and Floridians, people in different nations will be better off if they specialize in the goods and services they can produce at a low cost and trade them for goods they produce at a high cost. See the addendum to this chapter for additional evidence on this point.

Law of comparative advantage
A principle that states that individuals, firms, regions, or nations can gain by specializing in the production of goods that they produce cheaply (at a low opportunity cost) and exchanging them for goods they cannot produce cheaply (at a high opportunity cost).

Trade channels goods to those who value them most. Trade also helps disseminate ideas for improved products and makes production methods such as specialization, the division of labor, and mass production more feasible. Over the years, trade has enabled us to produce more with our limited resources, dramatically improving our living standards.

REUTERS/Carlos Barria

GAINS FROM MASS PRODUCTION METHODS

Trade also promotes economic progress by making it possible for firms to lower their per-unit costs with mass production. Suppose a nation isolated itself and refused to trade with other countries. In an economy like this, self-sufficiency and small-scale production would be the norm. If trade were allowed, however, the nation's firms could sell their products to customers around the world. This would make it feasible for the firms to adopt more efficient, large-scale production processes. Mass production often leads to labor and machinery efficiencies that increase enormously the output per worker. But without trade, these gains could not be achieved.

GAINS FROM INNOVATION

Trade also makes it possible to realize gains from the discovery and dissemination of innovative products and production processes. Economic growth involves brain power, innovation, and the application of technology. Without trade, however, the gains derived from the discovery of better ways of doing things would be stifled. Furthermore, observing and interacting with other people using different and better technologies often encourage others to copy successful approaches. People also modify the technology they observe, adapting it for their own purposes. This sometimes results in new, and even better, technologies. Again, gains from these sources would be far more limited in a world without trade.

Can you imagine the difficulty involved in producing your own housing, clothing, and food, to say nothing of radios, television sets, dishwashers, automobiles, and telephone services? Yet, most families in North America, Western Europe, Japan, and Australia enjoy all these conveniences. They are able to do so largely because their economies are organized in such a way that individuals can cooperate, specialize, and trade, thereby reaping the benefits of the enormous increases in output—in both quantity and diversity—that can be generated. In contrast, countries that impose obstacles that retard exchange—either domestic or international—hinder their citizens from achieving these gains and more prosperous lives.

HUMAN INGENUITY AND THE CREATION OF WEALTH

keys to economic prosperity

iStockphoto.com/Scott Dunlap

Human Ingenuity

Economic goods are the result of human ingenuity and action; thus, the size of the "economic pie" is variable, not fixed.

The size of a country's "economic pie" is most easily thought of as the total dollar value of all goods and services produced during some period of time. This economic pie is the grand total of the wealth (or value) created by each member of the society. It is not some fixed total waiting to be divided up among people. On the contrary, the size of the economic pie reflects the physical effort and ingenuity of human beings. It is not an endowment from nature.

Economic output expands as we discover better ways of doing things. So over time, it is human knowledge and ingenuity—perhaps more than anything else—that limit our economic progress. If Jim, a local farmer who normally produces $30,000 worth of corn each year, finds a better growing method enabling him to produce $40,000 of corn per year, he has created additional wealth. But Jim has actually created more than the $10,000 in extra wealth. The $10,000 is only his share of the gains from the additional trades made possible by the extra corn he grew. Exchange makes both buyer and seller better off, so the total wealth created by Jim includes not only his $10,000 but also the gains of all of the buyers who purchased his additional output of corn.

This highlights an important point: in a market economy, a larger income for one person does not mean a smaller income for a trading partner. In fact, it is just the opposite. When a person earns income, he or she expands the economic pie by more than the amount of the slice that he or she gets, making it possible for the rest of us to have a bigger slice, too. When a wealthy entrepreneur, such as Bill Gates or Stephen King, has an income of, say, $100 million per year earned through voluntary exchanges in the marketplace, he has enlarged the economic pie by an even larger amount. Here's why: Suppose that Linda, a freelance graphic artist, pays $175 for a new software program developed by Bill Gates. As a result, she can do twice as much work in the same amount of time. Because she's more productive, Linda can earn more than enough additional income with the software to justify her purchase. In addition, the businesses she serves are also likely to be better off because the software makes it possible for her to give them more and better service and a lower price. More is produced in total. Thus, while Bill Gates gained, so, too, did Linda and her customers.

Similarly, had Stephen King never written a novel, not only would he not be as rich, but we would also all be poorer for never having had the opportunity to read his novels. When income is acquired through voluntary exchange, people who earn income also help others earn more income and live better, too.

ECONOMIC ORGANIZATION

Every economy faces three basic questions: (1) What will be produced? (2) How will it be produced? and (3) For whom will it be produced? These questions are highly interrelated. Throughout the book, we will consider how different types of economies solve them. There are two broad ways that an economy can be organized: markets and government (political) planning. Let us briefly consider each.

MARKET ORGANIZATION

Private ownership of productive assets, voluntary exchange, and market prices are the distinguishing features of market organization. Market organization is also known as capitalism.[8] Under market organization, private parties are permitted to buy and sell ownership rights of their assets at mutually acceptable prices. The government plays the limited role of rule maker and referee. It develops the rules, or the legal structure, that recognizes, defines, and protects private ownership rights. It helps individuals enforce contracts and protects people from violence and fraud. But in this role, the government is not an active player in the economy. Ideally, it avoids modifying market outcomes in an attempt to favor some people at the expense of others. For example, it doesn't prevent sellers from slashing prices or improving the quality of their products to attract customers from other competitors. Nor does it prevent buyers from outbidding others for products and productive resources. No legal restraints limit potential buyers or sellers from producing, selling, or buying in the marketplace.

Under market organization, no single individual or group of individuals guides the economy. There is no central planning authority, only individual planning. The three basic questions are solved independently in the marketplace by individual buyers and sellers making their own decentralized decisions. Buyers and sellers decide on their own what to produce, how to produce it, and whom to trade it to, based on the prices they themselves decide to charge.

In markets, individual buyers and sellers communicate their desires and preferences both directly and indirectly. They communicate directly through their buying and selling choices, by advertising, word of mouth and letters of request and complaint, and other means. They communicate indirectly by exiting or entering exchange relationships, as when they stop purchasing Coca-Cola and switch to Pepsi. The indirect, or "exit," option gives special power to their voiced, or direct, communication.

POLITICAL ORGANIZATION

The major alternative to market organization is collective decision-making, whereby the government, through the political process, makes decisions for buyers and sellers in an attempt to solve the basic economic questions facing the economy. The government may maintain private ownership but uses taxes, subsidies, and regulations to resolve the basic economic

Market organization A method of organization in which private parties make their own plans and decisions with the guidance of unregulated market prices. The basic economic questions of consumption, production, and distribution are answered through these decentralized decisions.

Capitalism An economic system in which productive resources are owned privately and goods and resources are allocated through market prices.

Collective decision-making The method of organization that relies on public-sector decision-making (voting, political bargaining, lobbying, and so on) to resolve basic economic questions.

[8]*Capitalism* is a term coined by Karl Marx.

Socialism
A system of economic organization in which (1) the ownership and control of the basic means of production rest with the state and (2) resource allocation is determined by centralized planning rather than market forces.

questions. Alternatively, an economic system in which the government also owns the income-producing assets (machines, buildings, and land) and directly determines what goods will be produced is called **socialism**. Either way, individual planning and decisions are replaced by central planning and decisions made through the political process. These decisions can be made by a single dictator or a group of experts, or through democratic voting. Political rather than market forces direct the economy, and government officials and planning boards hand down decisions to expand or contract the output of education, medical services, automobiles, electricity, steel, consumer durables, and thousands of other commodities.

While the market and political process can be used to address the same basic economic questions, there are fundamental differences between the two. The market system relies on voluntary exchange, price signals, and freedom of entry. This results in wider variety of products, a more competitive environment, and more dynamic change. On the other hand, the democratic political process responds primarily to the votes of the majority. In varying degrees, all economies use a combination of both of these methods of economic organization. Even predominantly market economies will still use taxes, subsidies, and some government ownership to direct and control resources. Similarly, predominantly socialist economies will, to some degree, use markets to allocate certain goods and services.

As we proceed, the tools of economics will be used to analyze both the market and political sectors. We think this approach is important and that you will find it both interesting and enlightening.

iStockphoto.com/gaspr13

Looking Ahead

The next two chapters present an overview of the market sector and explain how supply and demand for goods and services work. Chapters 5 and 6 focus on potential shortcomings of the market and how the collective decision-making process works in a democracy.

KEY POINTS

- The highest valued activity sacrificed when a choice is made is the opportunity cost of the choice; differences (or changes) in opportunity costs help explain human behavior.

- Mutual gain is the foundation of trade. When two parties engage in voluntary exchange, they are both made better off. Trade creates value because it channels goods and resources to those who value them the most.

- Transaction costs—the time, effort, and other resources necessary to search out, negotiate, and conclude an exchange—hinder the gains from trade in an economy. Middlemen perform a productive function by reducing transaction cost.

- Private-property rights motivate owners to use their resources in ways that benefit others and avoid doing harm to them. Private ownership also motivates owners to maintain and care for items they own and conserve valuable resources for the future.

- The production possibilities curve shows the maximum combination of any two products that can be produced with a fixed quantity of resources.

- Over time, the production possibilities curve of an economy can be shifted outward by (1) investment,

(2) technological advances, (3) improved institutions, and (4) greater work effort (forgoing leisure).

- The law of comparative advantage indicates that the joint output of individuals, regions, and nations will be maximized when each productive activity is undertaken by the low-opportunity-cost supplier. When a good can be acquired through trade more economically than it can be produced directly, it makes sense to trade for it.

- In addition to the gains that occur when goods are moved toward those who value them most, trade also makes it possible to expand output through specialization, division of labor, mass production processes, and innovation. These improved production techniques have contributed greatly to our modern living standards.

- The size of the economic pie is variable, not fixed. Human ingenuity can expand output by discovering lower cost methods of production and new products that are highly valued relative to cost.

- Economies can either be organized by decentralized markets (capitalism) or they can be centrally planned by government through political decision-making.

CRITICAL ANALYSIS QUESTIONS

1. "If Jones trades a used car to Smith for $5,000, nothing new is created. Thus, there is no way the transaction can improve the welfare of people." Is this statement true? Why or why not?

2. *Economists often argue that wage rates reflect productivity. Yet, the wages of house painters have increased nearly as rapidly as the national average, even though these workers use approximately the same production methods as they did 50 years ago. Can you explain why the wages of painters have risen substantially even though their productivity has changed so little?

3. It takes one hour to travel from New York City to Washington, D.C., by air, but it takes five hours by bus. If the airfare is $110 and the bus fare is $70, which would be cheaper for someone whose opportunity cost of travel time is $6 per hour? For someone whose opportunity cost is $10 per hour? $14 per hour?

4. *"People in business get ahead by exploiting the needs of their consumers. The gains of business are at the expense of suffering imposed on their customers." Evaluate this statement.

5. What is the major function of the middleman? Would people be better off if there were no middlemen? Why or why not?

6. If you have a private-ownership right to something, what does this mean? Does private ownership give you the right to do anything you want with the things that you own? Explain. How does private ownership influence the incentive of individuals to (a) take care of things, (b) conserve resources for the future, and (c) develop and modify things in ways that are beneficial to others? Explain.

7. What is the law of comparative advantage? According to the law of comparative advantage, what should be the distinguishing characteristics of the goods a nation produces? What should be the distinguishing characteristics of the goods a nation imports? How will international trade influence people's production levels and living standards? Explain.

8. *Does a 60-year-old tree farmer have an incentive to plant and care for Douglas fir trees that will not reach optimal cutting size for another 50 years?

9. *What forms of competition does a private-property, market-directed economy authorize? What forms does it prohibit?

10. Why is exchange important to a nation's prosperity? How does trade influence the quantity of output that trading partners are able to produce? In a market economy, will there be a tendency for both resources and products to be supplied by low-cost producers? Why or why not? Does this matter? Explain.

11. *Chick-fil-A's "Eat Mor Chikin" advertising campaign features three cows holding signs that say things like: "Save the cows, eat more chicken." If consumers began eating more chicken and less beef, would the cattle population increase or decrease? Explain.

12. *In many states, ticket scalping, or reselling tickets to entertainment events at prices above the original purchase price, is prohibited. Who is helped and who is hurt by such prohibitions? How can owners who want to sell their tickets get around the prohibition? Do you think it would be a good idea to prohibit the resale of other things—automobiles, books, works of art, or stock shares—at prices higher than the original purchase price? Why or why not?

13. Two centuries ago, there were more buffalo than cattle in the United States. Even though millions of cattle are killed for beef consumption each year, the cattle population continues to grow while the buffalo are virtually extinct. Why?

14. Consider the following questions:
   a. Do you think that your work effort is influenced by whether there is a close link between personal output and personal compensation (reward)? Explain.
   b. Suppose the grades in your class were going to be determined by a random drawing at the end of the course. How would this influence your study habits?
   c. How would your study habits be influenced if everyone in the class was going to be given an A grade? How about if grades were based entirely on examinations composed of the multiple-choice questions in the coursebook for this textbook?
   d. Do you think the total output of a nation will be influenced by whether or not there is a close link between the productive contribution of individuals and their personal reward? Why or why not?

15. In this chapter, it was stated that a private-property right also involves having the right to transfer or exchange what you own with others. However, selling your organs is a violation of federal law, a felony punishable by up to five years in prison or a $50,000 fine. In 1999, eBay intervened when a person put one of his kidneys up for sale on the auction site (the bidding reached $5.7 million before the auction was halted). Does this lack of legal ability to exchange mean that individuals do not own their own organs? Explain.

16. During the last three decades, entrepreneurs like Steve Jobs, Sam Walton, and Michael Dell have earned billions of dollars. Do you think the average American is better or worse off as the result of the economic activities of these individuals? Explain your response.

17. *As the skill level (and therefore earnings rate) of, say, an architect, computer specialist, or chemist increases, what happens to his or her opportunity cost of doing other things? How is the time spent on leisure likely to change?

18. *This question pertains to the addendum to Chapter 2.* The following tables show the production possibilities for two hypothetical countries, Italia and Nire. Which country has the comparative advantage in producing butter? Which country has the comparative advantage in producing guns? What would be a mutually agreeable rate of exchange between the countries?

Italia		Nire	
Guns	Butter	Guns	Butter
12	0	16	0
8	2	12	1
4	4	8	2
0	6	4	3
		0	4

*Asterisk denotes questions for which answers are given in Appendix B.

ADDENDUM

COMPARATIVE ADVANTAGE, SPECIALIZATION, AND GAINS FROM TRADE

This addendum is for instructors who want to assign a more detailed numerical example demonstrating comparative advantage, specialization, and mutual gains from trade. Students who are uncertain about their understanding of these topics may also find this material enlightening. The international trade chapter later in the text provides still more information on trade and how it affects our lives.

We begin with hypothetical production possibilities curves for two countries, Slavia and Lebos, shown in **Exhibit A-1**. The numerical tables represent selected points from each country's production possibilities curve. To make calculations easier, we have assumed away increasing opportunity costs in production so that the production possibilities curves are linear.

Without trade, each country would be able to consume only what it can produce for itself. Let's arbitrarily assume that for survival, Slavia requires three units of food and Lebos requires six units of food. As can be seen by point A

Exhibit A-1

Production Possibilities for Slavia and Lebos

For Slavia, the opportunity cost of producing one unit of clothing is equal to three units of food (1C = 3F). For Lebos, the opportunity cost of producing three units of clothing is equal to three units of food (3C = 3F or 1C = 1F). The difference in the opportunity costs of production will make possible mutually beneficial trade between the countries, with each specializing in its area of comparative advantage.

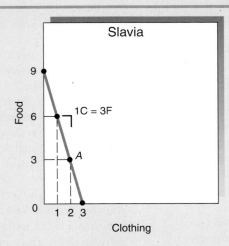

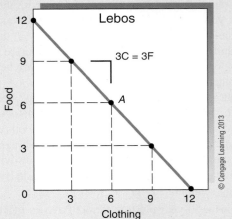

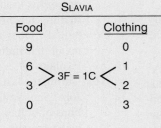

SLAVIA	
Food	Clothing
9	0
6	1
3	2
0	3

3F = 1C

LEBOS	
Food	Clothing
12	0
9	3
6	6
3	9
0	12

3F = 3C

© Cengage Learning 2013

in the exhibit, if Slavia were to produce the three units of food it requires, it would have enough resources remaining to produce two units of clothing. Similarly, if Lebos were to produce the six units of food it requires, it would have enough resources left to produce six units of clothing, again shown by point *A* in the exhibit. As we proceed, we will use this outcome as our benchmark outcome that occurs in the absence of specialization and trade between the countries.

Economic analysis suggests that both countries could gain if each were to specialize in the production of the good for which it has the comparative advantage and then trade for the other. First, let's figure out which country has a comparative advantage in the production of clothing. Doing so requires calculating the opportunity cost of producing clothing for each country. Because, in this example, the opportunity costs are constant at all points along the production possibilities curve, rather than increasing, this can be found by first selecting any two points on the production possibilities curve (or equivalently by comparing any two rows of numbers in the numerical tables given in the exhibit). For Slavia, moving from the point of producing six food units and one clothing unit to the alternative point of producing three food units and two clothing units, we see that Slavia gains one clothing unit but must give up three units of food. For simplicity, the opportunity cost for Slavia can be written as $1C = 3F$, where C stands for clothing and F for food. You might note that this same numerical trade-off is true for Slavia anywhere along its production possibilities curve (for example, beginning from nine food units and zero clothing units, it would also have to give up three food units to gain one unit of clothing).

Using a similar approach (taking any two points or two rows in the table) for Lebos shows that for every three units of clothing the country wishes to produce, it must give up three units of food ($3C = 3F$). This can be treated as any other mathematical equation, and can be simplified by dividing both sides by three, resulting in an opportunity cost of one clothing unit equals one food unit ($1C = 1F$). Now, compare this to the opportunity cost for Slavia ($1C = 3F$). Slavia must give up the production of three units of food for every one unit of clothing it produces, whereas Lebos must give up only one unit of food for every one unit of clothing it produces. Thus, Lebos gives up the production of *less* food for every unit of clothing. Lebos is the low-opportunity-cost producer of clothing, and thus it has a comparative advantage in the production of clothing.

Because comparative advantage is a relative comparison, if one country has the comparative advantage in the production of one of the products, the other country must have the comparative advantage for the other good. Thus, because Lebos has the comparative advantage in clothing, it will be true that Slavia has the comparative advantage in food. However, it is worthwhile to show this here as well. To produce one unit of food, Lebos must give up one unit of

clothing (recall the $1C = 1F$ opportunity cost). To produce one unit of food, Slavia must give up the production of only one-third of a unit of clothing (recall the $1C = 3F$ opportunity cost and rewrite the equation as $1/3\ C = 1F$ by dividing both sides of the equation by 3). Thus, Slavia gives up the production of *less* clothing for every unit of food produced. Slavia is the low-opportunity-cost producer of food, and thus has a comparative advantage in the production of food.

Suppose that, according to their comparative advantages, Lebos specializes in producing clothing and Slavia in food. From the last row of the table for Lebos, you can see that it can produce twelve units of clothing (and zero food) if it specializes in producing only clothing. From the top row of the table for Slavia, you can see that it can produce nine units of food (and zero clothing) if it specializes in producing only food. Note that this joint output (nine food and twelve clothing) is greater than the benchmark joint output (nine food and eight clothing) produced and consumed without trade.

If they are to trade, the countries now must find a mutually agreeable rate of exchange. Any rate of exchange *between* the two opportunity costs of $1C = 3F$ and $3C = 3F$ would be mutually agreeable. Here we will use $2C = 3F$.

Recall that Slavia requires three units of food for survival. Now, however, they are specializing and producing nine units of food. Using this rate of exchange, Slavia would send its extra six units of food to Lebos in exchange for four units of clothing. After trade, Slavia would then have three units of food and four units of clothing. Compare this to the situation that existed before specialization and trade, in which Slavia had only three units of food and two units of clothing to consume. Specialization and trade have created two additional units of clothing for Slavia that it would not have had without trade.

With specialization, Lebos is producing twelve units of clothing. In the trade with Slavia, Lebos gave up four units of clothing to obtain six units of food. After trade, Lebos has eight units of clothing remaining and six units of food imported from Slavia. Compare this to the situation that existed before specialization and trade, in which Lebos had only six units of food and six units of clothing to consume. For Lebos, specialization and trade have also created two additional units of clothing that it would not have had without trade.

As this simple example shows, total output is greater and *both* countries are better off when they specialize in the area in which they have a comparative advantage. By doing so, each is able to consume a bundle of goods and services that exceeds what it could have achieved in the absence of trade. This concept applies equally to individuals, states, or nations. The typical worker could not begin to produce alone all of the things he or she can afford to buy with the money earned in a year by specializing and working in a single occupation. As our world has become more integrated over the past several hundred years, the gains that have occurred from specialization and trade are at the root of the significant improvements in well-being that we have experienced.

Markets and Government

Economics has a great deal to say about how both markets and governments allocate scarce resources. It gives us insight about the conditions under which each will likely work well (and each will likely work poorly). The next four chapters will focus on this topic.

PART 2

Market Allocation of Resources

Business firms purchase resources like materials, labor services, tools, and machines from households in exchange for income, bidding the resources away from their alternate uses. The firms then transform the resources into products like shoes, automobiles, food products, and medical services and sell them to households. In a market economy, businesses will continue to supply a good or service only if the revenues from the sale of the product are sufficient to cover the cost of the resources required for its production.

Government Allocation of Resources

Resource allocation by the government involves a more complex, three-sided exchange. In a democratic political setting, a legislative body levies taxes on voter–citizens, and these revenues are subdivided into budgets, which are allocated to government bureaus and agencies. In turn, the bureaus and agencies use the funds from their budgets to supply goods, services, and income transfers to voter–citizens. The legislative body is like a board of directors elected by the citizens. Legislators have an incentive to take action that will attract votes. Voters have an incentive to support legislators who provide them with goods, services, and transfers that are highly valued relative to their tax payments. When decisions are made democratically, political action will require the approval of a legislative majority.

This section will first analyze the operation of markets and then turn to the political process.

There are two primary methods of allocating scarce resources: markets and government.

CHAPTER

3

Supply, Demand, and the Market Process

CHAPTER FOCUS

- What are the laws of demand and supply?
- How do consumers decide whether to purchase a good? How do producers decide whether to supply it?
- How do buyers and sellers respond to changes in the price of a good?
- What role do profits and losses play in an economy? What must a firm do to make a profit?
- How is the market price of a good determined?
- How do markets adjust to changes in demand? How do they adjust to changes in supply?
- What is the "invisible hand" principle?

I am convinced that if [the market system] were the result of deliberate human design, and if the people guided by the price changes understood that their decisions have significance far beyond their immediate aim, this mechanism would have been acclaimed as one of the greatest triumphs of the human mind.

—Friedrich Hayek, Nobel Laureate[1]

From the point of view of physics, it is a miracle that [7 million New Yorkers are fed each day] without any control mechanism other than sheer capitalism.

—John H. Holland, scientist, Santa Fe Institute[2]

[1]Friedrich Hayek, "The Use of Knowledge in Society," *American Economic Review* 35 (September 1945): 519–30.
[2]As quoted by Russell Ruthen in "Adapting to Complexity," *Scientific American* 268 (January 1993): 132.

To those who study art, the *Mona Lisa* is much more than a famous painting of a woman. Looking beyond the overall picture, they see and appreciate the brush strokes, colors, and techniques embodied in the painting. Similarly, studying economics can help you to gain an appreciation for the details behind many things in your everyday life. During your last visit to the grocery store, you probably noticed the fruit and vegetable section. Next time, take a moment to ponder how potatoes from Idaho, oranges from Florida, apples from Washington, bananas from Honduras, kiwi fruit from New Zealand, and other items from around the world got there. Literally thousands of different individuals, *working independently*, were involved in the process. Their actions were so well coordinated, in fact, that the amount of each good was just about right to fill exactly the desires of your local community. Furthermore, even the goods shipped from halfway around the world were fresh and reasonably priced.

How does all this happen? The short answer is that it is the result of market prices and the incentives and coordination that flow from them. To the economist, the operation of markets—including your local grocery market—is like the brush strokes underlying a beautiful painting. Reflecting on this point, Friedrich Hayek speculates that if the market system had been deliberately designed, it would be "acclaimed as one of the greatest triumphs of the human mind." Similarly, computer scientist John H. Holland argues that, from the viewpoint of physics, the feeding of millions of New Yorkers day after day with very few shortages or surpluses is a miraculous feat (see the chapter-opening quotations).

Amazingly, markets coordinate the actions of millions of individuals *without* central planning. There is no individual, political authority, or central planning committee in charge. Considering that there are more than 300 million Americans with widely varying skills and desires, and roughly 27 million businesses producing a vast array of products ranging from diamond rings to toilet paper, the coordination derived from markets is indeed an awesome achievement.

This chapter focuses on supply, demand, and the determination of market prices. For now, we will analyze the operation of competitive markets—that is, markets in which buyers and sellers are free to enter and exit. We will also assume that the property rights are well defined. Later, we will consider what happens when these conditions are absent.

On eBay, sellers enter their reserve prices—the minimum prices they will accept for goods; buyers enter their

The produce section of your local grocery store is a great place to see economics in action. Literally millions of individuals from around the world have been involved in the process of getting these goods to the shelves in just the right quantities. Market prices underlie this feat.

maximum bids—the maximum prices they are willing to pay for goods. The process works the same way when a person runs a newspaper ad to sell a car. The seller has in mind a minimum price he or she will accept for the car. A potential buyer, on the other hand, has in mind a maximum price he or she will pay for the car. If the buyer's maximum price is greater than the seller's minimum price, the exchange will occur at a price somewhere in between. As these examples show, the buyers' and sellers' desires and incentives determine prices and make markets work. We will begin with the demand (buyer's) side, and then turn to the supply (seller's) side of the market.

CONSUMER CHOICE AND THE LAW OF DEMAND

Clearly, prices influence our decisions. As the price of a good increases, we have to give up more of *other* goods if we want to buy it. Thus, as the price of a good rises, its opportunity cost increases (in terms of other goods that must be forgone to purchase it).

A basic principle of economics is that if something becomes more costly, people will be less likely to buy it. This principle is called the law of demand. ***The law of demand states that there is an inverse (or negative) relationship between the price of a good or service and the quantity of it that consumers are willing to purchase.*** This inverse relationship means that price and the quantity consumers wish to purchase move in opposite directions. As the price increases, buyers purchase less—and as the price decreases, buyers purchase more.

The availability of substitutes—goods that perform similar functions—helps explain this inverse relationship. No single good is absolutely essential; everything can be replaced with something else. A chicken sandwich can be substituted for a cheeseburger. Wood, aluminum, bricks, and glass can take the place of steel. Going to the movies, playing tennis, watching television, and going to a football game are substitute forms of entertainment. When the price of a good increases, people cut back on their purchases of it and turn to substitute products.

THE MARKET DEMAND SCHEDULE

The lower portion of **Exhibit 1** shows a hypothetical *demand schedule* for cellular telephone service.[3] A demand schedule is simply a table listing the various quantities of something consumers are willing to purchase at different prices. In Exhibit 1, notice that the price is the average monthly cost of purchasing cellular phone service. The quantity demanded is the number of people willing to subscribe to cellular service at each price. When the price of cell phone service is $143 per month, slightly more than 2 million people subscribe. As the price falls to $85, the quantity of subscribers rises to 11 million; when the price falls to $41 per month, the quantity of subscribers increases to slightly more than 69 million.

The upper portion of Exhibit 1 shows what the demand schedule would look like if the various prices and corresponding quantity of subscribers were plotted on a graph and connected by a line. This is called the *demand curve*. When representing the demand schedule graphically, economists measure price on the vertical or *y*-axis and the amount demanded on the horizontal or *x*-axis. Because of the inverse relationship between price and amount purchased, the demand curve will have a negative slope—that is, it will slope downward to the right. More of a good will be purchased as its price decreases. This is the law of demand.

Read horizontally, the demand curve shows how much of a particular good consumers are willing to buy at a given price. Read vertically, the demand curve shows how much consumers value the good. The height of the demand curve at any quantity shows the maximum price consumers are willing to pay for an additional unit. If consumers value highly an additional unit of a product, they will be willing to pay a large amount for it. Conversely, if they place a low value on the additional unit, they will be willing to pay only a small amount for it.

Because the amount a consumer is willing to pay for a good is directly related to the good's value to them, the demand curve indicates the marginal benefit (or value) consumers receive from additional units. (Recall that we briefly discussed marginal benefit in Chapter 1.) When viewed in this manner, the demand curve reveals that as consumers have more and more of a good or service, they value additional units less and less.

---

[3]These data are actual prices (adjusted to 2000 dollars) and quantities annually for 1988 to 1998 taken from *Statistical Abstract of the United States* (Washington, DC: U.S. Bureau of the Census, various years). *If we could assume that other demand determinants (income, prices of related goods, and so on) had remained constant,* then this hypothetical demand schedule would be accurate for that time period. Because it is possible that some of these other factors changed, we treat the numbers as hypothetical, depicting alternative prices and quantities *at a given time.*

Law of demand
A principle that states there is an inverse relationship between the price of a good and the quantity of it buyers are willing to purchase. As the price of a good increases, consumers will wish to purchase less of it. As the price decreases, consumers will wish to purchase more of it.

Substitutes
Products that serve similar purposes. An increase in the price of one will cause an increase in demand for the other (examples are hamburgers and tacos, butter and margarine, Chevrolets and Fords).

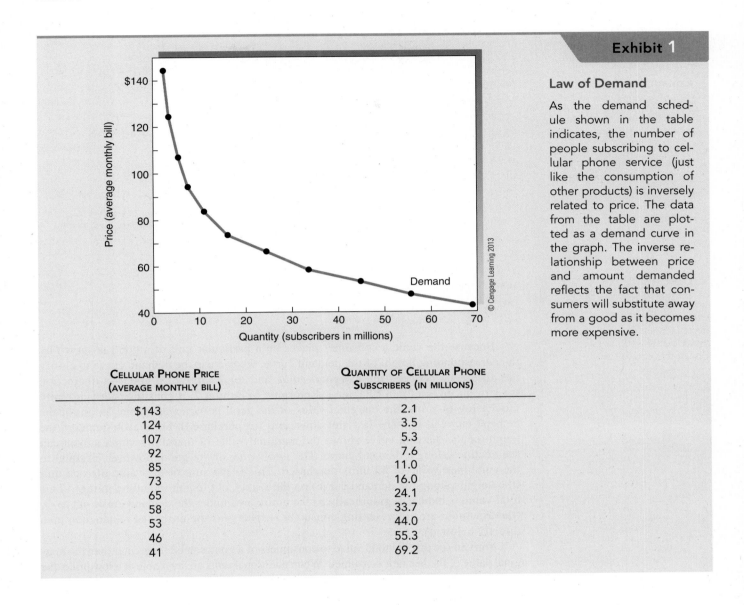

© Cengage Learning 2013

Exhibit 1

Law of Demand

As the demand schedule shown in the table indicates, the number of people subscribing to cellular phone service (just like the consumption of other products) is inversely related to price. The data from the table are plotted as a demand curve in the graph. The inverse relationship between price and amount demanded reflects the fact that consumers will substitute away from a good as it becomes more expensive.

CELLULAR PHONE PRICE (AVERAGE MONTHLY BILL)	QUANTITY OF CELLULAR PHONE SUBSCRIBERS (IN MILLIONS)
$143	2.1
124	3.5
107	5.3
92	7.6
85	11.0
73	16.0
65	24.1
58	33.7
53	44.0
46	55.3
41	69.2

CONSUMER SURPLUS

Previously, we indicated that voluntary exchanges make both buyers and sellers better off. The demand curve can be used to illustrate the gains to consumers. Suppose you value a particular good at $50, but you are able to purchase it for only $30. Your net gain from buying the good is the $20 difference. Economists call this net gain of buyers **consumer surplus**. Consumer surplus is simply the difference between the maximum amount consumers would be willing to pay and the amount they actually pay for a good.

Exhibit 2 shows the consumer surplus for an entire market. The height of the demand curve measures how much buyers in the market value each unit of the good. The price indicates the amount they actually pay. The difference between these two—the triangular area below the demand curve but above the price paid—is a measure of the total consumer surplus generated by all exchanges of the good. The size of the consumer surplus, or triangular area, is affected by the market price. If the market price for the good falls, more of it will be purchased, resulting in a larger surplus for consumers. Conversely, if the market price rises, less of it will be purchased, resulting in a smaller surplus (net gain) for consumers.

Consumer surplus
The difference between the maximum price consumers are willing to pay and the price they actually pay. It is the net gain derived by the buyers of the good.

Exhibit 2

Consumer Surplus

Consumer surplus is the area below the demand curve but above the actual price paid. This area represents the net gains to buyers from market exchange.

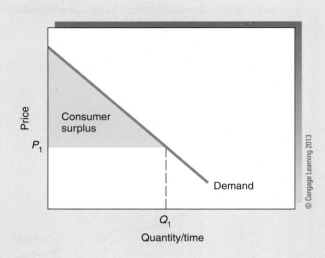

Because the value a consumer places on a particular unit of a good is shown by the corresponding height of the demand curve, we can use the demand curve to clarify the difference between the *marginal value* and *total value* of a good—a distinction we introduced briefly in Chapter 1. Returning to Exhibit 2, if consumers are currently purchasing Q_1 units, the marginal value of the good is indicated by the height of the demand curve at Q_1—the last unit consumed (or purchased). So at each quantity, the height of the demand curve shows the marginal value of that unit, which as you can see declines along a demand curve. The *total value* of the good, however, is equal to the combined value of all units purchased. This is the sum of the value of each unit (the heights along the demand curve) on the x-axis, out to and including unit Q_1. This total value is indicated graphically as the entire area under the demand curve out to Q_1 (the triangular area representing consumer surplus *plus* the unshaded rectangular area directly below it).

You can see that the total value to consumers of a good can be far greater than the marginal value of the last unit consumed. When additional units are available at a low price, the marginal value of a good may be quite low, even though its total value to consumers is exceedingly high. This is usually the case with water, for example, because it is essential for life. The value of the first few units of water consumed per day will be exceedingly high. The consumer surplus derived from these units will also be large when water is plentiful at a low price. As more and more units are consumed, however, the *marginal value* of even something as important as water will fall to a low level. When water is cheap, then, people will use it not only for drinking, cleaning, and cooking but also for washing cars, watering lawns, flushing toilets, and maintaining fish aquariums. Thus, although the total value of water is rather large, its marginal value is quite low.

Consumers will tend to expand their consumption of a good until its price and *marginal value* are equal (which occurs at Q_1 in Exhibit 2 at a price of P_1). Thus, the price of a good (which equals marginal value) reveals little about the *total value* derived from the consumption of it. This is the reason that the market price of diamonds (which reflects their high marginal value) is greater than the market price of water (which has a low marginal value), even though the total value of diamonds is far less than the total value of water. Think of it this way: Beginning from your current levels of consumption, if you were offered a choice between one diamond or one gallon of water right now, which would you take? You would probably take the diamond, because at the margin it has more value to you than additional water. However, if given a choice between giving up *all* of the water you use or *all* of the diamonds you have, you would probably keep the water over diamonds, because water has more total value to you.

RESPONSIVENESS OF QUANTITY DEMANDED TO PRICE CHANGES: ELASTIC AND INELASTIC DEMAND CURVES

As we previously noted, the availability of substitutes is the main reason why the demand curve for a good slopes downward. Some goods, however, are much easier than others to substitute away from. As the price of tacos rises, most consumers find hamburgers a reasonable substitute. Because of the ease of substitutability, the quantity of tacos demanded is quite sensitive to a change in their price. Economists would say that the demand for tacos is relatively *elastic* because a small price change will cause a rather large change in the amount purchased. Alternatively, goods like gasoline and electricity have fewer close substitutes. When their prices rise, it is harder for consumers to find substitutes for these products. When close substitutes are unavailable, even a large price change may not cause much of a change in the quantity demanded. In this case, an economist would say that the demand for such goods is relatively *inelastic*.

Graphically, this different degree of responsiveness is reflected in the steepness of the demand curve, as shown in **Exhibit 3**. The flatter demand curve (D_1, left frame) is for a product like tacos, for which the quantity purchased is highly responsive to a change in price. As the price increases from $2.00 to $4.00, the quantity demanded falls sharply from ten to four units. The steeper demand curve (D_2, right frame) is for a product like gasoline, for which the quantity purchased is much less responsive to a change in price. For gasoline, an increase in price from $2.00 to $4.00 results in only a small reduction in the quantity purchased (from ten to eight units). An economist would say that the flatter demand curve D_1 is "relatively elastic," whereas the steeper demand curve D_2 is "relatively inelastic." The availability of substitutes is the main determinant of a product's elasticity or inelasticity and thus how flat or steep its demand curve is.

What would a demand curve that was perfectly vertical represent? Economists refer to this as a "perfectly" inelastic demand curve, meaning that the quantity demanded of the product never changes—regardless of its price. Although it is tempting to think that the demand curves are vertical for goods essential to human life (or goods that are addictive), this is inaccurate for two reasons. First, in varying degrees, there are substitutes for everything. As the price of a good rises, the incentive increases for suppliers to invent even more substitutes. Thus, even for goods that currently have few substitutes, if the price were to rise high enough, alternatives would be invented and marketed, reducing the

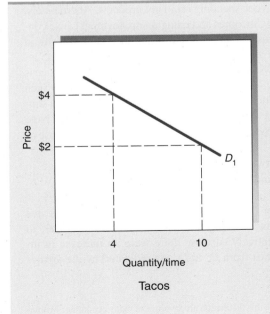

Tacos

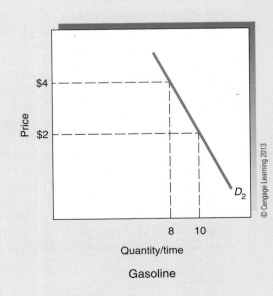

Gasoline

Exhibit 3

Elastic and Inelastic Demand Curves

The responsiveness of consumer purchases to a change in price is reflected in the steepness of the demand curve. The flatter demand curve (D_1) for tacos shows a higher degree of responsiveness and is called relatively elastic, while the steeper demand curve (D_2) for gasoline shows a lower degree of responsiveness and is called relatively inelastic

© Cengage Learning 2013

quantity demanded of the original good. Second, our limited incomes restrict our ability to afford goods when they become very expensive. As the price of a good rises to higher and higher levels, if we do not cut back on the quantity purchased, we will have less and less income to spend on other things. Eventually, this will cause us to cut back on our purchases of it. Because of these two reasons, the demand curve for every good will slope downward to the right.

CHANGES IN DEMAND VERSUS CHANGES IN QUANTITY DEMANDED

The purpose of the demand curve is to show what effect a price change will have on the quantity demanded (or purchased) of a good. Economists refer to a change in the quantity of a good purchased in response solely to a price change as a "change in *quantity demanded*." A change in quantity demanded is simply a movement along a demand curve from one point to another.

Changes in factors other than a good's price—such as consumers' income and the prices of closely related goods—will also influence the decisions of consumers to purchase a good. If one of these other factors changes, the entire demand curve will *shift* inward or outward. Economists refer to a shift in the demand curve as a "change in *demand*."

Failure to distinguish between a change in demand and a change in quantity demanded is one of the most common mistakes made by beginning economics students.[4] *A change in demand is a shift in the entire demand curve. A change in quantity demanded is a movement along the same demand curve.* The easiest way to distinguish between these two concepts is the following: If the change in consumer purchases is caused by a change in the price of the good, it is a change in quantity demanded—a movement along the demand curve; if the change in consumer purchases is due to a change in anything other than the price of the good (a change in consumer income, for example), it is a change in demand—a shift in the demand curve.

Let us now take a closer look at some of the factors that cause a "change in demand"—an inward or outward shift in the entire demand curve.

1. Changes in consumer income. An increase in consumer income makes it possible for consumers to purchase more goods. If you were to win the lottery, or if your boss were to give you a raise, you would respond by increasing your spending on many products. Alternatively, when the economy goes into a recession, falling incomes and rising unemployment cause consumers to reduce their purchases of many items. A change in consumer income will result in consumers buying more or less of a product at all possible prices. When consumer income increases, in the case of most goods, individuals will purchase more of the good even if the price is unchanged. This is shown by a shift to the right—an outward shift—in the demand curve. Such a shift is called an *increase in demand*. A reduction in consumer income generally causes a shift to the left—an inward shift—in the demand curve, which is called a *decrease in demand*. Note that the appropriate terminology here is an increase or a decrease in demand, not an increase or a decrease in quantity demanded.

Exhibit 4 highlights the difference between a change in demand and a change in quantity demanded. The demand curve D_1 indicates the initial demand curve for DVDs. At a price of $30, consumers will purchase Q_1 units. If the price were to decline to $10, the *quantity demanded* would increase from Q_1 to Q_3. The arrow in panel (a) indicates the change in *quantity demanded*—a movement along the original demand curve D_1 in response to the change in price. Now, alternatively suppose there were an increase in income that caused the *demand* for DVDs to shift from D_1 to D_2. As indicated by the arrows

---

[4]Questions designed to test the ability of students to make this distinction are favorites of many economics instructors. A word to the wise should be sufficient.

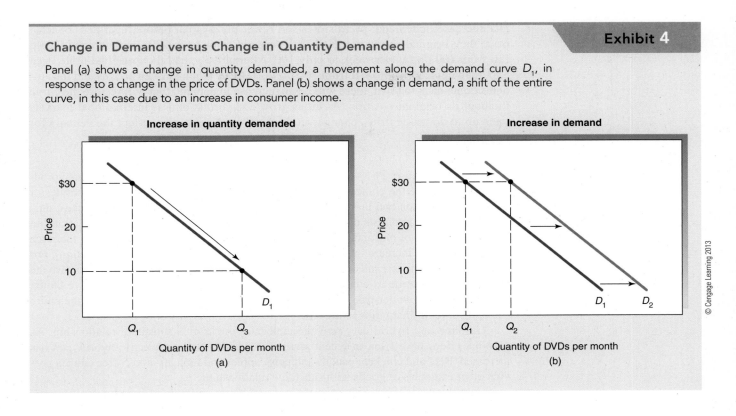

Exhibit 4

Change in Demand versus Change in Quantity Demanded

Panel (a) shows a change in quantity demanded, a movement along the demand curve D_1, in response to a change in the price of DVDs. Panel (b) shows a change in demand, a shift of the entire curve, in this case due to an increase in consumer income.

Increase in quantity demanded

(a)

Quantity of DVDs per month

Increase in demand

(b)

Quantity of DVDs per month

© Cengage Learning 2013

in panel (b), the entire demand curve would shift outward. At the higher income level, consumers would be willing to purchase more DVDs than before. This is true at a price of $30, $20, $10, and every other price. The increase in income leads to an increase in *demand*—a shift in the entire curve.

2. Changes in the number of consumers in the market. Businesses that sell products in college towns are greatly saddened when summer arrives. As you might expect in these towns, the demand for many items—from pizza delivery to beer—falls during the summer. **Exhibit 5** shows how the falling number of consumers in the market caused by students going home for the summer affects the demand for pizza delivery. With fewer customers, the demand curve shifts inward from D_1 to D_2. There

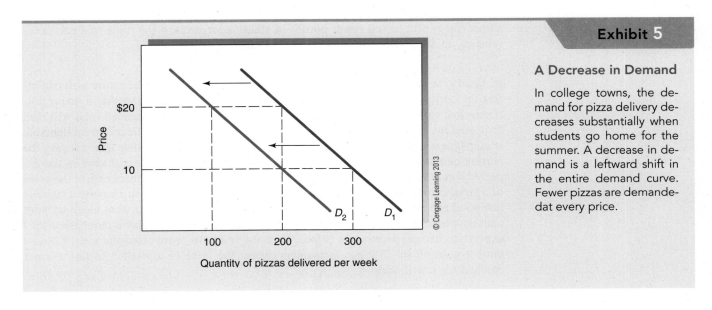

Exhibit 5

A Decrease in Demand

In college towns, the demand for pizza delivery decreases substantially when students go home for the summer. A decrease in demand is a leftward shift in the entire demand curve. Fewer pizzas are demanded at every price.

Quantity of pizzas delivered per week

© Cengage Learning 2013

is a decrease in demand; pizza stores sell fewer pizzas than before regardless of what price they originally charged. Had their original price been $20, then demand would fall from 200 pizzas per week to only 100. Alternatively, had their original price been $10, then demand would fall from 300 pizzas to 200. When autumn arrives and the students come back to town, there will be an increase in demand that will restore the curve to about its original position. As cities grow and shrink, and as international markets open up to domestic firms, changes in the number of consumers affect the demand for many products.

3. Changes in the price of a related good. Changes in prices of closely related products also influence the choices of consumers. Related goods may be either substitutes or complements. When two products perform similar functions or fulfill similar needs, they are substitutes. Economists define goods as substitutes when there is a direct relationship between the price of one and the demand for the other—meaning an increase in the price of one leads to an increase in demand for the other (they move in the same direction). For example, margarine is a substitute for butter. If the price of butter rises, it will increase the demand for margarine as consumers substitute margarine for the more expensive butter. Conversely, lower butter prices will reduce the demand for margarine, shifting the entire demand curve for margarine to the left.

Gasoline and hybrid cars provide another example of a substitute relationship. As gasoline prices have risen in recent years, the demand for gas–electric hybrid cars has increased. Beef and chicken, pencils and pens, apples and oranges, and coffee and tea provide other examples of goods with substitute relationships.

Note that although a change in the price of butter shifts the demand curve for *margarine* (a change in demand), it will only result in a movement along the demand curve for *butter* (a change in the quantity demanded). The reason is that the demand curve for butter already shows the relationship between the price of butter and the quantity of butter desired. An increase in the price of butter makes consumers willing to purchase more margarine, holding constant the price of margarine.

Other products are consumed jointly, so the demands for them are linked together as well. Examples of goods that "go together" include peanut butter and jelly, DVDs and DVD players, hot dogs and hot dog buns, and tents and other camping equipment. These goods are called **complements**. For complements, a decrease in the price of one will not only increase its quantity demanded; it will also increase the demand for the other good. For example, lower prices for DVD players over the past decade have substantially increased the demand for movies on DVD. The reverse is also true. As a complement becomes more expensive, the quantity demanded of it will fall, and so will the demand for its complements. For example, if the price of steak rises, grocery stores can expect to sell fewer bottles of steak sauce, even if the price of steak sauce remains unchanged.

Complements
Products that are usually consumed jointly (for example, bread and butter, hot dogs and hot dog buns). A decrease in the price of one will cause an increase in demand for the other.

4. Changes in expectations. Consumers' expectations about the future also can affect the current demand for a product. If consumers begin to expect that a major hurricane will strike their area, the current demand for batteries and canned food will rise. Expectations about the future direction of the economy can also affect current demand. If consumers are pessimistic about the economy, they start spending less, causing the current demand for goods to fall. Perhaps most important is how a change in the expected future price of a good affects current demand. When consumers expect the price of a product to rise in the near future, their current demand for it will increase. Gasoline is a good example. If you expect the price to increase soon, you'll want to fill up your tank now before the price goes up. In contrast, consumers will delay a purchase if they expect the item to decrease in price. No doubt you have heard someone say, "I'll wait until it goes on sale." When consumers expect the price of a product to fall, current demand for it will decline.

Thumbnail Sketch

Factors That Cause Changes in Demand and Quantity Demanded

This factor changes the quantity demanded of a good:

1. The price of the good: A higher price decreases the quantity demanded; a lower price increases the quantity demanded.

These factors change the demand for a good:

1. Consumer income: Lower consumer income decreases demand; higher consumer income increases demand.
2. Number of consumers in the market: Fewer consumers decreases demand; more consumers increases demand.
3a. Price of a substitute good: A decrease in the price of a substitute decreases the demand for the original good; an increase in the price of a substitute increases the demand for the original good.
3b. Price of a complementary good: An increase in the price of a complement decreases the demand for the original good; a decrease in the price of a complement increases the demand for the original good.
4. Expected future price of the good: If the price of a good is expected to fall in the future, the current demand for it will decrease; if the price of a good is expected to rise in the future, the current demand for it will increase.
5. Demographic changes: Population trends in age, gender, race, and other factors can increase or decrease demand for specific goods.
6. Consumer preferences: Changes in consumer tastes and preferences can increase or decrease demand for specific goods.

5. Demographic changes. The demand for many products is strongly influenced by the demographic composition of the market. An increase in the elderly population in the United States in recent years has increased the demand for medical care, retirement housing, and vacation travel. The demand curves for these goods have shifted to the right. During the 1980s, the number of people aged 15 to 24 fell by more than 5 million. Because young people are a major part of the U.S. market for jeans, the demand for jeans fell by more than 100 million pairs over the course of the decade.[5] More recently, the increased use of cell phones and iPods among teenagers has led to a dramatic reduction in the demand for wristwatches.

6. Changes in consumer tastes and preferences. Why do preferences change? Preferences change because people change and because people acquire new information. Consider how consumers are responding to the popularity of the Atkins diet. The demand for high-carbohydrate foods like white bread has fallen substantially, whereas the demand for low-carbohydrate foods like beef has risen. This is a major change from the 1990s, when the demand for beef fell because of the "heart-healthy" eating habits consumers preferred then. Trends in the markets for clothing, toys, collectibles, and entertainment are constantly causing changes in the demand for these products as well. Firms may even try to change consumer preferences for their own products through advertising and information brochures.

The accompanying **Thumbnail Sketch** summarizes the major factors that cause a change in *demand*—a shift of the entire demand curve—and points out that quantity *demanded* (but not demand) will change in response to a change in the price of a good.

---

[5]These figures are from Suzanne Tregarthen, "Market for Jeans Shrinks," *The Margin* 6, no. 3 (January–February 1991): 28.

PRODUCER CHOICE AND THE LAW OF SUPPLY

Now let's shift our focus to producers and the supply side of the market. How does the market process determine the amount of each good that will be produced? To figure this out, we first have to understand what influences the choices of producers. Producers convert resources into goods and services by doing the following:

1. organizing productive inputs and resources, like land, labor, capital, natural resources, and intermediate goods;
2. transforming and combining these inputs into goods and services; and
3. selling the final products to consumers.

Producers have to purchase the resources at prices determined by market forces. Predictably, the owners of these resources will supply the resources only at prices at least equal to what they could earn elsewhere. Put another way, each resource the producers buy to make their product has to be bid away from all other potential uses. Its owner has to be paid its opportunity cost. The sum of the producer's cost of each resource used to produce a good will equal the **opportunity cost of production**.

Opportunity cost of production
The total economic cost of producing a good or service. The cost component includes the opportunity cost of all resources, including those owned by the firm. The opportunity cost is equal to the value of the production of other goods sacrificed as the result of producing the good.

There is an important difference between the opportunity cost of production and standard accounting measures of cost. Accountants generally do not count the cost of assets owned by the firm when they calculate the firm's cost. But economists do. Economists consider the fact that the assets owned by the firm could be used some other way—in other words, that they have an opportunity cost. Unless these opportunity costs are covered, the resources will eventually be used in other ways.

The opportunity cost of the assets owned by the firm is the earnings these assets could have generated if they were used in another way. Consider a manufacturer that invests $10 million in buildings and equipment to produce shirts. Instead of buying buildings and equipment, the manufacturer could simply put the $10 million in the bank and let it draw interest. If the $10 million were earning, say, 10 percent interest, the firm would make $1 million on that money in a year's time. This $1 million in forgone interest is part of the firm's opportunity cost of producing shirts. Unlike an accountant, an economist will take that $1 million opportunity cost into account. If the firm plans to invest the money in shirt-making equipment, it had better earn more from making the shirts than the $1 million it could earn by simply putting the money in the bank. If the firm can't generate enough to cover all of its costs, including the opportunity cost of assets owned by the firm, it will not continue in business. If the firm were earning only $7 million producing shirts, it might be earning profit on its accounting statements, but it would be suffering a $3 million economic loss relative to simply putting the money in the bank.

THE ROLE OF PROFITS AND LOSSES

keys to economic prosperity

Profits and Losses

Profits direct producers toward activities that increase the value of resources; losses impose a penalty on those who reduce the value of resources.

iStockphoto.com/Scott Dunlap

Profit
An excess of sales revenue relative to the opportunity cost of production. The cost component includes the opportunity cost of all resources, including those owned by the firm. Therefore, profit accrues only when the value of the good produced is greater than the value of the resources used for its production.

Firms earn a **profit** when the revenues from the goods and services that they supply exceed the opportunity cost of the resources used to make them. Consumers will not buy goods and services unless they value them at least as much as their purchase price. For example, Susan would not be willing to pay $40 for a pair of jeans unless she valued them by at least that amount. At the same time, the seller's opportunity cost of supplying a good will reflect the value consumers place on *other* goods that could have been produced with those same resources. This is true precisely because the seller has to bid those resources away from other producers wanting to use them.

Think about what it means when, for example, a firm is able to produce jeans at a cost of $30 per pair and sell them for $40, thereby reaping a profit of $10 per pair. The $30 opportunity cost of the jeans indicates that the resources used to produce the jeans could have been used to produce other items worth $30 to consumers (perhaps a denim backpack). In turn, the profit indicates that consumers value the jeans more than other goods that might have been produced with the resources used to supply the jeans.

The willingness of consumers to pay a price greater than a good's opportunity cost indicates that they value the good more than other things that could have been produced with the same resources. Viewed from this perspective, profit is a reward earned by entrepreneurs who use resources to produce goods consumers value more highly than the other goods those resources could have produced. In essence, this profit is a signal that an entrepreneur has increased the value of the resources under his or her control.

Business decision makers will seek to undertake production of goods and services that will generate profit. However, things do not always turn out as expected. Sometimes business firms are unable to cover their costs. Losses occur when the revenue derived from sales is insufficient to cover the opportunity cost of the resources used to produce a good or service. Losses indicate that the firm has reduced the value of the resources it has used. In other words, consumers would have been better off if those resources had been used to produce something else. In a market economy, losses will eventually cause firms to go out of business, and the resources they previously utilized will be directed toward other things valued more highly, or to other firms who can produce those same goods at a lower cost.

Profits and losses play a very important role in a market economy. They determine which products (and firms) will expand and survive and which will contract and be driven from the market. Clearly, there is a positive side to business failures. As our preceding discussion highlights, losses and business failures free up resources being used unwisely so they can be put to use by other firms providing consumers with more value.

Loss
A deficit of sales revenue relative to the opportunity cost of production. Losses are a penalty imposed on those who produce goods even though they are valued less than the resources required for their production.

SUPPLY AND THE ENTREPRENEUR

Entrepreneurs organize the production of new products. In doing so, they take on significant risk in deciding what to produce and how to produce it. Their success or failure depends on how much consumers eventually value the products they develop relative to other products that could have been produced with the resources. Entrepreneurs figure out which projects are likely to be profitable and then try to persuade a corporation, a banker, or individual investors to invest the resources needed to give their new idea a chance. Studies indicate, however, that only about 55 to 65 percent of the new products introduced are still on the market five years later. Being an entrepreneur means you have to risk failing.

To prosper, entrepreneurs must convert and rearrange resources in a manner that will increase their value. A person who purchases 100 acres of raw land, puts in streets and a sewage-disposal system, divides the plot into 1-acre lots, and sells them for 50 percent more than the opportunity cost of all resources used is clearly an entrepreneur. This entrepreneur profits because the value of the resources has increased. Sometimes entrepreneurial activity is less complex, though. For example, a 15-year-old who purchases a power mower and sells lawn services to his neighbors is also an entrepreneur seeking to profit by increasing the value of his resources—time and equipment.

An entrepreneur who buys raw land, puts in streets and sewer lines, and divides up the land into lots for sale will earn a profit because he or she has increased the value of the resources under his or her control.

MARKET SUPPLY SCHEDULE

How will producer–entrepreneurs respond to a change in product price? Other things constant, a higher price will increase the producer's incentive to supply the good. Established producers will expand the scale of their operations, and over time new entrepreneurs, seeking personal gain, will enter

the market and begin supplying the product, too. *The law of supply states that there is a direct (or positive) relationship between the price of a good or service and the amount of it that suppliers are willing to produce. This direct relationship means that the price and the quantity producers wish to supply move in the same direction. As the price increases, producers will supply more—and as the price decreases, they will supply less.*

Like the law of demand, the law of supply reflects the basic economic principle that incentives matter. Higher prices increase the reward entrepreneurs get from selling their products. The more profitable it is to produce a product, the more of it entrepreneurs will be willing to supply. Conversely, as the price of a product falls, so do its profitability and the incentive to supply it. Just think about how many hours of tutoring services you would be willing to supply for different prices. Would you be willing to spend more time tutoring students if instead of $8 per hour, tutoring paid $50 per hour? The law of supply suggests you would, and producers of other goods and services are no different.

Exhibit 6 illustrates the law of supply. The curve shown in the exhibit is called a *supply curve*. Because there is a direct relationship between a good's price and the amount offered for sale by suppliers, the supply curve has a positive slope. It slopes upward to the right. Read horizontally, the supply curve shows how much of a particular good producers are willing to produce and sell at a given price. Read vertically, the supply curve reveals important information about the cost of production. The height of the supply curve indicates both (1) the minimum price necessary to induce producers to supply that additional unit and (2) the opportunity cost of producing that additional unit. These are both measured by the height of the supply curve because the minimum price required to induce a supplier to sell a unit is precisely the marginal cost of producing it.

PRODUCER SURPLUS

We previously used the demand curve to illustrate consumer surplus, the net gains of buyers from market exchanges. The supply curve can be used in a similar manner to illustrate the net gains of producers and resource suppliers. Suppose that you are an aspiring musician and are willing to perform a two-hour concert for $500. If a promoter offers to pay you $750 to perform the concert, you will accept, and receive $250 more than your minimum price. This $250 net gain represents your producer surplus. In effect, producer surplus is the difference between the amount a supplier actually receives (based on the market price) and the minimum price required to induce the supplier to produce the given units (their marginal cost). The shaded area of *Exhibit 7* illustrates the measurement of producer surplus for an entire market.

It's important to note that producer surplus represents the gains received by all parties contributing resources to the production of a good. In this respect, producer surplus is fundamentally different from profit. Profit accrues to the owners of the business firm producing the good,

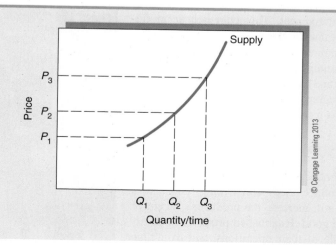

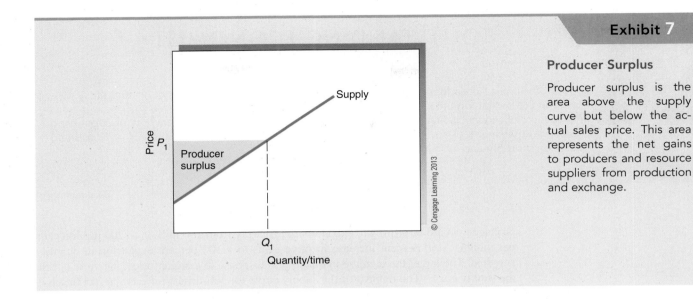

© Cengage Learning 2013

Exhibit 7

Producer Surplus

Producer surplus is the area above the supply curve but below the actual sales price. This area represents the net gains to producers and resource suppliers from production and exchange.

whereas producer surplus encompasses the net gains derived by all people who help produce the good, including those employed by or selling resources to the firm.

RESPONSIVENESS OF QUANTITY SUPPLIED TO PRICE CHANGES: ELASTIC AND INELASTIC SUPPLY CURVES

Like the quantity demanded, the responsiveness of the quantity supplied to a change in price is different for different goods. The supply curve is said to be elastic when a modest change in price leads to a large change in quantity supplied. This is generally true when the additional resources needed to expand output can be obtained with only a small increase in their price. Consider the supply of soft drinks. The contents of soft drinks—primarily carbonated water, sugar, and flavoring—are abundantly available. A sharp increase in the use of these ingredients by soft drink producers is unlikely to push up their price much. Therefore, as **Exhibit 8** illustrates, if the price of soft drinks were to rise from $1 to $1.50,

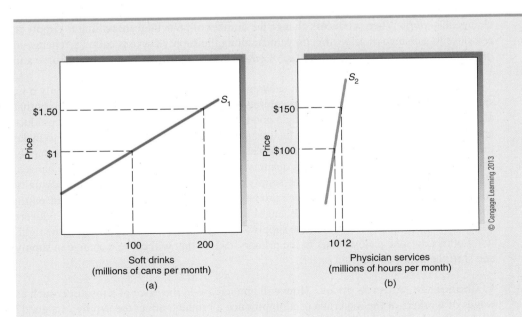

© Cengage Learning 2013

Exhibit 8

Elastic and Inelastic Supply Curves

Frame (a) illustrates a supply curve that is relatively elastic and therefore the quantity supplied is highly responsive to a change in price. Soft drinks provide an example. Frame (b) illustrates a relatively inelastic supply curve, one in which the quantity supplied increases by only a small amount in response to a change in price. This is the case for physician services.

OUTSTANDING ECONOMIST

Alfred Marshall (1842–1924)

British economist Alfred Marshall was one of the most influential economists of his era. Many concepts and tools that form the core of modern microeconomics originated with Marshall in his famous *Principles of Economics*, first published in 1890. Marshall introduced the concepts of supply and demand, equilibrium, elasticity, consumers' and producers' surplus, and the idea of distinguishing between short-run and long-run changes.

producers would be willing to expand output sharply from 100 million to 200 million cans per month. A 50 percent increase in price leads to a 100 percent expansion in quantity supplied. The larger the increase in quantity in response to a higher price, the more elastic the supply curve. The flatness of the supply curve for soft drinks reflects the fact that it is highly elastic.

In contrast, when the quantity supplied is not very responsive to a change in price, supply is said to be inelastic. Physicians' services are an example. If the earnings of doctors increase from $100 to $150 per hour, there will be some increase in the quantity of the services they provide. Some physicians will work longer hours; others may delay retirement. Yet, these adjustments are likely to result in only a small increase in the quantity supplied because it takes a long time to train a physician and the number of qualified doctors who are working in other occupations or who are outside of the labor force is small. Therefore, as Exhibit 8 (right frame) shows, a 50 percent increase in the price of physician services leads to only a 20 percent expansion in the quantity supplied. Unlike soft drinks, higher prices for physician services do not generate much increase in quantity supplied. Economists would say that the supply of physician services is relatively inelastic.

CHANGES IN SUPPLY VERSUS CHANGES IN QUANTITY SUPPLIED

Like demand, it is important to distinguish between a change in the *quantity supplied* and a change in *supply*. When producers change the number of units they are willing to supply in response to a change in price, this movement along the supply curve is called a "change in *quantity supplied*." A change in any factor *other than the price* shifts the supply curve and is called a "change in *supply*."

As we previously discussed, profit-seeking entrepreneurs will produce a good only if its sales price is expected to exceed its opportunity cost of production. Therefore, changes that affect the opportunity cost of supplying a good will also influence the amount of it producers are willing to supply. These other factors, such as the prices of resources used to make the good and the level of technology available, are held constant when we draw the supply curve. The supply curve itself reflects quantity changes only in response to price changes. Changes in these other factors shift the supply curve. Factors that increase the opportunity cost of providing a good will discourage production and decrease supply, shifting the entire curve inward to the left. Conversely, changes that lower the opportunity cost of producers will encourage production and increase supply, shifting the entire curve outward to the right.

Let us now take a closer look at the primary factors that will cause a change in supply and shift the entire curve right or left.

1. Changes in resource prices. How will an increase in the price of a resource, such as wages of workers or the materials used to produce a product, affect the supply of a good? Higher resource prices will increase the cost of production, reducing the profitability of

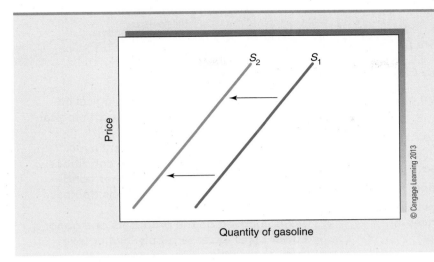

© Cengage Learning 2013

Exhibit 9

A Decrease in Supply

Crude oil is a resource used to produce gasoline. When the price of crude oil rises, it increases the cost of producing gasoline and results in a decrease in the supply of gasoline.

firms supplying the good. The higher cost will induce firms to reduce their output. With time, some may even be driven out of business. As **Exhibit 9** illustrates, higher resource prices will reduce the supply of the good, causing a shift to the left in the supply curve from S_1 to S_2. Alternatively, a reduction in the price of a resource used to produce a good will cause an increase in supply—a rightward shift in the supply curve—as firms expand output in response to the lower costs and increased profitability of supplying the good.

2. Changes in technology. Like lower resource prices, technological improvements— the discovery of new, lower-cost production techniques—reduce production costs, and thereby increase supply. Technological advances have affected the cost of almost everything. Before the invention of the printing press, books had to be handwritten. Just imagine the massive reduction in cost and increase in the supply of books caused by this single invention. Similarly, improved farm machinery has vastly expanded the supply of agricultural products through the years. The field of robotics has reduced the cost of producing airplanes, automobiles, and other types of machinery. Better computer chips have drastically reduced the cost of producing electronics. Forty years ago, a simple calculator cost more than $100 and a microwave oven almost $500. When introduced in the mid-1980s, a cellular telephone cost more than $4,000. You have probably noticed that the prices of flat-screen computer monitors and plasma-screen televisions have fallen substantially in recent years. Again, technological advances explain these changes.

3. Elements of nature and political disruptions. Natural disasters and changing political conditions can also alter supply, sometimes dramatically. In some years, good weather leads to "bumper crops," increasing the supply of agricultural products. At other times, freezes or droughts lead to poor harvests, reducing supply. War and political unrest in the Middle East region have had a major impact on the supply of oil several times during the past few decades. Factors such as these will alter supply.

4. Changes in taxes. If the government increases the taxes on the sellers of a product, the result will be the same as any other increase in the cost of doing business. The added tax that sellers have to pay will reduce their willingness to sell the product at any given price. Each unit must now be sold for a price that covers not only the opportunity cost of production, but also the tax. For example, a special tax is levied on commercial airline tickets, partially to cover the cost of airport security. This tax increases the cost of air travel and thereby reduces the supply (a shift to the left in the supply curve.)

The accompanying **Thumbnail Sketch** summarizes the major factors that change *supply* (a shift of the entire supply curve) and quantity supplied (a movement along the supply curve).

Thumbnail sketch

Factors That Cause Changes in Supply and Quantity Supplied

This factor changes the quantity supplied of a good:

1. The price of the good: A lower price decreases the quantity supplied; a higher price increases the quantity supplied.

These factors change the supply of a good:

1. Resource prices (the prices of things used to make the good): Lower resource prices increase supply; higher resource prices decrease supply.

2. Technological change: A technological improvement increases supply; a technological setback decreases supply.

3. Weather or political conditions: Favorable weather or good political conditions increase supply; adverse weather conditions or poor political conditions decrease supply.

4. Taxes imposed on the producers of a good: Lower taxes increase supply; higher taxes decrease supply.

HOW MARKET PRICES ARE DETERMINED: SUPPLY AND DEMAND INTERACT

Market
An abstract concept encompassing the forces of supply and demand and the interaction of buyers and sellers with the potential for exchange to occur.

Consumer–buyers and producer–sellers make decisions independent of each other, but market prices coordinate their choices and influence their actions. To the economist, a **market** is not a physical location but an abstract concept that encompasses the forces generated by the decisions of buyers and sellers. A market may be quite narrow (for example, the market for grade A jumbo eggs), or it may be quite broad like when we lump diverse goods into a single market, such as the market for all "consumer goods." There is also a wide range of sophistication among markets. The New York Stock Exchange is a highly formal, computerized market. Each weekday, buyers and sellers, who seldom meet, electronically exchange corporate shares they own worth billions of dollars. In contrast, a neighborhood market for babysitting services or tutoring in economics may be highly informal, bringing together buyers and sellers primarily by word of mouth.

Equilibrium
A state in which the conflicting forces of supply and demand are in balance. When a market is in equilibrium, the decisions of consumers and producers are brought into harmony with one another, and the quantity supplied will equal the quantity demanded.

Equilibrium *is a state in which the conflicting forces of supply and demand are in balance. When a market is in equilibrium, the decisions of consumers and producers are brought into harmony with one another, and the quantity supplied will equal the quantity demanded.* In equilibrium, it is possible for both buyers and sellers to realize their choices simultaneously. What could bring these diverse interests into harmony? We will see that the answer is market prices.

MARKET EQUILIBRIUM

As we have learned, a higher price will reduce the quantity of a good demanded by consumers. Conversely, a higher price will increase the quantity of a good supplied by producers. The market price of a good will tend to change in a direction that will bring the quantity of a good consumers want to buy into balance with the quantity producers want to sell. If the price is too high, the quantity supplied by producers will exceed the quantity demanded. Producers will be unable to sell as much as they would like unless they reduce their price. Alternatively, if the price is too low, the quantity demanded by consumers will exceed the quantity supplied. Some consumers will be unable to get as much as they would like, unless they are willing to pay a higher price to bid some of the good away from other potential customers. Thus, there will be a tendency for the price in a market to move toward the price that brings the two into balance.

People have a tendency to think of consumers wanting lower prices and producers wanting higher prices. Although this is true, price changes frequently trend toward the middle of the two extremes. When a local store has an excess supply of a particular item, how does it get rid of it? By having a sale or otherwise lowering its price (a "blue-light special"). Firms often lower their prices in order to get rid of excess supply.

In contrast, excess demand is solved by consumers bidding up prices. Children's toys around Christmas provide a perfect example. When first introduced, items such as the Nintendo Wii, Webkinz, and the video game Rock Band were immediate successes. The firms producing these products had not anticipated the overwhelming demand; every child wanted one for Christmas. Some stores raised their prices, but the demand was so strong that lines of parents were forming outside stores before they even opened. Often, only the first few in line were able to get the toys (a sure sign that the store had set the price below equilibrium). Out in the parking lots, in the classified ads, and on eBay, parents were offering to pay even higher prices for these items. If stores were not going to set the prices right, parents in these informal markets would! These examples show that rising prices are often the result of consumers bidding up prices when excess demand is present. A similar phenomenon can be seen in the market for tickets to a World Series game or a popular music group's upcoming concert, as the immediate value of a ticket on the resale market can be much higher than the original retail price if, at that price, the original quantity supplied is not adequate to meet the quantity demanded.

As these examples illustrate, whenever quantity supplied and quantity demanded are not in balance, there is a tendency for price to change in a manner that will correct the imbalance. It is possible to show this process graphically with the supply and demand curves we have developed in this chapter. Exhibit 10 shows the supply and demand curves in the market for a basic calculator. At a high price—$12, for example—producers will plan to supply 600 calculators per day, whereas consumers will choose to purchase only 450. An excess supply of 150 calculators (shown by distance *ab* in the graph) will result. Unsold calculators will push the inventories of producers upward. To get rid of some of their calculators in inventory, some

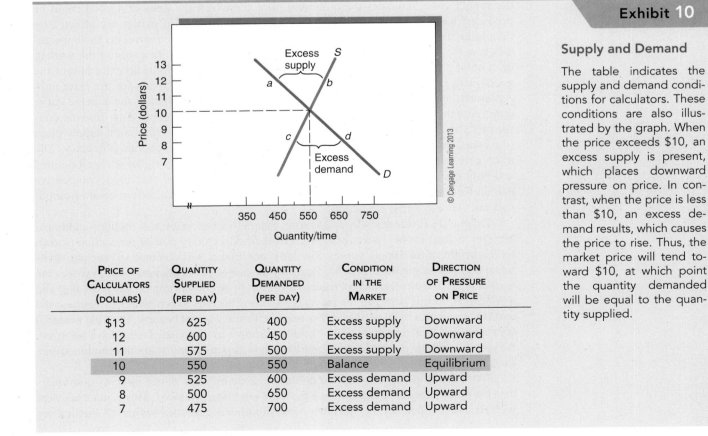

Exhibit 10

Supply and Demand

The table indicates the supply and demand conditions for calculators. These conditions are also illustrated by the graph. When the price exceeds $10, an excess supply is present, which places downward pressure on price. In contrast, when the price is less than $10, an excess demand results, which causes the price to rise. Thus, the market price will tend toward $10, at which point the quantity demanded will be equal to the quantity supplied.

Price of Calculators (dollars)	Quantity Supplied (per day)	Quantity Demanded (per day)	Condition in the Market	Direction of Pressure on Price
$13	625	400	Excess supply	Downward
12	600	450	Excess supply	Downward
11	575	500	Excess supply	Downward
10	550	550	Balance	Equilibrium
9	525	600	Excess demand	Upward
8	500	650	Excess demand	Upward
7	475	700	Excess demand	Upward

producers will cut their price to increase their sales. Other firms will have to lower their price, too, as a result, or sell even fewer calculators. This lower price will make supplying calculators less attractive to producers. Some of them will go out of business. Others will reduce their output or perhaps produce other products. How low will the price of calculators go? As the figure shows, when the price has declined to $10, the quantity supplied by producers and the quantity demanded by consumers will be in balance at 550 calculators per day. At this price ($10), the quantity demanded by consumers just equals the quantity supplied by producers, and the choices of the two groups are brought into harmony.

What will happen if the price per calculator is lower—$8, for example? In this case, the amount demanded by consumers (650 units) will exceed the amount supplied by producers (500 units). An excess demand of 150 units (shown by the distance *cd* in the graph) will be the result. Some consumers who are unable to purchase the calculators at $8 per unit because of the inadequate supply would be willing to pay a higher price. Recognizing this fact, producers will raise their price. As the price increases to $10, producers will expand their output and consumers will cut down on their consumption. At the $10 price, equilibrium will be restored.

EFFICIENCY AND MARKET EQUILIBRIUM

Economic efficiency
A situation in which all of the potential gains from trade have been realized. An action is efficient only if it creates more benefit than cost. With well-defined property rights and competition, market equilibrium is efficient.

When a market reaches equilibrium, all the gains from trade have been fully realized and **economic efficiency** is present. Economists often use economic efficiency as a standard to measure outcomes under alternative circumstances. The central idea of efficiency is a cost-versus-benefit comparison. On the one hand, undertaking an economic action will be efficient only if it generates more benefit than cost. On the other hand, undertaking an action that generates more cost than benefit is inefficient. For a market to be efficient, all trades that generate more benefit than cost need to be undertaken. In addition, economic efficiency requires that no trades creating more cost than benefit be undertaken.

A closer look at the way that markets work can help us understand the concept of efficiency. The supply curve reflects producers' opportunity cost. Each point along the supply curve indicates the minimum price for which the units of a good could be produced without a loss to the seller. Assuming no other third parties are affected by the production of this good, then the height of the supply curve represents the opportunity cost to society of producing and selling the good. On the other side of the market, each point along the demand curve indicates how consumers value an extra unit of the good—that is, the maximum amount the consumer is willing to pay for the extra unit. Again assuming that no other third parties are affected, the height of the demand curve represents the benefit to society of producing and selling the good. Any time the consumer's valuation of a unit (the benefit) exceeds the producer's minimum supply price (the cost), producing and selling the unit is consistent with economic efficiency. The trade will result in mutual gain to both parties. When property rights are well defined and only the buyers and sellers are affected by production and exchange, competitive market forces will automatically guide a market toward an equilibrium level of output that satisfies economic efficiency.

Exhibit 11 illustrates why this is true. Suppliers of bicycles will produce additional bicycles as long as the market price exceeds their opportunity cost of production (shown by the height of the supply curve). Similarly, consumers will continue to purchase additional bikes as long as their benefit (shown by the height of the demand curve) exceeds the market price. Eventually, market forces will result in an equilibrium output level of Q and a price of P. At this point, all the bicycles providing benefits to consumers that exceed the costs to suppliers will be produced. Economic efficiency is met because all of the potential consumer and producer gains from exchange (shown by the shaded area) have occurred. As you can see, the point of market equilibrium is also the point where the combined area showing consumer and producer surplus is the greatest.

When fewer than Q bicycles are produced, some bicycles valued more by consumers than the opportunity cost of producing them are not being produced. This is not consistent with economic efficiency. On the other hand, if output is expanded beyond Q, inefficiency

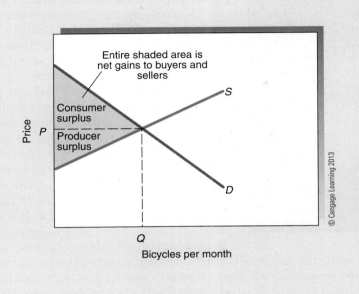

© Cengage Learning 2013

Exhibit 11

Economic Efficiency

When markets are competitive and property rights are well defined, the equilibrium reached by a market satisfies economic efficiency. All units that create more benefit (the buyer's valuation shown by the height of the demand curve) than cost (opportunity cost of production shown by the height of the supply curve) are produced. This maximizes the total gains from trade, the combined area represented by consumer and producer surplus.

will also result because some of the bicycles cost more to produce than consumers are willing to pay for them. Prices in competitive markets eventually guide producers and consumers to the level of output consistent with economic efficiency.

HOW MARKETS RESPOND TO CHANGES IN DEMAND AND SUPPLY

How will a market adjust to a change in demand? **Exhibit 12** shows the market adjustment to an increase in the demand for eggs around Easter. Demand D_1 and supply S are typical throughout much of the year. During the two weeks before Easter, however, consumer demand for eggs rises because people purchase them to decorate, too. This shifts egg demand

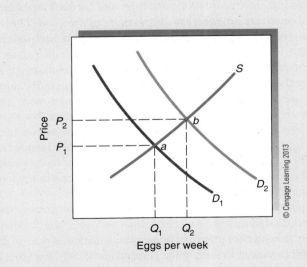

© Cengage Learning 2013

Exhibit 12

Market Adjustment to Increase in Demand

Here, we illustrate how the market for eggs adjusts to an increase in demand such as generally occurs around Easter. Initially (before the Easter season), the market for eggs reflects demand D_1 and supply S. The increase in demand (shift from D_1 to D_2) pushes price up and leads to a new equilibrium at a higher price (P_2 rather than P_1) and larger quantity traded (Q_2)

The tradition of coloring and hunting for eggs causes an increase in demand for eggs around Easter. As Exhibit 12 illustrates, this leads to higher egg prices and costly actions by producers to supply a larger quantity during this period.

from D_1 to D_2 during that time of year. As you can see, the increase in demand pushes the price upward from P_1 to P_2 (typically by about 20 cents per dozen) and results in a larger equilibrium quantity traded (Q_2 rather than Q_1—an increase of typically around 600 million eggs). There is a new equilibrium at point b around Easter (versus point a during the rest of the year).

Although consumers may not be happy about paying a higher price for eggs around Easter, the higher price serves two essential purposes. First, it encourages consumers to conserve on their usage of eggs. Some consumers may purchase only two dozen eggs to color, rather than three; other consumers may skip having an omelet for breakfast and have yogurt instead. These steps on the consumer side of the market help make the eggs that are available around Easter go further. Second, the higher price is precisely what results in the additional 600 million eggs being supplied to the market to satisfy this increased consumer demand. Without the price increase, excess demand would be present, and many consumers would simply be unable to find eggs to purchase around Easter. If the price remained at P_1 (the equilibrium price throughout most of the year), consumers at Easter-time would want to purchase more eggs than producers would be willing to supply. At the higher P_2 price, however, the quantity suppliers are willing to sell is again in balance with the quantity consumers wish to purchase.

Why were suppliers unwilling to supply the additional 600 million eggs at the original price of P_1? Because at the original equilibrium price of P_1, suppliers were already producing and selling all the eggs that cost less to produce than that price. The additional eggs desired by consumers around Easter all cost more to produce than the old market price of P_1. The higher price of P_2 is what allows suppliers to cover their higher production costs associated with these extra eggs. Around Easter, farmers take costly steps to avoid having the hens molt because hens lay fewer eggs when they are molting. They do this by changing the quantity and types of feed and by increasing the lighting in the birds' sheds—both of which mean higher production costs. Farmers also try to build up larger than normal inventories of eggs before Easter. Eggs are typically about two days old when consumers buy them at the store, but can be up to seven days old around Easter time. Building up and maintaining this additional inventory are costly, too.

In a market economy, when the demand for a good increases, its price will rise, which will (1) motivate consumers to search for substitutes and cut back on additional purchases of the good and (2) motivate producers to supply more of the good. These two forces will eventually bring the quantity demanded and quantity supplied back into balance.

It's important to note that this response on the supply side of the egg market is not a shift in the supply curve. The supply curve remains unchanged. Rather, there is a movement along the original supply curve—a change in *quantity* supplied. The only reason suppliers are willing to alter their behavior (produce more eggs) is because the increased demand has pushed up the price of eggs. Notice that it is the change in demand (a shift of the demand curve) that leads to the change in quantity supplied (a movement along the supply curve). Producers are simply responding to the price movement caused by the change in demand. A movement along one curve (a change in quantity supplied *or* a change in quantity demanded) happens in response to a shift in the other curve (a change in demand or a change in supply).

When the demand for a product declines, the adjustment process sends buyers and sellers just the opposite signals. Take a piece of paper and see if you can diagram a decrease in demand and how it will affect price and quantity in a market. If you've done it correctly, a decline in demand (a shift to the left in the demand curve) will lead to a lower price and a lower quantity traded. What's going on in the diagram is that the lower price (caused by lower consumer demand) is reducing the incentive of producers to supply the good. When

consumers no longer want as much of a good, falling market prices signal producers to cut back production. The reduced output allows these resources to be freed up to go into the production of other goods consumers want more.

How will markets respond to changes in supply? **Exhibit 13** shows the market's adjustment to a decrease in the supply of lemons, such as happened during January 2007 when freezing temperatures in California destroyed a large portion of the lemon crop. A reduction in supply (shift from S_1 to S_2) will cause the price of lemons to increase sharply (P_1 to P_2). Because of the higher price, consumers will cut back on their consumption of lemons (the movement along the demand curve from a to b). Some will switch to substitutes—in this case, probably other varieties of citrus. The higher price also encourages the remaining lemon suppliers to take additional steps—like more careful harvesting techniques or using more fertilizer—that allow them to produce more lemons than otherwise would be the case. The higher prices will rebalance the quantity demanded and quantity supplied.

As the lemon example illustrates, a decrease in supply will lead to higher prices and a lower equilibrium quantity. How do you think the market price and quantity would adjust to an increase in supply, as might be caused by a breakthrough in the technology used to harvest the lemons? Again, try to draw the appropriate supply and demand curves to illustrate this case. If you do it correctly, the graph you draw will show an increase in supply (a shift to the right in the supply curve) leading to a lower market price and a larger equilibrium quantity.

The accompanying **Thumbnail Sketch** summarizes the effect of changes—both increases and decreases—in demand and supply on the equilibrium price and quantity. The cases listed in the sketch, however, are for when only a single curve shifts. But sometimes market conditions simultaneously shift both demand and supply. For example, consumer income might increase at the same time that a technological advance in production occurs. These two changes will cause both demand and supply to increase at the same time—both curves will shift to the right. The new equilibrium will definitely be at a larger quantity, but the direction of the change in price is indeterminate. The price may either increase or decrease, depending on whether the increase in demand or increase in supply is larger—which curve shifted the most, in other words.

What will happen if supply increases but demand falls at the same time? Price will definitely fall, but the new equilibrium quantity may either increase or decrease. Draw the supply and demand curves for this case and make sure that you understand why.

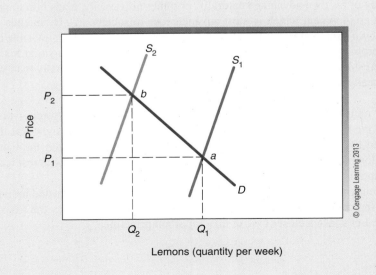

Exhibit 13

Market Adjustment to a Decrease in Supply

Here, using lemons as an example, we illustrate how a market adjusts to a decrease in supply. Assume adverse weather conditions substantially reduce the supply (shift from S_1 to S_2) of lemons. The reduction in supply leads to an increase in the equilibrium price (from P_1 to P_2) and a reduction in the equilibrium quantity traded (from Q_1 to Q_2).

Thumbnail Sketch

How Changes in Demand and Supply Affect Market Price and Quantity

Changes in Demand

1. An increase in demand—shown by a rightward shift of the demand curve—will cause an increase in both the equilibrium price and the equilibrium quantity.
2. A decrease in demand—shown by a leftward shift of the demand curve—will cause a decrease in both the equilibrium price and the equilibrium quantity.

Changes in Supply

1. An increase in supply—shown by a rightward shift of the supply curve—will cause a decrease in the equilibrium price and an increase in the equilibrium quantity.
2. A decrease in supply—shown by a leftward shift of the supply curve—will cause an increase in the equilibrium price and a decrease in the equilibrium quantity.

iStockphoto.com/mart_m

INVISIBLE HAND PRINCIPLE

keys to economic prosperity

iStockphoto.com/Scott Dunlap

Invisible Hand Principle

Market prices coordinate the actions of self-interested individuals and direct them toward activities that promote the general welfare.

More than 235 years ago, Adam Smith, the father of economics, stressed that personal self-interest *when directed by market prices* is a powerful force promoting economic progress. In a famous passage in his book *An Inquiry into the Nature and Causes of the Wealth of Nations*, Smith put it this way:

> Every individual is continually exerting himself to find out the most advantageous employment for whatever [income] he can command. It is his own advantage, indeed, and not that of the society which he has in view. But the study of his own advantage naturally, or rather necessarily, leads him to prefer that employment which is most advantageous to society. . . . He intends only his own gain, and he is in this, as in many other cases, led by an invisible hand to promote an end which was not part of his intention. By pursuing his own interest he frequently promotes that of the society more effectually than when he really intends to promote it.[6]

The "invisible hand" to which Smith referred was the pricing system—prices determined by the forces of supply and demand. Smith's fundamental insight was that market prices tend to bring the self-interest of individuals into harmony with the betterment of society. Moreover, when it is directed by market prices, personal self-interest is a powerful force promoting growth and prosperity.

The tendency of market prices to channel the actions of self-interested individuals into activities that promote the prosperity of the society is now known as the **invisible hand principle**. Let's take a closer look at this important principle.

Invisible hand principle
The tendency of market prices to direct individuals pursuing their own interests to engage in activities promoting the economic well-being of society.

---

[6]Adam Smith, *An Inquiry into the Nature and Causes of the Wealth of Nations* (New York: Modern Library, 1937), 423.

PRICES AND MARKET ORDER

The invisible hand principle can be difficult to grasp because there is a natural tendency to associate order with central direction and control. Surely some central authority must be in charge. But this is not the case. The pricing system, reflecting the choices of literally millions of consumers, producers, and resource owners, provides the direction. Moreover, the market process works so automatically that most of us give little thought to it. We simply take it for granted.

Perhaps an example from your everyday life will help you better understand the invisible hand principle. Visualize a busy retail store with 10 checkout lanes. No one is assigning shoppers to checkout lanes. Shoppers are left to choose for themselves. Nonetheless, they do not all try to get in the same lane. Why? Individuals are always alert for adjustment opportunities that offer personal gain. When the line at one lane gets long or is held up by a price check, some shoppers will shift to other lanes and thereby smooth out the flow among the lanes. Even though central planning is absent, this process of mutual adjustment by self-interested individuals results in order and social cooperation. A similar phenomenon occurs on busy interstate highways as drivers switch between lanes for personal gain, with the end result being the quickest flow of traffic for everyone and for the group as a whole.

The incentive structure generated by markets is a lot like that accompanying the checkout at a busy retail store or driving on the freeway. Like the number of people in a lane, profits and losses provide market participants with information about the advantages and disadvantages of different economic activities. Losses indicate that an economic activity is congested, and, as a result, producers are unable to cover their costs. In such a case, successful market participants will shift their resources away from such activities toward other, more valuable uses. Conversely, profits are indicative of an open lane, the opportunity to experience gain if one shifts into an activity in which the price is high relative to the per-unit cost. As producers and resource suppliers shift away from activities characterized by congestion and into those characterized by the opportunity for profit, they enlarge the flow of economic activity.

Consider the following three vitally important functions performed by market prices.

1. Market prices communicate information to both buyers and sellers that will promote efficient use of resources and proper response to changing conditions. Prices provide producers with up-to-date information about which goods consumers most intensely desire and with important information about the abundance of the resources used in the production process. The cost of production, driven by the opportunity cost of resources, tells the business decision-maker the relative importance others place on the alternative uses of those resources. A boom in the housing market might cause lumber prices to rise. In turn, furniture-makers seeing these higher lumber prices will utilize substitute raw materials such as metal and plastic in their production processes. Because of market prices, furniture-makers will conserve on their use of lumber, just as if they had known that lumber was now more urgently needed for constructing new housing.

Consider another example. Suppose a drought in Brazil severely reduces the supply of coffee. Coffee prices will rise. Even if consumers do not know about the drought, the higher prices will provide them with all the information they need to know—it's time to cut back on coffee consumption. *Market prices register information derived from the choices of millions of consumers, producers, and resource suppliers, and provide them with everything they need to know to make wise decisions*.

2. Market prices coordinate the actions of market participants. Market prices also coordinate the choices of buyers and sellers, bringing their decisions into line with each other. Excess supply will lead to falling prices, which discourage production and encourage consumption until the excess supply is eliminated. Alternatively, excess demand will lead to price increases, which encourage consumers to economize on their uses of the good and suppliers to produce more of it, eliminating the excess demand. Changing market prices induce responses on both sides of the market that will correct imbalances.

3. Market prices motivate economic players. Market prices establish a reward–penalty (profit–loss) structure that encourages people to work, cooperate with others, use efficient production methods, supply goods that are intensely desired by others, and invest for the future. Self-interested entrepreneurs will seek to produce only the goods consumers value enough to pay a price sufficient to cover production cost. Self-interest will also encourage producers to use efficient production methods and adopt cost-saving technologies because lower costs will mean greater profits. Firms that fail to do so will be unable to compete successfully in the marketplace.

At the beginning of this chapter, we asked you to reflect on why the grocery stores in your local community generally have on hand about the right amount of milk, bread, vegetables, and other goods. Likewise, how is it that refrigerators, automobiles, and CD players, produced at different places around the world, make their way to stores near you in approximately the same numbers that they are demanded by consumers? The invisible hand principle provides the answer, and it leads to an amazing degree of social cooperation.

Is the concept of the invisible hand really valid? Next time you sit down to have a nice dinner, think about all the people who help make it possible. It is unlikely that any of them, from the farmer to the truck driver to the grocer, was motivated by a concern that you have an enjoyable meal. Market prices, however, bring their interest into harmony with yours. Farmers who raise the best beef or turkeys receive higher prices; truck drivers and grocers earn more money if their products are delivered fresh and in good condition; and so on. An amazing degree of cooperation and order is created by market exchanges—all without the central direction of any government official.

COMPETITION AND PROPERTY RIGHTS

As we noted earlier in this chapter, our focus so far has been on markets in which rival firms can freely enter and exit, and private-property rights are clearly defined and enforced. ***The efficiency of market organization is, in fact, dependent upon these two things: (1) competitive markets and (2) well-defined and enforced private-property rights.***

Competition, the great regulator, can protect both buyer and seller. It protects consumers from sellers who would charge a price substantially above the cost of production or withhold a vital resource for an exorbitant amount of money. Similarly, it protects employees (sellers of their labor) from the power of any single employer (the buyers of labor). When markets are competitive, both buyers and sellers have alternatives and these alternatives provide them with protection against ill treatment by others.

When property rights are well defined, secure, and tradable, suppliers of goods and services have to pay resource owners for their use. They will not be permitted to seize and use scarce resources without compensating the owners. Neither will they be permitted to use violence (for example, to attack or invade the property of another) to get what they want. The efficiency of markets hinges on the presence of property rights—after all, people can't easily exchange or compete for things they don't have or can't get property rights to. Without well-defined property rights, markets simply cannot function effectively.

iStockphoto.com/gaspr13

Looking Ahead

Although we incorporated numerous examples designed to enhance your understanding of the supply-and-demand model throughout this chapter, we have only touched the surface. In various modified forms, this model is the central tool of economics. The next chapter will explore several specific applications and extensions of this important model.

KEY POINTS

- The law of demand states that there is an inverse (or negative) relationship between the price of a good or service and the quantity of it that consumers are willing to purchase. The height of the demand curve at any quantity shows the maximum price that consumers are willing to pay for that unit.

- The degree of responsiveness of consumer purchases to a change in price is shown by the steepness of the demand curve. The more responsive buyers are to a change in price, the flatter, or more elastic, the demand curve will be. Conversely, the less responsive buyers are to a change in price, the steeper, or more inelastic, the demand curve will be.

- A movement along a demand curve is called a change in quantity demanded. A shift of the entire curve is called a change in demand. A change in *quantity demanded* is caused by a change in the price of the good (generally in response to a shift of the supply curve). A change in *demand* can be caused by several things, including a change in consumer income or a change in the price of a closely related good.

- The opportunity cost of producing a good is equal to the cost of bidding away the resources needed for its production from alternative uses. Profit indicates that the producer has increased the value of the resources used, whereas a loss indicates that the producer has reduced the value of the resources used.

- The law of supply states that there is a direct (or positive) relationship between the price of a good or service and the quantity of it that producers are willing to supply. The height of the supply curve at any quantity shows the minimum price necessary to induce suppliers to produce that unit—that is, the opportunity cost of producing it.

- A movement along a supply curve is called a change in quantity supplied. A change in *quantity supplied* is caused by a change in the price of the good (generally in response to a shift of the demand curve). A shift of the entire supply curve is called a change in supply. A change in *supply* can be caused by several factors, such as a change in resource prices or an improvement in technology.

- The responsiveness of supply to a change in price is shown by the steepness of the supply curve. The more willing producers are to alter the quantity supplied in response to a change in price, the flatter, or more elastic, the supply curve. Conversely, the less willing producers are to alter the quantity supplied in response to a change in price, the steeper, or less elastic, the supply curve.

- Prices bring the conflicting forces of supply and demand into balance. There is an automatic tendency for market prices to move toward the equilibrium price, at which the quantity demanded equals the quantity supplied.

- Consumer surplus represents the net gain to buyers from market trades. Producer surplus represents the net gain to producers and resource suppliers from market trades. In equilibrium, competitive markets maximize these gains, a condition known as economic efficiency.

- Changes in the prices of goods are caused by changes in supply and demand. An increase in demand will cause the price and quantity supplied to rise. Conversely, a decrease in demand will cause the price and quantity supplied to fall. An increase in supply, however, will cause the price to fall and quantity demanded to rise. Conversely, a decrease in supply will cause the price to rise and quantity demanded to fall.

- Market prices communicate information, coordinate the actions of buyers and sellers, and motivate decision makers to act. As the invisible hand principle indicates, market prices are generally able to bring the self-interest of individuals into harmony with the general welfare of society. The efficiency of the system is dependent upon two things, however: (1) competitive market conditions and (2) well-defined and secure property rights.

CRITICAL ANALYSIS QUESTIONS

1. *Which of the following do you think would lead to an increase in the current demand for beef?
   a. higher pork prices
   b. higher consumer income
   c. higher prices of feed grains used to feed cattle
   d. widespread outbreak of mad cow or hoof-and-mouth disease
   e. an increase in the price of beef

2. What is being held constant when a demand curve for a specific product (shoes or apples, for example) is constructed? Explain why the demand curve for a product slopes downward to the right.

3. What is the law of supply? How many of the following "goods" do you think conform to the general law of supply? Explain your answer in each case.
   a. gasoline
   b. cheating on exams
   c. political favors from legislators
   d. the services of heart specialists
   e. children
   f. legal divorces

4. *Are prices an accurate measure of a good's total value? Are prices an accurate measure of a good's marginal value? What's the difference? Can you think

of a good that has high total value but low marginal value? Use this concept to explain why professional wrestlers earn more than nurses, despite the fact that it is virtually certain that nurses create more total value for society than do wrestlers.

5. What is being held constant when the supply curve is constructed for a specific good like pizza or automobiles? Explain why the supply curve for a good slopes upward to the right.

6. Define consumer surplus and producer surplus. What is meant by economic efficiency, and how does it relate to the gains of consumers and producers?

7. How is the market price of a good determined? When the market for a product is in equilibrium, how will consumers value an additional unit compared to the opportunity cost of producing that unit? Why is this important?

8. *"The future of our industrial strength cannot be left to chance. Somebody has to develop notions about which industries are winners and which are losers." Is this statement by a newspaper columnist true? Who is the "somebody"?

9. What factors determine the cost of producing a good or service? Will producers continue to supply a good or service if consumers are unwilling to pay a price sufficient to cover the cost?

10. *"Production should be for people and not for profit." Answer the following questions concerning this statement:
    a. If production is profitable, are people helped or harmed? Explain.
    b. Are people helped more if production results in a loss than if it leads to profit? Is there a conflict between production for people and production for profit?

11. What must an entrepreneur do to earn a profit? How do the actions of firms earning profits influence the value of resources? What happens to the value of resources when losses are present? If a firm making losses goes out of business, is this bad? Why or why not?

12. *What's wrong with this way of thinking? "Economists claim that when the price of something goes up, producers increase the quantity supplied to the market. But last year, the price of oranges was really high and the supply of them was really low. Economists are wrong!"

13. What is the invisible hand principle? Does it indicate that self-interested behavior within markets will result in actions that are beneficial to others? What conditions are necessary for the invisible hand to work well? Why are these conditions important?

14. *What's wrong with this way of thinking? "Economists argue that lower prices will result in fewer units being supplied. However, there are exceptions to this rule. For example, in 1972, a very simple 10-digit electronic calculator sold for $120. By 2000, the price of the same type of calculator had declined to less than $5. Yet business firms produced and sold many more calculators in 2000 than they did in 1972. Lower prices did not result in less production or in a decline in the number of calculators supplied."

15. What is the difference between substitutes and complements? Indicate two goods that are substitutes for each other. Indicate two goods that are complements.

16. *Do business firms operating in competitive markets have a strong incentive to serve the interest of consumers? Are they motivated by a strong desire to help consumers? Are "good intentions" necessary if individuals are going to engage in actions that are helpful to others? Discuss.

*Asterisk denotes questions for which answers are given in Appendix B.

CHAPTER 4

Supply and Demand: Applications and Extensions

CHAPTER FOCUS

- How are the markets for products and resources related?
- What happens when prices are set by law above or below the market equilibrium level?
- How do rent controls affect the maintenance and quality of rental housing? How do minimum-wage rates influence the job opportunities of low-skilled workers?
- What are "black markets"? How does the lack of a well-structured legal environment affect their operation?
- How does a tax or subsidy affect a market? What determines the distribution of the tax burden (or subsidy benefit) between buyers and sellers?
- What is the Laffer curve? What does it indicate about the relationship between tax rates and tax revenues?

iStockphoto.com/sorendls

The division of labour, from which so many advantages are derived, is not originally the effect of any human wisdom, which foresees and intends that general opulence to which it gives occasion. It is the necessary, though very slow and gradual consequence of a certain propensity in human nature . . .; the propensity to truck, barter, and exchange one thing for another.

—*Adam Smith*[1]

Nations stumble upon establishments, which are indeed the result of human action, but not the execution of any human design.

—*Adam Ferguson*[2]

[1]Adam Smith, *An Inquiry into the Nature and Causes of the Wealth of Nations* (New York: Modern Library, 1937), 13.
[2]Adam Ferguson, *An Essay on the History of Civil Society* (Edinburgh: A. Millar and T. Caddel, London, 1767), 187.

arkets are everywhere. They exist in many different forms and degrees of sophistication. In elementary schools, children trade Baseball cards and Silly Bandz; in households, individuals trade chores ("I'll clean the bathroom, if you'll clean the kitchen"); and in the stock market, individuals who have never met exchange shares of corporate stock and other financial assets worth billions of dollars each business day. Even making an activity illegal does not eliminate the market for it. Instead, the market is merely pushed underground. The exchange of illegal drugs or tickets to a big game at illegal prices illustrates this point.

Trading with other individuals is a natural part of human behavior that exists regardless of legal and societal conditions. As Adam Smith put it more than 230 years ago, human beings have a natural propensity "to truck, barter, and exchange one thing for another" (see the quotation at the chapter opening). We all want to improve our standard of living, and trade with others helps us achieve this goal—by allowing us to get the goods and services we really want and giving us the opportunity to earn the income necessary to buy them. Further, as Adam Ferguson points out, markets are a result of human action, not human design.[3] They arise because people can improve their lives by trading with others.

Market prices coordinate the actions of buyers and sellers, but sometimes the "price" of a good or service in a particular market is called something different. For example, in the labor market, the price is often called the "wage rate." In the loanable funds market, the price is generally referred to as the "interest rate." However, as Juliet observes in Shakespeare's *Romeo and Juliet*, "What's in a name? That which we call a rose by any other name would smell as sweet." The same is true for prices. When the price of something is referred to by another term, such as the wage or interest rate, it will still play the same role. Therefore, when these special terms are used, we put them along the vertical axes of supply and demand diagrams, just as we do "price"—because that's what they are.

In the previous chapter, we saw how the forces of supply and demand determine market prices and coordinate the actions of buyers and sellers in the absence of government intervention. In this chapter, we turn our attention to using the supply and demand model to understand more fully what happens when governments intervene in markets by implementing price controls, taxes, and subsidies.

iStockphoto.com/nicoolay

THE LINK BETWEEN RESOURCE AND PRODUCT MARKETS

Understanding the interrelationship among markets is vitally important. A change in one market will also lead to changes in other markets. This section addresses the link between the resource and product markets.

The production process generally involves (1) the purchase of resources—like raw materials, labor services, tools, and machines; (2) transformation of the resources into products (goods and services); and (3) sale of the goods and services in a product market. Production is generally undertaken by business firms. Typically, business firms will demand resources, and households will supply them. Firms demand resources *because* they contribute to the production of goods and services. In turn, households supply them in order to earn income.

Resource market
The market for inputs used to produce goods and services.

Just as in product markets, the demand curve in a **resource market** is typically downward-sloping and the supply curve upward-sloping. The inverse relationship between the amount of a resource demanded and its price exists because businesses will substitute away from a resource as its price rises. In contrast, there will be a direct relationship between the amount of a resource supplied and its price because a higher price means greater rewards to those who provide more. As in product markets, prices will coordinate

---

[3]This theme was a focus of much of the work of Nobel Prize–winning economist Friedrich Hayek.

the choices of buyers and sellers in resource markets, bringing the quantity demanded into balance with the quantity supplied.

The labor market is a large component of the broader resource market. Actually, there is not just one market for labor, but rather there are many labor markets, one for each different skill–experience–occupational category. Let's look at the labor market for waitstaff (waiters and waitresses). **Exhibit 1** shows how resource and product markets are linked. The supply of young workers in many occupations, including waitstaff, has declined in recent years in many areas of the United States. This lower supply has caused the wages (tip-inclusive wages) of waitstaff to increase (for example, from $8 to $10 in Exhibit 1a). The higher price of this resource increases the cost of producing restaurant meals. This higher cost, in turn, reduces the supply (shifting S_1 to S_2) of restaurant meals, pushing the price upward (Exhibit 1b). When the price of a resource increases, it will lead to higher production costs, lower supply, and higher prices for the goods and services produced with the resource.

Of course, lower resource prices have the opposite effect. Lower resource prices reduce costs and expand the supply of consumer goods made with the lower-priced resources (shifting the supply curve to the right). The increase in supply will lead to a lower price in the product market. ***Thus, when the price of a resource—such as labor—changes, the prices of goods and services produced with that resource will change in the same direction.***

Changes in product markets will also influence resource markets. There is a close relationship between the demand for products and the demand for the resources required for their production. An increase in demand for a consumer good—automobiles, for example—will lead to higher auto prices, which will increase the profitability of producing automobiles and give automakers an incentive to expand output. But the expansion in automobile output will require additional resources, causing an increase in the demand for, and prices of, the resources required for their production (steel, rubber, plastics, and the labor services of autoworkers, for example). The higher prices of these resources will cause other industries to conserve on their use, freeing them up for more automobile production.

The process will work in reverse if demand for a product falls. A decrease in demand will not only reduce the price of the product but will also reduce the demand for and prices of the resources used to produce it. ***Thus, when the demand for a product changes, the demand for (and prices of) the resources used to produce it will change in the same direction.***

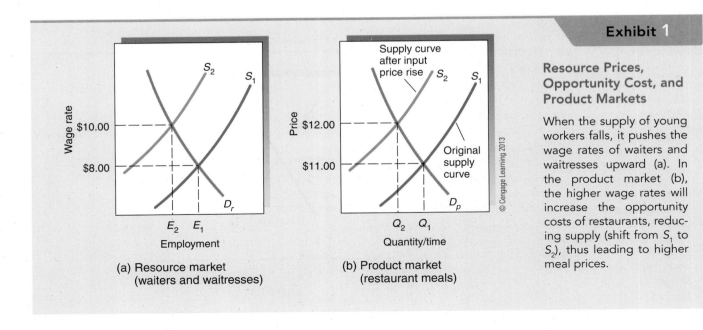

© Cengage Learning 2013

Exhibit 1

Resource Prices, Opportunity Cost, and Product Markets

When the supply of young workers falls, it pushes the wage rates of waiters and waitresses upward (a). In the product market (b), the higher wage rates will increase the opportunity costs of restaurants, reducing supply (shift from S_1 to S_2), thus leading to higher meal prices.

(a) Resource market
(waiters and waitresses)

(b) Product market
(restaurant meals)

THE ECONOMICS OF PRICE CONTROLS

Price controls
Government-mandated prices that are generally imposed in the form of maximum or minimum legal prices.

Buyers often complain that prices are too high, while sellers complain that they are too low. Unhappy with the prices established by market forces, various groups might try to persuade the government to intervene and impose **price controls**. Price controls force buyers or sellers to alter the prices of certain products. Price controls may be either price ceilings, which set a maximum legal price for a product, or price floors, which impose a minimum legal price. Imposing price controls may look like a simple, easy way for the government to help buyers at the expense of sellers (or vice versa). However, price controls reduce the gains from trade, and they generate secondary effects that often harm even the intended beneficiaries. Let's consider this issue in more detail.

THE IMPACT OF PRICE CEILINGS

Price ceiling
A legally established maximum price sellers can charge for a good or resource.

Shortage
A condition in which the amount of a good offered for sale by producers is less than the amount demanded by buyers at the existing price. An increase in price would eliminate the shortage.

Exhibit 2 shows the impact of imposing a **price ceiling** (P_1) for a product below its equilibrium level (P_0). At the lower price, the quantity supplied by producers is lower on the supply curve, at Q_S, while the quantity demanded by consumers is greater, at Q_D, on the demand curve. A **shortage** ($Q_D - Q_S$) of the good will result because the quantity demanded by consumers exceeds the quantity supplied by producers at the new controlled price. After the price ceiling is imposed, the quantity of the good exchanged declines from the equilibrium quantity to Q_S, and the gains from trade (consumer and producer surplus) fall as well.

Normally, a higher price would ration the good to the buyers most willing to pay for it. Because the price ceiling keeps this from happening, though, other means must be used to allocate the smaller quantity Q_S among consumers wanting to purchase Q_D. Predictably, nonprice factors will become more important in the rationing process. Sellers will ration their goods and services to eager buyers on the basis of factors other than their willingness to pay. For example, sellers will be more inclined to sell their products to their friends, to buyers who do them favors, and even buyers willing to make illegal "under-the-table" payments. (The accompanying Applications in Economics box, "The Imposition of Price Ceilings After Hurricanes," highlights this point.) Time might also be used as the rationing device, with those willing to wait in line the longest being the ones able to purchase the good. In addition, the below-equilibrium price reduces the incentive of sellers to expand the future supply of the good. At the lower price, suppliers will direct resources away from production of the good and into other, more profitable areas. As a result, the product shortage will worsen over time.

Exhibit 2

The Impact of a Price Ceiling

When a price ceiling like P_1 pushes the price of a product (rental housing, for example) below the market equilibrium, a shortage will develop. Because prices are not allowed to direct the market to equilibrium, nonprice elements will become more important in rationing the good.

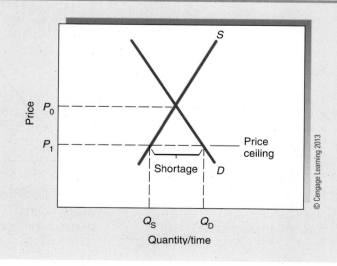

© Cengage Learning 2013

What other secondary effects can be expected? *In the real world, there are two ways that sellers can raise prices. First, they can raise their money price, holding quality constant. Or, second, they can hold the money price constant while reducing the quality of the good.* (The latter might also include reducing the size of the product, say, for example, a candy bar or a loaf of bread.) Faced with a price ceiling, sellers will use quality reductions as a way to raise their prices. Because of the government-created shortage, many consumers will buy the lower-quality good rather than do without it.

It is important to note that a shortage is not the same as scarcity. *Scarcity is inescapable.* Scarcity exists whenever people want more of a good than nature has provided. This means, of course, that almost everything of value is scarce. *Shortages, on the other hand, are a result of prices being set below their equilibrium values—a situation that is avoidable if prices are permitted to rise.* Removing the price ceiling will allow the price to rise back to its equilibrium level (P_0 rather than P_1 in Exhibit 2). This will stimulate additional production, discourage consumption, and increase the incentive of entrepreneurs to search for and develop substitute goods. This combination of forces will eliminate the shortage.

APPLICATIONS IN ECONOMICS

The Imposition of Price Ceilings after Hurricanes

Major hurricanes, such as Katrina (Gulf Coast in 2005), Andrew (south Florida in 1992), and Hugo (Charleston, South Carolina, in 1989), not only cause massive property damage and widespread power outages but also dramatically increase the local demand for items such as lumber, gasoline, ice, batteries, chain saws, and gasoline-powered generators. As a result, the prices of these items rise significantly in the wake of a hurricane. After Hurricane Hugo, for example, a bag of ice went up in price to as much as $10, the price of plywood rose to about $200 per sheet, chain saws soared to the $600 range, and gasoline sold for as much as $10.95 per gallon.

The higher prices play two important roles. First, they encourage suppliers to bring more of these items quickly to the disaster area. Second, they allocate the supplies to those deriving the greatest value from their use. The higher prices will begin to subside as additional quantities of critically needed supplies flow into the disaster area, but it is precisely these higher prices that encourage this response.

It is a natural reaction to think that the higher prices are unfair and that price controls should be imposed to prevent "price gouging." State and local officials have often imposed price controls for precisely these reasons. After Hurricane Hugo, the mayor of Charleston signed emergency legislation making it a crime, punishable by up to 30 days in jail and a $200 fine, to sell goods in the city at prices higher than their pre-hurricane levels. Similarly, Mississippi's attorney general announced a crackdown on price gouging after Hurricane Katrina.

While price ceilings may be motivated by a desire to help consumers by keeping prices low, they still exert secondary

Eric Gay/Associated Press

effects that retard the recovery process. At the lower mandated prices, consumer demand quickly outstrips the available supplies creating artificial shortages. The controls also slow the flow of goods into the area. Shipments that do arrive are greeted by long lines of consumers, many of whom end up without anything after waiting for hours.

The price controls result in serious misallocation of resources. Electric generators provide one of the best examples. The lack of electric power after a hurricane means that gasoline pumps, refrigerators, cash registers, ATMs, and other electrical equipment do not work. Grocery stores can't open and thousands of dollars' worth of food spoils. Although gas stations have gasoline in their underground storage tanks, it can't be pumped out. ATMs and banks can't operate without electricity, so people can't get to their money, which is critical because almost all transactions in post-hurricane environments are made with cash.

(continued)

Hardware stores that sell gasoline-powered electric generators typically have only a few in stock, but after a hurricane suddenly hundreds of businesses and residents want to buy them. In the absence of price controls, the price of these generators would rise and individual homeowners would generally be outbid by businesses, which can put the generators to use operating stores, gas stations, and ATMs. It is these uses that would yield enough revenue to cover the high price of the generators because they facilitate the provision of other goods and services that people desperately want. Given the large sums such businesses would be willing to pay, some with generators at home would even find it attractive to sell or lease them to buyers willing to pay attractive prices.

Market prices would allocate generators and other urgently needed supplies to those most willing to pay for them. Price ceilings keep this from happening. In the absence of price rationing people keep their generators at home, and it is commonplace for hardware store owners with a few generators on hand to take one home for their family and then sell the others to their close friends, neighbors, and relatives to run televisions and hair dryers. Moreover, the incentive of people to take action and bring generators in from other areas is slowed. For example, John Shepperson of Kentucky took time away from his normal job to buy 19 generators, rent a truck, and drive it 600 miles to the Katrina-damaged area of Mississippi. He thought he would be able to sell the generators at high enough prices to cover his cost and earn a profit. Instead his generators were confiscated, Shepperson was arrested for price gouging, held by police for four days, and the generators kept in police custody. They never made it to consumers with urgent needs who desperately wanted to buy them.

The dramatic change in conditions that often accompany a hurricane highlights the role prices play. It also illustrates how the secondary effects accompanying price controls can magnify the damage generated by hurricanes.

RENT CONTROL: A CLOSER LOOK AT A PRICE CEILING

Rent controls are a price ceiling intended to protect residents from high housing prices. Rent controls are currently in place in many U.S. cities, including New York City; Washington, D.C.; Newark, New Jersey; and San Jose, California. Most of these measures were enacted during either World War II or the 1970s, when inflation was high. Rent controls peaked in the mid-1980s. At that time, more than 200 cities, encompassing about 20 percent of the nation's population, imposed rent controls.

Because rent controls push the price of rental housing below the equilibrium level, the amount of rental housing demanded by consumers will exceed the amount landlords will make available. Initially, if the mandated price is only slightly below equilibrium, the impact of rent controls may be barely noticeable. Over time, however, the effects will worsen. Inevitably, rent controls that continue will lead to the following results.

Rent controls lead to shortages, poor maintenance, and deterioration in the quality of rental housing.

Denis Tangney Jr./Jupiter Images

1. Shortages and black markets will develop. Because the quantity of housing demanded will exceed the quantity supplied, some people who value rental housing highly will be unable to find it. Frustrated by the shortage, they will try to induce landlords to rent to them. Some will agree to prepay their rent, including a substantial damage deposit. Others might agree to rent or buy the landlord's furniture at exorbitant prices in order to get an apartment. Still others will make under-the-table (black market) payments to secure housing.

2. The future supply of rental housing will decline. The below-equilibrium price will discourage entrepreneurs from constructing new rental housing units, and private investment will flow elsewhere. In the city of Berkeley, rental units available to students at the University of California dropped by 31 percent in the first five years after the city adopted rent controls in 1978.[4] In contrast, removal of rent controls will often lead to a sharp increase in rental housing construction, as builders seek to expand the supply that lagged behind as the result of the controls. This happened in both Boston and Santa Monica following repeal of controls in the late 1990s.

3. The quality of rental housing will deteriorate. When apartment owners are not allowed to raise their prices, they will use quality reductions to achieve this objective. Normal maintenance and repair service will deteriorate. Tenant parking lots will be eliminated (or rented out). Eventually, the quality of the rental housing will reflect the controlled price. Cheaper housing will be of cheaper quality.

4. Nonprice methods of rationing will become more important. Because price no longer rations rental housing, other forms of competition will develop. Landlords will rely more heavily on nonmonetary discriminating devices. They will favor friends, people of influence, and those whose lifestyles resemble their own. In contrast, applicants with many children or unconventional lifestyles, and perhaps racial minorities, will find fewer landlords who will rent to them. In New York City, where rent controls are in force, a magazine article suggested that "joining a church or synagogue" could help people make the connections they need to get an apartment. Can you imagine having to devote this amount of effort to finding an apartment? If your city enacts rent controls, you just might have to.

5. Inefficient use of housing space will result. The tenant in a rent-controlled apartment will think twice before moving. Why? Even though the tenant might want a larger or smaller space or an apartment closer to work, he or she will be less likely to move because it will be much more difficult to find a unit that's vacant. Turnover will be lower, and many people will find themselves in locations and in apartments not well suited to their needs.

Imposing rent control laws may sound like a simple way to deal with high housing prices. However, the secondary effects are so damaging that many cities have begun repealing them. In the words of Swedish economist Assar Lindbeck: "In many cases, rent control appears to be the most efficient technique presently known to destroy a city—except for bombing."[5] Though this may overstate the case, both economics and experience show that the controls adversely impact the quantity and quality of rental housing.

THE IMPACT OF PRICE FLOORS

A **price floor** establishes a minimum price that can legally be charged. The government imposes price floors on some agricultural products, for example, in an effort to artificially increase the prices that farmers receive. When a price floor is imposed above the current market equilibrium price, it will alter the market's operation. **Exhibit 3** illustrates the impact of imposing a price floor (P_1) for a product above its equilibrium level (P_0). At the higher price, the quantity supplied by producers increases along the supply curve to Q_S, while the quantity demanded by consumers decreases along the demand curve to Q_D. A **surplus** ($Q_S - Q_D$) of the good will result, as the quantity supplied by producers exceeds the quantity demanded by consumers at the new controlled price. Just like a price ceiling, a price floor reduces the quantity of the good exchanged and reduces the gains from trade.

Price floor
A legally established minimum price buyers must pay for a good or resource.

Surplus
A condition in which the amount of a good offered for sale by producers is greater than the amount that buyers will purchase at the existing price. A decline in price would eliminate the surplus.

[4]William Tucker, *The Excluded Americans* (Washington, DC: Regnery Gateway, 1990), 162. For additional information on rent controls, see William Tucker, "Rent Control Drives Out Affordable Housing," in *USA Today Magazine* (July 1998) and Walter Block, "Rent Controls," in *Fortune Encyclopedia of Economics*, ed. David Henderson (New York: Warner Books, 1993). The latter publication can also be found online at http://www.econlib.org.

[5]Assar Lindbeck, *The Political Economy of the New Left* (New York: Harper & Row, 1972), 39.

Exhibit 3

The Impact of a Price Floor

When a price floor such as P_1 keeps the price of a good or service above the market equilibrium, a surplus will result.

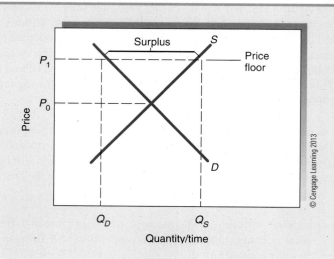

As in the case of the price ceiling, nonprice factors will play a larger role in the rationing process. But because there is a surplus rather than a shortage, this time buyers will be in a position to be more selective. Buyers will purchase from sellers willing to offer them nonprice favors—better service, discounts on other products, or easier credit terms, for example. When it's difficult to alter the product's quality—in this case, improve it to make it more attractive for the price that must be charged—some producers will be unable to sell it.

It is important to note that a surplus doesn't mean the good is no longer scarce. People still want more of the good than is freely available from nature, even though they want less of it *at the controlled price* than sellers want to bring to the market. A decline in price would eliminate the surplus, but the item will be scarce in either case.

MINIMUM WAGE: A CLOSER LOOK AT A PRICE FLOOR

Minimum wage
Legislation requiring that workers be paid at least the stated minimum hourly rate of pay.

In 1938, Congress passed the Fair Labor Standards Act, which mandated a national **minimum wage** of 25 cents per hour. During the past 70 years, the minimum wage has been increased many times. Most recently, in July 2009, the minimum wage was increased to $7.25 per hour. Numerous states, including California, Washington, Oregon, and Connecticut, have their own higher minimum-wage rates ranging to more than $8.50 per hour.

A minimum wage is a price floor. Because most employees in the United States earn wages in excess of the minimum, their employment opportunities are largely unaffected by the minimum wage law. However, low-skilled and inexperienced workers whose equilibrium wage rates are lower than the minimum wage will be affected.

Exhibit 4 shows the direct effect of a $7.25-per-hour minimum wage on the employment opportunities of a group of low-skilled workers. Without a minimum wage, the supply of and demand for these low-skilled workers would be in balance at some lower wage rate; here we use $5.00. Because the minimum wage makes low-skilled labor more expensive, employers will substitute machines and more highly skilled workers for the now more expensive low-skilled employees. Fewer low-skilled workers will be hired when the minimum wage pushes their wages up. Graphically, this is reflected in the movement up along the demand curve in Exhibit 4 from the equilibrium point to the point associated with the higher, $7.25 wage rate (point A). The result will be a reduction in employment of low-skilled workers from E_0 to E_1.

On the supply side of the market, as the wages of low-skilled workers are pushed above equilibrium, there will be more unskilled workers looking for jobs. Graphically, this is reflected in the movement up along the supply curve in Exhibit 4 from the equilibrium point to the point associated with the higher, $7.25 wage rate (point B). At the $7.25 wage

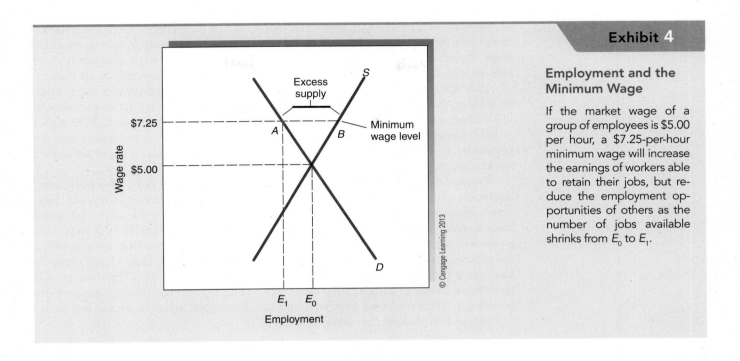

© Cengage Learning 2013

Exhibit 4

Employment and the Minimum Wage

If the market wage of a group of employees is $5.00 per hour, a $7.25-per-hour minimum wage will increase the earnings of workers able to retain their jobs, but reduce the employment opportunities of others as the number of jobs available shrinks from E_0 to E_1.

rate, the quantity of workers searching for jobs will exceed the quantity of jobs available, causing excess supply.

In a labor market, an excess supply will take the form of an abnormally high rate of unemployment. Thus, *economic analysis indicates that minimum-wage legislation will lead to high unemployment rates among low-skilled workers.* The exceedingly high unemployment rate of teenagers in the United States (a group with limited skills because they lack work experience) is consistent with this analysis. In 2010, the unemployment rate of teenagers was 25.9 percent, compared to 8.2 percent for workers age 25 and over. The unemployment rate of teenagers in recent years has persistently been about three times the average rate for other workers. Of course, the higher unemployment rate of teenagers reflects their shifts back and forth between schooling and the labor force, but detailed studies indicate that the minimum wage is also a contributing factor.

It is important to remember that the market price—the wage rate—is only one dimension of the transaction. When a price floor pushes the wage rate above equilibrium, employers will have less incentive to offer nonwage benefits to employees because they will have no trouble hiring low-skilled workers. Predictably, a higher minimum wage will lead to a deterioration of the nonwage attributes of minimum-wage jobs, and so workers in these jobs will experience less convenient working hours, fewer training opportunities, and less continuous employment.

The adverse impact of minimum wage laws on the work experience and training opportunities of youthful workers is particularly important. Low-paying, entry-level jobs often provide workers with experience that will help them move up the job ladder to higher-paying positions. Employment experience obtained at an early age, even on menial tasks, can help people acquire self-confidence, good work habits, and skills that make them more valuable to future employers. Mandated minimum wages will make it more difficult for youthful workers to acquire work experience and jobs with training opportunities. In order to pay the higher wage rate required by the law, employers will have to find other ways to cut employment costs, like reducing the amount of job training.[6]

---

[6] For evidence that the minimum wage limits training opportunities, see David Neumark and William Wascher, "Minimum Wages and Training Revisited," *Journal of Labor Economic* 19 (July 2001): 563–95.

Workers who are able to maintain their employment at the higher minimum-wage rate—most likely the better qualified among those with low skill levels—gain from a minimum wage. But other low-skilled workers are harmed by the minimum wage, particularly those with the lowest skill levels who will find it more difficult to both find jobs and acquire training.

How many fewer low-skilled workers are hired because of the minimum wage? Studies indicate that a 10 percent increase in the minimum wage reduces the employment of low-skilled workers by 1 to 3 percent. Minimum-wage supporters argue that the higher wages for low-skilled workers are worth this reduction in employment and job-training opportunities. Critics argue, however, that the reduced job opportunities for the lowest-skilled workers are reason enough to eliminate the minimum wage.

Proponents of minimum wage laws argue that they help the poor. Is this really true? According to the U.S. Department of Labor, most minimum wage earners are young, part-time workers and relatively few live below the poverty line. About one-half of minimum wage workers are between the ages of 16 to 24 years and approximately three-fifths hold a part-time job. Fewer than 20 percent of minimum wage workers are from families below the poverty line, and only about one out of every four is married. Only 15 percent are a sole earner providing support for a family with one or more children. Therefore, even if the adverse effects of a higher minimum wage on employment and training opportunities are small, a higher minimum wage does little to help the poor, making it a much less attractive antipoverty program than other alternatives.[7]

BLACK MARKETS AND THE IMPORTANCE OF THE LEGAL STRUCTURE

When price controls are imposed, exchanges at prices outside of the range set by the government are illegal. Governments may also make it entirely illegal to buy and sell certain products. This is the case with drugs like marijuana and cocaine in the United States. Similarly, prostitution is illegal in all states except Nevada. However, controlling prices and making a good or service illegal doesn't eliminate market forces. When demand is strong and gains from trade can be had, markets will develop and exchanges will occur in spite of the restrictions. People will also engage in illegal exchanges in order to evade taxes. For example, the $5.85 per-pack cigarette tax in New York City has made cigarette smuggling into that city a thriving business.

Black market
A market that operates outside the legal system in which either illegal goods are sold or legal goods are sold at illegal prices or terms.

Markets that operate outside the legal system are called **black markets**. How do black markets work? Can markets function without the protection of the law? As in other markets, supply and demand will determine prices in black markets, too. However, because black markets operate outside the official legal structure, enforcement of contracts and the dependability of quality will be less certain. Furthermore, participation in black markets involves greater risk, particularly for suppliers. Prices in these markets will have to be higher than they otherwise would be to compensate suppliers for the risks they are taking—the threat of arrest, possibility of a fine or prison sentence, and so on. Perhaps most important, in black markets there are no legal channels for the peaceful settlement of disputes. When a buyer or a seller fails to deliver, it is the other party who must try to enforce the agreement, usually through the use or threat of physical force.

Compared with normal markets, economic analysis indicates that black markets will be characterized by a higher incidence of defective products, higher profit rates (for those who do not get caught), and more violence. The incidence of phony tickets purchased from street dealers selling them at illegal prices and deaths caused by toxic, illicit drugs are reflections of the high presence of defective goods in these markets. The expensive clothes and automobiles

[7]See David Neumark and William Wascher, "The Effects of Minimum Wages Throughout the Wage Distribution," Journal of Human Resources 39 (April 2004): 425–50; David Neumark and William Wascher, Minimum Wages. (Cambridge, MA: MIT Press, 2008); and Joseph J. Sabia and Richard V. Burkhauser, "Minimum Wages and Poverty: Will a $9.50 Federal Minimum Wage Really Help the Working Poor?" Southern Economic Journal 76 (January 2010): 592–623, for evidence on this point.

of many drug dealers provide evidence of the high monetary profits present in black markets. Crime statistics indicate that violence is often used to settle disputes arising from black-market transactions. In urban areas, a high percentage of the violent crimes, including murder, are associated with illegal trades gone bad and competition among dealers in the illegal drug market.

The prohibition of alcohol in the United States from 1920 to 1933 provides additional evidence that violence, deception, and fraud plague markets that operate outside the law. When the production and sale of alcohol were illegal during the Prohibition era, gangsters dominated the alcohol trade, and the murder rate soared to record highs. There were also problems with product quality (tainted or highly toxic mixtures, for example) similar to the ones present in modern-day illegal-drug markets. When Prohibition was repealed and the market for alcoholic beverages began operating once again within the legal framework, these harmful secondary effects disappeared.

The operation of black markets highlights a point often taken for granted: *A legal system that provides for secure private-property rights, contract enforcement, and access to an unbiased court system for settling disputes is vitally important for the smooth operation of markets.* Markets will exist in any environment, but they can be counted on to function efficiently only when property rights are secure and contracts are impartially enforced.

THE IMPACT OF A TAX

How do taxes affect market exchange? When governments tax goods, who bears the burden? Economists use the term **tax incidence** to indicate how the burden of a tax is *actually* shared between buyers (who pay more for what they purchase) and sellers (who receive less for what they sell). When a tax is imposed, the government can make either the buyer or the seller legally responsible for payment of the tax. The legal assignment is called the *statutory incidence* of the tax. However, the person who writes the check to the government—that is, the person statutorily responsible for the tax—is not always the one who bears the tax burden. The *actual incidence* of a tax may lie elsewhere. If, for example, a tax is placed statutorily on a seller, the seller might simply increase the price of the product. In this case, the buyers end up bearing some, or all, of the tax burden through the higher price.

To illustrate, **Exhibit 5** shows how a $1,000 tax placed on the sale of used cars would affect the market. (To simplify this example, let's assume all used cars are identical.) Here, the tax has statutorily been placed on the seller. When a tax is imposed on the seller, it shifts the supply curve upward by exactly the amount of the tax—$1,000, in this example. To understand why, remember that the height of the supply curve at a particular quantity shows the minimum price required to cause enough sellers to offer that quantity of cars for sale. Suppose you were a potential seller, willing to sell your car for any price over $6,000, but you would keep it unless you could pocket at least $6,000 from the sale. Because you now have to pay a tax of $1,000 when you sell your car, the minimum price you will accept *from the buyer* will rise to $7,000, so that after paying the tax, you will retain $6,000. Other potential sellers will be in a similar position. The tax will push the minimum price each seller is willing to accept upward by $1,000. Thus, the after-tax supply curve will shift vertically by this amount.

Sellers would prefer to pass the entire tax on to buyers by raising prices by the full amount of the tax, rather than paying any part of it themselves. However, as sellers begin to raise prices, customers respond by purchasing fewer units. At some point, to avoid losing additional sales, some sellers will find it more profitable to accept part of the tax burden themselves (in the form of a lower price net of tax), rather than to raise the price by the full amount of the tax. This process is shown in Exhibit 5.

Before the tax was imposed, used cars sold for a price of $7,000 (at the intersection of the original supply and demand curves shown by point *A*). After the $1,000 tax is imposed, the equilibrium price of used cars will rise to $7,400 (to point *B,* the intersection of the new supply curve including the tax, and the demand curve). Thus, despite the tax being

Black markets like those for illegal drugs are characterized by less dependable product quality and the greater use of violence to settle disputes between buyers and sellers.

Tax incidence
The way the burden of a tax is distributed among economic units (consumers, producers, employees, employers, and so on). The actual tax burden does not always fall on those who are statutorily assigned to pay the tax.

Exhibit 5

The Impact of a Tax Imposed on Sellers

When a $1,000 tax is imposed statutorily on the sellers of used cars, the supply curve shifts vertically upward by the amount of the tax. The price of used cars to buyers rises from $7,000 to $7,400, resulting in buyers bearing $400 of the burden of this tax. The price received by a seller falls from $7,000 to $6,400 ($7,400 minus the $1,000 tax), resulting in sellers bearing $600 of the burden.

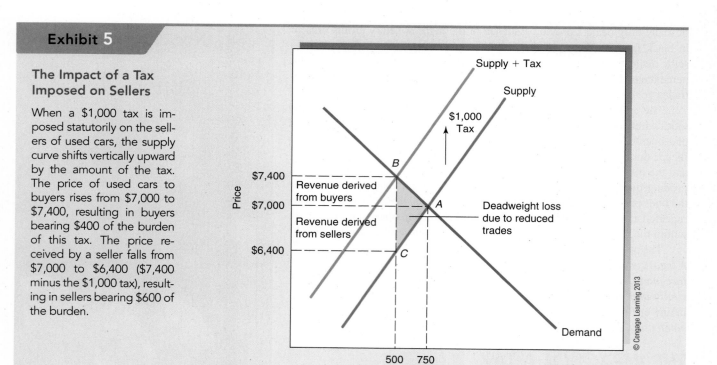

statutorily imposed on sellers, the higher price shifts some of the tax burden to buyers. Buyers will now pay $400 more for used cars. Sellers now receive $7,400 from the sale of their used cars. However, after sending $1,000 in taxes to the government, they retain only $6,400. This is exactly $600 less than the seller would have received had the tax not been imposed. Because the distance between the supply curves is exactly $1,000, this net price can be found in Exhibit 5 by following the vertical line down from the new equilibrium (point *B*) to the original supply curve (point *C*) and over to the price axis. In this case, each $1,000 of tax revenue transferred to the government imposes a burden of $400 on buyers (in the form of higher used-car prices) and a $600 burden on sellers (in the form of lower net receipts from a car sale), even though sellers are responsible for actually sending the $1,000 tax payment to the government.

The tax revenue derived from a tax is equal to the **tax base** (in this case, the number of used cars exchanged) multiplied by the **tax rate**. After the tax is imposed, the quantity exchanged will fall to 500,000 cars per month because some buyers will choose not to purchase at the $7,400 price, and some sellers will decide not to sell when they are able to net only $6,400. Given the after-tax quantity sold, the monthly revenue derived from the tax will be $500 million (500,000 cars multiplied by $1,000 tax per car).

THE DEADWEIGHT LOSS CAUSED BY TAXES

As Exhibit 5 shows, a $1,000 tax on used cars causes the number of units exchanged to fall from 750,000 to 500,000. It reduces the quantity of units exchanged by 250,000 units. Remember, trade results in mutual gains for both buyers and sellers. The loss of the mutual benefits that would have been derived from these additional 250,000 units also imposes a cost on buyers and sellers. But this cost—the loss of the gains from trade eliminated by the tax—does not generate any revenue for the government. Economists call this the **deadweight loss** of taxation. In Exhibit 5, the size of the triangle *ABC* measures the deadweight loss. The deadweight loss is a burden imposed on buyers and sellers over and above the cost of the revenue transferred to the government. Sometimes it is referred to as the

Tax base
The level or quantity of an economic activity that is taxed. Higher tax rates reduce the level of the tax base because they make the activity less attractive.

Tax rate
The per-unit amount of the tax or the percentage rate at which the economic activity is taxed.

Deadweight loss
The loss of gains from trade to buyers and sellers that occurs when a tax is imposed. The deadweight loss imposes a burden on both buyers and sellers over and above the actual payment of the tax.

excess burden of taxation. It is composed of losses to both buyers (the lost consumer surplus consisting of the upper part of the triangle *ABC*) and sellers (the lost producer surplus consisting of the lower part of the triangle *ABC*).

The deadweight loss to sellers includes an indirect cost imposed on the people who supply resources to that industry (such as its suppliers and employees). The 1990 luxury-boat tax provides a vivid illustration of this point. Supporters of the luxury-boat tax assumed the tax burden would fall primarily on wealthy yacht buyers. The actual effects were quite different, though. Because of the tax, luxury-boat sales fell sharply and thousands of workers lost their jobs in the yacht-manufacturing industry. The deadweight loss triangle might seem like an abstract concept, but it wasn't so abstract to the employees in the yacht industry who lost their jobs! Their losses are part of what is reflected in the triangular area. Moreover, because luxury-boat sales declined so sharply, the tax generated only a meager amount of revenue. The large deadweight loss (or excess burden) combined with meager revenue for the government eventually led to the repeal of the tax.

ACTUAL VERSUS STATUTORY INCIDENCE

Economic analysis indicates that the actual burden of a tax—or more precisely, the split of the burden between buyers and sellers—does not depend on whether the tax is statutorily placed on the buyer or the seller. To see this, we must first look at how the market responds to a tax statutorily placed on the buyer. Continuing with the auto tax example, let's suppose that the government places the $1,000 tax on the buyer of the car, rather than the seller. After making a used-car purchase, the buyer must send a check to the government for $1,000. Imposing a tax on buyers will shift the demand curve downward by the amount of the tax, as shown in **Exhibit 6**. This is because the height of the demand curve represents the maximum price a buyer is willing to pay for the car. If a particular buyer is willing and able to pay only $5,000 for a car, the $1,000 tax would mean that the most the buyer would be willing to pay *to the seller* would be $4,000. This is because the total cost to the buyer is now the purchase price plus the tax.

As Exhibit 6 shows, the price of used cars falls from $7,000 (point *A*) to $6,400 (point *B*) when the tax is statutorily placed on the buyer. Even though the tax is placed on buyers, the reduction in demand that results causes the price received by sellers to fall by $600. Thus, $600 of the tax is again borne by sellers, just as it was when the tax was placed statutorily on them. From the buyer's standpoint, a car now costs $7,400 ($6,400 paid to the seller plus $1,000 in tax to the government). Just as when the tax was imposed on the seller, the buyer now pays $400 more for a used car.

A comparison of Exhibits 5 and 6 makes it clear that the actual burden of the $1,000 tax is independent of its statutory incidence. In both cases, buyers pay a total price of $7,400 for the car (a $400 increase from the pretax level), and sellers receive $6,400 from the sale (a $600 decrease from the pretax level). Correspondingly, the revenue derived by the government, the number of sales eliminated by the tax, and the size of the deadweight loss are identical whether the law requires payment of the tax by the sellers or by the buyers. A similar phenomenon occurs with any tax. The 15.3 percent Social Security payroll tax, for example, is statutorily levied as 7.65 percent on the employee and 7.65 percent on the employer. The impact is to drive down the net pay received by employees and raise the employers' cost of hiring workers. Economic analysis tells us that the actual burden of this tax will probably differ from its legal assignment and that it will be the same regardless of how the tax is statutorily assigned. Because market prices (here, workers' gross wage) will adjust, the incidence of the tax will be identical regardless of whether the 15.3 percent is levied on employees or on employers or is divided between the two parties. (Note: The share of the payroll tax imposed on employees was temporarily reduced by 2 percentage points in 2011.)

ELASTICITY AND THE INCIDENCE OF A TAX

If the actual incidence of a tax is independent of its statutory assignment, what does determine the incidence? The answer: The incidence of a tax depends on the responsiveness of

Excess burden of taxation Another term for deadweight loss. It reflects losses that occur when beneficial activities are forgone because they are taxed.

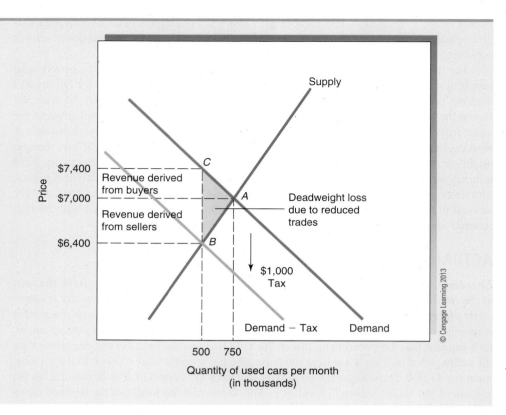

Exhibit 6

The Impact of a Tax Imposed on Buyers

When a $1,000 tax is imposed statutorily on the buyers of used cars, the demand curve shifts vertically downward by the amount of the tax. The price of used cars falls from $7,000 to $6,400, resulting in sellers bearing $600 of the burden. The buyer's total cost of purchasing the car rises from $7,000 to $7,400 ($6,400 plus the $1,000 tax), resulting in buyers bearing $400 of the burden of this tax. The incidence of this tax on used cars is the same regardless of whether it is statutorily imposed on buyers or sellers.

© Cengage Learning 2013

buyers and of sellers to a change in price. When buyers respond to even a small increase in price by leaving the market and buying other things, they will not be willing to accept a price that is much higher than it was prior to the tax. Similarly, if sellers respond to a small reduction in what they receive by shifting their goods and resources to other markets, or by going out of business, they will not be willing to accept a much smaller payment, net of tax. The burden of a tax—its incidence—tends to fall more heavily on whichever side of the market has the least attractive options elsewhere—the side of the market that is less sensitive to price changes, in other words.

The actual burden of a tax is independent of whether it is imposed on buyers or sellers.

In the preceding chapter, we saw that the steepness of the supply and demand curves reflects how responsive producers and consumers are to a price change. Relatively inelastic demand or supply curves are steeper (more vertical), indicating less responsiveness to a change in price. Relatively elastic demand or supply curves are flatter (more horizontal), indicating a higher degree of responsiveness to a change in price.

Using gasoline as an example, part (a) of **Exhibit 7** illustrates the impact of a tax when demand is relatively inelastic and supply is relatively elastic. It will not be easy for gasoline consumers to shift—particularly in the short run—to other fuels in response to an increase in the price of gasoline. The inelastic demand curve shows this. When a 50-cent per-gallon tax is imposed on gasoline (roughly the current average of combined federal and state taxes), buyers end up paying 40 cents more per gallon ($3.00 instead of $2.60), while the net price received by sellers is only 10 cents less ($2.50 instead of $2.60). *When demand is relatively inelastic, or supply is relatively elastic, buyers will bear the larger share of the tax burden.*

"THIS NEW TAX PLAN SOUNDS PRETTY GOOD... WE GET A 9% CUT AND BUSINESS PICKS UP THE BURDEN...."

By John Trever, Albuquerque Journal. Reprinted by permission.

Exhibit 7

How the Burden of a Tax Depends on the Elasticities of Demand and Supply

In part (a), when demand is relatively more inelastic than supply, buyers bear a larger share of the burden of the tax. In part (b), when supply is relatively more inelastic than demand, sellers bear a larger share of the tax burden.

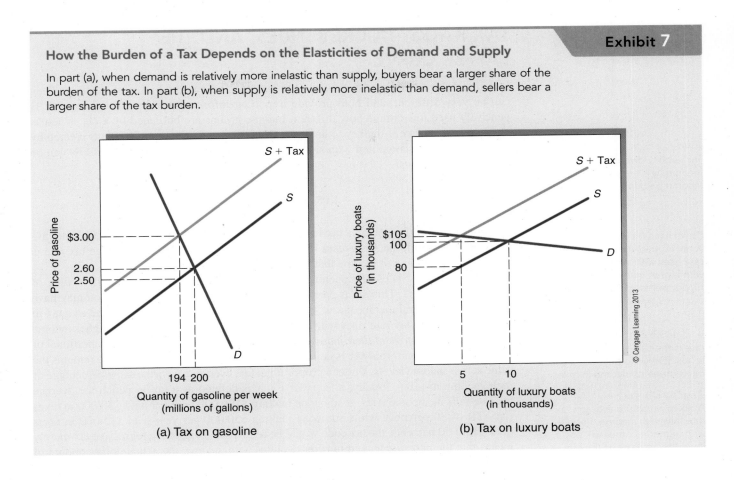

(a) Tax on gasoline

(b) Tax on luxury boats

© Cengage Learning 2013

Conversely, when demand is relatively elastic and supply is inelastic, more of the tax burden will fall on sellers and resource suppliers. The luxury-boat tax illustrates this point. As we mentioned earlier, Congress imposed a tax on the sale of luxury boats in 1990. Later, the tax was repealed because of its adverse impact on sales and employment in the industry. There are many things wealthy potential yacht owners can spend their money on other than luxury boats *sold in the United States.* For one thing, they can buy a yacht someplace else, perhaps in Mexico, England, or the Bahamas. Or they can spend more time on the golf course, travel to exotic places, or purchase a nicer car or a vacation home. Because there are attractive substitutes, the demand for domestically produced luxury boats is relatively elastic compared with supply. Therefore, as Exhibit 7b illustrates, when a $25,000 tax is imposed on luxury boats, prices rise by only $5,000 (from $100,000 to $105,000), but output falls substantially (from 10,000 to 5,000 boats). The net price received by sellers falls by $20,000 (from $100,000 to $80,000 per boat). *When demand is relatively elastic, or supply is relatively inelastic, sellers (including resource suppliers) will bear the larger share of the tax burden.*

ELASTICITY AND THE DEADWEIGHT LOSS

We have seen that the elasticities of supply and demand determine how the burden of a tax is distributed between buyer and seller. They also influence the size of the deadweight loss caused by the tax because they determine the total reduction in the quantity exchanged. When either demand or supply is relatively inelastic, fewer trades will be eliminated by the tax, so the deadweight loss will be smaller. From a policy perspective, the excess burden of a tax system will therefore be lower if taxes are levied on goods and services for which either demand or supply is highly inelastic.

TAX RATES, TAX REVENUES, AND THE LAFFER CURVE

It is important to distinguish between the average and marginal rates of taxation. They can be very different, and both provide important information. The average tax rate is generally used to examine how different income groups are burdened by a tax, whereas the marginal tax rate is the key to understanding the negative economic effects created by a tax. Both can be computed with simple equations. The average tax rate (ATR) can be expressed as follows:

Average tax rate (ATR)
Tax liability divided by taxable income. It is the percentage of income paid in taxes.

$$ATR = \frac{\text{Tax liability}}{\text{Taxable income}}$$

For example, if a person's tax liability was $3,000 on an income of $20,000, her average tax rate would be 15 percent ($3,000 divided by $20,000). The average tax rate is simply the percentage of income that is paid in taxes.

In the United States, the personal income tax provides the largest single source of government revenue. This tax is particularly important at the federal level. You may have heard that the federal income tax is "progressive." A progressive tax is defined as a tax in which the average tax rate rises with income. In other words, people with higher income pay a larger *percentage of their income* in taxes. Alternatively, taxes can be proportional or regressive. A proportional tax is defined as a tax in which the average tax rate remains the same across income levels. Under a proportional tax, everyone pays the same percentage of their income in taxes. Finally, a regressive tax is defined as a tax in which the average tax rate falls as income rises. If someone making $100,000 per year paid $30,000 in taxes (an ATR of 30 percent), while someone making $30,000 per year paid $15,000 in taxes (an ATR of 50 percent), the tax code would be regressive. Note that a regressive tax merely means that the *percentage* paid in taxes declines with income; the actual dollar amount of the tax bill might still be higher for those with larger incomes.

Progressive tax
A tax in which the average tax rate rises with income. People with higher incomes will pay a higher percentage of their income in taxes.

Proportional tax
A tax in which the average tax rate is the same at all income levels. Everyone pays the same percentage of income in taxes.

Regressive tax
A tax in which the average tax rate falls with income. People with higher incomes will pay a lower percentage of their income in taxes.

Although the average tax rate is useful in determining whether an income tax is progressive, proportional, or regressive, it is the marginal tax rate that is most relevant when individuals are making choices. It is the marginal tax rate that determines how much of an additional dollar of income must be paid in taxes (and thus, also, how much one gets to keep). An individual's marginal tax rate can be very different from his or her average tax rate. The marginal tax rate (MTR) can be expressed as follows:

Marginal tax rate (MTR)
The additional tax liability a person faces divided by his or her additional taxable income. It is the percentage of an extra dollar of income earned that must be paid in taxes. It is the marginal tax rate that is relevant in personal decision-making.

$$MTR = \frac{\text{Change in tax liability}}{\text{Change in taxable income}}$$

The MTR reveals both how much of one's *additional* income must be turned over to the tax collector and how much is retained by the individual taxpayer. For example, when the MTR is 25 percent, $25 of every $100 of additional earnings must be paid in taxes. The individual is permitted to keep only $75 of his or her additional income, in other words. The marginal tax rate is vitally important because it affects the incentive to earn additional income. The higher the marginal tax rate, the less incentive individuals have to earn more income. At high marginal rates, for example, many spouses will choose to stay home rather than take a job, and others will choose not to take on second jobs or extra work. **Exhibit 8** shows the calculation of both the average and marginal tax rates within the framework of the 2010 federal income tax tables. In addition to the federal income tax, there are also state and local income taxes and payroll taxes. The taxpayer's marginal tax rate will reflect the combine impact of all taxes that reduce the take-home pay derived from additional earnings.

Governments generally levy taxes to raise revenue. The revenue derived from a tax is equal to the tax base multiplied by the tax rate. As we previously noted, taxes will reduce the level of the activity. When an activity is taxed more heavily, people will choose to do less of it. The higher the tax rate, the greater the shift away from the activity. If taxpayers can easily escape the tax by altering their behavior (perhaps by shifting to substitutes), the tax base will shrink significantly as rates are increased. This erosion in the tax base in

Average and Marginal Tax Rates in the Income Tax Tables

This excerpt from the 2010 federal income tax table shows that in the 25 percent federal marginal income tax bracket, each $100 of additional taxable income a single taxpayer earns ($35,000 versus $35,100, for example) causes his or her tax liability to increase by $25 (from $4,938 to $4,963). Note that the average tax rate for a single taxpayer at $35,000 is about 14 percent ($4,938 divided by $35,000), even though the taxpayer's marginal rate is 25 percent.

2010 Tax Table–*Continued*

If line 43 (taxable income) is–		And you are–			
At Least	But Less Than	Single	Married Filing Jointly	Married Filing Separately	Head of a Household
			Your tax is–		
35,000					
35,000	35,050	4,938	4,416	4,938	4,656
35,050	35,100	4,950	4,424	4,950	4,664
35,100	35,150	4,963	4,431	4,963	4,671
35,150	35,200	4,975	4,439	4,975	4,679
35,200	35,250	4,988	4,446	4,988	4,686
35,250	35,300	5,000	4,454	5,000	4,694
35,300	35,350	5,013	4,461	5,013	4,701
35,350	35,400	5,025	4,469	5,025	4,709
35,400	35,450	5,038	4,476	5,038	4,716
35,450	35,500	5,050	4,484	5,050	4,724
35,500	35,550	5,063	4,491	5,063	4,731
35,550	35,600	5,075	4,499	5,075	4,739
35,600	35,650	5,088	4,506	5,088	4,746
35,650	35,700	5,100	4,514	5,100	4,754
35,700	35,750	5,113	4,521	5,113	4,761
35,750	35,800	5,125	4,529	5,125	4,769
35,800	35,850	5,138	4,536	5,138	4,776
35,850	35,900	5,150	4,544	5,150	4,784
35,900	35,950	5,163	4,551	5,163	4,791
35,950	36,000	5,175	4,559	5,175	4,799

$100 of additional income . . . . . . results in $25 of additional tax liability.

© Cengage Learning 2013

response to higher rates means that an increase in tax rates will generally lead to a less-than-proportional increase in tax revenue.

Economist Arthur Laffer popularized the idea that, beyond some point, higher tax rates will shrink the tax base so much that tax revenue will eventually decline as tax rates are pushed to higher and higher levels. The curve illustrating the relationship between tax rates and tax revenues is called the **Laffer curve. Exhibit 9** illustrates the concept of the Laffer curve as it applies to income taxes. Obviously, tax revenue would be zero if the income tax rate were zero. What isn't so obvious is that tax revenue would also be zero (or at least very close to zero) if the tax rate were 100 percent. Confronting a 100 percent tax rate, most individuals would go fishing or find something else to do rather than engage in taxable productive activity, since the 100 percent tax rate would eliminate all personal reward derived from earning taxable income. Why work when you have to give every penny of your earnings to the government?

Laffer curve
A curve illustrating the relationship between the tax rate and tax revenues. Tax revenues will be low at both very high and very low tax rates. When tax rates are quite high, lowering them can increase tax revenue.

Exhibit 9

Laffer Curve

Because taxing an activity affects the amount of it people will do, a change in tax rates will not lead to a proportional change in tax revenues. As the Laffer curve indicates, beyond some point (*B*), an increase in tax rates will cause tax revenues to fall. At high tax rates, revenue can be increased by lowering tax rates. The tax rate that maximizes tax revenue is higher than the ideal tax rate for the economy as a whole because of the large deadweight loss of taxation as tax rates increase toward point *B*.

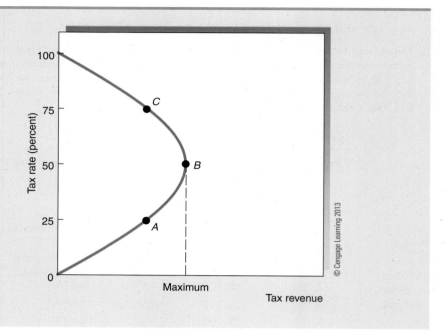

As tax rates are reduced from 100 percent, the incentive to work and earn taxable income increases, income expands, and tax revenue rises. Similarly, as tax rates increase from zero, tax revenue expands. Clearly, at some rate greater than zero but less than 100 percent, tax revenue will be maximized (point *B* in Exhibit 9). This is not to imply that the tax rate that maximizes revenue is the ideal, or optimal, tax rate from the standpoint of the economy as a whole. Although it might be the tax rate that generates the most revenue for government, we must also consider the welfare reductions imposed on individuals by the deadweight loss created by the tax. As rates are increased and the maximum revenue point (*B*) is approached, relatively large tax rate increases will be necessary to expand tax revenue by even a small amount. In this range, the deadweight loss of taxation in the form of reductions in gains from trade will be exceedingly large relative to the additional tax revenue. Far from being ideal, the revenue maximizing tax rate will be highly inefficient.

The Laffer curve shows that it is important to distinguish between changes in tax rates and changes in tax revenues. Higher rates will not always lead to more revenue for the government. Similarly, lower rates will not always lead to less revenue. ***When tax rates are already high, a rate reduction may increase tax revenues. Correspondingly, increasing high tax rates may lead to less tax revenue.***

Evidence from the sharp reduction in marginal tax rates imposed on those with high incomes during the 1980s supports the Laffer curve. The top marginal rate was reduced from 70 percent at the beginning of the decade to 33 percent by the end of the decade. Even though the top rates were cut sharply, tax revenues and the share of the personal income tax paid by high-income earners actually rose as a result. During the decade, revenue collected from the top 1 percent of earners rose a whopping 51.4 percent (after adjusting for inflation). In 1980, 19 percent of the personal income tax was collected from the top 1 percent of earners. By 1990, at the lower tax rates, the top 1 percent of earners accounted for more than 25 percent of income tax revenues. The top 10 percent of earners paid just over 49 percent of total income taxes in 1980, but by 1990 the share paid by these earners had risen to 55 percent. Thus, the reduction in the exceedingly high rates increased the revenue collected from high-income taxpayers. Additional evidence on the impact of these tax changes in the 1980s is provided in Special Topic 1.

Many politicians advocate higher marginal tax rates on high-income earners in order to raise additional revenue and reduce the size of the federal budget deficit. When considering

APPLICATIONS IN ECONOMICS

The Laffer Curve and Mountain-Climbing Deaths

The Laffer curve can be used to illustrate many other relationships besides just tax rates and tax revenues. Economists J. R. Clark and Dwight Lee have used it to analyze the relationship between the safety of mountain climbing and mountain-climbing deaths on Mt. McKinley, North America's highest peak. As the risk of dying from climbing Mt. McKinley fell due to greater search-and-rescue efforts by national park personnel, the number of people seeking to "conquer the mountain" rose significantly. The increase in the number of climbers attempting to conquer the mountain offset the lower risk, leading to a Laffer curve-type relationship. In other words, greater search-and-rescue efforts led to a *higher* number of total deaths on the mountain.

Let's look at the problem numerically. Assume that if the probability of death from an attempted climb were 90 percent, only 100 people would attempt to climb the mountain each year, leading to an annual death rate of 90.

Now suppose that greater search-and-rescue efforts lower the probability of death to 50 percent. Because incentives matter, the increased safety will result in an increase in the number of people attempting to climb the mountain. Suppose that the number of climbers increases from 100 to 200. With 200 climbers and a 50 percent probability of death, the annual number of fatalities would increase to 100, 10 more than before rescue efforts were improved. The total number of mountain-climbing deaths is actually lowest when there is both a very high and a very low probability of death—just as the Laffer curve predicts. The number of deaths is largest in the middle probability ranges. Making a very risky mountain safer can therefore result in more rather than fewer fatalities.[1]

[1]See J. R. Clark and Dwight R. Lee, "Too Safe to Be Safe: Some Implications of Short- and Long-Run Rescue Laffer Curves," *Eastern Economic Journal* 23, no. 2 (Spring 1997): 127–37.

such proposals, it is important to keep in mind that higher marginal tax rates will lead to a smaller amount of taxable income produced by high earners. Predictably, such proposals will raise less revenue than their proponents envision as the tax base shrinks in response to the higher marginal tax rate.

THE IMPACT OF A SUBSIDY

The supply and demand framework can also be used to analyze the impact of a government subsidy. A subsidy is a payment to either the buyer or seller of a good or service, usually on a per-unit basis. When a subsidy is granted to buyers, proponents typically argue that the subsidy will make the purchase of the good more affordable. Correspondingly, subsidies to sellers are generally thought to improve the profitability of the producers in the industry. As we have seen in other cases, however, the effect of government programs often differ substantially from the stated intentions of their proponents. Because prices change when subsidies are imposed (just as when taxes are imposed), the benefit of a subsidy can be partially, or totally, shifted from buyer to seller, or vice versa.

Suppose that the government, in an effort to make the cost of college more affordable, granted full-time students a subsidy of $4,000 per year. What impact would this subsidy have on the price and quantity in the market for a college education? **Exhibit 10** provides insight on the answer to this question. Prior to the subsidy, the market price was determined by the intersection of the initial demand (D_1) and supply (S_1). Thus, the pre-subsidy equilibrium price for a year of college was $10,000. The subsidy to the student-buyers increases demand, causing the demand curve to shift upward by $4,000 from D_1 to D_2. A new equilibrium will occur at a higher price ($12,000 in our example) and larger output (Q_2 rather than Q_1). The net price to students will fall to $8,000, the $12,000 new market price minus the $4,000.

Subsidy
A payment the government makes to either the buyer or the seller, usually on a per-unit basis, when a good or service is purchased or sold.

Exhibit 10

The Impact of a Subsidy Granted to Buyers

Here we illustrate how a $4,000 subsidy granted to full-time college students would impact the price and quantity of a year of college education. Prior to the subsidy, the equilibrium price of a year of college was $10,000 and Q_1 students attended college. The subsidy to students would cause demand to shift from D_1 to D_2, pushing the equilibrium price of a year of college to $12,000. Students would gain $2,000 in the form of a lower net cost of a year of college (the new net price after the subsidy is $8,000), but the suppliers would also gain $2,000 in the form of higher prices for their services. If the supply curve was more inelastic relative to the demand curve, the gains of the students would be smaller and those of the suppliers larger.

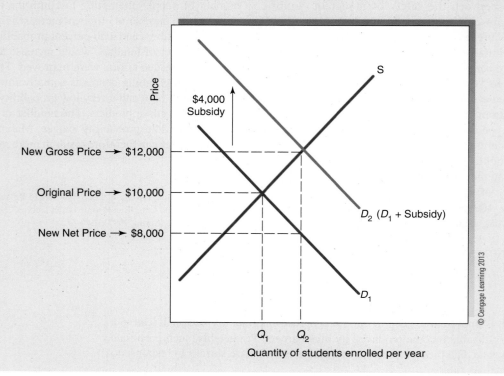

Interestingly, even though the students received an educational subsidy of $4,000, their net gain was only $2,000. The rest of the benefits went to the educational suppliers in the form of higher prices for their services.

As we previously discussed, the burden of a tax does not necessarily fall entirely or even primarily on the party writing out the check to the taxing authority. The same is true for subsidies. Parties other than the direct subsidy recipients may benefit substantially from the subsidies. Moreover, the direct recipients of the subsidy may gain less, and often substantially less, than their grant from the government.

ELASTICITY AND THE BENEFIT OF GOVERNMENT SUBSIDY PROGRAMS

What determines the allocation of the benefits derived from a subsidy? In the example of Exhibit 10, the benefit of the $4,000 subsidy granted to students was split evenly between buyers and sellers. However, the actual distribution of this benefit will depend on the elasticity of supply and demand—just as it does with a tax. Consider the case where the subsidy is granted to the buyers, causing the demand curve for the product to shift upward by the amount of the subsidy. If the supply curve is highly inelastic relative to demand, the increase in demand will lead primarily to higher prices and most of the benefits will be derived by the suppliers of the good or service. In contrast, if the supply curve is elastic and the demand curve inelastic, the increase in demand will lead to only a small increase in price and the primary beneficiaries of the subsidy will be consumers in the form of lower prices.

The greater share of the benefit of a subsidy will always be shifted toward the more inelastic side of the market. Thus, the more inelastic the supply, the larger the share of the benefit that will accrue to sellers. Conversely, the more inelastic the demand, the larger the share of the benefit that will accrue to buyers. Sometimes the subsidies will be granted to sellers rather than buyers. Nonetheless, the benefits will still flow primarily toward the more inelastic side of the market.

REAL-WORLD SUBSIDY PROGRAMS

The federal government now operates more than 2,000 separate subsidy programs, twice the number of the mid-1980s. Spending on these programs and the taxes that finance them are major items in the government budget. Some subsidy programs, such as Medicare and food stamps, provide payments to buyers. Others, such as the subsidies to the arts, public broadcasting, sports stadiums, and ethanol are directed toward suppliers. As we discussed, however, the party granted the subsidy may not be the one who captures the larger share of the actual benefit from the subsidy.

Let's take a closer look at the subsidies granted to college students. There has been a substantial increase in federal and state subsidies to college students since 1990. Measured in constant 2009 dollars, federal and state grants directly to college students rose from $1,402 per full-time equivalent student in 1990 to $3,229 in 2009–2010, an increase of 130 percent over the two decades. Federal loans to college students increased even more rapidly. Adjusted for inflation, federal loans per full-time student more than tripled, soaring from $2,034 in 1990 to $6,249 in 2009–2010.

As Exhibit 10 illustrated, subsidies in the form of grants and loans to students will increase the demand for college education and thereby push up its price. Indeed, this has been the case. Measured in constant 2009 dollars, the average price of a year of college approximately doubled, increasing from $5,305 in 1990 to $10,219 in 2009–2010. In 1990, the price of a year of college was 9.4 percent of the median income in the United States, but by 2009–2010, the figure had risen to 17 percent.[8]

Most students perceive that government aid in the form of grants and low-interest loans make it more economical for them to attend college. But there is another side to this issue: The subsidies are a driving force underlying the soaring cost of a college education. Moreover, colleges themselves are major beneficiaries of the student subsidies. Thus, it is not surprising that college administrators are at the forefront of those lobbying for additional subsidies.

Subsidies for medical care have had a similar impact. The Medicare and Medicaid programs were introduced in the mid-1960s. Since the large subsidies accompanying these programs were initiated, prices of medical services have persistently increased at twice the rate of the general level of prices. Again, this suggests that the suppliers of these services derived a substantial share of the benefits in the form of higher prices for their services. Given that the supply of most medical services is highly inelastic, this is precisely what one would expect from an increase in the subsidies granted to buyers.

Both the educational and medical care subsidies are allocated to a subset of the population. For example, the Medicare program subsidizes the healthcare purchases of senior citizens, and the Medicaid program provides subsidies to low-income households. These subsidies increase the demand for health care and drive up the prices of medical service for all consumers, including those ineligible for either program. When only some of the buyers in a market are subsidized, groups that are ineligible for the subsidies will generally be harmed because they will have to pay higher prices than would be the case in the absence of the subsidies.

---

[8]The figures presented here are from Sandy Baum, et al., "Trends in Student Aid 2010," The College Board, Washington D.C., 2010 and the U.S. Department of Education, National Center for Education Statistics. For additional details on the impact of subsidies to students on the cost of college, see Robert E. Martin and Andrew Gillen, "How College Pricing Undermines Financial Aid," The Center for College Affordability and Productivity, Washington, DC, March 2011.

Ethanol, a bio-fuel alternative to gasoline made from corn, provides another example of a product that is heavily subsidized in the United States. Ethanol subsidies, which amount to approximately $1.75 per gallon, have a direct cost to taxpayers of approximately $6 billion per year. Ethanol is significantly more costly to produce than gasoline. In effect, the ethanol subsidies channel resources into production of a good that is valued less than its production cost. Ethanol's environmental benefits over gasoline are highly questionable. Why does the government subsidize ethanol? The ethanol subsidies increase the demand for corn, driving up its price. Corn farmers derive major benefits from the program, while the cost is spread thinly across taxpayers (who fund the subsidies) and consumers (who pay higher prices for the many products made from corn—from tortillas to soft drinks). As we will discuss later, politicians can derive political gain by supporting programs of this type even when the programs are inefficient.

Subsidy programs are often highly complex, and their primary beneficiaries are often quite different than those stressed by their proponents. As in the case of ethanol, many subsidy programs are driven by political considerations, the desire of politicians to favor various groups, particularly those that are well organized, in exchange for their votes and other forms of political support. As we proceed, we will analyze several of these programs in more detail.

iStockphoto.com/gaspr13

Looking Ahead

This chapter focused on how government-mandated price controls, taxes, subsidies, and prohibitions affect market outcomes. The next two chapters will apply the basic tools of economics to the political process more generally. In the chapters that follow, we will analyze how the political process works and explain why it sometimes works poorly.

KEY POINTS

- Resource markets and product markets are closely linked. A change in one will generally result in changes in the other.

- Legally imposed price ceilings result in shortages, and legally imposed price floors will cause surpluses. Both also cause other harmful secondary effects. Rent controls, for example, will lead to shortages, less investment, poor maintenance, and deterioration in the quality of rental housing.

- The minimum wage is a price floor for low-skilled labor. It increases the earnings of some low-skilled workers but also reduces employment and leads to fewer training opportunities and nonwage job benefits for many low-skilled workers.

- Because black markets operate outside the legal system, they are often characterized by deception, fraud, and the use of violence as a means of enforcing contracts. A legal system that provides secure private-property rights and unbiased enforcement of contracts enhances the operation of markets.

- The division of the actual tax burden between buyers and sellers is determined by the relative elasticities of

demand and supply rather than on whom the tax is legally imposed.

- In addition to the cost of the tax revenue transferred to the government, taxes will reduce the level of the activity taxed, eliminate some gains from trade, and thereby impose an excess burden, or deadweight loss.

- As tax rates increase, the size of the tax base will shrink. Initially, rates and revenues will be directly related—revenues will expand as rates increase. However, as higher and higher rates are imposed, eventually an inverse relationship will develop—revenues will decline as rates are increased further. The Laffer curve illustrates this pattern.

- The division of the benefit from a subsidy is determined by the relative elasticities of demand and supply rather than to whom the subsidy is actually paid. For example, when the buyers of a good are subsidized, the subsidy will increase demand and lead to higher prices. If the supply is more elastic than the demand, the providers of the services will derive most of the benefits even though the subsidy was granted to the purchasers.

CRITICAL ANALYSIS QUESTIONS

1. *How will a substantial increase in demand for housing affect the wages and employment of carpenters, plumbers, and electricians?

2. Suppose that college students in your town persuaded the town council to enact a law setting the maximum price for rental housing at $400 per month. Will this help or hurt college students who rent housing? In your answer, address how this price ceiling will affect (a) the quality of rental housing; (b) the amount of rental housing available; (c) the incentive of landlords to maintain their properties; (d) the amount of racial, gender, and other types of discrimination in the local rental housing market; (e) the ease with which students will be able to find housing; and, finally, (f) whether a black market for housing would develop.

3. What is the difference between a price ceiling and a price floor? If a price ceiling for a good is set below the market equilibrium, what will happen to the quality and future availability of the good? Explain.

4. *To be meaningful, a price ceiling must be below the market price. Conversely, a meaningful price floor must be above the market price. What impact will a meaningful price ceiling have on the quantity exchanged? What impact will a meaningful price floor have on the quantity exchanged? Explain.

5. The tax on cigarettes in New York City is the highest in the nation—$5.85 per pack. Does this tax raise a lot of revenue for New York City? Why or why not? What are some of the secondary effects of this tax?

6. *Analyze the impact of an increase in the minimum wage from the current level to $10 per hour. How would the following be affected?
   a. employment of people previously earning less than $10 per hour
   b. the unemployment rate of teenagers
   c. the availability of on-the-job training for low-skilled workers
   d. the demand for high-skilled workers who are good substitutes for low-skilled workers

7. What is a black market? What are some of the main differences in how black markets operate relative to legal markets?

8. How do you think the markets for organ donation and child adoption would be affected if they were made fully legal with a well-functioning price mechanism? What would be the advantages and disadvantages relative to the current system?

9. What is meant by the incidence of a tax? Explain why the statutory and actual incidence of a tax often differ.

10. What impact do government grants and loans to college students have on the cost of going to college? Are students the primary beneficiary of these subsidies? Discuss.

11. *What is the nature of the deadweight loss accompanying taxes? Why is it often referred to as an "excess burden"?

12. *Suppose Congress were to pass legislation requiring that businesses employing workers with three or more children pay these employees at least $15 per hour. How would this legislation affect the employment level of low-skilled workers with three or more children? Do you think some workers with large families might attempt to conceal the fact? Why?

13. "We should impose a 20 percent luxury tax on expensive automobiles (those with a sales price of $50,000 or more) in order to collect more tax revenue from the wealthy." Will the burden of the proposed tax fall primarily on the wealthy? Why or why not?

14. *Should policy makers seek to set the tax on an economic activity at a rate that will maximize the revenue derived from the tax? Why or why not? Explain.

*Asterisk denotes questions for which answers are given in Appendix B.

CHAPTER

5

Difficult Cases for the Market, and the Role of Government

CHAPTER FOCUS

- What is economic efficiency and how can it be used to evaluate markets?
- Why is it generally undesirable to pursue any goal to perfection?
- What is the role of government in a market economy?
- What are externalities? What are public goods?
- Why might markets fail to allocate goods and services efficiently?
- If the market has shortcomings, does this mean that government intervention will improve things?

The principal justification for public policy intervention lies in the frequent and numerous shortcomings of market outcomes.

—*Charles Wolf, Jr.*[1]

---

[1]Charles Wolf, Jr., *Markets or Government* (Cambridge, MA: MIT Press, 1988), 17.

As we previously discussed, market allocation and political decision-making are the two main alternatives for the organization of economic activity. Chapters 3 and 4 introduced you to how markets work and analyzed the impact of government intervention in the form of price controls, taxes, and subsidies. We noted that when property rights are well defined, and competition present, markets will tend to direct self-interested individuals into activities that promote the general welfare. But this will not always be the case. In this chapter, we turn our attention to potential problem areas when a conflict arises between personal self-interest and getting the most out of the available resources. We will also consider the implications of these problem areas with regard to the role of government. In the following chapter, we will analyze how the political process works and will compare it more directly with markets.

iStockphoto.com/nicoolay

A CLOSER LOOK AT ECONOMIC EFFICIENCY

Economists use the standard of **economic efficiency** to assess the desirability of economic outcomes. We briefly introduced the concept in Chapter 3. We now want to explore it in more detail. The central idea of economic efficiency is straightforward. For any given level of cost, we want to obtain the largest possible benefit. Alternatively, we want to obtain any particular benefit for the least possible cost. Economic efficiency means getting the most value from the available resources—making the largest pie from the available set of ingredients, so to speak.

Economists acknowledge that individuals generally do not regard the efficiency of the entire economy as a primary goal for themselves. Rather, each person is interested in enlarging the size of his or her own slice. But if resources are used more efficiently, the overall size of the pie will be larger, and therefore, at least potentially, *everyone* could have a larger slice. For an outcome to be consistent with ideal economic efficiency, two conditions are necessary:

Rule 1. *Undertaking an economic action is efficient if it produces more benefits than costs.* To satisfy economic efficiency, all actions generating more benefits than costs must be undertaken. Failure to undertake all such actions implies that a potential gain has been forgone.

Rule 2. *Undertaking an economic action is inefficient if it produces more costs than benefits.* To satisfy economic efficiency, no action that generates more costs than benefits should be undertaken. When such counterproductive actions are taken, society is worse off because even better alternatives were forgone.

Economic efficiency results only when both of these conditions have been met. *Either failure to undertake an efficient action (Rule 1) or the undertaking of an inefficient action (Rule 2) will result in economic inefficiency.* To illustrate, consider **Exhibit 1**, which shows the benefits and costs associated with expanding the amount of any particular activity. We have avoided using a specific example here to ensure you understand the general idea of efficiency without linking it to a specific application. As we will show, the concept has wide-ranging applications, from the evaluation of government policy to how long you choose to brush your teeth in the morning.[2]

> **Economic efficiency**
> A situation that occurs when (1) all activities generating more benefit than cost are undertaken, and (2) no activities are undertaken for which the cost exceeds the benefit.

---

[2]Note to students who may pursue advanced study in economics: Using the concept of efficiency to compare alternative policies typically requires that the analyst estimate costs and benefits that are difficult or impossible to measure. Costs and benefits are the values of opportunities forgone or accepted by individuals, *as evaluated by those individuals.* Then, these costs and benefits must be added up across all individuals and compared. But does a dollar's gain for one individual really compensate for a dollar's sacrifice by another? Some economists simply reject the validity of making such comparisons. They say that neither the estimates by the economic analyst of subjectively determined costs and benefits nor the adding up of these costs and benefits across individuals is meaningful. Their case may be valid, but most economists today nevertheless use the concept of efficiency as we present it. No other way to use economic analysis to compare policy alternatives has been found.

Exhibit 1

Economic Efficiency

As we use more time and resources to expand the level of an activity, the marginal benefits will generally decline and the marginal costs rise. From the viewpoint of efficiency, the activity should be expanded as long as the marginal benefits exceed the marginal costs. Therefore, quantity Q_2 is the economically efficient level of this activity. Q_1 is inefficient because some production that could generate more benefits than costs is not undertaken. Q_3 is also inefficient because some units are produced even though their costs exceed the benefits they create. Thus, either too much or too little of an activity will result in inefficiency.

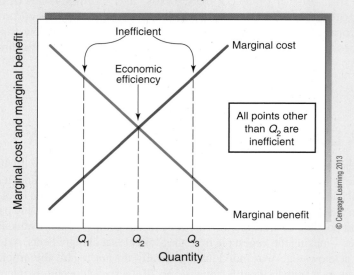

In Exhibit 1, the marginal benefit curve shows the additional benefit associated with expanding the activity. The marginal cost curve shows the cost—including any opportunity costs—of spending additional time, effort, and resources on the activity. At Q_1, the height of the marginal benefit curve exceeds the height of the marginal cost curve. Thus, at that point, the additional benefits of expanding the activity past Q_1 exceed the additional costs. According to Rule 1 of economic efficiency, we should continue to expand the activity until we reach Q_2. Beyond Q_2 (at Q_3, for example), the height of the marginal benefit curve is less than the height of the marginal cost curve. The additional benefits of expanding the activity beyond Q_2 to Q_3 are smaller than the additional costs. According to Rule 2, at Q_3, we have gone too far and should cut back on the activity. Q_2 is the only point consistent with both rules of economic efficiency.

IF IT'S WORTH DOING, IT'S WORTH DOING IMPERFECTLY

Eliminating pollution. Earning straight As. Being completely organized. Cleaning your apartment until it sparkles. Making automobiles completely safe. Making airplanes fully secure against terrorist attacks. All of these are worthwhile goals, right? Well, they are until you consider the costs of actually achieving them. The heading for this section is, of course, a play on the old saying "If it's worth doing, it's worth doing to the best of your ability." Economics suggests, however, that this is not a sensible guideline. At some point, the gains from doing something even better will not be worth the cost. It will make more sense to stop short of perfection.

Exhibit 1 can also be used to illustrate this point. As more resources are dedicated to an activity, the marginal improvements (benefits) will become smaller and smaller, while the marginal costs will rise. The optimal time and effort put into the activity will be achieved at Q_2, and this will nearly always be well below one's best effort. Note that inefficiency results when either too little (for example, Q_1) or too much (for example, Q_3) time and effort are put into the activity.

Do you make decisions this way? Last time you cleaned your car or apartment, why did you decide to leave some things undone? Once the most important areas were clean, you likely began to skip over other areas (like on top of the refrigerator or under the bed), figuring that the benefits of cleaning these areas were simply not worth the cost. Very few people live in a perfectly organized and clean house, wash their hands enough to prevent all colds, brush their teeth long enough to prevent all cavities, or make their home as safe as Fort Knox. They recognize that the benefit of perfection in these, and many other areas, is simply not worth the cost.

Economics is about trade-offs; it is possible to pursue even worthy activities beyond the level that is consistent with economic efficiency. People seem to be more aware of this in their personal decision-making than when evaluating public policy. It is not uncommon to hear people say things like, "We ought to eliminate all pollution" or "No price is too high to save a life."

Universal/Jersey Films/The Kobal Collection/ Bennett, Tracy

In the movie, "Along Came Polly" (2004), Ben Stiller and Jennifer Aniston struggle to find the efficient (optimal) amount of organization in their lives. Aniston believes the eight minutes a day Stiller spends arranging decorative pillows on his bed (that nobody else sees) isn't worth the effort—he's over-organized. Meanwhile, Aniston can't find her car keys because of her inefficiently low level of organization. At the margin, Stiller would be better off organizing less, and Aniston would be better off organizing more.

If we want to get the most out of our resources, we need to think about both marginal benefits and marginal costs and recognize that there are alternative ways of pursuing objectives. Consequently, economists do not ask whether eliminating pollution or saving lives is worth the cost *in terms of dollars* per se, but whether it is worth the cost in terms of giving up other things that could have been done with those dollars—the opportunity cost. Spending an extra $10 billion on worker safety requirements to save 100 lives isn't efficient if the funds could have been spent differently and saved 500 lives. It is no more efficient for the government to pursue perfection than for individuals to do so. Regardless of sector, achievement of perfection is virtually never worth the cost.

THINKING ABOUT THE ECONOMIC ROLE OF GOVERNMENT

For centuries, philosophers, economists, and other scholars have debated the proper role of government. While the debate continues, there is substantial agreement that at least two functions of government are legitimate: (1) protecting individuals and their property against invasions by others and (2) providing goods that cannot easily be provided through private markets. These two functions correspond to what Nobel laureate James M. Buchanan conceptualizes as the protective and productive functions of government.

PROTECTIVE FUNCTION OF GOVERNMENT

The most fundamental function of government is the protection of individuals and their property against acts of aggression. As John Locke wrote more than three centuries ago, individuals are constantly threatened by "the invasions of others." Therefore, each individual "is willing to join in society with others, who are already united, or have a mind to unite, for the mutual preservation of their lives, liberties, and estates."[3] *The protective function of government involves the maintenance of a framework of security and order—an infrastructure of rules within which people can interact peacefully with one another.* Protection of person and property is crucial. It entails providing police protection and prosecuting aggressors who take things that do not belong to them. It also involves providing for a national defense designed to protect against foreign invasions. The legal enforcement of contracts and rules against fraud are also central elements of the protective function. People and businesses that write bad checks, violate contracts, or knowingly supply others with false information, for example, are therefore subject to legal prosecution.

---

[3]John Locke, *Treatise of Civil Government*, 1690, ed. Charles Sherman (New York: Appleton-Century-Crofts, 1937), 82.

© Bettmann/Corbis

The English philosopher John Locke argued that people own themselves and, as a result of this self-ownership, they also own the fruits of their labor. Locke stressed that individuals are not subservient to governments. On the contrary, the role of governments is to protect the "natural rights" of individuals to their person and property. This view, also reflected in the "unalienable rights" section of the U.S. Declaration of Independence, is the basis for the protective function of government.

It is easy to see the economic importance of the protective function. When it is performed well, the property of citizens is secure, freedom of exchange is present, and contracts are legally enforceable. When people are assured that they will be able to enjoy the benefits of their efforts, they will be more productive. In contrast, when property rights are insecure and contracts unenforceable, productive behavior is undermined. Plunder, fraud, and economic chaos result. Governments set and enforce the "rules of the game" that enable markets to operate smoothly.

PRODUCTIVE FUNCTION OF GOVERNMENT

The nature of some goods makes them difficult to provide through markets. Sometimes it is difficult to establish a one-to-one link between the payment and receipt of a good. If this link cannot be established, the incentive of market producers to supply these goods is weak. In addition, high transaction costs—particularly, the cost of monitoring use and collecting fees—can sometimes make it difficult to supply a good through the market. When either of these conditions is present, it may be more efficient for the government to supply the good and impose taxes on its citizens to cover the cost.

One of the most important productive functions of government is providing a stable monetary and financial environment. If markets are going to work well, individuals have to know the value of what they are buying or selling. For market prices to convey this information, a stable monetary system is needed. This is especially true for the many market exchanges that involve a time dimension. Houses, cars, consumer durables, land, buildings, equipment, and many other items are often paid for over a period of months or even years. When the purchasing power of money fluctuates wildly, previously determined prices do not represent their intended values. Under these circumstances, exchanges involving long-term commitments are hampered, and the smooth operation of markets is undermined.

The government's tax, spending, and monetary policies exert a powerful influence on the stability of the overall economy. If properly conducted, these policies contribute to economic stability, full and efficient utilization of resources, and stable prices. However, improper stabilization policies can cause massive unemployment, rapidly rising prices, or both. For those pursuing a course in macroeconomics, these issues will be central to that analysis.

POTENTIAL SHORTCOMINGS OF THE MARKET

As we previously discussed, the invisible hand of market forces generally gives resource owners and business firms a strong incentive to use their resources efficiently and undertake projects that create value. Will this always be true? The answer to this question is "No." There are four major factors that can undermine the invisible hand and reduce the efficiency of markets: (1) lack of competition, (2) externalities, (3) public goods, and (4) poorly informed buyers or sellers. We will now consider each of these factors and explain why they may justify government intervention.

LACK OF COMPETITION

Competition is vital to the proper operation of the pricing mechanism. The existence of competing buyers and sellers reduces the power of both to rig or alter the market in their own favor. Although competition is beneficial from a social point of view, individually each of us would prefer to be loosened from its grip. Students do not like stiff competitors in their romantic lives, at exam time, or when they're trying to get into graduate school. Buyers on eBay hope for few competing bidders so they can purchase the items they're bidding on at lower prices. Similarly, sellers prefer fewer competing sellers so they can sell at higher prices.

Exhibit 2 illustrates how sellers can gain from restricting competition. In the absence of any restrictions on competition in the market, the price P_1 and output Q_1 associated with the competitive supply curve (S_1) will prevail. Here, Q_1 is the level of output consistent with

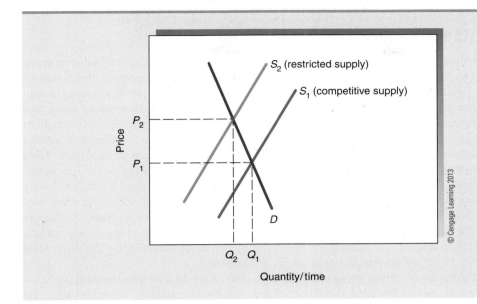

Exhibit 2

Lack of Competition and Problems for the Market

If a group of sellers can restrict competition, the group may be able to gain by reducing supply (to S_2, for example) and raising the price (to P_2, for example) rather than charging the competitive market price of P_1. Under these circumstances, output will be less than the economically efficient level.

economic efficiency. If a group of sellers is able to restrict competition, perhaps by forcing some firms out of the market and preventing new firms from entering, the group would be able to gain by raising the price of the product. This is illustrated by the price P_2 and output Q_2 associated with the restricted supply (S_2). Even though the output is smaller, the total revenue (price P_2 times quantity Q_2) derived by the sellers at the restricted output level is greater than at the competitive price P_1. Clearly, the sellers gain because, at the higher price, they are being paid more to produce less.

The restricted output level, however, is clearly less efficient. At the competitive output level Q_1, all units that were valued more than their cost are produced and sold. But this is not the case at Q_2. The additional units between Q_2 and Q_1 are valued more than their cost. Nonetheless, they will not be produced if suppliers are able to limit competition and restrict output. When competition is absent, there is a potential conflict between the interests of sellers and the efficient use of resources.

What can the government do to ensure that markets are competitive? The first guideline might be borrowed from the medical profession: Do no harm. A productive government will refrain from using its powers to impose licenses, discriminatory taxes, price controls, tariffs, quotas, and other entry and trade restraints that lessen the intensity of competition. In the vast majority of markets, sellers will find it difficult or impossible to limit the entry of rival firms (including rival producers from other countries). Thus, most suppliers will not be able to limit competition unless they get the government to impose various types of entry restrictions or mandates that provide them with an advantage relative to rivals. Predictably, private firms and interest groups will lobby for government action of this type. When governments succumb to these pressures and engage in actions that limit competition, however, economic inefficiency will result.

When entering a market is very costly and there are only a few existing sellers, it may be possible for these sellers by themselves to restrict competition. In an effort to deal with cases like this, the United States has enacted a series of "antitrust laws," most notably the Sherman Antitrust Act (1890) and the Clayton Act (1914), making it illegal for firms to collude or attempt to monopolize a market.

Virtually all economists favor competitive markets, but there is considerable debate about the impact of government action in this area. Many economists believe that, by and large, government policy in this area has been ineffective. Others stress that government policies have often been misused to actually limit competition, rather than promote it. Laws are often adopted that restrict entry into markets, protect existing producers from competitors, and limit price competition. For those taking a microeconomics course, noncompetitive markets and related policy alternatives will be analyzed in greater detail later.

EXTERNALITIES—A FAILURE TO ACCOUNT FOR ALL COSTS AND BENEFITS

Externalities
Spillover effects of an activity that influence the well-being of nonconsenting third parties.

When property rights are unclear or poorly enforced, the actions of an individual or group may "spill over" onto others and thereby affect their well-being without their consent. These spillover effects are called **externalities**. You are probably familiar with externalities. For example, when your neighbor's loud stereo makes it hard for you to study, you are experiencing an externality firsthand. Although your neighbors do not have a right to come in to your apartment and turn on your stereo, they do have a right to listen to their own stereo, and their listening may interfere with the quietness in your apartment. Their actions impose a cost on you, and they also raise an issue of property rights. Do your neighbors have a property right to play their stereo as loudly as they please? Or do you have a property right to quietness in your own apartment? When questions like these arise, how should the boundaries of property rights be determined, and what steps should be taken to ensure adequate enforcement? Although the volume of your neighbor's stereo may not be a major economic issue, it nonetheless illustrates the nature of the problems that arise when property rights are unclear and externalities are present.

External cost
Spillover effects that reduce the well-being of nonconsenting third parties.

External benefit
Spillover effects that generate benefits for nonconsenting third parties.

The spillover effects may either impose a cost or create a benefit for third parties—people not directly involved in the transaction, activity, or exchange. Economists use the term **external cost** to describe a situation in which the spillover effects harm third parties. If the spillover effects enhance the welfare of the third parties, an **external benefit** is present. We will analyze both external costs and external benefits and consider why both of them can lead to problems.

EXTERNAL COSTS

Economists worry about external costs because they may result in economic inefficiency. For example, resources may be used to produce goods that are valued less than their production costs, including the costs imposed on the nonconsenting third parties. Consider the production of paper. The firms in the market operate mills and purchase labor, trees, and other resources to produce the paper. But they also emit pollutants into the atmosphere that impose costs on residents living around the mills. The pollutants cause paint on buildings to deteriorate more rapidly. They make it difficult for some people to breathe normally, and perhaps cause other health hazards. If the residents living near a pulp mill can prove they have been harmed, they could take the mill to court and force the paper producer to cover the cost of their damages. But it might be difficult to prove that they were harmed and that the pulp mill is responsible for the damage. As you can see, the residents' property rights to clean air may be difficult to enforce, particularly if there are many parties emitting pollutants into the air.

If the residents are unable to enforce their property rights, the production of paper will result in an external cost that will not be registered through markets. **Exhibit 3** illustrates the implications of these external costs within the supply and demand framework. As the result of the external cost, the market supply curve S_1 will understate the true cost of producing paper. It reflects only the cost actually paid by the firms, and ignores the uncompensated costs imposed on the nearby residents. Under these circumstances, the firm will expand output to Q_1 (the intersection of the demand curve D and supply curve S_1) and the market price P_1 will emerge. Is this price and output consistent with economic efficiency? The answer is clearly "No." If all of the costs of producing the paper, including those imposed on third parties, were taken into account, the supply curve S_2 would result. From an efficiency standpoint, only the smaller quantity Q_2 should be produced. The units beyond Q_2 on out to Q_1 cost more than their value to consumers. People would be better off if the resources used to produce those units (beyond Q_2) were used to produce other things. Nonetheless, profit-maximizing firms will expand output into this range. Thus, when external costs are present, the market supply curve will understate production costs, and output will be expanded beyond the quantity consistent with economic efficiency. Moreover, resources for which property rights are poorly enforced will be overutilized and

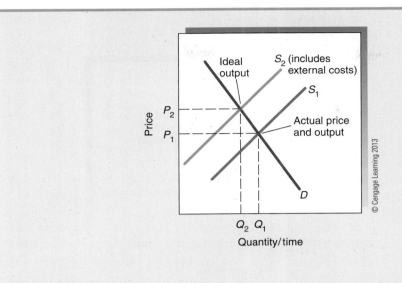

© Cengage Learning 2013

Exhibit 3

External Costs and Output That Is Greater Than the Efficient Level

When an activity such as paper production imposes external costs on nonconsenting third parties, these costs will not be registered by the market supply curve (S_1). As a result, output will be beyond the economically efficient level. The units between Q_2 and Q_1 will be produced, even though their cost exceeds the value they provide to consumers.

sometimes polluted. This is often the case with air and water when the property rights to these resources are poorly enforced.

What should be done about external costs? These costs arise because property rights are poorly defined or imperfectly enforced. Initially, therefore, it makes sense to think seriously about how property rights might be better defined and enforced. However, the nature of some goods will make the defining and enforcement of property rights extremely difficult. This will certainly be the case for resources like clean air and many fish species in the ocean. In cases that involve a relatively small number of people, the parties involved may be able to agree to rules and establish procedures that will minimize the external effects. For example, property owners around a small lake will generally be able to control access to the lake and prevent each other, as well as outsiders, from polluting or overfishing the lake.

However, in cases that involve large numbers of people, the transaction costs of arriving at an agreement will often be prohibitively high, so it is unrealistic to expect that private contracts among the parties will handle the situation satisfactorily. For example, this will be the case when a large number of automobiles and firms emit pollutants into the atmosphere. In these "large-number" cases, government regulations may be the best approach. At this point, we want you to see the nature of the problem when external costs are present. As we proceed, we will analyze a number of problems in this area in detail and will consider alternative approaches that might improve economic efficiency.

External costs resulting from poorly defined and enforced property rights underlie the problems of excessive air and water pollution.

EXTERNAL BENEFITS

As we mentioned, sometimes the actions of individuals and firms generate external benefits for others. The homeowner who keeps a house in good condition and maintains a neat lawn improves the beauty of the entire community. A flood-control dam built by upstream residents for their benefit might also generate gains for those who live downstream. Scientific theories benefit their authors, but the knowledge can also help others who did not contribute to the development of them.

Exhibit 4

External Benefits and Output That Is Less Than the Efficient Level

A vaccine that protects users against the flu will also help nonusers by making it less likely that they will catch it. But this benefit will not be registered by the market demand curve (D_1). In cases where external benefits like this are present, output will be less than the economically efficient level. Even though the units between Q_1 and Q_2 generate more benefits than costs, they will not be supplied because sellers are unable to capture the value of these external benefits.

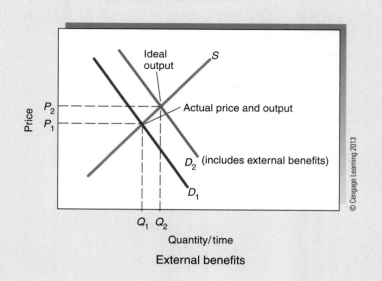

From the standpoint of efficiency, why might external benefits be a problem? Here, inefficiency may arise because potential producers may fail to undertake productive activities because they are unable to fully capture the benefits their actions create for others. Suppose a pharmaceutical company develops a vaccine protecting users against a contagious virus or some other communal disease. Of course, the vaccine can easily be marketed to users who will benefit directly from it. However, because of the communal nature of the virus, as more and more people take the vaccine, nonusers will also be less likely to get the flu. But it will be very difficult for the pharmaceutical companies to capture any of the benefits derived by the nonusers. As a result, too little of the vaccine may be supplied.

Exhibit 4 illustrates the impact of external benefits like those generated by the vaccine within the framework of supply and demand. The market demand curve reflects the benefits derived by the users of the vaccine, while the supply curve reflects the opportunity cost of providing it. Market forces result in an equilibrium price of P_1 and output of Q_1. Is this outcome consistent with economic efficiency? Again, the answer is "No." The market demand curve D_1 will register only the benefits derived by the users. Those benefits that accrue to nonusers, who are now less likely to contract the flu, will not be taken into account by decision-makers. The producer of the vaccine makes it more likely that these people will not get sick, but it doesn't derive any benefit (sales revenue) from having done so. Thus, market demand D_1 understates the total benefits derived from the production and use of the vaccine. Demand D_2 provides a measure of these total benefits, including those that accrue to the nonusers. The units between Q_1 and Q_2 are valued more highly than what it costs to produce them. Nonetheless, they will not be supplied because the suppliers of the vaccine will be unable to capture the benefits that accrue to the nonusers. Thus, when external benefits are present, market forces may supply less than the amount consistent with economic efficiency.

While external benefits are a potential source of inefficiency, entrepreneurs have a strong incentive to figure out ways to capture more fully the gains their actions generate for others. In some cases, they are able to capture what would otherwise be external benefits by extending the scope of the firm. The accompanying Application in Economics, "Capturing External Benefits: The Case of Walt Disney World," provides an interesting and informative illustration of this point.

APPLICATIONS IN ECONOMICS

Capturing External Benefits: The Case of Walt Disney World

REUTERS/Charles W. Luzier/Landov

Sometimes projects that generate more benefits than cost are still unattractive because a substantial share of the benefits is external and therefore difficult to capture. If an entrepreneur could figure out a way to capture more of these benefits, an otherwise unprofitable project might be transformed into a profitable one. Sometimes this can be done by extending the scope of a project.

The development of golf courses is an example. Because of the beauty and openness of the courses, many people find it attractive to live nearby. Thus, constructing a golf course typically generates an external benefit—an increase in the value of the nearby property. In recent years, golf course developers have figured out how to capture this benefit. Now, they typically purchase a large tract of land around the planned course *before it is built.* This lets them resell the land at a higher price after the golf course has been completed and the surrounding land has increased in value. By extending the scope of their activities to include real estate as well as golf course development, they are able to capture what would otherwise be external benefits.

Florida's Walt Disney World is an interesting case study in entrepreneurial ingenuity designed to capture external benefits more fully. When Walt Disney developed Disneyland

in California, the market value of the land in the immediate area soared as a result of the increase in demand for services (food, lodging, gasoline, and so on). Because the land in the area was owned by others, the developers of Disneyland were unable to capture these external benefits. In addition, Disney felt as if some of the adult nightclubs that had opened around his existing Disneyland park were imposing external costs on him by detracting from the family image his park was trying to attain.

Because of his experience with these externalities, when Walt Disney World was developed outside of Orlando, Florida, in the mid-1960s, Walt Disney purchased far more land than was needed for the amusement park. This enabled him to capture the increased land value surrounding his development (when he resold the land for a higher price) and reduce the negative externalities imposed on him via his control of the surrounding property.

The purchases were made as secretly as possible to prevent speculators from driving up the land prices if Disney's actions were detected. Disney even created a handful of smaller companies, with names like the Latin-American Development and Managers Corporation and the Reedy Creek Ranch Corporation, to purchase the land. After his first major land purchase of 12,400 acres, Walt Disney was at a meeting at which he was offered an opportunity to purchase an additional 8,500 acres. Walt Disney's assistant was rumored to have said, "But Walt, we already own 12,000 acres, enough to build the park." Disney replied, "How would you like to own 8,000 acres around our existing Disneyland facility right now?" His assistant immediately responded, "Buy it!"

After another major acquisition of 1,250 acres, Disney began concentrating on buying smaller land parcels around his main property. By June 1965, Disney had purchased 27,400 acres, or about 43 square miles—an area 150 times larger than his existing Disneyland park, and about twice as big as Manhattan. In October 1965, when an Orlando newspaper finally broke the story that Disney was behind the land purchases, the remaining land prices around his property jumped from $183 an acre to $1,000 an acre overnight. But by then, except for several small parcels he was unable to acquire, Walt Disney had purchased all of the land he wanted.

Florida eventually gave Walt Disney permission to create an autonomous Reedy Creek Improvement District, outside the authority of any local government in Florida. In a very real sense, Walt Disney World is a jurisdiction of its own, separate from any other local government authority. Because of this, Walt Disney World can write its own zoning restrictions and building codes. It can also plan its own roadways, lakes, security, sidewalks, airports, and recreational areas. Walt Disney World is able to provide

(continued)

goods and services like these—that might normally be considered public goods—by charging general admission fees to its park. This helped Disney overcome the potential free-rider problems sometimes associated with producing these goods.

Just as Disney expected, the value of the land surrounding Walt Disney World soared as the demand for hotels, restaurants, and other businesses increased along with the development of the amusement park. Through the years, the resale of land near the park has been a major source of revenue for the company. To a large degree, the success of the Disney Corporation reflects Walt Disney's entrepreneurial ability to deal with externality and public-good problems.

PUBLIC GOODS AND WHY THEY POSE A PROBLEM FOR THE MARKET

Public goods
Goods for which rivalry among consumers is absent and exclusion of nonpaying customers is difficult.

What are public goods? **Public goods** have two distinguishing characteristics; they are: (1) nonrival in consumption and (2) nonexcludable. Let's take a closer look at both of these characteristics.

Nonrivalry in consumption means that making the good available to one consumer does not reduce its availability to others. In fact, providing it to one person simultaneously makes it available to other consumers. A radio broadcast signal provides an example. The same signal can be shared by everyone within the listening range. Having additional listeners tune in does not detract from the availability of the signal. Clearly, most goods do not have this shared consumption characteristic, but are instead rival-in-consumption. For example, two individuals cannot simultaneously consume the same pair of jeans. Further, if one person purchases a pair of jeans, there is one less pair available for someone else.

The second characteristic of a public good—nonexcludability—means that it is impossible (or at least very costly) to exclude nonpaying customers from receiving the good. Suppose an antimissile system were being built around the city in which you live. How could some people in the city be protected by the system and others excluded? Most people will realize there is no way the system can protect their neighbors from incoming missiles without providing similar protection to other residents. Thus, the services of the antimissile system have the nonexcludability characteristic.

It is important to note that it is the characteristic of the good, not the sector in which it is produced, that determines whether it qualifies as a public good. There is a tendency to think that if a good is provided by the government, then it is a public good. This is not the case. Many of the goods provided by governments clearly do not have the characteristics of public goods. Medical services, education, mail delivery, trash collection, and electricity come to mind. Although these goods are often supplied by governments, they do not have either nonrivalry or nonexcludability characteristics. Thus, they are not public goods.

Free riders
A person who receives the benefit of a good without paying for it. Because it is often virtually impossible to restrict the consumption of public goods to those who pay, these goods are subject to free-rider problems.

Why are public goods difficult for markets to allocate efficiently? The nonexcludability characteristic provides the answer. Because those who do not pay cannot be excluded, sellers are generally unable to establish a one-to-one link between the payment and receipt of these goods. Realizing they cannot be excluded, potential consumers have little incentive to pay for these goods. Instead, they have an incentive to become **free riders**, people who receive the benefits of the good without helping to pay for its cost. But, when a large number of people become free riders and revenues thus are low, not very much of the good is supplied. This is precisely the problem: Markets will tend to undersupply public goods, even when the population in aggregate values them highly relative to their cost.

Suppose national defense were provided entirely through the market. Would you voluntarily help to pay for it? Your contribution would have little impact on the total supply of defense available to each of us, even if you made a large personal contribution. Many citizens, even though they might value defense highly, would become free riders, and few funds would be available to finance national defense.

For most goods, it is easy to establish a link between payment and receipt. If you do not pay for a gallon of ice cream, an automobile, a television set, a DVD player, and literally thousands of other items, suppliers will not provide them to you. Thus, there are very few public goods. National defense is the classic example of a public good. Radio and TV signals, software programs, flood-control projects, mosquito abatement programs, and perhaps some scientific theories also have public good characteristics. But beyond this short list, it is difficult to think of additional goods that qualify.

Just because a good is a public good does not necessarily mean that markets will fail to supply it. When the benefit of producing these goods is high, entrepreneurs will attempt to find innovative ways to gain by overcoming the free-rider problem. For example, radio and television broadcasts, which have both of the public good characteristics, are still produced well by the private sector. The free-rider problem is overcome through the use of advertising (which generates indirect revenue from listeners), rather than by directly charging listeners. Private entrepreneurs have developed things like scrambling devices (so nonpaying customers can't tune into broadcasts free of charge), copy protection on DVDs, and tie-in purchases (for example, tying the purchase of a software instruction manual to the purchase of the software itself) to overcome the free-rider problem. The marketing of computer software provides an interesting illustration. Because the same software program can be copied without reducing the amount available to others, and it is costly to prevent consumption by nonpayers, software clearly has public good characteristics. Nonetheless, Bill Gates became the richest man in the world by producing and marketing it!

In spite of the innovative efforts of entrepreneurs, however, the quantity of public goods supplied strictly through market allocation might still be smaller than the quantity consistent with economic efficiency. This creates a potential opportunity for government action to improve the efficiency of resource allocation.

POTENTIAL INFORMATION PROBLEMS

Like other goods, information is scarce. Thus, when making purchasing decisions, people are sometimes poorly informed about the price, quality, durability, and side effects of alternative products. Imperfect knowledge is not the fault of the market. In fact, the market provides consumers with a strong incentive to acquire information. If they mistakenly purchase a "lemon," they will suffer the consequences. Furthermore, sellers have a strong incentive to inform consumers about the benefits of their products, especially in comparison with competing products. However, circumstances will influence the incentive structure confronted by both buyers and sellers.

The consumer's information problem is minimal if the item is purchased regularly. Consider the purchase of soap. There is little cost associated with trying different brands. Because soap is a regularly purchased product, trial and error is an economical means of determining which brand is most suitable to one's needs. Regularly purchased items such as toothpaste, most food products, lawn service, and gasoline provide additional examples of repeat-purchase items. When purchasing items like these, the consumer can use past experience to acquire accurate information and make wise decisions.

Repeat-purchase items
An item purchased often by the same buyer.

Furthermore, the sellers of repeat-purchase items also have a strong incentive to supply consumers with accurate information about them because failing to do so will adversely affect future sales. Because future demand is directly related to the satisfaction level of current customers, sellers of repeat-purchase items will want to help their customers make satisfying long-run choices. This helps harmonize the interests of buyers and sellers.

But harmony will not always occur. Conflicting interests, inadequate information, and unhappy customers can arise when goods are either (1) difficult to evaluate on inspection and seldom repeatedly purchased from the same producer, or (2) potentially capable of serious and lasting harmful side effects that cannot be predicted by a typical consumer. Under these conditions, consumers might make decisions they will later regret.

When customers are unable to distinguish between high-quality and low-quality goods, business entrepreneurs have an incentive to cut costs by reducing quality. Businesses that follow this course may survive and even prosper. Consider the information problem when an automobile is purchased. Are consumers capable of properly evaluating the safety equipment? Most are not. Of course, some consumers will seek the opinion of experts, but this information will be costly and difficult to evaluate. In this case, it might be more efficient to have the government regulate automobile safety and require certain safety equipment.

Similar issues arise with regard to product effectiveness. Suppose a new wonder drug promises to reduce the probability a person will be stricken by cancer or heart disease. Even if the product is totally ineffective, many consumers will waste their money trying it. Verifying the effectiveness of the drug will be a complicated and lengthy process.

Consequently, it may be better to have experts certify its effectiveness. The federal Food and Drug Administration was established to perform this function. However, letting the experts decide is also a less than ideal solution. The certification process is likely to be costly and lengthy. As a result, the introduction of products that are effective may be delayed for years, and they are likely to be more costly than they would be otherwise.

INFORMATION AS A PROFIT OPPORTUNITY

Consumers are willing to pay for information that will help them make better decisions. This presents a profit opportunity. Entrepreneurial publishers and other providers of information help consumers find what they seek by offering product evaluations by experts. For example, dozens of publications provide independent expert opinions about automobiles and computers at a low cost to potential purchasers. Laboratory test results and detailed product evaluations on a wide variety of goods are provided by *Consumer Reports* and other publications.

Franchises are another way entrepreneurs have responded to the need of consumers for more and better information. A **franchise** is a right or license granted to an individual to market a company's goods or services (or use their brand name). Fast-food restaurants like McDonald's and Wendy's are typically organized as franchises. The individual restaurants are independently owned, but the owner pays for the right to use the company name and must offer specific products and services in a manner specified by the franchiser. Franchises help give consumers reliable information. The tourist traveling through an area for the first time with very little time to search out alternatives may find that eating at a franchised restaurant and sleeping at a franchised motel are the cheapest ways to avoid annoying and costly mistakes that might come from patronizing an unknown local establishment. The franchiser sets the standards for all firms in the chain and establishes procedures, including continuous inspections designed to maintain the standards. Franchisers have a strong incentive to maintain their reputation for quality, because if it declines, their ability to sell new franchises and to collect ongoing franchise fees is adversely affected. Even though the tourist may visit a particular establishment only once, the franchise turns that visit into a "repeat purchase" because the reputation of the entire national franchise operation is at stake.

Similarly, advertising a brand name nationally puts the brand's reputation at stake each time a purchase is made. How much would the Coca-Cola Company pay to avoid the sale of a dangerous bottle of Coke? Surely, it would be a large sum. Interbrand, a branding consulting agency that evaluates and ranks the top brand names in the world, estimated that Coca-Cola's brand name was worth $70 billion in 2010. The value of that brand name is a hostage to quality control. The firm would suffer enormous damage if it failed to maintain the quality of its product. For example, in 2000 and 2001, Firestone's brand name suffered an immense reduction in value after only a few Firestone tires were suspected of being defective. Firestone is still attempting to recover fully from its loss in brand name value.

Enterprising entrepreneurs have found ways to assure buyers that products meet high standards of quality, even when the producer is small and not so well known. Consider the case of Best Western Motels.[4] Best Western owns no motels; however, building on the franchise idea, it publishes rules and standards with which motel owners must comply if they are to use the Best Western brand name and the reservation service that the company also operates. To protect its brand name, Best Western sends out inspectors to see that each Best Western Motel meets these standards. Every disappointed customer harms the reputation and reduces the value of the Best Western name, which reduces the willingness of motel owners to pay for use of the name. The standards are designed to keep customers satisfied. Even though each motel owner has only a relatively small operation, renting the Best Western name provides the small operator with the kind of international reputation formerly available only to large firms. In effect, Best Western acts as a regulator of all motels bearing its name. It profits by requiring efficient standards—those that produce maximum visitor satisfaction for every dollar spent by the motels utilizing the franchise name. As it does so, it helps eliminate problems in the market that result from imperfect information.

Franchise
A right or license granted to an individual to market a company's goods or services or use its brand name. The individual firms are independently owned but must meet certain conditions to continue to use the name.

---

[4]This section draws from Randall G. Holcombe and Lora P. Holcombe, "The Market for Regulation," *Journal of Institutional and Theoretical Economics* 142, no. 4 (1986): 684–96.

Brand names (like Coca-Cola), franchises (like McDonald's or Best Western), consumer-ratings magazines (like Consumer Reports), and private-sector certification firms (like Underwriters Laboratories, Inc.) are ways the private sector helps buyers overcome potential information problems.

Underwriters Laboratories Inc. (UL) is another example of private-sector regulation aimed at overcoming potential information problems. UL is a private-sector corporation that has been testing and certifying products for more than 100 years based on its own set of quality standards. You have probably seen the UL mark on many of your household appliances. Sellers pay a fee to have UL evaluate their products for possible certification. The value of the UL brand depends on its careful evaluation of every product it certifies. If UL allows defective products to carry its mark, its brand value will diminish.

Information published by reliable sources, franchising, and brand names can help consumers make better-informed decisions. Although these options are effective, they will not always provide an ideal solution. Government regulation may sometimes be able to improve the situation, but this, too, has some predictable shortcomings. As with other things, there is no general solution to imperfect information problems.

MARKET AND GOVERNMENT FAILURE

Throughout this textbook, we stress that a sound legal system—one that protects individuals and their property and provides access to evenhanded courts for the enforcement of contracts and settlement of disputes—is vitally important for the smooth operation of markets. So, too, is a monetary regime that provides people with access to a sound currency—money that maintains its value through time. Beyond these functions, however, there is little justification for government action when there is reason to expect that markets will allocate resources efficiently.

However, as we have shown in this chapter, a lack of competition, externalities, public goods, and information problems often pose challenges and sometimes undermine the efficient operation of markets. Economists use the term **market failure** to describe the situation where there is reason to believe that markets will fail to achieve the conditions implied by idealized economic efficiency. Private entrepreneurs can profit, however, from solving these problems so markets can sometimes overcome these potential challenges on their own.

It is tempting to jump to the conclusion that if the market fails to achieve economic efficiency, then the government can intervene and improve the situation. Indeed, even professional economists often make this error. But we must not forget that government directed by political decision-making is merely an alternative form of economic organization. It is not a corrective device that can be counted on to make choices that will promote economic efficiency. There is government failure, as well as market failure. **Government failure** is present when political choices lead to outcomes that conflict with the efficient allocation of resources. In order to evaluate the potential of political decision-making to improve on the shortcomings of the market and allocate resources efficiently, we need better knowledge about how the political process works. This will be the focal point of the next chapter.

Market failure
A situation in which the structure of incentives is such that markets will encourage individuals to undertake activities that are inconsistent with economic efficiency.

Government failure
A situation in which the structure of incentives is such that the political process, including democratic political decision-making, will encourage individuals to undertake actions that conflict with economic efficiency.

Looking Ahead

Political decision-making is complex, but the tools of economics can enhance our understanding of how it works. This is the subject matter of the next chapter.

KEY POINTS

- Economists use the standard of economic efficiency to assess the desirability of economic outcomes. Efficiency requires (1) that all actions generating more benefit than cost be undertaken, and (2) that no actions generating more cost than benefit be undertaken.

- Although perfection is a noble goal, it is rarely worth achieving because additional time and resources devoted to an activity generally yield smaller and smaller benefits and cost more and more. Inefficiency can result when either too little or too much effort is put into an activity.

- Governments can enhance economic well-being by performing both protective and productive functions. The protective function involves (1) the protection of individuals and their property against aggression and (2) the provision of a legal system for the enforcement of contracts and settlement of disputes. The productive function of government can help people obtain goods that would be difficult to supply through markets.

- When markets fail to meet the conditions for ideal economic efficiency, the problem can generally be traced to one of four sources: absence of competition, externalities, public goods, or poor information.

- Externalities reflect a lack of fully defined and enforced property rights. When external costs are present, output can be too large—units are produced even though their costs exceed the benefits they generate. In contrast, external benefits can lead to an output that is too small—some units are not produced even though the benefits of doing so would exceed the cost.

- Public goods are goods for which (1) rivalry in consumption is absent and (2) it is difficult to exclude those who do not pay. Because of the difficulties involved in establishing a one-to-one link between payment and receipt of such goods, the market supply of public goods will often be less than the economically efficient quantity.

- Entrepreneurs in markets have an incentive to find solutions to each market problem, and new solutions are constantly being discovered. But problems remain that can potentially be improved through government action.

- Both markets and government can have problems in achieving the efficient allocation of resources. The term market failure describes the situation where markets will fail to achieve the conditions implied by idealized economic efficiency. But political action may also result in outcomes that are inefficient, a situation known as government failure.

CRITICAL ANALYSIS QUESTIONS

1. *Why is it important for producers to be able to prevent nonpaying customers from receiving a good?

2. In response to the terrorist attacks of September 11, 2001, airline security screening increased dramatically. As a result, the travel time of airline passengers has increased substantially. Would it make economic sense to devote enough resources to completely prevent any such future attacks? Why or why not?

3. What are the distinguishing characteristics of "public goods"? Give two examples of a public good. Why are public goods difficult for markets to allocate efficiently?

4. *Which of the following are public goods? Explain, using the definition of a public good.
   a. an antimissile system surrounding Washington, D.C.
   b. a fire department
   c. tennis courts
   d. Yellowstone National Park
   e. elementary schools

5. Explain in your own words what is meant by external costs and external benefits. Why may market outcomes be less than ideal when externalities are present?

6. English philosopher John Locke argued that the protection of each individual's person and property (acquired without the use of violence, theft, or fraud) was the primary function of government. Why is this protection important to the efficient operation of an economy?

7. "If it's worth doing, it's worth doing to the best of your ability." What is the economic explanation for why this statement is frequently said but rarely followed in practice? Explain.

8. "Unless quality and price are regulated by government, travelers would have no chance for a fair deal. Local people would be treated well, but the traveler would have no way to know, for example, who offers a good night's lodging at a fair price." Is this true or false? Explain.

9. *If sellers of toasters were able to organize themselves, reduce their output, and raise their prices, how would economic efficiency be affected? Explain.

10. What are external costs? When are they most likely to be present? When external costs are present, what is likely to be the relationship between the market output of a good and the output consistent with ideal economic efficiency?

11. *"Elementary education is obviously a public good. After all, it is provided by the government." Evaluate this statement.

12. What are the necessary conditions for economic efficiency? In what four situations might a market fail to achieve ideal economic efficiency?

13. What is market failure? If market failure is present, does this imply that government intervention will lead to a more efficient allocation of resources? Why or why not?

14. *Apply the economic efficiency criterion to the role of government. When would a government intervention be considered economically efficient? When would a government intervention be considered economically inefficient?

*Asterisk denotes questions for which answers are given in Appendix B.

CHAPTER

6

The Economics of Collective Decision-Making

CHAPTER FOCUS

- How large is the government sector, and what are the main activities undertaken by government?

- What are the similarities and differences between governments and markets with regard to how they allocate goods?

- What insights can economics provide about the behavior of voters, politicians, and bureaucrats? How will their actions affect political outcomes?

- When is democratic representative government most likely to lead to economic efficiency?

- Why will there sometimes be a conflict between winning politics and economic efficiency?

- What is crony capitalism, and is it an increasing problem in the United States?

[Public choice] analyzes the motives and activities of politicians, civil servants and government officials as people with personal interests that may or may not coincide with the interest of the general public they are supposed to serve. It is an analysis of how people behave in the world as it is.

—*Arthur Seldon*[1]

A s we have previously discussed, the protection of property rights, evenhanded enforcement of contracts, and provision of a stable monetary environment are vital for the smooth and efficient operation of markets. Governments that perform these functions well will help their citizens prosper and achieve higher levels of income. Governments may also help allocate goods difficult for markets to handle. However, it is crucially important to recognize that government is simply an alternative form of economic organization. In most industrialized nations, the activities of governments are directed by the democratic political process. In this chapter, we will use the tools of economics to analyze how this process works.

iStockphoto.com/nicoolay

THE SIZE AND GROWTH OF THE U.S. GOVERNMENT

What exactly does government do? Has its role in the economy shrunk or grown over time? Data on government spending shed light on these questions. As **Exhibit 1** illustrates, total government expenditures (federal, state, and local combined) were only 9.4 percent of the U.S. economy in 1930. (*Note:* GDP, or Gross Domestic Product, is generally how economists measure the size of the economy. The term will be explained more fully in a macroeconomics course.) In that year, federal government spending by itself was only 3 percent of the economy. At the time, this made the federal government about half the size of all state and local governments combined.

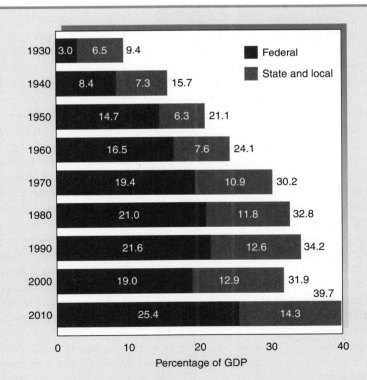

Exhibit 1

The Growth of Government Spending between 1930 and 2010

U.S. government expenditures as a share of the economy's gross domestic product have risen dramatically over the past eighty years. They are now over one-third of the U.S. economy.

Source: Bureau of Economic Analysis, http://www.bea.gov. Grants to state and local governments are included in federal expenditures. Individual data may not add to total due to rounding.

Government Spending by Category

The major categories of federal government spending are health care, Social Security, national defense, and income security (welfare programs). The major categories of state and local government spending are education, health and welfare programs, and administration.

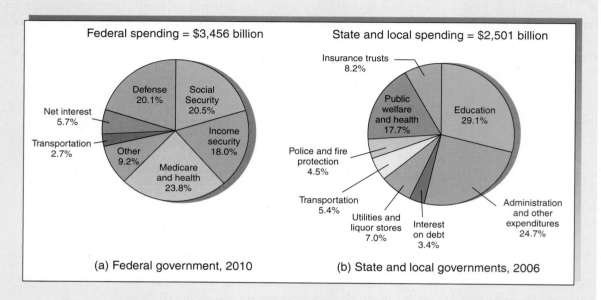

(a) Federal government, 2010

(b) State and local governments, 2006

Source: Economic Report of the President, 2011, and Statistical Abstract of the United States, 2010.

Between 1930 and 1980, the size of government grew very rapidly. By 1980, government expenditures had risen to 32.8 percent of the economy, *more than three times* the level of 1930. Moreover, the federal government grew to about twice the size of all state and local governments combined, despite the fact that they were growing rapidly, too. After remaining fairly constant between 1980 and 2000, the size of government increased dramatically between 2000 and 2010 to almost 40 percent of the U.S. economy.

Exhibit 2 shows the major categories of government spending for both the federal government and state and local governments. The major categories of federal spending are health care, Social Security, national defense, and other income transfers. Education, administration, and public welfare and health constitute the largest areas of spending for state and local governments.

Transfer payments are transfers of income from some individuals (who pay taxes) to others (who receive government payments). Social Security, unemployment benefits, and welfare are examples of transfer payments. Direct income transfers now account for almost half of the total spending of the government. As Exhibit 3 illustrates, government spending on income transfers has grown rapidly. In 1930, income transfers summed to only 1.1 percent of total income. By 1970, the figure had jumped to 7.7 percent; by 2010, it had risen to 19.5 percent of national income. In 2010 the figure was higher than usual because of the economic downturn, but it had already risen to 15.9 percent of total income in 2008. Obviously, the government has become much more involved in tax-transfer activities during the past 80 years.

Given the size and growth of government, understanding how the political process works and how it is likely to affect the economy is vitally important. The remainder of this chapter will address this issue.

Transfer payments
Payments to individuals or institutions that are not linked to the current supply of a good or service by the recipient.

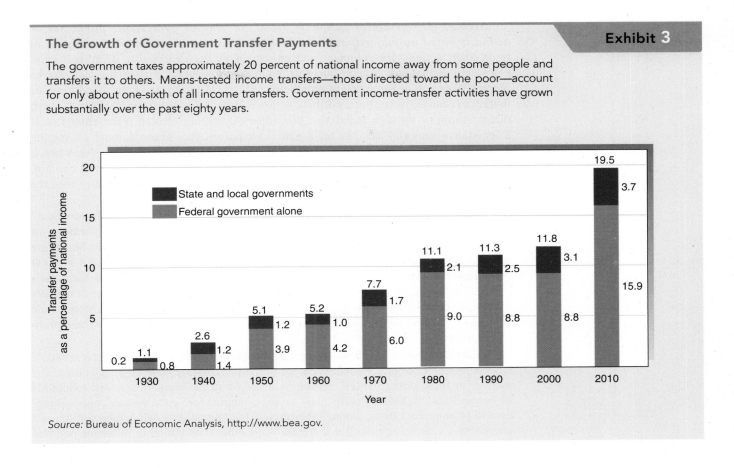

The Growth of Government Transfer Payments

Exhibit 3

The government taxes approximately 20 percent of national income away from some people and transfers it to others. Means-tested income transfers—those directed toward the poor—account for only about one-sixth of all income transfers. Government income-transfer activities have grown substantially over the past eighty years.

Source: Bureau of Economic Analysis, http://www.bea.gov.

SIMILARITIES AND DIFFERENCES BETWEEN GOVERNMENTS AND MARKETS

This chapter will focus on the analysis of how the political process works. Let's begin by considering some of the major similarities and differences between the two sectors. Competition is present in the government sector, just as it is in the market sector. The nature of the competition and criteria for success differ, but intense competition is present in both. In the government sector, politicians compete for elective office. Bureau chiefs and agency heads compete for larger budgets. Government employees compete for promotions and higher pay rates. Perhaps most importantly, business, labor, and other special interest groups compete for program funding, favorable bureaucratic rulings, and other political favors that serve their narrow interests.

Scarcity and the opportunity cost of resource use are present in both sectors. If the government uses resources to achieve one goal, those resources are unavailable to achieve others. Thus, just as in the market sector, provision of goods through government is costly, and this is true even if the good is provided free of charge to certain consumers.

But there are also important differences between market and political allocation, and these differences shed light on how the two processes allocate resources. Let's consider four of the key differences.

First, public sector organization can break the linkage between payment and consumption of a good. In the market sector, goods are allocated to those who are willing to pay the price: there is a one-to-one relationship between a person's payment and receipt of a good. This is often not the case when decisions are made politically. Sometimes goods are allocated to people even if they have paid little or nothing to cover their cost. In other instances, however, individuals are required to pay dearly for a government program even though they derive few, if any, benefits from it.

Second, private-sector action is based on mutual agreement; public-sector action is based on majority rule. In the market sector, when two parties engage in trade, their actions are voluntary and motivated by the expectation of mutual gain. Corporations like Exxon and Microsoft, no matter how large or powerful, cannot take income from you or force you to buy their products. Mutual gain is the foundation for market exchange. In contrast, political action is based on majority rule, either through direct voting or through legislative procedures involving elected representatives. If a legislative majority decides on a particular policy, the minority must accept the policy and help pay for it, even if they strongly object. Political action, even when it is democratic, creates "losers" as well as "winners." Further, as we will explain, there is no assurance that the gains the winners derive from a project will exceed the losses imposed on the losers.

Third, when political choices are made legislatively, voters face a "bundle purchase" problem. They must choose among candidates who represent a bundle of positions on issues. On election day, the voter cannot choose the views of one politician on healthcare and agricultural subsidies for example, and simultaneously choose the views of a different politician on social security reform and national defense. This greatly limits the voter's power to make his or her preferences count on specific issues. The situation in markets is quite different. A buyer can purchase some groceries or clothing from one store, while choosing related items from different suppliers. There is seldom a bundle-purchase problem in markets.

Fourth, income and influence are distributed differently in the two sectors. People who supply more highly valued resources in the marketplace have larger incomes. The number of these dollar "votes" earned by a person in the marketplace will reflect his or her abilities, ambitions, skills, past savings, inheritance, good fortune, and willingness to produce for others, among other things. In contrast, in a democratic setting, one citizen, one vote is the rule. But there are ways other than voting to influence political outcomes. People can donate their money and time to help a campaign. They can also try to influence friends and neighbors, write letters to legislators, and speak in public on behalf of a candidate or cause. The greatest rewards of the political process go to those best able and most willing to use their time, persuasive skills, organizational abilities, and financial contributions to help politicians get votes. People who have more money and skills of this sort—and are willing to spend them in the political arena—can expect to benefit themselves and their favorite causes more handsomely. Thus, while the sources of success and influence differ between sectors, the allocation of income and influence is unequal in both.

OUTSTANDING ECONOMIST

James Buchanan (1919–)

James Buchanan is a key figure in the development of public-choice theory. Buchanan's most famous work, *The Calculus of Consent* (1962), coauthored with Gordon Tullock, argues that unless constitutional rules are structured in a manner that will bring the self-interests of the political players into harmony with the wise use of resources, government action will often be counterproductive.[1] With growing government involvement and favoritism in the economy, public-choice theory is more relevant than ever and helps us to understand why government actions often conflict with the efficient use of resources. This and related contributions won him the 1986 Nobel Prize in economics. Buchanan is the founder of the Center for the Study of Public Choice and a longtime professor of economics at George Mason University.

[1]J. M. Buchanan and G. Tullock, *The Calculus of Consent* (Ann Arbor: University of Michigan Press, 1962).

POLITICAL DECISION-MAKING: AN OVERVIEW

When political decisions are made democratically, or in a representative democracy, as we assume in this chapter, the choices of individuals will influence outcomes in the government sector, just as they do in the market sector. **Public-choice analysis** is a branch of economics that applies the principles and methodology of economics to the operation of the political process. Public-choice analysis links the theory of *individual* behavior to political action, analyzes the implications of the theory, and tests them against events in the real world. Over the past 50 years, research in this area has greatly enhanced our understanding of how the political process works and the structure of the outcomes it generates.[2] Just as economists use self-interest and the structure of incentives to analyze markets, public-choice economists use them to analyze political choices and the operation of government. After all, the same people make decisions in both sectors. If self-interest and the structure of incentives influence market choices, there is good reason to expect that they will also influence choices in a political setting.

The collective decision-making process can be thought of as a complex interaction among voters, legislators, and bureaucrats. Voters elect a legislature, which levies taxes and allocates budgets and regulatory authority to various government agencies and bureaus. The bureaucrats in charge of these agencies utilize the funds to supply government services and income transfers, and to exercise regulatory authority as well. In a representative democracy, voter support determines who is elected to the legislature. A majority vote of the legislature is generally required for the passage of taxes, budget allocations, and regulatory legislation. Let's take a closer look at the incentive structure confronting the three primary political players—voters, legislators, and bureaucrats—and consider how they affect the operation of the political process.

Public-choice analysis
The study of decision-making as it affects the formation and operation of collective organizations, like governments. In general, the principles and methodology of economics are applied to political science topics.

INCENTIVES CONFRONTED BY THE VOTER

How do voters decide whom to support? Self-interest dictates that voters, like market consumers, will ask, "What can you do for me and my goals, and how much will it cost me?" The greater the voter's perceived net personal gain from a particular candidate's election, the more likely it is that the voter will favor that candidate. In contrast, the greater the perceived net economic cost imposed on the voter by the positions of a candidate, the less inclined the voter will be to support the candidate. Other things being equal, voters will tend to support those candidates who they believe will provide the most government services and transfer benefits to them and their favorite causes, net of costs.

How well will voters be informed about political issues and candidates? When decisions are made collectively, the choices of a single person will not be decisive. The probability that an individual vote will decide a city, state, or national election is virtually zero. Realizing that their votes will not affect the outcome, individual voters have little incentive to spend much effort seeking the information needed to cast an informed ballot. Economists refer to this lack of incentive as the **rational ignorance effect**.

As the result of the rational ignorance effect, most voters simply rely on information supplied to them freely by candidates (via political advertising) and the mass media, as well as conversations with friends and coworkers. Surveys, in fact, indicate that huge numbers of voters are unable even to identify their own congressional representatives, much less know where they stand on issues like Social Security reform, tariffs, and agricultural price supports. Given that voters gain little from casting a more informed vote, their meager knowledge of political candidates and issues is not surprising.

Rational ignorance effect
Because it is highly unlikely that an individual vote will decide the outcome of an election, a rational individual has little or no incentive to search for and acquire the information needed to cast an informed vote.

---

[2]The contributions of Kenneth Arrow, James Buchanan, Duncan Black, Anthony Downs, William Niskanen, Mancur Olson, Robert Tollison, and Gordon Tullock have been particularly important. Public choice is something of a cross between economics and political science. Thus, advanced courses are generally offered in both departments.

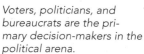

Voters, politicians, and bureaucrats are the primary decision-makers in the political arena.

When people can put information to good use in serving their own goals, they will put forth more effort to acquire it. Consider the incentive of auto purchasers to make well-informed choices. They often shop at several dealerships, take different models for test drives, review consumer publications, and consult with various car experts as they make their purchasing decisions. Most important, if an auto buyer makes a bad choice, he or she will personally bear the consequences. In contrast, voters gain little or nothing if they cast a more informed vote. It is a virtual certainty that their vote will not decide the outcome of an election, and therefore there will be no adverse consequences of casting a poorly informed vote. Thus, it is actually *reasonable* to expect people to be far better informed when choosing a car than a senatorial, congressional, or other political candidate.

The fact that citizens recognize that their individual vote will not sway the outcome also helps explain why many do not vote. Even in a presidential election, only about half of all voting-age Americans take the time to register and vote. The turnout for state and local elections is generally still lower. Given the low probability that one's vote will be decisive, low voter turnout is an expected result.

INCENTIVES CONFRONTED BY THE POLITICIAN

What motivates political candidates and officeholders? Economics indicates that their actions and political positions will be heavily affected by the pursuit of votes. No doubt, many of them genuinely care about the "public interest" and the quality of government, but they need to be elected to achieve their objectives, whatever they might be. Moreover, if a candidate is going to be successful, their positive attributes must be brought to the attention of rationally ignorant voters focused on their families, jobs, various civic activities, and local sports teams (which are probably more entertaining). The successful candidate needs an expert staff, sophisticated polling techniques to uncover popular issues and positions, and high-quality advertising to shape his or her image favorably. This, of course, will be costly. It is not unusual for an incumbent candidate to the U.S. Senate to spend $15 million or more seeking to win an election. In other words, votes are the necessary objective of politicians, but money helps them get those votes. Predictably, the pursuit of campaign contributions then shapes the actions of politicians, too.

Are we implying that politicians are selfish, caring only for their pocketbooks and re-election chances? The answer is "No." Factors other than personal political gain, narrowly defined, may well influence their actions. Sometimes an elected official may feel so strongly about an issue that he or she will knowingly take a position that is politically unpopular and damaging to his or her future electoral prospects. None of this is inconsistent with the economic view of the political process. Over time, however, the politicians most likely to remain in office are the ones who focus on how their actions will influence their

Just as the general does not want his Camp Swampy budget cut, most heads of agencies want expanded budgets to help them do more and do it more comfortably.

reelection prospects. Just as profits are the lifeblood of the market entrepreneur, votes are the lifeblood of the politician.

Politicians face competition for elected office from other candidates. Like market suppliers, political suppliers have an incentive to find ways to gain an advantage over their competitors. Catering to the strongly held views of voters and contributors is one way of doing that. Enacting rules that put potential challengers at a disadvantage is another. When geographic political districts are redrawn, for example, politicians frequently manipulate the process to increase their chances of reelection—a process known as "gerrymandering." Incumbents can also attempt to use government resources for their reelection campaigns, an advantage challengers do not have. Campaign finance "reforms" that make it more difficult for a challenger to raise funds may also provide incumbents with an additional advantage.

INCENTIVES CONFRONTED BY THE GOVERNMENT BUREAUCRAT

Like other people, bureaucrats who staff government agencies, especially those who rise to decision-making levels, have narrowly focused interests. They usually want to see their own agency's goals furthered. Doing so, however, requires larger budgets or greater authority to regulate or both. In turn, larger budgets and more authority lead to more satisfaction, prestige, and career opportunities for the bureaucrats. Economic analysis suggests there is a strong tendency for government bureaucrats and employees to want to expand their budgets and their authority well beyond what would be economically efficient. Indeed, analysts recognize that bigger programs often have strong, organized political backing. In contrast "efficiency has no political constituency."

Legislative bodies are in charge of overseeing these bureaus, but the individual legislators themselves generally know little about the true costs of agency decisions, especially the costs to those regulated. This makes it even more likely that bureaucrats will be able to get funding and authority beyond what's economically efficient.

In summary, the political process, which begins with voter-driven elections and proceeds to legislative decisions and bureaucratic actions, brings about results that please some voters and displease others. The goals of the three major categories of participants—voters, politicians, and bureaucrats—frequently conflict with one another. Each group wants more of the government's limited supply of resources. Coalitions form and the members of each coalition hope to enhance their ability to get the government to do what they want. Sometimes this results in productive activities on the part of the government, and sometimes it does not.

WHEN THE POLITICAL PROCESS WORKS WELL

Under what conditions are voting and representative government most likely to result in productive actions? People have a tendency to believe that support by a majority makes a political action productive. However, if a project is truly productive, it will always be possible to allocate its costs such that *all* voters gain. This would mean that, even if

Exhibit 4

The Benefits Derived by Voters from a Hypothetical Road Construction Project

When taxes are levied in proportion to benefits received (tax plan B), any efficient project can pass unanimously (and any inefficient project will fail unanimously). When taxes are not levied in accordance with benefits received (tax plan A), efficient projects can fail to win a majority vote (or inefficient projects can pass in a majority vote).

		Tax Payment	
Voter	Benefits Received (1)	Plan A (2)	Plan B (3)
Adams	$20	$5	$12.50
Chan	12	5	7.50
Green	4	5	2.50
Lee	2	5	1.25
Diaz	2	5	1.25
Total	**$40**	**$25**	**$25.00**

© Cengage Learning 2013

voting rules required unanimity or near unanimity, all truly productive government projects would pass if the costs were allocated in the right manner. **Exhibit 4** helps illustrate this point. Column 1 presents hypothetical data on the distribution of benefits from a government road construction project. These benefits sum to $40, which exceeds the $25 cost of the road, so the project is productive. But if the project's $25 cost were allocated equally among the voters (plan A), Adams and Chan gain substantially, but Green, Lee, and Diaz lose. If the fate of the project is decided by majority vote, the project will be defeated by the "no" votes of Green, Lee, and Diaz. This productive government project fails to obtain a majority vote in this case because of the way that the costs have been allocated.

Because the project is indeed productive, there is an alternative way to allocate its costs so that Adams, Chan, Green, Lee, and Diaz all benefit. This can be accomplished by allocating the cost of the project among voters in proportion to the benefits that they receive (plan B). Under this arrangement, Adams would pay half ($12.50) of the $25 cost, because he receives half ($20) of the total benefits ($40). The other voters would all pay in proportion to the benefits they receive. Under this plan, all voters would gain from the proposal. Even though the proposal could not secure a majority when the costs were allocated equally among voters, it will be favored by all five voters when they are taxed in proportion to the benefits they receive (plan B).

This simple illustration highlights an extremely important point about voting and the efficiency of government action. *When voters pay in proportion to benefits received, all voters will gain if the government action is productive, and all will lose if it is unproductive.*[3] *When the benefits and costs derived by individual voters are closely related, the voting process will enact efficient projects while rejecting inefficient ones. When voters pay in proportion to the benefits they receive, there will tend to be harmony between good politics and sound economics.*

---

[3]The principle that productive projects generate the potential for political unanimity was initially articulated by Swedish economist Knut Wicksell in 1896. See Wicksell, "A New Principle of Just Taxation," in *Public Choice and Constitutional Economics*, James Gwartney and Richard Wagner (Greenwich, CT: JAI Press, Inc., 1988). Nobel laureate James Buchanan has stated that Wicksell's work provided him with the insights that led to his large role in the development of modern public-choice theory.

Distribution of Benefits and Costs among Voters

Exhibit 5

It is useful to visualize four possible combinations for the distribution of benefits and costs among voters to consider how the alternative distributions affect the operation of representative governments. When the distribution of benefits and costs is both widespread among voters (type 1) or both concentrated among voters (type 3), representative government will tend to undertake projects that are productive and reject those that are unproductive. In contrast, when the benefits are concentrated and the costs are widespread (type 2), representative government is biased toward the adoption of inefficient projects. Finally, when benefits are widespread but the costs concentrated (type 4), the political process may reject projects that are productive.

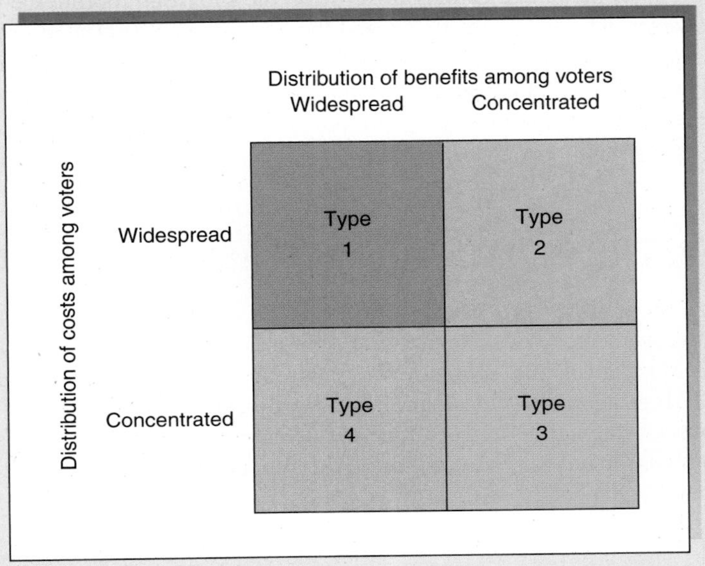

How might the cost of a government service be linked to the benefits received? **User charges**, which require people who use a service more to pay a larger share of the cost, provide one way. User charges are most likely to be levied at the local level. Local services such as electricity, water, and garbage collection are generally financed with user charges. Sometimes the intensity of the use of a service and the amount paid for it can be linked by specifying that the revenue from a specific tax be used for a designated purpose. For example, many states finance road construction and maintenance with the revenue collected from taxes on gasoline and other motor fuels. The more an individual drives—getting more benefits from the roads—the more that individual pays.

Exhibit 5 provides a useful way to look at the possible linkage between the benefits and costs of government programs. The benefits from a government action may be either widespread among the general public or concentrated among a small subgroup (for example, farmers, students, business interests, senior citizens, or members of a labor union). Similarly, the costs may be either widespread or highly concentrated among voters. Thus, as the exhibit shows, there are four possible patterns of voter benefits and costs: (1) widespread benefits and widespread costs, (2) concentrated benefits and widespread costs, (3) concentrated benefits and concentrated costs, and (4) widespread benefits and concentrated costs.

When both the benefits and costs are widespread among voters (type 1 issue), essentially everyone benefits and everyone pays. Although the costs of type 1 measures may not

User charges
Payments users (consumers) are required to make if they want to receive certain services provided by the government.

be precisely proportional to the benefits individuals receive, there will be a rough relationship. When type 1 measures are productive, almost everyone gains more than they pay. There will be little opposition, and political representatives have a strong incentive to support such proposals. In contrast, when type 1 proposals generate costs in excess of benefits, almost everyone loses, and representatives will face pressure to oppose such issues. Thus, for type 1 projects, the political process works pretty well. Productive projects will tend to be accepted and unproductive ones rejected.

Similarly, there is reason to believe that the political process will work fairly well for type 3 measures—those for which both benefits and costs are concentrated on one or more small subgroups. In some cases, the concentrated beneficiaries may be the same group of people paying for the government to provide them a service. In other cases, the subgroup of beneficiaries may differ from the subgroup footing the bill. Even in this case, however, when the benefits exceed the costs, the concentrated group of beneficiaries will have an incentive to expend more resources lobbying for the measure than those harmed by it will expend opposing it. Thus, when the benefits and costs are both concentrated, there will be a tendency for productive projects to be adopted and unproductive ones to be rejected.

WHEN THE POLITICAL PROCESS WORKS POORLY

Although the political process yields reasonable results when there is a close relationship between the receipt of benefits and the payment of costs, the harmony between good politics and sound economics breaks down when the beneficiaries differ from those bearing the costs (type 2 and type 4 projects). Inefficiency may also arise from other sources when governments undertake economic activities. In this section, we consider four major reasons why the political allocation of resources will often result in inefficiency.

SPECIAL-INTEREST EFFECT

Special-interest issue
An issue that generates substantial individual benefits to a small minority while imposing a small individual cost on many other citizens. In total, the net cost to the majority might either exceed or fall short of the net benefits to the special-interest group.

Trade restrictions that limit the import of steel and lumber from abroad; subsidies for sports stadiums, the arts, and various agricultural products; federal spending on an indoor rain forest in Coralville, Iowa; a tattoo-removal program in San Luis Obispo County, California; a golf awareness program in St. Augustine, Florida; and therapeutic horseback riding in Apple Valley, California: These seemingly diverse programs funded by tax dollars from the federal government have one thing in common—they reflect the attractiveness of special interests issues to vote-seeking politicians. A **special-interest issue** is one that generates substantial personal benefits for a small number of constituents while the costs are spread widely across the bulk of citizens (type 2 projects). Individually, a few people gain a great deal, but many others lose a small amount. In aggregate, the losses may exceed the benefits.

How will a vote-seeking politician respond to special-interest issues? Because their personal stake is large, members of the interest group (and lobbyists representing their interests) will feel strongly about such issues. Many of the special-interest voters will vote for or against candidates strictly on the basis of whether they are supportive of their positions. In addition, interest groups are generally an attractive source of campaign resources, including financial contributions. In contrast, most other rationally ignorant voters will either not know or will care little about special-interest issues. Even if voters know about some of these programs, it will be difficult for them to punish their legislators because each politician represents a bundle of positions on many different issues. Politicians have little to gain by supporting the rationally ignorant and unorganized majority, but organized interest groups are eager to provide cooperative politicians with vocal supporters, campaign workers, and, most important, financial contributions.

Exhibit 6

VOTERS OF DISTRICT[a]	NET BENEFITS (+) OR COSTS (−) TO VOTERS IN DISTRICT			
	CONSTRUCTION OF POST OFFICE IN A	DREDGING HARBOR IN B	CONSTRUCTION OF MILITARY BASE IN C	TOTAL
A	+$10	−$ 3	−$ 3	+$ 4
B	−$ 3	+$10	−$ 3	+$ 4
C	−$ 3	−$ 3	+$10	+$ 4
D	−$ 3	−$ 3	−$ 3	−$ 9
E	−$ 3	−$ 3	−$ 3	−$ 9
Total	−$ 2	−$ 2	−$ 2	−$ 6

[a]We assume the districts are of equal size.

© Cengage Learning 2013

Trading Votes and Passing Counterproductive Legislation

All three projects are inefficient and would not pass majority vote individually. However, representatives from districts A, B, and C could trade votes (logrolling) or put together pork-barrel legislation that would result in all three projects passing.

As a result, politicians have a strong incentive to support legislation that provides concentrated benefits to special-interest groups at the expense of disorganized groups (like the bulk of taxpayers and consumers). Even if supporting such legislation is counterproductive economically, politicians can often gain by supporting programs favored by special interests. For a real-world illustration of how the special-interest effect works, see Applications in Economics, "Sweet Subsidies to Sugar Growers: A Case Study of the Special-Interest Effect."

The power of special interests is further strengthened by logrolling and pork-barrel legislation. **Logrolling** involves the practice of vote trading by politicians in order to get the necessary support to pass desired legislation. **Pork-barrel legislation** is the term used to describe the bundling of unrelated projects benefiting many interests into a single bill. Both logrolling and pork-barrel legislation will often make it possible for special-interest projects to gain legislative approval, even though each project is counterproductive and individually could not muster the needed votes.

Exhibit 6 provides a numeric illustration of the forces underlying logrolling and pork-barrel legislation. Here we analyze the operation of a five-member legislature considering three projects: construction of a post office in district A, dredging of a harbor in district B, and spending on a military base in district C. For each district, the net benefit or cost is shown—that is, the benefit to the district minus the tax cost imposed on it. The total cost of each of the three projects exceeds the benefits (as shown by the negative number in the total row at the bottom of the table); therefore, each is counterproductive. If the projects were voted on separately, each would lose by a 4-to-1 vote because only one district would gain, and the other four would lose. However, when the projects are bundled together through either logrolling (representatives A, B, and C could agree to trade votes) or pork-barrel legislation (all three programs put on the same bill), they can all pass, despite the fact that all are inefficient.[4] This can be seen by noting that the total combined net benefit is positive for representatives A, B, and C.

The political incentive to support special interest projects, including those that are counterproductive, is even stronger than the simple numeric example of Exhibit 6 implies.

Logrolling
The exchange between politicians of political support on one issue for political support on another.

Pork-barrel legislation
A package of spending projects bundled into a single bill. It is often used as a device to obtain funding for a group of projects intensely desired by regional or interest groups that would be unlikely to pass if voted on separately.

---

[4]Logrolling and pork-barrel policies can sometimes lead to the adoption of productive measures. However, if a project is productive, there would always be a pattern of finance that would lead to its adoption even if logrolling and pork-barrel policies were absent. Thus, the tendency for logrolling and pork-barrel policies to result in the adoption of inefficient projects is the more significant point.

Earmarking
The direction of budgeted funds to specific projects, programs, and locations. The technique is costly but provides major benefits to business firms and other concentrated constituent groups, and to the districts where the spending takes place. The benefits are often targeted to those willing to make substantial campaign contributions.

As the result of the rational ignorance effect, those harmed by pork-barrel and other special-interest policies will often be unaware of the adverse impact the projects exert on their welfare. Moreover, the power of special interests is further enhanced by **earmarking**, detailed directives written into spending bills that require budgeted funds to be spent in specific locations, or on specific projects or programs. In effect, earmarks let members of Congress direct federal spending to specific firms, districts, and states. These directives are often inserted into bills late in the legislative process by powerful committee members or through logrolling as a means of obtaining needed votes for legislative passage. Not surprisingly, firms and groups benefiting substantially from the earmarks are often those making large contributions to the political campaigns of the senators and representatives inserting the earmarks. In recent years, the national defense, transportation, energy, and homeland security bills have been "stuffed" with earmark spending.

Political leaders often criticize the use of earmarking when they are in the minority and therefore less able to use it effectively. Earmarking was widely criticized during the 2010 election and many current members of Congress have pledge not to use it in the future. However, earmarking helps incumbents raise more campaign funds, which provides them with a competitive advantage relative to challengers. Given this incentive structure, the recent cutback on the use of the technique is likely to be temporary.

APPLICATIONS IN ECONOMICS

Sweet Subsidies to Sugar Growers: A Case Study of the Special-Interest Effect

For many years, the price of sugar in the United States has been two or three times as high as the world price. Why? Because the U.S. government severely restricts the quantity of sugar imported. This keeps the domestic price of sugar high. As a result, the roughly 60,000 sugar growers in the United States gain about $1.9 billion. That's more than $30,000 per grower! Most of these benefits are reaped by large growers with incomes far above the national average. In contrast, these subsidies cost the average American household about $20 in the form of higher prices for products containing sugar. Even more important, the resources of Americans are wasted producing a good we are ill suited to produce and one that could be obtained at a substantially lower cost through trade. As a result, Americans are worse off.

Why does Congress support this program year after year? Given the sizable impact the restrictions have on the personal wealth of sugar growers, it is perfectly sensible for the growers, particularly the large ones, to use their wealth and political clout to help politicians who support their interests. This is precisely what they have done. During the 2008 and 2010 election cycles, the sugar lobby contributed nearly $10 million to candidates and political action committees. One company alone, American Crystal Sugar, contributed $4.1 million. During the same period, the industry spent another $26 million lobbying for continuation of the subsidies. In contrast, it makes no sense for the average voter to

Glow Images/Getty Images

investigate this issue or give it any significant weight when deciding for whom to vote. In fact, most voters are unaware that this program is costing them money. Here, as in several other areas, politicians have a strong incentive to support policies favored by special interests, solicit those parties for political contributions, and use the funds to attract the support of other voters, most of whom know nothing about the sugar program. Even though the sugar program is counterproductive, it is still a political winner.

Why don't representatives oppose measures that force their constituents to pay for projects that benefit others? There is some incentive to do so, but the constituents of any one elected representative would capture only a tiny portion of the benefits of tax savings from improved efficiency. The savings, after all, would be spread nationwide among all taxpayers. We would not expect the president of a corporation to devote any significant amount of the firm's resources toward projects that chiefly benefit other firms. Neither should we expect an elected representative to devote political resources to projects like defeating pork-barrel programs when the bulk of the benefits derived from spending reductions and tax savings will accrue to constituents in other districts. Instead, representatives have a strong incentive to fight for more spending for their constituents and not worry much about the spending pushed by other members of Congress.

When the benefits of a governmental action are spread far and wide among the unorganized, and the costs are highly concentrated (type 4 of Exhibit 5), special-interest groups—those who stand to bear the cost—are likely to oppose and lobby strongly against even an efficient project. Most other voters will be largely uninformed and uninterested. Once again, politicians will have an incentive to respond to the views of the concentrated interests. A proposal to reduce or eliminate a tariff (tax) on an imported good would be an example of this type of legislation. Although many thousands of consumers would benefit from the lower prices that result, the domestic firms that compete with the imported good would devote substantial resources toward lobbying to keep the tariff in place. Projects of this type will tend to be rejected even when they are productive, that is, when they would generate larger benefits than costs.

There is a tendency to believe that if a project or program can muster a political majority, it will be good for the society. The special interest effect illustrates that this is not necessarily the case. *Majority voting and representative democracy work poorly when concentrated interests can benefit at the expense of disorganized groups such as taxpayers and consumers. In the case of special-interest issues, there is a conflict between good politics—getting elected—and the efficient use of resources.* The special-interest effect helps explain the presence of numerous government programs that increase the size of government but reduce the overall size of the economic pie. As we discuss diverse topics throughout this text, counterproductive political action that has its foundation in the special-interest effect will arise again and again.

SHORTSIGHTEDNESS EFFECT

Current economic conditions will have a major impact on the choices of voters on election day. As a result, incumbent politicians will want to institute programs that will provide visible results prior to the next major election. Thus, legislators have a strong incentive to favor projects that yield highly visible current benefits at the expense of cost that will be difficult to identify and mostly observable in the future. In contrast, politicians will find projects unattractive when they generate visible cost now with the expectation of future gain. Economists refer to this bias inherent in the political process as the **shortsightedness effect**.

As the result of the shortsightedness effect, political decision-makers will often engage in actions that are counterproductive and even dangerous. *The popularity of debt financing has its foundation in the shortsightedness effect. Politicians like to spend on programs designed to provide highly visible benefits prior to the next election, but they are reluctant to levy taxes for their finance. Borrowing makes it possible for them to undertake the spending without having to impose current taxation, which would make the cost more visible.* Since 1960, the federal budget has been in deficit 46 times; there have been only five surpluses (1969 and 1998–2001). During the fiscal years 2009–2011, the federal government has financed approximately 40 percent of its expenditures through borrowing. The outstanding federal debt has now been pushed to nearly 100 percent of the economy, a level not seen since the aftermath of World War II.

The shortsightedness effect also explains why vote-seeking politicians find it attractive to promise future benefits without levying the taxes that are sufficient for their

Shortsightedness effect
The misallocation of resources that results because public-sector action is biased (1) in favor of proposals yielding clearly defined current benefits in exchange for difficult-to-identify future costs and (2) against proposals with clearly identifiable current costs that yield less concrete and less obvious future benefits.

finance. This has been the case with both the Social Security and Medicare programs. The unfunded liabilities of these two programs are now more than *four times* the size of the official outstanding federal debt. By the time the higher taxes (or benefit cuts) for these programs are confronted, the politicians who gained votes from the promised benefits will be long gone.

It is worth taking a moment to consider the differences between the public and private sectors in terms of how future benefits and costs are considered in current decisions. As we explained in Chapter 2, private-property rights provide a means by which the value of future benefits can be immediately captured (and costs must be borne) by a property owner. Owners who do not invest now to properly maintain their homes or cars, for example, will bear the consequences of the reduced value of those assets. Correspondingly, the value of a firm's stock will immediately rise (or fall), depending on the shareholders' perception of the expected future benefits and costs of an action taken by the company's executives today. In contrast, there is no such market indicator or incentive in the public sector, so decision-makers there naturally tend to place more weight on current benefits and costs and less weight on the future.

RENT-SEEKING

There are two ways individuals can acquire wealth: production and plunder. When individuals produce goods or services and exchange them for income, they not only enrich themselves, but they also enhance the wealth of the society. Sometimes the rules—or lack of rule enforcement—also allow people to get ahead by taking, or plundering, from others. This method not only fails to generate additional income—the gain of one is a loss to another—but it also consumes resources and thereby reduces the wealth of the society.

Rent-seeking
Actions by individuals and groups designed to restructure public policy in a manner that will either directly or indirectly redistribute more income to themselves or the projects they promote.

Rent-seeking is the term economists use to describe actions taken by individuals and groups seeking to use the political process to take the wealth of others.[5] Perhaps "favor seeking" would be a more descriptive term for this type of activity, which generally involves "investing" resources in lobbying and other activities designed to gain favors from the government. The incentive for individuals to spend time and effort in rent-seeking will be determined by how rewarding it is. Rent-seeking will be unattractive when constitutional constraints prevent politicians from taking the property of some and transferring it to others (or forcing some to pay for things desired by others).

However, when the government becomes heavily involved in income transfer activities and the granting of favors to some at the expense of others (instead of simply acting as a neutral force protecting property rights and enforcing contracts), people will spend more time rent seeking and less time producing goods and services. Rather than competing by offering consumers more for their money, rent-seekers compete by using resources to obtain more funds from taxpayers. As a result, more resources are squandered on plunder activities and fewer are available for productive use. Most importantly, output and income levels will be less than their potential.

To get elected (or reelected), politicians have a strong incentive to provide spending programs to important interest groups to secure their support.

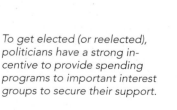

[5]See the classic work of Charles K. Rowley, Robert D. Tollison, and Gordon Tullock, *The Political Economy of Rent-Seeking* (Boston: Kluwer Academic Publishers, 1988) for additional details on rent-seeking.

INEFFICIENCY OF GOVERNMENT OPERATIONS

Will government enterprises and agencies be operated efficiently? The incentive to keep cost low and provide customers with highly valued goods and services differs substantially between the market and government sectors. In the market sector, there is a strong incentive to produce efficiently because lower costs mean higher profits. The profit motive also provides private firms with a strong incentive to supply goods and services that are highly valued relative to their cost. Bankruptcy weeds out private sector firms that have high costs and serve their customers poorly.

In the public sector, the structure of incentives is much different. There is nothing like profit and loss that might be used to evaluate the performance of public sector managers and bureaus. Neither is there a mechanism like bankruptcy that can be counted on to eventually bring inefficient public sector operations to a halt. In fact, failure to achieve a targeted objective (for example, a lower crime rate or improvement in student achievement scores) is often used as an argument for *increased* public-sector funding of an agency or its programs. Furthermore, public-sector managers are seldom in a position to gain personally from measures that reduce costs. The opposite is often true, in fact. If an agency fails to spend its entire budget for a given year, not only does it have to return the extra money, but its budget for the next year is likely to be cut. Because of this, government agencies typically go on a spending spree near the end of a budget period if they discover they have failed to spend all the current year's allocated funds.

It is important to note that the argument of internal inefficiency is not based on the assumption that employees of a bureaucratic government are lazy or less capable. Many agency managers are highly capable, diligent, and focused strongly on their mission within the agency. Rather, the inefficiency stems from the incentives and opportunities that such managers and workers confront. Government enterprises do not have owners that are risking their wealth on the future success of the firm. No decision-maker in the firm can reap substantial economic gain if the firm produces more efficiently or incorporates a new product or service highly valued relative to its costs. In the public sector, there is no test like profit and loss that might be used to measure inefficiency, much less eliminate it. Given this incentive structure, inefficient use of resources is the predicted result.

The empirical evidence is consistent with this view. Economies dominated by government control, like those of the former Soviet bloc, Indonesia, Syria, and Nigeria (and many other African countries), have performed poorly. The level of output per unit of resource input in countries with numerous government enterprises is low. Similarly, when private firms are compared with government agencies providing the same goods or services (like garbage collection, hospitals, electric and water utilities, weather forecasting, and public transportation), studies indicate that private firms generally provide the services more economically.

POLITICAL FAVORITISM, CRONY CAPITALISM, AND GOVERNMENT FAILURE

Public-choice analysis indicates that as government spending, subsidies, income transfers, and regulatory favors grow, businesses and other well-organized groups have a greater incentive to expend resources seeking to obtain the government favors. As a result, crony capitalism tends to expand relative to market allocation. **Crony capitalism** is the situation where the allocation of resources, and winners and losers in business, are determined by political favors rather than by consumer preferences translated through the market profit and loss system. Under crony capitalism, rather than providing equal treatment of individuals and businesses under the law, government uses spending, subsidies, and regulations to favor those most willing to provide political decision-makers with campaign contributions and other forms of political support.

Is crony capitalism an emerging problem in the United States? There is reason to believe that it is. As Exhibit 1 shows, federal, state, and local government expenditures now sum to

Crony Capitalism
A situation where the institutions of markets are maintained, but the allocation of resources, and winners and losers in business, is determined by political decision-making rather than consumer purchases, market prices, and profit and loss. To a large degree, the activities of business firms are directed and controlled by government spending, subsidies, tax credits, regulations, and other forms of political favoritism. In turn, many of the business firms will use contributions and other forms of political support to fight for these favors.

nearly 40 percent of income, up from 32 percent as recently as 2000. Transfers and subsidies accounted for 19.5 percent of national income in 2010, compared to 11.8 percent in 2000 (see Exhibit 3). Social Security and healthcare comprise the bulk of the transfers, but there were more than 2,000 federal subsidy programs in 2010, compared to 1,425 just a decade earlier.

A substantial portion of government spending is driven by what Clemson University economist Bruce Yandle calls the "bootleggers and Baptists" coalition.[6] During the era when many states and counties had bans on the sale of alcoholic beverages, the bootleggers and Baptists both supported the bans, the former because it increased the demand for their product and the latter for moral reasons. Like the bootleggers, opportunistic rent-seekers often frame their programs in a manner designed to attract support from naïve idealists. They argue their programs will enhance child safety, promote energy independence, save family farms, or some other widely supported goal. But when one looks below the surface, you note that the programs provide favoritism that generates handsome profits for the rent-seekers.

Let's consider some examples that illustrate special-interest politics, rent-seeking, and bootlegger–Baptist-type coalitions at work. The Consumer Product Safety Improvement Act of 2008 (CPSIA) and the role played by giant toy manufacturer Mattel in its passage provide an example. The bill imposed new lead testing requirements on manufacturers of products ranging from apparel to home furnishings and toys. Between 1998 and 2007, Mattel had 36 costly recalls, which both damaged its reputation and added to its legal expenses. By 2008, however, it had completed its own product-testing lab. Mattel played a central role in the writing of the CPSIA, and the act permitted Mattel to test its own products because, unsurprisingly, its lab met the specifications of the legislation it helped to formulate. The act also provided Mattel with a sizeable advantage relative to its smaller rivals, who had to submit their products for costly testing at independent laboratories. Equally important, the testing virtually eliminated the secondhand toy and children's clothing market. Clearly, Goodwill and other retailers of used toys and clothing with zippers, buttons, or other accessories with even a touch of paint could not afford to test these products and still make them available at economical prices. Literally, tens of millions of dollars of used toys and clothing were rendered useless and eliminated from the market. This made it possible for Mattel to charge higher prices than would have otherwise been the case. Like many other rent-seekers, Mattel used the bootlegger–Baptist strategy to achieve their goals. They argued that the requirement would protect children from suffering great harm and benefitted from the support of consumer lobby groups. Controversy over these claims helped to divert attention away from the cost that the program was sure to impose on taxpayers and consumers. There was no evidence that even one child had suffered health damage from lead paint on toys or clothing. Nonetheless, Mattel was able to reap huge benefits from the child safety legislation.[7]

General Electric, the nation's sixth largest corporation derives major benefits from ties to government, while Goodwill suffered greatly from restrictions imposed on the sale of items containing lead that were pushed by toy-maker Mattel.

General Electric, the nation's sixth-largest corporation, is heavily involved in crony capitalism activities. It derives major benefits from government subsidies for wind farms, wind turbine engines, high-speed rail, solar panels, and tax advantages for export products. Jeffrey Immelt, GE's CEO, is a close friend and major supporter of President Obama. In March

[6]See Bruce Yandle, "Bootleggers and Baptists: The Education of a Regulatory Economist," *Regulation* 7, no. 3 (May/June 1983): 12–16 and "Bootleggers and Baptists in Retrospect," *Regulation* 22, no. 3 (1999): 5–7.

[7]Timothy P. Carney, "Mattel Exempted from Toy Safety Law It Helped Write," *Washington Examiner*, September 4, 2009.

of 2011, the president named Immelt chairman of his Council on Jobs and Competitiveness, and before that Immelt was on the President's Economic Recovery Advisory Board. He's a regular companion when President Obama travels abroad to promote American exports. In 2010, GE managed to rack up worldwide profits of $14.2 billion, $5.1 billion from its U.S. operations. Its U.S. corporate income tax bill was zero. In fact, GE received a tax benefit of $3.2 billion. This did not happen by chance. Over the past decade the company has pursued "an aggressive strategy that mixes fierce lobbying for tax breaks and innovative accounting that enables it to concentrate its profits offshore." The GE tax division, including lobbyists, had 975 employees in 2010. The team includes former officials from the Treasury, the IRS and virtually all the tax-writing committees in Congress. Over the last decade, GE has spent tens of millions of dollars pushing for tax savings and subsidies ranging from more generous depreciation schedules on jet engines to "green energy" credits for its wind turbines.[8]

Perhaps the financial crisis provides the most vivid example of how crony capitalism affects the lives of ordinary Americans. Banking and finance is one of the most, if not the most, heavily regulated and politicized sectors of the economy. Since the mid-1990s, two huge government-sponsored corporations, Fannie Mae and Freddie Mac, have dominated mortgage lending. These corporations have a competitive advantage relative to other lenders because their bonds are backed by the federal government, and they are therefore able to obtain funds cheaper than are rivals. Following congressional mandates that proponents argued would promote more affordable housing, the policies of Fannie and Freddie undermined lending standards and promoted subprime loans that contributed heavily to the housing price boom and bust and the soaring default rate that followed. Seeking to maintain their government favors, Fannie and Freddie were among the biggest spenders on lobbying activities. Their expenditures on lobbying summed to $174 million during 1998–2008.[9] As a whole, the heavily regulated banking and finance sector spent 2.9 billion on lobbying and political contributions between 2004 and 2010, far more than any other sector except healthcare. Citigroup and five large investment banks (Goldman Sachs, Merrill Lynch, Bear Stearns, Morgan Stanley, and Lehman Brothers), key banks at the center of the crisis, spent more than $100 million on lobbying and political contributions during the four years prior to the 2008 crisis.[10] One of the most important decision-makers in the Republican Bush administration at the time was Secretary of the Treasury Henry Paulson. Prior to his appointment, he was CEO of Goldman Sachs. One of the most highly respected voices by the Democratic congressional majority was that of Robert Rubin, a former secretary of the treasury during the Clinton Administration. At the time of the crisis, Rubin was vice-chairman of the Board of Citigroup. Special Topic 5 examines the financial crisis in considerable detail. For now, we merely want to note that banking and mortgage finance was and continues to be a highly politicized sector characterized by incestuous crony capitalist relationships among the key business and political decision-makers.

The examples presented here are indicative of how modern political allocation works. It is driven by special interest spending, rent-seeking, and a cozy relationship between political leaders and the interest groups that both benefit from their decisions and provide them with the lion's share of the contributions for their political campaigns. The box feature in this chapter explained the inefficiency generated by the sugar subsidy program, but the grain, cotton, peanut, wool, and dairy programs all have a similar impact. Together, these subsidy programs cost taxpayers and consumers more than $20 billion per year. Special interest and rent-seeking politics also explain the presence of tariffs and quotas on steel, shoes, brooms, textiles, and many other products. Subsidies for ethanol, irrigation of arid lands, exports, small business start-ups, sports stadiums, high-speed rail

---

[8]See David Kocieniewski, "G.E.'s Strategies Let It Avoid Taxes Altogether," *New York Times*, March 24, 2011. Data from the Center for Responsive Politics indicates that General Electric spent $160 million on lobbying and political contributions during 2004–2010.

[9]Center for Responsive Politics, "Lobbying: Top Spenders" (2008), available at http://www.opensecrets.org/lobby/top.php?indexType=s.

[10]Ibid.

systems, (the list goes on and on) are all policies motivated by perverse political incentives rather than the net benefits to Americans. While each such program individually imposes only a small drag on our economy, together they exert a major impact on the efficiency of resource use.

Spending on projects like these is not about correcting market failure. Pure and simple, it is driven by government favoritism in exchange for political support. This spending is illustrative of government failure: political forces that channel resources into wasteful, counterproductive activities. It is interesting to consider the difference in the incentive structure confronted by business firms directed by markets compared to crony capitalists directed by political decision-making. In both cases, pursuit of profit will direct the actions of the firm. Market entrepreneurs have a strong incentive to serve the interests of consumers spending their own money. In order to be successful, market entrepreneurs must produce goods and services that consumers value more than the resources required for their production. When they do so, their actions are productive. In contrast, crony capitalists have a strong incentive to serve the interests of political decision-makers spending someone else's money. Crony capitalists succeed by providing political players with campaign contributions and other political resources in exchange for government contracts, subsidies, tax benefits, and other forms of political favoritism. Their activities will often be counterproductive.

While the cozy relationship between government contractors and political leaders is nothing new, the expanded role of the government provides reason for additional concern. Can political decision-makers really be evenhanded when they derive substantial political support from those benefiting from their spending, regulatory, and tax policies? The answer to this question exerts an impact on not only economic efficiency, but also the legitimacy of the democratic process.

THE ECONOMIC WAY OF THINKING ABOUT MARKETS AND GOVERNMENT

When analyzing the operation of markets and government, it is vitally important to keep two points in mind. First, the government's protective role provides the foundation for the smooth operation of markets. A government that protects private property, enforces contracts evenhandedly, maintains monetary stability, and refrains from regulations that restrict entry into markets is central to the efficient operation of markets.

Second, both the market and the political process have shortcomings. In Chapter 5, we focused on the shortcomings of the market and explained why markets sometimes fail to achieve the efficient use of resources. This chapter provides a parallel analysis for the political process. The accompanying **Thumbnail Sketch** lists the major deficiencies of both sectors. It indicates the conditions that underlie both market and government failure.

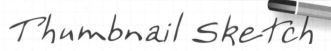

Thumbnail Sketch

What Weakens the Case for Market-Sector Allocation Versus Public-Sector Intervention, and Vice Versa?

These factors weaken the case for market-sector allocation:

1. lack of competition
2. externalities
3. public goods
4. poor information

These factors weaken the case for public-sector action:

1. the special-interest effect
2. the shortsightedness effect
3. rent-seeking
4. weak incentives for operational efficiency

There is a tendency to idealize democratic governance—to focus on the stated objectives of political officials rather than the actual effects of their policies. Public-choice analysis warns against this naïve view. It focuses on how the political process really works, even if that is not how we might like for it to work. Public choice also highlights the importance of institutions, constitutional rules, and procedures that encourage productive political actions and restrain those that are counterproductive. Higher income levels and living standards can be achieved if institutions more consistent with economic progress are adopted. This will be a recurring theme throughout this book.

Looking Ahead

iStockphoto.com/gaspr13

Cases involving potential government intervention will be discussed repeatedly throughout this book. The tools presented in this chapter and the previous one will help us better understand both the potential and the limitations of public policy as a source for economic progress.

KEY POINTS

- In recent years, government spending has increased, and it is now nearly 40 percent the size of the economy

- There are both similarities and differences between markets and governments. Competition is present in both sectors. Both involve the use of scarce resources. The government can use its taxing power to break the link between payment and receipt of a good for an individual, but not for the economy as a whole. In the public sector, voters face a "bundle" purchase problem; they are unable to vote for some policies favored by one candidate and other policies favored by the candidate's opponent. Power and income are unequal in both the market and government sectors, but the factors influencing their distribution differ between the two.

- In a representative democracy, government is controlled by voters who elect politicians to set policy and hire bureaucrats to run government agencies. The incentives faced by all three classes of participants influence political outcomes.

- Voters have a strong incentive to support the candidate who offers them the greatest gain relative to their personal costs. Because collective decisions break the link between the choice of the individual and the outcome of the issue, voters are likely to be poorly informed on most political matters.

- Politicians have a strong incentive to follow a strategy that will enhance their chances of getting elected (and reelected). Political competition more or less forces them to focus on how their actions influence their support among voters and potential contributors.

- The distribution of the benefits and costs among voters influences how the political process works. When voters pay in proportion to the benefits they receive from a public-sector project, productive projects tend to be approved and counterproductive ones rejected. When the costs of a policy are distributed among voters differently than are the benefits, democratic decision-making will tend to be less efficient.

- Government actions will often lead to economic inefficiency as the result of (1) the special-interest effect, (2) the shortsightedness effect, (3) rent-seeking, and (4) weak incentives to keep costs low within government enterprises and agencies. Thus, just as the market sometimes fails to allocate goods efficiently, so, too, will the political process.

- As the size and scope of government grow, public-choice analysis indicates that political activity involving the exchange of government favors for political support will become more widespread. More resources will be channeled into rent-seeking and inefficient government programs, particularly those favored by special interest groups.

CRITICAL ANALYSIS QUESTIONS

1. Are voters likely to be well informed on issues and the positions of candidates? Why or why not?

2. *"The government can afford to take a long view when it needs to, while a private firm has a short-term outlook. Corporate officers, for example, typically care about the next 3 to 6 months, not the next 50 to 100 years. Government, not private firms, should own things like forests, which take decades to develop." Evaluate this view.

3. "If there are problems with markets, government will generally be able to intervene and correct the situation." Is this statement true? Explain your response.

4. *"The political process sometimes leads to economic inefficiency because we elect the wrong people to political office. If the right people were elected, a democracy governed by majority rule would allocate resources efficiently." Evaluate this statement.

5. What is rent-seeking? When is it likely to be widespread? How does it influence economic efficiency? Explain.

6. *"The average person is more likely to make a well-informed choice when purchasing a personal computer than when voting for a congressional candidate." Is this statement true? Why or why not?

7. "Government action is based on majority rule, whereas market action is based on mutual consent. The market allows for proportional representation of minorities, but minorities must yield to the views of the majority when activities are undertaken through government." In your own words, explain the meaning of this statement. Is the statement true? Why or why not?

8. *"Voters should simply ignore political candidates who play ball with special-interest groups and vote instead for candidates who will represent all the people when they are elected. Government will work far better when this happens." Evaluate this view.

9. If a project is efficient (its total benefits exceed its total costs), would it be possible to allocate the cost of the project in a manner that would provide net benefits to each voter? Why or why not? Explain. Will efficient projects necessarily be favored by a majority of voters? Explain.

10. *"When an economic function is turned over to the government, social cooperation replaces personal self-interest." Is this statement true? Why or why not?

11. What is the shortsightedness effect? How does it influence the attractiveness of government borrowing? Explain.

12. *What's wrong with this way of thinking? "Public policy is necessary to protect the average citizen from the power of vested interest groups. In the absence of government intervention, regulated industries such as airlines, railroads, and trucking will charge excessive prices; products will be unsafe; and the rich will oppress the poor. Government curbs the power of special-interest groups."

13. "Because government-operated firms do not have to make a profit, they can usually produce at a lower cost and charge a lower price than privately owned enterprises." Evaluate this view.

14. If a senator trades his or her vote on an issue for a $10,000 payment, would you consider this corruption? If a senator votes a certain way in "exchange" for a $10,000 contribution to his political campaign, would you consider this corruption? Is there a major difference between the two? Discuss.

15. *The United States imposes highly restrictive sugar import quotas that result in a domestic price that is generally two or three times the world price. The quotas benefit sugar growers at the expense of consumers. Given that there are far more sugar consumers than growers, why aren't the quotas abolished? Has government action in this area improved the living standards of Americans? Why or why not?

*Asterisk denotes questions for which answers are given in Appendix B.

Core Microeconomics

Consumers are the ultimate judge of both products and business firms. Their choices determine which survive and which fail. The competitive process is highly dynamic. Numerous businesses come and go. Each year, newly incorporated businesses account for approximately 10 percent of the total. However, about 60 percent of the new businesses will fail within the first six years. Microeconomics analyzes the dynamic interaction among consumers, business firms, and resource suppliers, and how it affects the quality of our lives.

PART

3

Microeconomics focuses on the choices of consumers, the operation of firms, the structure of markets, and the choices of resource suppliers and employers.

CHAPTER

7

Consumer Choice and Elasticity

CHAPTER FOCUS

- What are the fundamental postulates underlying consumer choice?
- How does the law of diminishing marginal utility help explain the law of demand?
- How do the demand curves of individuals translate into a market demand curve?
- What is demand elasticity? What does it measure? Why is it important?

The most famous law in economics, and the one economists are most sure of, is the law of demand. On this law is built almost the whole edifice of economics.

—*David R. Henderson*[1]

A thing is worth whatever a buyer will pay for it.

—*Publilius Syrus, first century B.C.*[2]

[1]David R. Henderson, "Demand," in *The Concise Encyclopedia of Economics*, ed. David R. Henderson (http://www.econlib.org/library/CEE.html).
[2]Quoted in Michael Jackman, ed., *Macmillan Book of Business and Economic Quotations* (New York: Macmillan, 1984), 150.

The statement of David Henderson highlights the central position of the law of demand in economics. As Publilius Syrus noted more than 2,000 years ago, demand reflects the willingness of individuals to pay for what is offered in the marketplace. In this section, we begin our examination of microeconomic markets for specific products with an analysis of the demand side of markets. In essence, we will be going "behind" the market demand curve to see how it is made up of individual consumer demands and what factors determine the choices of individual consumers.[3]

FUNDAMENTALS OF CONSUMER CHOICE

Each of us must decide how to allocate our limited income among the many possible things we would like to buy. The prices of goods, *relative to each other,* are important determining factors. If your favorite cereal doubled in price, would you switch to a different brand? Would your decision be different if all cereals, not just yours, doubled in price? Your choice *between* brands of cereal will be affected only by the change in relative prices. If the prices of all cereals rose by a proportional amount, you might quit purchasing cereal, but this would not give you a strong reason to switch to a different brand. Relative prices measure opportunity cost. If cereal is $5 per box when movie tickets are $10, you must give up two boxes of cereal to purchase one movie ticket.

Several fundamental principles underlie the choices of consumers. Let's take a closer look at the key factors influencing consumer behavior.

1. Limited income necessitates choice. Because of scarcity, we all have limited incomes. The limited nature of our income requires us to make choices about which goods we will and will not buy. When more of one good or service is bought, we must buy less of some other goods if we are to stay within our budget.

2. Consumers make decisions purposefully. The goals that underpin consumer choice can usually be met in alternative ways. If two products cost the same, a consumer will choose to buy the one expected to have the higher benefit. Conversely, if two products yield equal benefits, the consumer will choose to buy the less expensive one. Fundamentally, economics assumes that consumers are rational—that they are able to weigh the costs and benefits of alternative choices.

3. One good can be substituted for another. Consumers can achieve *utility*—that is, satisfaction—from many different alternatives. Either a hamburger or a taco might satisfy your hunger, whereas going either to a movie or to a football game might satisfy your desire for entertainment. With $600, you might either buy a new TV set or take a short vacation. No single good is so precious that some of it will not be given up in exchange for a large enough quantity of other goods. Even seemingly unrelated goods are sometimes substituted one for another. For example, high water prices in Southern California have led residents there to substitute cactus gardens and reduced flow showerheads for water.

4. Consumers must make decisions without perfect information, but knowledge and past experience will help. In Chapter 1, we noted that information is costly to acquire. Asking family and friends, searching through magazines such as *Consumer Reports,* and contacting your local Better Business Bureau are all ways of gathering information about products and potential sellers. The time and effort consumers spend

---

[3]You may want to review the section on demand in Chapter 3 before proceeding with this chapter.

Consumers will seek to spend their income in a manner that will provide them with the maximum value (total utility).

Law of diminishing marginal utility
The basic economic principle that as the consumption of a product increases, the marginal utility derived from consuming more of it (per unit of time) will eventually decline.

Marginal utility
The additional utility, or satisfaction, derived from consuming an additional unit of a good.

Marginal benefit
The maximum price a consumer will be willing to pay for an additional unit of a product. It is the dollar value of the consumer's marginal utility from the additional unit, and therefore it falls as consumption increases.

acquiring information will be directly related to the value derived from it. Predictably, consumers will spend more time and money to inform themselves when they are buying "big ticket" items such as automobiles or air-conditioning systems than when they are buying pencils or paper towels.

While no one has perfect foresight, your own experiences—and those of others—will help you make better-informed choices. You have a pretty good idea of what to expect when you buy a cup of coffee and a bagel at your favorite restaurant. Your expectations might not always be fulfilled precisely the same way every time (for example, the coffee may be weak or the bagel too crispy), but even then, you will gain valuable information that will help you project the outcome of future choices more accurately.

5. The law of diminishing marginal utility applies: As the rate of consumption increases, the marginal utility gained from consuming additional units of a good will decline. Utility is a term economists use to describe the subjective personal benefits that result from taking an action. The law of diminishing marginal utility states that the marginal (or additional) utility derived from consuming successive units of a product will eventually decline as the rate of consumption increases. For example, the law says that even though you might like ice cream, your marginal satisfaction from additional ice cream will eventually decline as you eat more and more of it. Ice cream at lunchtime might be great. An additional helping for dinner might also be good. However, after you have had it for lunch and dinner, another serving as a midnight snack will be less attractive. When the law of diminishing marginal utility sets in, the additional utility derived from still more units of ice cream declines.

The law of diminishing marginal utility explains why, even if you really like a certain product, you will not spend your entire budget on it. As you increase your consumption of any good, the utility you derive from each additional unit will become smaller and smaller, eventually becoming less than the price. At that point, you will not want to purchase any more units of the good.

MARGINAL UTILITY, CONSUMER CHOICE, AND THE DEMAND CURVE OF AN INDIVIDUAL

The law of diminishing marginal utility helps us understand the law of demand and the shape of the demand curve. The height of an individual's demand curve at any specific unit is equal to the maximum price the consumer would be willing to pay for that unit—its marginal benefit to the consumer—given the number of units he or she has already purchased. Although marginal benefit is measured in dollars, the dollar amount reflects the opportunity cost of the unit in terms of other goods forgone. If a consumer is willing to pay, at most, $5 for an additional unit of the product, this indicates a willingness to give up, at most, $5 worth of other goods. ***Because a consumer's willingness to pay for a unit of a good is directly related to the utility derived from consuming the unit, the law of diminishing marginal utility implies that a consumer's marginal benefit, and thus the height of the demand curve, falls as the quantity consumed increases.***

Exhibit 1 shows this relationship for a hypothetical consumer Jones, relative to her weekly consumption of pizza. Because of the law of diminishing marginal utility, each additional pizza consumed per week will generate less marginal utility for Jones than did the previous pizza. For this reason, Jones's maximum willingness to pay—her marginal

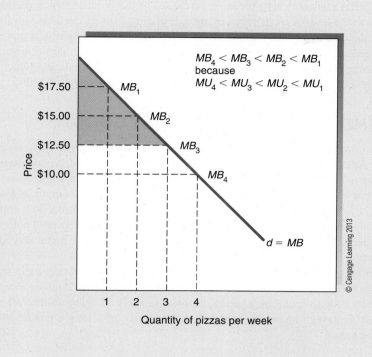

Exhibit 1

Diminishing Marginal Utility and the Individual's Demand Curve

An individual's demand curve, Jones's demand for personal pizzas in this case, reflects the law of diminishing marginal utility. Because marginal utility (*MU*) falls with increased consumption, so does the consumer's maximum willingness to pay—marginal benefit (*MB*). A consumer will purchase until *MB* = Price, so at a price of $12.50 per pizza, Jones would purchase three pizzas and receive a consumer surplus shown by the shaded triangle.

benefit—will fall as the quantity consumed increases. In addition, the steepness of Jones's demand curve, or its responsiveness to a change in price—its elasticity—is a reflection of how rapidly Jones's marginal utility diminishes with additional consumption. An individual's demand curve for a good whose marginal value declines more rapidly, will be steeper.

Given what we now know about a consumer's maximum willingness to pay for additional units of a good, we are in a position to discuss how many units the consumer will choose to purchase at various prices. ***At any given price, consumers will purchase all units of a good for which their maximum willingness to pay—their marginal benefit—is greater than the price.*** They will stop at the point at which the marginal benefit of the next unit would be less than the price. Although there are some problems related to dividing up certain kinds of goods (for example, it is hard to purchase half a car), we can generally say that a consumer will purchase all units of a good up to the point at which the marginal benefit from it equals the price of the good (*MB = P*).

Returning to Exhibit 1, if the price of pizza were $12.50, Jones would purchase three pizzas per week.[4] Remember from Chapter 3 that consumer surplus is defined as the difference between the maximum price the consumer is willing to pay and the price actually paid, summed over all units consumed. Because the height of the demand curve reflects Jones's maximum willingness to pay for pizza, the shaded triangle that lies above the price shows the total consumer surplus derived from her consumption of the three pizzas. When a consumer has purchased all units to the point at which *MB = P*, total consumer surplus is maximized.

---

[4]Jones would certainly purchase the first and second pizzas because *MB > P*. For the third pizza, *MB = P*, so Jones would be indifferent to buying the unit or not purchasing it. For a good that is easily divisible, say, pounds of roast beef, the consumer could continue purchasing up to 2.9999 pounds at a deli counter. Thus, economists are comfortable with simply concluding that the consumer will purchase this final unit, implying that Jones will purchase three pizzas.

Within this framework, how would a consumer respond to a decrease in the price of a good? The consumer will increase purchases to the point at which marginal benefit diminishes to the level of the new lower price. If marginal utility declines rapidly with consumption, the consumer will expand his or her purchases only slightly. If marginal utility declines less rapidly, it will take a larger expansion in purchases to reach this point. The law of diminishing marginal utility underlies a person's demand curve for a product. The shape and steepness of the curve, for example, depend on his or her marginal utility.

CONSUMER EQUILIBRIUM WITH MANY GOODS

The last time you were at the mall, you probably saw something that you liked, perhaps a nice shirt. After all, there are many things we would like—many different alternatives that would give us utility. Next, you looked at the price tag: "Fifty dollars, wow! That's too much." What you were really saying was, "I like the shirt, but not as much as the $50 worth of other goods that I would have to give up for it." Consumer choice is a constant comparison of value relative to price. Consider another example: Perhaps you prefer expensive steak to a hamburger. Even if you do, your happiness may often be better served if you buy the hamburger and then spend the savings on something else.

The idea that consumers choose among products by comparing their relative marginal utility (MU) to price (P) can be expressed more precisely. A consumer with a limited amount of income to spend on a group of products is not likely to do the following math, but will act as though he or she had, and will end up consuming a bundle of goods and services such that

$$\frac{MU_A}{P_A} = \frac{MU_B}{P_B} = \cdots = \frac{MU_n}{P_n}$$

In this formula, MU represents the marginal utility derived from the last unit of a product, and P represents the price of the good. The subscripts $_{A, B, \ldots, n}$ indicate the different products available to the consumer. *This formula implies that the consumer will maximize his or her satisfaction (or total utility) by ensuring that the last dollar spent on each good purchased yields an equal degree of marginal utility.* Alternatively stated, the last unit of each item purchased should provide the same marginal utility *per dollar spent on it*. Thus, if the price of a gallon of ice cream is twice as high as the price of a smoothie, the ice cream should provide twice the marginal benefits to justify its purchase. Thus, a consumer will purchase these items to the point at which the marginal utility of the last gallon of ice cream is exactly twice as high as the marginal utility derived from the last smoothie.

Perhaps the best way to grasp this point is to think about what happens when your ratios of marginal utility to price are not equal for two goods. Suppose that you are at a local restaurant eating buffalo chicken wings and drinking Coke. For simplicity, assume that a large Coke and an order of wings each costs $2. With your $10 budget, you decide to purchase four orders of wings and one large Coke. When you finish your Coke, there are still lots of wings left. You have already eaten so many wings, though, that those remaining do not look as attractive. You could get more utility with fewer wings and another Coke, but it is too late. You have not spent your $10 in a way that gets you the most for your money. Instead of satisfying the preceding condition, you find that the marginal utility of wings is lower than the marginal utility of a Coke, and because they both have the same price ($2), this implies that

$$\frac{MU_{WINGS}}{P_{WINGS}} < \frac{MU_{COKE}}{P_{COKE}}$$

If you had purchased fewer wings and more Coke, your total utility would have been higher. Consuming the added Coke would have lowered its marginal utility, decreasing the value of the right side of the equation. Simultaneously, spending less on wings would have raised the marginal utility of wings, increasing the value of the left side of the equation. You will maximize your utility—and get the most "bang for the buck" from your budget—when you make these values (the ratios) equal.

The equation can also be used to illustrate the law of demand. Beginning with a situation in which the two sides were equal, suppose that the price of wings increased. It would lower the value of *MU/P* for wings below the *MU/P* for Coke. In response, you would reallocate your budget, purchasing fewer of the more costly wings and more Coke. Thus, we have the law of demand—as the price of wings rises, you will purchase less of them. When people try to spend their money in a way that gives them the greatest amount of satisfaction, the consumer decision-making theory outlined here is difficult to question. In the next section, we will take the theory a little further.

PRICE CHANGES AND CONSUMER CHOICE

The demand curve or schedule shows the amount of a product that consumers are willing to buy at alternative prices during a specific time period. The law of demand states that the amount of a product bought is inversely related to its price. We have seen how the law of demand can be derived from fundamental principles of consumer behavior. Now, we go further and distinguish two different phenomena underlying a consumer's response to a price change. First, as the price of a product declines, the lower opportunity cost will induce consumers to buy more of it—even if they have to give up some other products, whose price had not fallen. This tendency to substitute a product that has become cheaper for goods that are now relatively more expensive is called the **substitution effect** of a price change.

Second, if a consumer's money income is unchanged, a reduction in the price of a product they consume will increase his or her real income—the amount of goods and services he or she is able to purchase with that fixed amount of money income. If your rent were to decline by $100 per month, for example, that would allow you to buy more of many other goods. This increase in your real income has the same effect as if the rent had remained the same but your income had risen by $100 per month. As a result, this second way in which a price change affects consumption is called the **income effect**. Typically, consumers will respond to the income effect by buying more of the cheaper product and other products as well because they can better afford to do so. Substitution and income effects generally work in the same direction: They both cause consumers to purchase more of a good as its price falls and less of a good as its price rises.[5]

Substitution effect
That part of an increase (decrease) in amount consumed that is the result of a good being cheaper (more expensive) in relation to other goods because of a reduction (increase) in price.

Income effect
That part of an increase (decrease) in amount consumed that is the result of the consumer's real income being expanded (contracted) by a reduction (rise) in the price of a good.

TIME COSTS AND CONSUMER CHOICE

You may have heard the saying that "time is money." It is certainly true that time has value and that this value can sometimes be measured in dollars. As we have learned, the monetary price of a good is not always a complete measure of its cost to the consumer. Consuming most goods requires not only money but also time; and time, like money, is scarce to the consumer. So a lower time cost, like a lower money price, will make a product more attractive. For example, one study showed that patients in a dentist's office are willing to pay more than $5 per minute saved to shorten their time spent in waiting rooms.[6] Similarly, fast food and air travel are demanded mainly for the time savings they offer.

Time costs, unlike money prices for goods, differ among individuals. They are higher for people with higher wage rates, for example. Other things being equal, high-wage consumers choose more time-saving commodities than do people with lower time costs and wages. For example, high-wage consumers are overrepresented

---

[5]The substitution effect will always work in this direction. The income effect, however, may work in the reverse direction for some types of goods known as inferior goods. These will be addressed later in this chapter.
[6]Rexford E. Santerre and Stephen P. Neun, *Health Economics: Theories, Insights and Industry Studies* (Orlando, FL: Harcourt, 2000), 113.

among airplane and taxicab passengers but underrepresented among television watchers, chess players, and long-distance bus travelers.

Failure to account for time costs can lead to bad decisions. For example, which is cheaper for consumers: (1) waiting in line three hours to purchase a $25 concert ticket or (2) buying the same ticket for $40 without standing in line? A consumer whose time is worth more than $5 per hour will find that $40 without the wait in line is less costly. As you can see, time costs matter. For example, when government-imposed price ceilings (discussed in Chapter 4) create shortages, rationing by waiting occurs. For many consumers, the benefit of the lower price due to the ceiling will be largely, if not entirely, offset by their increased time cost of having to wait in line.

MARKET DEMAND REFLECTS THE DEMAND OF INDIVIDUAL CONSUMERS

The market demand schedule is the relationship between the market price of a good and the amount demanded by all the individuals in the market area. Because individual consumers purchase less at higher prices, the amount demanded in a market area as a total is also inversely related to price.

Exhibit 2 shows the relationship between individual demand and market demand for a hypothetical two-person market. The individual demand curves for both Jones and Smith are shown. Jones and Smith each consume three pizzas per week at a price of $12.50. The amount demanded in the two-person market is six pizzas. If the price rises to $17.50 per pizza, the amount demanded in the market will fall to three pizzas, one demanded by Jones and two by Smith. *The market demand is simply the horizontal sum of the individual demand curves of consumers—in this case, Smith and Jones.*

In the real world, there can be millions of consumers in a market. But the relationship between the demand curves of individuals and the market demand curve will still be just like the one shown in Exhibit 2. At any given price, the amount purchased in the market will be the sum of the amounts purchased by each consumer in the market. Furthermore, the total amount demanded in the market will decline as price increases because individual consumers will purchase fewer units at the higher prices. The market demand curve reflects the collective choices of the individual consumers.

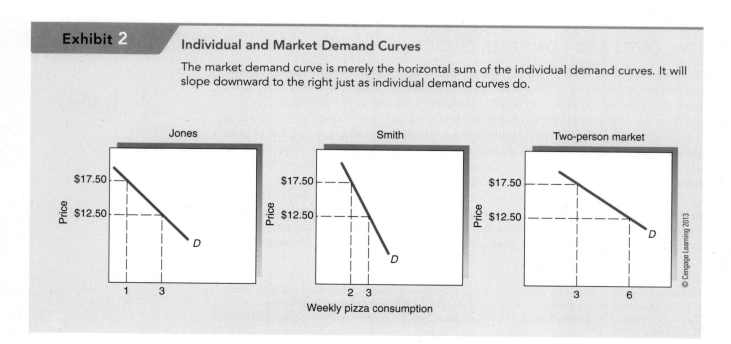

Exhibit 2   **Individual and Market Demand Curves**

The market demand curve is merely the horizontal sum of the individual demand curves. It will slope downward to the right just as individual demand curves do.

© Cengage Learning 2013

ELASTICITY OF DEMAND

Although it is important to recognize that consumers will buy less of a product as its price increases, it is also often important to know whether the increase will lead to a large or small reduction in the amount purchased. Economists have designed a tool called the price elasticity of demand to measure this sensitivity of amount purchased in response to a change in price. The equation for the **price elasticity of demand** is as follows:

$$\text{Price elasticity of demand} = \frac{\text{Percentage change in quantity demanded}}{\text{Percentage change in price}} = \frac{\%\Delta Q}{\%\Delta P}$$

Price elasticity of demand The percentage change in the quantity of a product demanded divided by the percentage change in the price that caused the change in quantity. The price elasticity of demand indicates how responsive consumers are to a change in a product's price.

This ratio is often called the *elasticity coefficient*. To express it more briefly, we use the notation $\%\Delta Q$ to represent percentage change in quantity and $\%\Delta P$ to represent percentage change in price. (The Greek letter delta [Δ] means "change in.") The law of demand states that an increase in a product's price lowers the quantity of it purchased, whereas a decrease in price raises it. *Because a change in price causes the quantity demanded to change in the opposite direction, the price elasticity coefficient is always negative, although economists often ignore the sign and use the absolute value of the coefficient.*

To see how the concept of elasticity works, suppose that the price of the Ford Explorer rises 10 percent, while other prices remain the same. Ford could expect Explorer sales to fall substantially—perhaps 30 percent—as sport-utility vehicle (SUV) buyers respond by switching to other SUVs whose prices have not changed. This strong response by buyers means that the demand for the Explorer is elastic.

Now consider a different situation. Suppose that, because of a new tax, the price of not only the Explorer *but of all new SUVs* rises 10 percent. In this case, consumers' options are much more limited. They can't simply switch to a cheaper close substitute as they could when the price of the Explorer alone rose. They might either simply pay the extra money for a new SUV or settle for a used SUV instead. Because of this, the 10 percent rise in the price of all new SUVs will lead to a smaller consumer response, perhaps a 5 percent decline in sales of new SUVs.

To calculate the elasticity coefficient for the Explorer in the initial example, we begin with the 30 percent decline in quantity demanded and divide it by the 10 percent increase in the price. Thus, the elasticity of demand for the Explorer would be

$$\frac{\%\Delta Q}{\%\Delta P} = \frac{-30\%}{+10\%} = -3$$

(or 3.0 if we ignore the minus sign). This means that the percentage change in quantity demanded is three times the percentage change in price.

To calculate the demand elasticity for *all* SUVs (our second example), we see that the percentage change in quantity, 5 percent, divided by the percentage change in price, 10 percent, gives us –1/2, or –0.5. When it comes to the price elasticity of demand for all SUVs, the percentage change in quantity demanded (using our hypothetical numbers) is only half the percentage change in price, not three times the percentage change in price as it was with the Explorer.

Often, we will have to derive the percentage change in quantity and price. If you know the quantities that will be purchased at two different prices, you can then derive the percentage change in both the price and the quantity. For example, suppose that a price change from P_0 to P_1 causes a change in quantity demanded from Q_0 to Q_1. The change in quantity demanded would therefore be $Q_0 - Q_1$. To calculate the percentage change in quantity, we divide the actual change by the midpoint (or average) of the two quantities.[7] Although it is often easy to find the midpoint without a formula (halfway between $4 and $6 is $5), it can

---

[7]This formula uses the average of the starting point and the ending point of the change so that it will give the same result whether we start from the lower or the higher price. This arc elasticity formula is not the only way to calculate elasticity, but it is the most frequently used.

also be found as $(Q_0 + Q_1)/2$. Finally, because 0.05 is simply 5 percent, we multiply by 100. Thus, we can express the percentage change in quantity demanded as

$$\frac{(Q_0 - Q_1)}{[(Q_0 + Q_1)/2]} \times 100$$

Similarly, when the change in price is $P_0 - P_1$, the *percentage* change in price is

$$\frac{(P_0 - P_1)}{[(P_0 + P_1)/2]} \times 100$$

Dividing the resulting percentage change in quantity by the percentage change in price gives us the elasticity.

Using substitution, it is possible to derive a version of the elasticity formula that incorporates these two percentage calculations. Because each term is multiplied by 100 and the denominator of each term contains a 2, these factors cancel out of the final expression. After simplification this version is

$$\frac{[(Q_0 - Q_1)/(Q_0 + Q_1)]}{[(P_0 - P_1)/(P_0 + P_1)]}$$

A numerical example will help you understand this. Suppose that Trina's Cakes can sell fifty specialty cakes per week at $7 each, or it can sell seventy specialty cakes per week at $6 each. The percentage difference in quantity is the difference in the quantity demanded $(50 - 70 = -20)$ divided by the midpoint (60) times 100. The result is a -33.33 percent change in quantity $(-20 \div 60 \times 100 = -33.33)$.

Now that we've calculated the percentage change in quantity demanded of cakes, let's calculate the percentage change in the price. The percentage change in price is the difference in the two prices ($7 - $6 = $1) divided by the midpoint price ($6.50) times 100, or a 15.38 percent change in price $(1 \div 6.5 \times 100 = 15.38)$. Dividing the percentage change in quantity by the percentage change in price $(-33.33 \div 15.38)$ gives an elasticity coefficient of -2.17. Alternatively, we could have expressed this directly as

$$\frac{[(50 - 70)/(50 + 70)]}{[(7 - 6)/(7 + 6)]} = \frac{(-20/120)}{(1/13)} = \frac{(-1/6)}{(1/13)} = \frac{-13}{6} = -2.17$$

The same result is obtained either way. The elasticity of 2.17 (ignoring the sign) indicates that the percentage change in quantity is just over twice the percentage change in price.

The elasticity coefficient lets us make a precise distinction between elasticity and inelasticity. When the elasticity coefficient is greater than 1 (ignoring the sign), as it was for the demand for Trina's Cakes, demand is elastic. When it is less than 1, demand is inelastic. Demand is said to be of *unitary elasticity* if the price elasticity is exactly 1.

GRAPHIC REPRESENTATION OF PRICE ELASTICITY OF DEMAND

Exhibit 3 presents demand curves of varying elasticity. A demand curve that is completely vertical is said to be *perfectly inelastic*, shown in part (a) of Exhibit 3. In the real world, such demand does not exist because the substitutes for a good become more attractive as the price of that good rises. Moreover, because of the income effect, we should expect that a higher price will always reduce the quantity demanded, other things remaining the same.

The more inelastic the demand, the steeper the demand curve *over any specific price range*. As you can see, the demand for cigarettes (shown in part b of Exhibit 3) is highly inelastic; a big change in price doesn't change quantity demanded much. People who crave nicotine will be willing to pay the higher price. Conversely, the demand for apples (shown in part d) is relatively elastic. People will find it easy to switch to oranges or bananas, for example, if the price of apples increases dramatically.

Price Elasticity of Demand

Exhibit 3

(a) Perfectly inelastic: Despite an increase in a product's price, consumers still purchase the same amount of it. Substitution and income effects prevent this from happening in the real world, though.

(b) Relatively inelastic: A percentage increase in a product's price results in a smaller percentage reduction in its sales. The demand for cigarettes has been estimated to be highly inelastic.

(c) Unit elastic: The percentage change in quantity demanded of a product is equal to the percentage change in its price. A curve with a decreasing slope results. Sales revenue (price times quantity sold) is constant.

(d) Relatively elastic: A percentage increase in a product's price leads to a larger percentage reduction in purchases of it. When good substitutes are available for a product (as in the case of apples), the amount of it purchased will be highly sensitive to price changes.

(e) Perfectly elastic: Consumers will buy all of Farmer Jones's wheat at the market price, but none will be sold above the market price.

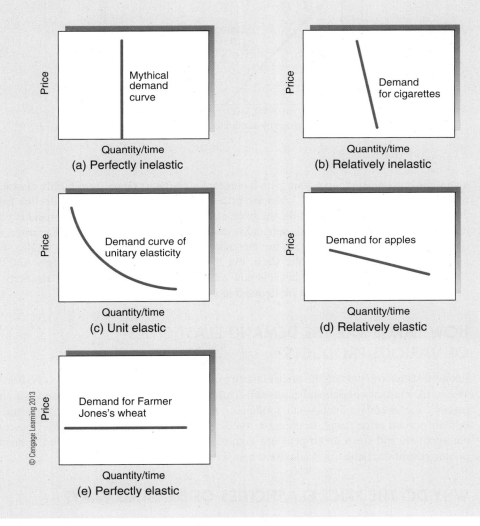

(a) Perfectly inelastic

(b) Relatively inelastic

(c) Unit elastic

(d) Relatively elastic

(e) Perfectly elastic

© Cengage Learning 2013

When demand elasticity is unitary, as part (c) shows, a demand curve that is convex to the origin will result. When a demand curve is completely horizontal, an economist would say that it is *perfectly elastic*. Demand for the wheat marketed by a single wheat farmer, for example, would approximate perfect elasticity (part e).

Because elasticity is a relative concept, the elasticity of a straight-line demand curve will differ at each point along the demand curve. As Exhibit 4 shows, the elasticity of

Exhibit 4

Slope of the Demand Curve versus Price Elasticity

With this straight-line (constant slope) demand curve, demand is more elastic in the high price range. The formula for elasticity shows that, when price rises from $1 to $2 and quantity falls from 110 to 100, demand is inelastic. A price rise of the same magnitude (but of a smaller percentage), from $10 to $11, leads to a decline in quantity of the same size (but of a larger percentage), so that elasticity is much greater. (Price elasticities are negative, but economists often ignore the sign and look only at the absolute value.)

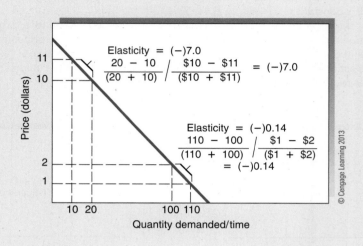

a straight-line demand curve (one with a constant slope) will range from highly elastic to highly inelastic. In this exhibit, when the price rises from $10 to $11, sales decline from 20 to 10. According to the formula, the price elasticity of demand is –7.0. Demand is very elastic in this region. In contrast, demand is quite inelastic in the $1 to $2 price range. As the price increases from $1 to $2, the amount demanded declines from 110 to 100. The ten-unit change in quantity is the same, but it is a smaller *percentage* change. And the $1 change in price is the same, but it is now a larger *percentage* change. The elasticity of demand in this range is only –0.14; demand in this case is highly inelastic.

HOW LARGE ARE THE DEMAND ELASTICITIES OF VARIOUS PRODUCTS?

Economists have estimated the price elasticity of demand for many products. As **Exhibit 5** shows, the elasticity of demand varies substantially among products. The demand is highly inelastic for several products—salt, toothpicks, matches, coffee, and gasoline (short-run)—in their normal price range. In contrast, the demand curves for fresh tomatoes, Chevrolet automobiles, and fresh green peas are highly elastic. The demand for movies, housing, private education, radios, and television sets is near 1.0 (unitary).

WHY DO THE PRICE ELASTICITIES OF DEMAND VARY?

The primary determinants of a product's price elasticity of demand are the availability of good substitutes and to the share of the typical consumer's total budget expended on a product. Let's consider each of these factors.

AVAILABILITY OF SUBSTITUTES

The most important determinant of the price elasticity of demand is the availability of substitutes. When good substitutes for a product are available, a price increase induces

INELASTIC		APPROXIMATELY UNITARY ELASTICITY		Exhibit 5
Salt	– 0.1	Movies	– 0.9	**Estimated Price Elasticity of Demand for Selected Products**
Matches	– 0.1	Housing, owner occupied, long run	– 1.2	
Toothpicks	– 0.1	Shellfish, consumed at home	– 0.9	
Airline travel, short run	– 0.1			
Gasoline, short run	– 0.2	Oysters, consumed at home	– 1.1	
Gasoline, long run	– 0.7	Private education	– 1.1	
Residential natural gas, short run	– 0.1	Tires, short run	– 0.9	
Residential natural gas, long run	– 0.5	Tires, long run	– 1.2	
Coffee	– 0.25	Radio and television receivers	– 1.2	
Fish (cod), consumed at home	– 0.5	ELASTIC		
Tobacco products, short run	– 0.45	Restaurant meals	– 2.3	
Legal services, short run	– 0.4	Foreign travel, long run	– 4.0	
Physician services	– 0.6	Airline travel, long run	– 2.4	
Dental services	– 0.7	Fresh green peas	– 2.8	
Taxi, short run	– 0.6	Automobiles, short run	– 1.2–1.5	
Automobiles, long run	– 0.2	Chevrolet automobiles	– 4.0	
Cigarette consumption, long run, Canada	– 0.3	Fresh tomatoes	– 4.6	
		Hospital care in California	– 4.8	

Sources: Hendrick S. Houthakker and Lester D. Taylor, *Consumer Demand in the United States, 1929–1970* (Cambridge, MA: Harvard University Press, 1966, 1970); Douglas R. Bohi, *Analyzing Demand Behavior* (Baltimore: Johns Hopkins University Press, 1981); Hsaing-tai Cheng and Oral Capps Jr., "Demand for Fish," *American Journal of Agricultural Economics* 70, no. 3 (1988): 533–42; Rexford E. Santerre and Stephen P. Neun, *Health Economics: Theories, Insights and Industry Studies* (Orlando, FL: Harcourt, 2000); Martin Gaynor and William Vogt, "Competition among Hospitals," *The RAND Journal of Economics* (Winter 2003): 764–85; and Nikolay Gospodinov and Ian Irvine, "A 'Long March' Perspective on Tobacco use in Canada," *Canadian Journal of Economics* 38, no. 2 (2005): 366–93.

many consumers to switch to other products. Demand is elastic. For example, if the price of apples increases consumers might substitute oranges or bananas.

When good substitutes for a product are unavailable, the demand for it will tend to be inelastic. Medical services are an example. When we are sick, most of us find witch doctors, faith healers, palm readers, and aspirin to be highly imperfect substitutes for the services of a physician. Not surprisingly, the demand for physician services is inelastic.

The availability of substitutes increases as the product class becomes more specific, thus increasing price elasticity. For example, as Exhibit 5 shows, the price elasticity of Chevrolets, a narrow product class, exceeds that of the broad class of automobiles in general. If the price of Chevrolets alone rises, many substitute cars are available. But if the prices of all automobiles rise together, consumers have fewer good substitutes.

PRODUCT'S SHARE OF THE CONSUMER'S TOTAL BUDGET

If the expenditures on a product are quite small relative to the consumer's budget, the income effect will be small even if there is a substantial increase in the price of the product. This will make demand less elastic. Compared to one's total budget, expenditures on some commodities are minor. Matches, toothpicks, and salt are good examples. Most consumers spend less than a couple of dollars per year on each of these items. A doubling of their price would exert little influence on a family's budget. Therefore, even if the price of such a product were to rise sharply, consumers would still not find it worthwhile to spend much time and effort looking for substitutes.

Exhibit 6 provides a graphic illustration of both elastic and inelastic demand curves. In part (a), the demand curve for fast-food hamburgers is elastic because there are good substitutes—for example, tacos, burritos, salads, chicken, and other sandwiches. Therefore, when the price of the hamburgers increases from $4.00 to $6.00, the quantity purchased declines sharply from 100 million to only 25 million. The calculated price elasticity equals –3.0. The fact that the absolute value of the coefficient is greater than 1 confirms that the demand for hamburgers is elastic over the price range shown.

Part (b) of Exhibit 6 shows the demand curve for cigarettes. Because most smokers do not find other products to be a good substitute, the demand for cigarettes is highly inelastic. As the price of cigarettes increases from $4.00 to $6.00, the number of packs purchased falls by only a small amount (from 100 million to 90 million). The price elasticity coefficient is –0.26, substantially less in absolute value than 1, confirming that the demand for cigarettes is inelastic. (*Exercise:* Use the price elasticity formula to verify the values of these elasticity coefficients.)

TIME AND DEMAND ELASTICITY

As changing market conditions raise or lower the price of a product, both consumers and producers will respond. However, the response will not be instantaneous, and it is likely to become larger over time. *In general, when the price of a product increases, consumers will reduce their consumption by a larger amount in the long run than in the short run. Thus, the demand for most products will be more elastic in the long run than in the short run. This relationship between elasticity and the length of the adjustment period is sometimes referred to as the second law of demand.*

The first law of demand says that buyers will respond predictably to a price change, purchasing more when the price is lower than when the price is higher, if other things remain the same. The second law of demand says that the response of buyers will be greater after they have had time to adjust more fully to a price change.

Exhibit 6

Inelastic and Elastic Demand

As the price of fast-food hamburgers (a) rose from $4 to $6, the quantity purchased fell sharply from 100 million to 25 million. The percentage reduction in quantity is larger than the percentage increase in price. Thus, the demand for the hamburgers is elastic. In contrast, an increase in the price of cigarettes from $4 to $6 leads to only a small reduction in the number of packs purchased (b). Because the percentage reduction in quantity is smaller than the percentage increase in price, demand is inelastic.

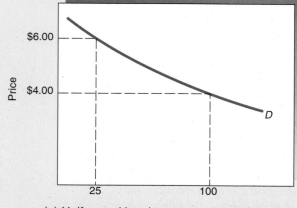

(a) Half-pound hamburgers per week (in millions)

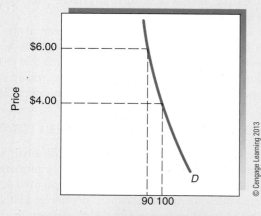

(b) Cigarette packs per week (in millions)

© Cengage Learning 2013

HOW DEMAND ELASTICITY AND PRICE CHANGES AFFECT TOTAL EXPENDITURES (OR REVENUES) ON A PRODUCT

By looking at demand elasticity, we can determine changes in total consumer spending on a product when its price changes. We can do this in three different ways: by looking at (1) changes in an individual's total spending, using the demand elasticity from his or her demand curve for the product; (2) changes in the total combined spending of all consumers, using the elasticity from the total market demand curve; or (3) changes in total consumer spending on the product, using the demand curve facing the firm that produces it. This third method allows us to look at elasticity based not on what consumers spend, but on what the producer receives from selling the product.

Total expenditures (or revenues) simply amount to the price of the product times the number of units of it purchased (or sold). Because total expenditures are equal to the price times the quantity, and because the price and the quantity move in opposite directions, the net effect of a price change on the total spending on a product depends on whether the (percentage) price change or the (percentage) quantity change is greater.

Change in Total Expenditures	=	Price	×	Quantity
?	=	↑	×	↓
?	=	↓	×	↑

When demand is inelastic, the price elasticity coefficient is less than 1. This means that the percentage change in price is greater than the percentage change in quantity. *Therefore, when demand is inelastic, the change in the price will dominate and, as a result, the price and total expenditures will change in the same direction.* In other words, when the price of an inelastic product (say, cigarettes) increases, spending on it will increase, too—and vice versa. Conversely, when demand is elastic, the change in quantity will be greater than the change in the price. *As a result, the impact of the change in quantity will dominate, and therefore the price and expenditures will move in opposite directions.* In other words, when the price of a product with an elastic demand (say, fast-food hamburgers) increases, spending on it will decrease.

When demand elasticity is unitary, the change in quantity demanded will be equal in magnitude to the change in price. With regard to their impact on total expenditures, these two effects will exactly offset each other. *Thus, when price elasticity of demand is equal to 1, total expenditures will remain unchanged as price changes.*

Exhibit 7 summarizes the relationship between changes in the price of a product and changes in total spending on it when demand is elastic, inelastic, and unit elastic. The demand curves shown in Exhibit 6 can also be used to show the link between elasticity and changes in total spending. When the price of cigarettes (part b), increases from $4.00 to $6.00, the price elasticity of demand is 0.26, indicating that demand is inelastic. This

Exhibit 7

Demand Elasticity and How Changes in Price Affect Total Consumer Expenditures or a Firm's Total Revenue

Price Elasticity of Demand	Numerical Elasticity Coefficient (in absolute value)	Impact of Raising Price on Total Consumer Expenditures or a Firm's Total Revenue	Impact of Lowering Price on Total Consumer Expenditures or a Firm's Total Revenue
Elastic	1 to ∞	decrease	increase
Unit Elastic	1	unchanged	unchanged
Inelastic	0 to 1	increase	decrease

© Cengage Learning 2013

increase in cigarette prices leads to an increase in spending on the product from $400 million ($4.00 × 100 million units) to $540 million ($6.00 × 90 million units). If the change had occurred in the opposite direction, with the price falling from $6.00 to $4.00, total expenditures would have declined.

The price elasticity of demand for fast-food hamburgers when the price increases from $4.00 to $6.00 (part a of Exhibit 6) is 3.0, indicating that demand is elastic. In this case, price and expenditures will move in opposite direction. The increase in the price of hamburgers lowers total consumer spending on the product from $400 million ($4.00 × 100 million hamburgers) to $150 million ($6.00 × 25 million hamburgers). If the price change had been in the opposite direction, with the price falling from $6.00 to $4.00, total expenditures would have risen.

When a firm increases the price of its product, its revenues may rise, fall, or remain the same. If the demand for the firm's product is inelastic, the higher price will expand the firm's total revenue. However, if the demand for the firm's product is elastic, a price increase will lead to substantially lower sales and a decline in total revenue. In the case of unitary elasticity, the price increase will leave total revenue unchanged.

Beyond the price elasticity of demand, two other elasticity relationships are important. We therefore end this chapter with a brief discussion of income elasticity of demand and price elasticity of supply.

INCOME ELASTICITY

Increases in consumer income will increase the demand (the quantity demanded at each price) for most goods. Income elasticity tells us how responsive the demand for a product is to income changes. **Income elasticity** is defined as

$$\text{Income elasticity} = \frac{\text{Percentage change in quantity demanded}}{\text{Percentage change in income}}$$

Income elasticity
The percentage change in the quantity of a product demanded divided by the percentage change in consumer income that caused the change in quantity demanded. It measures the responsiveness of the demand for a good to a consumer's change in income.

Normal good
A good that has a positive income elasticity, so that as consumer income rises, demand for the good rises, too.

As **Exhibit 8** shows, although the income elasticity coefficients for products vary from one good to another, they are normally positive. In fact, the term **normal good** refers to any good with a positive income elasticity of demand. Some normal goods have lower income elasticities than others, however. In general, goods that people regard as "necessities" will have low income elasticities (between 0 and 1). Significant quantities are purchased even at low incomes, and, as income increases, spending on these items will increase by less than a proportional amount. It is understandable that items such as fuel, electricity, bread, tobacco, economy clothing, and potatoes have a low income elasticity.

Goods that consumers regard as "luxuries" generally have a high (greater than 1) income elasticity. For example, private education, new automobiles, swimming pools, and

Exhibit 8	LOW-INCOME ELASTICITY		HIGH-INCOME ELASTICITY	
Estimated Income Elasticity of Demand for Selected Products	Margarine	−0.20	Private education	2.46
	Fuel	0.38	New cars	2.45
	Electricity	0.20	Recreation and amusements	1.57
	Fish (haddock)	0.46	Alcohol	1.54
	Food	0.51		
	Tobacco	0.64		
	Hospital care	0.69		

Sources: Hendrick S. Houthakker and Lester D. Taylor, *Consumer Demand in the United States, 1929–1970* (Cambridge, MA: Harvard University Press, 1966); L. Taylor, "The Demand for Electricity: A Survey," *Bell Journal of Economics* 6, no. 1 (1975): 74–110; F. W. Bell, "The Pope and the Price of Fish," *American Economic Review* 58, no. 5 (1968): 1346–50; and Rexford E. Santerre and Stephen P. Neun, *Health Economics: Theories, Insights and Industry Studies* (Orlando, FL: Harcourt, 2000).

vacation travel are all highly income-elastic. As the consumer's income increases, the demand for these goods expands even more rapidly, and therefore spending on these items increases as a proportion of income.

A few commodities, such as margarine, low-quality meat cuts, and bus travel, actually have a negative income elasticity. Economists refer to goods with a negative income elasticity as **inferior goods**. As income expands, the demand for inferior goods will decline. Conversely, as income declines, the demand for inferior goods will increase.

Inferior good
A good that has a negative income elasticity, so that as consumer income rises, the demand for the good falls.

PRICE ELASTICITY OF SUPPLY

The **price elasticity of supply** is the percentage change in quantity supplied, divided by the percentage change in the price causing the supply response. Because this measures the responsiveness of sellers to a change in price, it is analogous to the price elasticity of demand. However, the price elasticity of supply will be positive because the quantity producers are willing to supply is directly related to price. As in demand elasticity, time plays a role. In the next two chapters, we will discuss more fully the factors that determine supply elasticity. For now, it is important simply to recognize the concept of supply elasticity and the fact that suppliers (like buyers) will be more responsive to a price change when they have had more time to adjust to it.

Price elasticity of supply
The percentage change in quantity supplied, divided by the percentage change in the price that caused the change in quantity supplied.

Looking Ahead

Market demand indicates how strongly consumers desire a good or service. In the following chapter, we will turn to a firm's costs of production—costs that arise because resources are demanded for alternative uses. These two topics—consumer demand and the cost of production—are central to understanding how markets work and the conditions necessary for the efficient allocation of resources.

iStockphoto.com/gaspr13

KEY POINTS

- Consumers will try to allocate their limited incomes among a multitude of goods in a way that maximizes their utility. The role of relative prices, information, and preferences, as well as the law of diminishing marginal utility, help explain the choices consumers make and the downward slope of a person's demand curve for products.

- The market demand curve for a product is the horizontal sum of the demand curve of the individuals for the product.

- The price elasticity of demand measures the responsiveness of the quantity of a product purchased to a change in its price.

- The availability of substitutes is the primary determinant of the price elasticity of demand for a product. When there are good substitutes available, and the item is a sizable component of the consumer's budget, its demand will tend to be elastic. When only poor substitutes are available, demand will tend to be inelastic.

- Typically, the price elasticity of a product will increase as consumers have had more time to adjust to a change in its price. This direct relationship between the size of the elasticity coefficient and the length of the adjustment period is often referred to as the *second law of demand*.

- The concept of elasticity helps us determine how a change in price will affect total consumer expenditures on a product or a firm's total revenues derived from it. When the demand for a product is elastic, a price change will cause total spending on it to change in the opposite direction. When demand for a product is inelastic, a change in price will cause total spending on it to change in the same direction.

- The concept of elasticity can also be applied to consumer income (which is called the income elasticity of demand) and supply (which is called the price elasticity of supply).

CRITICAL ANALYSIS QUESTIONS

1. *Suppose that, in an attempt to raise more revenue, Nowhere State University (NSU) increases its tuition. Will this necessarily result in more revenue? Under what conditions will revenue (a) rise, (b) fall, or (c) remain the same? Explain this, focusing on the relationship between the increased revenue from students who enroll at NSU despite the higher tuition and the lost revenue from lower enrollment. If the true price elasticity were −1.2, what would you suggest the university do to expand revenue?

2. *A bus ticket between two cities costs $50 and the trip will take 28 hours, whereas an airplane ticket costs $300 and takes three hours. Mary values her time at $12 per hour, and Michele values her time at $8 per hour. Will Mary take the bus or the plane? Which will Michele take? Explain.

3. *Recent research confirms that the demand for cigarettes is not only inelastic, but it also indicates that smokers with incomes in the lower half of all incomes respond to a given price increase by reducing their purchases by amounts that are more than four times as large as the purchase reductions made by smokers in the upper half of all incomes. How can the income and substitution effects of a price change help explain this finding?

4. A consumer is currently purchasing three pairs of jeans and five T-shirts per year. The price of jeans is $30, and T-shirts cost $10. At the current rate of consumption, the marginal utility of jeans is 60, and the marginal utility of T-shirts is 30. Is this consumer maximizing his or her utility? Would you suggest that he buy more jeans and fewer T-shirts, or more T-shirts and fewer jeans?

5. When residential electricity in the state of Washington cost about half as much as in nearby Montana, the average household in Washington used about 1,200 kilowatt-hours per month, whereas Montanans used about half that much per household. Do these data provide us with two points on the average household's demand curve for residential electricity in this region? Why or why not?

6. *People who are wealthy are widely believed to have more leisure time than people who are poor. However, even though we are a good deal wealthier today than our great-grandparents were 100 years ago, we appear to live more hectic lives and have less free time. Can you explain why?

7. What are the major determinants of a product's price elasticity of demand? Studies indicate that the demand for Florida oranges, Bayer aspirin, watermelons, and airfares to Europe are elastic. Why?

8. Most systems of medical insurance substantially lower the out-of-pocket costs consumers have to pay for additional units of physician services and hospitalization. Some reduce these costs to zero. How does this method of payment affect the consumption levels of medical services? Might this method of organization result in "too much" consumption of medical services? Discuss.

9. *Are the following statements true or false? Explain your answers.
   a. A 10 percent reduction in price that leads to a 15 percent increase in the amount purchased indicates a price elasticity of more than 1.
   b. A 10 percent reduction in price that leads to a 2 percent increase in total expenditures indicates a price elasticity of more than 1.
   c. If the percentage change in price is less than the resultant percentage change in quantity demanded, demand is elastic.

10. *Respond to the following questions: If you really like pizza, should you try to consume as much pizza as possible? If you want to succeed, should you try to make the highest possible grade in your economics class?

11. *Sue loves ice cream but cannot stand frozen-yogurt desserts. In contrast, Carole likes both foods and can hardly tell the difference between the two. Who will have the more elastic demand for yogurt?

12. *Patsy's Specialty Bakery projects the following demand for Patsy's pies:

Price ($)	Quantity Purchased (per Night)
9	130
10	110
11	95

   a. Calculate the price elasticity of demand between $9 and $10. Is demand in this range elastic or inelastic?
   b. Calculate the price elasticity of demand between $10 and $11. Is demand in this range elastic or inelastic?

13. Suppose Bobby, the owner–manager of Bobby's Red Hot BBQ restaurant, projects the following demand for his Baby Back Rib platter:

Price ($)	Quantity Purchased (per Night)
9	110
11	100
13	80

   a. Calculate the price elasticity of demand between $9 and $11.

b. Is the price elasticity of demand between $9 and $11 elastic, unit elastic, or inelastic?

c. Will Bobby's total revenue rise if he increases the price from $9 to $11?

d. Calculate the price elasticity of demand between $11 and $13.

e. Is the price elasticity of demand between $11 and $13 elastic, unit elastic, or inelastic?

f. Will Bobby's total revenue rise if he increases the price from $11 to $13?

*Asterisk denotes questions for which answers are given in Appendix B.

CHAPTER

Costs and the Supply of Goods

CHAPTER FOCUS

- Why are business firms used to organize production? How do market incentives influence the operation of businesses?
- What are explicit and implicit costs, and how do they guide the behavior of the firm?
- How does economic profit differ from accounting profit? Why is this difference important?
- How will increases in output influence the firm's costs in the short run? How will costs vary with output in the long run?
- What are the major factors that would cause the firm's costs to change?

From the standpoint of society as a whole, the "cost" of anything is the value that it has in alternative uses.

—Thomas Sowell[1]

―――――――

[1]Thomas Sowell, *Basic Economics* (New York: Basic Books, 2000), 10.

Demand and supply interact to determine the market price of a product. In the preceding chapter, we showed that the demand for a product reflects the strength of consumer desire for that product. In this chapter, we will focus on the cost of production. The resources needed to produce one good could be used to produce other goods instead. As Thomas Sowell says in the quotation that begins this chapter, the cost to society of anything is the value that it has in alternative uses. The market price for resources makes that cost clear to producers as they must bid resources away from alternative uses. The maker of soccer balls, for example, must compete against producers of other goods when purchasing the machines, raw materials, and labor needed to produce the balls.

Costs carry an important message: They tell producers the value of the resources if left in their alternative uses. If the per-unit cost of producing a good exceeds its price, producers will suffer losses, reduce output, and some may go out of business. Only when a producer can generate enough value for consumers to allow the price to exceed production costs, will the firm be profitable and survive. This chapter lays the foundation for a detailed investigation of the links between costs, business output, and market supply.

THE ORGANIZATION OF THE BUSINESS FIRM

The business firm is an entity designed to organize raw materials, labor, and machines with the goal of producing goods and/or services. Firms (1) purchase productive resources from households and other firms, (2) transform them into a different commodity, and (3) sell the transformed product or service to consumers. In market economies, business firms choose their own price, output level, and methods of production. They not only reap the benefits of sales revenues, but they also must pay the costs of the resources they use.

INCENTIVES, COOPERATION, AND THE NATURE OF THE FIRM

In privately owned firms, owners risk their wealth on the success of the business. If the firm is successful and earns profits, these financial gains go to the owners. Conversely, if the firm suffers losses, the owners must bear the consequences.

The property right of owners to the residual income of the firm plays a very important role: It provides owners with a strong incentive to organize and operate their business in a manner that will maximize the value of their output to consumers while keeping the cost of producing output low. The wealth of these residual claimants is directly influenced by the success or failure of the firm. Thus, they have both the authority and a strong incentive to see that resources under their direction are used efficiently and directed toward production of goods that are valued more highly than their costs.

There are two ways of organizing productive activity: contracting and team production. In principle, all production could be accomplished solely through contracting. For example, a builder might have a house built by contracting with one person to pour the concrete, another to construct the wooden part of the house, a third to install the roofing, a fourth to do the electrical wiring, and so on. No employees would have to be involved in such a project. More commonly, though, goods and services are produced with some combination of contracting and the use of team production.

Team production involves the employment of workers operating under the supervision of the owner, or the owner's representative—a manager. While team production can often reduce transaction costs, it leads to another set of problems. Team members—the employees working for the firm—must be monitored and given incentives to avoid shirking, or working at less than the expected rate of productivity. Taking long work breaks, paying more attention to their own convenience than to work results, and wasting time when

Residual claimants
Individuals who personally receive the excess, if any, of revenues over costs. Residual claimants gain if the firm's costs are reduced or revenues increase.

Team production
A production process in which employees work together under the supervision of the owner or the owner's representative.

Shirking
Working at less than the expected rate of productivity, which reduces output. Shirking is more likely when workers are not monitored, so that the cost of lower output falls on others.

Principal–agent problem
The incentive problem that occurs when the purchaser of services (the principal) lacks full information about the circumstances faced by the seller (the agent) and cannot know how well the agent performs the purchased services. The agent may to some extent work toward objectives other than those sought by the principal paying for the service.

diligence is called for are examples of shirking. Hired managers, even including those at the top, must be monitored and given incentives to avoid shirking.

Imperfect monitoring and imperfect incentives are always a problem with team production. It is part of a larger class of what economists call principal–agent problems. If you have ever taken a car to an auto mechanic, you have confronted this problem. The mechanic wants to get the job done quickly and make as much money as possible. The car owner not only wants to get the job done quickly also, but wants the problem fixed in a lasting way, at the lowest possible cost. Because the mechanic typically knows far more about the job than the customer, it is hard for the customer to monitor the mechanic's work. Therefore, the mechanic (the agent) may not act in the best interest of the customer (the principal).

The owner of a firm is in a similar situation. It is often difficult to monitor the performance of individual employees and motivate them to work together productively. If it is going to keep costs low and the value of output high, a firm must discover and adopt an incentive structure that motivates executives, managers, and workers to cooperate productively and discourages shirking. Ultimately, it is the job of the owners, as residual claimants, to develop an incentive structure that will minimize the principal–agent problem.

THREE TYPES OF BUSINESS FIRMS

Business firms can be organized in one of three ways: as a proprietorship, a partnership, or a corporation. The structure chosen determines how the owners share the risks and liabilities of the firm and how they participate in making decisions.

A **proprietorship** is a business firm owned by a single individual who is fully liable for the debts of the firm. In addition to assuming the responsibilities of ownership, the proprietor often works directly for the firm, providing managerial and other labor services. Many small businesses, including restaurants, barbershops, and farms, are business proprietorships. As Exhibit 1 shows, proprietorships account for 72 percent of the business firms in the United States. Because most proprietorships are small, however, they account for only 4 percent of all business revenues.

A **partnership** consists of two or more people who are co-owners of a business firm. The partners share risks and responsibilities in an agreed-upon manner. There is no difference between a proprietorship and a partnership in terms of owner liability. In both cases, the owners are fully liable for all business debts incurred by the firm. Many law, medical, and accounting

Proprietorship
A business firm owned by an individual who possesses the ownership right to the firm's profits and is personally liable for the firm's debts.

Partnership
A business firm owned by two or more individuals who possess ownership rights to the firm's profits and are personally liable for the debts of the firm.

Exhibit 1

How Business Firms Are Organized

Nearly three out of every four firms are proprietorships, but only 4 percent of all business revenue is generated by proprietorships. Corporations account for about one out of every five firms but generate 82 percent of all revenues.

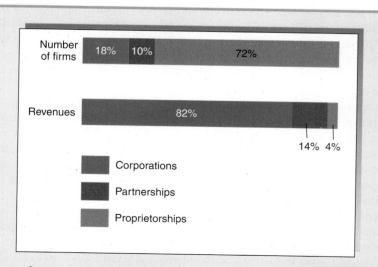

Source: *Statistical Abstract of the United States* (2011), table 744. (Data are for 2007.)

firms are organized along partnership lines. However, this form of business structure accounts for only 10 percent of the total number of firms and 14 percent of all business revenues.

The business firms that are **corporations** account for 82 percent of total business revenue, even though they constitute only 18 percent of all firms. What accounts for the attractiveness of this business structure? From its start, by an act of the British Parliament in 1862, the corporation, or "joint stock company," as it is also called, grew in importance for two main reasons. First, although the stockholders of the corporation are the legal owners, their liability is limited to the value of their shares of the corporation. If a corporation owes you money, you cannot directly sue the stockholders. Of course, you can sue the corporation. However, if a corporation goes bankrupt, you and others to whom the firm owes money may simply be out of luck. This limited liability makes it possible for corporations to attract investment funds from a large number of "owners" who do not participate in the day-to-day management of the firm.

Second, ownership can easily be transferred under the corporate structure. The shares, or ownership rights, of an owner who dies can be sold by the heirs to another owner without disrupting the business firm. Because of this, the corporation is an ongoing concern. Similarly, stockholders who become unhappy with the way a corporation is run can bail out simply by selling their stock.

While there are advantages to the corporate form of business organization, large corporations with many stockholders—millions in some cases—are also more likely to suffer from principal–agent problems. The stockholders elect a board of directors, which in turn appoints the company's high-level managers. Internal corporate policies and competition for control of the firm by outsiders can be used to reduce these principal–agent problems.

Corporation
A business firm owned by shareholders who possess ownership rights to the firm's profits, but whose liability is limited to the amount of their investment in the firm.

COSTS, COMPETITION, AND THE CORPORATION

Three major factors in a market economy promote cost efficiency and customer service within the corporation, limiting the power of corporate managers to shirk on their duties to shareholders.

1. Competition among firms for investment funds and for customers. Even without direct control of their corporation, stockholders (and the investment advisers, pension fund managers, and others hired to help them) have an incentive to monitor the corporation's management in order to anticipate problems and search for constructive changes. Investors who are the first to spot a profitable new management strategy can buy stock early, before others realize the opportunity, and bid the price up. A rising stock price is both a signal of approval to good managers and an incentive to manage the corporation well. Conversely, when managers' decisions are contrary to the interests of stockholders, the opposite occurs: The stock price will fall. Thus, managers get constant feedback via stock price changes, which can be just as important as current profits to stockholders and boards of directors.

Similarly, consumers have an incentive to monitor the quality and price of the firm's output. No one forces them to buy the product of a corporation, so if other firms supply superior products or offer lower prices, consumers can take their business elsewhere. Because investors are free to buy and sell the company's shares and customers to buy its products or those of other firms, the ability of managers to benefit personally at the expense of either customers or stockholders is limited. While some managers are still able to enrich themselves at stockholders' expense, at least temporarily, the recent cases of corporations like Enron, Qwest, and Countrywide show that their actions tend to catch up with them.

2. Compensation and management incentives. The compensation of managers can be structured to bring the interests of managers more into harmony with those of shareholders. Corporations usually tie the compensation of managers to the market success of the business. The salary increases and bonuses of most high-level managers are directly related to the firm's profitability and the price of its shares.

How important are these incentives? In recent years, salaries have constituted only about 10 percent of the compensation of chief executive officers (CEOs). The other 90 percent has been in the form of bonuses, often stock awards and stock options (the right to buy shares at a certain price). Both forms of payment have a "vesting period," which means they will be granted only if the CEO stays with the firm for a certain amount of time and meets specific goals. Policies like these promote shareholders' interests by encouraging corporate managers to maximize the firm's profits and, not coincidentally, the value of its shares.

However, incentive pay can generate an unwanted side effect: the potential for managers to derive personal gain by manipulating the firm's accounting records to make its financial performance look better than it really is. But stockholders and portfolio managers, and especially investors who specialize in selling stocks short when they think the firm is overvalued, will be scrutinizing the records to detect phony accounting designed to mislead investors. In addition, criminal penalties await those found to have participated in fraudulent behavior.

3. The threat of corporate takeover. Managers who do not serve the interests of their shareholders leave the firm vulnerable to a takeover, a move by an outside person or group to gain control of the firm. As we previously noted, shareholders who lose confidence in the firm's management can exit the arrangement by selling their shares. When a significant number of shareholders follow this course of action, the market value of the firm's stock will decline. This will make it an attractive prospect for takeover specialists shopping for a poorly run business, the value of which could be substantially increased by a new and better management team.

Consider a firm currently earning $1.50 per share. At present, the market value of the firm's stock is $15 per share, ten times its earnings. If the firm's earnings are low because the current management team is pursuing its own objectives at the expense of profitability, then a corporate takeover could lead to substantial gain for someone. Suppose outsiders believe they can restructure the firm, improve the management, and double the firm's earnings. They then "tender" a takeover bid—make an offer to buy the shareholders' stock or persuade them to pressure the board of directors to sell out. Suppose they offer $20 per share. This is more than the current market value of the firm, so shareholders and the board will be tempted to accept the offer and gain wealth from the sale. If the takeover team gains control of the firm, improves its performance, and increases its earnings to $3 per share, then the stock value of the firm will rise accordingly (to $30 per share, ten times its higher earnings just as was initially the case).

Of course, the current managers have an incentive to resist the takeover. After all, they are likely to lose their jobs if the potential new owners are successful. Unfortunately for them, though, the shareholders or their board of directors will ultimately decide whether to accept the offer. The takeover threat helps keep current managers from straying too far from a profit maximization strategy.

Corporate managers are more likely to serve the interests of customers and stockholders because of the following: competition for investment funds and consumer sales, the threat of takeover, and managerial compensation packages based on stock and stock options.

Moshe Milner/GPO via Getty Images

HOW WELL DOES THE CORPORATE STRUCTURE WORK?

If the corporate structure were not an effective form of business organization, it would not have continued to survive and be so prevalent today. Rival forms of business organization, including proprietorships, partnerships, consumer cooperatives, employee ownership, and mutually owned companies, can and do compete in the marketplace for investment funds and customers. In certain industries, some of these alternative forms of business organization are dominant. Nonetheless, across the economy, the corporate structure is the dominant form of business organization (see Exhibit 1). This is strong evidence that, despite its defects, the corporation is generally a cost-efficient, consumer-sensitive form of organization.

THE ECONOMIC ROLE OF COSTS

Consumers would like to have more economic goods, but resources to produce them are scarce. How much of each desired good should be produced? In a market economy, consumer demand and production costs are central to performing this balancing function. *The demand for a product represents the voice of consumers instructing firms to produce the good. Conversely, a firm's costs represent the desire of consumers not to sacrifice goods that could be produced if the same resources were employed elsewhere.* A profit-seeking firm will try to produce only those units of output for which buyers are willing to pay full cost. Proper measurement and interpretation of costs by the firm are critical to both the firm's profitability and its efficient use of resources.

CALCULATING ECONOMIC COSTS AND PROFITS

Profit directs the actions of business firms. Profit is simply the firm's total revenue minus its total costs. But to calculate profit correctly, costs must be measured properly. Most people think of costs as amounts paid for raw materials, labor, machines, and similar inputs. However, this concept of cost, which stems from accounting procedures, excludes some important components.

The key to understanding the economist's concept of profit is to remember the idea of *opportunity cost*—the highest valued alternative forgone by the resource owner when the resource is used. These costs may be either explicit or implicit. Explicit costs result when the firm makes a monetary payment to resource owners. Money wages, interest, and rental payments are a measure of what the firm gives up to employ the services of labor and capital resources. These are relatively easy to track. But firms also incur implicit costs—those associated with the use of resources owned by the firm. For example, the owners of small proprietorships often work for their own businesses, for little or no pay. These businesses incur an implicit cost—an opportunity cost—associated with the use of this resource (the owners' labor services). The highest valued alternative forgone in this case is the maximum amount of money the owners could have earned doing something else. The total cost of production is the sum of these explicit and implicit costs incurred by the employment of all resources involved in the production process.

Accounting statements generally omit the implicit cost of equity capital—the cost of funds supplied by the firm's owners. If a firm borrows financial capital from a bank or other private source, it will have to pay interest. Accountants properly record this interest expense as a cost. In contrast, when the firm acquires financial capital by issuing shares of stock, accountants don't record this as an expense. Essentially, this is because the stockholders *are* the firm's owners. Either way, acquiring capital has an opportunity cost. Banks will demand interest payments, and shareholders will expect a return from their investment in the form of dividend payments or rising share value.

Economists use the normal return on financial capital as a basis for determining the implicit opportunity cost of equity capital. If the normal rate of return on financial capital is 10 percent, for example, investors will not continue to supply equity capital unless they can earn this normal return. Thus, it is an opportunity cost of equity capital.

Explicit costs
Payments by a firm to purchase the services of productive resources.

Implicit costs
The opportunity costs associated with a firm's use of resources that it owns. These costs do not involve a direct money payment. Examples include wage income and interest forgone by the owner of a firm who also provides labor services and equity capital to the firm.

Total cost
The costs, both explicit and implicit, of all the resources used by the firm. Total cost includes a normal rate of return for the firm's equity capital.

Opportunity cost of equity capital
The rate of return that must be earned by investors to induce them to supply financial capital to the firm.

HOW DO ECONOMIC AND ACCOUNTING PROFIT DIFFER?

Economic profit
The difference between the firm's total revenues and its total costs, including both the explicit and implicit cost components.

Normal profit rate
Zero economic profit, providing just the competitive rate of return on the capital (and labor) of owners. An above-normal profit will draw more entry into the market, whereas a below-normal profit will lead to an exit of investors and capital.

Accounting profits
The sales revenues minus the expenses of a firm over a designated time period, usually one year. Accounting profits typically make allowances for changes in the firm's inventories and depreciation of its assets. No allowance is made, however, for the opportunity cost of the equity capital of the firm's owners, or other implicit costs.

Economic profit is total revenues minus total costs, including both the explicit and implicit cost components. Economic profit will be positive only if the earnings of the business exceed the opportunity cost of all the resources used by the firm, *including the opportunity cost of assets owned by the firm and any unpaid labor services supplied by the owner.* In contrast, economic losses result when the earnings of the firm are insufficient to cover explicit and implicit costs. That is why the **normal profit rate** is zero economic profit, yielding just the competitive rate of return on the capital (and labor) of owners. A higher rate would draw more competitors and their investors into the market; a lower rate would cause competitors and their investors to exit the market.

Remember, zero economic profits do not imply that the firm is about to go out of business. On the contrary, they indicate that the owners are receiving exactly the normal profit rate, or the competitive market rate of return on their investment.

Whenever accounting procedures omit implicit costs, like those associated with owner-provided labor services or equity capital, the firm's opportunity costs of production will be understated. This understatement of cost leads to an overstatement of profits. Therefore, the **accounting profits** of a firm are generally greater than the firm's economic profits (see the Applications in Economics feature on accounting costs). For most large corporations, though, omitting the implicit costs of services provided by an owner isn't an issue. In this case, the accounting profits approximate the returns to the firm's equity capital. High accounting profits (measured as a rate of return on a firm's assets), relative to those of other firms, suggest that a firm is earning an economic profit. Correspondingly, a low rate of accounting profit implies economic losses. Either positive or negative economic profits, of course, call for a change in output. Such a change, however, will take time.

APPLICATIONS IN ECONOMICS

Economic and Accounting Costs: A Hypothetical Example

The revenue–cost statement for a corner grocery store owned and operated by Emily Blake is presented here.

TOTAL REVENUE	
Sales (groceries)	$170,000
Costs (explicit)	
Groceries, wholesale	$76,000
Utilities	4,000
Taxes	6,000
Advertising	2,000
Labor services (employees)	12,000
Total (explicit) costs	$100,000
Net (accounting) profit	$70,000
Additional (implicit) costs	
Interest (personal investment)	$7,000
Rent (Emily's building)	18,000
Salary (Emily's labor)	50,000
Total (implicit) costs	$75,000
TOTAL EXPLICIT AND IMPLICIT COSTS	$175,000
ECONOMIC PROFIT (TOTAL REVENUE MINUS EXPLICIT AND IMPLICIT COSTS)	–$5,000

Emily works full-time as the manager, chief cashier, and janitor. She has $140,000 worth of refrigeration and other equipment invested in the store. Last year, her total sales were $170,000, and suppliers and employees were paid $100,000. Emily's revenues therefore exceeded explicit costs by $70,000. This is what was recorded on the accounting statements as profit.

But did Emily really make a profit last year? Let's look at her opportunity costs and see: If Emily didn't have $140,000 of her own money invested in equipment, she could be earning 5 percent interest on the money in the bank, which would add up to $7,000 each year. Similarly, if the building she owns weren't being used as a grocery store, it could be rented to someone else for $1,500 per month. Rental income forgone is therefore $18,000 per year. In addition, because Emily is tied up working in the grocery store, a $50,000 managerial position she could hold at another local grocery store is forgone. Considering the interest, rental, and salary income that Emily had to forgo to operate the grocery store last year, her implicit costs were $75,000. This makes her total costs—both explicit and implicit—$175,000. (Recall that explicit costs were $100,000.) That's $5,000 *less* than her actual revenues of $170,000. As a result, Emily incurred an economic loss of $5,000, despite the accounting profit of $70,000 recorded on the store's books.

SHORT-RUN AND LONG-RUN TIME PERIODS

Time plays an important role in the production process. All of a firm's resources can be expanded (or contracted) over time, but for specialized equipment, expanding (and contracting) availability quickly is likely to be very expensive or even impossible. Economists often speak of the **short run** as a time period so short that the firm is unable to alter its present plant size. In the short run, the firm is typically stuck with its existing plant and heavy equipment. These assets are "fixed" for a given time period, in other words. The firm can alter output, however, by applying larger or smaller amounts of "variable" resources, like labor and raw materials. In this way, the existing plant capacity can be used more or less intensively in the short run.

How long is the short run? The short run is that period of time during which at least one factor of production, usually the size of the firm's plant, cannot be changed. The length varies across industries and firms. A trucking firm might be able to hire more drivers and buy or rent more trucks and double its hauling capacity in a few months. In other industries, particularly those that use assembly lines and mass-production techniques, increasing production capacity may take several years.

The **long run** is a time period long enough for existing firms to alter the size of their plants and for new firms to enter (or exit) the market. All of the firm's resources are variable in the long run. In the long run, firms can expand their output by increasing the sizes of their plants—perhaps by adding on to them or by constructing entirely new facilities.

An example may help you understand the distinction between the short- and long-run time periods: If a battery manufacturer hired 200 additional workers and ordered more raw materials in order to squeeze more production out of its existing plant, it would be making a short-run adjustment. In contrast, if the manufacturer built an additional plant (or expanded the size of its current facility) and installed additional heavy equipment, it would be making a long-run adjustment.

Short run (in production)
A time period so short that a firm is unable to vary some of its factors of production. The firm's plant size typically cannot be altered in the short run.

Long run (in production)
A time period long enough to allow the firm to vary all of its factors of production.

CATEGORIES OF COSTS

In the short run, we can break a firm's costs into two categories—fixed and variable. Each category of costs behaves differently. Seeing that behavior graphically will help us understand how the profit-maximizing level of the firm's output is determined. It will also be important to distinguish between a firm's total costs and its per-unit costs, which we call "average" costs.

Each of the firm's fixed costs, and their sum, called **total fixed cost** (*TFC*), will remain unchanged when output rises or falls in the short run. For example, a firm's insurance premiums; its property taxes; and, most significantly, the opportunity cost of using its fixed assets will be present whether the firm produces a large or small amount of output. These costs will not vary with output. They can be avoided only if the firm goes out of business.

What will happen to **average fixed cost** (*AFC*), which is fixed cost *per unit*, as output expands? Remember that the firm's fixed cost will be the same whether output is 1, or 100, or 1,000. The *AFC* is simply fixed cost divided by output. As output increases, *AFC* declines because the fixed cost will be spread over more and more units (see part a of **Exhibit 2**).

Some costs vary with output. For example, additional output can usually be produced by hiring more workers and buying more raw materials. The sum of those and other costs that rise as output increases is the firm's **total variable cost** (*TVC*). At any given level of output, the firm's **average variable cost** (*AVC*), which is variable cost *per unit*, is the total variable cost divided by output.

A firm's total cost (*TC*) is the sum of the fixed and variable costs. At zero output a firm has no variable costs, thus total cost will be equal to total fixed cost. As output expands from zero, variable costs begin to increase, causing total cost to rise with output even though fixed costs are remaining unchanged. **Average total cost** (*ATC*), sometimes referred to as unit cost, can be found by dividing total cost by the total number of units produced. *ATC* is also equal to the sum of the average fixed and average variable costs. One way to look at ATC is that it is the amount of revenue needed per unit of output to cover total cost.

The economic way of thinking focuses on what happens "at the margin." How much does it cost to produce an additional unit? **Marginal cost** (*MC*) is the change in total

Total fixed cost
The sum of the costs that do not vary with output. They will be incurred as long as a firm continues in business and the assets have alternative uses.

Average fixed cost
Total fixed cost divided by the number of units produced. It always declines as output increases.

Total variable cost
The sum of those costs that rise as output increases. Examples of variable costs are wages paid to workers and payments for raw materials.

Average variable cost
The total variable cost divided by the number of units produced.

Average total cost
Total cost divided by the number of units produced. It is sometimes called per-unit cost.

Marginal cost
The change in total cost required to produce an additional unit of output.

Exhibit 2

The General Characteristics of Short-Run Cost Curves

Average fixed costs (a) will be high for small rates of output, but they will always decline as output expands. Marginal cost (b) will rise sharply as the plant approaches its production capacity, q. As graph (c) shows, ATC will be a U-shaped curve because AFC will be high for small rates of output, and MC will be high as the plant's production capacity is approached.

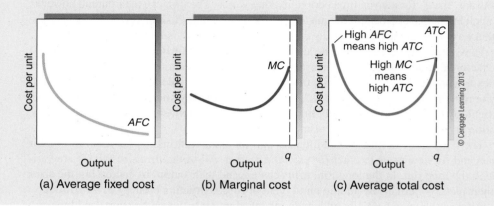

(a) Average fixed cost   (b) Marginal cost   (c) Average total cost

© Cengage Learning 2013

cost that results from the production of one additional unit. The profit-conscious decision-maker recognizes *MC* as the addition to cost that must be covered by additional revenue if producing the marginal unit is to be profitable. In the short run, as illustrated by part (b) of Exhibit 2, *MC* will generally decline at first if output is increased, reach a minimum, and then increase. The rising *MC* simply reflects the fact that it becomes increasingly difficult to squeeze additional output from a plant as the facility's maximum capacity (the dotted line of part b of Exhibit 2) is approached. The accompanying **Thumbnail Sketch** summarizes how the firm's various costs are related to one another.

Thumbnail Sketch

Compact Glossary on Cost

Term	Symbol	Equation	Definition
Fixed cost			Cost that is independent of the output level
Variable cost			Cost that varies with the output level
Total fixed cost	TFC		Cost of the fixed inputs (equals sum of quantity times unit price for each fixed input)
Total variable cost	TVC		Cost of the variable inputs (equals sum of quantity times unit price for each variable input)
Total cost	TC	$TC = TFC + TVC$	Cost of all inputs (equals fixed costs plus variable costs)
Marginal cost	MC	$MC = \Delta TC \div \Delta q$	Change in total cost resulting from a one-unit rise in output (q) [equals the change in total cost divided by the change in output]
Average fixed cost	AFC	$AFC = TFC \div q$	Total fixed cost per unit of output (equals total fixed cost divided by total output)
Average variable cost	AVC	$AVC = TVC \div q$	Total variable cost per unit of output (equals total variable cost divided by total output)
Average total cost	ATC	$ATC = AFC + AVC$	Total cost per unit of output (equals average fixed cost plus average variable cost)

OUTPUT AND COSTS IN THE SHORT RUN

As a firm changes its rate of output in the short run, how will its unit cost be affected? In the short run, the firm can vary its output by using its fixed plant size more (or less) intensively. Exhibit 2 shows two ways that this can result in high unit costs. First, when the output rate of a plant is small relative to its capacity, the facility is being underutilized, causing *AFC* to be high and *ATC* to be high, too. It will be costly to operate a large plant, with its high fixed costs, substantially below its production capacity. Alternatively, overutilization can also cause high unit costs. An overutilized plant will mean congestion—time spent by workers waiting for machines and similar costly delays. Requiring output beyond the least-cost, or designed, output level of a plant will lead to high *MC* and therefore to high *ATC*.

*Thus, the **ATC** curve will be U-shaped, as pictured in part (c) of Exhibit 2. **ATC** will be high for both an underutilized plant and an overutilized plant. It will be high for an underutilized plant because average fixed cost will be high. It will be high for an overutilized plant because marginal cost will be high.*

DIMINISHING RETURNS AND PRODUCTION IN THE SHORT RUN

Our analysis of the changes in unit cost as the output rate rises reflects a long-established economic law. This **law of diminishing returns** states that, as more and more units of a variable factor are applied to a fixed amount of other resources, output will eventually increase by smaller and smaller amounts. Therefore, the impact on output of additional units of the variable factor will diminish. The cost per unit of adding the variable factor may be the same, but the added output per dollar spent falls. The impact on cost per unit of output is clear: When the returns to the variable factor are rising, marginal costs (the additions to total variable cost needed to add a unit of output) are falling. Similarly, when the returns to the variable factor are falling, marginal cost is rising.

The law of diminishing returns is as famous in economics as the law of gravity is in physics. It is based on common sense and real-life observation. Have you ever noticed that as you apply a single resource more intensively, the resource eventually tends to accomplish less and less? Consider a wheat farmer who applies fertilizer (a variable resource) more and more intensively to an acre of land (a fixed factor). At some point, the application of additional 100-pound units of fertilizer will expand the wheat yield by successively smaller amounts.

Essentially, the law of diminishing returns is a constraint imposed by nature. If it were not valid, it would be possible to raise all the world's food in a flowerpot. We would be able to increase output simply by applying another unit of labor and fertilizer to the world's most fertile flowerpot! In the real world, of course, this is not the case; the law of diminishing returns is valid, reflecting a constraint we all must face.

Exhibit 3 illustrates the law of diminishing returns numerically. Column 1 indicates the quantity of the variable resource, labor in this example, which is combined with a specified amount of the fixed resource. Column 2 shows the **total product** that will result as the utilization rate of labor increases. Column 3 provides data on the **marginal product**, the change in total output associated with each additional unit of labor. Without the application of labor, output will be zero. As additional units of labor are applied, total product (output) rises. As the first three units of labor are applied, total product increases by successively larger amounts (8, then 12, then 14). Beginning with the fourth unit, however, diminishing returns are confronted. When the fourth unit of labor is added, marginal product—the change in the total product—declines to 12 (down from 14, when the third unit was applied). As additional units of labor are applied, marginal product continues to decline. It is increasingly difficult to squeeze a larger total product from the fixed resources (for example, plant size and equipment). Eventually, marginal product becomes negative (beginning with the tenth unit).

Column 4 of Exhibit 3 provides data for the **average product** of labor, which is simply the total product divided by the units of labor applied. Note that the average product increases as long as the marginal product is greater than the average product. Whenever the marginal unit's contribution is greater than the average, it must cause the average to rise.

Law of diminishing returns
The postulate that as more and more units of a variable resource are combined with a fixed amount of other resources, using additional units of the variable resource will eventually increase output only at a decreasing rate. Once diminishing returns are reached, it will take successively larger amounts of the variable factor to expand output by one unit.

Total product
The total output of a good that is associated with each alternative utilization rate of a variable input.

Marginal product
The increase in the total product resulting from a unit increase in the employment of a variable input. Mathematically, it is the ratio of the change in total product to the change in the quantity of the variable input.

Average product
The total product (output) divided by the number of units of the variable input required to produce that output level.

	Exhibit 3	(1) UNITS OF THE VARIABLE RESOURCE, LABOR (PER DAY)	(2) TOTAL PRODUCT (OUTPUT)	(3) MARGINAL PRODUCT	(4) AVERAGE PRODUCT
The Law of Diminishing Returns (Hypothetical Data)		0	0		—
		1	8	8	8.0
		2	20	12	10.0
		3	34	14	11.3
		4	46	12	11.5
		5	56	10	11.2
		6	64	8	10.7
		7	70	6	10.0
		8	74	4	9.3
		9	75	1	8.3
		10	73	−2	7.3

© Cengage Learning 2013

(A good analogy would be your grade point average. If the grade you get in this course is higher than your overall grade point average, your grade in this class will increase your overall average.) Here, marginal product rises through the first four units. The marginal product of the fifth unit of labor, though, is 10, less than the average product for the first four units of labor (11.5). Therefore, beginning with the fifth unit, the average product declines as additional labor is applied. When marginal productivity is below the average, it brings down the average product.

Using the data from Exhibit 3, Exhibit 4 illustrates the law of diminishing returns graphically. Initially, the total product curve (part a) increases quite rapidly. As diminishing marginal returns are confronted (beginning with the fourth unit of labor), total product increases more slowly. Eventually, a maximum output (75) is reached with the application of the ninth unit of labor. The marginal product curve (part b) reflects the total product curve. Geometrically, marginal product is the slope—the rate of increase—of the total product curve. That slope, the marginal product, reaches its maximum here with the application of three units of labor. Beyond three units, diminishing returns are present. Eventually, at ten units of labor, the marginal product becomes negative. When marginal product becomes negative, total product is necessarily declining. The average product curve rises as long as the marginal product curve is above it, because each added unit of labor is raising the average. The average product reaches its maximum at four units of labor. Beyond that, each additional unit of labor brings down the average product, and the curve slopes downward.

DIMINISHING RETURNS AND THE SHAPE OF THE COST CURVES

What impact will diminishing returns have on a firm's costs? Once a firm confronts diminishing returns, larger and larger additions of the variable factor are required to expand output by one unit. This will cause marginal cost (MC) to rise. As MC continues to increase, eventually it will exceed average total cost. Until that point, MC is below ATC, bringing ATC down. When MC is greater than ATC, the additional units cost more than the average, and ATC must increase. Think about what happens when you get a grade on an exam above your current class average. Your class average goes up. What happens if a unit of above-average cost is added to output? Average total cost rises. The firm's *MC* curve therefore crosses the *ATC* curve at the *ATC*'s lowest point. For output rates beyond the minimum *ATC*, the rising *MC* causes *ATC* to increase.

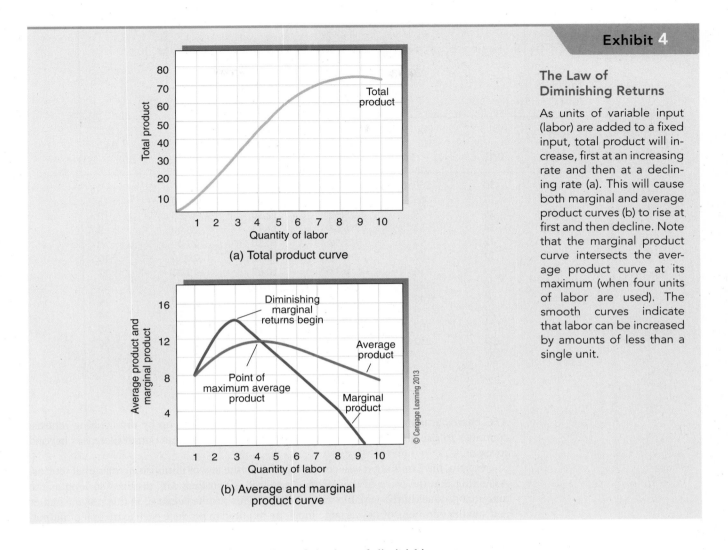

Exhibit 4

The Law of Diminishing Returns

As units of variable input (labor) are added to a fixed input, total product will increase, first at an increasing rate and then at a declining rate (a). This will cause both marginal and average product curves (b) to rise at first and then decline. Note that the marginal product curve intersects the average product curve at its maximum (when four units of labor are used). The smooth curves indicate that labor can be increased by amounts of less than a single unit.

Exhibit 5 numerically illustrates the effect of the law of diminishing returns on a firm's short-run cost curve. Here, we assume that Royal Roller Blades, Inc., combines units of a variable input with a fixed factor to produce units of output (pairs of inline skates). Columns 2, 3, and 4 indicate how the total cost schedules vary as output is expanded. Total fixed costs (TFC), representing the opportunity cost of the fixed factors of production, are $50 per day at all levels of output. For the first four units of output, total variable costs (TVC) increase at a decreasing rate—by $15 with the production of the first unit, $10 with the production of the second unit, $9 with the third, and so on. Why? In this range, there are increasing returns to the variable input. Beginning with the fifth unit of output, however, diminishing marginal returns are present. From this point on, TVC and TC increase by successively larger amounts as output is expanded.

Columns 5 through 8 of Exhibit 5 are the average and marginal cost schedules. For small output rates, the ATC of producing roller blades is high, primarily because of the high AFC. Initially, MC is less than ATC, so ATC is falling. When diminishing returns set in for output rates beginning with five units, however, MC rises. Beginning with the sixth unit of output, MC exceeds AVC, causing AVC to rise. Beginning with the eighth unit of output, MC exceeds ATC, causing it also to rise. ATC thus reaches its minimum at seven units of output. Look carefully at the data of Exhibit 5 to be sure that you fully understand the relationships among the various cost curves. Do you understand how columns 4 to 8 are derived from columns 1 to 3?

Using the numeric data of Exhibit 5, Exhibit 6 graphically illustrates the total, the average, and the marginal cost curves. Note that the MC curve intersects both the AVC and

Exhibit 5   The Numerical Short-Run Cost Schedules of Royal Roller Blades, Inc.

	TOTAL COST DATA (PER DAY)			AVERAGE/MARGINAL COST DATA (PER DAY)			
(1) OUTPUT PER DAY	(2) TFC	(3) TVC	(4) TC (2) + (3)	(5) AFC (2) ÷ (1)	(6) AVC (3) ÷ (1)	(7) ATC (4) ÷ (1)	(8) MC Δ(4) ÷ Δ(1)
0	$50	$0	$50	—	—	—	—
1	50	15	65	$50.00	$15.00	$65.00	$15
2	50	25	75	25.00	12.50	37.50	10
3	50	34	84	16.67	11.33	28.00	9
4	50	42	92	12.50	10.50	23.00	8
5	50	52	102	10.00	10.40	20.40	10
6	50	64	114	8.33	10.67	19.00	12
7	50	79	129	7.14	11.29	18.43	15
8	50	98	148	6.25	12.25	18.50	19
9	50	122	172	5.56	13.56	19.11	24
10	50	152	202	5.00	15.20	20.20	30
11	50	202	252	4.55	18.36	22.91	50

© Cengage Learning 2013

ATC curves at their minimum points (part b). As *MC,* driven up by diminishing returns, continues to rise above *ATC,* unit costs rise higher and higher as output increases beyond seven units.

In sum, the firm's short-run cost curves reflect the law of diminishing marginal returns. Assuming that the price of the variable resource is constant, *MC* declines so long as the marginal product of the variable input is rising. This results because, in this range, smaller and smaller additions of the variable input are required to produce each extra unit of output. The situation is reversed, however, when diminishing returns are confronted. Once diminishing returns set in, more and more units of the variable factor are required to generate each additional unit of output. *MC* will rise because the marginal product of the variable resource is declining. Eventually, *MC* exceeds *AVC* and *ATC,* causing these costs also to rise. A U-shaped, short-run average total cost curve results.

OUTPUT AND COSTS IN THE LONG RUN

The short-run analysis relates costs to output *for a specific size of plant.* Firms, though, are not committed forever to their existing plants. In the long run, all resources used by the firm are variable, thus there are no long-run fixed costs.

How will the firm's choice of plant size affect per-unit production costs? **Exhibit 7** illustrates the short-run *ATC* curves for three different plant sizes, ranging from small to large. If these three plant sizes were the only possible choices, which one should the firm choose as it plans for the future? The answer depends on the rate of output the firm expects to produce from the plant. The smallest plant would have the lowest cost if an output rate of less than q_1 were produced. The medium-size plant would provide the least cost method of producing output rates between q_1 and q_2. For any output level greater than q_2, the largest plant would be the most cost efficient.

*The long-run **ATC** curve shows the minimum average cost of producing each output level when the firm is free to choose among all possible plant sizes. It can best be thought of as a planning curve because it reflects the expected per-unit cost of producing alternative rates of output while plants are still in the blueprint stage.*

Costs in the Short Run

Exhibit 6

Using data from Exhibit 5, this exhibit shows the general shape of the firm's short-run total cost curves (a), and average and marginal cost curves (b). Note that when output is small (for example, two units), ATC will be high because the AFC is so high. Similarly, when output is large (for example, eleven units), per-unit cost (ATC) will be high because additional units will be extremely costly to produce at this point. Thus, the short-run ATC curve will be U-shaped.

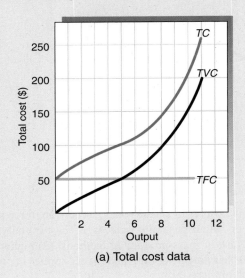

(a) Total cost data

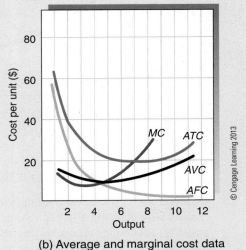

(b) Average and marginal cost data

© Cengage Learning 2013

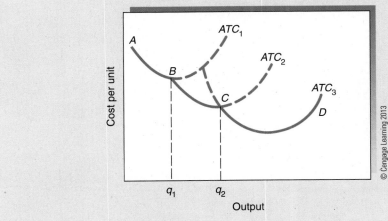

© Cengage Learning 2013

Exhibit 7

Long-Run Average Total Cost

The short-run average total cost curves are shown for three alternative plant sizes. If these three were the only possible plant sizes, the long-run average total cost curve would be *ABCD*.

Exhibit 7 illustrates the long-run *ATC* curve when only three plant sizes are possible, and the planning curve *ABCD* is thus mapped out. Of course, given sufficient time, firms can usually choose among many plants of various sizes. Exhibit 8 presents the long-run planning curve under these circumstances. It is a smooth curve, with each short-run *ATC* curve tangent to it.

It is important to keep in mind that no single plant size could produce the alternative output rates at the costs indicated by the planning curve *LRATC* in Exhibit 8. Any of the planning curve options are, of course, available to the firm before a plant size is chosen and the plant is built. But it can *operate* in the short run only *after* a plant size has been chosen and put in place. The *LRATC* curve outlines the *possibilities* available in the planning stage. It shows the expected output and average total costs of production for the firm depending on the plant size it chooses.

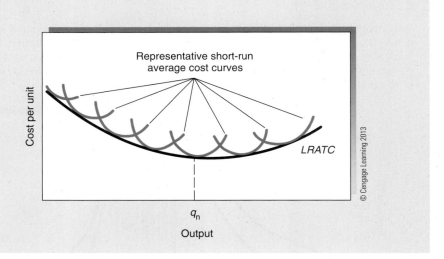

Exhibit 8

The Planning Curve (LRATC)

When many different plant sizes are possible, the long-run average total cost curve (*LRATC*) can be mapped out. When firms are able to plan large volumes of output, using mass-production methods will generally lead to lower per-unit costs. This helps explain why the *LRATC* has a downward-sloping portion.

ECONOMIES AND DISECONOMIES OF SCALE

Do larger firms have lower minimum unit costs than smaller ones?[2] There are three major reasons why planning a larger volume of output generally reduces, at least initially, unit costs: (1) economies accompanying the use of mass-production methods, (2) higher productivity as a result of specialization and "learning by doing," and (3) economies in promotion and purchasing.[3] Let's consider each of these factors.

Mass-production methods can often reduce average costs for firms planning higher output volumes.

---

[2]Throughout this section, we assume that firms with larger plants necessarily plan a larger volume of output than do their smaller counterparts. Reality approximates these conditions. Firms choose large plants because they are planning to produce a large volume.

[3]Note the distinction between rate and volume of output. Rate of output is the number of units produced during a specific period (for example, the next six months). Volume is the total number of units produced during all time periods. For example, Boeing might produce two 787 airplanes per month (rate of output) while planning to produce a volume of two hundred 787s during the expected life of the model. Increasing the rate (reducing the time period during which a given output is produced) tends to raise costs, whereas increasing the volume (total amount produced) tends to lower costs per unit.

Mass-production techniques usually are economical only when large volumes of output are planned, because they tend to involve large development and setup costs. Once the production methods are established, though, marginal costs are low. For example, the use of molds, dies, and assembly line production methods reduce the per-unit cost of automobiles only when the planned volume of output is in the millions. High-volume methods, although cheaper to use for high rates of output and high volumes, will typically require high fixed costs and therefore cause unit costs to be far higher for low volumes of production.

Large-scale operation also allows the specialized use of labor and machines. In a giant auto plant, hundreds of different jobs must be done, and many of them require a training period for each worker. In a small plant, a single worker might do ten or twenty of these jobs, so each worker would have a much longer, more costly training period. Even then, the worker doing so many tasks might never fully develop the same level of proficiency of the more specialized worker. Baseball players improve by playing baseball, and pianists by playing the piano. Similarly, the employees of a firm improve their skills as they experience "learning by doing" in their jobs. Even better, concentration on a narrower range of tasks can help workers discover or develop cost-reducing techniques. The result of greater size and specialization is often more output per unit of labor.

Large firms are also able to achieve lower costs by spreading fixed costs (like the costs of advertising, developing specialized equipment, and searching out and negotiating better input prices, for example) over many more units. For example, both McDonald's and General Motors are able to spread these costs over a large number of stores and volume of sales. The cost advantages of scale come in many forms.

Economic theory explains why, at least initially, larger firms have lower unit costs than comparable smaller firms. Declining unit costs mean that **economies of scale** are present over the initial range of outputs. The long-run *ATC* curve is falling.

What about *dis*economies of scale? As output continues to expand, is there reason to believe that larger firms will eventually have higher average total costs than smaller ones? The underlying causes of diseconomies of scale are less obvious, but they do occur. As a firm gets bigger and bigger, beyond some point bureaucratic inefficiencies *may* result. Inflexible procedures tend to replace managerial genius. Innovation requires clearance from more levels of management and becomes more difficult and costly. Motivating the workforce, carrying out managerial directives, and monitoring results of plans are also more complex when the firm is larger, and principal–agent problems grow as the number of employees increases and more levels of communication and monitoring are needed.

Circumstances vary, so diseconomies of scale set in at smaller firm sizes for some kinds of firms than for others. For example, firms in the fast-food industry can be very large and remain efficient; economies of scale apparently outweigh the diseconomies, even for giants like McDonald's. But in the fine-dining segment of the restaurant industry, the best restaurants seem to be small. Customers demand individual attention, and a constantly changing, innovative menu that takes advantage of the continually changing array of locally available fresh ingredients—with consistently high quality as the only constant—is important. There are few truly gourmet restaurant chains because diseconomies seem to set in at a much smaller size at these firms. The bottom line for diseconomies of scale is this: For some firms, bureaucratic inefficiencies, principal–agent problems, difficulties with innovation, and similar problems that increase with firm size cause long-run average total costs to rise beyond some output level. However, there is considerable variation among industries and even among firms in the same industry concerning the precise output level at which diseconomies of scale begin to occur.

Economies of scale
Reductions in the firm's per–unit costs associated with the use of large plants to produce a large volume of output.

The consistently high quality of gourmet restaurants like 18 Seaboard in Raleigh, North Carolina, can seldom be duplicated by chain restaurants, in part because a gourmet chef must make decisions daily about which locally available fresh ingredients will be used and how they will be used to produce a constantly innovative menu, delivered by an attentive and dedicated staff. Thus, diseconomies of scale limit the size of firms like 18 Seaboard.

Rick Stroup/18 Seaboard

It is important to note that scale economies and diseconomies stem from sources different from those of increasing and diminishing returns. ***Economies and diseconomies of scale are long-run concepts. They relate to conditions of production when all factors are variable. In contrast, increasing and diminishing returns are short-run concepts, applicable only when the firm has at least one fixed factor of production.***

ALTERNATIVE SHAPES OF THE *LRATC*

Exhibit 9 outlines three different long-run average total cost (*LRATC*) curves, each describing real-world conditions in differing industries. For a firm described by the cost curve in part (a), both economies and diseconomies of scale are present. Higher per-unit costs will result if the firm chooses a plant size other than the one that minimizes the cost of producing output *q*. If each firm in an industry faces the same cost conditions, we can generalize and say that all plants larger or smaller than this ideal size will experience higher unit costs. A very narrow range of plant sizes would be expected in industries with the *LRATC* depicted by part (a). Some agricultural products and retail lines approximate these conditions.

Part (b) demonstrates the general shape of the *LRATC* that economists believe is present in most industries. Initially, economies of scale exist, but once a minimum efficient scale is reached, wide variation in firm size is possible. Firms smaller than the minimum efficient size would have higher per-unit costs, but firms larger than that would not gain a cost advantage. Constant returns to scale are present for a broad range of output rates (between q_1 and q_2), in other words. This situation is consistent with real-world conditions in many industries. For example, small firms can be as efficient as larger ones in the apparel, lumber, and publishing industries, as well as in several retail industries.

In part (c) of Exhibit 9, economies of scale exist for all relevant output levels. The larger the firm size, the lower the per-unit cost. The *LRATC* for local telephone service can approximate the curve shown here.

Constant returns to scale
Unit costs that are constant as the scale of the firm is altered. Neither economics nor diseconomies of scale are present.

WHAT FACTORS CAUSE COST CURVES TO SHIFT?

When we drew the general shapes of a firm's cost curves in both the long run and short run, we assumed that certain other factors—resource prices, taxes, regulations, and technology—remained constant as the firm altered its rate of output. Let's now consider how changes in these factors affect the firm's costs.

PRICES OF RESOURCES

If the price of resources used should rise, the firm's cost curves will shift upward, as Exhibit 10 shows. Higher resource prices will increase the cost of producing each alternative output level. For example, what happens to the cost of producing automobiles when the price of steel rises? The cost of producing automobiles also rises. Conversely, lower resource prices will reduce costs and shift the cost curves downward at each level of output.

TAXES

Taxes are a component of a firm's cost. Suppose that an excise tax of 20 cents were levied on the seller for each gallon of gasoline sold. What would happen to the seller's costs? They would increase, just as they did in Exhibit 10. The firm's average total and marginal cost curves would shift upward by the amount of the tax. If the tax were an annual business license fee instead, it would raise the average cost, but not the variable cost. Can you explain why?

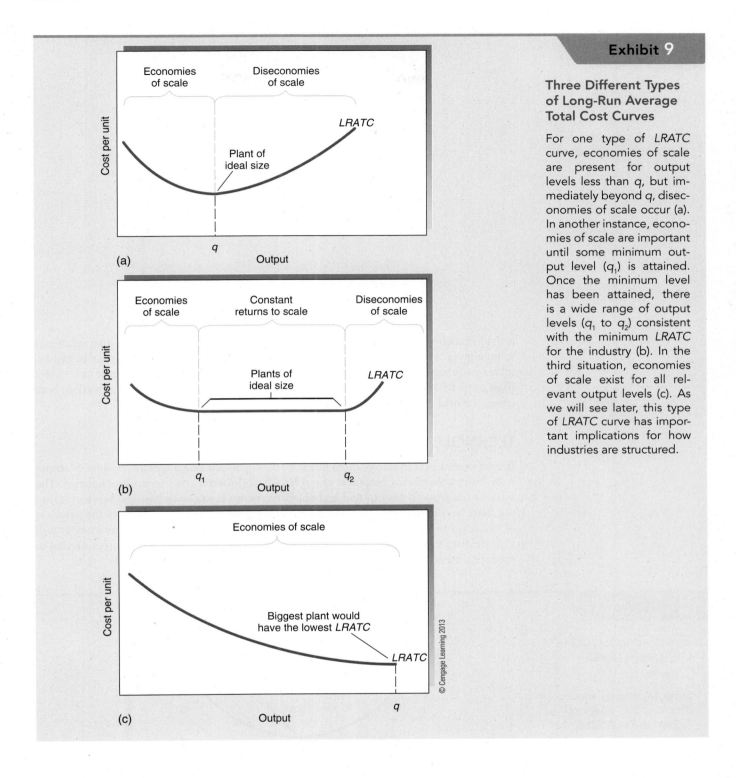

© Cengage Learning 2013

Exhibit 9

Three Different Types of Long-Run Average Total Cost Curves

For one type of *LRATC* curve, economies of scale are present for output levels less than *q*, but immediately beyond *q*, diseconomies of scale occur (a). In another instance, economies of scale are important until some minimum output level (q_1) is attained. Once the minimum level has been attained, there is a wide range of output levels (q_1 to q_2) consistent with the minimum *LRATC* for the industry (b). In the third situation, economies of scale exist for all relevant output levels (c). As we will see later, this type of *LRATC* curve has important implications for how industries are structured.

REGULATIONS

The government often imposes health, safety, environmental, and production regulations on business firms. Regulations might require businesses to provide a certain number of water fountains and restrooms for customers and workers. Federal regulations under the Americans with Disabilities Act compel many firms to make their facilities accessible to people in wheelchairs. Other regulations force firms to build certain features into their products. Strong bumpers and air bags in automobiles are examples. Although regulations

Exhibit 10

Higher Resource Prices and Cost

An increase in resource prices will cause the firm's cost curves to shift upward.

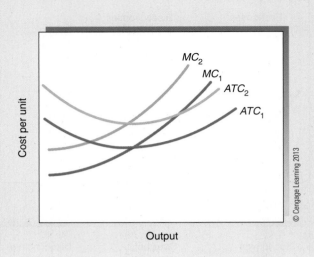

provide benefits, they are also costly. Just processing the paperwork that must be submitted to regulators is costly, and so are the compulsory changes themselves. Like tax increases, increases in regulatory compliance costs will shift cost curves upward. In some cases, only fixed costs will be affected; in other instances, variable costs will be altered as well. In both cases, the firm's *ATC* will be higher.

TECHNOLOGY

Improvements in technology often make it possible to produce a specific amount of output with fewer resources. Computers and robots have lowered costs in many industries. The Internet has made it easy to find and outsource many business-to-business services, ranging from building maintenance and bookkeeping to software development to the purchase of manufacturing components. As **Exhibit 11** shows, a technological improvement will shift the firm's cost curves downward, reflecting the lower amount of resources needed to produce different levels of output.

Exhibit 11

Egg Production Costs and Technological Change

Suppose an egg producer discovers (or develops) a "super" mineral water that makes it possible to get more eggs from the same number of chickens. Because of this technological improvement, various output levels of eggs can now be produced with less feed, space, water, and labor. Costs will be reduced. The egg producer's *ATC* and *MC* curves will shift downward.

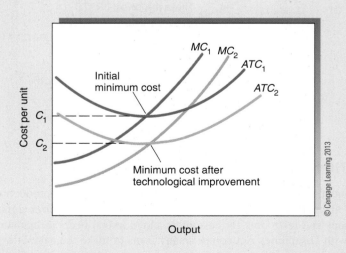

THE ECONOMIC WAY OF THINKING ABOUT COSTS

While focusing on the relationship between costs and output, it is important to keep in mind that costs are associated with choices and that they are forward looking. Business decision-makers incur costs when they choose to purchase raw materials, hire new employees, or renew the lease on a plant. Like other choices, these decisions must be made under conditions of uncertainty. Of course, past experience can help business decision-makers anticipate the likely costs of various choices. But the world is constantly changing; the future may differ substantially from the past.

Think for a moment about what the cost curves developed in this chapter really mean. The firm's short-run *MC* curve represents the opportunity cost of expanding output, *given the firm's current plant size*. The firm's long-run *ATC* curve represents the opportunity cost per unit of output associated with varying plant sizes and rates of output, *given that the alternative plants are still on the drawing board*. Opportunity costs look forward, reflecting expectations of what will be forgone as a result of current decisions. At the time decisions must be made, neither the short-run *MC* nor the long-run *ATC* can be determined from accounting records, because accounting costs look backward. Accounting figures yield valuable information about historical costs, but, as the following section illustrates, they must be interpreted carefully when they are used to forecast future costs.

WHAT ARE SUNK COSTS?

Sunk costs are the historical costs of past decisions that cannot be reversed. Sunk costs give managers hindsight when it comes to making current decisions, but the specific costs themselves are no longer relevant. When past choices cannot be reversed—no refund is available, for example—money that has been spent is gone for good. Today's choices must be based on the costs and benefits expected under *current and future* market conditions, if mistakes are to be avoided (see the accompanying Myths of Economics feature).

Sunk costs
Costs that have already been incurred as a result of past decisions. They are sometimes referred to as historical costs.

MYTHS OF ECONOMICS

"A Good Business Decision-Maker Will Never Sell a Product for Less Than Its Production Costs."

This statement contains a grain of truth. A profit-seeking entrepreneur will not undertake a project knowing the costs can't be covered. However, the statement fails to emphasize (1) the time dimension of the production process and (2) the uncertainty associated with business decisions. The production process takes time. Raw materials must be purchased, employees hired, and plants equipped. Retailers must contract with suppliers. As these decisions are made, costs result. Many of the firm's costs of production are incurred long before its product is ready for marketing.

Even a good business decision-maker is not always able to predict the future because market conditions can change quickly and unexpectedly. At the time the product is ready for sale, buyers might be unwilling to pay a price that will cover the seller's past costs of production. These past costs, however, are now sunk costs and no longer relevant. Decisions must now be made on the basis of the firm's current costs of delivering value to buyers, and the revenues to be gained by doing so.

Should a grocer refuse to sell oranges that are about to spoil because their wholesale cost cannot be covered? The grocer's current opportunity cost of selling the oranges at this point is nearly zero. The alternative would be to throw them in the garbage next week. Almost any price, even one far below past costs, will be better than letting the oranges spoil.

Consider another example. Suppose a couple that owns a house plans to relocate temporarily. Should they refuse to rent the house they're moving out of for $500 (if this is the best offer available) because their monthly house payment is $800? Of course not. The house payment will go on, regardless of whether they rent the house. If the homeowners can cover their opportunity costs (perhaps the expected wear and tear plus a $60 monthly fee for a property management service), they will gain by renting rather than leaving the house vacant.

Past mistakes provide useful lessons for the future, but they cannot be reversed. Bygones are bygones, even if they resulted in business loss. There is no need to fret over spilt milk, burnt toast, or yesterday's business losses.

To minimize costs, business decision-makers need to realize that sunk costs are, indeed, *sunk*. A simple example will emphasize this point. Suppose that the firm in Exhibit 5 pays $100,000 to purchase and install a roller blade–producing machine. The machine is expected to last ten years. The company's books record the cost of the machine as $10,000 each year under the heading of depreciation. The machine can be used only to make roller blades, though. Because dismantling and reinstallation costs are high, it cannot be leased or sold to another firm. Also, it has no scrap value. In other words, there are no alternative uses for the machine. The machine's annual production of roller blades will generate $50,000 of revenues for the firm when it is employed with raw materials and other factors of production that cost $46,000. Thus, the net revenue generated by the machine is $4,000.

Should the firm continue to use the machine? Its depreciation figures suggest that the machine is costing the firm $10,000 annually, compared to the $4,000 net revenue it generates. Put another way, accounting costs indicate that the machine is reducing the firm's profit by $6,000 annually. The machine's depreciation cost, however, is a sunk cost. It was incurred when the machine was purchased and installed, which is over and done with now. The *current* opportunity cost of the machine is therefore precisely zero. In other words, the firm is not giving up anything by continuing to use it today. Because using the machine generates $4,000 of additional net revenue, the firm can gain by continuing to use it. Of course, if market conditions are not expected to improve, the firm will not purchase a similar machine or replace the machine when it wears out, but this should not influence its decision whether to continue operating the one it already has. As this example illustrates, sunk costs help to explain why it will often make sense to continue using older equipment (it has a low opportunity cost), even if it would not be wise to purchase similar equipment again.

HOW WILL COST INFLUENCE SUPPLY?

Costs underpin the firm's supply decisions. A strictly profit-maximizing firm will compare the expected revenues derived from a decision or a course of action with the expected costs. If the anticipated revenues exceed costs, then the course of action will be chosen because it is expected to expand profits (or reduce losses).

For short-run supply decisions, the marginal cost of producing additional units is the relevant cost to consider. To maximize profits, the decision-maker should compare the expected marginal costs with the expected additional revenue from larger sales. If the latter exceeds the former, output (the quantity supplied) should be expanded.

While marginal costs are central in the short run, average total costs are the relevant cost consideration in the long run. Before entering an industry (or purchasing capital assets for expansion or replacement), a profit-maximizing decision-maker will compare the expected market price with the expected long-run average total cost. Profit-seeking potential entrants will supply the product if, and only if, they expect the market price to exceed their long-run average total cost. Similarly, existing firms will continue to supply a product in the long run only if they expect that the market price will enable them at least to cover their long-run average total cost.

Looking Ahead

This chapter focused on the relationship between output and cost in both the short and long runs. The next three chapters will use these general principles to analyze the price and output decisions of firms under alternative market conditions.

KEY POINTS

- The business firm is used to organize productive resources and transform them into goods and services. There are three major types of business structure—proprietorships, partnerships, and corporations.

- The principal–agent problem tends to reduce efficiency within the firm. Monitoring and the structure of incentives can be used to minimize inefficiencies arising from this source.

- The demand for a product indicates the intensity of consumers' desires for the item. The (opportunity) cost of producing the item indicates the intensity of consumers' desires for other goods that could have been produced instead, with the same resources.

- In economics, total cost includes not only explicit payments for resources employed by the firm, but also the implicit costs associated with the use of productive resources owned by the firm (like the opportunity cost of the firm's equity capital or owner-provided services) that could be used elsewhere.

- Because accounting methods omit the cost of equity capital (and sometimes other implicit costs), they tend to understate the opportunity cost of producing a good and overstate the firm's economic profit.

- Economic profit (or loss) results when a firm's sales revenues exceed (or are less than) its total costs, both explicit and implicit. Firms that are earning the market (or "normal") rate of return on their assets will therefore make zero economic profit.

- The firm's short-run average total cost (ATC) curve will tend to be U-shaped.

- The law of diminishing returns explains why a firm's short-run marginal and average total costs will eventually rise. When diminishing marginal returns are present, successively larger amounts of the variable input will be required to increase output by one more unit. As this happens, marginal cost will rise.

- The long-run ATC ($LRATC$) reflects the costs of production for plants of various sizes. When economies of scale are present, $LRATC$ will decline. When constant returns to scale are experienced, $LRATC$ will be constant. When diseconomies of scale are present, $LRATC$ will rise.

- Changes in (1) resource prices, (2) taxes, (3) regulations, and (4) technology will cause the cost curves of firms to shift.

- Sunk costs are costs that have already been incurred and cannot be recovered. Sunk costs give managers hindsight when it comes to making current decisions, but the specific costs themselves are no longer directly relevant for current and future decisions.

CRITICAL ANALYSIS QUESTIONS

1. The owners of a firm are residual income claimants. How does their property right to the residual income affect their incentive to (a) produce efficiently and keep cost low and (b) supply goods that consumers value highly relative to cost? Why is this important?

2. *Which of the following statements do you think reflect sound economic thinking? Explain your answer.
   a. "I paid $400 for this economics course. Therefore, I'm going to attend the lectures even if they are useless and boring."
   b. "Because we own rather than rent, and the house is paid for, housing doesn't cost us anything."
   c. "I own 100 shares of stock that I can't afford to sell until the price goes up enough for me to get back at least my original investment."
   d. "Private education is costly to produce, whereas public schooling is free."

3. Suppose a firm produces bicycles. Will the firm's accounting statement reflect the opportunity cost of the bicycles? Why or why not? What costs would an accounting statement reveal? Should current decisions be based on accounting costs? Explain.

4. What is the principal–agent problem? When will the principal–agent problem be most severe? Why might there be a principal–agent problem between the stockholder owners and the managers of a large corporation?

5. *"If a firm maximizes profit, it must minimize the cost of producing the profit-maximizing output." Is this statement true or false? Explain your answer.

6. What are some of the advantages of the corporate business structure of ownership for large business firms? What are some of the disadvantages? Is the corporate form of business ownership cost efficient? In a market economy, how would you tell whether the corporate structural form was efficient?

7. *Explain the factors that cause a firm's short-run average total costs initially to decline but eventually to increase as the rate of output rises.

8. Which of the following are relevant to a firm's decision to increase output: (a) short-run average total cost,

(b) short-run marginal cost, (c) long-run average total cost? Justify your answer.

9. Economics students often confuse (a) diminishing returns related to the variable factors of production and (b) diseconomies of scale. Explain the difference between the two, and give one example of each.

10. "Firms that make a profit have increased the value of the resources they used; their actions created wealth. In contrast, the actions of firms that make losses reduce wealth. The discovery and undertaking of profit-making opportunities are key ingredients of economic progress." Evaluate the statement.

11. *Is profit maximization consistent with the self-interest of corporate owners? Is it consistent with the self-interest of corporate managers? Is there a conflict between the self-interests of owners and those of managers?

12. *What is the opportunity cost of (a) borrowed funds and (b) equity capital? Under current tax law, firms can record as an expense the opportunity cost of borrowed funds, but not equity capital. How does this tax law affect the amount of debt the firm wants to incur, compared with the amount of money it raises by selling equity?

13. Why do economists consider normal returns to capital to be a cost? How does economic profit differ from normal profit?

14. *Draw a U-shaped, short-run *ATC* curve for a firm. Construct the accompanying *MC* and *AVC* curves.

15. What is shirking? If the managers of a firm are attempting to maximize its profits, will they have an incentive to limit shirking? How might they go about doing so?

16. What are implicit costs? Do implicit costs contribute to the opportunity cost of production? Should an implicit cost be counted as cost? Give three examples of implicit costs. Does the firm's accounting statement take implicit costs into account? Why or why not?

17. *Consider a machine purchased one year ago for $12,000. The machine is being depreciated $4,000 per year over a three-year period. Its current market value is $5,000, and the expected market value of the machine one year from now is $3,000. If the interest rate is 10 percent, what is the expected cost of holding the machine during the next year?

18. *Investors seeking to take over a firm often bid a positive price for the business even though it is currently experiencing losses. Why would anyone ever bid a positive price for a firm operating at a loss?

19. Fill in the blanks in the accompanying table shown at the bottom of page and answer the following questions:
   a. What happens to total product when marginal product is negative?
   b. What happens to average product when marginal product is greater than average product?
   c. What happens to average product when marginal product is less than average product?
   d. At what point does marginal product begin to decrease?
   e. At what point does marginal cost begin to increase?
   f. Summarize the relationship between marginal product and marginal cost.
   g. What happens to marginal costs when total product begins to fall?
   h. What is happening to average variable costs when they equal marginal costs?
   i. Marginal costs equal average variable costs between what output levels?
   j. What is happening to average total costs when they equal marginal costs?
   k. Marginal costs equal average total costs between what output levels?

*Asterisk denotes questions for which answers are given in Appendix B.

Units of Variable Input	Total Product	Marginal Product	Average Product	Price of Input	Total Variable Cost	Average Variable Cost	Total Fixed Cost	Total Cost	Average Total Cost	Marginal Cost
0	0	___	___	$1	___	___	$2	___	___	___
1	6	___	___	$1	___	___	$2	___	___	___
2	15	___	___	$1	___	___	$2	___	___	___
3	27	___	___	$1	___	___	$2	___	___	___
4	37	___	___	$1	___	___	$2	___	___	___
5	45	___	___	$1	___	___	$2	___	___	___
6	50	___	___	$1	___	___	$2	___	___	___
7	52	___	___	$1	___	___	$2	___	___	___
8	50	___	___	$1	___	___	$2	___	___	___

CHAPTER

Price Takers and the Competitive Process

CHAPTER FOCUS

- How do firms that are price takers differ from those that are price searchers?
- What determines the output of a price taker?
- How do price takers respond to changes in price in the short run? In the long run?
- How does time influence the elasticity of supply?
- What must firms do in order to make profits? How do profits and losses influence the supply and market price of a product?
- Does competition provide an incentive for producers to supply goods that consumers want at a low cost?

Competition means decentralized planning by many separate persons.

—*Friedrich A. von Hayek*[1]

[I]t is competition that drives down costs and prices, induces firms to produce the goods consumers want, and spurs innovation and the expansion of new markets...

—*President's Council of Economic Advisers*[2]

[1]Friedrich A. von Hayek, "The Use of Knowledge in Society," *American Economic Review* 35 (September 1945): 521.
[2]President's Council of Economic Advisers, *Economic Report of the President, 1996* (Washington, DC: U.S. Government Printing Office, 1996), 155.

In the previous chapter, we focused on cost conditions of business firms. In this chapter and the next two, we will take a closer look at the price and output decisions of the firm, and how they are influenced by costs and market conditions. The importance of profits, losses, and competition will be addressed. As we proceed, we will also analyze how the structure of a market—for example, the number of firms, the control they have over price, and the ease of entry into the market—influences both the decision making of firms and the operation of markets.

Price takers
Sellers who must take the market price in order to sell their product. Because each price taker's output is small relative to the total market, price takers can sell all their output at the market price, but they are unable to sell any of their output at a price higher than the market price.

PRICE TAKERS AND PRICE SEARCHERS

This chapter will focus on markets in which the firms are price takers: They simply take the price that is determined in the market. *In a price-taker market, the firms all produce identical products (for example, wheat, eggs, or regular unleaded gasoline), and each seller is small relative to the total market. Thus, the output of any single firm has no effect on the market price. Each firm can sell all its output at the market price but cannot sell any of its output at a higher price.* When a firm is a price taker, there is no pricing decision to be made. Price takers try to choose the output level that will maximize profit, given their costs and the price determined by the market.

APPLICATIONS IN ECONOMICS

Netherlands Flower Auctions Illustrate Competitive Markets[1]

The FloraHolland and Bloemenveiling Aalsmeer flower auctions in the Netherlands, each run by a growers' cooperative, operate as highly competitive markets with a large number of both buyers and sellers. FloraHolland itself has 98 percent of the Netherlands' trade, and the Netherlands has 60 percent of the world's trade. Thousands of growers from the Netherlands and around the world sell their products in these auctions. Each business day, several thousand buyers representing wholesale florists around the world, participate in the auction. Many bid by computer from outside the Netherlands. These auctions sell more than 17 million flowers each day from their locations in the Netherlands. This high volume is made possible by the speed of the Dutch auction system. Under this system, each lot of flowers is displayed and a "clock" runs backward from the highest to the lowest price per unit. The buyer pushes a button indicating his or her willingness to purchase when the clock reaches an acceptable per-unit price. The purchaser is the first buyer to push the button. There are 39 such clocks operated by these two firms. Flowers and plants auctioned in the morning will be available in shops around the world within 24 hours. Competition is

increasing, as large flower markets of this kind develop all over the world. Very large retailers like Walmart have also begun buying flowers directly from growers in the tropics.

[1]Information in this feature came in part from "Petal Power," *Economist* 383, no. 8528 (May 12, 2007): 73; and "Dutch Flower Auctions," *Economist* (downloaded June 3, 2009), from http://www.Economist.com.

Price takers, like all other profit-seeking firms, cannot survive in a competitive environment unless they are sensitive to cost. However, price-taker markets and price-searcher markets have differing methods of competition, differing ease of entry for competitors, and perhaps differing scale economies, too. To compete, each firm has to provide a high level of benefits per dollar relative to what consumers can find elsewhere.

In the real world, most firms are not price takers. They are usually able to increase their prices, at least a little, without losing all their customers. For example, if Nike increased the price of its athletic shoes by 10 percent, the number of shoes sold would decline, but it would not fall to zero. Firms like Nike are not price takers. They are price searchers: They choose the price that they will charge for their product, but the quantity that they are able to sell is very much related to that price. To maximize their profits, price searchers must not only decide how much to produce but also what price to charge. We will examine markets in which the firms are price searchers in the next two chapters.

If most real-world firms are price searchers, why is it important to analyze price-taker markets? There are several reasons. First, even though most firms are not price takers, there are a number of important markets, particularly in agriculture, in which the firms do essentially take the price determined in the market. Second, the price-taker model helps clarify the relationship between the decision making of individual firms and the market supply. Finally, and perhaps most important, the study of markets in which firms are price takers enhances our knowledge of **competition as a dynamic process**, *including its operation in markets other than those that are price takers*.

Historically, the term **pure competition** has been used to refer to markets in which firms are price takers. However, the expression "price-taker market" is more descriptive. Furthermore, this label avoids the implication that competitive forces are necessarily less pure or less intense in price-searcher markets. Often, this is not the case. When **barriers to entry** are low, the competitive process is just as important in price-searcher markets as it is when the firms are price takers.

Nonetheless, it should be noted that price-taker markets and purely competitive markets are really alternative names for the same thing. So when you hear people talk about pure competition or purely competitive markets, they mean markets with characteristics like those analyzed in this chapter.

WHAT ARE THE CHARACTERISTICS OF PRICE-TAKER MARKETS?

Consider the situation of Andy, a Texas cattle rancher. In the financial pages of the local newspaper, he finds that the current market price of quality steers is 94 cents per pound. Even if his ranch is quite large, there is little that Andy can do to change the market price of beef cattle. After all, there are tens of thousands of farmers who raise cattle. Thus, Andy supplies only a small portion of the total cattle market. The amount that he sells will exert little or no effect on the market price of cattle. Andy is a price taker.

Price searchers
Firms that face a downward-sloping demand curve for their product. The amount the firm is able to sell is inversely related to the price it charges.

Competition as a dynamic process
Rivalry or competitiveness between or among parties (for example, producers or input suppliers) to deliver a better deal to buyers in terms of quality, price, and product information.

Pure competition
A market structure characterized by a large number of small firms producing an identical product in an industry (market area) that permits complete freedom of entry and exit. Also called price-taker markets.

Barriers to entry
Obstacles that limit the freedom of potential rivals to enter and compete in an industry or market.

Producers in the wheat-farming and beef cattle markets are price takers. If they are going to sell their output, they must do so at the price determined by the market. Because individual producers are small relative to the total market, they can sell as many units as they like at the market price.

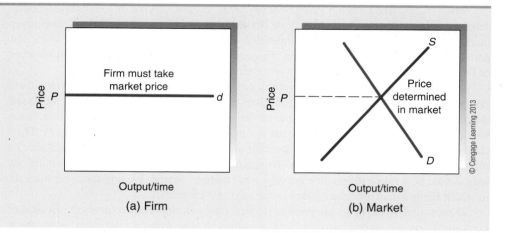

Exhibit 1

The Price Taker's Demand Curve

The market forces of supply and demand determine price (b). Price takers have no control over price. Thus, the demand for the product of the firm is perfectly elastic (a).

Firm must take market price

d

P

Price

Output/time

(a) Firm

S

P

Price

Price determined in market

D

Output/time

(b) Market

The firms in a market will be price takers when the following four conditions are met:

1. All the firms in the market are producing an identical product (for example beef, or eggs of a given grade).
2. A large number of firms exist in the market.
3. Each firm supplies only a very small portion of the total amount supplied to the market.
4. No barriers limit the entry or exit of firms in the market.

Exhibit 1 illustrates the relationship between the market forces (part b) and the demand curve facing the price-taking firm (part a). If the firm sets a price above the market level, consumers will simply buy from other sellers. Why pay the higher price when the identical good is abundantly available elsewhere at the lower market price? For example, if the market price of wheat were $5.00 per bushel, a farmer would be unable to find buyers for wheat if he tried to sell his at $5.50 per bushel. A firm would gain nothing by setting its price below the market level, because any small firm in the market can already sell as much as it wants at the market price. A price reduction would only reduce revenue and profit. A firm that is a price taker thus faces a perfectly elastic demand for its product. (In Exhibit 1, note that a lowercase *d* is used to denote the demand curve faced by the *firm,* whereas an uppercase *D* indicates the *market* demand curve.)

HOW DOES THE PRICE TAKER MAXIMIZE PROFIT?

The firm's output decision is based on maximizing profit, which requires comparing revenue with cost. A firm will continue to expand output as long as the additional revenues from the production and sales of the additional units exceed their marginal costs, thereby increasing profit. In the preceding chapter, we discovered that the law of diminishing returns assures that a firm's short-run marginal costs will eventually increase as the firm expands its output. As the firm continues to add additional variable resources to its fixed plant facilities, marginal productivity falls, and marginal costs rise, and eventually increase to the point where it is no longer profitable to further expand output.

Marginal revenue (*MR*)
The incremental change in total revenue derived from the sale of one additional unit of a product.

What about the benefits or additional revenues from output expansion? **Marginal revenue (*MR*)** is the change in the firm's total revenue per unit of output. It is the additional revenue derived from the sale of an additional unit of output. Mathematically,

$$MR = \frac{\textbf{Change in total revenue}}{\textbf{Change in output}}$$

Because the price taker sells all units at the same price, its marginal revenue will be equal to the market price. That is, producing and selling one more unit of output increases the firm's revenue by exactly the amount of the current market price. The firm's marginal revenue

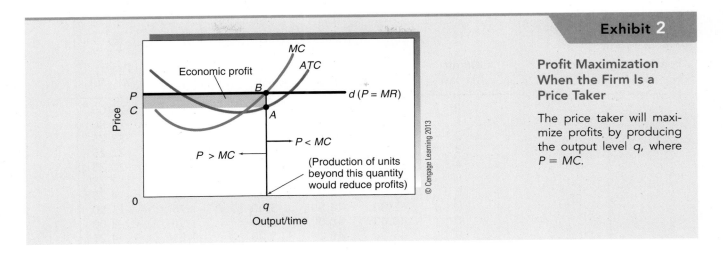

Exhibit 2

Profit Maximization When the Firm Is a Price Taker

The price taker will maximize profits by producing the output level q, where $P = MC$.

curve is a horizontal line at the market price. For a price-taker firm the marginal revenue curve is also the demand curve faced by the price-taker firm shown in Exhibit 1.

To maximize profits, in the short run, the price taker will expand its output until marginal cost just equals marginal revenue (price). **Exhibit 2** illustrates this decision. The firm will continue to expand output as long as the marginal revenue curve (*MR*) lies above the marginal cost (*MC*) curve. The profit of the price taker is maximized at the output rate at which $P = MR = MC$. In Exhibit 2, this occurs at output q. The firm will not expand output beyond q because those units would add more to the firm's costs than to its revenue, thus reducing profit.

Using Exhibit 2 it is also possible to illustrate the firm's total revenue, total cost, and profit as areas in the diagram. The total revenue of the firm would be the sales price of each unit, P, multiplied by output sold, q. Total revenue is represented by the area $P0qB$. The firm's total cost, in contrast, can be found by multiplying the average total cost (*ATC*) by the output level. Total cost is represented by the area $C0qA$. Because the firm's total revenues exceed its total costs, it is making short-run economic profit shown by the area of excess revenue over cost (the shaded area $PCAB$).

In the real world, of course, decisions are not made by entrepreneurs who spend time drawing demand and marginal cost curves. However, business firms do attempt to maximize their profits, producing units only when it is profitable to do so. Experimentation, trial and error, and strong competitive forces will eventually lead firms to seek out the level of output consistent with this rule for profit maximization.

PROFIT MAXIMIZING—A NUMERIC EXAMPLE

Exhibit 3 uses numeric data to illustrate profit-maximizing decision-making for a firm that is a price taker. As column 6 of Exhibit 3 shows, the firm maximizes profit at an output of fifteen units.

There are two ways to look at this profit-maximizing output rate. First, profit is equal to the difference between total revenue and total cost. Thus, profit will be maximized at the output rate where this difference (*TR* minus *TC*) is greatest. For output rates less than eleven units the firm would actually experience losses. But at fifteen units of output, an $11 profit is earned ($75 total revenue minus $64 total cost). A look at the profit figures of column 6 shows that it's impossible to earn a profit larger than $11 at any other rate of output.

In **Exhibit 4**, part (a) presents the total revenue and total cost approach in graph form. (However, the curves are drawn smoothly, as though output could be increased by tiny amounts, not just in whole-unit increments like those shown in Exhibit 3.) Profits will be greatest when the total revenue line lies above the total cost curve by the largest vertical amount, at 15 units of output.

You can also use the marginal approach to determine the profit-maximizing rate of output for the firm. Remember, as long as price (marginal revenue) exceeds marginal cost,

	(1) OUTPUT (PER DAY)	(2) TOTAL REVENUE (TR)	(3) TOTAL COST (TC)	(4) MARGINAL REVENUE (MR)	(5) MARGINAL COST (MC)	(6) PROFIT (TR − TC)
Exhibit 3 Profit Maximization for a Price Taker: A Numeric Illustration	0	$0.00	$25.00	$0.00	$0.00	$−25.00
	1	5.00	29.80	5.00	4.80	−24.80
	2	10.00	33.75	5.00	3.95	−23.75
	3	15.00	37.25	5.00	3.50	−22.25
	4	20.00	40.25	5.00	3.00	−20.25
	5	25.00	42.75	5.00	2.50	−17.75
	6	30.00	44.75	5.00	2.00	−14.75
	7	35.00	46.50	5.00	1.75	−11.50
	8	40.00	48.00	5.00	1.50	−8.00
	9	45.00	49.25	5.00	1.25	−4.25
	10	50.00	50.25	5.00	1.00	−0.25
	11	55.00	51.50	5.00	1.25	3.50
	12	60.00	53.25	5.00	1.75	6.75
	13	65.00	55.75	5.00	2.50	9.25
	14	70.00	59.25	5.00	3.50	10.75
	15	75.00	64.00	5.00	4.75	11.00
	16	80.00	70.00	5.00	6.00	10.00
	17	85.00	77.25	5.00	7.25	7.75
	18	90.00	85.50	5.00	8.25	4.50
	19	95.00	95.00	5.00	9.50	0.00
	20	100.00	108.00	5.00	13.00	−8.00
	21	105.00	125.00	5.00	17.00	−20.00

© Cengage Learning 2013

production and sale of additional units will add to the firm's profit (or reduce its losses). A look at columns 4 and 5 of Exhibit 3 reveals that *MR* is greater than *MC* for the first 15 units of output. Producing these units will expand the firm's profit. In contrast, producing any unit beyond fifteen adds more to cost than to revenue. Profit will therefore decline when output is expanded beyond fifteen units. Given the firm's cost and revenue schedule, profits are maximized by producing fifteen, and only fifteen, units per day.

Part (b) of Exhibit 4 graphically illustrates the marginal approach. Note here that the output rate at which the marginal cost and marginal revenue curves intersect (15 units) coincides with the output rate in part (a) at which the total revenue curve exceeds the total cost curve by the largest amount. Beyond that output rate, *MR* is less than *MC*, so profit will decline.

LOSSES AND WHEN TO GO OUT OF BUSINESS

Suppose that changes in the bigger marketplace cause the price to drop below a firm's average total cost at all possible output levels. How will a profit-maximizing firm respond to this situation? The answer to this question depends both on the firm's revenues relative to its *variable* cost and on its expectations about the future. The firm's owner has three options: (1) continue to operate in the short run, (2) shut down temporarily, or (3) go out of business.

A Temporary Shutdown
A firm will temporarily shut down if it cannot cover its variable cost but does not want to go out of business because it expects to be able to operate profitably in the future. This ice-cream store in Morgantown, West Virginia, closes for several months each winter and re-opens during the summer. During these short-run shutdowns, the store still pays its fixed costs, such as its rent, taxes, and insurance. The store avoids only variable costs during the winter months.

© Russell Sobel

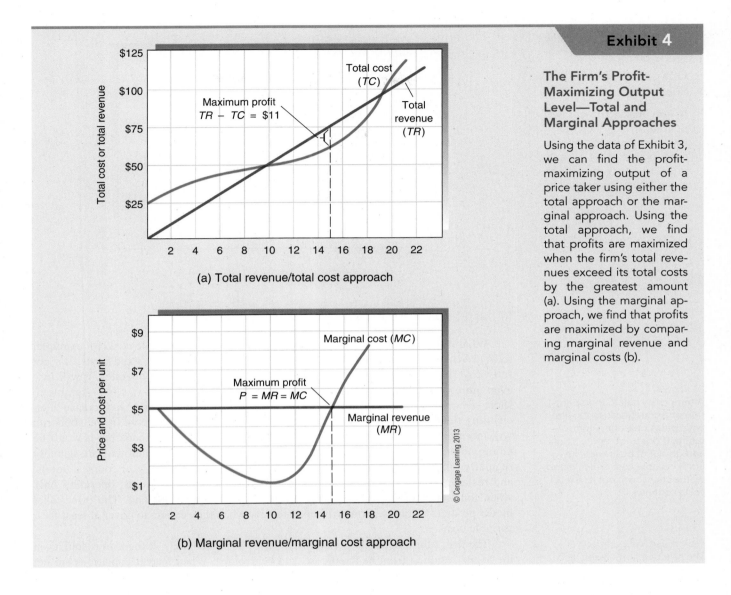

(a) Total revenue/total cost approach

(b) Marginal revenue/marginal cost approach

© Cengage Learning 2013

Exhibit 4

The Firm's Profit-Maximizing Output Level—Total and Marginal Approaches

Using the data of Exhibit 3, we can find the profit-maximizing output of a price taker using either the total approach or the marginal approach. Using the total approach, we find that profits are maximized when the firm's total revenues exceed its total costs by the greatest amount (a). Using the marginal approach, we find that profits are maximized by comparing marginal revenue and marginal costs (b).

If the firm anticipates that the lower market price is temporary, it may want to continue operating in the short run as long as it can cover its variable cost.[3] **Exhibit 5** illustrates why. The firm shown in this exhibit would minimize its loss at output level q, where $P = MR = MC$. But at q, total revenues ($0qBP_1$) are less than total costs ($0qAC$). The firm faces short-run economic losses. Even if it shuts down completely, it will still incur fixed costs, *unless the firm goes out of business*. If it anticipates that the market price will increase enough to allow the firm to cover its average total costs in the future, it may not want to terminate operations and sell its assets. It may choose to produce q units in the short run, even though it will incur losses. At price P_1, producing output q is more advantageous than shutting down, because the firm is able to cover its variable costs and have revenue remaining to pay some of its fixed costs. If it were to shut down but not sell out, the firm would lose the entire amount of its fixed cost.

---

[3]Keep in mind the opportunity-cost concept. The firm's fixed costs are opportunity costs that do not vary with the level of output. They can be avoided if, and only if, the firm goes out of business. To specify fixed costs, we need to know (1) how much the firm's fixed assets would bring if they were sold or rented to others and (2) any other costs, such as operating license fees and debts, that could be avoided if the firm declared bankruptcy and/or went out of business. Because fixed costs can be avoided if the firm goes out of business, the firm will foresee greater losses from operating even in the short run if it does not expect conditions to improve.

Exhibit 5

Operating with Short-Run Losses

A firm making losses will operate in the short run if it (1) can cover its variable costs now and (2) expects price to be high enough in the future to cover all its costs.

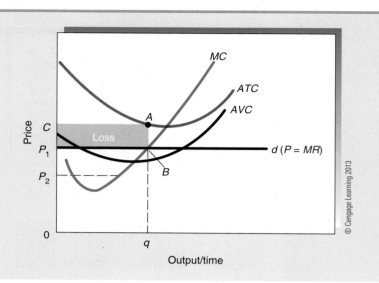

Shutdown
A temporary halt in the operation of a firm. Because the firm anticipates operating in the future, it does not sell its assets and go out of business. The firm's variable cost is eliminated by the shutdown, but its fixed costs continue.

Going out of business
The sale of a firm's assets and its permanent exit from the market. By going out of business, a firm is able to avoid its fixed costs, which would continue during a shutdown.

What if the market price drops below the firm's average variable cost (for example, to P_2)? When this happens, not only is the firm not covering its fixed costs, it's not fully covering its variable costs either. In other words, if the firm operates, it will lose even more money. Under these circumstances, a temporary **shutdown** is preferable to short-run operation. Even if the firm's owner expects the market price to increase later, enabling the firm to survive and prosper in the future, shutting down in the short run will minimize its losses. The firm will still have to pay its fixed costs, but it won't be taking an additional loss on each unit it produces. Temporary shutdowns are actually regularly planned in some markets. For example, many ski resorts, golf courses, hotels, and restaurants in vacation areas plan to shut down in slow seasons, operating only when tourists or other seasonal purchasers provide enough demand. The price-taker model predicts that these firms will operate only when they expect to cover at least their variable costs.

The firm's third option is **going out of business** immediately. If the firm is sold, even the losses resulting from its fixed costs can be avoided. When market conditions are not expected to change for the better, going out of business is the preferred option.

THE FIRM'S SHORT-RUN SUPPLY CURVE

The price taker that intends to stay in business will maximize profits (or minimize losses) when it produces the output level at which P = MR = MC and variable costs are covered. Therefore, the portion of the firm's short-run marginal cost curve that lies above its average variable cost is the short-run supply curve of the firm.

Exhibit 6 illustrates that, as the market price increases, the firm will expand output along its *MC* curve. If the market price were less than P_1, the firm would shut down immediately and produce zero output. If the market price is P_1, a price equal to the firm's minimum average variable cost, the firm may supply output q_1 in the short run. Economic losses will result, but the firm would incur similar losses if it shut down completely. As the market price increases to P_2, the firm will happily expand output along its *MC* curve to q_2. At P_2, price is equal to average total costs. At this point, the firm is making a "normal rate of return," or zero economic profits. Higher prices will result in a still larger short-run output. For example, when the price rises to P_3, the firm will supply q_3 units. At this price, economic profits will result. As long as price exceeds average variable cost, higher prices will cause the firm to expand output along its *MC* curve, which therefore becomes the firm's short-run supply curve.

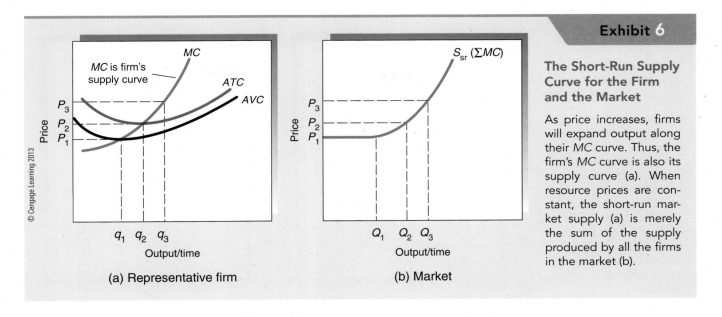

© Cengage Learning 2013

(a) Representative firm

(b) Market

Exhibit 6

The Short-Run Supply Curve for the Firm and the Market

As price increases, firms will expand output along their *MC* curve. Thus, the firm's *MC* curve is also its supply curve (a). When resource prices are constant, the short-run market supply (a) is merely the sum of the supply produced by all the firms in the market (b).

THE SHORT-RUN MARKET SUPPLY CURVE

The short-run market supply curve shows the total quantity supplied at alternative market prices. *When the firms are price takers, the short-run market supply curve is the horizontal summation of the marginal cost curves (ΣMC) above the level of average variable cost for all of the firms in the market. Because individual firms will supply a larger amount at a higher price, the short-run market supply curve will slope upward to the right.*

Exhibit 6 illustrates this relationship. As the price of the product rises from P_1 to P_2 to P_3, the individual firms expand their output along their marginal cost curves. Because the individual firms supply a larger output as the market price increases, the total amount supplied to the market also expands.

PRICE AND OUTPUT IN PRICE-TAKER MARKETS

The short-run market supply curve, together with the demand curve for the industry's product, will determine the market price. At the short-run equilibrium market price, each firm will have expanded output until marginal costs are equal to the market price, and they may be earning either economic profits or losses.

LONG-RUN EQUILIBRIUM

In the long run, existing firms will have the opportunity to expand (or contract) the sizes of their plants, and firms will also be able to enter and exit the industry. As these long-run adjustments are made, output in the whole industry may either expand or contract. If economic profit is present, new firms will enter the industry to capture some of those profits. Current producers will have an incentive to expand the scale of their operations to capture some of the additional profits, too. This increase in supply will put downward pressure on prices. In contrast, if firms in the industry are suffering economic losses, they will leave the market. This decrease in supply will put upward pressure on prices. This process of entry and exit will continue until the profit rate in the industry has returned to a normal level ("zero economic profit") consistent with the profit rates in other competitive industries. Therefore, as **Exhibit 7** shows, when a price-taker market is in long-run equilibrium, the quantity supplied and the quantity demanded will be equal at the market price (part b) and each firm in the industry will be earning normal (zero) economic profit (that is, its minimum *ATC* will just equal the market price [part a]).

Exhibit 7

Long-Run Equilibrium in a Price-Taker Market

The two conditions necessary for long-run equilibrium in a price-taker market are depicted here. First, quantity supplied and quantity demanded must be equal in the market (b). Second, the firms in the industry must earn zero economic profit (the "normal rate of return") at the established market price (a).

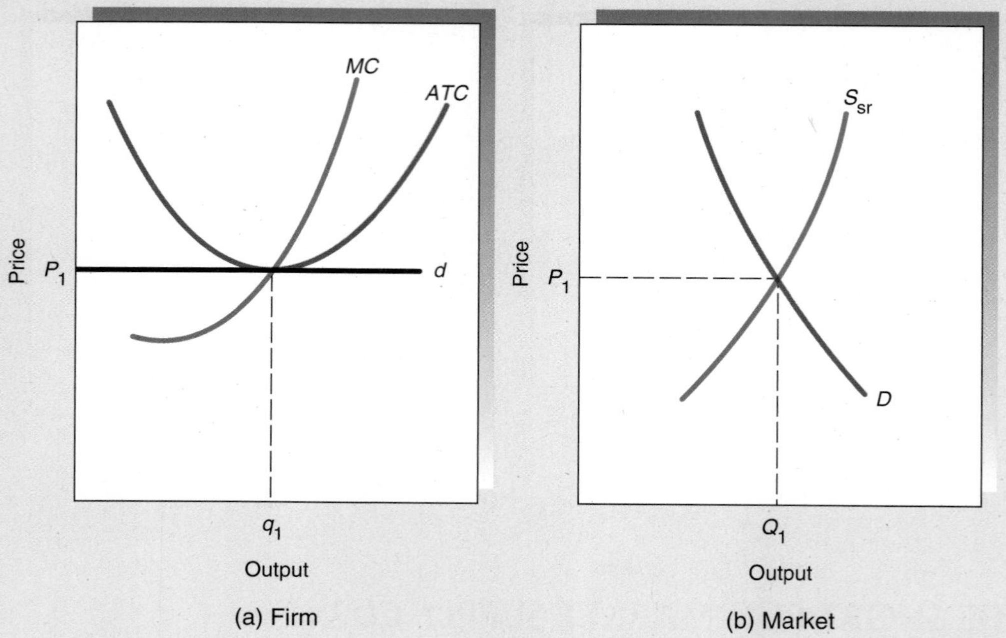

(a) Firm

(b) Market

In price-taker markets, a single price will emerge and all of the potential gains from trade between the buyer-consumers and seller-suppliers will be realized. Does the price-taker model really work in the real world? As the Applications in Economics feature on experimental economics and the significance of competition indicates, the general implications of the price-taker model are approximated even when the restrictive assumptions of the model are not fully met.

When long-run equilibrium is present, firms will have no incentive to alter either their output levels or their plant sizes. Neither will there be incentive for net investment to flow into or away from the industry. Thus, the market price and output will persist into the future. This is why it is referred to as a long-run equilibrium.

APPLICATIONS IN ECONOMICS

Experimental Economics and the Significance of Competition

In fields like physics and chemistry, scientists use controlled laboratory experiments to test and verify the basic principles on which their science is built. Historically, it was thought that experiments of this type were not an option for economists. But this changed during the middle part of the twentieth century and over the past 50 years, economists have conducted numerous experiments investigating key elements of economic theory.

Vernon Smith, currently at Chapman University, won the 2002 Nobel Prize in Economics for his path-breaking work in experimental economics. In one of his early experiments, Smith brought individuals into a laboratory setting

and arbitrarily assigned them roles as buyers and sellers in a game-like activity. Each buyer was assigned a maximum value representing the maximum price he or she would be willing to pay for a hypothetical commodity. If the buyer could purchase the commodity at a price less than their maximum value, they would receive a cash payment equal to the difference between the two. Each buyer gained financially by purchasing at lower prices—just as buyers do in real markets. The sellers were treated similarly. All sellers were assigned a minimum value representing their cost, and if they were able to sell the commodity for more than this minimum, they would receive a cash payment for the difference.

Buyers and sellers were free to make verbal offers and enter into exchanges at any mutually agreeable price.

The competitive price-taker model predicts that all mutually advantageous trades among buyers and sellers will be undertaken and that, as trades occur, the price will tend to converge toward a single price—the market price. Smith and other experimental researchers confirmed that this was indeed the case. After the experiments, participants often describe the experience as disorganized and chaotic. Thus, many are startled when shown that their actions (trades) achieved the maximum income for the group and that a sealed envelope, given to them prior to the experiment, approximated both the price of most trades and the maximum joint gains achieved by the group. The competitive model presented in this chapter provided the foundation for these predictions.

Prior to the work in experimental economics, many economists thought this model was relevant only under highly restrictive conditions. Experimental researchers, however, have found that outcomes approximating those of the competitive price-taker model generally emerge even when the strict assumptions of the model are not fully met. For example, even if the number of sellers is relatively small,

say ten to fifteen, outcomes similar to those predicted by the price-taker model generally occur.

At first, Smith himself was surprised that efficient outcomes were achieved under a wide variety of conditions, but after numerous experiments, he stated that

In many experimental markets, poorly informed, error-prone, and uncomprehending human agents interact through the trading rules to produce social algorithms which demonstrably approximate the wealth maximizing outcomes traditionally thought to require complete information and cognitively rational actors.[1]

In addition to analyzing the exchange process, experimental research has addressed numerous other topics, including the impact of alternative auction rules, the likelihood of a stock market or real estate bubble, and the provision of public goods. Experimental economics is one of the most exciting and fruitful areas of current economic research.

[1]Vernon L. Smith, "Economics in the Laboratory," *Journal of Economic Perspectives* 8, no. 1 (Winter 1994): 118.

HOW WILL THE MARKET RESPOND TO AN INCREASE IN DEMAND?

Suppose that a price-taker market is in long-run equilibrium. What will happen if there is an increase in demand? Exhibit 8 shows us. Suppose that an entrepreneur introduces a fantastic new candy. However, because it sticks to people's teeth, the market demand for toothpicks increases from D_1 to D_2, pushing toothpick prices upward from P_1 to P_2. What impact will the higher market price have on the output level of toothpick-producing firms? The firms will expand output (from q_1 to q_2 in part a of the exhibit) along their MC curves. In the short run, the toothpick producers will make economic profits. The profits will attract new toothpick producers to the industry and cause the existing firms to expand the scale of their plants. Hence, the market supply will increase (shift from S_1 to S_2) and eventually eliminate the short-run profits. If the prices of resources supplied to the industry are unchanged, the market supply will continue to expand (shift to the right) until the price of toothpicks returns to its initial level (P_1), even though output has expanded to Q_3.

HOW WILL THE MARKET RESPOND TO A DECREASE IN DEMAND?

Economic profits attract new firms to an industry. In contrast, economic losses encourage firms to move out of the industry and into other areas where the profitability potential is more favorable. Economic losses mean firms are earning less than a normal market rate of return. The opportunity cost of continuing in the industry exceeds the gain.

Exhibit 9 shows market forces reacting to economic losses. Initially, assume that an equilibrium price exists in the industry. The firms are able to cover their average costs of production. Now suppose that consumer incomes fall, lowering the product's demand and its market price. At the new, lower price, firms in the industry will not be able to cover their costs of production. In the short run, they will reduce output along their MC curves. The lower output by the individual firms results in a lower quantity supplied in the market.

Exhibit 8

Market Response to Increased Demand

A new candy that sticks to people's teeth causes the demand for toothpicks to increase to D_2 (b). Toothpick prices rise to P_2, inducing firms to expand output. Toothpick firms make short-run profits (a), which draw new competitors into the industry. The toothpick supply then expands (shifts from S_1 to S_2). If cost conditions are unchanged, the expansion in supply will continue until the market price of toothpicks declines to its initial level of P_1.

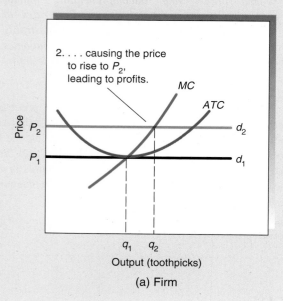

(a) Firm

2. . . . causing the price to rise to P_2, leading to profits.

MC

ATC

Price

P_2 d_2

P_1 d_1

q_1 q_2

Output (toothpicks)

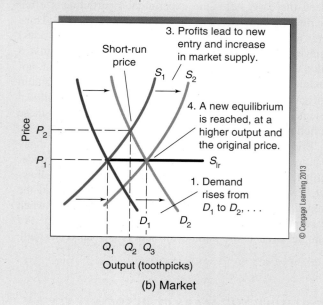

(b) Market

3. Profits lead to new entry and increase in market supply.

Short-run price

S_1 S_2

4. A new equilibrium is reached, at a higher output and the original price.

S_{lr}

1. Demand rises from D_1 to D_2, . . .

Price

P_2

P_1

Q_1 Q_2 Q_3

D_1 D_2

Output (toothpicks)

© Cengage Learning 2013

Exhibit 9

The Impact of a Fall in Demand

Lower market demand will cause the price to fall and short-run losses to occur. The losses will cause some firms to go out of business and others to reduce their output. In the long run, the market supply will fall, causing the market price to rise. The supply will continue to decline and price will continue to rise until the short-run losses have been eliminated.

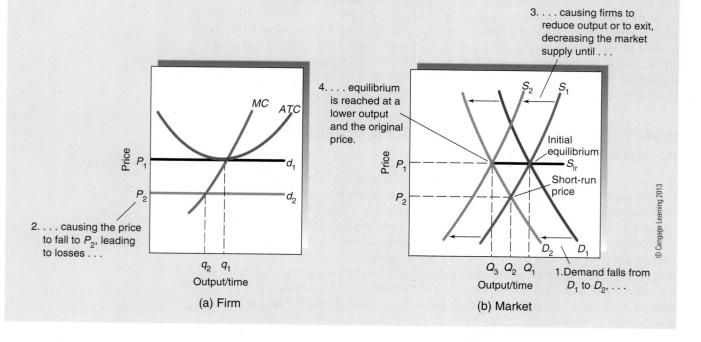

(a) Firm

MC   ATC

Price

P_1 d_1

P_2 d_2

2. . . . causing the price to fall to P_2, leading to losses . . .

q_2 q_1

Output/time

(b) Market

3. . . . causing firms to reduce output or to exit, decreasing the market supply until . . .

S_2 S_1

4. . . . equilibrium is reached at a lower output and the original price.

Initial equilibrium

S_{lr}

Short-run price

Price

P_1

P_2

Q_3 Q_2 Q_1

D_2 D_1

1. Demand falls from D_1 to D_2, . . .

Output/time

© Cengage Learning 2013

In the face of short-run losses, some firms will leave the industry, causing the industry supply to decline, indicated by the shift from S_1 to S_2. Firms will continue to exit until the price rises enough that the firms remaining in the industry can once again earn a normal rate of return, or zero economic profit. At that point, a new long-run equilibrium is established. For a real-world example of how a market adjusts to changing demand and cost conditions, see the Applications in Economics feature on coffee production in a price takers' market.

APPLICATIONS IN ECONOMICS

Coffee Production in a Price Takers' Market

Sellers in the world's coffee market are price takers. Hundreds of thousands of farmers produce coffee beans, and no grower has a significant impact on the world price. Each grower selling in the world market takes the price as given and is free to respond to any price change. Changes can be dramatic in the coffee market. The monthly average market price reported by the International Coffee Organization rose from the $0.45 to $0.75 range in the early 1990s to over $1.80 in May of 1997.

As growing coffee became more profitable, coffee production around the world expanded. For example, Vietnamese growers more than quadrupled their coffee production, from 92,000 tons in 1990 to 487,000 tons in 1999. By 2000, Vietnam had become the world's second-largest coffee-producing nation.

But the greater supply of coffee turned out to be more than consumers were willing to buy at the high 1997 prices. The market price began to fall. By August 2000, coffee bean prices were averaging less than $0.60 per pound and stayed that way until 2004. Many growers couldn't cover their costs at such low prices and began growing other crops.

Some landowners in Indonesia, for example, planted rice. Others, especially in Central and Latin America, began to plant organic and other specialty coffees, with lower yields but higher prices. Still other producers, including some in Vietnam, simply abandoned the least profitable plantations, at least temporarily. In Mexico, more than an estimated 300,000 coffee farmers—unable to cover even their variable costs—left their farms to seek other opportunities. The price rose slowly to an average of $1.24 for 2008, and production that year was nearly back to its 1999 high. [1]

The world coffee market illustrates very clearly how producers in price-taker markets can quickly expand production when rising prices are seen or expected but also contract production when prices and profits fall.

[1] The data presented in this feature are from Howard LaFranchi, "Economic Upheaval over Coffee," *Christian Science Monitor* (August 15, 2001, the BBC Web site, http://www.bbc.co.uk/worldservice/business/story_fdh200301.shtml, accessed September 17, 2001), and the Web site of the International Coffee Organization (http://www.ico.org/, "Statistics: Historical Data" section).

iStockphoto.com/sorendls

THE LONG-RUN MARKET SUPPLY CURVE

The *long-run market supply curve* shows how the quantity supplied in an industry varies with the market price, given enough time for firms to adjust the sizes of their plants (or other fixed factors) and to enter or exit the industry. Because the curve is constructed from points of long-run equilibrium, at each point the market price is equal to the minimum average total cost for firms in the industry. Therefore, the shape of the curve depends on what happens to the cost of production as the *industry's* output is altered; there are three possibilities.

Long-run supply in constant-cost industries If resource prices remain unchanged, the long-run market supply curve will be horizontal, or perfectly elastic. In terms of economics, this describes a **constant-cost industry**. Exhibits 8 and 9 both depict constant-cost industries. As Exhibit 8 shows, in these industries an increase in market demand for the product results in only a temporary increase in the price of the product. With time, the higher price and profits will stimulate expansion and additional production, which will push the market price back down precisely to its initial level (and profitability back to its normal rate).

Constant-cost industry
An industry for which factor prices and costs of production remain constant as market output is expanded. The long-run market supply curve is therefore horizontal in these industries.

Similarly, Exhibit 9 illustrates the impact of a decline in demand in a constant-cost industry. Here, market price falls inducing losses and the exit of firms. Assuming resource prices and production costs are unaffected by the change in market output, the reduction in demand lowers the price in the short run, but it returns to its original level in the long run. Thus, in a constant-cost industry, the *long-run market supply curve* (S_{lr}) is perfectly elastic.

A constant-cost industry is most likely to arise when the industry's demand for resource inputs is quite small relative to the total demand for these resources. For example, the demand of the toothpick industry for wood, chemicals, and labor is very small relative to the total demand for these resources. Thus, doubling the output of toothpicks would have very little effect on the price of the resources used by the industry. Toothpicks, therefore, approximate a constant-cost industry.

Long-run supply in increasing-cost industries In most industries, an increase in *industry* output will lead to higher resource prices and per-unit production costs for all the firms in the industry. Economists refer to such industries as increasing-cost industries. **Exhibit 10** depicts an increasing-cost industry. The rising resource costs cause the firms' average and marginal cost curves to shift upward (to ATC_2 and MC_2) as the industry expands. For an increasing-cost industry, the market price necessary to result in zero economic profit (long-run equilibrium) will have to be higher as the industry gets larger (now P_2). The long-run market supply curve for the product will therefore slope upward to the right.

Long-run supply in decreasing-cost industries Sometimes, resource prices will decline when an industry expands, causing the cost curves to shift downward as new firms enter the industry. For example, as the electronics industry expands, suppliers of certain components may be able to adopt large-scale production techniques that will lead to lower component prices. In such decreasing-cost industries, the long-run (but not the short-run) market supply curve will slope downward to the right. Decreasing-cost industries are rare.

Increasing-cost industry
An industry for which costs of production rise as output is expanded. In these industries, even in the long run, higher market prices will be needed to induce firms to expand total output. As a result, the long-run market supply curve in these industries will slope upward to the right.

Decreasing-cost industry
An industry for which costs of production decline as the industry expands. The market supply is therefore inversely related to price. Such industries are atypical.

Exhibit 10   **Increasing Costs and Long-Run Supply**

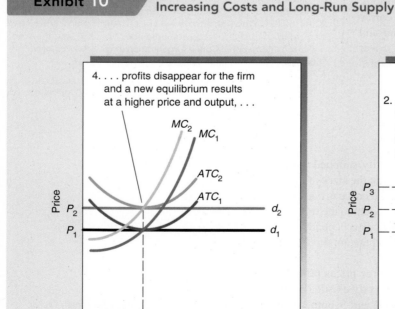

4. . . . profits disappear for the firm and a new equilibrium results at a higher price and output, . . .

(a) Firm

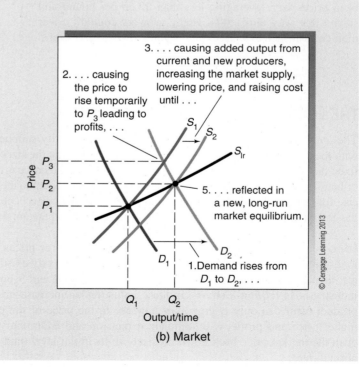

2. . . . causing the price to rise temporarily to P_3 leading to profits, . . .

3. . . . causing added output from current and new producers, increasing the market supply, lowering price, and raising cost until . . .

5. . . . reflected in a new, long-run market equilibrium.

1. Demand rises from D_1 to D_2, . . .

(b) Market

© Cengage Learning 2013

In central areas of large cities, the supply of parking spaces can be expanded only by using higher-cost space and higher-cost techniques, such as taller parking garages that use a large portion of the building for access ramps. As a result, the unit cost of parking spaces increases as the total number is expanded. Thus, provision of parking space is an increasing-cost industry.

SUPPLY ELASTICITY AND THE ROLE OF TIME

The short- and long-run supply curve distinction offers a convenient two-stage analysis, but in the real world there are many intermediate production "runs." The delivery rates for some factor inputs that could not be easily increased in a one-week time period can be increased over a two-week period. It might take two weeks, for example, to hire reliable workers who need no special skills. Expanding other factors might take a month, and still others, six months. More precisely, the cost penalty for quicker availability is greater for some productive resources than others. In any case, a faster expansion usually means that greater cost penalties are encountered in order to obtain the earlier availability of the resources needed to expand production.

When a firm has a longer time period to plan its output and adjust all of its productive inputs to their desired utilization levels, it will be able to produce any specific new rate of output at a lower cost. *Because it is less costly to expand output slowly in response to a demand increase, the expansion of output by firms will increase with time, as long as the price exceeds the cost. Therefore, the supply curve for products is typically more elastic over a longer time period than over a shorter period.*

Exhibit 11 shows a more continuous view of the impact of time on producers' responses to an increase in price caused by greater market demand. When the price of a product increases from P_1 to P_2, the immediate supply response of the firms is small, reflecting the high cost of hasty expansion. After one week, firms are willing to expand output only from Q_1 to Q_2. After one month, cost reductions made possible by the longer production-planning period allow firms to offer Q_3 units at the price P_2. After three months, the rate of output expands to Q_4. In the long run, when it is possible to adjust all inputs to the desired utilization levels (after a six-month time period, for example), firms are willing to supply Q_5 units of output at the market price of P_2.

THE ROLE OF PROFITS AND LOSSES

Profit is a reward that business owners will earn if they produce a good that consumers value more (as measured by their willingness to pay) than the alternative goods that could have been produced with those same resources (as measured by the cost of bidding the resources away from their alternative uses). In contrast, losses are a penalty imposed on businesses that reduce the value produced from resources. Losses are a signal that

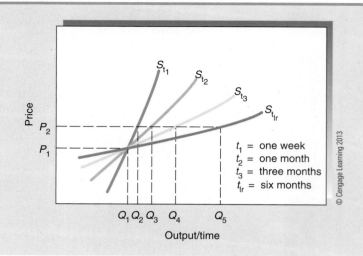

Exhibit 11

Time and the Elasticity of Supply

The elasticity of the market supply curve usually increases when suppliers have more time to adjust to a change in the price.

t_1 = one week
t_2 = one month
t_3 = three months
t_{lr} = six months

© Cengage Learning 2013

the other goods that could have been produced with those same resources were of greater value than what is currently being produced. Losses and bankruptcies are the market's way of providing signals and incentives to bring such wasteful activities to a halt, releasing those resources for use in other more highly valued uses.

The price-taker model also highlights the role of profits and losses in directing the actions of entrepreneurs and resource suppliers in an economy. When consumer demand for a product increases, higher economic profits result in the entry of new firms to satisfy this increased demand. Additional resources flow into the production of the now more highly valued good and away from other industries. In contrast, when consumer demand for a product decreases, economic losses result in firms going out of business and reallocation of resources toward other industries where they are now more valuable. It is the profit and loss mechanism, driven by consumer demand and the costs of production that steers the allocation of resources in a market economy.

We live in a world of changing tastes and technology, imperfect knowledge, and uncertainty. Business decision-makers cannot be sure of either future market prices or costs of production. Their decisions must be based on expectations. Nonetheless, the reward–penalty structure of a market economy is clear. *Firms that anticipate correctly the products and services for which future demand will be most urgent (relative to production costs) and produce and market them efficiently will make economic profits. Those that are inefficient and allocate resources incorrectly to areas of weak demand (relative to costs) will be penalized with losses.*

The firms most adept at giving consumers value for their money thrive and expand. Those less successful in doing so tend to shrink or even to disappear from the market. Free entry and the competitive process will protect the consumer from arbitrarily high prices. When profits are present, profit-seeking entrepreneurs will put more resources into these markets, supply will expand, and eventually the price will be driven down to the unit cost.

COMPETITION PROMOTES PROSPERITY

keys to economic prosperity

Competition

Competition motivates businesses to produce efficiently, cater to the views of consumers, and search for innovative improvements.

OUTSTANDING ECONOMIST

Friedrich A. von Hayek (1899–1992)

The writings of this 1974 Nobel Prize recipient spanned seven decades. Friedrich von Hayek's analysis on knowledge and markets greatly enhanced the understanding of how the competitive market process works. Hayek also made important contributions in the areas of monetary theory, law and economics, business cycles, and capital theory. He is also well known for the idea that market exchanges create an "extended order" in which perfect strangers who never meet nonetheless cooperate with one another to achieve their individual goals. The market process described in this chapter is an integral part of that cooperative network.

Apic/Getty Images

iStockphoto.com/sorendls

The price-taker model highlights the importance of the competitive process. Competition puts pressure on producers to operate efficiently and use resources wisely. Each competing firm will have a strong incentive to produce its products as economically as possible. Holding quality constant, lower costs will mean more profit. Therefore, pursuit of profit will encourage each firm to minimize its cost of production—to use the set of resources least valued in other uses to produce the desired output. Firms that fail to keep costs low will be driven from the market.

Similarly, firms in competitive markets have a strong incentive to discover and produce goods and services that consumers value highly relative to cost. Thus, resources will be drawn to those uses where they are most productive, as judged by the consumers' willingness to pay. The ability of firms freely to expand or contract their businesses and enter or exit markets means that resources will not be trapped unproductively in a particular industry when they're valued more highly elsewhere.

If firms are going to be successful in competitive markets, they must also be innovative and forward-looking. The production techniques and product offerings that lead to success today will not necessarily pass the competitive market test tomorrow. Producers who survive in a competitive environment cannot become complacent. On the contrary, they must be willing to experiment and quick to adopt improved methods.

In competitive markets, business firms must serve the interests of consumers. As Adam Smith noted more than 200 years ago, competition harnesses personal self-interest and channels it into activities that enhance our living standards. Smith stated that

> *It is not from the benevolence of the butcher, the brewer, or the baker, that we expect our dinner, but from their regard to their own self-interest. We address ourselves, not to their humanity but to their self-love, and never talk to them of our own necessities, but of their advantages.*[4]

Sellers profit when they supply products valued more highly than the resources needed to make them. But their actions also help the rest of us get more value from those resources than we would otherwise. As Smith properly noticed, personal self-interest is a powerful source of economic progress when it is directed by the competitive market process.

Looking Ahead

Consumers often seek variety in product design, style, durability, service, and location. Differentiating products gives firms some control over the prices they can charge. In the next two chapters, we will examine markets in which the firms are price searchers. We will also consider the impact entry barriers have on markets and pricing.

iStockphoto.com/gaspr13

---

[4]Adam Smith, *An Inquiry into the Nature and Causes of the Wealth of Nations* (1776; Cannan's ed., Chicago: University of Chicago Press, 1976), 18.

KEY POINTS

- A firm facing a perfectly elastic demand for its product is a price taker. A firm that can raise its price without losing all of its customers (and that must lower its price in order to sell more units) is a price searcher.

- To maximize profit, a price taker will expand its output as long as the sale of additional units adds more to revenues than to costs. Therefore, the profit-maximizing price taker will produce the output level at which marginal revenue (and price) equals marginal cost.

- A firm that experiences losses but that anticipates being able to cover its costs in the long run will operate in the short run if it can cover its average variable costs. Conversely, the firm will shut down if it cannot cover its average variable costs. A firm that does not anticipate being able to cover its average total cost even in the long run will minimize losses by immediately going out of business.

- The price taker's short-run marginal cost curve (above its average variable cost) is its supply curve. The short-run market supply curve is the horizontal summation of the marginal cost curves (above *AVC*) of the firms in the industry.

- When the market price exceeds the firm's average total cost, it will earn an economic profit. When entry barriers are absent, profits will attract new firms into the industry and stimulate the existing firms to expand. This increasing market supply continues and puts downward pressure on the price until it reaches the level of average total cost, eliminating the economic profit.

- When the market price is less than the firm's average total cost, the resulting losses imply that the resources could be used elsewhere to produce more value. Losses will cause firms to leave the industry or to reduce the scale of their operations. This declining market supply continues and puts upward pressure on price until the firms remaining in the market are once again able to earn normal returns (zero economic profit).

- As the output of an industry expands in response to rising demand, "fixed" resources like the size of the firm's plant will make it costly for firms to expand output quickly. The diminishing returns and rising marginal costs of firms explain why the short-run market supply curve slopes upward to the right.

- Normally, as industry output expands, rising factor prices push the costs of each firm upward, causing the long-run market supply curve to slope upward to the right also. However, in the long run, firms can alter the size of their plants and other resources that are fixed in the short run. As a result, the market supply curve is generally more elastic in the long run than the short run.

- Firms earn economic profit by producing goods that can be sold for more than the cost of the resources required to produce them. Profit is a reward people get for increasing the value of resources. Conversely, losses are a penalty imposed on those who use resources in a way that reduces their value.

- Competition motivates producers to operate efficiently, heed the views of consumers, and discover better products and lower-cost production methods. In competitive markets, self-interested producers will be directed toward wealth-creating activities that generate economic progress.

CRITICAL ANALYSIS QUESTIONS

1. *Farmers are often heard to complain about the high costs of machinery, labor, and fertilizer, suggesting that these costs drive down their profits. Does it follow that if, for example, the price of fertilizer fell by 10 percent, farming (a highly competitive industry with low barriers to entry) would be more profitable? Explain.

2. *If the firms in a price-taker market are making short-run profits, what will happen to the market price in the long run? Explain.

3. "In a price-taker market, if a business operator produces efficiently—that is, if the cost of producing the good is minimized—the operator will be able to make at least a normal profit." True or false? Explain.

4. Suppose the government of a large city levies a 5 percent sales tax on hotel rooms. How will the tax affect (a) prices of hotel rooms, (b) the profits of hotel owners, and (c) gross expenditures (including the tax) on hotel rooms?

5. *If coffee suppliers are price takers, how will an unanticipated increase in demand for their product affect each of the following, in a market that was initially in long-run equilibrium?
   a. the short-run market price of the product

b. industry output in the short run
c. profitability in the short run
d. the long-run market price in the industry
e. industry output in the long run
f. profitability in the long run

6. *Suppose that the development of a new drought-resistant hybrid seed corn leads to a 50 percent increase in the average yield per acre without increasing the cost to the farmers who use the new technology. If the producers in the corn production industry were price takers, what would happen to the following?
   a. the price of corn
   b. the profitability of corn farmers who quickly adopt the new technology
   c. the profitability of corn farmers who are slow to adopt the new technology
   d. the price of soybeans, a substitute product for corn

7. "When the firms in the industry are just able to cover their cost of production, economic profit is zero. Therefore, if demand falls, causing prices to go down even a little bit, all of the firms in the industry will be driven out of business." True or false? Explain.

8. Why does the short-run market supply curve for a product slope upward to the right? Why does the long-run market supply curve generally slope upward to the right? Why is the long-run market supply curve generally more elastic than the short-run supply curve?

9. *How does competition among firms affect the incentive of each firm to (a) operate efficiently (produce at a low per-unit cost) and (b) produce goods that consumers value? What happens to firms that fail to do these two things?

10. Will firms in a price-taker market be able to earn profits in the long run? Why or why not? What determines profitability? Discuss.

11. *During 2011, drought conditions throughout much of Europe substantially reduced the size of the corn, wheat, and soybean crops, three commodities for which demand is inelastic. Use the price-taker model to determine how the drought affected (a) prices of the three commodities, (b) revenue from the three crops, and (c) the profitability of those farming the three crops.

12. Why is competition in a market important? Is there a positive or negative effect on the economy when strong competitive pressures drive various firms out of business? Discuss.

13. Do business firms in competitive markets have a strong incentive to serve the interests of consumers? Are they motivated by a strong desire to help consumers? Are "good intentions" necessary if individuals are going to engage in actions that are helpful to others? Discuss.

14. A combination of high crude oil prices and government subsidies for ethanol have led to a sharp increase in the demand for corn in recent years. How will this increase in demand for corn influence (a) the price of corn; (b) the quantity of corn supplied; (c) the cost of producing soybeans and wheat, crops that are often produced on land suitable for production of corn; (d) the price of cereals, tortillas, and other products produced from corn; and (e) the price of beef, chicken, and pork, meats produced from animals that are generally fed large quantities of corn? Explain each of your answers.

15. *The accompanying table presents the expected cost and revenue data for the Tucker Tomato Farm. The Tuckers produce tomatoes in a greenhouse and sell them wholesale in a price-taker market.
   a. Fill in the firm's marginal cost, average variable cost, average total cost, and profit schedules.
   b. If the Tuckers are profit maximizers, how many tomatoes should they produce when the market price is $500 per ton? Indicate their profits.
   c. Indicate the firm's output level and maximum profit if the market price of tomatoes increases to $550 per ton.
   d. How many units would the Tucker Tomato Farm produce if the price of tomatoes fell to $450 per ton? What would be the firm's profits? Should the firm stay in business? Explain.

Cost and Revenue Schedules for Tucker Tomato Farm, Inc.

OUTPUT (TONS PER MONTH)	TOTAL COST	PRICE PER TON	MARGINAL COST	AVERAGE VARIABLE COST	AVERAGE TOTAL COST	PROFITS (MONTHLY)
0	$1,000	$500	—	—	—	—
1	1,200	500	—	—	—	—
2	1,350	500	—	—	—	—
3	1,550	500	—	—	—	—
4	1,900	500	—	—	—	—
5	2,300	500	—	—	—	—
6	2,750	500	—	—	—	—
7	3,250	500	—	—	—	—
8	3,800	500	—	—	—	—
9	4,400	500	—	—	—	—
10	5,150	500	—	—	—	—

16. In the accompanying table, you are given information about two firms that compete in a price-taker market. Assume that fixed costs for each firm are $20.
    a. Complete the table.
    b. What is the lowest price at which firm A will produce?
    c. How many units of output will it produce at that price? (Assume that it cannot produce fractional units.)
    d. What is the lowest price at which firm B will produce?
    e. How many units of output will it produce?
    f. How many units will firm A produce if the market price is $20?

g. How many units will firm B produce at the $20 price? (Assume that it cannot produce fractional units.)
h. If each firm's total fixed costs are $20 and the price of output is $20, which firm would earn a higher net profit or incur a smaller loss?
i. How much would that net profit or loss be?

*Asterisk denotes questions for which answers are given in Appendix B.

FIRM A

Quantity	Total Variable Cost	Marginal Cost	Average Variable Cost
1	$24	—	—
2	30	—	—
3	38	—	—
4	48	—	—
5	62	—	—
6	82	—	—
7	110	—	—

FIRM B

Quantity	Total Variable Cost	Marginal Cost	Average Variable Cost
1	$8	—	—
2	10	—	—
3	16	—	—
4	24	—	—
5	36	—	—
6	56	—	—
7	86	—	—

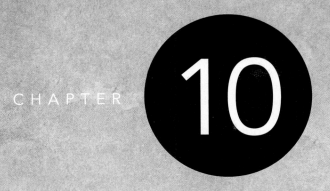

CHAPTER

10

Price-Searcher Markets with Low Entry Barriers

CHAPTER FOCUS

- What are the characteristics of competitive price-searcher markets? How are price and output determined in such markets?

- How will profit and loss influence the choices of price searchers?

- Why do some economists criticize price-searcher behavior when entry barriers are low, while others like the results?

- Is price discrimination bad?

- Why is the role of the entrepreneur left out of economic models? How do the actions of entrepreneurs influence innovation and development of improved products?

- Does successful innovation by some businesses lead to the failure of others? Is this bad?

[T]he price to the price searcher is not determined for him as if by some impersonal market mechanism. Instead he must search out the optimal (wealth-maximizing) price. And, not knowing the demand schedule exactly, he will have to resort to retrial-and-error search processes.

—Armen A. Alchian and William R. Allen[1]

[1]Armen A. Alchian and William R. Allen, *University Economics,* 2nd ed. (Belmont, CA: Wadsworth Publishing, 1967), 113.

As we noted in the previous chapter, price-taker firms decide what output to produce, but they do not have a pricing decision to make. They must take the market-determined price for their output, and they operate in a market with low entry barriers. In this chapter, we will focus on markets in which entry barriers are also low, but firms can instead decide the price they charge. These firms differ in that they face a downward sloping demand curve. If they increase their price they will sell fewer units, and if they reduce their price they will sell more units. This is in contrast to a price-taker firm whose horizontal demand curve means they lose all their sales if they raise price.

COMPETITIVE PRICE-SEARCHER MARKETS

Competitive price-searcher market
A market in which the firms have a downward-sloping demand curve, and entry into and exit from the market are relatively easy.

Differentiated products
Products distinguished from similar products by characteristics like quality, design, location, and method of promotion.

Markets that are characterized by (1) low entry barriers and (2) firms that face a downward-sloping demand curve are called **competitive price-searcher markets**.[2] The low entry barriers ensure that these markets are competitive, and the firm's downward-sloping demand curve means that the sellers in these markets have to search for the price and output combination that will maximize their profits.

In contrast with price-taker markets, in which the firms produce identical products, price searchers produce **differentiated products**. For example, a hamburger from Burger King is not identical to one from McDonald's or Five Guys. The products supplied by the alternative sellers may differ in their design, dependability, location, packaging, and a multitude of other factors. This product differentiation explains why the firms confront a downward-sloping demand curve. Because some consumers are willing to pay more to get the specific product they like best, the firm will lose some but not all its customers to rivals if it raises its price.

Rival firms, however, supply products that are quite similar. Because good substitutes are readily available from other suppliers, the demand curve faced by the firms in competitive price-searcher markets will be downward sloping, but highly elastic.

Given the low entry barriers, new entrants will be attracted if an activity is profitable. Thus, sellers in competitive price-searcher markets face competition from both firms already in the market and potential new firms that might be attracted.

Monopolistic competition
A term often used by economists to describe markets characterized by a large number of sellers that supply differentiated products to a market with low barriers to entry. Essentially, it is an alternative term for a competitive price-searcher market.

Sometimes economists use the term **monopolistic competition** to describe markets quite similar to those of the competitive price-searcher model, but because there is nothing "monopolistic" about these markets, we believe that this term is misleading. Competitive price searcher is much more descriptive of the conditions in these markets. However, students should be aware that the expression "monopolistic competition" is often used to describe markets like those analyzed in this chapter.

For the price searcher, demand is not simply a given. Price searchers must try to estimate how buyers will respond to the various prices that might be charged. In essence, the firm must try to figure out what the demand curve for its product looks like. The firm, by changing product quality, style, location, and service (among many other factors), and by advertising, can also alter the demand for its products. It can increase demand by drawing customers from rivals if it can convince consumers that its products provide more value. In the real world, most firms occupy the complex and risky territory of the price searcher.

PRICE AND OUTPUT IN COMPETITIVE PRICE-SEARCHER MARKETS

How does a price searcher decide what price to charge and what level of output to produce? For the price searcher, reducing price in order to expand output and sales has two conflicting

---

[2]It is important to distinguish between the demand curve faced by the firm and the market demand curve. The competitive price-searcher model focuses on the *firm's* demand curve.

influences on total revenue, illustrated by areas in **Exhibit 1**. First, the increase in sales (from q_1 to q_2) due to the lower price will, by itself, add to the revenue of the price searcher as revenue is obtained on the additional units sold. Second, the price reduction, because it applies to all units sold—*including those that could otherwise have been sold at a higher price* (P_1, rather than the lower price, P_2) reduces the revenue received on the original q_1 units of output.

A numerical example will help to illustrate. Suppose a firm could sell three units at $5 for total revenue of $15, or at a reduced price of $4 it could sell 4 units for a total revenue of $16. When the firm lowers price to $4 to sell the fourth unit, this additional unit sold adds $4 to revenue. But there is an offsetting factor: The three units that could have been sold at $5 now only sell for $4, so the firm loses $1 in revenue on each of those original three units. Thus, the net addition to the firm's revenue (the marginal revenue from the sale of the fourth unit) is only $1, as the loss of $3 is deducted from the gain of $4. This can also be seen in the firm's total revenue, which was $15 at an output of three units (sold at $5) and only $16 at an output of four units (sold at $4).

As price is lowered, these two conflicting forces will result in marginal revenue (a change in total revenue) that is less than the selling price of the additional units. The price searcher's marginal revenue will always be less than price because the prices of units that could have been sold for more will be reduced as price is lowered in order to expand sales. Therefore, as Exhibit 1 shows, the price searcher's marginal revenue curve will always lie below the firm's demand curve.[3] (Remember, the lowercase d is used when the reference is to the *firm's* demand curve.)

In the highly competitive market for custom-fitted golf clubs, firms use competitive weapons such as style, swingweight, variable length and club-shaft flexibility, advertising, and celebrity endorsements. Firms in this market are price searchers.

Ed Honowitz/Stone/Getty images

Exhibit 1

Marginal Revenue of a Price Searcher

When a firm faces a downward-sloping demand curve, a price reduction that increases sales will exert two conflicting influences on total revenue. First, total revenue will rise because of an increase in the number of units sold (from q_1 to q_2). However, revenue losses from the lower price (P_2) on units that could have been sold at a higher price (P_1) will at least partially offset the additional revenues from increased sales. Therefore, the marginal revenue curve will lie inside the firm's demand curve.

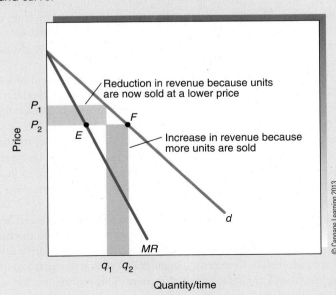

© Cengage Learning 2013

---

[3]For a straight-line demand curve, the marginal revenue curve will bisect any line from the *y*-axis to the demand curve, drawn parallel to the *x*-axis. For example, in Exhibit 1, the *MR* curve will divide the line P_2F into two equal parts, P_2E and EF.

Exhibit 2

The Price Searcher's Price and Output

A price searcher maximizes its profits by producing output q, for which $MR = MC$, and charging price P. The firm is making economic profits. What impact will these profits have if this is a typical firm?

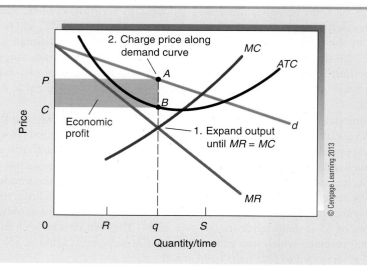

2. Charge price along demand curve

1. Expand output until $MR = MC$

Economic profit

All firms maximize profits by producing all units for which marginal revenue is greater than marginal cost. Therefore, a price searcher will continue to lower price and expand output until marginal revenue is equal to marginal cost.

Exhibit 2 illustrates the profit-maximizing price and output. The price searcher will maximize profit by producing the level of output q, where marginal revenue is equal to marginal cost ($MC = MR$). For any output level less than q (for example, R), a price reduction and resulting sales expansion will add more to revenues than to costs, increasing profit. In contrast, all units beyond q (for example, S), add more to costs than to revenues, reducing profit. Profits will therefore be maximized by producing the output level q. The price the firm should charge is simply the price that will result in exactly q units being sold, which is a price of P. This price can be found by going up to the demand curve (to point A) at the profit maximizing level of output.

The firm in Exhibit 2 is making an economic profit in the short run. Total revenues $PAq0$ exceed the firm's total costs $CBq0$ at the profit-maximizing output level q. Given low barriers to entry in these markets, in the long run economic profits will result in other firms entering the market. These new rivals will draw customers away from existing firms and thereby reduce their demand. This entry of new firms into the market will continue until competition among rivals shifts the demand curve in far enough to eliminate the economic profit earned by the firms in the industry.

As Exhibit 3 illustrates, when long-run equilibrium is present in a competitive price-searcher market, the price will equal per-unit cost. Firms will produce at the $MR = MC$ output level, but they will be unable to earn economic profits because competitive pressures will force the price down to the per-unit cost level.

If losses are present in a specific market, with time, some of the firms in the market will go out of business. As firms leave, some of their previous customers will buy from other firms. The demand curve facing the remaining firms in the industry will then shift outward until the economic losses are eliminated and the long-run, zero-profit equilibrium illustrated by Exhibit 3 is restored.

Consider the role of profits and losses in competitive price-searcher markets. Profits will attract both new firms and additional investment capital into the market. In turn, the increased availability of the product (and similar products) will drive down the price until the profits are eliminated. Conversely, economic losses will cause competitors to exit the market and investment capital to move elsewhere. This will reduce the supply of the product and eventually make it possible for the firms remaining in the market to charge a price sufficient to cover their unit costs. *Thus, firms in competitive price-searcher markets can make either economic profits or losses in the short run. But, after long-run adjustments occur, only a normal profit (that is, zero economic profit) will be possible because entry barriers are low and competition is strong.*

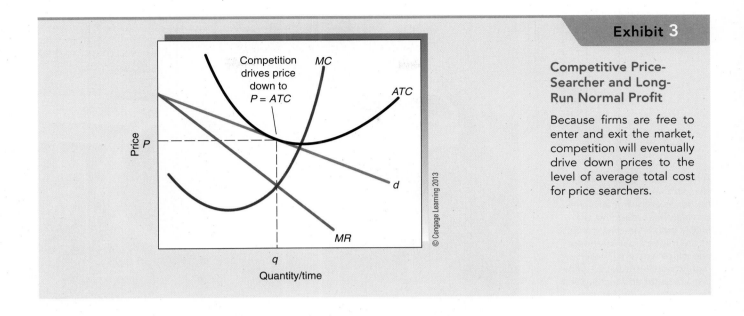

© Cengage Learning 2013

Exhibit 3

Competitive Price-Searcher and Long-Run Normal Profit

Because firms are free to enter and exit the market, competition will eventually drive down prices to the level of average total cost for price searchers.

CONTESTABLE MARKETS AND THE COMPETITIVE PROCESS

If firms can easily enter a market with little risk of suffering a substantial loss if they later exit the market, competition is likely to be intense, even if there are only a few firms operating within it. Markets in which firms can enter and exit with minimal risk are known as contestable markets.[4] Even if entering a contestable market requires a substantial amount of capital, this won't be a major deterrent if the funds can largely be recovered should the firm need to exit. This will be the case when the assets necessary to compete in a market can be either leased for short time periods or resold at something near their original purchase price.

When airport landing rights and facilities are available, an airline route is a classic example of a contestable market. Consider the case of the airline route between Salt Lake City, Utah, and Albuquerque, New Mexico. For many years, only Delta Airlines provided nonstop service on this route, because there is relatively little traffic. Furthermore, there would seem to be high barriers to entry, because it takes multimillion-dollar airplanes to compete, as well as a workforce, facilities for reservations, ticketing, baggage handling, and so on. Given that Delta was the only supplier on the route, one might have expected the price to be high and service relatively poor. However, if firms can easily rent facility space at airports, then the barriers to entry are much lower than the equipment costs suggest. The nonstop Salt Lake City–Albuquerque market, for example, can be entered by other airlines simply by shifting aircraft, personnel, and equipment from other routes and locations. Moreover, airlines often rent or lease their planes. This reduces both the amount of initial capital needed to enter a market and the risk of losing it should the venture fail. Indeed, recently US Airways has offered some service now in competition to Delta on the route. All along, several other airlines have served customers with connecting service, which requires a stop and perhaps a plane change at another city before completing the route connecting Albuquerque and Salt Lake City.

In a contestable market, potential competition, as well as actual entry, will discipline sellers. When entry and exit are not expensive, even a firm alone in a market faces the serious prospect of competition. Two important conditions will be present in contestable

Contestable market
A market in which the costs of entry and exit are low, so a firm risks little by entering. Efficient production and zero economic profits should prevail in a contestable market.

[4]The classic article on this topic is William J. Baumol's "Contestable Markets: An Uprising in the Theory of Industry Structure," *American Economic Review* 72 (March 1982): 1–15.

iStockphoto.com/Bim

Airliners are extremely expensive, so their cost might be a barrier to entry. But airplanes can also be leased and are highly mobile among markets, as are pilots, flight attendants, and office workers. These highly mobile resources allow firms to enter and exit a given transportation market with relative ease. Such a market is contestable.

markets: (1) Prices above the level necessary to achieve zero economic profits will not be sustained, and (2) the costs of production will be kept to a minimum. This is because production inefficiencies and prices that are above costs present a profitable opportunity for new entrants. Predictably, profit-seeking rivals will enter and drive the price down to the level of per-unit costs.

The contestable market model has important policy implications. If policy-makers are concerned that a market is not sufficiently competitive, they should take a close look at its entry barriers and what might be done to make it contestable. Much of economists' enthusiasm for deregulation can be traced to the fact that regulation often impedes market entry. Many economists believe that deregulating markets to make entry easier can lead to lower prices and better performance than other alternatives, including directly regulating prices.

EVALUATING COMPETITIVE PRICE-SEARCHER MARKETS

Because the long-run equilibrium conditions in price-taker markets are generally consistent with ideal economic efficiency, it is useful to compare and contrast them with long-run conditions in competitive price-searcher markets.

First, let us consider the similarities. Because of the low entry barriers, both price takers and competitive price searchers will have a strong incentive to serve the interests of consumers. Neither will be able to earn long-run economic profits. In the long run, competition will drive prices down to the level of average total cost in both price-taker and competitive price-searcher markets. Furthermore, entrepreneurs in both price-taker and price-searcher markets have a strong incentive to manage and operate their businesses efficiently. In both cases, operational inefficiency will lead to higher costs, losses, and forced exit from the market. Similarly, price takers and competitive price searchers alike will be motivated to develop and adopt new, cost-reducing procedures and techniques because lower costs will lead to higher short-run profits (or at least smaller losses).

The responses to changing demand conditions in price-taker and competitive price-searcher markets are also similar. In both cases, any increase in market demand that was not already expected leads to higher prices, short-run profits, expanded output, and the entry of new firms. With the entry of new producers and the expanded output of existing firms, the market supply will increase, putting downward pressure on the price. Profits drive this process until the market price falls to the level of average total cost, squeezing out all economic profit. Correspondingly, lower demand will lead to lower prices and short-run losses, causing output to fall and some firms to exit. As the market supply declines, prices will rise until the short-run losses are eliminated and the firms remaining in the market can again cover their costs. Thus, profits and losses direct the output decisions and market supply in both price-taker and competitive price-searcher markets.

What are some of the differences between the two market structures? As **Exhibit 4** shows, the price taker confronts a horizontal demand curve, while the demand curve of the price-searcher firm is downward sloping. This is important: It means that the marginal revenue of the price-searcher will be less than, not equal to, the price charged for the product sold. So, when the price searcher expands output until $MR = MC$, the price will still exceed the marginal cost (part b). In contrast, the price charged by a profit-maximizing price taker will equal the marginal cost (part a). In addition, when a price searcher is in long-run equilibrium, the firm's output rate will be less than the rate that minimizes average total cost. The price searcher would have a lower per-unit cost ($0.97 rather than $1.00) if a larger output were produced, but MR would be even less.

Some argue that the slightly higher prices (and unit costs) in competitive price-searcher markets indicate that these markets allocate goods and services inefficiently. However, it is important to recognize that the higher prices reflect the fact that it is costly to provide the greater product variety and diversity found in competitive price-searcher markets. But a broader range of choices also provides benefits. The greater variety makes it possible for

Comparing Price-Taker and Price-Searcher Markets

Exhibit 4

Here, we illustrate the long-run equilibrium conditions of a price taker and a price searcher when entry barriers are low. In both cases, the price is equal to the average total cost, and economic profit is zero. However, because the price searcher confronts a downward-sloping demand curve for its product, its profit-maximizing price exceeds marginal cost, and output is not large enough to minimize average total cost when the market is in long-run equilibrium. For identical cost conditions, the price of the product in a price-searcher market will be slightly higher than in a price-taker market. Some argue that this higher price is indicative of inefficiency, whereas others believe that it merely reflects the higher cost accompanying greater variety and convenience.

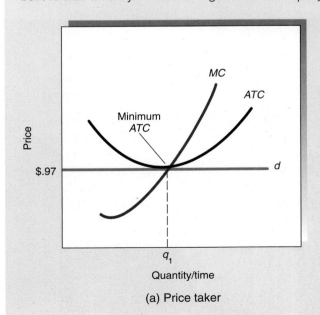

(a) Price taker

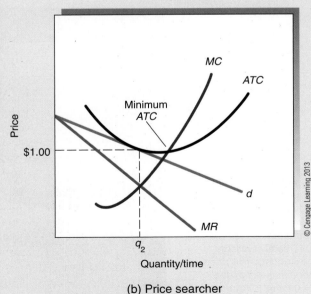

(b) Price searcher

© Cengage Learning 2013

a wider range of consumers to obtain the quality, style, and accompanying service that best fit their preferences and specific situation.

Are the higher prices accompanying the greater diversity worth the cost? This question can't be answered with certainty, but in some cases it is clear that consumers are willing to pay for it. For example, many consumers patronize small, conveniently located stores, even though they know that the same items are available at lower prices at large supermarkets.

The two market structures also differ with regard to advertising: Price searchers often advertise, but price takers do not. Like variety, advertising is costly, and in the long run, consumers cover this cost in the form of higher prices. Do advertised products provide enough information and variety to justify the higher cost from the consumer's viewpoint? We cannot know for certain. However, we do know that producers are always free to use low-priced, more uniform, and less-advertised products to lure buyers away from firms that advertise and provide variety at a higher price. Some firms do, and sometimes the strategy works; yet many consumers choose to buy advertised goods and pay the higher prices. This result suggests that many customers do find that advertised products and greater variety are worth the added cost.

A SPECIAL CASE: PRICE DISCRIMINATION

So far, we have assumed that all sellers of a product will charge each customer the same price. Sometimes, though, price searchers can increase their revenues (and profits) by charging different prices to different groups of consumers. Businesses like hotels, restaurants, and drugstores often charge senior citizens less than other customers. Students and children are often given discounts at movie theaters and athletic events. Bars offer "ladies' night" discounts on drinks for women. Colleges often give financial aid (reduced tuition) to students from low-income families, or scholarships to students with good grades. These practices are called **price discrimination**. *To gain from such a practice, price searchers must be able to do two things: (1) identify and separate at least two groups with differing elasticities of demand and (2) prevent those who buy at the low price from reselling to the customers charged higher prices.*

Let us take a closer look at how sellers may gain from price discrimination. Suppose that a seller has two groups of customers: one with an inelastic demand for its product and the other with an elastic demand. An increase in the price charged the first group will

Price discrimination
A practice whereby a seller charges different consumers different prices for the same product or service.

Students from low-income families are likely to be more sensitive to tuition charges than those from high-income families. Colleges often make scholarships and other forms of financial aid more readily available to low-income students. This price discrimination makes it possible for them to generate larger revenues from tuition than would otherwise be the case.

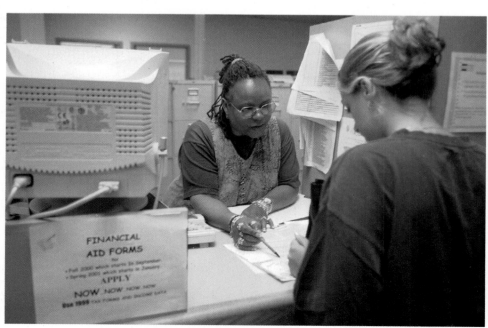

Andrew Holbrooke/The Image Works

increase the total revenue derived from that group. At the same time, a reduction in price will increase revenues derived from the latter. Thus, a seller may be able to increase total revenue and profit by charging the first group a higher price than the second.

The pricing of airline tickets illustrates the potential of price discrimination. The airline industry has found that the demand of business fliers is substantially less elastic than the demand of vacationers, students, and other travelers. Thus, airlines often charge higher fares to people who are unwilling to stay over a weekend, who spend only a day or two at their destination, and who make reservations a short time before their flight. These high fares fall primarily on business travelers, who are less sensitive to price. In contrast, discount fares are offered to fliers willing to make reservations well in advance, travel during off-peak hours, and stay at their destinations over a weekend before returning home. Such travelers are likely to be vacationers and students, who are highly sensitive to price.

Exhibit 5 illustrates the logic of this policy. Part a shows what would happen if a single price were charged to all customers. Given the demand, the profit-maximizing firm expands output to 100, where *MR* equals *MC*. The profit-maximizing price on coast-to-coast flights is $400, which generates $40,000 of revenue per flight. Because the marginal cost per passenger is $100, this provides the airline with net operating revenue of $30,000 with which to cover other costs.

However, as part b shows, although the market demand schedule is unchanged, the airline can do even better if it uses price discrimination. When it charges business travelers $500, most of these passengers continue to use the airline, because their demand is highly inelastic. Conversely, a $100 price cut generates substantial additional ticket sales from price-sensitive vacationers, students, and others whose demands are more

---

Exhibit 5

Price Discrimination

As part (a) illustrates, a $400 ticket price will maximize profits on coast-to-coast flights if an airline charges a single price. However, the airline can do still better if it raises the price to $500 for passengers with a highly inelastic demand (business travelers) and reduces the price to $300 for travelers with a more elastic demand (for example, students and vacationers). When sellers can segment their market, they can gain by (1) charging a higher price to consumers with a less elastic demand and (2) offering discounts to customers whose demand is more elastic.

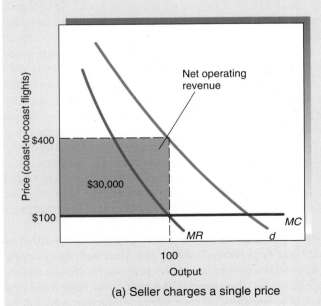

(a) Seller charges a single price

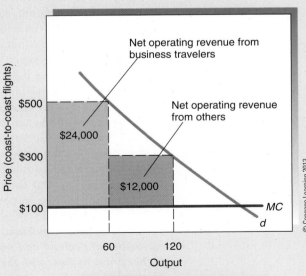

(b) Seller uses price discrimination

© Cengage Learning 2013

elastic. Therefore, with price discrimination, the airline can sell sixty tickets (primarily to business travelers) at $500 and sixty additional tickets to others at $300. Total revenue jumps to $48,000 and leaves the airline with $36,000 ($48,000 minus 120 times the $100 marginal cost per passenger) of revenue in excess of variable cost. Compared with the single-price outcome (part a), the price discrimination strategy expands profit by $6,000.

When sellers can segment their market (at a low cost) into groups with differing price elasticities of demand, price discrimination can increase profits. For *each group*, the seller will maximize profit by equating marginal cost and marginal revenue. This rule will lead to higher prices for groups with a less elastic demand and lower prices for those with a more elastic demand. Compared with the single-price situation, price discrimination increases profitability because a higher price increases the net revenue from groups with an inelastic demand, while a lower price increases the net revenue from price-sensitive customers. With price discrimination, the number of units sold also increases (compare part a with part b) because the discounts provided to price-sensitive groups increase the quantity sold more than the higher prices charged the less-price-sensitive groups reduce sales.

Of course, this will work only if the two groups can't trade with each other. Movie theaters sell children's tickets to kids, and the tickets cannot be used by adults. Notice, though, that they don't try to sell popcorn at lower prices to children because popcorn could be too easily resold to adults.

How do buyers fare when a seller can price discriminate? Some buyers pay more than they would if a single, intermediate price were offered. They purchase fewer units, and they are worse off. In contrast, those for whom the price-discrimination process lowers the price are better off. Of course, with some products, such as airline transportation, a single buyer might be better off with some purchases and worse off with others.

On balance, however, we can expect that output will be greater with price discrimination than it would be with a single price. The market is not as understocked as it would have been in the absence of the price discrimination. So from an allocative efficiency standpoint, price discrimination gets high marks; it allows more trades, reducing the inefficiency due to price being set above marginal cost. Some of the gains that would accrue to consumers with an inelastic demand are transferred to the price searcher as increased revenue, but additional gains from trade are created by the increased output of goods that would be lost if price discrimination were absent.

In some markets, there is an additional gain from price discrimination: Production may occur that would be lost entirely if only a single price could be charged. With price discrimination, some otherwise unprofitable firms may be able to generate enough additional revenue to operate successfully in the marketplace. For example, some small towns in Montana might not provide enough revenue at a single price to enable a local physician to cover her opportunity costs. However, if she is able to discriminate on the basis of income, charging higher-income patients more than normal rates and lower-income patients less, the resulting revenues from practicing in the small town may enable her to stay in the community. In this case, all residents of the town may be better off because of the price discrimination, since it makes it possible for them to access a local physician. After all, even those being charged the highest prices are not disadvantaged if the price discrimination keeps the physician in town. They are just as able to seek physician services elsewhere as they would have been in the absence of the price-discriminating local doctor. With or without price discrimination, access to competing sellers (or buyers) protects market participants from unfair treatment.

In summary, if potential customers can be segmented into groups with different elasticities of demand and resale can be prevented, sellers can often gain by charging higher prices to those with the less elastic demand (and lower prices to those with a more elastic demand). Price discrimination can also increase the total gains from trade and thereby reduce allocative inefficiency. Sometimes it even allows production where none would have otherwise occurred.

ENTREPRENEURSHIP AND ECONOMIC PROGRESS

Entrepreneurship
Entrepreneurial discovery and the development of improved products and production processes provide a central element of economic progress.

keys to economic prosperity

iStockphoto.com/Scott Dunlap

Scientific models simplify conditions in order to help us understand complex relationships. Economic models like the price-taker and price-searcher models are no exception. But these models are not rich enough to fully capture all aspects of the dynamic process of competition. Competitive markets provide entrepreneurs with a strong incentive to innovate and discover better ways of doing things. However, if we are going to get the most from the available resources, they must be directed toward the activities that create the most value. This target, however, is an ever-shifting one. Discovery of new products, technologies, and organizational structures creates opportunities for some and diminishes them for others. To a large degree, market economies are successful because they provide entrepreneurs with a strong incentive to search for and act on opportunities to move resources toward higher valued uses in a world of constant change.[5]

Entrepreneurs must make choices about how much output and what kind of output to produce and what price to charge. They also must figure out the type of business structure, scale of operation, and combination of jointly supplied goods and services that will keep per-unit costs low. The entry of firms into an industry earning short-run economic profit also reflects the decisions and behavior of entrepreneurs searching for profit opportunities. Moreover, all of these choices must be made with imperfect information under conditions of uncertainty. While the assumptions and operational elements of the price-taker and price searcher models incorporate these elements, they do not reflect the central role of entrepreneurial decision-making. Therefore, the picture is incomplete.

The role of the entrepreneur cannot be fully captured by the profit maximization assumption of a model. Better ways of doing things do not just happen; they must be discovered and developed by entrepreneurs. Further, the actions of entrepreneurs often cause entirely new markets to appear, and others to disappear. A hypothetical newspaper ad to hire an entrepreneur might read something like this:

> *Wanted: Entrepreneur.* Diverse skills required. Must be (1) alert to new business opportunities and new problems before they become obvious; (2) willing to back judgments with hard work and creative effort before others recognize the correctness of judgments; (3) able to make correct decisions and convince others of their validity, so as to attract additional financial backing; and (4) able to recognize own inevitable mistakes and to back away from incorrect decisions without wasting additional resources. Exciting, exhausting, high-risk position. Pay will be very good for success and very poor for failure.

Entrepreneurship is a process in which individual entrepreneurs discover previously unnoticed profit opportunities and act on them. In this framework profit opportunities always exist in the marketplace, but they must be discovered. The rate of discovery will depend on the reward. In economies where it is attractive to discover better ways of doing things, the discovery rate of wealth creating opportunities will be higher and human progress more rapid.

---

[5]For a more complete overview of entrepreneurship and references on the topic, see Mark Crosson, "Entrepreneurship," in *The New Palgrave: A Dictionary of Economics,* ed. John Eatwell et al. (New York: Stockton Press, 1987), 151–153; and Russell Sobel, "Entrepreneurship," in David R. Henderson, ed., *The Concise Encyclopedia of Economics,* 2nd ed. (Indianapolis: Liberty Fund, 2007).

Entrepreneurship and discovery can happen within existing business firms (often called "intrapreneurship") or from new entrants into the marketplace. Research shows that large existing corporations are more likely to make marginal improvements on existing products, while breakthrough ideas are more likely to come from new start-up firms.

An entrepreneur is someone who finds new combinations of resources and creates products and production methods that did not previously exist. Sifting through these many combinations is a complex task fraught with uncertainty because the number of ways of combining resources is almost limitless. A growing, vibrant economy will be characterized by the constant introduction of new products and services. Think of the new products that have been introduced during the last fifty years: microwave ovens, personal computers, cellular telephones, DVD players, video games, better coronary artery bypass techniques, and computerized social networks come to mind. Innovations like these have had an enormous impact on our lives.

But no one knows what the next innovative breakthrough will be or who will discover and develop it. Even smart professors, business leaders, and government officials are unable to pre-evaluate business ideas and differentiate between those that will succeed and the ones destined for failure. For example, Fred Smith, the founder of Federal Express Corporation, developed the business plan for FedEx as a class project while he was a student at Yale University. His business professor gave him a "C" because he thought the idea was infeasible. (See Applications in Economics Box on "Five Entrepreneurs Who Have Changed Our Lives.") Not even entrepreneurs themselves can know for certain in advance whether their business idea will be profitable. The only real test is to try it out within the framework of the competitive market process.

DYNAMIC COMPETITION, INNOVATION, AND BUSINESS FAILURES

Business failures are often painful for the parties directly involved. From the standpoint of the entire economy, however, business failures and the shrinkage of other firms play an important role: They weed out less efficient, high-cost producers and production, and release resources to be employed more productively elsewhere. The assets and workers of firms that shrink or fail become available for use by others, supplying goods that are more highly valued by consumers, relative to their costs. Without this release of resources, the expansion of both profitable firms and the entire economy would be slowed. Viewed from this perspective, business failures are often the flip side of consumers shifting their spending toward firms offering improved products and/or lower prices.

While business failures occur for a variety of reasons, including poor management and misjudgment of market conditions, innovative actions by rivals is also a major contributing factor. When a firm introduces a new, improved product or comes up with a lower-cost method of supplying a good, it will attract buyers away from other firms. Entrepreneurship is inherently a disruptive force in an economy because the introduction of new products leads to the obsolescence of others, a process known as "creative destruction." Examples abound. The digital camera has virtually eliminated the use and production of film. The introduction of digital music has resulted in the closure of stores selling CDs like Tower Records and Music Den. The innovations of on-demand movies, Netflix, and Redbox have driven traditional movie rental stores like Blockbuster and Movie Gallery (which ran Hollywood Video) into bankruptcy.

Even giant firms can be brought down by innovative rivals. During the 1990s, Microsoft's dominance of the computer industry was overwhelming. Between January 1990 and January 2000, Microsoft's stock price rose by about 8,000 percent. Apple lagged far behind Microsoft in both market share and brand name recognition. But things soon began to change. Apple introduced the iPod in 1996, which revolutionized how consumers purchased and listened to music, and gained substantial brand name recognition among consumers, especially younger consumers. In 2007, Apple introduced the iPhone, again changing the game, but this time in the market for cell phones. The innovative behavior of Apple continued, in 2008 the MacBook Air was introduced, and in 2010 the iPad again unleashed a wave of creative destruction, altering the way consumers receive news, read books, and play games. During the first decade of this century, the stock value of Microsoft fell by more than 40 percent, while that of Apple soared. By 2010, the market value of Apple surpassed that of the previously dominant Microsoft.

In a competitive economy, numerous businesses come and go. Each year, newly incorporated businesses account for about 10 percent of the total, but about 60 percent of them will fail within six years. Even during good economic times, approximately 1 percent of businesses file for bankruptcy each year, and many others close their doors or sell their assets to other, more successful (or at least more optimistic) operators.

From an economic standpoint then, business failure has a positive side; it gets rid of bad or outdated ideas, freeing up resources to be used in other endeavors. A vibrant economy will have both a large number of new business start-ups and a large number of business failures. However, as more ideas are tried, it will be more likely that we will stumble on to that one-in-a-million new innovation that will substantially improve our lives.

Let's summarize the importance of entrepreneurship. Discovery of new products and better ways of doing things is an important source of economic growth and improved living standards. These discoveries often come from unexpected sources and there is no way to tell in advance which will succeed and which will fail. Thus, it is vitally important that new ideas can be tested. Many will fail, but a few will succeed and transform our lives. This discovery process is too complex to be captured, at least not fully, by models, but it is nonetheless a central ingredient of a healthy, growing economy.

APPLICATIONS IN ECONOMICS

Five Entrepreneurs Who Have Changed Our Lives

Compared with movie stars and athletes, business entrepreneurs seldom command quite as much respect in our society. Often, their contributions are either overlooked or misunderstood. Everyone knows that highly successful entrepreneurs make a lot of money. But their innovative ideas and product improvements enhance the lives of others. If they did not, people would not buy their products and services. Entrepreneurs are a major source of economic progress and higher living standards. Their impact on our lives is far greater than most realize. Let's take a closer look at the impact of five leading entrepreneurs.

Fred Smith

In 2010, FedEx had 141,000 employees and generated $35 billion in revenues. Fred Smith was the founder of the path-breaking firm. The idea behind FedEx came to him when he was in college in the 1960s, with his observation that computers were going to become a major part of people's lives. More important, he predicted a logical consequence: If computers were going to replace people for many tasks, the computers would have to be in good working order every day. If something went wrong, it would need to be fixed immediately. This would create a strong demand for a delivery system capable of getting parts and materials whenever and wherever they were needed.

Beginning in 1973, FedEx created a giant network of airplane and truck transportation capable of providing overnight delivery around the world. Smith's chief innovation was the development of a transportation system with a "central switch" or "central junction." For FedEx, that was Memphis, Tennessee. When one looks at moving an item from Detroit to Minneapolis via Memphis, it seems inefficient, says Smith. "But when you take all of the transactions on the network together, it's tremendously efficient."

Smith developed the idea and described the system in a paper for a business strategy course while studying in the M.B.A. program at Yale. Perhaps because it seemed far-fetched at the time, he reports that the professor gave him a "gentleman's C." In the following decade, however, Smith founded Federal Express and created the express delivery system outlined in his paper. FedEx has revolutionized the express mail and package delivery system. It has forced competitors, from the U.S. Postal Service to United Parcel Service, to become more efficient and to make major changes in their operations. Smith can take great pride in the fact that the market gave him a much higher grade than his old M.B.A. professor.

(continued)

Oprah Winfrey

Oprah Winfrey is a billionaire, a successful entrepreneur, and a one-person conglomerate. Winfrey overcame personal difficulties to achieve her success. Her parents never married, and her childhood was spent traveling among temporary homes with family members in Mississippi, Nashville, and Milwaukee. She attended Tennessee State University in Nashville but left early to take a job at a local radio station.

In 1984, she started as a talk-show host in Chicago, but her program was soon the top talk show in the country. It has held that rating for nearly two decades and is now broadcast in more than 100 countries. Always inspirational, she decided in the mid-1990s that her show, which was often about dysfunctional relationships, was too negative. She began to make it more upbeat and also began to develop "lifestyle" products that were attractive and uplifting. As a child, Winfrey loved to read, so she formed Oprah's Book Club, which existed for 25 years and created many bestsellers. She has two of her own magazines, *O, the Oprah Magazine* as well as *O at Home*, about personal home decorating. She was a cofounder of the Oxygen Network, a cable television network, and in January 2011 she launched a new network called OWN. Winfrey is an astute business executive, with her own company, Harpo, Inc. (that's Oprah spelled backward). Few entrepreneurs have changed more lives than Oprah has. She changed television by winning an international audience through candid and heartfelt discussion and she has expanded her influence through many other businesses. Most important perhaps, she has encouraged women to advance both emotionally and intellectually.

Peter Thiel

Many of you have probably never heard of this entrepreneur, but if you have ever used PayPal or Facebook, you have benefited from his entrepreneurial skills. Thiel was a cofounder of PayPal in 1998, and served as its CEO. He sold it to eBay in 2002 for $1.5 billion, personally netting $60 million. In 2004, Thiel invested $500,000 in Facebook. This stake now makes up the bulk of his net worth, reported to be $1.5 billion in March of 2011. As with many entrepreneurs, he has not had a perfect record in his still-young investment career (he will turn 45 in 2012). In 2005 he opened a hedge fund, Clarium Capital in New York, but the assets of that fund, once as high as $6 billion in mid-2008, have since fallen to just $460 million.

Thiel has many and varied talents and interests, from human rights, philosophy, and technology to film. He coproduced a film, *Thank You for Smoking*. As a student at Stanford, he founded *The Stanford Review* newspaper.

Earlier in life he was a chess champion, ranking seventh in the U.S. under-13 age bracket.

His creativity even carries over to his charitable giving. In 2008, he pledged $500,000 to the new Seasteading Institute, to support their mission "to establish permanent, autonomous ocean communities to enable experimentation and innovation with diverse social, political, and legal systems." In 2010 he established a "Thiel Fellowship" that would award $100,000 to each of 20 people less than 20 years of age who promised to quit college and create their own entrepreneurial ventures. If the awardees have a fraction of the creativity of this imaginative entrepreneur, the future world will be an exciting place to live.

Sergey Brin and Larry Page

For years, Internet users struggled to find billions of bits of information scattered across the World Wide Web. Two Stanford computer science graduate students—Sergey Brin and Larry Page—dramatically simplified that process. Brin and Page were in their early twenties when they dropped out of graduate school. Using their credit cards and those of their parents and friends, they formed Google, Inc., in a garage in Menlo Park, California. ("Googol" is the number 1 followed by 100 zeros.)

Google's computers are constantly searching the Web, downloading a huge number of files into the company's databases, and updating them regularly. The sophisticated programs sort and quickly bring the most important and reliable information to the top of users' screens. Information seekers love it. The keywords they type in for their searches also target the advertising that generates the firm's revenue. Unlike, say, a newspaper, which delivers the same ads to every reader, Google links advertising to the user's particular interests according to the topic being searched. Users see fewer ads, but advertisers get more targeted exposure of their messages.

In 2004, Google's stock went public. Even the stock offering was innovative—a "Dutch auction," whereby anyone, including individual investors, could bid on the shares. The bidder specified a price as high or low as he or she wanted and the number of shares to be purchased at that price. Following the auction, the stock opened on the market at just over $100 per share. While there have been ups and downs in the price, the stock was trading in the $600 per share range during the first quarter of 2011. The two founders of Google have not yet earned their doctorates, but they *have* earned a fortune. They did it by designing a system that benefits millions of people every day.

Looking Ahead

In this chapter, we have analyzed the choices facing price searchers and their behavior when barriers to entry are low. The following chapter will analyze the performance of price-searcher markets when the barriers to entry are relatively high.

iStockphoto.com/gaspr13

KEY POINTS

- Firms in price-searcher markets with low barriers to entry face a downward-sloping demand curve. They are free to set the prices for the products that they sell but face strong competitive pressure from existing and potential rivals.

- Firms in price searcher markets with low entry barriers use product quality, style, convenience of location, advertising, and price as competitive weapons. Because each firm competes with rivals offering similar products, each confronts a highly elastic demand curve for its products.

- A profit-maximizing price searcher will expand output as long as marginal revenue exceeds marginal cost, lowering its price in the process, until $MR = MC$. The price charged by the profit-maximizing price searcher will be greater than its marginal cost.

- Firms in competitive price-searcher markets can experience either profits or losses in the short run. Profits will attract rival firms into the market until supply increases and the profit-maximizing price falls to the level of per-unit price. Losses will cause firms to exit the market until the price increases enough that the remaining firms can once again cover their per-unit costs. Because of the low entry barriers, the firms in competitive price-searcher markets will earn only normal returns (zero economic profit) in long-run equilibrium.

- Competition can come from potential as well as actual rivals. If entry and exit can be arranged at low cost, and if there are no legal barriers to entry, the theory of contestable markets indicates that competitive results will be approximated, even if there are only a few firms actually in the market.

- Competitive price-searcher markets provide more variety but may raise costs relative to price-taker markets because (1) price exceeds marginal cost at the profit-maximizing output level, (2) long-run average cost is not minimized, and (3) advertising is costly. When barriers to entry are low, however, price searchers have an incentive to (1) produce efficiently; (2) undertake production if, and only if, their actions are expected to increase the value of the resources used; and (3) be innovative in offering new product options.

- When a price searcher can (1) identify groups of customers that have different price elasticities of demand and (2) prevent customers from retrading the product, price discrimination may emerge. Sellers may be able to gain by charging higher prices to groups with a less elastic demand and lower prices to those with a more elastic demand. The practice generally leads to a larger output and more gains from trade than would otherwise occur.

- Entrepreneurs discover previously unnoticed profit opportunities and act on them. By discovering and developing new products that are highly valued relative to cost, entrepreneurs promote economic progress. The profit and loss system provides entrepreneurs with quick and persuasive feedback on the merit of their idea.

- Entrepreneurship is an inherently disruptive force in an economy as new products often cause the failure of old ones. But this creative destruction is an important source of improved products, lower costs production methods, and higher living standards.

CRITICAL ANALYSIS QUESTIONS

1. Price searchers can set the prices of their products. Does this mean that they will charge the highest possible price for their products? Why or why not?

2. Because price searchers can set their prices, does this mean that their prices are unaffected by market conditions? In price-searcher markets with low barriers to

entry, will the firms be able to make economic profit in the long run? Why or why not?

3. *What determines the *variety* of styles, designs, and sizes of different products? Why do you think there are only a few different varieties of toothpicks but lots of different types of napkins on the market?

4. What do competitive price searchers have to do to make economic profit?

5. What must an entrepreneur do in order to introduce a new innovative product? What determines whether the new product will be a success or failure?

6. Is quality and style competition as important as price competition? Would you like to live in a country where government regulation restricted the use of quality and style competition? Why or why not? Do you think you would get more or less for your consumer dollar under restrictions like these? Discuss.

7. *Suppose that a price searcher is currently charging a price that maximizes the firm's total revenue. Will this price also maximize the firm's profit? Why or why not? Explain.

8.* a. What determines whether corporations, individual proprietorships, employee-owned firms, consumer cooperatives, or some other form of business structure will dominate in a market?

  b. What determines whether small firms, medium-size firms, or large firms will dominate in a market?

9. Would our standard of living be higher if the government "bailed out" troubled businesses? If a firm goes out of business, what happens to the firm's assets, workers, and customers? Are business failures bad for the economy? Why or why not?

10. *Suppose that a group of investors wants to start a business operated out of a popular Utah ski area. The group is considering either building a new hotel complex or starting a new local airline serving that market. Each new business would require about the same amount of capital and personnel hiring. The group believes each endeavor has the same profit potential. Which is the safer (less likely to result in a substantial capital loss) investment? Why? Is there an offsetting advantage to the other investment?

11. Is price discrimination harmful to the economy? How does price discrimination affect the total amount of gains from exchange? Explain. Why do colleges often charge students different prices based on their family income?

12. *"When competition is intense, only the big firms survive. The little guy has no chance." True or false? Explain.

13. What is the primary requirement for a market to be competitive? Is competition necessary for markets to work well? Why or why not? How does competition influence the following: (a) the cost efficiency of producers, (b) the quality of products, and (c) the

discovery and development of new products? Explain your answers.

14. *What keeps McDonald's, Walmart, General Motors, or any other business firm from raising prices, selling shoddy products, and providing lousy service?

15. "The superiority of the competitive market is the positive stimuli it provides for constantly improving efficiency, innovating, and offering consumers diversity of choice." This quotation is from Alfred Kahn, the architect of transportation deregulation during the 1970s. Evaluate the statement. Is it true? Discuss.

16. The accompanying graph shows the short-run demand and cost situation for a price searcher in a market with low barriers to entry.

  a. What level of output will maximize the firm's profit level?

  b. What price will the firm charge?

  c. How much revenue will the firm receive in this situation? How much is total cost? Total profit?

  d. How will the situation change over time?

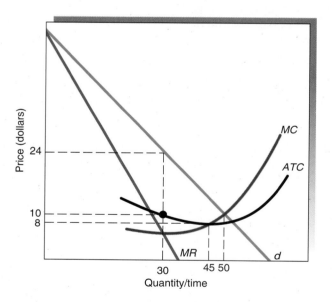

17. *Rod N. Reel owns a dealership that sells fishing boats in an open, price-searcher market. To develop his pricing strategy, Rod hired an economist to estimate his demand curve. Columns (1) and (2) of the chart on the next page provide the data for the expected weekly quantity demanded for Rod's fishing boats at alternative prices. Rod's marginal (and average) cost of supplying each boat is constant at $5,000 per boat no matter how many boats he sells per week in this range. This cost includes all opportunity costs and represents the economic cost per boat.

  a. Find Rod's economic profits at each alternative price by calculating the difference between total revenue and total cost.

b. Find Rod's marginal revenue and marginal cost from the sale of each additional boat.

c. If Rod wants to maximize his profits, what price should he charge per boat?

d. How many boats will Rod sell per week at the profit-maximizing price?

e. What will Rod's profits be per week at this price and sales volume?

f. At the price and sales level where profits are maximized, has Rod sold all boats that have higher marginal revenue than marginal cost?

g. If Rod's profits are typical of all firms in the boat sales business, what might be expected to happen in the future? Will more boat dealers open in the area, or will some of the existing ones go out of business? What will happen to the profitability of the boat dealers in the future once the entry/exit has occurred?

h. Challenge Question: Recall the relationship between elasticity of demand, price changes, and their impact on total revenues. As Rod lowers his price from $9,000 to $5,000, his total revenues keep increasing. Is demand in this price range elastic, inelastic, or unit elastic? When Rod lowers his price from $5,000 to $4,000, his total revenues stay the same. Is demand in this price range elastic, inelastic, or unit elastic? Can you guess what might happen at prices below $4,000? Explain.

*Asterisk denotes questions for which answers are given in Appendix B.

Price of Fishing Boats (1)	Number of Fishing Boats Sold per Week (2)	Total Revenue per Week (3)	Total Cost per Week (4)	Economic Profit per Week (5)	Marginal Revenue (6)	Marginal Cost (7)
$9,000	0	—	—	—	n/a	n/a
8,000	1	—	—	—	—	—
7,000	2	—	—	—	—	—
6,000	3	—	—	—	—	—
5,000	4	—	—	—	—	—
4,000	5	—	—	—	—	—

Price-Searcher Markets with High Entry Barriers

CHAPTER FOCUS

- What are the major barriers to entry that limit competitiveness in some markets?

- What is a monopoly? Does it guarantee the ability to make a profit?

- What is an oligopoly? When are oligopolists likely to collude? Why is it impossible to construct a general theory of output and price for an oligopolist?

- Will competition keep large firms in check in markets that have high barriers to entry? What problems may arise in such markets?

- What policy alternatives might improve the operation of markets with high barriers to entry?

"When the monopolist raises prices above the competitive level in order to reap his monopoly profits, customers buy less of the product, less is produced, and society as a whole is worse off. In short, monopoly reduces society's income."

"… [C]ompetition is a tough weed, not a delicate flower."

—*George Stigler*[1]

---

[1] Both quotes are from George J. Stigler, "Monopoly," in *The Concise Encyclopedia of Economics*, 2nd ed., David R. Henderson, editor, (Indianapolis, Ind.: Liberty Fund, Inc., 2007), available online at http://www.econlib.org/library/Enc/Monopoly.html.

In the previous two chapters, we analyzed the way firms behave in markets with low barriers to entry. In those markets, short-run economic profits lead to the entry of new firms and expansion in supply that drive profits down to a normal level (zero economic profit). We now turn to the analysis of firm behavior when entry barriers are high and there are few, if any, rival firms offering the same or similar products. This chapter focuses on factors that make entry into a market more difficult, and how this can reduce the ability of markets to keep firms in check. We will also consider policy alternatives that might improve the efficiency of these markets.

iStockphoto.com/nicoolay

WHY ARE ENTRY BARRIERS SOMETIMES HIGH?

What makes it difficult for potential competitors to enter a market? Under certain conditions, four factors can be important: economies of scale, government licensing, patents, and control over an essential resource. Let's consider each.

ECONOMIES OF SCALE

When the fixed costs in an industry are large, bigger firms can generally achieve lower average total per-unit costs than can smaller ones. As our discussion of contestable markets indicated in the last chapter, however, economies of scale and high fixed costs are not a significant barrier to entry when the assets needed to enter the market can be leased, transferred to another location, or resold later without a major loss of value.

In some markets, however, this will not be the case. Airline routes may be contestable, but airplane manufacturing is not, because much of the equipment used to produce airplanes is of little use in the production of other things. Once it is in place, most of the equipment cannot be shifted to other uses. The cost of the equipment is a sunk cost. Under these circumstances, if necessary, the incumbent firm will continue operating for a lengthy period of time as long as it can cover its variable (operating) costs. Potential new entrants will recognize that this incentive structure will make it extremely difficult to displace the current incumbent. Thus, they will be reluctant to attempt entry, even if the current incumbent is earning economic profit. A dominant firm will tend to emerge in the industry, and if the market is not contestable, the cost advantages resulting from its size will protect it from potential rivals.

GOVERNMENT LICENSING AND OTHER LEGAL BARRIERS TO ENTRY

Government imposed legal barriers are the oldest and most prevalent method of protecting a business firm from potential competitors. Kings once granted exclusive business rights to favored citizens or groups. Tariffs that raise the price of imported goods and quotas that limit the quantity of imports have reduced the competitiveness of various markets for centuries. To compete in certain parts of the communications industry in the United States (for example, to operate a radio or television station), one must obtain a government license. Similarly, local governments often grant exclusive licenses for the local operation of cable television systems. Each of these measures reduces competition and protects the profits of favored firms, and often in effect provides a local monopoly franchise.

Licensing can also limit entry and reduce competitiveness even without the monopoly franchise feature. States and cities often require the operators of liquor stores, hairstyling shops, taxicabs, funeral homes, and many other businesses to obtain a license.

Licensing
A requirement that one obtain permission from the government in order to perform certain business activities or work in various occupations.

Sometimes, these licenses cost little and are designed to ensure certain minimum standards. Often, however, they are costly to obtain and a major deterrent to the entry of potential rivals.

PATENTS

Most countries have patent laws to give inventors a property right to their inventions. A patent grants the owner the exclusive legal right to the commercial use of a newly invented product or process for a limited period of time—twenty years in the United States. Others are not allowed to copy the product or procedure without the permission of the patent holder. For example, when a pharmaceutical company is granted a patent for a newly developed drug, other potential suppliers must obtain permission from the patent holder before producing and selling the product during the life of the patent. Others might be able to supply the drug more economically. During that time period though, if they want to do so while the patent is in effect, they will have to purchase the production and marketing rights from the originating firm.

A firm that develops a new drug can use patent protection to restrain production by others for twenty years from the time the patent is issued. Although consumers will pay higher prices than if open competition were permitted, they may benefit from additional investment in research and more rapid development of new products by firms seeking a market with patent protection.

Both costs and benefits for consumers come with a patent system. The entry barrier created by the grant of a patent generally leads to higher consumer prices for several years, for products that have already been developed. On the positive side, however, patents increase the potential returns to inventive activity, thus encouraging scientific research and technological improvements. As we noted in the previous chapter, entrepreneurial discovery will occur at a faster rate when it is more profitable. A study at the Federal Trade Commission estimated the average cost of developing and testing a new pharmaceutical drug at more than $1 billion.[2] Without the profit potential accompanying patents, the incentive to engage in research and develop new products would be reduced.

CONTROL OVER AN ESSENTIAL RESOURCE

Control over a resource essential to produce a product may also insulate a firm from direct competitors. An example often cited is the Aluminum Company of America, which before World War II controlled the known supply of bauxite conveniently available to American firms. Without this critical raw material, potential competitors could not produce aluminum. Over time, however, other supplies of bauxite were discovered, and the Aluminum Company of America lost its advantage. Resource monopolies are seldom complete or long lasting. Profit opportunities provide potential competitors with an incentive to search for mineral deposits, new technologies, and substitute resources. Over time, they are usually found.

Barriers to entry like the different ones we've just described are often temporary, but they do exist. Let's see what happens when, at least temporarily, there is a barrier to entry high enough to limit the market to only one seller.

Monopoly
A market structure characterized by (1) a single seller of a well-defined product for which there are no good substitutes and (2) high barriers to the entry of any other firms into the market for that product.

CHARACTERISTICS OF A MONOPOLY

The word *monopoly*, derived from two Greek words, means "single seller." We will define **monopoly** as a market characterized by (1) high barriers to entry and (2) a single seller of a well-defined product for which there are no good substitutes. Even this definition is ambiguous, because "high barriers" and "good substitutes" are both relative terms. Are the barriers to entry into the automobile or steel industries high? Many observers would argue that they

---

[2]See Christopher P. Adams and Van V. Brantner, "Estimating the Cost of New Drug Development: Is It Really $802 Million?" *Health Affairs* 25, no. 2 (March/April 2006): 421–28.

are. After all, it takes a great deal of capital to operate at the least-cost scale of output in both of these industries. However, there are no *physical* or *legal* restraints that prevent an entrepreneur from producing automobiles or steel. If price is well above cost and profit potential is present, it should not be too difficult to find the necessary investment capital. Thus, some would argue that entry barriers into these industries are not particularly high.

"Good substitute" is also a subjective term. There is always some substitutability among products, even those produced by a single seller. Is a letter a good substitute for a telephone or e-mail message? For some purposes—correspondence between law firms, for example—a letter delivered by mail is a very good substitute. In other cases, when the speed of communication and immediacy of response are important, the telephone and e-mail are far superior forms of communication.

Monopoly, then, is a matter of degree. Only a small fraction of all markets are served by just one seller. In a few markets, governments have allocated specific markets to a single seller. In many communities, this is the case with cable television and providers of electricity. The monopoly model we discuss next will illuminate the operation of these markets. It will also help us understand markets in which there are just a few sellers and little active rivalry. When there are only two or three producers in a market, firms may seek to collude rather than compete, and thus, together, they may behave much like a monopoly.

PRICE AND OUTPUT UNDER MONOPOLY

Because a monopolist is a price searcher like the firms we examined in the previous chapter, the graphical analysis is similar. The main difference is that because the monopolist is the only seller in the market, the demand curve facing the firm (d) is the entire market demand curve (D), and the firm's output (q) is the entire market output (Q). *Like other price searchers, the monopolist will expand its output until marginal revenue equals marginal cost. This profit-maximizing output rate can be sold at the price indicated on the firm's demand curve.*

Exhibit 1 graphically illustrates how a monopolist derives the profit-maximizing output rate.[3] Output will be expanded to Q, where MR = MC. The monopolist will set a price of P to sell exactly the desired profit-maximizing level of output Q (the height of the demand curve at Q). Thus, output rate Q and price P will maximize the firm's profit.

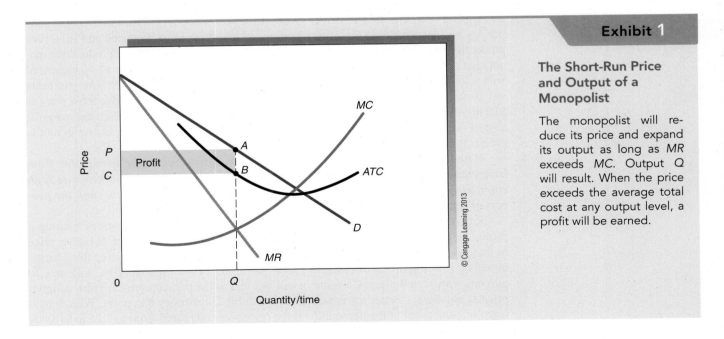

Exhibit 1

The Short-Run Price and Output of a Monopolist

The monopolist will reduce its price and expand its output as long as MR exceeds MC. Output Q will result. When the price exceeds the average total cost at any output level, a profit will be earned.

© Cengage Learning 2013

---

[3]In this chapter, we assume that firms are unable to use price discrimination to increase their revenues. If they could, the analysis of price discrimination from the previous chapter would be relevant to their decision-making.

Exhibit 2

Profit Maximization for a Monopolist

Rate of Output (Per Day) (1)	Price (Per Unit) (2)	Total Revenue (1) × (2) (3)	Total Cost (Per Day) (4)	Profit (3) − (4) (5)	Marginal Cost (6)	Marginal Revenue (7)
0	—	—	$50.00	$−50.00	—	—
1	$25.00	$25.00	60.00	−35.00	$10.00	$25.00
2	24.00	48.00	69.00	−21.00	9.00	23.00
3	23.00	69.00	77.00	−8.00	8.00	21.00
4	22.00	88.00	84.00	4.00	7.00	19.00
5	21.00	105.00	90.50	14.50	6.50	17.00
6	19.75	118.50	96.75	21.75	6.25	13.50
7	18.50	129.50	102.75	26.75	6.00	11.00
8	17.25	138.00	108.50	29.50	5.75	8.50
9	16.00	144.00	114.75	29.25	6.25	6.00
10	14.75	147.50	121.25	26.25	6.50	3.50
11	13.50	148.50	128.00	20.50	6.75	1.00
12	12.25	147.00	135.00	12.00	7.00	−1.50
13	11.00	143.00	142.25	.75	7.25	−4.00

The profits earned by the monopolist are also shown in Exhibit 1. At output Q and price P, the firm's total revenue is equal to $PAQ0$, the price times the number of units sold. The firm's total cost would be $CBQ0$, the average per-unit cost multiplied by the number of units sold. The firm's profits are total revenue less total cost, the shaded area of Exhibit 1 ($PABC$).

Exhibit 2 provides a numeric illustration of decision-making by a profit-maximizing monopolist. At low output rates, marginal revenue exceeds marginal cost. The monopolist will expand output as long as MR is greater than MC. Thus, an output rate of eight units per day will be chosen. (*Note:* If tiny portions of a unit could be produced and sold, then production would increase to where $MR = MC$.) Given the demand for the product, the monopolist can sell eight units at a price of $17.25 each. Total revenue will be $138, compared with a total cost of $108.50. The monopolist will make a profit of $29.50. The profit rate will be smaller at all other output rates. For example, if the monopolist reduces the price to $16 in order to sell nine units per day, revenue will increase by $6. However, the marginal cost of producing the ninth unit is $6.25. Because the cost of producing the ninth unit is greater than the revenue it brings in, profits will decline.

When high barriers to entry are present, they will insulate the monopolist from competition from new entrants producing a similar product. Thus, in markets with high entry barriers, short-run monopoly profits will not be competed away through the process of entry.

Protected by high entry barriers, a monopolist may be able to continue earning a profit, even in the long run. Does this mean that monopolists can charge as high a price as they want? Monopolists are often accused of price gouging. In evaluating this charge, however, it is important to recognize that, like other sellers, monopolists will seek to maximize *profit*, not *price*. Consumers will buy less as the price increases. Thus, a higher price is not always better for a monopolist. Exhibit 2 illustrates this point. What would happen to the profit of the monopolist if the price were increased from $17.25 to $18.50? At the higher price, only seven units would be sold, and total revenue would equal $129.50. The cost of producing seven units would be $102.75. Thus, when the price is

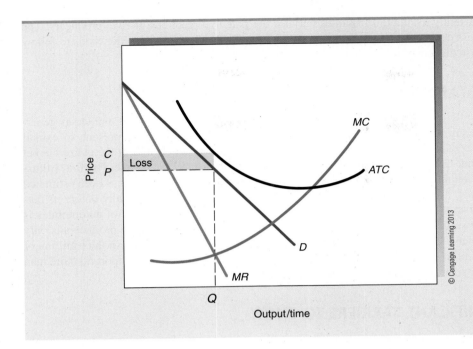

© Cengage Learning 2013

Exhibit 3

How a Monopolist Can Lose Money

Even a monopolist will lose money if its average total cost curve lies everywhere above the demand curve.

$18.50 and output seven units, profit is only $26.75—less than it would be at the lower price ($17.25) and larger output (eight units). The highest price is not usually the best price for the monopolist.

Will a monopolist always earn a profit? The ability of a monopolist to cover cost and make a profit is limited by the demand for the product that it produces. In some cases, a monopolist—even one protected by high barriers to entry—may be unable to sell its product for a profit. For example, there are thousands of clever, patented items that are never produced because demand–cost conditions are not favorable. Exhibit 3 illustrates this possibility. Here, the monopolist's average total cost curve is above its demand curve at every level of output. Even when operating at the $MR = MC$ rate of output, economic losses (shaded area) will occur. While output Q could be sold at price P, this price and quantity yield too little revenue to cover cost for the monopolist. This model explains why many small towns lack even a single bookstore, gourmet coffee shop, or any number of other specialty stores, even though if one opened up it would be the only one in town. Under these circumstances, not even a monopolist would want to operate—at least not for long.

THE CHARACTERISTICS OF AN OLIGOPOLY

In the United States, the domestic output in certain industries, such as the automobile, cigarette, and aircraft industries, is produced by five or fewer dominant firms. These industries are characterized by oligopoly. *Oligopoly* means "few sellers." ***The distinguishing characteristics of an oligopolistic market are (1) a small number of rival firms, (2) interdependence among the sellers because each is large relative to the size of the market, (3) substantial economies of scale, and (4) high entry barriers to the market.***

Oligopoly
A market situation in which a small number of sellers constitutes the entire industry. It is competition among the few.

INTERDEPENDENCE AMONG OLIGOPOLISTIC FIRMS

Because the number of sellers in an oligopolistic industry is small, the supply decisions of any one firm will significantly influence the demand, price, and profit of rival firms. This adds to the complexity of the firm's decision-making. A firm that is deciding what price to charge, output to produce, or quality of product to offer must consider not only the currently available substitutes but also the potential reactions of rival producers. The business decisions of each firm depend on the policies it expects its major rivals to follow because those will influence the demand for all the rivals' products.

SUBSTANTIAL ECONOMIES OF SCALE

In an oligopolistic industry, large-scale production (relative to the total market) is generally required to achieve minimum per-unit cost. Economies of scale are present, so a small number of large-scale firms can produce enough of the product to meet the entire market demand. Using the automobile industry in the recent past as an example, Exhibit 4 illustrates the importance of economies of scale as a source of oligopoly. It has been estimated that each firm must produce approximately 1 million automobiles annually before its per-unit cost of production is minimized. However, when the selling price of automobiles is barely sufficient to cover costs, the total quantity demanded from these producers is only 6 million. To minimize costs, then, each firm must produce at least one-sixth (1 million of the 6 million) of the output demanded. If this is true, the industry can support no more than five or six domestic firms of cost-efficient size.

SIGNIFICANT BARRIERS TO ENTRY

As with monopoly, barriers to entry limit the ability of new firms to compete effectively in oligopolistic industries. Except where a market is contestable, economies of scale are probably the most significant entry barrier protecting firms in an oligopolistic industry. A potential competitor may be unable to start out small and gradually grow to the optimal size, because it must gain a large share of the market before it can minimize its per-unit cost. The manufacture of refrigerators, diesel engines, and automobiles seems to fall into this category. Other factors, including patent rights, control over an essential resource, and government–imposed entry restraints, can also prevent new competitors from entering profitable oligopolistic industries.

IDENTICAL OR DIFFERENTIATED PRODUCTS

The products of sellers in an oligopolistic industry may be either similar or differentiated. On the one hand, when firms produce identical products, like milk or gasoline, there is less opportunity for nonprice competition. On the other hand, when rival firms produce differentiated products they are more likely to use style, quality, and advertising as competitive weapons. Each firm attempts to convince buyers that other products are poor substitutes.

Exhibit 4

Economies of Scale and Oligopoly

An oligopoly exists in the automobile industry because firms do not fully achieve the lower costs of large-scale operations until they are able to produce approximately one-sixth of the total market.

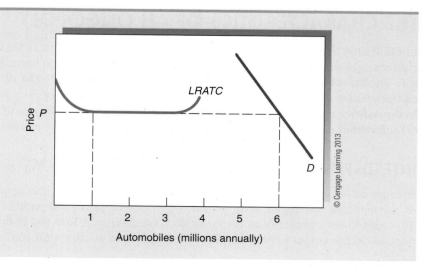

PRICE AND OUTPUT UNDER OLIGOPOLY

Unlike the other firms we have examined, an oligopolist cannot determine the product price that will deliver maximum profit simply by estimating only its own costs and the *existing* market demand. The demand facing an oligopolistic firm depends also on the pricing behavior of its rivals. Suppose, for example, that Ford is considering how to price a new hybrid car model when it comes on the market next year. The number of cars it can sell at each price will depend not only on buyer preferences but also on the prices (and quality) of substitutes available from Toyota, General Motors, and other rival firms. What pricing strategy will each rival use if Ford puts a low price on its new model? How will each rival firm react to a higher Ford price?

Economic models cannot predict these complex interactions among rivals without making some strong, simplifying assumptions about how each firm reacts when another firm makes a change in price or quality. These simplifying assumptions will not be realistic for the general case, and therefore we cannot precisely predict the price and output that will emerge in an oligopoly. We can, however, zero in on a potential range of prices and the factors that will determine whether prices in the industry will be high or low relative to costs of production.

Consider a typical oligopolistic industry in which seven or eight rival firms produce the entire market output because substantial economies of scale are present. The firms produce nearly identical products and have similar costs of production. **Exhibit 5** depicts the market demand conditions and long-run costs of production of the individual firms for such an industry.

What price will prevail? We can answer this question for two extreme cases. First, suppose that each firm sets its price independently of the other firms. There is no **collusion** (no agreement among the firms to limit output and keep the price high), so each competitive firm is free to seek additional customers and profits by offering buyers a slightly better deal than its rivals. Under these conditions, the market price would be driven down to P_c. Firms would be just able to cover their per-unit costs of production. If a single firm raised its price, its customers would switch to rival firms, which would now expand to accommodate the new customers. It would be self-defeating for any one firm to raise its price if the other firms didn't also raise theirs.

What happens if the current price is greater than P_c, perhaps because the market has not yet adjusted fully to a recent reduction in resource prices that lowered production costs? As a result, price is above per-unit cost, and the firms are making economic profit. However,

Collusion
Agreement among firms to avoid various competitive practices, particularly price reductions. It may involve either formal agreements or merely tacit recognition that competitive practices will be self-defeating in the long run. Tacit collusion is difficult to detect. In the United States, antitrust laws prohibit collusion and conspiracies to restrain trade.

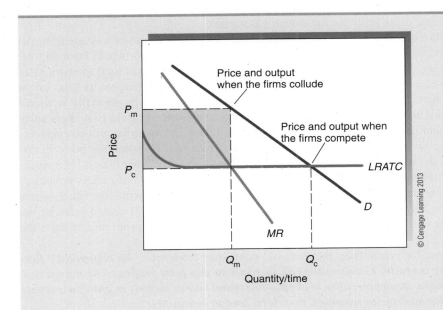

Price and Output in an Oligopoly

If oligopolists were to act independently and compete with one another, price cutting would drive price down to P_c. In contrast, perfect cooperation among firms would lead to a higher price of P_m and a smaller output (Q_m rather than Q_c). The shaded area shows profit if firms collude. Demand here is the market demand.

any *individual firm* that reduces its price slightly, by 1 or 2 percent, for example, will gain numerous customers if the other firms maintain the higher price. The price-cutting firm will attract some new buyers to the market, but more importantly, it will also lure many buyers away from rival firms charging higher prices. Thus, if the rival sellers act independently, each will have a strong incentive to reduce price in order to increase sales and gain a large share of the total market. Price will be driven down to P_c, and the economic profit will be eliminated.

However, oligopolists don't always compete with one another. They have a strong incentive to collude—to raise prices and restrict output in order to maximize their joint profits. The collusion may be either formal or informal. Formal collusion might even involve the formation of a **cartel**, like the Organization of the Petroleum Exporting Countries (OPEC). Under federal antitrust laws, both formal and informal collusive agreements to restrict output and raise prices are illegal in the United States. Nonetheless, let's see what would happen if oligopolists followed this course.

Exhibit 5 shows the marginal revenue curve that would accompany the market demand D for the product. Under perfect cooperation, the oligopolists would refuse to produce units for which marginal revenue to the group was less than marginal cost. Thus, they would restrict joint output to Q_m, where $MR = MC$. The market price would rise to P_m. With collusion, substantial joint profits (the shaded area of Exhibit 5) can be attained. If the collusion were perfect, the outcome would be identical to the one that would occur under monopoly.

Real-world outcomes are likely to be between the two polar case extremes of price competition and perfect collusion. Oligopolists generally recognize their interdependence and try to avoid vigorous price competition because they know it will drive down the price to the level of per-unit costs. But there are also obstacles to collusion, which is why prices in oligopolistic industries are unlikely to rise to the monopoly level. *As a result, oligopoly prices are typically above per-unit cost but below those a monopolist would charge.*

> **Cartel**
> An organization of sellers designed to coordinate supply decisions so that the joint profits of the members will be maximized. A cartel will seek to create a monopoly in the market.

THE INCENTIVE TO COLLUDE . . . AND TO CHEAT

Rival oligopolists can profit as a group by colluding to restrict output and raise price. To achieve the higher price, however, they must reduce total market output. Returning to Exhibit 5, from a competitive outcome of Q_c and P_c, output must be restricted toward the monopoly level of Q_m to achieve a higher price near P_m. This raises a point of conflict: None of the oligopolists want to reduce their output independently, especially at a higher price! Although the firms have an incentive to collude in order to achieve higher prices, each of them also has an incentive to cheat on the agreement by producing and selling more units than would maximize profit for the industry as a whole.

Exhibit 6 explains why this is the case. An undetected price cut by a single firm will have a larger percentage impact on its sales than a similar price cut would have on total industry sales. For example, if all firms lowered price by 10 percent total industry sales might only rise by 10 percent, but if one firm lowers price by 10 percent its sales might rise by 30 percent. Both price cuts attract additional customers who normally wouldn't buy at the higher price, but a price cut by one firm also attracts current customers away from the other firms. Therefore, the demand facing each *individual firm* will be considerably more elastic than the market demand curve. As Exhibit 6 shows, the price P_i that maximizes the industry's profits will be higher than the price P_F that is best for a single oligopolist when the others stay with the higher price. If a firm can use secret rebates or other ways to undercut the price set by the collusive agreement while the other sellers maintain the higher price, it can expand its sales (beyond the level agreed upon by the cartel). This will more than make up for the reduction in per-unit profit margin from the price cut.

In oligopolistic industries, there are two conflicting tendencies. *An oligopolistic firm has a strong incentive to cooperate with its rivals so that joint profit can be maximized. But it also has a strong incentive to cheat—to expand output secretly in order to increase its profit. Oligopolistic agreements, therefore, tend to be unstable.*

Gaining from Cheating

Exhibit 6

The industry demand (D_i) and marginal revenue (MR_i) curves show that the joint profits of oligopolists would be maximized at Q_i, where $MR_i = MC$. Price P_i would be best for the industry as a whole (a). However, as part (b) shows, the demand curve (d_F) facing each firm (under the assumption that no other firms cheat) will be much more elastic than D_i. Given the greater elasticity of its demand curve, an individual firm will have an incentive to cut its price to P_F and expand output to q_F, where $MR_F = MC$. In other words, an individual oligopolist can gain by secretly cutting its price and cheating on the collusive agreement—until the other firms find out and react by cutting their price.

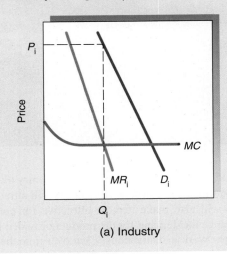

(a) Industry

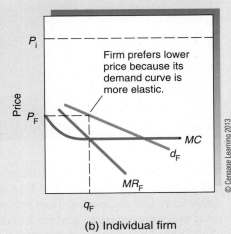

Firm prefers lower price because its demand curve is more elastic.

(b) Individual firm

© Cengage Learning 2013

OBSTACLES TO COLLUSION

There are certain situations in which it is more difficult for oligopolists to collude. Five major obstacles limit collusive behavior.

1. **As the number of firms in an oligopolistic market increases, the likelihood of effective collusion declines.** Other things being constant, an increase in the number of firms in an industry will make it more difficult for the oligopolists to communicate, negotiate, and enforce agreements among themselves. Opinions about the best collusive price arrangement are likely to differ because marginal costs, unused plant capacity, and estimates of market demand elasticity will often differ among the firms. As the number of firms expands, conflict arising from these and other sources will increase and make it more difficult to maintain collusive agreements.

2. **When it is difficult to detect and eliminate price cuts, collusion is less attractive.** Unless firms have a way of policing the pricing and output activities of rivals, effective collusion will be unlikely as firms will cheat on the agreement. The history of the oil cartel OPEC highlights this point. Cheating by members on production and sales quota agreements is not easy to monitor by the others, and it has been a persistent problem for the cartel.

Some forms of price cutting are difficult for the rival firms to identify. For example, a firm might freely provide better credit terms, faster delivery, and other related services that improve the package offered to the buyer. In an industry supplying differentiated products, oligopolists can hold money prices constant and still use improvements in quality and style to provide consumers with more value. "Price cuts" like this cannot be easily and quickly duplicated by rivals. As a result, collusive agreements on price are largely ineffective when quality and style are important competitive weapons. The bottom line is this: When cheating (price cutting) is profitable and difficult for rivals to detect and police, collusive agreements—both formal and informal—will be difficult to maintain.

Collusive agreements among oligopolists and cartels like OPEC are difficult to maintain because any individual cartel member would be better off if it could cheat on the agreement and charge a slightly lower price, so long as other members do not.

AP Photo/Bela Szandelszky

3. Low entry barriers are an obstacle to collusion. Without barriers to entry oligopolists will be unable to sustain long-run economic profits because the profits will attract new competitors into the market. High prices will also make it more attractive for potential rivals to develop substitutes, which will reduce the demand for the product provided by the oligopolists. Of course, these factors will not work instantaneously, but over time they will reduce the ability to charge abnormally high prices and earn economic profits.

Again, the experience of OPEC illustrates this point. When OPEC attempts to cut production and push up world oil prices, the non-OPEC producers develop new oil fields and expand their output from existing sources. The higher prices also encourage energy conservation and greater use of alternative energy sources, such as coal, natural gas, and nuclear energy, and make it more profitable for firms across many other industries to introduce substitutes like more fuel-efficient, hybrid-electric cars. These innovations from rival sellers who can enter and compete with OPEC for customers cause the demand for oil to decrease and make it difficult for OPEC to collude successfully.

4. Unstable demand conditions are an obstacle to collusion. Honest differences of opinion among oligopolists about what is best for the industry always exist, but unstable demand increases the likelihood of conflict. One firm might want to expand because it anticipates a sharp increase in future demand, whereas a more pessimistic rival may want to hold the line on existing industrial capacity. The larger the differences in expectations about future demand, the greater the potential for conflict among oligopolistic firms. When demand is more stable, successful collusion will be more likely.

5. Vigorous antitrust action increases the cost of collusion. Under existing antitrust laws in many nations, collusive behavior is prohibited by law. Secretive illegal agreements do, of course, happen. Simple informal cooperation might be conducted without having explicit discussions or collusive agreements. However, unlike formal (legal) collusive agreements, these informal agreements are not easily enforceable. Thus, vigorous antitrust action can discourage firms from making illegal agreements. As the threat of getting caught increases, participants will be less likely to attempt collusive behavior.

UNCERTAINTY AND OLIGOPOLY

Uncertainty and imprecision characterize the theory of oligopoly. We know that firms will gain if they successfully restrict output and raise prices. However, collusion is fraught with

APPLICATIONS IN ECONOMICS

Oligopolistic Decision-Making, Game Theory, and the Prisoner's Dilemma

In an oligopoly, a few firms compete in the same market, and the actions of each influence the demand faced by the others. One firm can gain customers at the expense of the others by cutting its price or increasing its advertising. The firms that fail to follow suit will lose customers. But if the other firms react competitively by doing the same, then all the firms lose. Thus, each firm finds itself on the horns of a dilemma—something like the classic "prisoner's dilemma."

Economists have increasingly used game theory like the prisoner's dilemma to analyze strategic choices made by competitors, particularly those in an oligopoly. To understand the prisoner's dilemma, consider the hypothetical case of Al and Bob, two touring Americans who just met at a train station in a small foreign country. Al and Bob are taken prisoner and hauled into the local police station to be questioned separately. They are suspected of being the two men who robbed a local merchant, and each is told that if he makes the job of the police easier by confessing immediately, he will get only a six-month sentence. But each is also told that if he says nothing while the other confesses, then the one who did not confess immediately will get a twelve-month sentence. If neither confesses, both will be held for three months while the investigation continues. Al and Bob will not be allowed to communicate with each other. Will they confess?

To analyze such a situation, the game theorist begins by laying out the alternative outcomes and showing how they are related to choices made by the players of the game, as we do in Exhibit 7. For each man individually, in this version of the dilemma, the box reveals that the best choice depends on what the other does. If Al confesses, then Bob can save six months of jail time by also confessing. The same holds for Al, if he thinks Bob will confess. But if neither confesses, both serve only three months in jail. The proper strategy for each prisoner depends heavily on his estimate of the likelihood that the other will confess. The problem becomes more complex if we consider prisoners who face a series of such decisions over time and each prisoner learns what the other has done before making his or her next choice.

Firms in an oligopoly must make decisions somewhat like those of the prisoners: Should a firm cut its price in order to attract more customers—luring some of them away from its competitors—or should it keep its price high and risk losing customers to competitors who cut *their* prices? If all firms keep the price high, then as a group they will reap more profit.

If all of them cut prices, then as a group they will reap less profit. But the firm that fails to cut price when the others do will lose many customers. The decision about whether or not to advertise has similar characteristics.

For example, consider the pricing policies or advertising strategies of large automakers, like Ford, Toyota, and General Motors. Suppose the profit rate of each would be 15 percent if all the major automobile producers raised their

---

Exhibit 7

The Prisoner's Dilemma

Al and Bob must each decide, without communicating with each other, whether to confess. Al knows that if Bob does not confess, then he can either confess and spend six months in jail, or not confess and spend three months. But if Bob does confess, then Al's failure to confess will cost him an additional six months in jail. Bob is in a similar situation, facing the same options under the same assumptions about whether Al confesses. Each man has an incentive to confess if he thinks the other one will, but an incentive not to confess if he thinks the other will also remain silent.

		Al's Choice	
		Confess	Not Confess
Bob's Choice	Confess	6 months each	Al: 12 months Bob: 6 months
	Not Confess	Al: 6 months Bob: 12 months	3 months each

© Cengage Learning 2013

(continued)

prices by a similar amount. In contrast, each would earn a profit rate of only 10 percent if intense competition led to lower prices. Industry profits are highest when all firms decide to charge high prices. However, if one automaker cuts prices, it will be able to steal customers away from its rivals and increase its profit rate to 20 percent. Thus, if the firm thinks its rivals will continue to charge the higher prices, it will be tempted to cut its price. If the other firms follow a similar course, however, the strategy will backfire and the profit rate of all the firms in the industry will be less than the level it would have achieved had they all charged the higher prices.

Although our simplified analysis highlights the interdependence among the firms and the importance of probability estimates concerning the strategy of rivals, the real world is much more complex. The choices of the rival firms will be repeated over and over again, although often in modified forms. A prior strategy will be modified in light of previous reactions on the part of rivals. How attractive a strategy will be depends on its likelihood of being detected by rivals and the speed with which they will respond. In addition, the strategies of oligopolistic firms will be influenced by market conditions and the threat of foreign competition—factors

that change with the passage of time. As you can see, additional assumptions will need to be made to account for these and other complex factors.

Economists have used game theory extensively to show how results change when the "rules of the game" change for the firms in an oligopolistic market, as well as for auction-bidding markets and other business decision-making situations. When the rules of the game are carefully defined and enforced, as they are in economic experiments held in laboratories, game theory has yielded interesting and important testable conclusions. But in open markets in the real world, empirical work using game theory has been less successful. The use of models is always difficult when the problem to be solved is complex and when human expectations about the changing strategic choices of other human beings must be taken into account. There is no question, however, that game theory can be useful for scholars and business practitioners alike, by helping them frame the issues involved in strategic decision-making.[1]

[1]For a further explanation of game theory and the prisoner's dilemma, see Avinash Dixit and Barry Nalebuff, "Game Theory," in *The Concise Encyclopedia of Economics*, ed. David R. Henderson (Indianapolis, IN: Liberty Fund, Inc., 2002), http://www.econlib.org/library/CEE.html.

Market power
The ability of a firm that is not a pure monopolist to earn persistently large profits, indicating that it has some monopoly power. Because the firm has few (or weak) competitors, it has a degree of freedom from vigorous competition.

Game theory
A tool used to analyze the strategic choices made by competitors in a conflict situation like the decisions made by firms in an oligopoly.

conflicts and difficulties. In some industries, these difficulties are so great that the **market power** of the oligopolists is relatively small. In other industries, oligopolistic cooperation, although not perfect, can raise prices significantly, indicating a higher degree of market power. The use of **game theory** to analyze the costs and benefits of collusive behavior, under varying degrees of cooperation and conflict, has become an important part of economics. (See the accompanying Applications in Economics feature on this topic.) Although this developing field of economics does not yield precise predictions on oligopoly pricing and output, it does suggest the conditions that make it more likely that an oligopolist will be kept in check by competitive pressures.

MARKET POWER AND PROFIT—THE EARLY BIRD CATCHES THE WORM

Our analysis of both monopoly and oligopoly indicates that because entry barriers into these markets are often high, firms can sometimes earn economic profits over lengthy periods of time. Does that mean that buying stock in one of these companies is a better investment? The answer is no because the price of a share of stock in such a corporation would long ago have risen to reflect the firm's expected future profitability. Many of the present stockholders paid high prices for their stock because they expected these firms to continue to be highly profitable. In other words, these shareholders paid for any above-normal economic profits generated by the firm's market power at the time they purchased their ownership shares.

DEFECTS OF MARKETS WITH HIGH ENTRY BARRIERS

From Adam Smith's time to the present, economists have generally considered monopoly to be a problem. The attitude toward markets with few sellers and high entry barriers has been only slightly more tolerant. Generally, economists offer three major criticisms. We will outline each of them.

1. When entry barriers are high and there are few, if any, alternative suppliers, the discipline of market forces is weakened. In contrast, when alternatives are present, consumers are in a position to direct the behavior of suppliers. If you do not like the food at a local restaurant, you eat elsewhere. If you think prices are high and the selection poor at a particular grocery store, you go to a different one. But consider your alternatives if you do not like the local cable television service. You can voice a complaint to the company or your legislative representative, but the only exit option might be to stop your cable service, perhaps to rely instead on satellite dish service. Cable and satellite service are imperfect substitutes, each with its own disadvantages. When consumers do not have good exit options, they must either take what the seller offers or do without. Consequently, their ability to keep sellers in check is greatly reduced.

2. Reduced competition results in allocative inefficiency. The formal condition for allocative efficiency requires that all units are produced that are valued more highly than what it costs to produce them. When barriers to entry are low, profit-seeking producers of each good expand their output until its price is driven down to the level of per-unit costs. Because price equals cost, all units of the good that consumers value higher than the cost of production will be produced and sold. With high barriers to entry, however, price may exceed per-unit costs, even over the long run. Therefore some units might not be produced, even though consumers value them more than their costs. These are the units valued by consumers more than cost, but less than the higher monopoly price.

3. Government grants of monopoly power will encourage rent seeking; resources will be wasted by firms attempting to secure and maintain grants of market protection. Special favors granted by the government will lead to costly activities for those who seek such favors. As we noted in Chapter 6, economists refer to such activities as rent seeking. When licenses or other entry barriers erected by the government enhance the profitability and provide protection from the rigors of market competition, people will expend scarce resources to secure and maintain these political favors. From an efficiency standpoint, these rent-seeking costs related to getting and keeping monopoly power add to the welfare losses resulting from the allocative inefficiencies we previously mentioned.

Suppose the government issues a license providing a single seller the exclusive right to sell liquor in a specific market. If this grant of monopoly power permits the licensee to earn monopoly profit, potential suppliers will compete, each trying to convince government officials that it should be the one firm granted the license. The potential monopolists will lobby government officials, make political contributions, hire representatives to do consulting studies, and undertake other actions designed to obtain the monopoly grant. Each firm may be willing to spend up to the present value of the future expected monopoly profits trying to obtain the monopoly license. With several potential suppliers, the total rent-seeking expenditures of all firms combined may even exceed the economic profit expected from the monopoly enterprise.

The resources devoted to rent seeking have an opportunity cost (for example, a cable company could have instead used the money to provide better service to customers), and thus are wasteful from a societal point of view. Therefore, the total losses to society from monopolies created through government favors can far exceed the losses caused by allocative inefficiency.

POLICY ALTERNATIVES WHEN ENTRY BARRIERS ARE HIGH

What government policies might be used to counteract the problems that result from high barriers to entry? Economists suggest four policy options:

1.   Control the structure of the industry to ensure the presence of rival firms.
2.   Reduce artificial barriers that limit competition.
3.   Regulate the price and output of firms in the market.
4.   Supply the market with goods produced by a government firm.

Each of these policies has been used to either reduce entry barriers or counteract their negative results. We will briefly consider each of them and analyze both their potential and limitations as tools that can be used to improve the efficiency of resource use.

ANTITRUST POLICY AND CONTROLLING THE STRUCTURE OF AN INDUSTRY

The major problems associated with high barriers to entry and monopoly power are not present when rival sellers are present and compete. The United States, to a greater degree than most Western countries, has adopted antitrust laws designed to prevent monopoly and promote competition. Antitrust legislation began in 1890 with the passage of the Sherman Antitrust Act. Additional legislation, including the Clayton Act and the Federal Trade Commission Act of 1914, has buttressed policy in this area.

Antitrust laws give the U.S. Department of Justice the power to prosecute firms engaging in collusive behavior or other actions designed to create a monopoly or cartel. They also give the government the power to break up an existing monopoly and prevent mergers that significantly reduce competition. The Federal Trade Commission (FTC) is allowed to bring charges under the Sherman Act. Private firms can also bring suits charging antitrust violations by a rival under the Sherman and Clayton acts and collect up to three times any actual damages caused by the rival firm. Each year, far more cases are brought by private firms against their competitors than by the two federal agencies. Rival firms can also ask the two agencies to bring antitrust cases against successful competitors who may have, or threaten to gain, monopoly power.

Economists do not fully agree on the usefulness of antitrust action to increase the number of rival firms in an industry. Those who support such policies believe that only by preserving numerous competitors in a market can we be confident that monopoly has been controlled. Opponents point to the danger of protecting high-cost firms at the expense of both consumers and the more aggressive and successful firm(s) in the market. Protection of less efficient firms from successful competitors, they say, is all too common in the actual practice of antitrust policy.

There is one situation in which the application of antitrust action would clearly be inappropriate. When substantial economies of scale are present, unit cost will be minimized only if the entire industry output is produced by a single firm, a case known as **natural monopoly**. Here, breaking up the one large firm in order to increase the number of rivals in the industry would lead to higher per-unit costs. Because of their higher costs, the prices charged by the smaller firms might even exceed those of the lower-cost natural monopoly. Therefore, using antitrust laws to expand the number of firms is not an attractive option when economies of scale in an industry produce a natural monopoly.

Natural monopoly
A market situation in which the average costs of production continually decline with increased output. In a natural monopoly, the average costs of production will be lowest when a single, large firm produces the entire output demanded by the marketplace.

REDUCE ARTIFICIAL BARRIERS TO TRADE

When government-imposed restrictions are the source of the monopoly power, the appropriate policy action is obvious: Remove the government restraints. But this is easier said than done. The restraints are generally in place because of the political influence of special-interest groups—the producers currently in the industry—who have a vested interest in restricting competition and keeping prices high. The politicians who supply these restrictions get political support from current producers in return, and removing them would be a costly political move. Thus, political considerations often make it difficult to remove government-imposed barriers to entry, such as licensing restrictions and tariff and quota restrictions on imported goods.

The interest groups behind government-imposed barriers to entry are highly concentrated and generally well organized politically. In contrast, the consumers who would benefit from more competitive markets are poorly organized, and the costs imposed on them by the restraints are nearly always thinly spread among them. As we discussed in Chapter 6, the political process often works to the advantage of the concentrated interests. As a result, even when lower barriers are needed to increase the competitiveness of an industry, political factors often prevent them.

REGULATE THE PRICE

Can government regulation improve the allocative efficiency of a monopoly or an oligopoly? Exhibit 8 illustrates why ideal government price regulation, in the case of a monopolist, could theoretically improve resource allocation. The firm illustrated here is a natural monopoly. Its *LRATC* falls over the entire relevant range of output. Antitrust action dividing the firm into several smaller rivals will not help consumers because the unit costs of the smaller firms will be higher than if the output were produced by the monopolist. The profit maximizing monopolist will set price at P_0 and produce output Q_0, where $MR = MC$. Consumers, however, would value additional units of output beyond Q_0 more than the cost of producing them violating the conditions for allocative efficiency. Let's consider the potential of two regulatory options and also analyze some of their real-world limitations.

AVERAGE COST PRICING

If a regulatory agency forces the firm in Exhibit 8 to reduce the price to P_1, at which point the *LRATC* curve intersects the market (and firm) demand curve, then the firm will expand output to Q_1. Because it cannot charge a price above P_1, the firm cannot increase its revenues by selling a smaller output at a higher price. Once the price ceiling is instituted, the firm can increase its revenues by P_1, and by only P_1, for each unit it sells. The regulated firm's *MR* is constant at P_1 for all units sold until output is increased to Q_1. Because the firm's *MC* is less than P_1 (and therefore less than *MR*), the profit-maximizing regulated firm shown here will expand output from Q_0 to Q_1. The benefits from the consumption of these units (ABQ_1Q_0) clearly exceed their costs (CEQ_1Q_0). Social welfare has improved as a result of the regulatory action (we will ignore the impact on the distribution of income). At this output level, revenues are sufficient to cover costs. The firm is making zero economic profit (or "normal" accounting profit).

MARGINAL COST PRICING

Even at the Q_1 output level, marginal cost is still less than price. Additional welfare gains could be achieved if output were increased to Q_2. However, if a regulatory agency forced the monopolist to reduce the price to P_2 (so the price would equal the marginal cost at the output level Q_2), economic losses would result. Even a monopolist, unless it is subsidized,

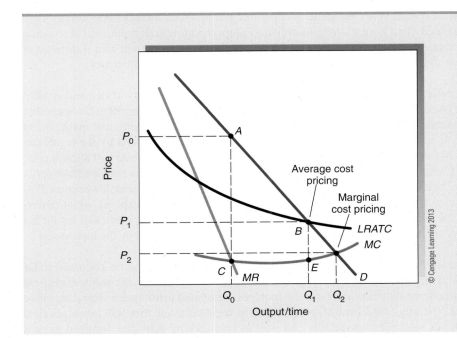

© Cengage Learning 2013

Exhibit 8

Regulating a Monopolist

If unregulated, a profit-maximizing monopolist with the costs indicated here will produce Q_0 units and charge P_0. If a regulatory agency forced the monopolist to reduce price to P_1, then the monopolist would expand output to Q_1. Ideally, we would like output to be expanded to Q_2, where $P = MC$, but regulatory agencies usually do not attempt to keep prices as low as P_2. Can you explain why?

wouldn't produce the product at P_2 or any price below P_1. But how large should a subsidy be? No one has the knowledge to set this subsidy, partly because prices, technologies, and the value of output change daily. Also, who has the incentive to fight the pressures on both sides for higher (or lower) subsidies? Marginal cost pricing is seldom practical.

PROBLEMS WITH REGULATION

Although regulating a monopoly might seem like a way to improve the efficiency of markets, both economic analysis and the history of regulation suggest that it has serious shortcomings. In practice, three factors tend to reduce the effectiveness of regulation and the probability that regulators will act on behalf of all citizens to control monopolies. Let's look at each of these factors.

1. Lack of information. When we discussed ideal regulation, we assumed that we knew what the firm's *ATC, MC,* and demand curves looked like. In reality, of course, regulators do not. Even the firms themselves will have difficulty knowing their costs, and especially their demand curves, with any precision. Furthermore, both supply and demand will vary over time and by location. The market for electricity is an excellent example. Because electricity cannot be stored for later use, the highly variable supply-and-demand conditions in that market cause the opportunity cost of power to change dramatically from one day, or even one hour, to the next. There is simply no way to have government-determined prices that are flexible and correct enough to avoid causing major shortages and surpluses of the good through time. In the summer of 2001, for example, sharply changing cost conditions for California utilities coupled with inflexible, regulated retail power rates combined to produce widespread power outages.

Because it is virtually impossible to estimate demand and marginal costs, regulatory agencies usually gauge profits (or the rate of return) to determine whether the regulated price is too high or too low. The regulatory agency seeks to impose a "fair" or "normal" rate of return on the firm. If the firm is making economic profits (that is, an abnormally high rate of return), the regulated price must be higher than P_1 in Exhibit 8, and therefore it should be reduced. Alternatively, if the firm is incurring losses (less than the fair, or normal, rate of return), this indicates that the regulated price is less than P_1 and that the firm should be permitted to charge a higher price.

The actual existence of profits, though, is not easily identifiable. Accounting profit, or the rate of return, is not the same as economic profit, which includes opportunity cost. Also, regulated firms have a strong incentive to adopt reporting techniques and accounting methods that conceal profits. Because of this, a regulatory agency will find it difficult or impossible to identify and impose a price consistent with allocative efficiency.

2. Cost shifting. Regulation changes incentives, so it can affect costs. If demand is sufficient, the owners of the regulated firm can expect the long-run rate of profit to be essentially fixed, regardless of whether efficient management reduces costs or inefficient management allows costs to increase. If costs decrease, the "fair return" rule imposed by the regulatory agency will force a price reduction; if costs increase, the "fair return" rule will allow a price increase. Compared to the managers of unregulated firms, managers of a regulated monopoly have more freedom to pursue personal objectives and less incentive to seek lower costs. Predictably, they will often fly first class, entertain lavishly at company expense, grant unwarranted wage increases, and so on. Production inefficiency and higher costs will result, but consumers are in a weak position to shift away from the good supplied by the monopolist.

3. Special-interest influence. The difficulties of government regulation discussed so far are practical limitations a regulatory agency confronts. Unfortunately, the political element of government regulation exacerbates the problem. Regulated firms have a strong incentive to see that "friendly," "reasonable" people serve as regulators, and they will invest political and economic resources toward this end. Just as rent-seeking activities designed to gain

monopoly privileges in the first place can be expected, so, too, can activities to influence regulators' decisions. Few consumers will invest the time and resources required to understand regulatory policy and make the political contributions needed to counteract the influence peddling. Over time, regulatory commissions are therefore likely to reflect the views and interests of the business and labor interests they regulate.

In summary, regulation not only has the potential to improve resource allocation in markets with few competitors, but it also generates adverse side effects. Both economic reasoning and decades of experience indicate that regulation is not a magic cure.

SUPPLY MARKET WITH GOVERNMENT PRODUCTION

Government-operated firms—like the U.S. Postal Service and many local public utilities—present an alternative to both private monopoly and regulation. Here, too, however, economic thinking and experience indicate that these firms will fail to counteract fully the problems that stem from high barriers to entry. The same perverse managerial incentives that regulated firms experience—incentives to ignore efficiency and pursue personal or professional objectives at the firm's expense—also tend to plague government-operated firms. In addition, the rational ignorance effect comes into play here. Individual voters have little incentive to acquire information about the operation of government firms because, unlike the case of a personal investment, the individual's choices will not decide which investment will be purchased with the voter's money. Predictably, the "owners" of a government-operated firm (voters) will be uninformed about how well the firm is run, how it might be run better, or if another firm has a better plan. This is especially true when there are no direct competitors against which the firm's performance might be compared.

The operation of enterprises by the government does not create an environment that rewards managers or investors for efficient management and reductions in cost. Unlike in the private sector, no small group of investors can increase their wealth by taking over the firm and improving its management. Even more than with monopoly or oligopoly in the private sector, customers of the socialized monopoly cannot easily switch their business to other sellers. Voter-taxpayers who do not even consume the product often have to pay taxes to support its provision. When the government operates a business there is typically less investor scrutiny, less reward for efficiency, and less penalty for inefficiency or the production of inferior goods. Higher costs and lower-valued outputs are predictable results.

Government ownership, like unregulated monopoly and government regulation, is a less-than-ideal solution. Even those who denounce private sector monopoly seldom point to a government-operated monopoly as an example of how an industry should be run.

PULLING IT TOGETHER

The policy alternatives available when high barriers to entry are present are less than satisfying. Most are just not very attractive. Economies of scale often make antitrust actions impractical. When larger firms have lower per-unit costs, restructuring the industry to increase the number of firms will be both costly and difficult to maintain. Furthermore, antitrust policy opens the door for firms to use it against successful rivals that have simply given consumers a better deal and captured a large part of the market in the process. Policy actions to stop or to punish such progress are counterproductive for customers and for economic efficiency. Lifting government restrictions such as licensing requirements, quotas, and tariffs that limit competition is perhaps the surest way to improve the performance of markets with few suppliers. But the nature of the political process, particularly its tendency to cater to the views of well-organized interest groups at the expense of the unorganized majority of consumer/voters, often undermines the feasibility of this option.

Price regulation is also a less-than-ideal solution. Regulators do not possess the information necessary to impose an efficient outcome, and as part of the political process, they will be susceptible to manipulation by special interests. When firms are operated by the government, political objectives will be pursued at the expense of consumer interests and economic efficiency. Thus, government operation of firms also has its problems. In short, when economies of scale lead to a tendency toward monopoly, there is no ideal solution.

THE COMPETITIVE PROCESS IN THE REAL WORLD

How competitive are markets today? As George Stigler points out in the second of his chapter-opening quotations, "Competition is a tough weed, not a delicate flower." Firms in markets that appear to be unrelated often compete with one another. For example, sellers of swimming pools compete with airlines, hotels, casinos, and automobile rental companies for the vacation and leisure time expenditures of consumers.

Over the past few decades, direct competition in almost all markets has increased. Lower transportation and communication costs have played an important role here. Lower transport costs make it more feasible for consumers to consider products offered by faraway suppliers. They also make it possible for producers to compete over a much larger geographic area, which often leads to lower per-unit costs and larger gains from economies of scale. Further, the Internet provides even those living in small towns with quick and easy access to worldwide markets. This widening of markets reduces the market power of both buyers and sellers and, at the same time, reduces potential problems related to economies of scale.

When workers can work at remote locations, via the Internet and by contract if they wish, they have more options, and firms who can hire them—even small firms—no longer need large-scale production to achieve some of the economies of specialization previously available only to large firms. Both workers and firms can have some of the benefits of being in a large urban market even if they operate far from such markets.

Technological change is also a powerful force for competitive markets. Innovation and nonprice competition on product quality, design, convenience, and other factors are used constantly by firms seeking greater market share and profitability. For a firm, innovation is the key to (temporary) profits. Successful innovation can give the innovating firm some degree of relief from competition while other firms struggle to catch up. Technical improvements, like newer and better computers or ways to make and sell them, cheaper and better inventory control methods, and 4G cell phones, have all made fortunes for the firms developing the information technology behind them. But the advantage is always temporary. Over time, each technical and business innovation becomes available to all firms, and the consumers of all products win, even as the profits of the innovating firms wane.

The competitiveness of markets is complex and difficult to measure directly. However, given the importance of quality competition, broader markets, and technological discoveries, most economists believe that the U.S. economy is more competitive today than it was, say, 50 or 75 years ago. Moreover, profit levels are considerably lower than many people think. A national sample poll of adults conducted by Opinion Research Corporation of Princeton, New Jersey, found that the average person thought profits constituted 29 percent of every dollar of sales in manufacturing. In reality, the after-tax accounting profits of manufacturing corporations are about 4 cents to 5 cents per dollar of sales. These figures also suggest that the U.S. economy, including the manufacturing sector, is relatively competitive.

Looking Ahead

The last several chapters have focused on product markets. Of course, resources are required to produce products. The following chapters will focus on resource markets and the employment decisions of both business firms and resource suppliers.

KEY POINTS

- The four major sources of barriers to entry are economies of scale, government licensing, patents, and control of an essential resource.

- A monopoly is present when there is a single seller of a well-defined product for which there are no good substitutes and the entry barriers into the market are high. Although there are only a few markets in which the entire output is supplied by a single seller, the monopoly model also helps us better understand the operation of markets dominated by a small number of firms.

- Like other price searchers, a profit-maximizing monopolist will lower the price and expand its output as long as marginal revenue exceeds marginal cost. At the maximum-profit output, *MR* will equal *MC*. The monopolist will charge the price on its demand curve consistent with that output.

- If a monopolist is earning a profit, high barriers to entry will shield the firm from direct competition, thereby enabling it to earn long-run economic profits. But sometimes demand and cost conditions will be such that even a monopolist will be unable to earn economic profit.

- An oligopolistic market is characterized by (1) a small number of rival firms, (2) interdependence among the sellers, (3) substantial economies of scale, and (4) high entry barriers into the market.

- There is no general theory for the determination of a unique price and output in an oligopolistic market. If rival oligopolists acted totally independently of their competitors, they would drive the price down to the per-unit cost of production. Alternatively, if they colluded perfectly, the price would rise to the level a monopolist would charge. The actual outcome under oligopoly will generally fall between these two extremes.

- Oligopolists have a strong incentive to collude and raise their prices. However, each firm will be able to gain if it (alone) can cut its price (or improve the quality of its product) because the demand curve confronted by the firm is more elastic than the industry demand curve. This introduces a conflict that makes it difficult to maintain collusive agreements, even where no law prohibits them.

- Oligopolistic firms are less likely to collude successfully against the interests of consumers if (1) there are more rival firms in the market; (2) it is costly to prohibit competitors from offering secret price cuts (or quality improvements) to customers; (3) entry barriers are low; (4) market demand conditions tend to be unstable; and/or (5) the threat of antitrust action is present.

- Economists criticize high barriers to market entry because (1) the ability of consumers to discipline producers is weakened, (2) the unregulated monopolist or oligopoly group can often gain by restricting output and raising price, and (3) legal barriers to entry encourage firms to engage in wasteful rent-seeking activities.

- When entry barriers are high and competition among rival firms weak, the major policy alternatives are (1) antitrust action designed to maintain or increase the number of firms in the industry, (2) relaxation of regulations that limit entry and trade, (3) price regulation, and (4) provision of output by government firms. When feasible, option (2) is the most attractive alternative. Under most circumstances, all the other options have shortcomings.

- Competitive forces are present and growing, even in markets with high barriers to entry. Quality competition, the widening of markets, and technological change are all-important elements of the competitive process.

CRITICAL ANALYSIS QUESTIONS

1. *"Barriers to entry are crucial to the existence of long-run profits, but they cannot guarantee the existence of profits." Evaluate.

2. "Monopoly is good for producers but bad for consumers. The gains of the former offset the losses of the latter. On balance, there is no reason to think that monopoly is bad for the economy." Is this statement true? Why or why not?

3. *Do monopolists charge the highest prices for which they can sell their products? Do they maximize their average profit per sale? Are monopolistic firms always profitable? Why or why not?

4. Compare the price and output policy of a purely competitive industry with the policy that would be established by a profit-maximizing monopolist or cartel. Who benefits and who is hurt? Construct the appropriate graphs to illustrate your answer.

5. Does economic theory indicate that an ideal regulatory agency that forces a monopolist to charge a price equal to either marginal or average total cost will improve economic efficiency? Explain. Does economic theory suggest that a regulatory agency will in fact regulate in a manner consistent with economic efficiency? What are some of the factors that complicate the regulatory function?

6. Is a monopolist subject to any competitive pressures? Explain. Would an unregulated monopolist have an incentive to operate and produce efficiently? Why or why not?

7. How will high entry barriers into a market influence (a) the long-run profitability of the firms, (b) the cost efficiency of the firms in the industry, (c) the likelihood that some inefficient (high-cost) firms will survive, and (d) the incentive of entrepreneurs to develop substitutes for the product supplied by the firms? Are competitive pressures present in markets with high barriers to entry? Discuss.

8. *Why is oligopolistic collusion more difficult when there is product variation than when the products of all firms are identical?

9. In large cities, taxi fares are often set above the market equilibrium rate. Sometimes, the number of licenses is limited in order to maintain the above-market price. Other times, licenses are automatically granted to anyone wanting to operate a taxi. When taxi fares are set above market equilibrium, compare and contrast resource allocation under the restricted license system (assume the licenses are tradable) and the free-entry system. In which case will it be easier for customers to get a taxi? In which case will the amount of capital required to enter the taxi business be greater?

10. We have a theory to explain the equilibrium price and output for monopoly, but not for oligopoly. Why? How can game theory help us understand the decisions made by oligopolists?

11. *Historically, the real costs of transporting both goods and people have declined substantially. What impact do lower transportation costs have on the market power of individual producers? Do you think the U.S. economy is more or less competitive today than it was 100 years ago? Explain.

12. *"My uncle just bought 1,000 shares of Apple, one of the largest and most profitable companies in the United States. Given Apple's high profit rate, he will make a bundle from this purchase." Evaluate this statement. Is it necessarily true? Explain.

13. *Gouge-em Cable Company is the only cable television service company licensed to operate in Backwater County. Most of its costs are access fees and maintenance expenses. These fixed costs total $640,000 monthly. The marginal cost of adding another subscriber to its system is constant at $2 per month. Gouge-em's demand curve can be determined from the data in the accompanying table.

SUBSCRIPTION PRICE	NUMBER OF SUBSCRIBERS (PER MONTH)
$25	20,000
20	40,000
15	60,000
10	80,000
5	100,000
1	150,000

a. What price will Gouge-em charge for its cable services? What are its profits at this price?

b. Now suppose the Backwater County Public Utility Commission has the data and believes that cable subscription rates in the county are too expensive and that Gouge-em's profits are unfairly high. What regulated price will it set so that Gouge-em makes only a normal rate of return on its investment?

14. Suppose that you produce and sell children's tables in a local market. Past experience enables you to estimate your demand and marginal cost schedules. This information is presented in the accompanying table.

a. Fill in the missing revenue and cost schedules.

b. Assuming you are currently charging $55 per table set, what should you do if you want to maximize profits?

c. Given your demand and cost estimates, what price should you charge if you want to maximize your weekly profit? What output should you produce? What is your maximum weekly profit?

Price	Quantity Demanded (per Week)	Marginal Cost	Total Revenue	Marginal Revenue	Fixed Cost	Total Cost
$60	1	$50	—	—	$40	—
55	2	20	—	—	—	—
50	3	24	—	—	—	—
45	4	29	—	—	—	—
40	5	35	—	—	—	—
35	6	45	—	—	—	—

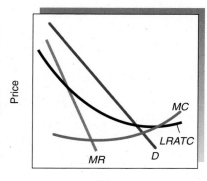

15. The accompanying diagram shows demand and long-run cost conditions in an industry.
   a. Explain why the industry is likely to be monopolized.
   b. Indicate the price that a profit-maximizing monopolist would charge and label it *P*.
   c. Indicate the monopolist's output level and label it *Q*.
   d. Indicate the maximum profits of the monopolist.
   e. Will the profits attract competitors to the industry? Why or why not? Explain.

*Asterisk denotes questions for which answers are given in Appendix B.

The Supply of and Demand for Productive Resources

CHAPTER FOCUS

- Why do business firms demand labor, machines, and other resources? Why is the demand for a productive resource inversely related to its price?

- How do business firms decide which resources to employ and the quantity of each that will be used?

- How is the quantity supplied of a resource related to its price in the short run? In the long run?

- What determines the market price of a resource? How do resource prices help a society allocate its resources efficiently among competing uses?

It is . . . necessary to attach price tags to the various factors of production . . . in order to guide those who have the day-to-day decisions to make as to what is plentiful and what is scarce.

—James Meade[1]

---

[1]James E. Meade was a longtime professor of economics at Cambridge University.

Recent chapters have focused on product markets, markets in which consumers purchase goods and services supplied by business firms. Our analysis now shifts to resource markets, markets in which firms hire productive resources like machines and workers and use them to produce goods and services. (*Note:* Because resources are often referred to as *factors or inputs*, these markets are also known as *factor markets* or *input markets*.)

As in product markets, the forces of supply and demand combine to determine prices in resource markets. The buyers and sellers in resource markets are just the reverse of what they are in product markets. In resource markets, business firms are the purchasers; they demand resources used to produce goods and services. Households are the sellers; they (and firms they own) supply resources in exchange for income. The income from supplying productive resources, like the wages received from the sale of labor services, is the major source of income for most of us. Prices in resource markets coordinate the choices of buyers and sellers and bring the amount of each resource demanded into harmony with the amount supplied. Resource prices also help to channel factors of production into the areas where they are most productive. This enables us to have higher incomes and a larger supply of consumer goods than would otherwise be the case.

As the circular flow diagram of **Exhibit 1** illustrates, there is a close relationship between product and resource markets. Households earn income by selling factors of production—for example, the services of their labor and capital—to business firms. Their offers to sell form the supply curve in resource markets (bottom loop). The income that households get from the sale of resources gives them the buying power they need to purchase goods and services in product markets. These expenditures by households generate revenue and motivate firms to produce goods and services (top loop). In turn, firms demand resources because they contribute to the production of goods and services that can be sold in product markets.

Exhibit 1

The Market for Resources

Until now, we have focused on product markets, in which households demand goods and services that are supplied by firms (upper loop). We now turn to resource markets, in which firms demand factors of production—human capital (like the skills and knowledge of workers) and physical capital (like machines, buildings, and land). Factors of production are supplied by households in exchange for income (bottom loop). In resource markets, firms are buyers and households are sellers—just the reverse of the case for product markets.

© Cengage Learning 2013

HUMAN AND NONHUMAN RESOURCES

Resource markets
Markets in which business firms demand factors of production (for example, labor, capital, and natural resources) from household suppliers. The resources are then used to produce goods and services. These markets are sometimes called factor markets or input markets.

Nonhuman resources
The durable, nonhuman inputs used to produce both current and future output. Machines, buildings, land, and raw materials are examples. Investment can increase the supply of nonhuman resources. Economists often use the term *physical capital* when referring to nonhuman resources.

Human resources
The abilities, skills, and health of human beings that contribute to the production of both current and future output. Investment in training and education can increase the supply of human resources.

Investment in human capital
Expenditures on training, education, skill development, and health designed to increase human capital and people's productivity.

Derived demand
The demand for a resource; it stems from the demand for the final good the resource helps produce.

Broadly speaking, there are two different types of productive inputs, nonhuman and human. Nonhuman resources can be further broken down into physical capital, land, and natural resources. *Physical capital* consists of human-made resources, like tools, machines, and buildings that are used to produce other things.

Investment involves the use of resources in a manner that will increase future production capacity. The use of resources to produce machines, upgrade the quality of land, or discover natural resources provide examples of investments in nonhuman resources. Of course, investments involve a cost because the resources used to expand future production capacity could have been used to produce consumption goods directly. Why take the roundabout path? Investment and the indirect method often expand total output. The investment will be attractive if the value of the future output exceeds the cost of the reduction in current output.

Human resources consist of the skills and knowledge of workers. Investments in education, training, health, and experience can enhance the skills, abilities, and ingenuity of individuals and thereby increase their productivity. Economists refer to activities like these as investment in human capital. Like physical capital, human capital also depreciates—people's skills, for example, can decline with age or lack of use. Education and training will add to the stock of human capital whereas depreciation detracts from it.

Decisions to invest in human capital are no different than other investment decisions we make. Consider your decision about going to college. As you know, an investment in a college education requires you to sacrifice some current earnings as well as pay for direct expenses, like tuition and books. However, you are making the investment anyway because you expect it to lead to a better job and other benefits later. A rational person will attend college only if the expected future benefits outweigh the current costs.

In competitive markets, the price of resources, like the price of products, is determined by supply and demand. We will begin our analysis of resource markets by focusing on the demand for resources, both human and nonhuman.

THE DEMAND FOR RESOURCES

Profit-seeking producers employ laborers, machines, raw materials, and other resources because they help produce goods and services. The demand for a resource exists because there is a demand for goods that the resource helps to produce. ***The demand for each resource is thus a*** derived demand***; it is derived from the demand of consumers for products.***

For example, the demand for inputs like carpenters, plumbers, lumber, and glass windows is derived from the demand of consumers for houses and other consumer products these resources help to make. Most resources contribute to the production of numerous goods. For example, glass is used to produce windows, lightbulbs, and mirrors, among other things. The total demand for a resource is the sum of the derived demands for each of its uses.

PHIL MCCARTEN/Landov

OUTSTANDING ECONOMIST

Gary Becker (1930–)

This 1992 Nobel Prize recipient is best known for his role in the development of human capital theory and his innovative application of that theory to areas as diverse as employment discrimination, family development, and crime. In his widely acclaimed book *Human Capital*,* Becker developed the theoretical foundation for human investment decisions in education, on-the-job training, migration, and health. Becker is a past president of the American Economic Association and a longtime professor at the University of Chicago.

*Gary Becker, *Human Capital* (New York: Columbia University Press, 1964).

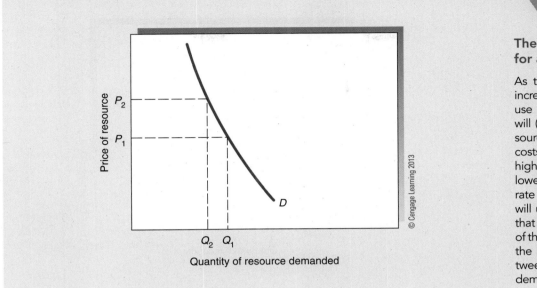

Exhibit 2

The Demand Curve for a Resource

As the price of a resource increases, producers that use the resource intensely will (1) turn to substitute resources and (2) face higher costs, which will lead to higher product prices and lower output. At the lower rate of output, producers will use less of the resource that increased in price. Both of these factors contribute to the inverse relationship between the price and amount demanded of a resource.

The demand curve for a resource shows the amount of the resource that will be used at different prices. As Exhibit 2 shows, there is an inverse relationship between the price of a resource and the quantity of it demanded. As the price of a resource increases there are two reasons why less will be demanded: (1) Producers will turn to substitute resources, and (2) consumers will buy less of goods that become more expensive as the result of higher resource costs. Let us take a closer look at each of these factors.

SUBSTITUTION IN PRODUCTION

Firms use the combination of resources that minimizes costs. When the price of one resource goes up, firms switch to other lower-cost substitute resources. If the price of oak lumber increases, furniture manufacturers will begin to use other types of wood (like maple) or metals and plastics more intensely. Sometimes, producers will alter the style and dimensions of a product, or even relocate the business, in order to use less of a more expensive resource. The degree to which firms will be able to cut back on a more expensive resource will depend on the availability of substitute resources. *Other things constant, the demand for a resource will be more elastic the more (and better) substitute resources are available for it.*

SUBSTITUTION IN CONSUMPTION

An increase in the price of a resource will lead to higher costs of production and thus higher prices for the products it helps to produce. Faced with these higher product prices, *consumers* will turn to substitute products and cut back on their purchases of the now more expensive products. In turn, fewer resources will be required to produce the smaller amount of the product demanded by consumers at the now higher price (including less of the resource that rose in price).

Other things constant, the more elastic the demand for a product is, the more elastic the demand for the resources used to make it. This relationship stems from the derived nature of resource demand. An increase in the price of a product for which consumer demand is highly elastic will cause a sharp fall in the sales of the good. As a result, there will be a relatively sharp fall in the demand for the resources used to produce it.

Exhibit 3

Time and the Demand Elasticity of Resources

The demand for a resource will be more elastic (1) the easier it is for firms to switch to substitute inputs and (2) the more elastic the consumer demand for the products the resource helps produce. As the graph here shows, demand for a resource in the long run (D_{lr}) is nearly always more elastic than demand in the short run (D_{sr}).

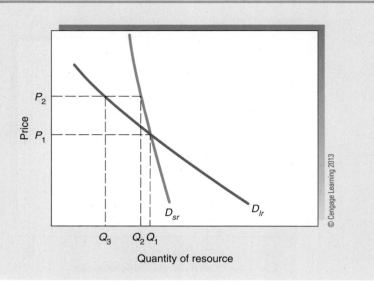

HOW TIME CHANGES THE DEMAND FOR RESOURCES

The elasticity of resource demand is also influenced by time. It takes time for both producers and consumers to make the adjustments described above after a resource price has changed. Producers may have to alter their plant and equipment, while consumers also need time to identify and utilize other substitutes. Thus, the demand for a resource generally becomes more elastic with the passage of time.

Exhibit 3 shows how time affects the elasticity of resource demand. The slope of the long-run demand curve (D_{lr}) is less steep, showing it is more elastic, than the slope of the short-run demand curve (D_{sr}). An increase in price from P_1 to P_2 will lead to only a small reduction in the quantity of the resource used (from Q_1 to Q_2) in the short run. Given more time, however, the increase in price to P_2 causes a much larger reduction in the quantity demanded (to Q_3).

SHIFTS IN THE DEMAND FOR A RESOURCE

Like the demand curve for a product, the entire demand curve for a resource may shift. There are three major reasons why.

1. A change in the demand for a product will cause a similar change in the demand for the resources used to produce it. Because the demand for a resource is a derived demand, an increase in the demand for a consumer good simultaneously increases the demand for resources needed to make it. For example, the demand for personal computers and other computerized equipment has increased substantially over the past couple of decades. In turn, this stronger demand for the equipment generated an increase in demand for computer chips required for its production. Of course, a reduction in the demand for a product will have the opposite impact. Lower demand for the product will lead to a reduction in demand for the resources required for its production.

2. Changes in the productivity of a resource will alter demand—the higher the productivity of a resource, the greater will be the demand for it. As the productivity of a resource increases, so does its value to potential users. Improvements in the quality of a resource—in the case of workers, their skill levels—will increase the productivity of the resource and therefore the demand for it. For example, as workers gain valuable new

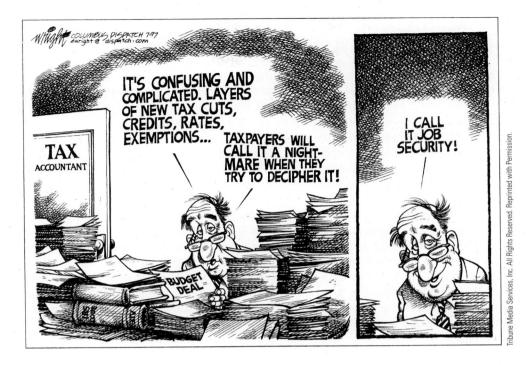

The demand for resources is a derived demand. A more complex tax code would increase the demand for (and thus the wages of) accountants, whereas a simpler tax code would have the opposite impact.

knowledge and/or upgrade their skills, they enhance their productivity and essentially move into a different skill category—one in which demand is greater.

The productivity of a resource will also depend on the amount of other resources used with it in the production process. In general, additional capital will tend to increase the productivity of labor. For example, someone with a dump truck can haul more material than can the same person with a shovel. The quantity and quality of the tools with which employees work will significantly affect their productivity. Technological advances in robotics and computing have substantially increased the productivity of a wide range of occupations including journalists, book authors, autoworkers, coal miners, and forensic scientists. The link between technological advances and worker productivity helps explain why improvements in technology generally do not simply displace workers and thereby exert a large negative impact on employment, even in the occupations most directly affected. Of course, when firms substitute new technology for labor services, the demand for labor will fall. However, the new technology both makes the labor more productive and lowers the cost of production and prices for consumers, which in turn increase the demand for labor. These positive impacts of technology on the employment of labor will partially, and sometimes more than completely, offset any negative effects.

The productivity–demand link sheds light on why wage rates in the United States, Canada, Western Europe, and Japan are higher than in most other areas of the world. Given the skill level of workers, the technology, and the capital equipment with which they work, individuals in these countries produce more goods and services per hour of labor than workers in most other countries. In turn, the demand for their labor (relative to supply) is greater because of their high productivity. Essentially, the workers' greater productivity leads to their higher wage rates.

3. A change in the price of a related resource will affect the demand for the original resource. A rise in the price of a resource will cause the demand for substitute resources to expand. For example, when the price of lumber increases, the demand for bricks will increase as homebuilders switch to building more brick homes and fewer wood homes. Conversely, an increase in the price of a resource that is a *complement* to a given resource will decrease the demand for the given resource. For example, higher lumber prices will tend to lower the demand for nails.

MARGINAL PRODUCTIVITY AND THE FIRM'S HIRING DECISION

Marginal revenue product (MRP)
The change in the total revenue of a firm that results from the employment of one additional unit of a resource. The marginal revenue product of an input is equal to its marginal product multiplied by the marginal revenue of the good or service produced.

How does a producer decide whether to employ additional units of a resource? As with other decisions, the marginal benefit relative to the marginal cost provides the answer. In resource markets, firms are mostly price takers, which means they can hire as many units of the resource as they wish without affecting the market price of the resource. Thus, the marginal cost of hiring one more worker is simply the worker's wage, while the marginal cost of purchasing a machine is its price. These represent the increase in the firm's costs from employing one more unit of each resource. But what about the marginal benefit of the resource to the firm? It is measured by the increase in the firm's revenue from employing one more unit of the resource. This is called the resource's **marginal revenue product (*MRP*)**. A profit-maximizing firm will only hire an additional unit of the resource if it generates more revenue for the firm than the cost of employing it. If the marginal revenue product of employing an additional unit of a resource is less than the cost, the firm will not employ it.

Suppose a retail store was considering hiring a security guard for $25 per hour to help reduce shoplifting. If the security guard could prevent $20 worth of shoplifting per hour, should the profit-maximizing firm hire the guard? Because the marginal cost of employing the security guard (the wage of $25) is higher than the guard's marginal revenue product (the $20 reduction in shoplifting per hour), the wise decision is for the firm not to hire the security guard. Hiring the guard will lower the firm's profit by $5 per hour. The guard should be employed only if the reduction in shoplifting exceeds the guard's wage cost. In most situations, the direct impact of hiring an additional resource on a firm's revenue is not as clear, so let's take a closer look at the firm's decision and how marginal revenue product is determined.

USING A VARIABLE RESOURCE WITH A FIXED RESOURCE

Marginal product (MP)
The change in total output that results from the employment of one additional unit of a resource.

Marginal revenue (MR)
The change in a firm's total revenue that results from the production and sale of one additional unit of output.

When an additional unit of the resource is used relative to a fixed amount of other resources, the firm's output will increase by an amount equal to the resource's **marginal product (*MP*)**. Because this is measured in units of physical output, it is sometimes referred to as marginal physical product. How much additional revenue can the firm derive from the employment of the resource? Recall that **marginal revenue (*MR*)** is the increase in the firm's revenue that results from the sale of each additional unit of output. Thus, a resource's marginal revenue product is equal to the marginal product of the resource multiplied by the marginal revenue of the good or service produced. *Because of the law of diminishing returns, the marginal product of a resource will fall as employment of the resource expands. As a result, the marginal revenue product of a resource will also decline as its employment expands.*

The relationship between the marginal revenue a firm gets from selling an additional unit of output and the price for which it is sold is different for *price-taker* firms than for *price searchers*, however. Because a price-taker firm sells all units produced at the same price, the price taker's marginal revenue will be equal to the market price of the product. The price searcher, however, must reduce the price of all units in order to expand the number of units sold. Consequently, the price searcher's marginal revenue will be less than the sales price of the units. The marginal product of a resource multiplied by the selling price of the product is called the resource's **value marginal product (*VMP*)**. *For a price-taker firm, the* **MRP** *of a resource is equal to its* **VMP** *because price and marginal revenue are equal. For a price-searcher firm, however, the* **MRP** *of a resource will be lower than its* **VMP** *because marginal revenue is less than price.*

Value marginal product (VMP)
The marginal product of a resource multiplied by the selling price of the product it helps produce. For a price-taker firm, marginal revenue product (*MRP*) will be equal to the value marginal product (*VMP*).

Using these measures, **Exhibit 4** illustrates how a firm decides how much of a resource to employ. Compute-Accounting, Inc., uses computer equipment and data entry operators to supply clients with monthly accounting statements. The firm is a price taker: It sells its service in a competitive market for $200 per statement. Given the fixed quantity of computer equipment owned by Compute-Accounting, column 2 shows how much total output

The Short-Run Demand Schedule of a Firm

Exhibit 4

Compute-Accounting, Inc., uses computer technology and data-entry operators to provide accounting services in a competitive market. For each accounting statement processed, the firm receives a $200 fee (column 4). Given the firm's current fixed capital, column 2 shows how total output changes as additional data entry operators are hired. The marginal revenue product (MRP) schedule (column 6) indicates how hiring an additional operator affects the total revenue of the firm. Because a profit-maximizing firm will hire an additional employee if, and only if, the employee adds more to revenues than to costs, the marginal revenue product curve is the firm's short-run demand curve for the resource (see Exhibit 5).

Units of Variable Factor (Data-Entry Operators) (1)	Total Output (Accounting Statements Processed Per Week) (2)	Marginal Product (Change in Column 2 Divided by Change in Column 1) (3)	Sales Price Per Statement (4)	Total Revenue (2) × (4) (5)	MRP (3) × (4) (6)
0	0.0	—	$200	$0	—
1	5.0	5.0	200	1,000	1,000
2	9.0	4.0	200	1,800	800
3	12.0	3.0	200	2,400	600
4	14.0	2.0	200	2,800	400
5	15.5	1.5	200	3,100	300
6	16.5	1.0	200	3,300	200
7	17.0	0.5	200	3,400	100

(quantity of accounting statements) the firm can produce with different numbers of data entry operators. One data entry operator can process five statements per week. When two operators are employed, nine statements can be completed. Column 2 indicates how total output is expected to change as additional data entry operators are employed. Column 3 presents the marginal product schedule for data entry operators. Column 6, the *MRP* schedule, shows how the employment of each additional operator affects total revenue. Both the marginal product and the *MRP* of workers decline as additional operators are employed due to the law of diminishing returns.

Because Compute-Accounting is a price taker, the marginal revenue product and the value marginal product of labor are equal. Thus, the marginal revenue product of labor (column 6) can be calculated by multiplying the marginal product (column 3) times the sales price of an accounting statement (column 4).

How does Compute-Accounting decide how many operators to employ? It analyzes the benefits relative to the costs. As additional operators are employed, the output of processed statements (column 2) will increase, which will expand total revenue (column 5). Employing additional operators, though, will also add to production costs because the operators must be paid. Applying the profit-maximization rule, Compute-Accounting will hire additional operators as long as their employment adds more to revenues than to costs. This will be the case as long as the *MRP* (column 6) of the data entry operators exceeds their wage rate. At a weekly wage of $1,000, Compute-Accounting would hire only one operator. If the weekly wage dropped to $800, two operators would be hired. At still lower wage rates, additional operators would be hired.

Profit-maximizing firms, both price takers and price searchers, will expand their employment of each variable resource until the **MRP** *of the resource (the firm's additional revenue generated by the resource) is just equal to the price of the resource (the firm's marginal cost of employing the resource).*

MRP AND THE FIRM'S DEMAND CURVE FOR A RESOURCE

Using the data in Exhibit 4, we can construct Compute-Accounting's demand curve for data entry operators. Recall that the height of a demand curve shows the maximum price (in this case, the wage) the buyer (the firm) would be willing to pay for the unit. Because the marginal revenue product of the first data entry operator is $1,000, the firm would be willing to hire this worker only up to a maximum price of $1,000. Because of this relationship, as **Exhibit 5** shows, a firm's short-run demand curve for a resource is precisely the *MRP* curve for the resource.[2] Using this demand curve yields the identical solutions as the table. Underlying the downward-sloping demand curve is the law of diminishing returns causing *MP*, and thus *MRP*, to fall as more workers are hired.

The location of the firm's *MRP* curve depends on (1) the price of the product, (2) the productivity of the resource, and (3) the amount of other resources with which the resource is working. Changes in any one of these three factors will cause the *MRP* curve to shift. For example, if Compute-Accounting purchased additional computer equipment making it possible for the operators to complete more statements each week, the *MRP* curve for labor would increase (shift outward). This increase in the quantity of the other resources working with labor would increase labor's productivity.

MULTIPLE RESOURCES AND HOW MUCH TO USE OF EACH

So far, we have analyzed the firm's hiring decision assuming that it used one variable resource (labor) and one fixed resource. Production, though, usually involves the use of many resources. How should these resources be combined to produce the product? We can answer this question by considering either the conditions for profit maximization or the conditions for cost minimization.

Exhibit 5

The Firm's Demand Curve for a Resource

The firm's demand curve for a resource will reflect the marginal revenue product (MRP) of the resource. In the short run, it will slope downward because the marginal product of the resource will fall as more of it is used with a fixed amount of other resources. The location of the MRP curve will depend on (1) the price of the product, (2) the productivity of the resource, and (3) the quantity of other factors working with the resource.

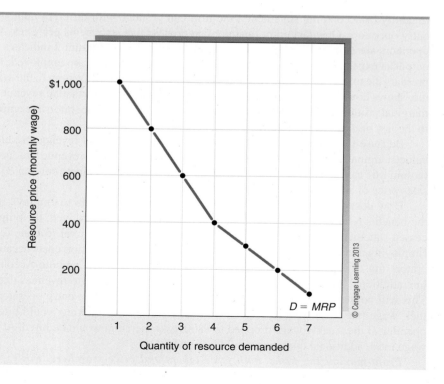

---

[2]Strictly speaking, this is true only for a variable resource that is employed with a fixed amount of another factor.

MAXIMIZING PROFITS WHEN MULTIPLE RESOURCES ARE USED

The same decision-making considerations apply when the firm employs several factors of production. The profit-maximizing firm will expand its use of a resource as long as the *MRP* of the resource exceeds its employment cost. If we assume that resources are perfectly divisible, the profit-maximizing decision rule implies that, in equilibrium, the *MRP* of each resource will be equal to the price of the resource. Therefore, the following conditions will exist for the profit-maximizing firm:

MRP of skilled labor = Price (wage rate) of skilled labor

MRP of unskilled labor = Price (wage rate) of unskilled labor

MRP of machine A = Price (explicit or implicit rental price) of machine A and so on, for all other factors

COST MINIMIZATION WHEN MULTIPLE RESOURCES ARE USED

To maximize its profits, the firm must produce the profit-maximizing output at the least possible cost. If the firm is minimizing costs, the marginal dollar expenditure for each resource will have the same impact on output as an additional dollar expenditure on other resources used to produce the product. Factors of production will be employed such that the marginal product *per last dollar spent* on each factor is the same for all factors.

To see why, consider a situation in which a $100 expenditure on labor caused output to rise by ten units, whereas an additional $100 expenditure on machines generated only a five-unit expansion in output. In this case, the firm could employ $100 less in machines, spend the $100 on labor instead, and produce five more units of output for the same total cost. By substituting labor for machines, it will reduce its *per-unit* cost.

If the marginal dollar spent on one resource increases output by a larger amount than a dollar expenditure on other resources, substituting the one with the high marginal product per dollar for the low one will always reduce costs. Substitution will continue to reduce unit costs (and increase profit) until the marginal product per dollar expenditure on each resource is equalized. This will occur because as additional units of a resource are hired, their marginal product will fall. Thus, the proportional relationship between the price of each resource and its marginal product will eventually be achieved.

Therefore, the following condition exists when per unit costs are minimized:

$$\frac{MP \text{ of skilled labor}}{\text{Price of skilled labor}} = \frac{MP \text{ of unskilled labor}}{\text{Price of unskilled labor}} = \frac{MP \text{ of machine A}}{\text{Price (rental value) of machine A}}$$

This relationship explains why workers with different skill levels earn different wages. If skilled workers are twice as productive as unskilled workers, their wage rates will tend to be twice those of unskilled workers. For example, suppose that a construction firm hiring workers to hang doors is choosing among skilled and unskilled workers. If skilled door hangers can complete four doors per hour, while unskilled workers can hang only two doors per hour, a cost-minimizing firm would hire only skilled workers—as long as their wages are less than twice the wages of unskilled workers. In contrast, only unskilled workers would be hired if the wages of skilled workers are more than twice that of unskilled workers. Because of competition, wages across skill categories will tend to mirror productivity differences.

It is important to note that low wages do not necessarily mean low cost. In other words, it is not always cheaper to hire the lowest-wage workers. It is not just wages, but rather wages *relative to productivity* that matter. If the wages of skilled workers are twice those of unskilled workers, it will still be cheaper to hire additional skilled workers if their marginal productivity (output per hour) is more than twice that of the unskilled workers.

Do employers in the real world really think in terms of equating the marginal product/price ratio (*MP/P*) for each factor of production? Probably not. Their thought process is likely going to be something more like this: "Can we reduce costs by using more of one resource and less of another?" However, regardless of how managers think about the problem, when a firm maximizes its profits and minimizes its costs, its marginal product/price ratio will be equal for all factors of production. The outcome will be *the same as if* the firm followed the cost-minimization, decision-making rule presented here.

Summing up, resources will only be employed if they generate enough revenue to cover the cost of their employment. Resources that are more productive will be able to command higher prices (or wage rates) because they generate more revenue for the firm. The marginal-productivity theory underlies the demand for resources. Of course, resource prices will also be influenced by supply. We now turn to that topic.

THE SUPPLY OF RESOURCES

Just as benefits and costs direct the choices of employers, so too will they guide the actions of resource suppliers. Resource owners will supply their services to an employer only if they perceive that the benefits of doing so exceed their costs (the value of the other things they could do with their time or resources). Because of this, employers must offer resource owners at least as good a deal as they can get elsewhere. For example, if an employer does not offer a potential employee pay, benefits, and working conditions as good as, or better than, others, the employer will be unable to hire that worker.

Resource owners will supply their services to those who offer them the best employment alternative. Other things constant, as the price of a specific resource increases, the incentive of potential suppliers to provide the resource increases.

An increase in the price of a resource will lure resource suppliers into the market. A decrease will cause them to shift into other activities. Therefore, as **Exhibit 6** illustrates, the supply curve for a specific resource will slope upward to the right.[3]

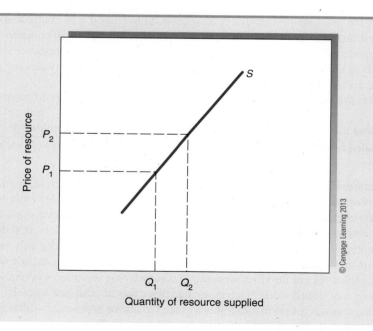

Exhibit 6

The Supply of a Resource

As the price of a resource increases, individuals have a greater incentive to supply it. Therefore, a direct relationship will exist between the price of a resource and the quantity supplied.

[3]Although the supply for nonhuman resources will always slope upward, the supply of labor at very high wage rates can become backward bending. As wages rise, individuals will substitute toward more work, but simultaneously the higher income will cause them to desire more leisure. At very high wage rates, the income effect might dominate, causing a negative relationship between wage rates and quantity of labor supplied in this range. For example, at a wage of $10,000 per hour, many individuals would probably supply fewer hours of work than at $500 per hour!

SHORT-RUN VERSUS LONG-RUN RESOURCE SUPPLY

Like demand, supply in resource markets can be different in the short run than in the long run. If the wage rate for certified public accountants (CPAs) rose, for example, we would expect more workers supplying their services as CPAs. But where do these additional CPAs come from? In the short run, the additional supply must come from those who are already qualified as CPAs but are currently doing other things. The higher wages might induce some college accounting professors and some stay-at-home spouses with accounting credentials to move into employment as CPAs. In the short run, however, there isn't enough time to alter the availability of a resource through investment in human and physical capital. In contrast, in the long run, resource suppliers have time to adjust their investment choices in response to a change in resource prices. With time, the higher wages and easier employment opportunities for CPAs will cause more students to major in accounting and other people to pursue the coursework needed to become a CPA. Higher resource prices will increase the quantity supplied in both the short run and the long run, but the response will be greater in the long run. Therefore, as **Exhibit 7** shows, the long-run supply of a resource will be more elastic than the short-run supply.

SHORT-RUN SUPPLY

The short-run supply response to a change in price is determined by how easily the resource can be transferred from one use to another—that is, **resource mobility**. The supply of resources with high mobility will be relatively elastic even in the short run. Conversely, resources that have few alternative uses (or are not easily transferable) are said to be immobile. The short-run supply of immobile resources will be highly inelastic.

Consider the mobility of labor. Within a skill category (for example, plumber, store manager, accountant, or secretary), labor will be highly mobile within the same geographic area. Movements between geographic areas and from one skill category to another are more costly to accomplish, though. Labor will thus be less mobile for movements of this variety. In addition, because it is easier for a highly skilled person to perform effectively in a lower-skill position than vice versa, short-run mobility will tend to decline as the skill

Resource mobility
The ease with which factors of production are able to move among alternative uses. Resources that can easily be transferred to a different use or location are said to be highly mobile. Resources with few alternative uses are immobile.

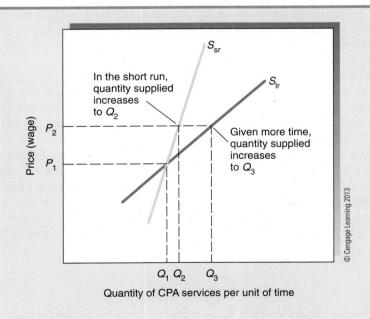

Exhibit 7

Time and the Elasticity of Supply for Resources

If the wage rate for CPAs rises, for example, to P_2, we would expect more workers to supply CPA services. Because it takes time to be trained as a CPA, though, the quantity of CPA services supplied in the short-run (S_{sr}) won't increase by much—just to Q_2. The supply of CPA services is therefore relatively inelastic in the short run. In the long run, though, it is more elastic and the quantity supplied increases to Q_3.

In the short run, quantity supplied increases to Q_2

Given more time, quantity supplied increases to Q_3

Price (wage)

P_2

P_1

Q_1 Q_2 Q_3

Quantity of CPA services per unit of time

© Cengage Learning 2013

The supply curve for truck drivers will be considerably more elastic than the supply curve for doctors. Can you explain why?

level of the occupation rises. Thus, the short-run supply curve in high-skill occupations like architect, mechanical engineer, and medical surgeon is usually quite inelastic.

What about the mobility of land? Land is highly mobile among uses when location doesn't matter. For example, the same land can often be used to raise corn, wheat, soybeans, or oats. As a result, the supply of land allocated to the production of each of these commodities will be highly responsive to changes in their relative prices. Undeveloped land on the outskirts of cities is particularly mobile among uses. It can be used for agriculture, but it can also quickly be subdivided and used for a housing development or a shopping center. Because land is totally immobile physically, you might think its supply is unresponsive to changes in price when it comes to how desirable it is (or isn't) due to its location. You can't move it to make it more desirable and get a better price, obviously. You can, however, expand its usable space by constructing multiple-story buildings, for instance. As the demand for a given location increases, higher and higher multilevel construction will be justified. This is why tall buildings are generally located in city centers, for example—because the demand for space is highest in these locations.

LONG-RUN SUPPLY

In the long run, the supply of resources can change substantially. Machines wear out, human skills depreciate, and even the fertility of land declines with use and erosion. These factors reduce the supply of resources. In contrast, investment can replace and expand the supply of productive resources, including machines, buildings, and durable assets. Correspondingly, investments in training and education can develop and improve the skills of future labor force participants. Thus, the supply of both physical and human resources in the long run is determined primarily by investment and depreciation.

As the price of a resource increases, more and more people will make the investments necessary to supply it. This will be true for human as well as physical resources. For example, higher salaries for lawyers stimulate law school enrollments. According to Harvard University economist Richard Freeman, a 1 percent increase in starting law salaries causes enrollment in the first year of law school to rise by 2 percent.[4]

The long run, of course, is not a specified length of time. Investment can increase the availability of some resources fairly quickly. For example, it does not take very long to train additional truck drivers. However, it takes a long time to train physicians, dentists, lawyers, and pharmacists. Higher earnings in these occupations may have only a small impact on their current availability. Additional investment will flow into these areas, but it will typically be several years before there is a substantial increase in the quantity supplied.

---

[4]Richard B. Freeman, "Legal Cobwebs: A Recursive Model of the Market for New Lawyers," *The Review of Economics and Statistics* 57, no. 2 (May 1975): 171–79.

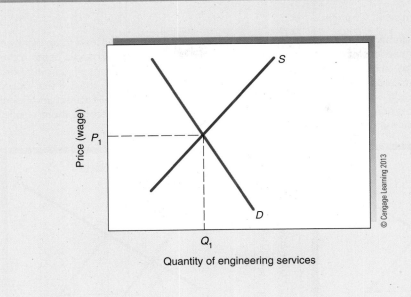

© Cengage Learning 2013

Exhibit 8

Equilibrium in a Resource Market

The market demand for a resource, such as engineering services, is a downward-sloping curve, reflecting the declining *MRP* of the resource. The market supply curve slopes upward because higher resource prices (wage rates) will motivate people to supply more of the resource. Market price will move toward equilibrium (P_1), where the quantity demanded and the quantity supplied are in balance.

SUPPLY, DEMAND, AND RESOURCE PRICES

In a market economy, resource prices will be determined by the forces of supply and demand and will bring the choices of buyers and sellers into line with each other. **Exhibit 8** illustrates how the forces of supply and demand push the market wage rates of engineers toward equilibrium, where quantity demanded and quantity supplied are equal. Equilibrium is achieved when the price (wage rate) for engineering services is P_1. Given the market conditions illustrated by Exhibit 8, an excess supply is present if the price of engineering services exceeds P_1. Some engineers will be unable to find jobs at the above-equilibrium wage. This excess supply of engineers will cause the wage rate for engineers to fall. This will cause some of the engineers to look for jobs in other fields, and quantity supplied will fall, pushing the market toward equilibrium. In contrast, if the resource price is less than P_1, excess demand is present. Employers are unable to hire the amount of engineering services they want at a below-equilibrium resource price. Rather than doing without the resource, employers will attempt to hire engineers away from other firms by bidding the price up to P_1 and thereby eliminating the excess demand.

How will a resource market adjust to an unexpected change in market conditions? Suppose there is a sharp increase in the demand for houses, apartments, and office buildings. The increase in demand for these products will also increase the demand for resources required for their construction. Thus, the demand for resources like steel, lumber, brick, and the labor services of carpenters, architects, and construction engineers will increase. **Exhibit 9** shows the increase in demand for new houses and buildings (part a) and the accompanying increase in demand for construction engineers. The market demand for the services of construction engineers increases from D_1 to D_2 (part b), and initially there is a sharp rise in their wages (price increases from P_1 to P_2). The higher wages will motivate additional people to get the education and training necessary to become construction engineers. Over time, the entry of the newly trained construction engineers will increase the elasticity of the resource supply curve. As these new construction engineers eventually enter the occupation, the supply curve will become more elastic (S_{lr} rather than S_{sr}), which will place downward pressure on wages in the occupation (the move from *b* to *c*). Therefore, as part (b) of Exhibit 9 illustrates, the long-run price increase (to P_3) will be less than the short-run increase (to P_2).

The market adjustment to an unexpected reduction in demand for a resource is the same. The price falls farther in the short run than in the long run. At the lower price, some

Exhibit 9   **Adjusting to Dynamic Change**

An increase in the demand for housing and commercial buildings (part a) will lead to an increase in demand for the services of construction engineers (part b) and other resources used in the construction industry. Initially, the increase in the resource price will be substantial, jumping from P_1 to P_2 (point a versus point b in the graph). The increase will be particularly sharp if the supply of the resource is highly inelastic in the short run. The higher resource price will attract additional human capital investment, and, with time, the resource supply curve will become more elastic, which will moderate the price (or wage) increase to P_3 (point c).

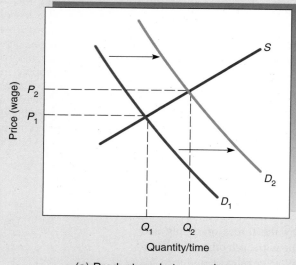

(a) Product market—new houses and commercial buildings

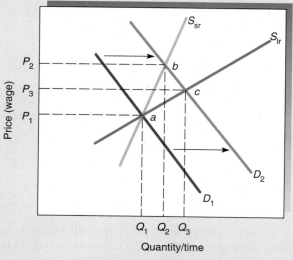

(b) Resource market—services of construction engineers

© Cengage Learning 2013

resource suppliers will use their talents in other areas, and the incentive for potential new suppliers to offer the resource will be less. With time, the quantity of the resource supplied will decline, moderating the reduction in its price. Those with the poorest alternatives (that is, lowest opportunity cost) will continue to provide the resource at the lower prices. Those with better alternatives will look for other opportunities.

Workers in occupations like nursing that require substantial skill and education will generally earn higher wages than will those in occupations requiring little training or experience.

Flying Colours Ltd/Jupiter Images

Mark Anderson/Rubberball Productions/Jupiter Images

THE COORDINATING FUNCTION OF RESOURCE PRICES

Our analysis indicates that prices in resource markets play a vitally important role. These prices coordinate the actions of the firms demanding factors of production and the households supplying them. ***Resource prices provide users with both information about the scarcity of the resources they're using and the incentive to conserve them in production. They also provide suppliers with an incentive to learn skills and provide resources—particularly those that are intensely demanded by users.*** Without the use of resource markets and the price incentives they provide, efficient use and wise conservation of resources would be extremely difficult to achieve.[5]

Looking Ahead

The analysis of this chapter can be applied to a broad range of economic issues. The next chapter will focus on the labor market and earnings differences among workers. Later, we will focus on the capital market and the allocation of resources over time. The operation of these two markets plays an important role in determining the distribution of income, a topic that will also be analyzed in detail in a subsequent chapter.

KEY POINTS

- Productive assets and services are bought and sold in resource markets. There are two broad classes of productive resources: (1) nonhuman capital and (2) human capital.

- The demand for resources is derived from the demand for products that the resources help produce. The quantity of a resource demanded is inversely related to its price because of substitutions made by both producers and consumers.

- The demand curve for a resource, like the demand for a product, can shift. The major factors that increase the demand for a resource are (1) an increase in demand for products that use the resource, (2) an increase in the productivity of the resource, and (3) an increase in the price of substitute resources.

- Profit-maximizing firms will hire additional units of a resource up to the point at which the marginal revenue product (*MRP*) of the resource equals its price. With multiple inputs, firms will expand their use of each until the marginal product divided by the price (*MP/P*) is equal across all inputs. When real-world decision makers minimize

per-unit costs, the outcome will be as if they had followed these mathematical procedures, even though they may not consciously do so.

- The amount of a resource supplied will be directly related to its price. The supply of a resource will be more elastic in the long run than in the short run. In the long run, investment can increase the supply of both physical and human resources.

- The prices of resources are determined by supply and demand. Changes in the market prices of resources will influence the decisions of both users and suppliers. Higher resource prices give users a greater incentive to turn to substitutes and suppliers a greater incentive to provide more of the resource.

- Resource prices coordinate the actions of resource owners and business firms demanding their services. Changes in resource prices in response to changing market conditions are essential for the efficient allocation of resources in a dynamic world.

---

[5]Analysis of energy consumption under central planning illustrates this point. The centrally planned economies both used more energy per unit of output and their energy consumption was less responsive to changes in price than was true for economies that used markets to allocate energy. For evidence on these points, see Mikhail S. Bernstam, *The Wealth of Nations and the Environment* (London: Institute of Economic Affairs, 1991).

CRITICAL ANALYSIS QUESTIONS

1. "The demand for resources is a derived demand." What is meant by that statement? Why is the employment of a resource inversely related to its price?

2. How does a firm decide whether or not to employ an additional unit of a resource? What determines the combination of skilled and unskilled workers employed by a firm?

3. *Use the information in Exhibit 4 of this chapter to answer the following:
   a. How many employees (operators) would Compute-Accounting hire at a weekly wage of $250 if it were attempting to maximize profits?
   b. What would the firm's maximum profit be if its fixed costs were $1,500 per week?
   c. Suppose there were a decline in demand for accounting services, reducing the market price per monthly statement to $150. At this demand level, how many employees would Compute-Accounting hire at $250 per week in the short run? Would Compute-Accounting be able to stay in business at the lower market price? Explain.

4. *Are productivity gains the major source of higher wages? If so, how does one account for the rising real wages of barbers, who, by and large, have used the same techniques for a half-century? (*Hint:* Do not forget opportunity cost and supply.)

5. Are the following statements both correct? Are they inconsistent with each other? Explain.
   a. "Firms will hire a resource only if they can make money by doing so."
   b. "In a market economy, each resource will tend to be paid according to its marginal product. Highly productive resources will command high prices, whereas less productive resources will command lower prices."

6. *Many school districts pay teachers on the basis of their highest degree earned and number of years of service (seniority). They often find it quite easy to fill the slots for English and history teachers, but very difficult to find the required number of math and science teachers. Can you explain why?

7. Suppose that you were the manager of a large retail store that was currently experiencing a shoplifting problem. Every hour, approximately $15 worth of merchandise was being stolen from your store. Suppose that a security guard would completely eliminate the shoplifting in your store. If you were interested in maximizing your profits, should you hire a security guard if the wage rate of security guards was $20 per hour? Why or why not? What does this imply about the relationship between av-erage shoplifting per hour in the economy and the wage rates of security guards?

8. *A dressmaker uses labor and capital (sewing machines) to produce dresses in a competitive market. Suppose the last unit of labor hired cost $1,000 per month and increased output by 100 dresses. The last unit of capital hired (rented) cost $500 per month and increased output by 80 dresses. Is the dressmaker minimizing costs? If not, what changes need to be made?

9. A firm is considering moving from the United States to Mexico. The firm pays its U.S. workers $12 per hour. Current U.S. workers have a marginal product of forty, whereas the Mexican workers have a marginal product of ten. How low would the Mexican wage have to be for the firm to reduce its wage cost per unit of output by moving to Mexico?

10. *"The earnings of engineers, doctors, and lawyers are high because lots of education is necessary to practice in these fields." Evaluate this statement.

11. Other things constant, what impact will a highly elastic demand for a product have on the elasticity of demand for the resources used to produce the product? Explain.

12. *The following chart provides information on a firm that hires labor competitively and sells its product in a competitive market.

Units of Labor	Total Output	Marginal Product	Product Price	Total Revenue	MRP
1	14	—	$5	—	—
2	26	—	$5	—	—
3	37	—	$5	—	—
4	46	—	$5	—	—
5	53	—	$5	—	—
6	58	—	$5	—	—

   a. Fill in the missing columns.
   b. How many units of labor would be employed if the market wage rate were $40? Why?
   c. What would happen to employment if the wage rate rose to $50? Explain.

13. Leisure Times, Inc., employs skilled workers and capital to install hot tubs. The capital includes the tools and equipment workers use to construct and install the tubs. The installation services are sold in a competitive market for $1,200 per hot tub. Leisure Times is able to hire workers for $2,200 per month, including the cost of wages, fringe benefits, and employment taxes. As additional workers are hired, the increase in the number of hot tubs installed is indicated in the table.

NUMBER OF WORKERS EMPLOYED	NUMBER OF HOT TUBS INSTALLED (PER MONTH)
1	5
2	12
3	18
4	23
5	27
6	30
7	32
8	33
9	34

a. Indicate the marginal product and *MRP* schedules of the workers.

b. What quantity of workers should Leisure Times employ to maximize its profit?

c. If a construction boom pushes the wages of skilled workers up to $2,500 per month, how many workers would Leisure Times employ to maximize its profit?

d. Suppose that strong demand for hot tubs pushes the price of installation services up to $1,500 per month. How would this affect employment of the skilled workers if the wage rate of the workers remained at $2,500 per month?

14. A recent flyer on a university campus stated that consumers should boycott sugar due to the low wages earned by laborers on sugar cane farms in Florida. Using the notion of derived demand, what impact would a boycott on sugar have on the wages of the farm laborers in the short run? In the long run?

*Asterisk denotes questions for which answers are given in Appendix B.

CHAPTER **13**

Earnings, Productivity, and the Job Market

CHAPTER FOCUS

- Why do some people earn more than others?
- Are earnings differences according to race and gender the result of employment discrimination?
- Why are wages higher in the United States than in India or China?
- What is the source of higher wages? How does the growth of productivity affect wages?
- Does automation destroy jobs?

How can I be overpaid? The boss wouldn't pay me that amount if I wasn't worth it.
—Jackie Gleason[1]

_____

[1]This statement was made in response to a question about the amount he was being paid for the popular television show *The Honeymooners*, which ran during the 1950s and 1960s.

The earnings of U.S. workers are among the highest in the world. However, they vary widely. An unskilled laborer may earn $12 per hour, or even less. Lawyers and physicians often earn $250 per hour, or more. Dentists and even economists might receive $200 per hour. How can these variations in earnings be explained? Why are the earnings of Americans so high? How have earnings changed in recent years, and what are the factors underlying these changes? This chapter will address these topics and related issues.

WHY DO EARNINGS DIFFER?

The earnings of individuals in the same occupation or with the same amount of education often differ substantially. So do the earnings of people in the same family. For example, one researcher found that the average annual earnings differential between brothers was $35,620, compared with $38,802 for men paired randomly.[2] The earnings of people with the same intelligence, level of training, or amount of experience also typically differ.

Several factors combine to determine a person's earning power. Some seem to be the result of good or bad luck. Others are clearly the result of conscious decisions people make. In the previous chapter, we analyzed how the market forces of supply and demand operate to determine resource prices. Wages are a resource price, and therefore the supply and demand model can be used to examine earnings differentials among workers.

For simplicity, we have proceeded as if employees earned only money payments. In reality, most workers receive a compensation package that includes **fringe benefits** as well as money wages. The fringe benefit component typically includes medical insurance, life insurance, pension benefits, and paid vacation days. When we use the terms *wages* and *earnings* in the following discussions, we are referring to the total compensation package that includes both wages and fringe benefits.

The **real earnings** of all employees in a competitive market economy would be equal if (1) all individuals were identical in preferences, skills, and background; (2) all jobs were equally attractive; and (3) workers were perfectly mobile among jobs. Given these conditions, if higher real wages existed in an area of the economy, the supply of workers in that area would expand until the wage differential was eliminated. Similarly, low wages in an area would cause workers to exit until wages there returned to normal. Of course, that's not the way things work in the real world. We all know that earnings differences are a fact of life. There are three reasons for this, and we'll discuss each one.

EARNINGS DIFFERENTIALS DUE TO NONIDENTICAL WORKERS

Workers differ in several important respects that affect both the supply of and demand for their services. In turn, these factors affect their wage rates. Let's consider these differences.

1. **Worker productivity and specialized skills.** The demand for employees who are highly productive is greater than the demand for those who are less productive. People who can operate a machine more skillfully, hit a baseball more consistently, or sell life insurance policies with greater regularity are more valuable to employers. Compared with their less skillful counterparts, these employees contribute more to the firm's revenue. Put another way, the marginal revenue product (*MRP*) of the more productive employees is higher than the *MRP* of less productive ones. In competitive labor markets, workers earn a wage equal to their marginal revenue product. As a result, the labor services of more productive workers will command higher wages in the marketplace.

Fringe benefits
Benefits other than normal money wages that are supplied to employees in exchange for their labor services. Higher fringe benefits come at the expense of lower money wages.

Real earnings
Earnings adjusted for differences in the general level of prices across time periods or geographic areas. When real earnings are equal, the same bundle of goods and services can be purchased with the earnings.

---

[2]Christopher Jencks, *Inequality* (New York: Basic Books, 1972), 220. The salary figures are in 2010 dollars.

Exhibit 1 — Demand, Supply, and Wage Rates for Skilled and Unskilled Workers

The productivity—and therefore marginal product (*MP*)—of skilled workers is greater than that of unskilled workers. As a result, as part (a) illustrates, the demand for skilled workers (D_s) will exceed the demand for unskilled workers (D_u). Education and training generally enhance skills. Because upgrading one's skills through investments in human capital is costly, the supply of skilled workers (S_s) is smaller than the supply of unskilled workers at any given wage (part b). As part (c) illustrates, the wages of skilled workers are high relative to those of unskilled workers due to the strong demand and small supply of skilled workers relative to unskilled workers. (*Note:* The quantity of skilled labor employed may be far smaller, far larger, or, by accident, equal to the quantity of unskilled labor hired.)

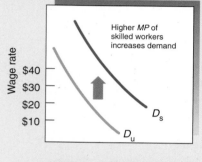

(a) Demand for skilled and unskilled labor

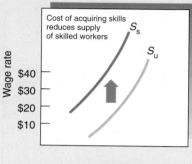

(b) Supply of skilled and unskilled labor

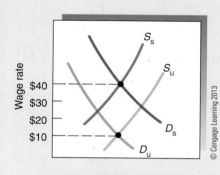

(c) Wages of skilled and unskilled labor

© Cengage Learning 2013

Worker productivity is the result of a combination of factors, including native ability, parental training, hard work, and investment in human capital. The link between higher productivity and higher earnings motivates people to invest in themselves in order to upgrade their knowledge and skills. If additional worker productivity didn't lead to higher earnings, people would have little incentive to incur the costs of skill development, including paying to go to college or get additional training.

Exhibit 1 shows the demand, supply, and wage rates for skilled versus unskilled workers. The productivity of skilled workers exceeds that of unskilled workers, and so does the demand for them. The vertical distance between the demand curve for skilled workers (D_s) and the demand curve for unskilled workers (D_u), shown in part (a), reflects the higher marginal product (*MP*) of skilled workers. Because human capital investments (education, training, and so on) are costly, the supply of skilled workers (S_s) will be smaller than the supply of unskilled workers (S_u). This is shown in part (b). The vertical distance between the two supply curves is the wage differential employers will need to pay skilled workers for the costs they incurred to acquire their skills.

Wages are determined by demand relative to supply (part c). Because the demand for skilled workers is large whereas their supply is small, the equilibrium wage of skilled workers will be high ($40 per hour). In contrast, because the supply of unskilled workers is large relative to the demand, their wage rates will be substantially lower ($10 per hour).

The skills that one person gains from a year of education, vocational school, or on-the-job training might be better or worse than those of someone else. Therefore, we should not expect a rigid relationship to exist between years of education (or training) and skill level. On average, however, there is a strong positive relationship between investment in education and earnings.

Exhibit 2 presents annual earnings data according to educational level for year-round, full-time workers in 2009. Notice that the earnings of both men and women increased consistently with additional schooling. High school graduates earned about 40 percent more than their counterparts with less than a high school education. Male college graduates working full-time, year-round earned $79,003, compared with $43,140

Education and Earnings

Exhibit 2

The accompanying graph presents data for the mean annual earnings of year-round, full-time workers based on their gender and education. Note that the earnings of both men and women increased with additional education. Even though the data are for full-time workers, the earnings of women were only about two-thirds those of men with similar education.

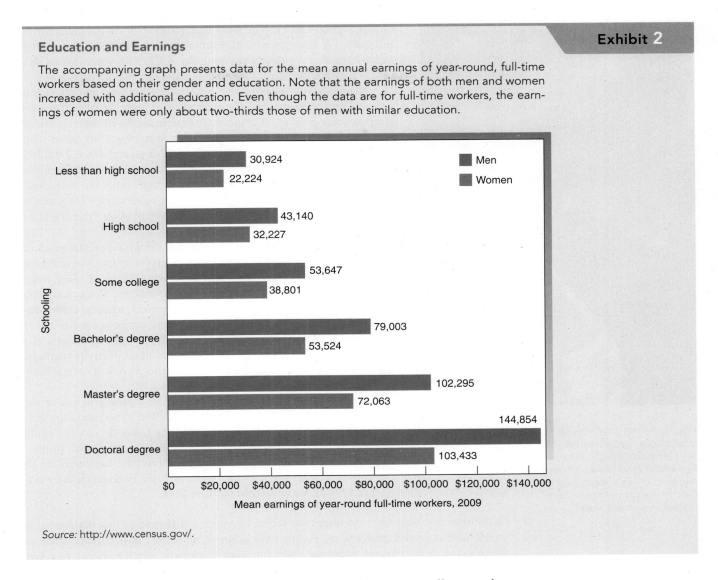

Men
Women

Less than high school — 30,924 / 22,224

High school — 43,140 / 32,227

Some college — 53,647 / 38,801

Bachelor's degree — 79,003 / 53,524

Master's degree — 102,295 / 72,063

Doctoral degree — 144,854 / 103,433

Schooling

$0 $20,000 $40,000 $60,000 $80,000 $100,000 $120,000 $140,000

Mean earnings of year-round full-time workers, 2009

Source: http://www.census.gov/.

for men with only a high school education. In the case of women, college graduates earned $53,524, compared with $32,227 for those who only graduated from high school. The earnings of both men and women continued to increase as they earned masters and doctoral degrees.

In addition to education, a person's intelligence, native ability, and motivation also affect his or her productivity and earnings. Research shows, however, that much of the extra income earned by high-wage earners is, in fact, the result of the knowledge and skills they acquired by making an investment in additional education. (See the accompanying Applications in Economics feature, "A College Degree as a Job Market Signal.") Other studies show that on-the-job training enhances the earnings of workers.

An investment in human capital and development of specialized skills can protect high-wage workers from the competition of others willing to offer their services at a lower price. Few people could develop the specialized skills of Steven Spielberg, LeBron James, or Oprah Winfrey. Similarly, the supply of heart surgeons, trial lawyers, engineers, business entrepreneurs, and many other specialized workers is limited in occupations in which specific skills, knowledge, and human capital investments contribute to job performance.

What about the large salaries received by CEOs of major corporations? Decisions made by CEOs can have a huge financial impact on their companies' profitability. Because

Hubert Boesl/dpa/Landov

What is the marginal revenue product of entertainment stars like Cameron Diaz? Do the earnings of star entertainers, athletes, and even business executives reflect the tournament pay nature of markets in these areas?

Tournament pay
A form of compensation in which the top performer (or performers) receives much higher rewards than do other competitors, even if the others perform at only a slightly lower level.

Employment discrimination
Unequal treatment of people on the basis of their race, gender, or religion, restricting their employment and earnings opportunities compared with others of similar productivity. Employment discrimination may stem from the prejudices of employers, customers, fellow employees, or all three.

of this, a good CEO can be particularly valuable when a company is in trouble, is facing new competitors, or is confronting a changing technological or regulatory environment. A CEO who turns losses into profits is worth millions to the stockholders of a major corporation.

The annual earnings of star athletes, entertainers, and television personalities often run into the millions of dollars. What is the marginal revenue product of a superstar entertainer like Cameron Diaz? How many more people will go see a movie starring Diaz rather than another actress less known or less talented? If an additional 2 million or 3 million people spend $10 to attend a movie, this will generate $20 million or $30 million of additional revenue. It is easy to see how hiring a "box office" star will generate a lot more money for a movie company. In turn, competitive labor markets will ensure that big stars get paid their marginal revenue product.

Economic studies have found that the marginal revenue product of many sports and entertainment superstars is pretty much in line with their salaries.[3] However, there may be another factor at work here. The earnings in some markets resemble tournaments. In tournaments, only the top-ranked person receives the big payoff, whereas those who finish second receive much less. This type of compensation is called **tournament pay**.[4] This name refers to reward systems structured like golf tournaments, in which a slight difference in productivity (perhaps one or two shots) is associated with a difference in pay of several hundred thousand dollars.

The tournament pay environment creates a strong incentive for potential superstars to expend considerable effort to become a top performer. As a result, many people spend long hours developing skills that will increase their chances of becoming a "star" in athletics, entertainment, professions, and business. The tournament system also encourages those who are unwilling to make such sacrifices to follow another path. Is this good or bad? Economics does not answer that question; it merely explains how these markets work.

2. Worker preferences. An important source of earnings differentials that is sometimes overlooked is worker preferences. People have different objectives in life. Some want to make a great deal of money. Many are willing to work two jobs or very long hours, undergo agonizing training and many years of education, or sacrifice social and family life to make money. Others might be "workaholics" because they enjoy their jobs. Still others might be satisfied with just enough money to get by, preferring to spend more time with their family, the Boy Scouts, watching television, on vacation, with a hobby, or at the local tavern.

Economics doesn't dictate that one set of worker preferences is more desirable than another any more than it suggests that people should eat more spinach and less pastrami. It does, however, show that worker preferences in the areas of money, work, and skill development will contribute to differences in earnings. Other things being constant, people who are more highly motivated by monetary objectives will be more likely to do the things necessary to command higher wage rates.

3. Race and gender. Discrimination on the basis of race or gender also contributes to earnings differences among people. **Employment discrimination** can directly limit the earnings opportunities of minority workers and women. Employment discrimination occurs when minority or female employees are treated differently from similarly productive white or male employees. Of course, the earnings of minorities or women can differ from

[3]Paul M. Sommers and Noel Quinton, "Pay and Performance in Major League Baseball: The Case of the First Family of Free Agents," *Journal of Human Resources* (Summer 1982): 426–35.
[4]Edward Lazear and Sherwin Rosen, "Rank Order Tournaments as an Optimum Labor Contract," *Journal of Political Economy* 89 (October 1981): 841–64; and Robert Frank and Phillip Cook, *The Winner-Take-All Society* (New York: The Free Press, 1995).

APPLICATIONS IN ECONOMICS

A College Degree as a Job Market Signal: Why You Should Take More Math

"Why should I take this difficult course?" "When will I ever use this?" Students often complain about taking courses not directly related to their future career. This complaint often reflects an incomplete understanding of exactly why college graduates do better in the job market than those without a college degree. A college degree increases a person's earnings because of both human capital (knowledge that will directly increase job productivity) and signaling ("signs" to employers about a person's attitude and motivational characteristics), as well as his or her general analytical skills.

Suppose that an employer is looking for an employee who is a very good analytical problem solver. Without a way to observe this ability directly, the employer will likely look for indicators that signal this attribute. For example, even if a job doesn't directly require calculus, people with a good calculus grade are likely to possess better problem-solving skills than those with a poor grade (or those who dodged the subject). Thus, employers may favor job applicants with good calculus grades, even if calculus isn't directly used on the job.

In other words, even if a college degree added nothing to the knowledge or skills required to do a particular job, it could still help employers identify people with abilities that are difficult to observe. Similarly, students who are admitted to and graduate from elite universities like Harvard and Yale are likely to have superior abilities relative to those attending lower-ranked schools. Because of this signaling device, even mediocre graduates from top universities often have better entry-level job market prospects than do exceptional students from lesser-known schools. The signaling function also explains why students who choose majors considered "hard" (like engineering, economics, or finance) generally do better in the job market than those choosing "easy" majors (like physical education, marketing, or social work).

"When will I ever use this stuff?" "When will a good grade in challenging courses like math and economics matter?" The answer to these questions is "Soon!" They will matter most when you're searching for a job at the beginning stages of your career—when it's still difficult for employers to judge your true abilities.

iStockphoto.com/sorendls

those of men, respectively, for reasons other than employment discrimination. Nonemployment discrimination—including access to high-quality education or specialized training, for example—can limit the opportunities of minority groups and women to acquire the human capital that would enhance their productivity and earnings. Other factors, like the limited opportunities that can result from growing up in a low-income or a single-parent family, can also influence skill development and educational achievement. In a later section in this chapter, we will analyze the impact of employment discrimination in more detail.

EARNINGS DIFFERENTIALS DUE TO NONIDENTICAL JOBS

When people evaluate employment alternatives, they consider working conditions as well as wage rates. Is a job dangerous? Does it offer the opportunity to acquire the experience and training that will enhance future earnings? Is the work strenuous and nerve wracking? Are the working hours, job location, and means of transportation convenient? These factors are what economists call **nonpecuniary job characteristics**. People will accept jobs with undesirable working conditions if the wages are high enough, compared to potential job alternatives with better working conditions. Because the higher wages, in essence, compensate workers for the unpleasant nonpecuniary attributes of a job, economists refer to wage differences stemming from this source as **compensating wage differentials**.

Examples abound of higher wages that compensate various workers for less-attractive working conditions. Because of the dangers involved, aerial window washers (those who hang from windows 20 stories up) earn higher wages than other window washers. Sales jobs involving a great deal of out-of-town travel typically pay more than similar jobs that aren't so inconvenient. Because the jobs are both physically demanding and sometimes dangerous, the wages of coal miners and oil rig workers are generally higher than those in other occupations available to low-skilled workers. Jobs in less attractive locations pay more than similar jobs in more-attractive areas. For example, American truck drivers in

Nonpecuniary job characteristics
Working conditions, prestige, variety, location, employee freedom and responsibilities, and other nonwage characteristics of a job that influence how employees evaluate the job.

Compensating wage differentials
Wage differences that compensate workers for risk, unpleasant working conditions, and other undesirable nonpecuniary aspects of a job.

war-torn Iraq often earned $100,000 per year tax free, which is much more than they could earn in the United States. This high rate of compensation is the result of the dangerous conditions they face in Iraq. Compensating factors even influence the earnings of economists. When economists work for colleges or universities, they generally enjoy a more independent and intellectually stimulating work environment than when they are employed in the business sector. Unsurprisingly, the earnings of academic economists are typically lower than those of business economists. However, it is important to remember that the academic economists with the lower earnings have chosen this job over business-sector employment. Thus, the lower earnings do not imply that they are worse off.

EARNINGS DIFFERENTIALS DUE TO THE IMMOBILITY OF LABOR

It is costly to move to a new location or train for a new occupation in order to get a job. As a result, labor, like other resources, isn't perfectly mobile. Some wage differentials therefore result because wages have not yet adjusted fully to changes in market conditions.

For example, as we've learned, when strong demand leads to wage increases, more and more people will train for the occupation in high demand. Eventually, supply will increase and moderate the wage increases. But this process will take time. Just the opposite will happen when demand falls. When the demand for workers in a given occupation or skill category falls, wages are likely to fall sharply in the short run. With time, some workers will move into other occupations, which eventually moderates the reduction in wages. But this will also take time. Some of the wage differences reflect the fact that this adjustment process doesn't happen instantly.

Institutional barriers can also limit the mobility of labor. Licensing requirements, for example, limit the mobility of labor into many occupations—medicine, taxicab driving, architecture, and mortuary science among them. Because minimum wages raise the cost to employers of hiring workers, they may retard the ability of low-skilled workers to obtain employment in certain sectors of the economy. These restrictions on labor mobility will also influence the size of wage differentials. Labor unions often promote policies designed to increase the demand for union labor and reduce the labor supply in unionized job categories. Their actions, though, often limit the ability of nonunionized workers (and firms) to enter and compete in the unionized sectors of the economy. To the extent that unions are successful, they hamper the mobility of nonunionized workers and create higher wages for those who are unionized. For more on this topic, see the special topic "Do Labor Unions Increase the Wages of Workers?" later in this book.

SOURCES OF WAGE DIFFERENTIALS: A SUMMARY

As the accompanying **Thumbnail Sketch** shows, wage differentials stem from many sources, which can be categorized in three main ways: differences in workers, differences in jobs, and immobility of resources. Many of the wage differentials in these categories play an important allocative role, compensating people for (1) human capital investments that increase their productivity or (2) unfavorable working conditions. Other wage differentials reflect, at least partially, locational preferences or the desires of individuals for higher money income rather than nonmonetary benefits. Still other differentials, like those related to discrimination and occupational restrictions, are unrelated to worker productivity or preferences and do not promote efficient production.

We have focused on why real earnings will differ. In addition to the factors contributing to differences in real earnings, nominal earnings will also vary because of cost of living differences. In a large, geographically diverse country like the United States, the cost of living varies substantially across cities, regions, and communities. In cities like New York

Thumbnail Sketch

What Are the Sources of Earnings Differentials?

Differences in Workers

1. Productivity and specialized skills that reflect native ability, parental training, and investment in human capital (education)
2. Worker preferences (the trade-off that workers are willing to make between money earnings and other factors)
3. Race and gender discrimination

Differences in Jobs

1. Location of job
2. Working conditions (such as job safety and comfort in the workplace)
3. Opportunity for training and skill-enhancing work experience

Immobility of Resources

1. Temporary disequilibrium resulting from market changes
2. Institutional restrictions (for example, occupational licensing and union-imposed restraints)

iStockphoto.com/mart_m

and San Francisco, the level of prices can be 50 percent or even 100 percent higher than in other parts of the country. Put another way, the quantity of goods and services that can be purchased with $50,000 of earnings is substantially less in New York City than in rural Georgia or Kansas. Therefore, differences in nominal wages will also reflect cost-of-living differences among geographic locations.

APPLICATIONS IN ECONOMICS

America's Millionaires[1]

The number of millionaires has expanded substantially in recent decades. In 1995, there were only 3 million households with a net worth (assets minus liabilities) of $1 million or more in 2004 dollars. By 2010, the figure had grown to 8.4 million or 7 percent of the total (1 out of every 14).

Who are these millionaires? In terms of age, millionaires are typically in their late 50s. They tend to be older than the general population because it takes time to accumulate wealth of this magnitude. In addition, older workers have higher earnings, enabling them to increase wealth more rapidly.

- Not surprisingly, millionaires tend to be well educated. About 80 percent have a college degree. In fact, nearly two-fifths have a graduate degree. Those with more education have higher earnings, which is an important source for acquiring wealth.

- Millionaires are disproportionately self-employed entrepreneurs. While less than one-fifth of the workforce is self-employed, two-thirds of the millionaires fall into this category. To a degree, the income and wealth of millionaires are rewards that compensate them for assuming the greater financial risks that accompany self-employment and business ownership than those that accompany working for a salary.

- The vast majority of millionaires achieved their status through saving and investment. They save on average 20 percent of their income. Most of them are first-generation rich. Less than 20 percent received more than 10 percent of their wealth through an inheritance.

[1]Based on Thomas J. Stanley and William D. Danko, *The Millionaire Next Door: The Surprising Secrets of America's Wealthy* (New York: Longstreet Press, 1996); and Spectrem Group, "U.S. Millionaire Population Grows by 600,000 in 2010," Press Release, March 15, 2011.

iStockphoto.com/sorendls

THE ECONOMICS OF EMPLOYMENT DISCRIMINATION

How does employment discrimination affect the job opportunities available to women and minorities? Do employers gain from discrimination? Economics sheds light on both these questions. There are two outlets for labor market discrimination: wage rates and employment exclusion.

Exhibit 3 illustrates the impact of wage discrimination. When nonminority workers are preferred to minority workers (or male to female workers), the demand for the latter groups falls and, as a result, their wages will be lower. Essentially, there are two labor markets—one market for the favored group and another for the group against which the discrimination is directed. The demand for the favored group, such as white workers, is higher, but the less expensive labor of minority workers is a substitute productive resource. Both white and minority employees are employed, but the white workers are paid a higher wage rate.

Exclusionary practices are another form of employment discrimination. Either in response to outside pressure or because of their own views, employers might primarily hire white workers and other men for certain types of jobs. When minority and female workers are excluded from a large number of occupations, they are crowded into a smaller number of remaining jobs and occupations. If entry restraints prevent people from becoming supervisors, plumbers, electricians, and airline pilots, they will be pushed elsewhere. As a result, the supply of labor in the unrestricted occupations increases, causing wage rates in these occupations to fall. In turn, the exclusionary practices reduce supply and push wages up in occupations and industries dominated by white men.

Discrimination is costly to employers when they merely reflect their own prejudices. *If employers can hire equally productive minority employees (or women) at a lower wage than whites (or men), then the profit motive gives them a strong incentive to do so. Hiring the higher-wage whites when similar minority employees are available will increase the costs of firms that discriminate.* Employers who hire employees regardless of their race or gender will have lower costs and higher profits than rival firms that try to fill positions with (mostly) white men. Thus, competitive forces tend to reduce the profitability of firms that discriminate.

Discriminatory hiring practices can stem from factors other than employer prejudice, however. If either the firm's employees or its customers have a preference for or against various groups, this may lead to discriminatory hiring, even if the employer is totally unbiased. When discrimination is customer based, a worker from a favored group will be able to bring in more revenue for the firm. For example, adult nightclubs that hire attractive young women as dancers will generate more revenue than those that hire dancers from all age and gender groups. Similarly, Chinese restaurants that hire all (or almost all) Chinese servers are likely to do better than if the ethnic and racial composition of their employees

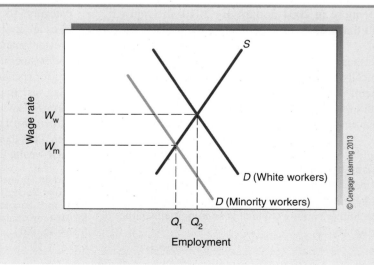

Exhibit 3

The Impact of Direct Wage Discrimination

If there is employment discrimination against minorities or women, then the demand for their services will decline, and their wage rate will fall from W_w to W_m.

© Cengage Learning 2013

mirrors that of the labor force. Historically, customer-based discrimination has often gone unchallenged. This appears to be changing. In a highly publicized case, the Hooters restaurant chain was charged with discriminating against male servers. Although the Equal Employment Opportunity Commission dropped its four-year investigation, Hooters agreed to pay $3.75 million in damages and begin hiring male servers as the result of privately filed lawsuits.

HOW MUCH IMPACT DOES EMPLOYMENT DISCRIMINATION HAVE ON EARNINGS?

If we want to isolate the impact of employment discrimination, we must (1) adjust for differences between groups in education, experience, and other productivity-related factors and (2) then make comparisons between similarly qualified groups of employees who differ only with regard to race (or gender).

How do the earnings of minority workers compare with those of similarly productive white workers? Exhibit 4 presents the actual wages of various minority groups relative to whites and the "productivity-adjusted" minority/white wage ratio. The adjusted ratio is an estimate of how the wages of minority workers would compare with those of whites if the two groups had the same productivity characteristics (schooling, work experience, marital status, regional location, and union and industry status). During 2007–2010, the actual wages of black men were 77 percent of the wages of white men. When the workforce characteristics of black men were taken into account, however, the adjusted hourly earnings of black men rose to 84 percent of the earnings of white men. This implies that productivity-related factors accounted for approximately one-third of the wage differential between the two groups. A 16 percent differential, which may well be the result of employment discrimination, remained after adjustment for the productivity characteristics.[5]

Mexican Americans constitute the second-largest minority group in the United States. Even though the actual wages of Mexican American men were only 65 percent of the wages of white men, their "adjusted" earnings were 87 percent of those for whites. Thus,

	MEN		WOMEN	
	ACTUAL	ADJUSTED	ACTUAL	ADJUSTED
White	100	100	100	100
African American	77	84	88	92
American Indian	79	92	84	97
Asian Americana	104	91	107	95
Mexican American	65	87	73	93
Other Hispanic	76	89	83	92

Exhibit 4

The Actual and Productivity-Adjusted Wages of Minority Workers Compared to White Workers: 2007–2010

Source: These data were supplied by David Macpherson. They were derived from the 2007–2010 *Current Population Surveys.* The four-year time period was used to increase the sample size for the various groups. The data were adjusted for years of schooling, work experience, region, industry, sector of employment, union status, and marital status.

---

[5]The figures presented in Exhibit 4 do not control for the lower average quality of schooling received by African Americans. Other researchers using more refined data have found that productivity factors account for a larger share of the earnings differential between whites and African Americans. For evidence on this point, see Francine D. Blau and Lawrence M. Kahn, "Race and Gender Pay Differentials," in *Research Frontiers in Industrial Relations and Human Resources*, ed. David Lewin, Olivia S. Mitchell, and Peter D. Scherer (Madison, WI: Industrial Relations Research Association, 1992), 381–416; and Derek A. Neal and William R. Johnson, "The Role of Premarket Factors in Black-White Wage Differences," *Journal of Political Economy* (October 1996): 869–95. For a detailed explanation of how the adjusted ratios of Exhibit 4 were derived and information on the significance of productivity factors and employment discrimination on the basis of gender, see David A. Macpherson and Barry T. Hirsch, "Wages and Gender Composition: Why Do Women's Jobs Pay Less?," *Journal of Labor Economics* (July 1995).

the productivity-related factors accounted for two-thirds of the earnings difference between white and Mexican American men. This figure was not adjusted for the ability to speak English. Adjustment for this factor would almost certainly further narrow the differential. Interestingly, adjustment for productivity factors reduces the wages of Asian Americans relative to whites. Asian Americans typically have more education and tend to live in large cities where nominal earnings and the cost of living are higher. As a result, the "adjusted" earnings of Asian Americans are lower than their actual earnings figures.

Turning to the data for women, the productivity-adjusted wage rates of minority women relative to white women are between 92 percent and 97 percent for each of the groups included in Exhibit 4. This implies that employment discrimination on the basis of race adds between 3 percent and 8 percent to earnings differentials that may reflect discrimination on the basis of gender. For an analysis of earnings differences according to gender, see the Special Topic 9: Earnings Differences Between Men and Women? in the final section of this book.

THE LINK BETWEEN PRODUCTIVITY AND EARNINGS

In a competitive market setting, productivity—that is, output per worker—and earnings are closely linked. When workers are more productive, the demand for their services will be higher, and therefore they will be able to command higher wages. ***High productivity provides the underlying source of high wages. When the output per hour of workers is high, the real wages of the workers will also be high.***

In turn, the link between productivity and earnings provides individuals with a strong incentive to develop their talents and utilize their resources in ways that are helpful to others. As the value of the services provided to others increases, so too will the amount they are willing to pay for those services. If you want to earn a lot of money, you had better figure out how to provide services that are highly valued by others.

Productivity differences are an important source of differences in earnings among individuals. They are also an important source of earnings differences across countries. For example, the earnings per worker are vastly greater in the United States than they are in India or China because the output of U.S. workers is much greater than the output of their counterparts in those countries. The average worker in the United States is better educated, works with more productive machines, and benefits from more efficient economic organization than the average worker in India or China. Thus, the value of the output produced by the average U.S. worker is eight to ten times that produced by the average worker in India or China. American workers earn more because they produce more. If they did not produce more, they would not be able to earn more.

Productivity differences also affect earnings across time. Today, American workers are substantially more productive than they were 50 years ago.[6] The output of goods and services per hour of U.S. workers in 2009 was approximately three times the level of the mid-1950s. Similarly, average real earnings (total compensation) per hour in 2009 were more than double those of fifty years ago. Earnings rose because productivity increased. If productivity had not increased, the increase in earnings would not have been possible.

keys to economic prosperity

Productivity and Earnings
In a market economy, productivity and earnings are closely linked. To earn a large income, one must provide large benefits to others.

iStockphoto.com/Scott Dunlap

[6]For more on productivity growth, see Kevin J. Stiroh, "What Drives Productivity Growth?," *Economic Policy Review* (Federal Reserve Bank of New York) (March 2001): 37–59.

Labor-saving equipment can improve productivity. But profit-maximizing firms will adopt automated production methods and high-tech equipment only when they reduce costs. Cost-effective automation releases labor and other resources so that they can be used to expand production in other areas. In turn, the higher worker productivity and expansion in production makes higher income levels and living standards possible.

Increased physical capital, improvements in the skill level of the labor force, and advances in technology drive productivity and earnings growth. For several decades, both the educational level of American workers and the capital equipment per worker have steadily increased. Technological advances have also enhanced productivity and contributed to the growth of output and income. Some people argue that technology and **automation** adversely affect workers (see the accompanying Myths in Economics feature). In fact, just the opposite is true. *Once you recognize that higher output is the source of higher earnings, the gains from capital formation and improvements in technology are apparent: Better machines and technological improvements make larger outputs possible. In turn, more productive workers will have higher earnings.*

Automation
A production technique that reduces the amount of labor required to produce a good or service. It is beneficial to adopt the new labor-saving technology only if it reduces the cost of production.

MYTHS IN ECONOMICS

"Automation Is the Major Cause of Unemployment. If We Keep Allowing Machines to Replace People, We Are Going to Run Out of Jobs."

Machines are substituted for people if, and only if, the machines reduce costs of production. Why did the automatic elevator replace human elevator operators or the power shovel virtually eliminate human ditch diggers? Because each is a cheaper method of accomplishing a task.

When automation and technological improvements reduce the cost of producing a good, they allow us to obtain each unit of the product with fewer resources. If the demand for the product is inelastic, consumers will spend less on the good and therefore have more of their income available for spending on other things. Consider the following example. Suppose that someone develops a new toothpaste that really prevents cavities and sells it for half the price of other brands. If the demand for toothpaste is inelastic, at the lower price consumers will spend less on this product than they did

before. Furthermore, the decline in cavities will lower the demand for and spending on dental services. Will the lower toothpaste and dental care expenditures reduce employment? Less spending on dental care will mean that households now have more income to spend on other goods and services. As a result, they will spend more on clothes, recreation, vacations, personal computers, education, and other items. This additional spending, which would not have taken place without lower dental costs, will generate additional demand and employment in these sectors. Employment will decline in the dental care sector, but it will increase in other sectors. Jobs will be reshuffled, but there's no reason to expect that total employment will decline.

What would happen to employment if a technological improvement reduced production costs and the demand for

(continued)

the product were elastic? Under these circumstances, a cost-saving invention can lead to higher employment, even in the industry affected by the invention. This was essentially what happened in the automobile industry when Henry Ford's mass-production techniques reduced the cost (and price) of cars. When the price of automobiles fell 50 percent, consumers bought three times as many cars. Even though the worker hours per car fell by 25 percent between 1920 and 1930, employment in the industry increased by approximately 50 percent during the decade.

More recently, the same thing happened in the computer-manufacturing industry. As technological improvements reduced the cost of producing various types of computer equipment, the lower costs and lower prices for computer products generated such a large increase in sales that employment in the computer-manufacturing sector actually increased.

Of course, technological advances can diminish the earnings of individual people or groups. Home appliances, like automatic washers and dryers, dishwashers, and microwave ovens, have reduced the job opportunities of maids. Voice recognition technology has lowered the demand for telephone operators. In the future, online courses and videotaped lectures may reduce the earnings and opportunities of college professors. It is understandable why groups directly affected in this manner often fear and oppose automation.

Focusing on the loss of specific jobs, however, can be misleading. Clearly, running out of jobs is not a problem. Jobs represent obstacles—tasks that must be accomplished to loosen the bonds of scarcity. As long as our ability to produce goods and services falls short of our consumption desires, there will be jobs. A society running out of jobs would be in an enviable position: It would be nearing the impossible goal—victory over scarcity!

Consider how machines and improved technology impact worker productivity. For example, accountants can handle more business accounts using microcomputers than they can with pencils and calculators. A secretary can prepare more letters with a word processor than a typewriter. Road construction workers can build roads more rapidly with bulldozers and grading equipment than with picks and shovels. Improvements in equipment and technology that increase worker productivity make larger outputs and higher incomes possible.

PRODUCTIVITY, WAGES, AND THE COMPUTER REVOLUTION

What has been happening to the growth of productivity, and how has this influenced the wages of workers? Exhibit 5 presents data on the change in both productivity (output per hour) and real hourly compensation of the United States for the periods 1948–1973, 1974–1995, and 1996–2010. Predictably, productivity growth and increases in real

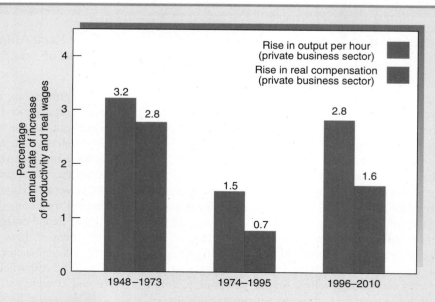

Exhibit 5

Productivity and Employee Compensation in the United States, 1948–2010

As shown in the graph, worker productivity and compensation per hour are closely linked. Between 1974 and 1995, the growth of both productivity and real compensation per hour slowed substantially compared with the growth figures achieved during the 1948–1973 period. However, worker productivity and real hourly compensation rebounded during the 1996–2010 period.

Source: Bureau of Labor Statistics (http://www.bls.gov/).

compensation per hour have moved together. During the period 1948–1973, both productivity and real hourly compensation grew at a rapid rate—approximately 3 percent annually. In contrast, both sagged badly during the period 1974–1995. Productivity growth averaged only 1.5 percent annually, and hourly real compensation rose at an annual rate of only 0.7 percent over the two decades (1974–1995). Although the reasons for slow productivity growth during this period are not entirely clear, most economists believe that slower improvement in the educational quality of the workforce, environmental regulations, and the inflation of the 1970s were contributing factors.

Beginning in the mid-1990s, both productivity and real compensation rebounded. Productivity per hour grew at an annual rate of 2.8 percent during 1996–2010, nearly twice the rate of 1974–1995. In turn, hourly compensation rose at an annual rate of 1.6 percent during 1996–2010, up from the 0.7 percent rate of the earlier period. Since the mid-1970s, Hourly compensation has lagged behind productivity growth. Why has this been the case? The answer to this question is not entirely clear. However, improvements in working conditions provide part of the answer. The hourly compensation measure does not account for movements toward less strenuous work, a more comfortable work environment, and greater job safety, all of which have improved steadily in recent decades. Consideration of these factors would tend to boost the growth of overall worker compensation.

What accounts for the rebound in the growth of productivity of the past 15 years? Most economists believe that the recent acceleration in productivity growth is largely the result of the computer revolution and related technological innovations.[7] Information technology and investment in computer equipment soared during the 1990s, and this substantially enhanced productivity in many occupations. Research indicates that nearly two-fifths of the productivity growth during 1995–2000 and about one-quarter of the growth during 2000–2006 was the result of higher levels of investment in computer equipment and information technology.[8]

Some believe that the pace of technological change has quickened and new technologies now spread throughout the economy more rapidly. There is evidence that this has been the case since the early 1980s. While automation and rapid improvements in technology do not destroy jobs, they do result in changing work requirements, more job switching, and less career stability. Earlier generations of workers could typically expect to have a long-term career with one firm. This is now less true. Today's workers switch employers more often than their parents did. In 1983, the average full-time male worker aged 22 to 59 expected to remain with his current employer for an additional 18.0 years. By 2001, this figure had fallen to 13.7 years. A similar pattern was present for women.[9]

Is the computer revolution going to continue, or have we already witnessed its major impact? Will the speedup of technological change continue at a rapid rate, or perhaps even accelerate, in the decades immediately ahead? It is too early to determine the precise answers to these questions. But one thing is for sure: The answers will exert a powerful impact on our future lives.

Looking Ahead

As we have learned, productivity and earnings are influenced by both human capital and physical capital investments. This chapter focused on the labor market. The following chapter will analyze investment choices and the operation of the capital market.

---

[7]For a discussion of the new-economy perspective, see Kevin J. Stiroh, "Is There a New Economy?," *Challenge* (July/August 1999): 82–101.

[8]Dale W. Jorgenson, Mun S. Ho, and Kevin J. Stiroh, "A Retrospective Look at the U.S. Productivity Growth Resurgence," *Journal of Economic Perspectives* 22 (Winter 2008): 3–24.

[9]Leora Friedberg, Michael Owyang, and Tara Sinclair, "Searching for Better Prospects: Endogenizing Falling Job Tenure and Pension Coverage," *Topics in Economic Analysis and Policy* 6, no.1 (2006): 1–40.

KEY POINTS

- The real earnings of individuals would be equal if (1) all individuals were identical in preferences, skills, and background; (2) all jobs were equally attractive; and (3) workers were perfectly mobile among jobs. Earnings differences among individuals result from the absence of these conditions.

- Wage differences play an important allocative role. They generally compensate people for (1) investments in education and training that enhance productivity and the development of highly specialized skills and (2) unfavorable working conditions and/or job locations. Wage differences can also result from differences in workers' preferences, employment discrimination, and institutional factors that restrict worker mobility.

- Employment discrimination reduces the wages of people being discriminated against by either lowering the demand for their services or restricting their entry into various job categories. Productivity differences also contribute to earnings differentials between groups. Research indicates that the earnings of African American and Mexican American men are, respectively, approximately 84 percent and 87 percent those of white men of similar productivity.

- Productivity is the ultimate source of high wages and earnings. Workers in the United States (and other high-income industrial countries) earn high wages because their output per hour is high as the result of (1) greater worker knowledge and skills (human capital) and (2) the use of modern machinery (physical capital).

- Automated methods of production will be adopted only if they reduce costs. Although automation might reduce employment in a specific industry, it also releases resources that can be employed in other areas. Improved technology permits us to achieve larger output and income levels than would otherwise be possible.

- The growth of productivity in the United States during 1996–2010 was more rapid than during the two prior decades. The computer revolution and lower cost of information technology equipment was a major contributor to the more rapid productivity growth of recent years.

CRITICAL ANALYSIS QUESTIONS

1. Why do some people earn higher wages than others? Why are wages in some occupations higher than in others? How do wage differentials influence the allocation of resources? Explain.

2. *Why are real wages in the United States higher than in other countries? Is the labor force itself responsible for the higher wages of American workers? Explain.

3. Indicate the major sources of earnings differences between (a) a lawyer and a minister; (b) an accountant and an elementary school teacher; (c) a business executive and a social worker; (d) a country lawyer and a Wall Street lawyer; (e) an experienced, skilled craftsperson and a 20-year-old high school dropout; and (f) an upper-story and a ground-floor window washer?

4. a. If minority employees are discriminated against, how will this affect their earnings? Use supply and demand analysis to explain your answer.

   b. If the average earnings differ between two groups of employees (for example, whites and blacks), does this mean that the group with the lower earnings is experiencing employment discrimination? Why or why not?

5. Is there a relationship between the growth of productivity and changes in wage rates? Can higher earnings be achieved without higher productivity? Why or why not? Discuss.

6. *"Jobs are the key to economic progress. Unless we create more jobs, our standard of living will fall." Is this statement true or false? Explain.

7. "If Jones has a skill that is highly valued, she will be able to achieve high market earnings. In contrast, Smith may work just as hard or even harder and still earn only a low income."

   a. Does hard work necessarily lead to a high income?

   b. Why are the incomes of some workers high and others low?

   c. Do you think the market system of wage determination is fair? Why or why not?

   d. Can you think of a more equitable system? If so, explain why it is more equitable.

8. *People who have invested heavily in human capital (for example, lawyers, doctors, and even college professors) generally have higher wages, but they also generally work more hours than other workers. Can you explain why?

9. *"If individuals had identical abilities and opportunities, earnings would be equal." Is this statement true or false?

10. *Other things being constant, how will the following influence the hourly earnings of employees? Explain your answer.
    a. The employee must work the midnight to 8:00 A.M. shift.
    b. The job involves split shifts (work three hours, off two hours, work three additional hours, and so on).
    c. The employer provides low-cost child care services on the premises.
    d. The job is widely viewed as prestigious.
    e. The job requires employees to move often from city to city.
    f. The job requires substantial amounts of out-of-town travel.

11. *Consider two occupations (A and B) in which people have the same skills and abilities. When employed, workers in the two occupations work the same number of hours per day. In occupation A, employment is stable throughout the year, whereas employment in B is characterized by seasonal layoffs. In which occupation will the hourly wage rate be highest? Why? In which occupation will the annual wage be highest? Why?

12. "Technological change eliminates thousands of jobs every year. Unless something is done to slow the growth of technology, ordinary workers will face a bleak future of low wages and high unemployment." Explain why you either agree or disagree with this statement.

13. If an individual is motivated primarily by the desire to make money, will he or she have an incentive to be helpful to others? Will he or she have an incentive to develop skills that others value highly? Why or why not?

*Asterisk denotes questions for which answers are given in Appendix B.

CHAPTER **14**

Investment, the Capital Market, and the Wealth of Nations

CHAPTER FOCUS

- Why do people invest? Why are capital resources often used to produce consumer goods?

- What is the interest rate? Why are investors willing to pay interest to get loanable funds? Why are lenders willing to loan funds?

- Why is the interest rate so important when evaluating costs and revenues across time periods?

- When is an investment profitable? How do profitable and unprofitable investments influence the creation of wealth?

- How does the capital market influence growth and prosperity?

To produce capital, people must forgo the opportunity to produce goods for current consumption. People can choose whether to spend their time picking apples or planting apple trees. In the first case there are more apples today; in the second, more apples tomorrow.
—*Steven Landsburg*[1]

---

[1]Steven E. Landsburg, *Price Theory and Applications* (Fort Worth: Dryden Press, 1992), 581.

In the previous chapter we noted that there was a close relationship between productivity and earnings. In turn, productivity is influenced by investment choices. Consider choices about whether to construct an office building, purchase a harvesting machine, or go to law school. The returns derived from investments like these are usually spread over years or even decades. Some costs, such as maintenance expenses, can also be incurred over time. How can people compare the benefits and costs of an activity when both are spread across lengthy periods of time? Why is the method of allocating investment in an economy a vitally important determinant of economic progress? This chapter will help you answer these questions.

iStockphoto.com/nicoolay

WHY PEOPLE INVEST

Capital is a term used by economists to describe long-lasting resources that are valued because they can help us produce goods and services in the future. As we previously discussed, there are two broad categories of capital: (1) *physical capital* (buildings, machines, tools, and natural resources) and (2) *human capital* (the knowledge and skills of people). **Investment** is the purchase, construction, or development of a capital resource. Thus, investment expands the availability of capital resources.

Saving is income not spent on current consumption. Investment and saving are closely linked. In fact, the two words describe different aspects of the capital formation process. *Saving refers to the nonconsumption of income, while investment refers to the use of the unconsumed income to produce a capital resource.* Sometimes saving and investment are conducted by the same person, like when a farmer saves current income (refrains from spending it on consumption goods) in order to purchase a new tractor (an investment good).

It is important to recognize that saving is required for investment. Someone must save—refrain from consumption—in order to provide the resources for investment. When investors finance a project with their own funds, they are also saving (refraining from current consumption). Investors, however, do not always use their own funds to finance investments. Sometimes they will borrow funds from others. When this is the case, it is the lender rather than the investor who is doing the saving.

Consumption is the goal of economic activity. Why would anyone want to delay consumption in order to undertake an investment? Sometimes more consumption goods can be produced by first using resources to produce capital resources and then using these resources to produce the desired consumer goods. Using capital to produce consumption goods makes sense, but only if it allows us to produce more consumption goods than we otherwise could.

For example, suppose that Robinson Crusoe can catch fish by either (1) combining his labor with natural resources (direct production) or (2) constructing a net and eventually combining his labor with this capital resource (indirect production). Let's assume that Crusoe can catch two fish per day by hand-fishing, but three fish per day if he constructs and uses a net that will last for 310 days. Now suppose it will take Crusoe 55 days to build the net. The opportunity cost of constructing the net will be 110 fish (two fish per day not caught for each of the 55 days he spends building the net). As the accompanying chart shows, if Crusoe invests in the capital resource (the net), his output during the next year (including the 55 days required to build the net) would be 930 fish (three per day for 310 days). Alternatively, hand-fishing during the year would lead to an output of only 730 fish (two fish per day for 365 days).

Capital
Resources that enhance our ability to produce output in the future.

Investment
The purchase, construction, or development of capital resources, including both nonhuman capital and human capital. Investments increase the supply of capital.

Saving
Current income that is not spent on consumption goods. Saving makes it possible for resources to be devoted to investments (like the making of tractors or other equipment used in production).

	NUMBER OF FISH CAUGHT	
	WITHOUT NET	WITH NET
Per day	2	3
Annually	730	930

In other words, Crusoe's investment will enhance his net productivity by 200 fish annually. In the short term, however, investing in the net will require a sacrifice. During the 55 days it takes to construct the net, Crusoe's production of consumption goods will decline.

How can Crusoe or any other investor know if the value of the larger future output is worth the short-term cost? Most of us have a preference for goods now rather than later. For example, if you are typical, you would prefer a sleek new sports car now rather than the same car ten years from now. On average, individuals possess a **positive rate of time preference**. That is, other things being the same, people subjectively value goods obtained sooner more highly than goods obtained later.

When only Crusoe is involved, the attractiveness of the investment in the fishing net depends on his rate of time preference. If he places a high value on a couple of fish per day during the next 55 days, as indeed he may if he is on the verge of starvation, the cost of the investment may well exceed the value of the larger future output. If Crusoe could find someone who would loan him fish while he built the net, however, he could consume the borrowed fish now while building the net and pay later with the extra fish made possible by the net. If such a loan is available, the attractiveness of the investment (building the net instead of hand-fishing now) will be influenced by the price of borrowing fish. Is the cost of borrowing fish in order to maintain his consumption while he constructs the net worth the extra cost? To answer this question, Crusoe must consider the cost of paying for earlier availability—he must consider, in effect, the interest rate.

Positive rate of time preference
The desire of consumers for goods now rather than in the future.

INTEREST RATES

The interest rate links the future to the present. It allows individuals to evaluate the value today—the present value—of future income and costs. In essence, it is the market price of earlier availability. From the viewpoint of a potential borrower, the interest rate is the premium that must be paid in order to acquire goods sooner and pay later. From the lender's viewpoint, it is a reward for waiting—a payment for supplying others with current purchasing power in terms of greater purchasing power in the future.

In a modern economy, people often borrow funds to finance current investments and consumption. Because of this, the interest rate is often defined as the price of loanable funds. But we should remember that it is the earlier availability of goods and services purchased, not the money itself, that is desired by the borrower.

HOW INTEREST RATES ARE DETERMINED

Interest rates are determined by the demand for and supply of loanable funds. Investors demand funds in order to finance capital assets they believe will increase output and generate profit. Simultaneously, consumers demand loanable funds because they have a positive rate of time preference: They prefer earlier availability.

The demand of investors for loanable funds stems from the productivity of capital. Investors are willing to borrow in order to finance the use of capital in production because they expect that expanding future output will provide them with more than enough resources to repay the amount borrowed—the principal—and interest on the loan. Our example of Robinson Crusoe illustrates this point. Remember, Crusoe could increase his output by 200 fish this year if he could take off 55 days from hand-fishing in order to build a net. But doing so would reduce Crusoe's fish production by 2 fish per day while he was constructing the net. Suppose a fishing crew from a neighboring island visited Crusoe and offered to lend him 110 fish so he could undertake the capital investment project (building the net). If Crusoe could borrow the 110 fish (the principal) in exchange for, say, 165 fish one year later (110 fish to repay the principal and 55 as interest on the loan), the investment project would be highly profitable. Crusoe could repay the funds borrowed, plus the 50 percent interest rate, and still have 145 additional fish (the 200 additional fish caught minus the 55 fish paid in interest).

Investors can gain by borrowing funds to undertake investment projects only when the capital assets they purchase permit them to expand output (or reduce costs) by enough to make the interest payments and still have more output than they would have without the investment.

As **Exhibit 1** illustrates, the interest rate brings the choices of investors and consumers wanting to borrow funds into harmony with the choices of lenders willing to supply funds. Higher interest rates make it more costly for investors to undertake capital spending projects and for consumers to buy now rather than later. Both investors and consumers will therefore curtail their borrowing as the interest rate rises. Investors will borrow less because some investment projects that would be profitable at a low interest rate will be unprofitable at higher rates. Some consumers will reduce their current consumption rather than pay the high interest premium when the interest rate increases. Therefore, the amount of funds demanded by borrowers is inversely related to the interest rate.

The interest rate also rewards people (lenders) willing to reduce their current consumption in order to provide loanable funds to others. If some people are going to borrow in order to undertake an investment project (or consume more than their current income), others must curtail their current consumption by an equal amount. In essence, the interest rate provides lenders with the incentive to reduce their current consumption so that borrowers can either invest or consume beyond their present income. Higher interest rates give people willing to save (willing to supply loanable funds) the ability to purchase more goods in the future in exchange for sacrificing current consumption. Even though people have a positive rate of time preference, they will give up current consumption to supply funds to the loanable funds market if the price is right. Higher interest rates will induce people to save more. Therefore, as the interest rate rises, the quantity of funds supplied to the loanable funds market will increase.

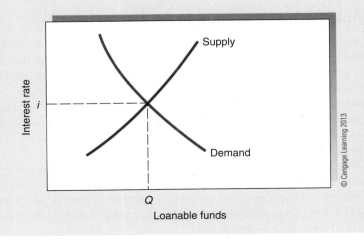

Exhibit 1

Determining the Interest Rate

The demand for loanable funds stems from the consumer's desire for earlier availability and the productivity of capital. As the interest rate rises, current goods become more expensive in comparison with future goods. Therefore, borrowers will demand fewer loanable funds. In contrast, higher interest rates will stimulate lenders to supply additional funds to the market.

As Exhibit 1 illustrates, the interest rate will bring the quantity of funds demanded into balance with the quantity supplied. ***At the equilibrium interest rate, the quantity of funds borrowers demand for investment and consumption will just equal the quantity of funds lenders save,*** so the interest rate brings the choices of borrowers and lenders into harmony.

THE MONEY RATE VERSUS THE REAL RATE OF INTEREST

Money rate of interest
The rate of interest in monetary terms that borrowers pay for borrowed funds. During periods when borrowers and lenders expect inflation, the money rate of interest exceeds the real rate of interest.

We have emphasized that the interest rate is a premium paid by borrowers for earlier availability and a reward received by lenders for delaying consumption of *goods and services*. However, during a period of inflation—a general increase in prices—the nominal interest rate, or **money rate of interest**, is a misleading indicator of really how much borrowers are paying and lenders are receiving. Inflation reduces the purchasing power of money. Rising prices mean that when the borrower repays the loan principal in the future, the money received by the lender will not be able to purchase as many goods and services as when the funds were initially loaned.

When inflation is common, lenders will recognize they are being repaid with dollars of less purchasing power. Unless they are compensated for the anticipated inflation by an upward adjustment in the interest rate, they will supply fewer funds to the loanable funds market. At the same time, when borrowers anticipate inflation, they will want to purchase goods and services now before they become even more expensive in the future. Thus, they are willing to pay an **inflationary premium**, an additional amount of interest that reflects the expected rate of future price increases. For example, if borrowers and lenders were willing to agree on a 4 percent interest rate when both anticipated price stability, they would have the same incentive to agree to a 9 percent interest rate when both anticipated a 5 percent rate of inflation.

Inflationary premium
A component of the money interest rate that reflects compensation to the lender for the expected decrease, due to inflation, in the purchasing power of the principal and interest during the course of the loan. It is determined by the expected rate of future inflation.

Real rate of interest
The money rate of interest minus the expected rate of inflation. The real rate of interest indicates the interest premium in terms of real goods and services that one must pay for earlier availability.

Therefore, when people anticipate inflation, the money interest rate will rise and it will overstate the "true" cost of borrowing and the yield from lending. This true cost is the **real rate of interest**, which is equal to the money rate of interest minus the inflationary premium. It reflects the real burden to borrowers and the payoff to lenders in terms of their being able to buy goods and services.

Our analysis indicates that high rates of inflation will lead to a high money rate of interest. The real world is consistent with this view. Money interest rates rose to historical highs in the United States as inflation soared to double-digit rates during the 1970s. Inflation rates have been much lower since the mid-1980s and, so too, have nominal interest rates. Cross-country comparisons also illustrate the link between inflation and high interest rates. The world's lowest money interest rates are found in nations such as Germany, Switzerland, and Japan, all with low rates of inflation. In contrast, the highest money interest rates have been present in Russia, Venezuela, Zimbabwe, and other countries with high rates of inflation.

INTEREST RATES AND RISK

So far, we've assumed there is only a single interest rate present in the loanable funds market. In the real world, of course, there are many interest rates. They include the mortgage rate, the prime interest rate (the rate charged to business firms with strong credit ratings), the consumer loan rate, and the credit card rate, to name but a few.

Interest rates in the loanable funds market will differ mainly because of differences in the risks associated with the loans. It is riskier, for example, to loan money to an unemployed worker than to a well-established business with substantial assets. Similarly, unsecured credit card loans are riskier than loans secured with an asset such as a house or a plot of land. Moreover, as recent experience vividly illustrates, a mortgage loan for the purchase of a house is far riskier when the down payment of the borrower is small. The risk also increases with the duration of the loan. The longer the time period of the loan, the more likely it is that the borrower's ability to repay the loan will deteriorate or market conditions change in a highly unfavorable manner.

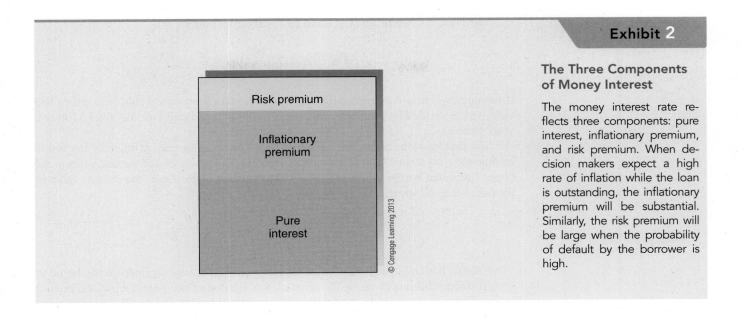

Exhibit 2

The Three Components of Money Interest

The money interest rate reflects three components: pure interest, inflationary premium, and risk premium. When decision makers expect a high rate of inflation while the loan is outstanding, the inflationary premium will be substantial. Similarly, the risk premium will be large when the probability of default by the borrower is high.

© Cengage Learning 2013

As **Exhibit 2** shows, the money rate of interest on a loan has three components. The pure-interest component is the real price one must pay for earlier availability. The inflationary-premium component reflects the expectation that the loan will be repaid with dollars of less purchasing power as the result of inflation. The risk-premium component reflects the probability of default—the risk imposed on the lender by the possibility that the borrower may be unable to repay the loan.

THE PRESENT VALUE OF FUTURE INCOME AND COSTS

If you deposited $100 today in a savings account earning 6 percent interest, you would have $106 one year from now. To put it another way, to have $106 one year from now requires that you invest $100 today. *The interest rate allows us to make this conversion from present to future dollars. The interest rate connects the value of dollars (and capital assets) today with the value of dollars (expected income and receipts) in the future. It is used to "discount" the value of a dollar received in the future so that its present worth can be determined today.*

The **present value** (*PV*) of a payment received one year from now can be expressed as follows:

$$PV = \frac{\text{Receipt One Year from Now}}{1 + \text{Interest Rate}}$$

If the interest rate is 6 percent, the current value of $100 to be received one year from now is

$$PV = \frac{100}{1.06} = \$94.34$$

If you put $94.34 in a savings account yielding 6 percent interest, during the year the account would earn $5.66 interest (6 percent of $94.34) and grow to $100 one year from now. Thus, the present value of $100 to be received a year from now is $94.34.

Economists use the term **discounting** to describe this procedure of reducing the value of a dollar to be received in the future to its present worth. Clearly, the value of a dollar in the future is inversely related to the interest rate. For example, if the interest rate is 10 percent, the present value of $100 received one year from now would be only $90.91 ($100 divided by 1.10). At still higher interest rates, the present value of $100 a year from now would be even lower.

Present value (PV)
The current worth of future income after it is discounted to reflect the fact that revenues in the future are valued less highly than revenues now.

Discounting
The procedure used to calculate the present value of future income, which is inversely related to both the interest rate and the amount of time that passes before the funds are received.

The present value of $100 received two years from now is

$$PV = \frac{100}{(1 + \text{Interest Rate})^2}$$

If the interest rate is 6 percent, $100 received two years from now would be equal to $89 today ($100 divided by 1.06^2). In other words, $89 invested today would yield $100 two years from now.

The present-value procedure can be used to determine the current value of any future income (or cost) stream. If R represents receipts received at the end of various years in the future (indicated by the subscripts) and i represents the interest rate, the present value of the future income stream is

$$PV = \frac{R_1}{(1 + i)} + \frac{R_2}{(1 + i)^2} + \ldots + \frac{R_n}{(1 + i)^n}$$

Exhibit 3 shows the present value of $100 received at various times in the future at several different discount rates. The chart clearly illustrates two points. First, the present value of income received in the future declines with the interest rate. The present value of the $100 received one year from now, when discounted at a 4 percent interest rate, is $96.15, compared with $98.04 when a 2 percent discount rate is used. Second, the present value of the $100 also declines as the date of its receipt is set farther into the future. If the discount rate is 6 percent, the present value of $100 received one year from now is $94.34, compared with $89 if the $100 is received two years from now. If the $100 is received five years from now, its current worth is only $74.73. *So the present value of a future dollar payment is inversely related both to the interest rate and to how far in the future the payment will be received.*

To see in a more personal way the importance of interest and the value of saving, consider what you could gain by saving just $1,000 per year ($83.33 per month) for ten years in a tax-free individual retirement account. If you begin at age 25 and continue only until age 35 (putting nothing into the account after that), and the account returns 8 percent annually, it will be worth $168,627 when you reach age 65. In contrast, if you wait until age 35 and then save $1,000 per year for thirty years (not ten years of savings as before) with the same 8 percent annual return, by age 65 your account will be worth only $125,228.

Exhibit 3

The Present Value of $100 to Be Received in the Future

The columns indicate the present value of $100 to be received a designated number of years in the future at different discount (interest) rates. For example, at a discount rate of 2 percent, the present value of $100 to be received five years from now is $90.57. Note that the present value of the $100 declines as either the interest rate or the number of years in the future increases.

PRESENT VALUE OF $100 TO BE RECEIVED
A DESIGNATED NUMBER OF YEARS
IN THE FUTURE AT ALTERNATIVE DISCOUNT RATES

YEARS IN THE FUTURE	2 PERCENT	4 PERCENT	6 PERCENT	8 PERCENT	12 PERCENT	20 PERCENT
1	98.04	96.15	94.34	92.59	89.29	83.33
2	96.12	92.46	89.00	85.73	79.72	69.44
3	94.23	88.90	83.96	79.38	71.18	57.87
4	92.39	85.48	79.21	73.50	63.55	48.23
5	90.57	82.19	74.73	68.06	56.74	40.19
6	88.80	79.03	70.50	63.02	50.66	33.49
7	87.06	75.99	66.51	58.35	45.23	27.08
8	85.35	73.07	62.74	54.03	40.39	23.26
9	83.68	70.26	59.19	50.02	36.06	19.38
10	82.03	67.56	55.84	46.32	32.20	16.15
15	74.30	55.53	41.73	31.52	18.27	6.49
20	67.30	45.64	31.18	21.45	10.37	2.61
30	55.21	30.83	17.41	9.94	3.34	0.42
50	37.15	14.07	5.43	2.13	0.35	0.01

Ten years of saving, starting with age 25, yields far more than 30 years of saving at the same amount each year but waiting until age 35 to start. Which savings plan is more attractive to you?

PRESENT VALUE, PROFITABILITY, AND INVESTMENT

Investment involves an up-front cost of acquiring a machine, skill, or other asset expected to generate additional output and revenue in the future. How can an investor know if the expected future revenues will be sufficient to cover the costs? The discounting procedure helps provide the answer. It permits the investor to place both the costs and the expected future revenues of an investment project into present-value terms. If the present value of the revenue derived from the investment exceeds the present value of the cost, it makes sense to undertake the investment. If the revenues and costs of such an investment turn out as expected, the investor will earn a profit, and the project will create wealth.

In contrast, if the cost of the project exceeds the discounted value of the future receipts, losses will be incurred. The losses reflect that the project diminished the value of the resources. Investments like these are counterproductive.

Let's pencil in the figures for a hypothetical investment option and determine whether it is a good investment. Suppose a truck rental firm is contemplating the purchase of a new $40,000 truck. Past experience indicates that after figuring in the truck's operational and maintenance expenses, the firm can rent it out for a net revenue of $12,000 annually (received at the end of each year). The firm will be able to do this every year for four years—the expected life of the vehicle.[2] Because the firm can borrow and lend funds at an interest rate of 8 percent, we will discount the future expected income at an 8 percent rate. Exhibit 4 illustrates the calculation. Column 4 shows how much $12,000, available at year-end for each of the next four years, is worth today. In total, the present value of the expected rental receipts is $39,744—less than the purchase price of the truck. Therefore, the project should not be undertaken.

If the interest rate in our example had been 6 percent, the results would have been different. The present value of the future rental income would have been $41,580.[3] It pays to

Year (1)	Expected Future Income Received at Year-End (2)	Discounted Value per Dollar (8 Percent Rate) (3)	Present Value of Income (4)
1	$12,000	$0.926	$11,112
2	12,000	0.857	10,284
3	12,000	0.794	9,528
4	12,000	0.735	8,820
Total			$39,744

© Cengage Learning 2013

Exhibit 4

The Discounted Present Value of $12,000 of Truck Rental for Four Years (Interest Rate = 8 Percent)

---

[2] For the sake of simplicity, we assume that the truck has no scrap value at the end of four years.

[3] The derivation of this figure is shown in the following tabulation:

Year	Expected Future Income (Dollars)	Discounted Value Per Dollar (6% rate)	Present Value of Income (Dollars)
1	12,000	0.943	11,316
2	12,000	0.890	10,680
3	12,000	0.840	10,080
4	12,000	0.792	9,504
Total			41,580

purchase a capital good whenever the present value of the income generated by it exceeds its purchase price. At the lower interest rate, the investment project would have been productive (and profitable).

EXPECTED FUTURE EARNINGS AND ASSET VALUES

The present value of the expected revenue from a project minus the cost of an investment will tell us whether the project should be undertaken. However, *once an investment project has been completed*, the present value of the expected future net earnings will determine the market value of the asset. If the present value of the expected net earnings rises (or falls), so too will the value of the asset.

The value of an asset is equal to the present value of the expected net revenues that can be earned by the asset. If the asset is expected to generate a constant annual net income each year in the future, its value would be equal to

$$\text{Asset Value} = \frac{\textbf{Annual Net Income from the Asset}}{\textbf{Interest Rate}}$$

What is the market value of a tract of land if it is expected to generate $1,000 of net rental income each year indefinitely into the future? If the market interest rate is 10 percent, investors would be willing to pay $10,000 for the land ($1,000 divided by 0.10). When purchased at this price, the land would provide an investor with the 10 percent market rate of return. Similarly, if an asset generates $2,500 of net earnings annually and the market interest rate is 10 percent, the asset would be worth $25,000 ($2,500 divided by 0.10). There is a direct relationship between the expected future earnings generated by an asset and the asset's market value. *As the present value of the future earnings of an asset increases, so too does the market value of the asset.*

This link between expected future earnings and the price of an asset motivates asset owners to make sure the assets are being used wisely. Some entrepreneurial investors are particularly good at (1) identifying a business that is poorly operated, (2) purchasing the business at a depressed price, (3) improving the operational efficiency of the firm, and then (4) reselling the business at a handsome profit. Suppose that a poorly run business currently has net earnings of $1 million per year. What is the market value of the business? If the firm is expected to continue earning $1 million per year, the market value of the firm would be $10 million if the interest rate is 10 percent. Suppose that an alert entrepreneur buys the business for $10 million and improves the operational efficiency of the firm. As the result of these changes, the annual net earnings of the firm increase to $2 million per year. Now how much is the firm worth? If the $2 million annual earnings are expected to continue into the future, the net present value of the firm would rise to $20 million. Thus, the entrepreneur would be able to sell the firm for a very substantial profit.

You can see from this example that business managers and asset owners have a strong incentive to use the resources under their control efficiently. If they fail to do so, the value of the assets will decline, and the business will be vulnerable to a takeover by those capable of using the resources more efficiently and thereby improving the firm's profitability.

INVESTORS AND CORPORATE INVESTMENTS

In modern market economies, investment choices are often made by corporate officers, under the scrutiny of corporate boards of directors. Nevertheless, individual investors (buyers and sellers of stock) influence that process through the stock market. Stock market investors who believe that a corporation is currently making decisions likely to increase its future profits will buy more of the corporation's stock, driving up its price. Similarly, stockholders who believe that the corporation's current investment decisions will reduce future profits have an incentive to "bail out" by selling their stock holdings, reducing the market value of the stock. Either way, the price of a corporation's shares gives corporate officers fast feedback on what investors think of their decisions.

Often corporate officers own stock themselves and the value of their pay package generally depends on the stock price. Also, the members of the corporate board (which hires and fires the officers) are typically large shareholders. Thus, the corporate officers have a strong incentive to act on the feedback from the stock market. The choices of consumers of the firm's products are the ultimate judge of its future profitability. However, the choices of investors and their fund managers provide early information today about the expected future success of business ventures.

INVESTING IN HUMAN CAPITAL

Investments in human capital (like the decision to go to college, for example) are the same as other investment decisions. Just like physical capital, discounting can also help us gauge whether or not to make a human capital investment.

Exhibit 5 shows the human capital decision confronting Juanita, an 18-year-old high school graduate thinking about pursuing a bachelor's degree in business administration. Just as an investment in a truck involves a cost in order to generate a future income, so does a degree in business administration. If Juanita does not go to college, she will be able to begin work immediately, starting at annual earnings of E_1. But if she goes to college, she will incur direct costs (C_d) in the form of tuition, books, transportation, and related expenses. She will also bear the opportunity cost (C_o) of lower earnings while she's in college. However, studying business will expand Juanita's knowledge and skills, and enable her to earn more money later (see the areas in the exhibit labeled "Earnings

---

Exhibit 5

Investing in Human Capital

Juanita, an 18-year-old who has just finished high school, is trying to decide whether or not to go to college and get a business degree. If Juanita goes to college and majors in business administration, she will incur the direct cost (C_d) of the college education—tuition, books, transportation, and so on—plus the opportunity cost (C_o) of earnings she forgoes while in college. However, with a business degree, she can expect to earn an additional amount of income (B) during her career. If the discounted present value of the additional future earnings exceeds the discounted value of the direct and indirect costs of a college education, the business degree will be a profitable investment for Juanita.

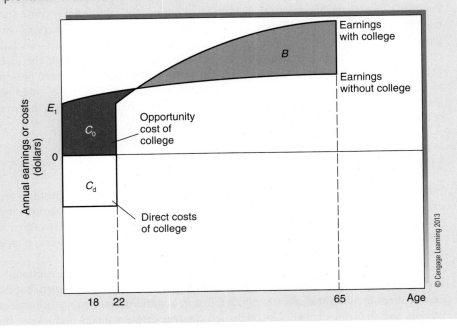

© Cengage Learning 2013

APPLICATIONS IN ECONOMICS

Does It Pay to Go to an Elite University?

Early research on this question found that students who attend highly selective schools like those of the Ivy League have higher subsequent earnings than similar students going to less selective colleges. This was true even after accounting for factors like the students' SAT score, the average SAT score of the school attended, race, gender, high school GPA, income of parents, and student athlete status. But there remained one question: Did the students attending the more selective schools earn more because they received a better education or because they were more ambitious and highly motivated?

A recent study by Princeton University economists Stacy Dale and Alan Krueger sheds light on this question.[1] In addition to controlling for the typical set of student characteristics, Dale and Krueger were able to make earnings comparisons between students (1) who were accepted by a more selective college but decided to attend a less selective one and (2) those who actually attended a more selective college. This technique enabled them to account more fully for the potential impact of motivation and ambition on earnings. Further, the earnings data used by Dale and Krueger were from actual Social Security records rather than the less accurate self-reported earnings.

Dale and Krueger found that students attending a more selective college such as Yale University did not earn more than similar students attending a less selective school such as Penn State University. However, minorities and students with poorly educated parents were exceptions. The latter groups did have higher earnings if they attended a more selective school. This is consistent with the view that going to more selective schools provides these groups with important contacts and connections that they would not otherwise be able to obtain.

The Dale and Krueger study also reports two other intriguing results. First, earnings were higher for those who applied to more selective schools. This suggests that ambition and a willingness to work hard are more important determinants of earnings than the selectivity of the school one actually attends. Second, students who attended schools with higher tuition did not earn more income than similar students who attended less expensive schools. Thus, students may want to think twice before attending an expensive school, particularly if they are borrowing money to do so.

[1]Stacy Dale and Alan B. Krueger. "Estimating the Return to College Selectivity over the Career Using Administrative Earning Data," Princeton University Industrial Relations Section Working Paper Number 563, February 2011.

iStockphoto.com/sorendls

with college" versus "Earnings without college"). Will the higher future income be worth the cost? To answer this question, Juanita must project the additional income she would earn by getting a business degree, discount each year's additional income, and compare the total with the discounted value of the cost of getting the degree—including the opportunity cost of the earnings she forgoes while attending college. If the discounted present value of Juanita's additional future income exceeds the discounted present value of the cost, acquiring the degree is a worthwhile investment. Of course, other nonmonetary considerations might also affect Juanita's decision, but the return on the investment is an important factor.

UNCERTAINTY, ENTREPRENEURSHIP, AND PROFIT

Firms and individual investors can sometimes earn persistent economic profits—returns in excess of the opportunity cost of funds—if they can restrict entry into various industries and occupations. Economic profits, however, can also be earned in competitive markets with no entry restrictions. *In competitive markets, there are two sources of economic profit: uncertainty and entrepreneurship.*

First, let's talk about how uncertainty enables people to earn an economic profit. Investment opportunities put people in a position to earn a handsome return, but they also expose them to additional uncertainty. We live in a world of uncertainty, imperfect information, and dynamic change. Unanticipated changes create winners and losers. If people didn't care about the uncertainty related to different investment projects, they wouldn't demand higher returns for higher risk projects. Most people, though, dislike uncertainty; they would prefer to know they'll collect $1,000 rather than take a 50-50 chance of collecting either nothing or $2,000. To accept the uncertainty accompanying riskier investments, they will demand a premium—an economic profit. For example, compared to government bonds, the returns on stocks are considerably more uncertain. This uncertainty of return is one reason why stocks have historically yielded a higher average return than bonds.

Entrepreneurship is a second source of economic profit. As we previously discussed, at any given time, there are an infinite number of potential investment projects from which to choose. Investing in some of them will increase the value of resources and lead to handsome returns. Successful entrepreneurship involves the identification of previously unnoticed profit opportunities. To finance their investments, would-be entrepreneurs usually have to use their own money and the money of co-venturers, in addition to whatever they can borrow. Entrepreneurs with successful track records will find it easier to get capital for their investment projects. Thus, over time, capital markets will allocate more control over investment dollars to those entrepreneurs with the most successful investment records.

The great Harvard economist Joseph Schumpeter believed that entrepreneurial discovery of new, improved ways of doing things drove economic progress and improved living standards. As Schumpeter put it, "The fundamental impulse that sets the capitalist engine

The introduction of new products often makes older ones obsolete. Examples abound: The personal computer replaced the typewriter, digital music players replaced the phonograph, and digital cameras are replacing film models. Joseph Schumpeter referred to outcomes of this type as "creative destruction." How does creative destruction influence the living standards of people like you?

© Bettmann/CORBIS

OUTSTANDING ECONOMIST

Joseph Schumpeter (1883–1950)

Born in Austria, Joseph Schumpeter was a longtime professor of economics at Harvard University. Generally recognized as one of the top five economists of the twentieth century, Schumpeter is perhaps best known for his views on entrepreneurship and the future of capitalism. He believed that the discovery and introduction of new and better products and organizational methods were constantly making the old ways of doing things obsolete. He referred to this process as "creative destruction" and argued that it was the primary fuel of economic progress.

iStockphoto.com/sorendls

in motion comes from the new consumer's goods, the new methods of production or transportation, and new markets, and the new forms of industrial organization that capitalist enterprise creates."[4]

RETURNS TO PHYSICAL AND HUMAN CAPITAL

Income reflects the returns from both human capital and physical capital. As **Exhibit 6** shows, approximately four-fifths of the national income in the United States is earned by employees and self-employed workers. The earnings in these two categories primarily reflect a return on human capital. The other one-fifth—income in the form of interest, corporate profits, and rents—reflects mostly returns to physical capital.[5] These shares of human and physical capital have been relatively constant for several decades.

Exhibit 6

The Income Shares of Human and Physical Capital

The share of national income earned by employees, self-employed proprietors, and owners of physical capital (interest, corporate profits, and rents) is shown here. Employee compensation and self-employment income represent primarily returns to human capital. These two components have composed approximately 80 percent of total national income in the United States for several decades.

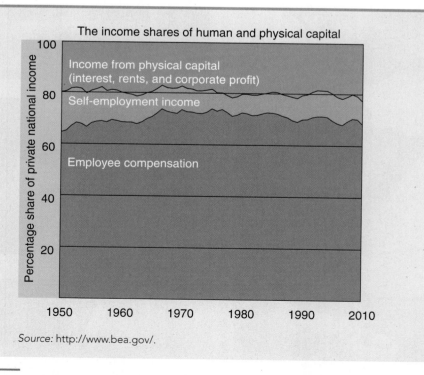

The income shares of human and physical capital

Source: http://www.bea.gov/.

---

[4]Joseph A. Schumpeter, *Capitalism, Socialism, and Democracy* (New York: Harper Torchbooks, 1950), 83.
[5]As used here, rent is income derived by owners who lease (rent) assets like buildings and equipment to another party for a period of time.

WHY IS THE CAPITAL MARKET SO IMPORTANT?

Innovation and the Capital Market

If the potential gains from innovative ideas and human ingenuity are going to be fully realized, it must be relatively easy for individuals to try their innovative and potentially ingenious ideas, but difficult to continue if the idea is a bad one.

keys to economic prosperity

iStockphoto.com/Scott Dunlap

If a nation is going to reach its full potential, it must have a mechanism that will attract savings and channel them into the investments that are most likely to create wealth. In a market economy, the capital market performs this function. Private investors, such as small business owners, corporate stockholders, and venture capitalists, place their own funds at risk in the capital market. Investors will sometimes make mistakes; sometimes they will undertake projects that prove to be unprofitable. However, if investors were unwilling to take such chances, many new ideas would go untested and many worthwhile but risky projects would not be undertaken.

In a world of uncertainty, mistaken investments are a necessary price that must be paid for fruitful innovations in new technologies and products. Such counterproductive projects, however, must be recognized and brought to a halt in a timely manner. In a market economy, the capital market performs this function. If a firm continues to experience losses, eventually investors will terminate the project and stop wasting their money.

New products, improved technologies, and lower cost production methods are a driving force that propels economic growth and higher living standards. But we do not know what they will be and who will discover and implement them during the next two or three decades. Based on the past, however, we can be pretty sure that many of the most successful new products and technologies will come from start-up businesses that are not even in existence today.

Measured on the basis of market capitalization, Microsoft, Cisco Systems, Walmart, and Intel all ranked among the ten largest companies in the world in 2000. Interestingly, all four were founded after 1967 and went public after 1970. None of them were ranked higher than 368th on the *Fortune* 500 in 1980. Thus, in the relatively short span of three decades, these companies grew from midgets to giants. As they did so, they were a powerful driving

iStockphoto.com/Dmitry Kalinovsky

The capital market will channel the savings of individuals into the finance of investment goods like trucks and earthmoving equipment. Does it make any difference whether these investment projects are profitable? Why or why not?

force for economic growth. This linkage between innovation and growth highlights why it is vitally important that entrepreneurs are both able to try out their new ideas but are forced to bring them to a halt if they do not generate revenues sufficient to cover cost.

Given the pace of change and the diversity of entrepreneurial talent, the knowledge required for sound decision-making about the allocation of capital is far beyond the scope of any single leader, industrial planning committee, or government agency. Without a private capital market, there is no mechanism that can be counted on to consistently channel investment funds into wealth-creating projects.

When investment funds are allocated by the government, rather than by the market, an entirely different set of factors comes into play. Political influence rather than market returns will decide which projects will be undertaken. Businesses will use contributions, lobbying, and other resources to curry favor with key political officials. In turn, the politicians will use subsidies, tax breaks, and "bailouts" to help those most willing to provide them with political support. Clearly, this system of crony capitalism will encourage rent-seeking and favor large firms with more lobbying clout at the expense of new start-up businesses. It will protect inefficient firms and slow the innovation and discovery process.

Profits and losses direct investors toward productive projects and away from those that are counterproductive. The political process does not have anything similar to profit and loss that can be counted on to direct funds toward wealth creation. As a result, inefficient allocation of capital is a predictable outcome.

The experiences of Eastern Europe and the former Soviet Union illustrate this point. For four decades (1950–1990), the investment rates in these countries were among the highest in the world. Central planners allocated approximately one-third of the national output into capital investment. Even these high rates of investment, however, did little to improve living standards because political rather than economic considerations determined which projects would be funded. Resources were often wasted on politically impractical projects and high visibility ("prestige") investments favored by important political leaders. Misdirection of investment and failure to keep up with dynamic change eventually led to the collapse of these systems.

Historically, the government of the United States has played a minor role in the allocation of capital. But this has changed in recent years. Beginning in the latter half of the 1990s, federal regulations and subsidies played a major role in directing capital toward the housing industry. Regulations imposed on the banking industry and the policies of two large government-sponsored corporations, Fannie Mae and Freddie Mac, expanded the availability of credit and promoted mortgage loans with little or no down payment. The policies were designed to increase the affordability of housing and promote home ownership among those with low and moderate incomes. These policies played a central role in the creation of a housing boom, followed by a bust and the 2008 financial crisis. (*Note:* For a detailed analysis of this issue, see Special Topic 5, "The Crisis of 2008: Causes and Lessons for the Future.")

Further, the government has become much more involved in the allocation of capital in other ways. During 2008–2011, approximately half of the saving flowing into the loanable funds market was consumed by federal borrowing to finance the budget deficit. In the energy area, the government has provided huge subsidies to high-cost energy sources such as ethanol, wind, and solar, while regulations have reduced the supply of lower-cost petroleum and natural gas. During the financial crisis, the government provided emergency loans to several companies, including large banks, the American Insurance Group, General Motors, and Chrysler. The operation of the capital market is undermined when investors are permitted to keep the revenues from profitable activities but bailed out by the government—that is, taxpayers—when they make unwise choices and experience losses. Under these circumstances, investors will have less incentive to evaluate risks and act prudently, and they will have more incentive to cater to political officials who can provide them with bailouts and subsidies.

Has the nature of the capital market been permanently altered? Will political considerations and centralized government decision-making play a much larger role in future allocation of capital? At this point, it is too early to know the answer to these questions. But one thing is for sure: How they are answered will exert a dramatic impact on America's future.

Looking Ahead

As the preceding two chapters have stressed, investment in physical and human capital will influence the wealth and income of both individuals and nations. Differences among individuals with regard to these factors will also contribute to income inequality. The next chapter will focus on this topic.

KEY POINTS

- We can often produce more consumption goods by first using our resources to produce physical and human capital resources and then using these capital resources to produce the desired consumption goods. Because resources used to produce capital goods will be unavailable for the direct production of consumption goods, saving is necessary for investment.

- The interest rate is the price of earlier availability. It is the premium that borrowers must pay to lenders to acquire goods now rather than later.

- The demand for loanable funds reflects the productivity of capital resources and the positive rate of time preference. The market interest rate will bring the quantity of funds demanded by borrowers into balance with the quantity supplied by lenders.

- During inflationary times, the money rate of interest incorporates an inflationary premium reflecting the expected future increase in the price level. When inflation is expected, the money rate of interest exceeds the real rate of interest.

- The money rate of interest on a specific loan reflects three basic factors—the pure interest rate, an inflationary premium, and a risk premium that is directly related to the probability of default by the borrower.

- The interest rate allows individuals to put a current value on future revenues and costs. The discounting procedure can be used to calculate the present value of an expected net income stream from a potential investment project. If the present value of the expected revenues exceeds the present value of the expected costs—and if things turn out as anticipated—the project will be profitable.

- The present value of expected future net earnings will determine the market value of existing assets. An increase in the expected future earnings of an asset will increase its market value.

- Economic profit plays a central role in allocating capital and determining which investment projects will be undertaken. In a competitive environment, economic profit reflects uncertainty and entrepreneurship—the ability to recognize and undertake profitable projects that have gone unnoticed by others.

- To grow and prosper, a nation must have a mechanism that will attract savings and channel them into investments that create wealth. The capital market performs this function in a market economy.

CRITICAL ANALYSIS QUESTIONS

1. *How would the following changes influence the rate of interest in the United States?
   a. an increase in the positive time preference of lenders
   b. an increase in the positive time preference of borrowers
   c. an increase in domestic inflation
   d. increased uncertainty about a nuclear war
   e. improved investment opportunities in Europe
2. What is capital investment? Why do business firms often use machinery and other capital assets to produce goods and services?
3. How are human and physical capital investment decisions similar? How do they differ? What determines the profitability of a physical capital investment? Do human capital investors make profits? If so, what is the source of the profit? Explain.
4. *A lender made the following statement to a borrower: "You are borrowing $1,000, which is to be repaid in twelve monthly installments of $100 each. Your total interest charge is $200, which means your interest rate is 20 percent." Is the effective interest rate on the loan really 20 percent? Explain.

5. In a market economy, investors have a strong incentive to undertake profitable investments. What makes an investment profitable? Do profitable investments create wealth? Why or why not? Do all investments create wealth? Discuss.

6. *Over long periods of time, the rate of return of an average investment in the stock market has exceeded the return on high-quality bonds. Is the higher return on stocks surprising? Why or why not?

7. The interest rates charged on outstanding credit card balances are generally higher than the interest rate that banks charge customers with a good credit rating. Why do you think the credit card rate is so high? Should the government impose an interest rate ceiling of, say, 10 percent? If it did, who would be hurt and who would be helped? Discuss.

8. *If the money rate of interest on a low-risk government bond is 10 percent and the inflation rate for the last several years has been steady at 4 percent, what is the estimated real rate of interest?

9. Suppose you are contemplating the purchase of a commercial lawn mower at a cost of $10,000. The expected lifetime of the machine is three years. You can lease the asset to a local business for $4,000 annually (payable at the end of each year) for three years. The lessee is responsible for the upkeep and maintenance of the machine during the three-year period. If you can borrow (and lend) money at an interest rate of 8 percent, will the investment be a profitable undertaking? Is the project profitable at an interest rate of 12 percent? Provide calculations in support of your answer.

10. *Alicia's philosophy of life is summed up by the proverb "A penny saved is a penny earned." She plans and saves for the future. In contrast, Mike's view is "Life is uncertain; eat dessert first." Mike wants as much as possible now.
    a. Who has the highest rate of time preference?
    b. Do people like Alicia benefit from the presence of people like Mike?
    c. Do people like Mike benefit from the presence of people like Alicia? Explain.

11. *Some countries with very low incomes per capita are unable to save very much. Are people in these countries helped or hurt by people in high-income countries with much higher rates of saving?

12. *According to a news item, the owner of a lottery ticket paying $3 million over twenty years is offering to sell the ticket for $1.2 million cash now. "Who knows?" the ticket owner explained. "We might not even be here in 20 years, and I do not want to leave it to the dinosaurs."
    a. If the ticket pays $150,000 per year at the end of each year for the next twenty years, what is the present value of the ticket when the appropriate rate for discounting the future income is thought to be 10 percent?
    b. If the discount rate is in the 10 percent range, is the sale price of $1.2 million reasonable?
    c. Can you think of any disadvantages of buying the lottery earnings rather than a bond?

13. Suppose you are moving into a new apartment you expect to rent for five years. The owner of the apartment offers to provide you with a used refrigerator for free and promises to maintain and repair the refrigerator during the next five years. You also have the option of buying a new energy-efficient refrigerator (with a five-year free maintenance agreement) for $700. The new refrigerator will reduce your electric bill by $150 per year and will have a market value of $200 after five years. If necessary, you can borrow money from the bank at an 8 percent rate of interest. Which option should you choose?

14. *Suppose that you are considering whether to enroll in a summer computer-training program that costs $2,500. If you take the program, you will have to give up $1,500 of earnings from your summer job. You figure that the program will increase your earnings by $500 per year for each of the next ten years. Beyond that, it is not expected to affect your earnings. If you take the program, you will have to borrow the funds at an 8 percent rate of interest. From a strictly monetary viewpoint, should you enroll in the program?

15. "In a world of uncertainty, it is important that entrepreneurs be able to introduce new products and try out innovative ideas. But it is also important that unproductive projects be brought to a halt." Evaluate this statement.

16. *Will political officials be more likely to channel funds into wealth-creating projects than private investors and entrepreneurs? Why or why not? Discuss.

*Asterisk denotes questions for which answers appear in Appendix B.

15

Income Inequality and Poverty

CHAPTER FOCUS

- How do resource prices and income differences influence the incentive of people to develop resources and use them productively?

- How much income inequality is there in the United States? Has the degree of inequality changed in recent years?

- How much income mobility exists? Do the rich stay rich whereas the poor stay poor?

- How widespread is poverty? How has the poverty rate changed in recent decades? Did the "War on Poverty" help reduce the poverty rate?

- Is there too much income inequality? Should the government try to reduce inequality? Why or why not?

All animals are equal, but some animals are more equal than others.
—*George Orwell*[1]

—————

[1]George Orwell, *Animal Farm* (New York: Harcourt and Brace Company, 1946), 112.

Differences in resource prices and the productivity of individuals will cause incomes to vary. Of course, economic inequality is present in all societies. Neither politics nor central planning will eliminate it. Nonetheless, most of us are troubled by the extremes of inequality—the extravagant luxury of some and the grinding poverty of others. How much inequality is there in the United States? Do wealthy families continually enjoy high incomes? What effect have income-transfer programs had on the welfare of the poor? Do these income-transfer programs lessen the incentive for both the poor and nonpoor to earn income? This chapter focuses on these questions and related issues.

HOW MUCH INCOME INEQUALITY EXISTS IN THE UNITED STATES?

Money income is only one component of economic well-being. Factors such as leisure, noncash-transfer benefits, the nonmonetary advantages and disadvantages of a job, and the expected stability of future income also affect people's economic welfare. Money income is quite important, however, because it makes it possible to buy market goods and services. It is also easy to measure and is therefore widely used as a yardstick of economic well-being and degree of inequality.

Exhibit 1 presents data on money income in the United States. First, look at the share of *before-tax* annual money income by quintile—that is, by each fifth of the total population of families—ranked from the lowest to the highest. If there were total income equality, each quintile (20 percent) of families would generate 20 percent of the aggregate income.

Exhibit 1	**Share of Money Income by Quintile during Selected Years, 1950–2009**				
	LOWEST 20 PERCENT OF RECIPIENTS	SECOND QUINTILE	THIRD QUINTILE	FOURTH QUINTILE	FIFTH QUINTILE
FAMILY INCOME BEFORE TAXES					
1950	4.5	12.0	17.4	23.4	42.7
1960	4.8	12.2	17.8	24.0	41.3
1970	5.4	12.2	17.6	23.8	40.9
1980	5.1	11.6	17.5	24.3	41.6
1990	4.6	10.8	16.6	23.8	44.3
2000	4.3	9.8	15.4	22.7	47.7
2004	4.0	9.6	15.4	23.0	47.9
2007	4.1	9.7	15.6	23.3	47.4
2009	3.9	9.4	15.3	23.2	48.2
IMPACT OF TAXES AND TRANSFERS ON HOUSEHOLD INCOME, 2009					
BEFORE	3.5	8.6	14.5	23.9	49.5
AFTER	4.6	10.8	16.3	23.9	44.4

Sources: Bureau of the Census, Current Population Survey, Series P-60; Statistical Abstract of the United States, 1995, table 733; Congressional Budget Office; 1994, Green Book; Bureau of the Census, The Effects of Taxes and Transfers on Income and Poverty in the United States: 2009; and. Bureau of the Census, Income, Poverty, and Health Insurance Coverage in the United States: 2009.

Given the differences in education, skills, ability, work effort, age, family size, and other factors among families, clearly we would not expect this to be the case. Some families will be able to generate more income than others. It is, however, informative to look at the shares of income by quintile.

The figures show that before-tax income inequality fell throughout the 1950s and 1960s. In other words, the income gap between the top and bottom earning quintiles closed. For example, in 1970, the top quintile earned 40.9 percent of the aggregate money income, down from 42.7 percent in 1950. During the same period, the share of income earned by the lowest quintile rose from 4.5 percent in 1950 to 5.4 percent in 1970.

Beginning in the 1970s, however, this trend has reversed. During the last three and a half decades, the share of income earned by the top quintile has steadily risen, whereas that earned by the bottom group has fallen.[2] By 2009, the share of before-tax money income of the top group had risen to 48.2 percent, whereas that earned by the bottom 20 percent of families had fallen to 3.9 percent. Thus, in 2009, the top quintile of families earned approximately twelve times as much before-tax money income as the bottom quintile of families.

Low-income families are the primary beneficiaries of noncash-transfer programs that provide people with food (food stamps), health care, and housing. Correspondingly, under a system of progressive taxation, which the United States has, taxes take a larger share of income as one's earnings increase. As a result, we would expect *after-tax* and *transfer* incomes to be more equal than before-tax incomes. Using household data, Exhibit 1 shows that this is indeed the case. After taxes and transfers, the bottom quintile of households received 4.6 percent of the total income in 2009 (compared with 3.5 percent of the before-tax income), and the top quintile of households received 44.4 percent (compared with 49.5 percent before taxes). Notice that taxes and transfers increased the income share of the bottom three quintiles. As you can see, taxes and transfers do, in fact, reduce income inequality. (*Note:* Household income is used here because after-tax and family transfer-income data are unavailable. In addition to families, households include individuals living by themselves and unrelated people living together.)

A market economy does not have a central distributing agency that carves up the economic pie and allocates slices to various individuals. Rather, each individual produces his or her own slice of the pie. If one person's income grows, it does not mean that another's must shrink. The distribution of income is actually a result of many individual efforts and decisions. We now turn to the consideration of the factors that underlie the distribution of income in the United States.

THE FACTORS AFFECTING INCOME DISTRIBUTION

How meaningful are the data of Exhibit 1? If all families (and households) were similar except with regard to the amount of income they earned, the use of annual income data as an index of inequality would be quite reasonable. However, the fact is that the aggregate data lump together (1) small and large families, (2) prime-age earners and elderly retirees, (3) multi-earner families and families without any current earners, and (4) husband–wife families and single-parent families.

Consider just one factor: the impact of age and the pattern of lifetime income. Typically, the annual income of young people is low, particularly if they are going to school or are getting training. Many people under 25 years of age studying to be lawyers, doctors, engineers, and economists will have low annual incomes during this phase of their lives. But this does not mean that they are poor—at least not in the usual sense. After completing their formal education and acquiring work experience, these people move into their prime working years. At this point, their annual incomes are generally quite high, particularly in families in which both spouses are employed outside the home. Remember, however, that

---

[2]A reduction in the share of income earned by the bottom quintile income group does not imply that their income level fell. It merely indicates that their income did not grow as rapidly as that of other groups, particularly the top quintile. The inflation-adjusted income of the bottom quintile of earners has increased in recent decades.

this is also a time when families are purchasing homes and providing for their children, which is costly. Consequently, the economic well-being of these people as measured by their earnings may well be overstated. In other words, although these people are earning more at this stage in their lives, they also have more responsibilities. Finally, people reach the retirement phase, characterized by less work, more leisure, and smaller family sizes. Even families that are quite well off tend to experience incomes well below average during the retirement phase. ***Given the life cycle of income, lumping together families of different ages (phases of their life-cycle earnings) results in substantial inequality in the annual income figures. This would be so even if the incomes of families over a lifetime were approximately equal.***

Exhibit 2 highlights major differences between high- and low-income families that underlie the distributional data of Exhibit 1. The typical high-income family (top 20 percent) is headed by a well-educated person in the prime working-age phase of life. His or her income is supplemented by the earnings of other family members, particularly working spouses. In contrast, people with little education, nonworking retirees, younger workers (under age 35), and single-parent families are substantially overrepresented among low-income families (the bottom 20 percent of income recipients). In 2009, 28 percent of the householders in the lowest income quintile failed to complete high school, compared with only 2 percent for the highest income quintile. Although only 10 percent of the household heads in the bottom quintile completed college, 63 percent of the householders in the top group did so. Seventy-eight percent of the high-income families had household heads in the prime working-age category (age thirty-five to sixty-four), compared with only 46 percent of the low-income families. Only one parent was present in 52 percent of the low-income families, whereas 93 percent of the high-income group were dual-parent families. High-income families are also larger than low-income families, which might surprise you. In 2009, there were 3.4 people per family in the top income quintile, compared to only 3.0 people per family in the bottom quintile.

Moreover, there was a striking difference between low- and high-income families in the percentage of hours each group worked. No doubt, much of this difference reflected

Exhibit 2		Bottom 20 Percent of Income Recipients	Top 20 Percent of Income Recipients
Differing Characteristics of High- and Low-Income Families, 2009	EDUCATION OF HOUSEHOLDER		
	Percent with less than high school	28	2
	Percent with college degree or more	10	63
	AGE OF HOUSEHOLDER (PERCENT DISTRIBUTION)		
	Under 35	33	12
	35–64	46	78
	65 and over	21	10
	FAMILY STATUS		
	Married couple family (percentage of total)	48	93
	Single parent family (percentage of total)	52	7
	PERSONS PER FAMILY	3	3.4
	EARNERS PER FAMILY	0.7	2.1
	Percent of married-couple families in which wife works full-time	12	64
	PERCENT OF TOTAL WORK HOURS SUPPLIED BY GROUP	7	31

Source: http://www.census.gov and author calculations from the March 2010 Current Population Survey.

factors like family size, the age of the wage earners, whether both spouses worked, and whether two spouses were present in the home. In high-income families, the average number of workers per family was 2.1, compared with 0.7 for low-income families. Among married-couple families, a wife working full time was present only 13 percent of the time in low-income families, compared with 64 percent of the time in high-income families. As we would expect, couples who decide not to have the wife work full-time pay for this choice by falling down the income distribution ladder.

In terms of their work effort, the top 20 percent of income recipients contributed 31 percent of the total number of hours worked in the economy, whereas the bottom 20 percent contributed only 7 percent of the total work time. In other words, high-income families worked 4.4 times as many hours as low-income families. As we noted earlier, they also earned approximately twelve times as much before-tax income. Clearly, differences in the amount of time worked were a major factor contributing to the income inequality of Exhibit 1. Less work time generally means more time for leisure. See Application in Economics: "The Increasing Leisure Time of Americans" for information on recent changes in this factor.

APPLICATIONS IN ECONOMICS

The Increasing Leisure Time of Americans

In the United States, men spend approximately 54 hours per week commuting to and from a job and performing work activities either in the marketplace or at home. The comparable figure for women is 47 hours per week. The rest of their time is available for leisure activities.

Leisure time is a valuable commodity. It is the time that you are not working at a job or at home performing tasks such as washing clothes and cutting the grass. Your leisure time is the time that you have simply to do things that you enjoy. It includes activities like watching TV, playing video games, visiting friends, going to bars, and attending sporting events.

Like an increase in market income, an increase in leisure makes us better off. The amount of leisure time available to the average American has increased substantially over the past four decades. After adjusting for demographic changes, Mark Aguiar and Erik Hurst find that leisure rose, between 1965 and 2003, on average by 7.9 hours per week for men and 6 hours per week for women.[1] This increase in leisure time is roughly equal to ten and eight extra weeks of vacation from work for men and women, respectively.

The source of the increased leisure time differs for men and women. Men now have more leisure because they have reduced their market work time more than they have increased their hours working at home. For women, the reverse is true. Women have more leisure because they have reduced their time devoted to housework more than they increased their time spent in market labor.

The increase in leisure has not been evenly spread out across education groups. In 1965, the amount of leisure was quite similar across various levels of education for both men and women. However, this situation has changed significantly during the last four decades. The average hours of leisure rose by 10.2 hours for men with a high school degree or less but by only 5.5 hours for men with more than a high school degree. This same pattern was also present for women. Women with a high school degree or less increased their leisure time by 9 hours per week compared with only 5.7 hours for those with schooling beyond the high school level. Given their higher hourly earnings, the opportunity cost of leisure time is greater for those with more education. Thus, it is not surprising that individuals with more education had smaller increases in leisure time than those with less schooling.

Interestingly, the increase in leisure inequality across education groups is the mirror image of the change in market income inequality. In recent decades, the market earnings of those with more education have increased more rapidly than have those with less schooling. However, just the opposite has been the case for the increase in leisure time. Thus, the increase in time worked (and reduction in leisure) has contributed to the growing income gap between college graduates and those with only a high school education that has been observed in recent decades.

[1]Mark Aguiar and Erik Hurst, "Measuring Trends in Leisure: The Allocation of Time over Five Decades," *Quarterly Journal of Economics* 122 (August 2007): 969–1006.

In summary, Exhibit 2 sheds a great deal of light on the distributional data presented in Exhibit 1. *Those with high incomes are far more likely to be well-educated, dual-parent families with both parents working outside the home in their prime earning years. In contrast, those with low incomes are often single-parent families headed by a poorly educated adult who is either youthful or elderly.* The household heads of those families with little income are often either out of the labor force or working only part-time. Given these factors, it is not surprising that the top 20 percent of recipients have substantially higher incomes, both before and after taxes, than the bottom quintile.

WHY HAS INCOME INEQUALITY INCREASED?

Exhibit 1 indicates that there has been an increase in income inequality in the United States during the last couple of decades. Why has the gap between the rich and the poor been growing? Research in this area shows that at least four factors have contributed to the rise in income inequality.

1. The increasing proportion of single-parent and dual-earner families.

The nature of the family and the allocation of work responsibilities within the family have changed dramatically in recent decades. In 2009, more than one-fourth (29 percent) of all families with children were headed by a single parent, double the figure of the mid-1960s. At the same time, the labor force participation rate of married women increased from 40 percent in 1970 to 59 percent in 2010.

As a result, today we have more single-parent families and more dual-earner families. Both of these changes tend to promote income inequality. Consider two hypothetical families, the Smiths and the Browns. In 1970, both were middle-income families with two children and one parent working earning $60,000 (in 2012 dollars). Now consider their 2012 counterparts. The Smiths of 2012 are divorced, and one of them, probably Mrs. Smith, is trying to work part-time and take care of the two children. The probability is very high that the single-parent Smith family of 2012 will be in the low-income rather than the middle-income category. The Smiths may well be in the bottom quintile of the income distribution. In contrast, the Browns of 2012 both work outside the home, and each earns $60,000 annually. Given their dual incomes, the Browns are now a high-income rather than a middle-income family. Along with many other dual-income families (see Exhibit 2), the Browns' 2012 family income will probably place them in the top quintile of income recipients.

Even if there were no changes in earnings between skilled and less-skilled workers, the recent changes within the family would increase the income inequality among families and households. Today, more single-parent families like the Smiths fall into the low-income quintile, whereas more dual-earner families like the Browns fall into the high-income quintile. The gap between the earnings of these two groups has therefore increased the overall income inequality in the United States.

2. Earnings differentials between skilled and less-skilled workers.

In 1970, workers with little education who were willing to work hard, often in a hot and sweaty environment, received high wages. This is less true today. In 1974, the annual earnings of men who graduated from college were only 27 percent higher than the earnings of male high school graduates—hardly a huge payoff for the time and cost of a college degree. Since 1974, however, things have changed dramatically. By the mid-1980s, the earnings premium of male college graduates relative to male high school grads rose to the 50–60 percent range, approximately twice the premium of 1974. By 2009, the income premium of male college graduates relative to high school graduates rose to 83 percent. Similarly, during the last two decades, the earnings of women college graduates have increased sharply relative to women with only a high school education.

Why have the earnings of people with more education (and skill) risen relative to those with less education (and skill)? As the Applications in Economics feature on page 553 indicates, an increase in the time worked of those with more education has played a role. Structural factors have also contributed. Deregulation of the transportation industry and the declining power of unions may have reduced the number of high-wage, blue-collar jobs available to workers with little education. International competition has also played a role because, increasingly, American workers must compete in a global economy. Furthermore, innovations and cost reductions in both communications and transportation have made it easier for firms to hire workers in different locations. Firms producing goods that require substantial amounts of less-skilled labor can easily move to places like Korea, Taiwan, and Mexico, where less-skilled labor is cheaper. In contrast, the United States is more attractive than most other countries to firms requiring substantial amounts of high-skilled, well-educated workers. Globalization has, therefore, reduced the demand for American workers with few skills and little education but increased the demand for high-skilled workers with college degrees. This has made for a wider earnings gap among workers in high-income countries like the United States. However, it is worth noting that this process enhances income levels in low-income countries and thereby reduces *worldwide* income inequality.

3. The increasing number of markets characterized by a few people at the top with very high earnings. As we discussed in the chapter on wage differentials, the market compensation of star entertainers and athletes, the most talented professionals, and top business executives is often like that of winner-take-all tournaments. At any point in time, a few people at the top have huge earnings, whereas most others in these areas have modest or even low incomes. As transportation and communication costs have declined, markets have increasingly become national and even global, rather than local. This not only increases the incomes of a few people at the top, but it also increases the degree of income inequality.

4. Sharply lower marginal tax rates than in the 1970s. Prior to 1981, high-income Americans confronted top marginal tax rates of up to 70 percent. This encouraged high-income earners to structure their business affairs and invest in ways that sheltered much of their income from the Internal Revenue Service. As we indicated in Chapter 4, the taxable incomes of the top 10 percent of earners expanded sharply when the top marginal tax rates were reduced to the 30 percent range during the 1980s. Some of this increase in income reflected greater work effort due to the increased incentive to earn. Much of it, however, merely reflected the fact that people were engaging in fewer activities to shelter their earnings from taxes. The flip side of fewer tax shelter activities accompanying lower marginal tax rates led to an increase in the visible income of the rich. As more of the income of the rich is observable, money income statistics such as those of Exhibit 1 will register an increase in income inequality.

INCOME MOBILITY AND INEQUALITY IN ECONOMIC STATUS

Statistics on the distribution of annual income do not reflect income mobility— movements up and down the income ladder. Therefore, they may be misleading. Consider two countries with identical distributions of annual income. In both cases, the annual income of the top quintile of income recipients is ten times greater than the bottom quintile. Now, suppose that in the first country—we will refer to it as Static—the same people are at the top of the income distribution year after year. Similarly, the poor people of Static remain poor year after year. Static is characterized by an absence of income mobility. In contrast, earners in the second country, which we will call Dynamic, are constantly changing places. Indeed, during every five-year period, each family spends one year in the upper-income quintile, one year in each of the three middle-income quintiles, and one year in the bottom-income quintile. In Dynamic, no one is rich for more than one year (out of

Income mobility
Movement of individuals and families either up or down income-distribution rankings when comparisons are made at two different points in time. When substantial income mobility is present, a person's current position in the rankings will not be a very good indicator of what his or her position will be a few years in the future.

Exhibit 3	Income Mobility–Income Ranking, 1994 and 2004

Percent Distribution by Income Status of Family in 1994	Percent Distribution by Income Status of Family in 2004				
	Highest Quintile	Next-Highest Quintile	Middle Quintile	Next-Lowest Quintile	Lowest Quintile
Highest quintile	53.0	25.0	12.0	5.5	4.5
Next-highest quintile	23.0	32.5	24.0	14.0	6.5
Middle quintile	14.0	22.5	28.0	24.0	12.0
Next-lowest quintile	5.5	12.5	25.5	33.5	23.5
Lowest quintile	5.0	7.5	10.0	24.5	53.5

Source: Katherine Bradbury and Jane Katz, Federal Reserve Bank of Boston (http://www.bos.frb.org/economic/dynamicdata/module2/index.htm).

each five), and no one is poor for more than a year. Obviously, the nature of economic inequality in Static is vastly different from that in Dynamic. You would not know it, though, by looking at their identical annual income distributions.

The contrast between Static and Dynamic highlights an important point: Income mobility is an important facet of economic inequality. Until recently, detailed data on income mobility were sparse. This is now beginning to change.[3] **Exhibit 3** presents data on the mobility of family income between 1994 and 2004 in the United States. The data compare the relative income positions of the *same families* at two different points in time. Based on their 1994 income, each family was placed into income quintiles ranked from highest to lowest. Later, the 2004 real-income level of the *same families* was used once again to group the income of each by quintiles.

The first row of Exhibit 3 shows the relative income position in 2004 of people in the top quintile of income recipients in 1994. Approximately one-half (53 percent) of those with incomes in the top quintile in 1994 were able to maintain this lofty position ten years later. Slightly less than one-half (47 percent) of the top income group in 1994 had fallen to a lower income quintile by 2004. However, only one in ten of the high-income individuals fell to one of the bottom two quintiles of the 2004 income distribution. This suggests that once families are able to achieve high-income status, they rarely fall back to a very low level of income.

The bottom row of Exhibit 3 tracks the experience of those in the lowest income quintile in 1994. Slightly more than half (53.5 percent) of the families in the lowest income quintile remained there in 2004. Nearly one-quarter (22.5 percent) moved up to one of the top three income quintiles in 2004. Among those in the next-to-lowest income quintile in 1994, more than two-fifths (43.5 percent) had moved up to one of the three higher income groupings by 2004.

The income mobility data reveal something concealed by the annual figures: There is considerable movement up and down the economic ladder. Relative income positions often change over time. A sizable portion of those with a high relative income during one year subsequently find themselves in a lower income position. At the same time, many of those with low relative incomes during a given year move up to higher income quintiles in subsequent years.

---

[3]For a review of the literature on income mobility, see Isabel V. Sawhill and Daniel P. McMurrer, *Income Mobility in the United States* (Washington, DC: Urban Institute, 1996). For an early classic work on this topic, see Greg J. Duncan et al., *Years of Poverty, Years of Plenty: The Changing Fortunes of American Workers and Families* (Ann Arbor: Institute for Social Research, University of Michigan, 1984).

Generational Mobility: There is a weak positive correlation between the earnings of fathers and sons. If a father has lifetime earnings 20 percent above the average of his generation, a son can expect to earn about 8 percent more. There is virtually no correlation between the earnings of grandparents and their grandchildren. Apparently, there is some truth in the old saying "From shirtsleeves to shirtsleeves in three generations."

Many economists argue that differences in household expenditures are a more accurate indicator of economic well-being than are the annual income figures. On the one hand, if your income or earnings prospects in the future are good, you're likely to spend more than your current income. On the other hand, if your future income is expected to be lower, you're likely to save more, causing spending to be less than your current income. To a large degree, current expenditures reflect long-term economic status.

What do expenditures reveal about the degree of inequality in the United States? The expenditure statistics indicate that the degree of inequality is significantly smaller than the corresponding figure for annual income. For example, in 2009, the household expenditures of the bottom 20 percent of households were approximately 8 percent of the total. This is substantially greater than their income share both before and after taxes. Correspondingly, the expenditures of the top 20 percent of households constituted approximately 39 percent of the total, well below their income share. Moreover, the share of household expenditures by quintile has been relatively constant during the last four decades. This suggests that the increase in inequality as measured by the annual income data is a reflection of dynamic change, temporary fluctuations in annual income, and measurement issues rather than a true increase in economic inequality.

POVERTY IN THE UNITED STATES

In an affluent country like the United States, income inequality and poverty are related issues. Poverty could be defined in strictly relative terms—the bottom one-fifth of all income recipients, for example. However, this definition would not be very helpful because it would mean that the poverty rate would never change, as 20 percent of the population would always be classified as poor.

The official definition of poverty in the United States is based on the perceived minimum income necessary to provide food, clothing, shelter, and basic necessities for a family to survive. This **poverty threshold income level** varies with family size and composition,

Poverty threshold income level
The level of money income below which a family is considered to be poor. It differs according to family characteristics (e.g., number of family members) and is adjusted when consumer prices change.

Exhibit 4

The Changing Composition of the Poor and Poverty Rates, Selected Groups: 1959, 1976, and 2009

	1959	1976	2009
NUMBER OF POOR FAMILIES (IN MILLIONS)	8.3	5.3	8.8
PERCENT OF POOR FAMILIES HEADED BY A:			
Female	23	48	51
Black	26	30	25
Elderly person (age 65 and over)	22	14	9
Person who worked at least some during the year[a]	70	55	46
POVERTY RATE			
All families	18.5	10.1	11.1
Married couple families	15.8	7.2	5.8
Female-headed families	42.6	32.5	29.9
All individuals	22.4	11.7	14.3
Whites	18.1	9.1	12.3
Blacks	55.1	31.1	25.8
Children (under age 18)	27.3	16.0	20.7

Source: U.S. Department of Commerce, Characteristics of the Population below the Poverty Level: 1982, Table 5; and http://www.census.gov/.

[a]The 2009 figure is the percentage of poor families headed by a person aged 15 to 64 who worked at least some during the year. The figures for the other years is the percentage of poor families headed by a person aged 15 and older who worked at least some during the year. The difference between the two measures is approximately two percentage points.

and it is adjusted annually for changes in prices. The official poverty threshold is based only on money income. (See the Measures of Economic Activity feature for additional details on how the poverty rate is measured.)

Who are the poor? **Exhibit 4** presents data on both the number of poor families and the poverty rate for 1959, 1976, and 2009. In 2009, 8.8 million families, 11.1 percent of the total, were classified as poor. As Exhibit 4 shows, there has been a substantial change in the composition of the poverty population during the last several decades. In 1959, elderly people and the working poor formed the core of the poverty population. Twenty-two percent of the poor families were headed by an elderly person in 1959 versus only 9 percent by 2009. In 1959, 70 percent of the heads of poor families worked at least part of the year, but in 2009, only 46 percent of them worked during the year.

In recent decades, the proportion of families headed by women in the United States has increased whereas the proportion of husband–wife families has declined. Because the poverty rate of families headed by women is several times higher than the rate for husband–wife families (29.9 percent compared with 5.8 percent in 2009), an increase in family instability tends to push the poverty rate upward. It also tends to increase the number of households headed by women among poor families. In 2009, 51 percent of the poor families were headed by a woman, compared with only 23 percent in 1959.

Rather than calculating the poverty rate of families, one could measure the poverty rate of individuals. The poverty rate of individuals is, in fact, somewhat higher than the poverty rate of families. In 2009, 14.3 percent of people in the United States were classified as poor, compared with 11.1 percent for families. The poverty rate of black individuals in 2009 was 25.8 percent, compared with 12.35 percent for white individuals. Nonetheless, more than two-thirds of the people in poverty were white. Perhaps the most tragic consequence of poverty is its impact on children. Moreover, the poverty rate among children has been increasing. In 2009, 21 percent of the children in the United States lived in poverty, up from 16 percent in 1976.

MEASURES OF ECONOMIC ACTIVITY

How Is the Poverty Rate Calculated?

Families and individuals are classified as poor or nonpoor based on the poverty threshold income level originally developed by the Social Security Administration (SSA) in 1964. Consumption survey data showed that low- and median-income families of three or more people spent approximately one-third of their income on food. Because of this, the SSA established the poverty threshold income level at three times the cost of an economical, nutritionally adequate food plan. A slightly larger multiple was used for smaller families and individuals living alone. The poverty threshold figure varies according to family size because the food costs vary by family size and composition. It is adjusted annually to account for rising prices. The following chart illustrates how the poverty threshold for a family of four has increased as prices have risen from 1959 to 2011.

1959	$2,973
1970	3,968
1980	8,414
1990	13,359
2000	17,603
2011	22,350

Even though the poverty threshold income level is adjusted for prices, it is actually an absolute measure of economic status. As real income increases, the poverty threshold declines relative to the income of the general populace.

The official poverty rate is the number of people or families living in households with a money income below the poverty threshold as a percentage of the total. Only money income is considered. Income received in the form of noncash benefits, like food stamps, medical care, and housing subsidies, is completely ignored in the calculation of the official poverty rate. Because of this omission, the official rate tends to overstate the degree of poverty. To remedy this deficiency, the Bureau of the Census has developed several alternative measures of poverty that count the estimated value of noncash benefits as income. In addition to the official poverty rate, the bureau now publishes annual data for the "adjusted" poverty rates that include a valuation for various noncash benefits. Of course, including these benefits reduces the poverty rate. For example, the official poverty rate for families was 11.1 percent in 2009, but the adjusted poverty rate that included the value of the noncash food, housing, and medical benefits was only 7.4 percent.

The poverty rate is calculated each year based on a survey of about 60,000 households designed to reflect the population of the United States. Two major sources for comprehensive data on this topic are the Bureau of the Census annual publications, *Income, Poverty, and Health Insurance Coverage in the United States.*

TRANSFER PAYMENTS AND THE POVERTY RATE

In the mid-1960s, it was widely believed that an increase in income transfers directed toward the poor would substantially reduce, if not eliminate, the incidence of poverty. The 1964 *Economic Report of the President* argued that poverty could be virtually eliminated if the federal government increased its expenditures on transfer programs by approximately 2 percent of aggregate income. Following the declaration of the "War on Poverty" by President Lyndon Johnson's administration, transfer expenditures increased rapidly. Measured in 1982–1984 dollars, means-tested income transfers—those limited to people with incomes below a certain cutoff point—tripled, expanding from $24 billion in 1965 to $70 billion in 1975. After 1975, transfer expenditures continued to expand, but the rate of increase was slower. Measured as a share of aggregate income, means-tested transfers jumped from 1.5 percent in 1965 to 5.3 percent in 2002.[4]

Did the expansion in government income transfers reduce the poverty rate as the 1964 *Economic Report of the President* anticipated? Exhibit 5 shows the poverty rate from 1947 through 2009. Interestingly, the poverty rate declined substantially during the period prior

Means-tested income transfers
Transfers that are limited to people or families with an income below a certain cutoff point. Eligibility is thus dependent upon low-income status.

---

[4]U.S. House of Representatives, Committee on Ways and Means, *Green Book, 2004: Background Material and Data on Programs within the Jurisdiction of the Committee on Ways and Means*, 18th ed. (Washington, DC: GPO, March 2004), appendix K.

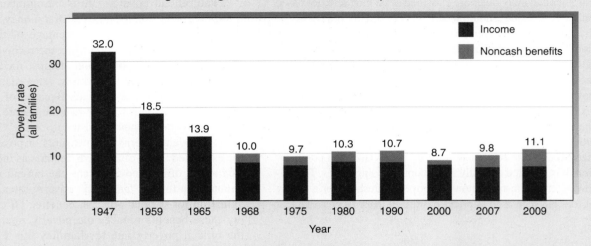

Exhibit 5

The Poverty Rate, 1947–2009

The official poverty rate of families fell sharply during the 1950s and 1960s, but it has remained near 10 percent since 1968. The shaded area of the bars shows the additional decline in the poverty rate when noncash benefits are counted as income. When the value of these noncash transfer benefits is added, the poverty rate ranges from 7 percent to 8 percent. This statistic remained unchanged throughout most of the 1968–2009 period.

Source: U.S. Department of Commerce, Characteristics of the Population below the Poverty Level: 1982, table 5; and http://www.census.gov/.

to the War on Poverty. It fell from 32 percent in 1947 to 13.9 percent in 1965. The downward trend continued for a few more years, reaching 10 percent in 1968. However, shortly after the War on Poverty was initiated, the downward trend in the poverty rate came to a halt. Since 1968, the poverty rate has fluctuated within a narrow band around the 10 percent level. In 2009, it was 11.1 percent—slightly higher than 1968. When noncash benefits like Medicaid and food stamps are counted as income, the poverty rate is lower, but the overall pattern is still much the same. The largely unchanged poverty rate during the last four decades is particularly remarkable when you consider that over this same time span, real income per person in the United States has approximately doubled.

Why wasn't the War on Poverty more effective? One reason is that means-tested income transfers generate two major side effects that reduce their effectiveness. ***First, transfer programs that significantly reduce the hardship of poverty also reduce the opportunity cost of choices that often lead to poverty.*** This factor is sometimes called the Samaritan's dilemma. To the extent that antipoverty programs reduce the negative effects of, for example, births by unmarried mothers, abandonment of children by fathers, dependence on drugs or alcohol, or dropping out of school, they inadvertently encourage people to make choices that result in these conditions. Of course, this is not the intent of the transfers, but nonetheless it is one of their side effects. In the short run, these secondary effects are probably not very important. Over the longer term, however, their negative consequences can be substantial.

Second, income-linked transfers reduce the incentive of low-income individuals to help themselves. When the size of transfers is linked to income, larger transfers tend to increase the implicit marginal tax rate imposed on the poor. The implicit marginal tax rate is the amount of additional (marginal) earnings that must be paid explicitly in taxes or—in the case of the poor—implicitly in the form of lower income supplements. The marginal tax rate determines the fraction of an additional dollar earned that an individual is permitted to keep, so it is an important determinant of the incentive to earn. Participants in the food stamp program, for example, have their food stamp benefits reduced by $30 for every $100

Samaritan's dilemma
The dilemma that occurs when assisting low-income citizens with transfers reduces the opportunity cost of choices that lead to poverty. Providing income transfers to the poor and discouraging behavior that leads to poverty are conflicting goals.

Implicit marginal tax rate
The amount of additional (marginal) earnings that must be paid explicitly in taxes or implicitly in the form of reduced income supplements. The marginal tax rate establishes the fraction of an additional dollar earned that an individual is permitted to keep, so it is an important determinant of the incentive to work and earn.

APPLICATIONS IN ECONOMICS

Implicit Marginal Tax Rates and the Incentive to Earn: A Real-World Example

High marginal tax rates reduce the incentive of people to earn and develop their skills. As low-income households increase their earnings, they will qualify for fewer and fewer benefits from food stamps, school lunch subsidies, Medicaid, and other means-tested transfer programs. As a result, the implicit marginal tax rates confronted by low-income households are often extremely high.

Exhibit 6 shows the implicit marginal tax rates facing a low-income mother with one child in West Virginia. Because state welfare programs vary, these numbers would be somewhat different for individuals living in other states (and households of different sizes and characteristics). But the pattern of the implicit marginal tax rates shown here is not atypical.

The exhibit shows the total transfer benefits the mother would receive and taxes she would owe at different levels of earned income. Her spendable income is calculated as her work earnings plus her benefits, minus her taxes. When she does not hold a job, and thus has zero earned income, she receives $8,976 in transfer benefits, which equals her spendable income. If she were to accept a part-time job earning $10,000 per year, her benefits would be reduced to $6,503 and she would now owe $765 in taxes, resulting in spendable income of $15,738.

Note how the implicit marginal tax rate rises with earnings. The combination of taxes and reductions in transfer benefits takes more than 40 percent of the increase in earnings

in the $5,000–$15,000 range. Here, the West Virginia mother gets to keep less than 60 percent of every dollar she earns. The implicit marginal tax rate peaks in the $15,000–$20,000 interval. In this range, the implicit marginal tax rate is 74 percent. Thus, additional earnings from employment in this range increase her spendable income by only 26 cents for every dollar earned. If you got to keep only 26 cents of every dollar you earned, how would this affect your incentive to work and develop your skills?

These numbers do not include the costs associated with her holding employment (such as transportation, clothing, and child care). If these work-related expenses summed to only 15 percent of earnings, this would mean that the combination of taxes, loss of transfers, and work-related expenses would take approximately 90 percent of her additional earnings in the $15,000–$20,000 range. Moreover, these numbers tend to understate the true work disincentives because other in-kind benefit programs, such as Medicaid and housing assistance, are not included in the calculations because they are difficult to quantify. However, they are also removed as earned income rises, compounding the work disincentives faced by transfer recipients. Clearly, high marginal tax rates like those of Exhibit 6 help explain why the transfer programs accompanying the War on Poverty were not very effective: The transfers reduced the incentive of those with low incomes to develop their skills and increase their earnings.

iStockphoto.com/sorendls

Earned Income from Work	Transfer Benefits	Income and Employment Taxes	Spendable Income	Implicit Marginal Tax Rate
$0	$8,976	$ 0	$ 8,976	
5,000	8,225	383	12,842	22.7%
10,000	6,503	765	15,738	42.1
15,000	4,955	1,420	18,535	44.1
20,000	1,914	2,072	19,842	73.9
25,000	1,115	2,697	23,419	28.5

Exhibit 6

The Effect of Transfer Benefits and Taxes on the Incentive of a West Virginia Mother with One Child to Earn Income (July 2007)

Source: Based on Anthony C. Gregory and J. Sebastian Leguizamon, "Quit Punishing the Working Poor: Reduce Work Disincentives in the Welfare System," in *Unleashing Capitalism: Why Prosperity Stops at the West Virginia Border and How to Fix It*, ed. Russell S. Sobel (Morgantown, WV: Public Policy Foundation of West Virginia, 2007).
Note: Transfer benefits include TANF, Earned Income Tax Credit, food stamps; taxes include Social Security, Medicare, and federal and state income taxes.

of income they earn. Consequently, every $100 of additional income leads to only a $70 increase in well-being (spendable net income) after the reduction in food stamp benefits is taken into account. When a person qualifies for several programs like food stamps, Medicaid, and housing benefits, the problem is compounded, and the combined implicit marginal tax rate can frequently exceed 50 or 60 percent. In some cases, the rate may exceed 100 percent. Under these circumstances, if recipients work, the money they make would actually reduce their spendable income. Because high implicit marginal tax rates reduce the incentive of poor families to work and earn, transfers often merely replace income that otherwise would have been earned. When this is the case, they add little or nothing to the *net* income of the poor. (See the Applications in Economics: "Implicit Marginal Tax Rates and the Incentive to Earn: A Real-World Example.")

ESTIMATING THE COSTS OF REDISTRIBUTION

The U.S. government has numerous income-transfer programs, including many that are unrelated to helping the poor. In 2010, income-transfers and subsidy programs intended to help various groups purchase food, housing, and health care summed to 15 percent of aggregate income.[5] As we discussed in Chapter 6, politicians will often be able to gain by proposing programs that provide concentrated benefits to readily identifiable groups (for example, farmers, senior citizens, or unemployed workers) while imposing a small personal cost on disparate groups like taxpayers and consumers in general. Because of this, the presence and size of transfer programs are not surprising.

Income transfers are also costly in terms of the economy's overall output level. The higher marginal tax rates needed to finance transfers and subsidies mean that taxpayers get to keep less of what they earn. Furthermore, recipients often qualify for larger transfers if their income is lower, which causes them to earn even less. Thus, transfer programs typically weaken the incentive of both taxpayer-donors and the subsidy recipients to work and earn. As a result, the cost of the transfers will be greater than the amount of income transferred. A study by economists Sam Allgood and Arthur Snow sought to measure the loss of output due to the lower supply of labor associated with higher marginal tax rates accompanying income transfers.[6] Allgood and Snow estimated that it costs between $1.26 and $3.22 in terms of lost output for every additional dollar redistributed from the top 60 percent of income recipients to the bottom 40 percent.

Helping transfer recipients achieve long-term well-being is also more difficult than it first appears. Competition for the transfers and subsidies will often erode much of the recipient's gain. See the Application in Economics: "Why Transfer Programs Will Not Help Their Intended Beneficiaries Very Much" for additional details about why this is the case.

INCOME INEQUALITY: SOME CONCLUDING THOUGHTS

Is there too much inequality in the United States? Should transfer programs be expanded or contracted? These are normative questions that positive economics cannot definitively answer. Economics can help identify and quantify the cost (in terms of lost output) and the expected effectiveness of alternative programs, but it can't make a judgment about whether that cost or amount is good or bad. Many people, including a good number of economists, would like to see income inequality reduced. This is a stated objective of many government

---

[5]http://www.bea.gov.
[6]See Sam Allgood and Arthur Snow, "The Marginal Cost of Raising Tax Revenue and Redistributing Income," *Journal of Political Economy* (December 1998). This study builds on earlier work by Edgar K. Browning and William Johnson, "The Trade-Off between Equality and Efficiency," *Journal of Political Economy* (April 1984), and Charles L. Ballard, "The Marginal Efficiency Cost of Redistribution," *American Economic Review* (December 1988).

programs. The progressive income tax system, the **Earned Income Tax Credit** (a tax credit that provides supplementary payments to workers with low incomes), and means-tested programs like food stamps, Medicaid, and housing subsidies are examples.

However, the political process is multidimensional. It represents a diverse set of forces, including powerful special-interest groups. Therefore, it shouldn't surprise you that the political record in this area, like others, is mixed. Social Security, the largest income-transfer program, redirects income toward the elderly, today a group with above-average levels of both income and wealth. Agriculture subsidies constitute another large transfer program; the bulk of these benefits go to large farmers with incomes well above the average. Another

Earned Income Tax Credit
A feature of the personal income tax system that provides supplementary payments to workers with low incomes.

APPLICATIONS IN ECONOMICS

Why Transfer Programs Will Not Help Their Intended Beneficiaries Very Much

As the data of this chapter show, the achievements of antipoverty transfer programs fell far short of the initial expectations. Indeed, the economic way of thinking would lead a person to believe that it's difficult to transfer income to a group of recipients in a way that will significantly improve their long-term well-being. The unintended consequences that alter people's incentives explain why this is true.

Governments must establish criteria to determine who should get the transfers, subsidies, and other political favors and who should not. Without these criteria, benefit programs would exhaust their budgets. Typically, governments require potential recipients to do something, own something, buy something, or be something in order to qualify for the transfer. However, as people take the steps necessary to qualify, they erode much of the benefit.

Consider the case in which the recipients have to do something (for example, fill out forms, take an exam, submit a detailed proposal, lobby government officials, endure delays, or contribute to selected political campaigns) in order to obtain the transfer. These actions are costly and will reduce the recipient's net gain. In some cases, almost all of the gain may be eroded. Perhaps a simple example will help illustrate this important point. Suppose the U.S. government decided to give away a $50 bill between 9 A.M. and 5 P.M. each weekday to anyone willing to show up at one of six teller windows at the U.S. Department of Treasury. Certainly, a line would emerge. How much time would people be willing to wait in the line? A person whose time was worth $5 per hour would be willing to spend up to 10 hours waiting in line for the $50. But it might take longer than 10 hours if there were enough other people, whose time was worth less, say $3 or $4 per hour. And everyone would find that the waiting consumed much of the value of the $50 transfer. If the government's objective is to make the recipients $50 richer, it will fail. In fact, some of those

waiting in line for the $50 bill will gain very little. For example, if the wait were 10 hours, the net benefit of a person with an opportunity cost of $4.90 would be only $1. So it is with real-world transfers. When you consider the cost of what has to be done for someone to qualify for the transfer, the net gain of the recipient is often small.

In other cases, the government will require recipients to own something (for example, land with an acreage allotment to grow wheat, a license to operate a taxicab, or a permit to sell in a restricted market) in order to qualify for a transfer or subsidy. Recipients will gain when programs like this are initiated or unexpectedly expanded. But once programs of this type are established, people will bid up the price of the asset needed to acquire the subsidy. The higher price of the asset, such as the taxicab license or the land with a wheat allotment, will capture the value of the expected future subsidy. Once this happens, the rate of return in the business or occupation (for example, farming or operating a taxicab) will be driven down to the normal level. The current recipients don't benefit from the subsidy program continuing at the expected benefit level. Essentially, they paid for the expected benefit of the subsidy when they purchased the asset needed to get it.

Interestingly, even though they don't benefit, current recipients will fight to keep the program going if it is threatened. Repealing (or reducing) the subsidies will be harmful because it will reduce the value of the asset they currently hold. This explains why eliminating farm subsidies, for example, is difficult even though the subsidies do not make farming more profitable for the current operators. Economist Gordon Tullock refers to this as the *transitional gains trap*, because once programs like these get started, they will be difficult to eliminate even though current recipients aren't benefiting from them.[1]

[1]See Gordon Tullock, "The Transitional Gains Trap," *Bell Journal of Economics* 6 (Autumn 1975): 671–78.

(continued)

Sometimes, recipients are required to purchase a good or service in order to qualify for a subsidy. For example, the Medicare and Medicaid programs subsidize health care purchases made by senior citizens and the poor. Several states provide educational subsidies for college tuition or the purchase of textbooks. As we discussed in Chapter 4, subsidizing the purchase of a good will increase its demand and lead to higher prices. As a result, some of the benefits of such subsidies will accrue to the suppliers rather than the purchasers. Again, the subsidized recipients will not gain as much as it might appear.

Finally, sometimes the government requires that recipients be something in order to qualify for the subsidy. Programs of this type are often intended to help protect people against the adverse effects of certain events such as unemployment or catastrophic storms. Unfortunately, the programs also encourage choices that increase the adverse effects of such events. For example, consider the impact of subsidized insurance premiums for those living in hurricane-prone areas. These subsidies reduce the owners' personal cost of rebuilding their properties after a hurricane. But the lower personal costs also encourage people to build in hurricane-prone areas. As more of them do so, the overall cost of damage from hurricanes increases. The secondary effects of unemployment insurance are much the same. The benefits paid to the unemployed will reduce the opportunity cost of continuing a job search while unemployed. As a result, periods of unemployment will be longer and the rate of unemployment higher than would have otherwise been the case.

Transfer programs can even exert an adverse impact on many of the intended beneficiaries. The Homestead Act of 1862 illustrates this point. Under this legislation, the federal government provided a land plot of 160 acres (later expanded to up to 640 acres in parts of the West) to settlers who staked their claim, built a house on the land, and stayed for five years. Many people were attracted by this opportunity, but it was not easy to survive in the early West, even with 160 acres. Thus, more than 60 percent of the land claims were abandoned before the five years were up.[2] In essence, this transfer program encouraged people to settle the land before it was economical to do so.

More recently, regulations imposed on two huge government-sponsored enterprises, Fannie Mae and Freddie Mac, forced them to extend more loans with little or no down payment to borrowers with low and moderate incomes. These regulatory subsidies were designed to help borrowers who could not qualify for conventional loans to nonetheless become homeowners. The results were much like those of the Homestead Act: high default rates, foreclosures, and financial troubles for many of the intended beneficiaries. See Special Topic 5, "The Crisis of 2008: Causes and Lessons for the Future," for additional details about housing regulations and their role in the crisis of 2008.

The ability of transfers to improve the well-being of a designated group is far more limited than is generally recognized. Transfer programs alter incentives and generate unintended consequences that erode some, if not most, of the benefits derived by the recipients. Thus, the net gains of the intended beneficiaries are often much less than they appear to be.

[2]Fred A. Shannon, "The Homestead Act and the Labor Surplus," *American Historical Review* 41 (July 1936): 637–51.

---

sizable share of government transfers is allocated to business interests, including many that are large and highly profitable. Thus, many of the income transfers are from those with modest incomes to those with incomes well above the average.

Finally, it is important to recognize that income in a market economy is not like manna from heaven. It is something people produce and earn by providing others with goods and services they are willing to pay for. The allocation of income reflects the choices of individuals with differing preferences, talents, educational levels, entrepreneurial skills, rate of saving, and so on. Wage differentials, profits, losses, and interest rates coordinate the choices of these vastly different individuals and bring them into harmony with one another. Income inequality is a natural outgrowth of this process. Indeed, policies that modify the process can generate perverse, counterproductive incentives.

When it comes to issues of fairness, some people argue that the process—the system, in other words—that generates the outcomes is more important than the actual result. Do all people in the economy have an opportunity to acquire education and training? Are people from all segments of society free to compete in business and labor markets? Do incomes reflect their choices, voluntary exchanges, and productive efforts? These questions are about opportunity, economic freedom, and how income is acquired. Many people believe that these things, rather than the income-distribution patterns that result from them, are the key elements of economic fairness.

Perhaps the following example will illustrate the difference between the process and pattern view. Suppose a million people purchase a $10 lottery ticket, and the proceeds are used to finance a $10 million jackpot for one person. This activity will clearly increase income inequality. But is it unfair? Those who adhere to the process view would stress that the outcome merely reflects the voluntary choices of participants who were well aware of the rules of the game prior to their purchasing a ticket. According to this view, it is the process rather than the outcome that is the primary determinant of fairness.

Economics provides insight into both the allocative role and sources of differences in income. It also indicates that it will be costly, in terms of lost output, to redistribute income through taxes and transfers. Of course, this does not reveal whether there is too much inequality or whether the government should play a larger or smaller role in the allocation of income. It does, however, enable us to address these normative issues in a more thoughtful way.

Looking Ahead

Income transfers are the focal point of many current policy issues, including Social Security and health care. The special topics in the final section of the book analyze this issue and other topics.

KEY POINTS

- In 2009, the bottom 20 percent of families earned 4.1 percent of aggregate income; the top 20 percent of families earned approximately twelve times that amount (48.2 percent). After taxes and transfers are taken into account, the top quintile of households earn nearly ten times the income of the bottom quintile.

- A substantial percentage of the inequality in annual income reflects differences in age, education, family size, marital status, number of earners in the family, and time worked. Young inexperienced workers, students, single-parent families, and retirees are overrepresented among those with low current incomes.

- Income inequality has risen during the last three decades. The following four factors contributed to this increase: (1) an increase in the proportion of both single-parent and dual-earner families, (2) an increase in earnings differentials on the basis of skill and education, (3) more "winner-take-all" markets, and (4) increases in the reported income of those in the top tax brackets due to lower marginal tax rates.

- The tracking of household income over time indicates that there is considerable movement of individuals both up and down the income spectrum. The data on the distribution of income at a particular point in time can be misleading because they do not reflect this movement up and down the income ladder.

- One-ninth of American families were officially classified as poor in 2009. Those living in poverty were generally younger, less educated, less likely to be working, and more likely to be living in families headed by a woman than those who were not poor. There is considerable movement both into and out of poverty. A relatively small proportion of families constitute the long-term poor.

- During the last several decades, income transfers—including means-tested transfers—have expanded rapidly both in real dollars and as a share of personal income. As a weapon against poverty, transfers have been largely ineffective. Even though per capita income more than doubled between 1965 and 2009, there was little reduction in the overall poverty rate during this period.

- Income transfers large enough to improve the economic status of the poor will (1) encourage behavior that increases the risk of poverty and/or (2) create high implicit marginal tax rates that reduce the recipient's incentive to earn.

- Positive economics cannot determine how much inequality should be present. The nature of the income-generating process as well as the pattern of income distribution is relevant to the issue of fairness.

CRITICAL ANALYSIS QUESTIONS

1. Do you think the current distribution of income in the United States is too unequal? Why or why not? What criteria do you think should be used to judge the fairness of the distribution of income? Is the final outcome more important than the process that generates the income?

2. *Is annual money income a good measure of economic status? Is a family with an $80,000 annual income able to purchase twice the quantity of goods and services as a family with $40,000 of annual income? Is the standard of living of the $80,000 family twice as high as that of the $40,000 family? Discuss.

3. What is income mobility? If there is substantial income mobility in a society, how does this influence the importance of income distribution data?

4. *Consider a table such as Exhibit 3 in which the family income of parents is grouped by quintiles down the first column, and that of their offspring is grouped by quintiles across the other columns. If there were no intergenerational mobility in this country, what pattern of numbers would appear in the table? If the nation had attained complete equality of opportunity, what pattern of numbers would emerge? Explain.

5. Do individuals have a property right to income they acquire from market transactions? Is it a proper function of government to tax some people in order to provide benefits to others? Why or why not? Discuss.

6. *Because income transfers to the poor typically increase the implicit marginal tax rate they confront, does a $1,000 transfer payment necessarily increase the income of poor recipients by $1,000? Why or why not?

7. *Sue is a single parent with two children. She is considering a part-time job that pays $800 per month. She is currently drawing monthly cash benefits of $300, food stamp benefits of $100, and Medicaid benefits valued at $80. If she accepts the job, she will be liable for employment taxes of $56 per month and lose all transfer benefits. What is Sue's implicit marginal tax rate for this job?

8. What groups are overrepresented among those with relatively low incomes? Do the poor in the United States generally stay poor? Why or why not?

9. Some people argue that taxes exert little effect on people's incentive to earn income. Suppose you were required to pay a tax rate of 50 percent on all money income you earn while in school. Would this affect your employment? How might you minimize the personal effects of this tax?

10. Large income transfers are targeted toward the elderly, farmers, and the unemployed, regardless of their economic condition. Why do you think this is so? Do you think there would be less income inequality if the government levied higher taxes in order to make larger income transfers? Why or why not?

11. The outcome of a state lottery game is certainly a very unequal distribution of the prize income. Some players are made very rich, whereas others lose their money. Using this example, discuss whether the fairness of the process or the fairness of the outcome is more important, and how they differ.

12. "Means-tested transfer payments reduce the current poverty rate. However, they also create an incentive structure that discourages self-sufficiency and self-improvement. Thus, they tend to increase the future poverty rate. Welfare programs essentially purchase a lower poverty rate today in exchange for a higher poverty rate in the future." Evaluate this statement.

13. Was the poverty rate increasing or decreasing prior to the War on Poverty initiated by the Johnson administration? As income-transfer programs accompanying the War on Poverty increased beginning in the latter half of the 1960s, what happened to the poverty rate?

14. Suppose one family has $100,000 whereas another has only $20,000. Is this outcome fair? What is your initial reaction? Compare and contrast your views depending on the following:
    a. The family with the higher income has both a husband and wife working, whereas the other family has chosen for the wife to remain home with the children rather than work in the labor force.
    b. The family with the higher income is headed by a person who completed a college degree, whereas the other family is headed by someone who dropped out of high school.
    c. The family with the higher income derived most of its income from the farm subsidy program.
    d. The family with the higher income received it as an inheritance from parents who just died.

*Asterisk denotes questions for which answers are given in Appendix B.

International Economics

The volume of international trade has grown dramatically in recent decades. Although the same general principles apply to both domestic and international trade, the latter also involves the exchange of one currency for another. Thus, this part will analyze the impact of both international trade and the operation of the foreign exchange market.

PART

4

The world is becoming a global village.

CHAPTER

16

Gaining from International Trade

CHAPTER FOCUS

- How has the volume of international trade changed in recent decades?

- Under what conditions can a nation gain from international trade?

- What effects do trade restrictions have on an economy?

- How have open economies performed relative to those that are more closed?

- What accounts for the political popularity of trade restraints?

- Do trade restrictions create jobs? Does trade with low-wage countries depress wage rates in high-wage countries like the United States?

The evidence is overwhelmingly persuasive that the massive increase in world competition—a consequence of broadening trade flows—has fostered markedly higher standards of living for almost all countries who have participated in cross-border trade. I include most especially the United States.

—*Alan Greenspan*[1]

[1]Alan Greenspan, speech before the Alliance for the Commonwealth Conference on International Business (Boston, Massachusetts, June 2, 1999).

We live in a shrinking world. Spurred by cost reductions in transportation and communications, the volume of international trade has grown rapidly in recent decades. The breakfast of many Americans includes bananas from Honduras, coffee from Brazil, or hot chocolate made from Nigerian cocoa beans. Americans often drive a car produced by a Japanese or European manufacturer that consumes gasoline refined from petroleum extracted in Saudi Arabia or Venezuela. Similarly, many Americans work for companies that sell a substantial number of their products to foreigners. Why do people engage in international trade? The expectation of gain provides the answer. If both parties did not expect to gain, they would not agee to the exchange.

iStockphoto.com/nicoolay

THE TRADE SECTOR OF THE UNITED STATES

As Exhibit 1 illustrates, the size of the trade sector of the United States has grown rapidly during the last several decades. In 1960, total exports of goods and services accounted for 3.6 percent of the U.S. economy, whereas imports summed to 4.1 percent. By 1980, both exports and imports were approximately 6 percent of the economy. In 2010, exports accounted for 12.5 percent of total output, while imports summed to 16.1 percent. Thus, U.S. international trade (exports + imports) in goods and services has more than doubled as a share of the economy since 1980 and more than tripled since 1960.

Who are the major trading partners of Americans? Exhibit 2 shows the share of U.S. trade (exports + imports) with each of its ten leading trading partners. These ten countries account for approximately two-thirds of the total volume of U.S. trade. Canada, China, Mexico, and Japan are the four largest trading partners of Americans. Nearly half of all

---

The Growth of the Trade Sector in the United States: 1960–2010   Exhibit 1

During the past several decades, international trade has persistently risen as a share of GDP. Imports of goods and services as a share of GDP rose from 4 percent in 1960 to 6 percent in 1980 and 16 percent in 2010. Similarly, exports increased from 4 percent of GDP in 1960 to 6 percent in 1980 and almost 13 percent in 2010.

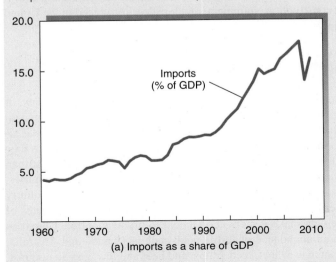

(a) Imports as a share of GDP

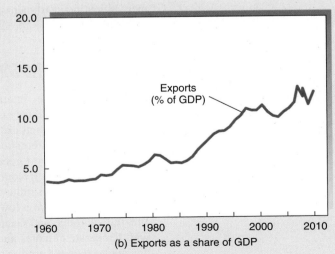

(b) Exports as a share of GDP

Source: http://www.economagic.com. The figures are based on data for real imports, exports, and GDP.

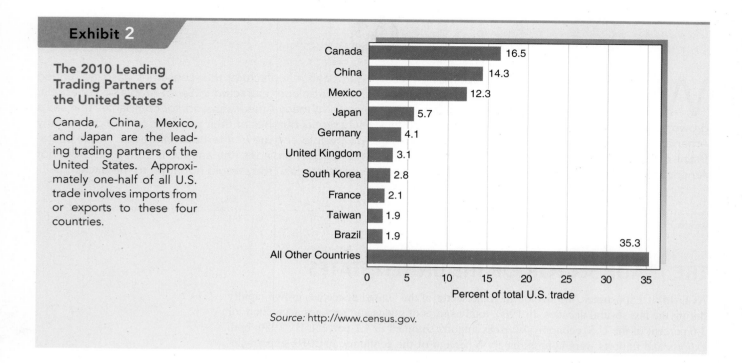

Exhibit 2

The 2010 Leading Trading Partners of the United States

Canada, China, Mexico, and Japan are the leading trading partners of the United States. Approximately one-half of all U.S. trade involves imports from or exports to these four countries.

	Percent of total U.S. trade
Canada	16.5
China	14.3
Mexico	12.3
Japan	5.7
Germany	4.1
United Kingdom	3.1
South Korea	2.8
France	2.1
Taiwan	1.9
Brazil	1.9
All Other Countries	35.3

Source: http://www.census.gov.

U.S. trade is with these four countries. The United States also conducts a substantial volume of trade with the nations of the European Union, particularly Germany, the United Kingdom, and France.

What are the leading imports and exports of the United States? Capital goods like automobiles, computers, semiconductors, telecommunications equipment, and industrial machines are bought and sold in worldwide markets. The United States both imports and exports substantial quantities of these goods. Civilian aircraft, electrical equipment, chemicals, and plastics are also among the leading products the United States exports. Crude oil, textiles, toys, sporting goods, and pharmaceuticals are major products it imports.

Clearly, the impact of international trade differs across industries. The majority of the television sets, diamonds, shoes, DVD players, and motorcycles consumed in the United States are imported. In contrast, a large proportion of the aircraft, power-generating equipment, scientific instruments, construction equipment, and fertilizers produced in the United States are exported to foreigners.

GAINS FROM SPECIALIZATION AND TRADE

Comparative advantage
The ability to produce a good at a lower opportunity cost than others can produce it. Relative costs determine comparative advantage.

Like domestic trade, international trade promotes growth and prosperity. The law of comparative advantage explains why a group of individuals, regions, or nations can gain from specialization and exchange. International trade leads to mutual gains because it allows residents of different countries to (1) specialize in the production of those things they do best, and (2) import goods foreign producers are willing to supply at a lower cost than domestic producers. Resources and labor-force skills differ substantially across countries, and these differences influence costs. A good that is quite costly to produce in one country might be produced at a lower cost in another. For example, the warm, moist climates of Brazil, Colombia, and Guatemala make it more economical to produce coffee. Countries with temperate climates and an abundance of fertile land, such as Canada and Australia, are able to produce products such as wheat, feed grains, and beef at a low cost. In contrast, land is scarce in Japan, a nation with a highly skilled labor force. The Japanese, therefore, specialize in manufacturing, using their comparative advantage to produce cameras, automobiles, and electronic products for export. With international trade, the residents of different countries can gain by specializing in the production of goods they can produce economically. They can then sell those goods in the world market and use the proceeds to import other goods that are expensive to produce domestically.

We will take the time to illustrate the principle in detail. To keep things simple, let's consider a case involving only two countries, the United States and Japan, and two products, food and clothing. Furthermore, let's assume that labor is the only resource used to produce these products. In addition, because we want to illustrate that gains from trade are nearly always possible, we are going to assume that Japan has an **absolute advantage**— that the Japanese workers are more efficient than the Americans—at producing both food and clothing. **Exhibit 3** illustrates this situation. Perhaps due to their prior experience or higher skill levels, Japanese workers can produce three units of food per day, compared with only two units per day for U.S. workers. Similarly, Japanese workers are able to produce nine units of clothing per day, compared with one unit of clothing per day for U.S. workers.

Can two countries gain from trade if one of them can produce both goods with fewer resources? The answer is "Yes." As long as the *relative* production costs of the two goods differ between Japan and the United States, gains from trade will be possible. Consider what would happen if the United States shifted three workers from the clothing industry to the food industry. This reallocation of labor would allow the United States to expand its food output by six units (two units per worker), while clothing output would decline by three units (one unit per worker). Suppose Japan reallocates labor in the opposite direction. When Japan moves one worker from the food industry to the clothing industry, Japanese clothing production expands by nine units, while food output declines by three units. The exhibit shows that this reallocation of labor *within* the two countries has increased their joint output by three units of food and six units of clothing.

Absolute advantage
A situation in which a nation, as the result of its previous experience and/or natural endowments, can produce more of a good (with the same amount of resources) than another nation can.

Exhibit 3

Gains from Specialization and Trade

Columns 1 and 2 indicate the daily output of either food or clothing of each worker in the United States and Japan. If the United States moves three workers from the clothing industry to the food industry, it can produce six more units of food and three fewer units of clothing. Similarly, if Japan moves one worker from food to clothing, clothing output will increase by nine units, while food output will decline by three units. With this reallocation of labor, the United States and Japan are able to increase their aggregate output of both food (three additional units) and clothing (six additional units).

COUNTRY	OUTPUT PER WORKER DAY		POTENTIAL CHANGE IN OUTPUT[a]	
	FOOD (1)	CLOTHING (2)	FOOD (3)	CLOTHING (4)
United States	2	1	+6	−3
Japan	3	9	−3	+9
Change in Total Output			+3	+6

© Cengage Learning 2013

[a]Change in output if the United States shifts three workers from the clothing to the food industry and if Japan shifts one worker from the food to the clothing industry.

The source of this increase in output is straightforward: Aggregate output expands because the reallocation of labor permits each country to specialize more fully in the production of the goods it can produce at a *relatively* low cost. Our old friend, the opportunity-cost concept, reveals the low-cost producer of each good. If Japanese workers produce one additional unit of food, they sacrifice the production of three units of clothing. Therefore, in Japan the opportunity cost of one unit of food is three units of clothing. Conversely, one unit of food in the United States can be produced at an opportunity cost of only a half-unit of clothing. American workers are therefore the low-opportunity-cost producers of food, even though they cannot produce as much food per day as the Japanese workers. Simultaneously, Japan is the low-opportunity-cost producer of clothing. The opportunity cost of producing a unit of clothing in Japan is only a third of a unit of food, compared with two units of food in the United States. The reallocation of labor illustrated in Exhibit 3 expanded joint output because it moved resources in both countries toward areas where they had a comparative advantage.

To reiterate: As long as the relative costs of producing the two goods differ in the two countries, gains from specialization and trade will be possible. Both countries will find it cheaper to trade for goods they can produce only at a high opportunity cost. For example, both countries will gain if the United States trades food to Japan for clothing at a trading ratio greater than one unit of food to one half-unit of clothing (the U.S. opportunity cost of food) but less than one unit of food to three units of clothing (the Japanese opportunity cost of food). Any trading ratio between these two extremes will permit the United States to acquire clothing more cheaply than it could be produced within the country and simultaneously permit Japan to acquire food more cheaply than it could be produced domestically.

HOW TRADE EXPANDS CONSUMPTION POSSIBILITIES

Because trade permits nations to expand their joint output, it also allows each nation to expand its consumption possibilities. The production possibilities concept can be used to illustrate this point. Suppose that there were 200 million workers in the United States and 50 million in Japan. Given these figures and the productivity of workers indicated in Exhibit 3, Exhibit 4 presents the production possibilities curves for the two countries. If the United States used all of its 200 million workers in the food industry, it could produce 400 million units of food per day—two units per worker—and zero units of clothing (N). Alternatively, if the United States used all its workers to produce clothing, daily output would be 200 million units of clothing and no food (M). Intermediate output combinations along the production possibilities line (MN) between these two extreme points also could be achievable. For example, the United States could produce 150 million units of clothing and 100 million units of food (US_1).

Part (b) of Exhibit 4 illustrates the production possibilities of the 50 million Japanese workers. Japan could produce 450 million units of clothing and no food (R), 150 million units of food and no clothing (S), or various intermediate combinations, like 225 million units of clothing and 75 million units of food (J_1). The slope of the production possibilities constraint reflects the opportunity cost of food relative to clothing. Because Japan is the high-opportunity-cost producer of food, its production possibilities constraint is steeper than the constraint for the United States.

In the absence of trade, the consumption of each country is constrained by its own production possibilities. Trade, however, expands the consumption possibilities of both. As we previously said, both countries can gain from specialization if the United States trades food to Japan at a price greater than one unit of food equals one half-unit of clothing but less than one unit of food equals three units of clothing. Suppose that they agree on an intermediate price of one unit of food equals one unit of clothing. As part (a) of Exhibit 5 shows, when the United States specializes in the production of food (where it has a comparative advantage) and trades food for clothing (at the price ratio where one unit of food equals one unit of clothing), it can consume along the line ON. If the United States insisted on self-sufficiency, it would be restricted to consumption possibilities like US_1 (100 million units of food and 150 million units of clothing) along its production possibilities constraint

Exhibit 4

The Production Possibilities of the United States and Japan before Specialization and Trade

Here, we illustrate the daily production possibilities of a U.S. labor force with 200 million workers and a Japanese labor force with 50 million workers, given the cost of producing food and clothing presented in Exhibit 3. In the absence of trade, consumption possibilities will be restricted to points such as US_1 in the United States and J_1 in Japan along the production possibilities curve of each country.

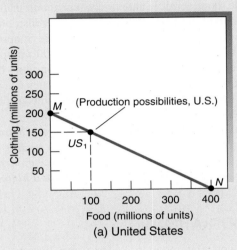

(a) United States

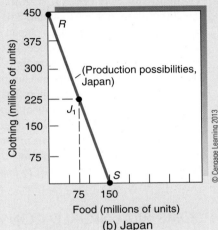

(b) Japan

© Cengage Learning 2013

Exhibit 5

Consumption Possibilities with Trade

The consumption possibilities of a country can be expanded with specialization and trade. If the United States can trade one unit of clothing for one unit of food, it can specialize in the production of food and consume along the ON line (rather than its original production possibilities constraint, MN). Similarly, when Japan is able to trade one unit of clothing for one unit of food, it can specialize in the production of clothing and consume any combination along the line RT. For example, with specialization and trade, the United States can increase its consumption from US_1 to US_2, gaining 50 million units of clothing and 100 million units of food. Simultaneously, Japan can increase consumption from J_1 to J_2, a gain of 125 million units of food and 25 million units of clothing.

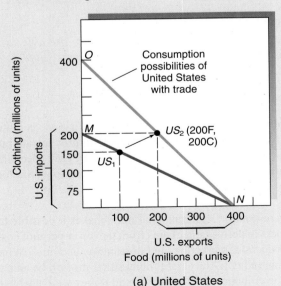

(a) United States

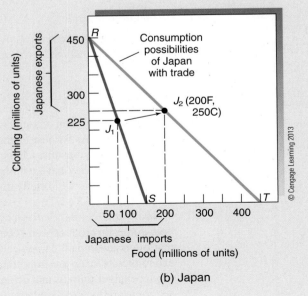

(b) Japan

© Cengage Learning 2013

of *MN*. With trade, however, the United States can achieve a combination like *US*$_2$ (200 million units of food and 200 million units of clothing) along the line *ON*. Trade permits the United States to expand its consumption of both goods.

Simultaneously, Japan is able to expand its consumption of both goods when it is able to trade clothing for food at the one-to-one price ratio. As part (b) of Exhibit 5 illustrates, Japan can specialize in the production of clothing and consume along the constraint *RT* when it can trade one unit of clothing for one unit of food. Without trade, consumption in Japan would be limited to points like *J*$_1$ (75 million units of food and 225 million units of clothing) along the line *RS*. With trade, however, it is able to consume combinations like *J*$_2$ (200 million units of food and 250 million units of clothing) along the constraint *RT*.

Look what happens when Japan specializes in clothing and the United States specializes in food. Japan can produce 450 million units of clothing, export 200 million to the United States (for 200 million units of food), and still have 250 million units of clothing remaining for domestic consumption. Simultaneously, the United States can produce 400 million units of food, export 200 million to Japan (for 200 million units of clothing), and still have 200 million units of food left for domestic consumption.

The implications of the law of comparative advantage are clear: Trade between nations will lead to an expansion in total output and mutual gain for each trading partner when each country specializes in the production of goods it can produce at a relatively low cost and uses the proceeds to buy goods that it could produce only at a high cost.

SOME REAL-WORLD CONSIDERATIONS

To keep things simple, we ignored the potential importance of transportation costs, which, of course, reduce the potential gains from trade. Sometimes transportation and other transaction costs, both real and artificially imposed, exceed the potential for mutual gain. In this case, exchange does not occur.

We also assumed that the cost of producing each good was constant in each country. This is seldom the case. Beyond some level of production, the opportunity cost of producing a good will often increase as a country produces more and more of it. Rising marginal costs as the output of a good expands will limit the degree to which a country will specialize in the production of a good. This situation would be depicted by a production possibilities curve that was convex, or bowed out from the origin. In a case like this, there will still be gains from trade, but generally such a situation won't lead to one country completely specializing in the production of the good.

keys to economic prosperity

International Trade

When people are permitted to engage freely in international trade, they are able to achieve higher income levels and living standards than would otherwise be possible.

Like trade within a country, trade between people living in different nations is mutually beneficial. As we just explained, the trading partners will be able to produce a larger joint output and consume a larger, more diverse bundle of goods when they each specialize in areas where they have a comparative advantage. Open markets also lead to gains from other sources. We will briefly discuss three of them.

1. More gains from large-scale production. International trade makes it possible for both domestic producers and consumers to derive larger gains from the lower per-unit costs that often accompany large-scale production, marketing, and distribution activities. When economies of scale are important in an industry, successful domestic firms will be able to produce larger outputs and achieve lower unit costs than they would if they were unable to sell their products internationally. This is particularly important for firms located in small countries. For example, textile manufacturers in Malaysia, Taiwan, and South Korea would face much higher per-unit costs if they could not sell abroad because the domestic markets of these countries are too small to support large-scale production. There simply aren't enough buyers. However, if the firms can access the world market, where there are many more buyers, they can operate on a large scale and compete quite effectively.

Domestic consumers also benefit because international trade often makes it possible for them to acquire goods at lower prices from large-scale producers in other countries. The aircraft industry vividly illustrates this point. Given the huge design and engineering costs it takes to produce a single jet, no firm would be able to produce them economically if it weren't able to sell them abroad. Because of international trade, however, consumers around the world are able to purchase planes economically from large-scale producers like Boeing, which is based in the United States.

2. Gains from more competitive markets. International trade promotes competition and encourages production efficiency and innovation. Competition from abroad keeps domestic producers on their toes and gives them a strong incentive to improve the quality of their products.

International trade also allows technologies and innovative ideas developed in one country to be disseminated to others. In many cases, local entrepreneurs will emulate production procedures and products that have been successful in other places and even further improve or adapt them for local markets. Dynamic competition of this type is an important source of growth and prosperity, particularly for less-developed countries (LDCs).

3. More pressure to adopt sound institutions. Not only do firms in open economies face more intense competition, so, too, do their governments. The gains from trade and the prosperity that results from free trade motivate political officials to establish sound institutions and adopt constructive policies. If they do not, both labor and capital will move toward more favorable environments. For example, neither domestic nor foreign investors will want to put their funds in countries characterized by hostile business conditions, monetary instability, legal uncertainty, high taxes, and inferior public services. When labor and capital are free to move elsewhere, implementing government policies that penalize success and undermine productive activities becomes more costly. This aspect of free trade is generally overlooked, but it may well be one of its most beneficial attributes.[2]

SUPPLY, DEMAND, AND INTERNATIONAL TRADE

Like other things, international trade can be analyzed within the supply and demand framework. An analysis of supply and demand in international markets can show us how trade influences prices and output in domestic markets.

Consider the market for a good that U.S. producers are able to supply at a low cost. Using soybeans as an example, **Exhibit 6** illustrates the relationship between the domestic and world markets. The price of soybeans is determined by the forces of supply and demand in the world market. In an open economy, domestic producers are free to sell and domestic consumers are free to buy the product at the world market price (P_w). At this price, U.S. producers will supply Q_p, and U.S. consumers will purchase Q_c. Reflecting their low cost (comparative advantage), U.S. soybean producers will export $Q_p - Q_c$ units at the world market price.

Let's compare this open-economy outcome with the outcome that would occur in the absence of trade. If U.S. producers were not allowed to export soybeans, the domestic price would be determined by the domestic supply (S_d) and demand (D_d) only. A lower "no-trade" price (P_n) would emerge.

---

[2]For evidence that trade openness helps improve the institutional quality of a country, see International Monetary Fund, "Building Institutions," *IMF World Economic Outlook* (September 2005).

Exhibit 6

Producer Benefits from Exports

The price of soybeans and other internationally traded commodities is determined by the forces of supply and demand in the world market (b). If U.S. soybean producers are prohibited from selling to foreigners, the domestic price will be P_n (a). Free trade permits the U.S. soybean producers to sell Q_p units at the higher world price (P_w). The quantity $Q_p - Q_c$ is the amount U.S. producers export. Compared with the no-trade situation, the producers' gain from the higher price ($P_w bc P_n$) exceeds the cost imposed on domestic consumers ($P_w ac P_n$) by the triangle abc.

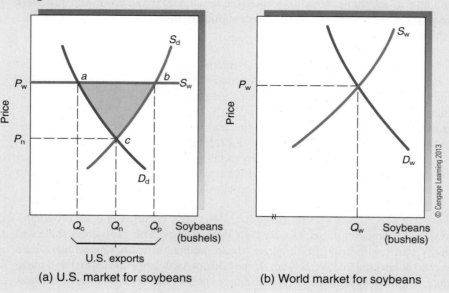

(a) U.S. market for soybeans

(b) World market for soybeans

© Cengage Learning 2013

Who are the winners and losers as the result of free trade in soybeans? Clearly, soybean producers gain. Free trade allows domestic producers to sell a larger quantity (Q_p rather than Q_n). As a result, the net revenues of soybean producers will rise by $P_w bc P_n$. In contrast, domestic consumers of soybeans will have to pay a higher price under free trade. Soybean consumers will lose (1) because they have to pay P_w rather than P_n for the Q_c units they purchase, and (2) because they lose the consumer surplus on the $Q_n - Q_c$ units now purchased at the higher price. Thus, free trade imposes a net cost of $P_w ac P_n$ on consumers. As you can see in Exhibit 6, however, the gains of soybean producers outweigh the losses to the consumers by the triangle abc. In other words, free trade leads to a net welfare gain.

This exporting example makes it seem like free trade benefits producers relative to consumers, but this ignores the secondary effects: If foreigners do not sell goods to Americans, they will not have the purchasing power necessary to purchase goods from Americans. U.S. imports—the purchase of goods from low-cost foreign producers—provide foreigners with the dollar purchasing power necessary to buy U.S. exports. In turn, the lower prices in the import-competitive markets will benefit the U.S. consumers who appeared at first glance to be harmed by the higher prices (compared with the no-trade situation) in export markets.

Using shoes as an example, **Exhibit 7** illustrates the situation when the United States is a net importer. In the absence of trade, the price of shoes in the domestic market would be P_n, the intersection of the domestic supply and demand curves. However, the world price of shoes is P_w. In an open economy, many U.S. consumers would take advantage of the low shoe prices available from foreign producers. At the lower world price, U.S. consumers would purchase Q_c units of shoes, importing $Q_c - Q_p$ from foreign producers.

Compared with the no-trade situation, free trade in shoes results in lower prices and greater domestic consumption. The lower prices lead to a net consumer gain of $P_n ab P_w$. Domestic producers lose $P_n ac P_w$ in the form of lower sales prices and reductions in output. However, the net gain of the shoe consumers exceeds the net loss of producers by abc.

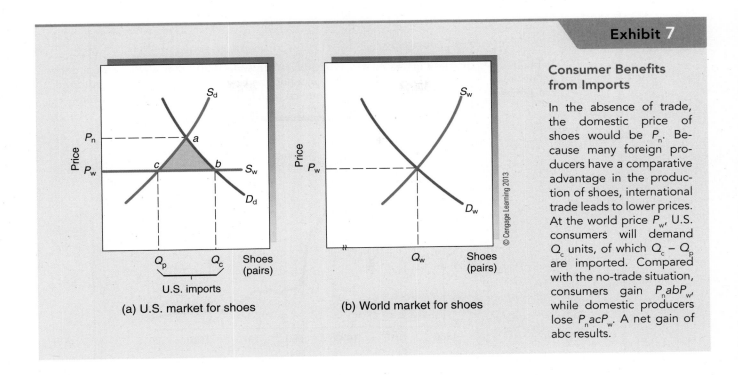

(a) U.S. market for shoes

(b) World market for shoes

Exhibit 7

Consumer Benefits from Imports

In the absence of trade, the domestic price of shoes would be P_n. Because many foreign producers have a comparative advantage in the production of shoes, international trade leads to lower prices. At the world price P_w, U.S. consumers will demand Q_c units, of which $Q_c - Q_p$ are imported. Compared with the no-trade situation, consumers gain $P_n abP_w$, while domestic producers lose $P_n acP_w$. A net gain of abc results.

International competition will direct resources toward those areas where they have a comparative advantage. If domestic producers have a comparative advantage in the production of a good—if they are a low opportunity cost producer, they will be able to compete effectively in the world market and profit from the export of goods to foreigners. In turn, the exports will generate the purchasing power necessary to buy goods that foreigners can supply more economically.

THE ECONOMICS OF TRADE RESTRICTIONS

Despite the potential benefits of free trade, almost all nations have erected trade barriers. Tariffs, quotas, and exchange rate controls are the most commonly used trade-restricting devices. Let's consider how various types of trade restrictions affect the economy.

THE ECONOMICS OF TARIFFS

A **tariff** is a tax on imports from foreign countries. As **Exhibit 8** shows, average tariff rates of between 30 percent and 50 percent of product value were often levied on products imported to the United States prior to 1945. The notorious Smoot-Hawley Tariff Act of 1930 pushed the average tariff rate upward to 60 percent. Many economists believe that this legislation contributed significantly to the length and severity of the Great Depression. During the past 70 years, however, tariff rates in the United States have declined substantially. In 2010, the average tariff rate on imported goods was only 3.5 percent.

Exhibit 9 shows the impact of a tariff on automobiles. In the absence of a tariff, the world market price of P_w would prevail in the domestic market. At that price, U.S. consumers purchase Q_1 units. Domestic producers supply Q_{d1}, while foreigners supply $Q_1 - Q_{d1}$ units to the U.S. market. When the United States levies a tariff, t, on automobiles, Americans can no longer buy cars at the world price. U.S. consumers now have to pay $P_w + t$ to purchase an automobile from foreigners. At that price, domestic consumers demand Q_2 units (Q_{d2} supplied by domestic producers and $Q_2 - Q_{d2}$ supplied by foreigners). The tariff results in a higher domestic price and lower level of domestic consumption.

The tariff benefits domestic producers and the government at the expense of consumers. Because domestic producers don't have to pay the tariff, they will expand their output

Tariff
A tax levied on goods imported into a country.

Exhibit 8

How High Are U.S. Tariffs?

Tariff rates in the United States spiked up sharply in the early 1930s, then declined during the period from 1935 to 1950. After rising slightly during the late 1950s, they have trended downward since 1960. In 2010, the average tariff rate on merchandise imports was 3.5 percent.

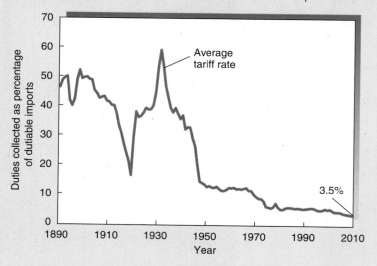

Source: http://dataweb.usitc.gov/scripts/AVE.PDF.

Exhibit 9

The Impact of a Tariff

Here, we illustrate the impact of a tariff on automobiles. In the absence of the tariff, the world price of automobiles is P_w. U.S. consumers purchase Q_1 units (Q_{d1} from domestic producers plus $Q_1 - Q_{d1}$ from foreign producers). The tariff makes it more costly for Americans to purchase automobiles from foreigners. Imports decline and the domestic price increases. Higher prices reduce consumer surplus by the areas $S + U + T + V$. Producers gain the area S, and the tariff generates T tax revenues for the government. The areas U and V are deadweight losses. Consumers lose the surplus associated with these two areas, but producers and the government don't gain it.

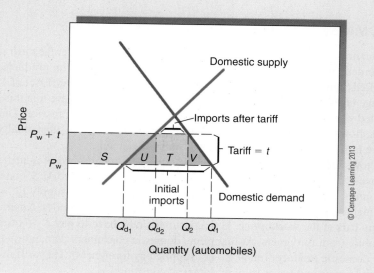

© Cengage Learning 2013

in response to the higher (protected) market price. In effect, the tariff acts as a subsidy to domestic producers. Domestic producers gain the area *S* (Exhibit 9) in the form of additional net revenues. The tariff raises revenues equal to the area *T* for the government. The areas *U* and *V* represent costs imposed on consumers and resource suppliers that do not benefit the government. Simply put, *U* and *V* represent *deadweight losses*: consumer and producer surpluses that could have been gained if the tariff hadn't been imposed.

As a result of the tariff, resources that could have been used to produce other U.S. goods more efficiently (compared with producing them abroad) are diverted to automobile production. Ultimately, we end up producing fewer products in areas where we have a comparative advantage and more products in areas where we are a high-cost producer. Because of this, potential gains from specialization and trade will go unrealized. In addition, most nations, including the United States, impose higher tariffs on some goods than others. This encourages producers in specific industries to lobby for higher tariffs on goods they produce. This diverts resources away from production and toward plunder, which also reduces the overall size of the economic pie.

THE ECONOMICS OF QUOTAS

An **import quota**, like a tariff, is designed to restrict foreign goods and protect domestic industries from foreign competition. A quota places a ceiling on the amount of a product that can be imported during a given period (typically a year). The United States imposes quotas on several products, including brooms, shoes, sugar, dairy products, and peanuts. For example, since 1953, the United States has imposed an annual peanut quota that in 2011 limited imports to 105.8 million pounds, about three-tenths of a pound per American.

Using peanuts as an example, **Exhibit 10** illustrates the impact of a quota. If there were no trade restraints, the domestic price of peanuts would be equal to the world market

Import quota
A specific limit or maximum quantity (or value) of a good permitted to be imported into a country during a given period.

Exhibit 10

The Impact of a Quota

Here, we illustrate the impact of a quota, such as the one the United States imposes on peanuts. The world market price of peanuts is P_w. If there were no trade restraints, the domestic price would also be P_w, and the domestic consumption would be Q_1. Domestic producers would supply Q_{d1} units, while $Q_1 - Q_{d1}$ would be imported. A quota limiting imports to $Q_2 - Q_{d2}$ would push up the domestic price to P_2. At the higher price, the amount supplied by domestic producers increases to Q_{d2}. Consumers lose the sum of the area $S + U + T + V$, while domestic producers gain the area S. In contrast with tariffs, quotas generate no revenue for the government. The area T goes to foreign producers, who are granted permission to sell in the U.S. market.

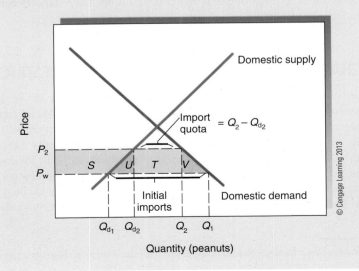

© Cengage Learning 2013

price (P_w). Under those circumstances, Americans would purchase Q_1 units. At the price P_w, domestic producers would supply Q_{d1}, and the amount $Q_1 - Q_{d1}$ would be imported from foreign producers.

Now consider what happens when a quota limits imports to $Q_2 - Q_{d2}$, a quantity well below the free-trade level of imports. Because the quota reduces the foreign supply of peanuts to the domestic market, the price of the quota-protected product increases (to P_2). At the higher price, U.S. consumers will reduce their purchases to Q_2, and domestic producers will happily expand their production to Q_{d2}. With regard to the welfare of consumers, the impact of a quota is similar to that of a tariff. Consumers lose the area $S + U + T + V$ in the form of higher prices and the loss of consumer surplus. Similarly, domestic producers gain the area S, while the areas U and V represent deadweight losses in the form of reductions in consumer surplus, gains that buyers would have derived in the absence of the quota.

While the adverse impact of a quota on consumer welfare is similar to that of a tariff, there is a big difference with regard to the area T. Under a tariff, the U.S. government would collect revenues equal to T, representing the tariff rate multiplied by the number of units imported. With a quota, however, these revenues will go to foreign producers, who are granted licenses (quotas) to sell various amounts in the U.S. market. Clearly, this right to sell at a premium price (because the domestic price exceeds the world market price) is extremely valuable. Thus, foreign producers will compete for the permits. They will hire lobbyists, make political contributions, and engage in other rent-seeking activities in an effort to secure the right to sell at a premium price in the U.S. market.

In many ways, quotas are more harmful than tariffs. With a quota, foreign producers are prohibited from selling additional units regardless of how much lower their costs are relative to those of domestic producers. In contrast to a tariff, a quota brings in no revenue for the government. Whereas a tariff transfers revenue from U.S. consumers to the Treasury, quotas transfer these revenues to foreign producers. Rewarding domestic producers with higher prices and foreign producers with valuable import permits will create *two* interest groups with a strong incentive to lobby for a quota. As a result, lifting the quota will often be more difficult than lowering a tariff would be.

In addition to tariffs and quotas, governments sometimes use regulations and political pressure to restrain foreign competition. For example, the United States prohibits foreign airlines from competing in the domestic air travel market. Japanese regulations make it illegal for domestic automobile dealers to sell both foreign and domestically produced vehicles; this makes it more difficult for foreign manufacturers to establish the dealer networks they need to penetrate the Japanese market effectively. Like tariffs and quotas, regulatory barriers such as these reduce the supply to domestic markets and the gains from potential trades. Overall output is reduced, and domestic producers benefit at the expense of domestic consumers.

EXCHANGE RATE CONTROLS AS A TRADE RESTRICTION

Some countries fix the exchange rate value of their currency above the market rate and impose restrictions on exchange rate transactions.[3] At the official (artificially high) exchange rate, the country's export goods will be extremely expensive to foreigners. As a result, foreigners will purchase goods elsewhere, and the country's exports will be small. In turn, the low level of exports will make it extremely difficult for domestic residents to obtain the foreign currency they need to purchase imports. Exchange rate controls both reduce the volume of trade and lead to black-market currency exchanges. Indeed, a large black-market premium indicates that the country's exchange rate policy is substantially

---

[3]The most common exchange rate restriction is that individuals are required to obtain approval from the government before they engage in transactions involving foreign currency.

limiting the ability of its citizens to trade with foreigners. While exchange rate controls have declined in popularity, they are still an important trade barrier in countries such as Myanmar, Venezuela, and Nigeria.

WHY DO NATIONS ADOPT TRADE RESTRICTIONS?

As social philosopher Henry George noted over a century ago, trade restraints act like blockades. Why would political officials want to erect blockades against their own people? As we consider this question, we will take a look at three arguments often raised by the proponents of trade restrictions: the national-defense, infant-industry, and antidumping arguments. Finally, we will look at the politics of trade restrictions and analyze how the nature of the restraints influences their political popularity.

THE NATIONAL-DEFENSE ARGUMENT

According to the national-defense argument, certain industries—aircraft, petroleum, and weapons, for example—are vital to a nation's defense. Therefore, these industries and their inputs should be protected from foreign competitors so that a domestic supply of necessary materials would be available in case of an international conflict. Would we want to be entirely dependent upon Arabian or Russian petroleum? Would complete dependence on French aircraft be wise? Many Americans would answer "no," even if it meant imposing trade restrictions that would lead to higher prices on products they buy.

   Although the national-defense argument has some validity, it is often abused. Relatively few industries are truly vital to our national defense. If a resource is important for national defense, often it would make more sense to stockpile the resource during peacetime rather than follow protectionist policies to preserve a domestic industry. Furthermore, fostering an economy robust enough to produce the mass quantity of goods necessary to sustain a war effort in the first place is, itself, part of a strong defense.

THE INFANT-INDUSTRY ARGUMENT

Infant-industry advocates believe that new domestic industries should be protected from foreign competition for a period of time so that they will have a chance to develop. As the new industry matures, it will be able to stand on its own feet and compete effectively with foreign producers, at which time the protection can be removed.

   The infant-industry argument has a long and often notorious history. Alexander Hamilton used it to argue for the protection of early U.S. manufacturing. The major problem with the argument is that the protection, once granted, will be difficult to remove. For example, a century ago, this argument was used to gain tariff protection for the newly emerging steel industry in the United States. Over time, the steel industry developed and became very powerful, both politically and economically. Despite its maturity, the tariffs remained. To this day, legislation continues to provide the steel industry with various protections that limit competition from abroad.

THE ANTIDUMPING ARGUMENT

Dumping involves the sale of goods by a foreign firm at a price below cost or below the price charged in the firm's home-base market. Dumping is illegal and if a domestic industry is harmed, current law provides relief in the form of antidumping duties (tariffs imposed against violators). Proponents of the antidumping argument argue that foreign producers will temporarily cut prices, drive domestic firms out of the market, and then use their

Protective tariffs are as much applications of force as are blockading squadrons, and their objective is the same—to prevent trade. The difference between the two is that blockading squadrons are a means whereby nations seek to prevent their enemies from trading; protective tariffs are a means whereby nations attempt to prevent their own people from trading.

—Henry George[4]

Dumping
Selling a good in a foreign country at a lower price than it's sold for in the domestic market.

---

[4]Henry George, *Protection or Free Trade* (Washington, DC: U.S. Government Printing Office, 1886), 37.

monopoly position to gouge consumers. However, there is reason to question the effectiveness of this strategy. After all, the high prices would soon attract competitors, including other foreign suppliers.

Antidumping cases nearly always involve considerable ambiguity. The prices charged in the home market generally vary, and the production costs of the firms charged with dumping are not directly observable. This makes it difficult to tell whether a dumping violation has really occurred. Furthermore, aggressive price competition is an integral part of the competitive process. When demand is weak and inventories are large, firms will often temporarily slash prices below per unit production cost in order to reduce excessively large inventories. Domestic firms are permitted to engage in this practice, and consumers benefit from it. Why shouldn't foreign firms be allowed to do the same?

One thing is for sure: Antidumping legislation gives politicians another way to channel highly visible benefits to powerful business and labor interests—another open invitation for rent seeking. The dumping charges are adjudicated by political officials in the International Trade Commission and the Department of Commerce. Consequently, it's naive to believe that political considerations won't be an important element underlying the charges that are levied and how they are resolved. Unsurprisingly, the number of claimants bringing charges of dumping has increased substantially over the past few decades.

APPLICATIONS IN ECONOMICS

Do More Open Economies Perform Better?

Economic theory indicates that more open economies will perform better than those with sizable trade restrictions. Is this really true? In order to address this question, a measure of trade openness—the freedom of individuals to engage in voluntary exchange across national boundaries—is needed. Economist Charles Skipton developed a trade openness index (TOI) for 81 countries during the 1980–2002 period.[1] To achieve a high rating on the zero-to-ten TOI scale (with ten indicating more openness to free trade), a country had to maintain low tariff rates, a freely convertible currency (no exchange rate controls), and refrain from imposing quotas and other regulations reducing the size of its trade sector.

Exhibit 11 shows the countries with the ten highest and ten lowest trade openness ratings. The ratings reflect the *average* degree of openness for the entire 1980–2002 period. This is important because the gains from increased openness can only be realized over time. Expanding the openness of trade is a long-term growth strategy, not a short-term "quick fix." Hong Kong, Singapore, Bahrain, Belgium, and Malaysia head the list of the most open of the 81 economies. By way of comparison, the United

States ranked sixteenth. At the other end of the spectrum, the TOI indicates that Bangladesh, Iran, Burundi, Sierra Leone, and Algeria were the least open economies during the period.

As Exhibit 11 shows, the 2005 average GDP per person of $28,251 of the ten most open economies was nearly ten times the comparable figure for the ten least open economies. Moreover, the more open economies also grew more rapidly. During 1980–2005, real GDP per person in the ten most open economies expanded at an annual rate of 3.1 percent, compared with 1.4 percent in the ten least open economies. Of course, the data of Exhibit 11 do not take into account other cross-country differences that theory indicates will influence growth. However, Skipton found that even after the differences in countries' inflation rates, legal structures, and similar factors were taken into account, trade openness continued to have a strong positive impact on both per capita GDP and growth rates.[2]

[1]Charles Skipton, "The Measurement of Trade Openness" (Ph.D. diss., Florida State University, 2003).

[2]For additional information on the relationship between international trade and economic growth, see Jeffrey A. Frankel and David Romer, "Does Trade Cause Growth?" *American Economic Review* (June 1999): 379–99; and Jeffrey D. Sachs and Andrew Warner, "Economic Reform and the Process of Global Integration," *Brookings Papers on Economic Activity*, no. 1 (1995): 1–95.

	TOI	GDP PER CAPITA (2005 DOLLARS)	GROWTH RATE, 1980–2005
Ten Most Open Economies			
Hong Kong	10.0	$30,989	3.9
Singapore	9.9	26,390	4.3
Bahrain	8.6	19,112	1.0
Belgium	8.6	28,575	1.7
Malaysia	8.6	9,681	3.6
Luxembourg	8.5	53,583	3.7
Netherlands	8.4	29,078	1.6
Taiwan	8.4	20,868	5.1
Ireland	8.1	34,256	4.5
Australia	7.9	29,981	1.9
Average	**8.7**	**$28,251**	**3.1**
Ten Least Open Economies			
India	4.3	$3,072	4.0
Tanzania	4.1	662	2.3
Egypt	4.1	3,858	2.5
Pakistan	3.9	2,109	2.4
Syria	3.8	3,388	0.6
Algeria	3.4	6,283	0.5
Sierra Leone	3.4	717	-1.1
Burundi	3.0	622	1.0
Iran	2.9	7,089	1.1
Bangladesh	2.5	1,827	2.2
Average	**3.5**	**$2,963**	**1.4**

Exhibit 11

Trade Openness, Income, and Growth

Source: The trade openness index data are from Charles Skipton, "The Measurement of Trade Openness" (Ph.D. diss., Florida State University, 2003), Table 4.6. The initial calculations were through 1999, but they were updated through 2002 by Skipton. The per capita GDP and growth rates are from the World Bank, *World Development Indicators*, CD-ROM, 2007. The per capita income figures were derived by the purchasing power parity method.

SPECIAL INTERESTS AND THE POLITICS OF TRADE RESTRICTIONS

Regardless of the arguments made by the proponents of trade restrictions, in truth, the restrictions are primarily special-interest related. (See the quotation from Weidenbaum.) *Trade restrictions typically provide highly visible, concentrated benefits for a small group of people, while imposing on the general citizenry costs that are widely dispersed and difficult to identify.* As we discussed in Chapter 6, the political process handles such issues poorly. It often leads to their adoption, even when they lower income levels and living standards.

The politics of trade restrictions are straightforward and play out over and over again. Well-organized business and labor interests gain substantially from restrictions that limit competition from abroad. Because their personal gain is large, they will feel strongly about the issue and generally vote for or against candidates on the basis of their positions on trade restrictions. Most important, the special-interest groups will be an attractive source of political contributions. When it comes to consumers, however, even if the total cost of the restrictions is quite large, it will be spread thinly among them; most consumers will be unaware that they are paying slightly higher prices for various goods because of the restrictions.

Protectionism is a politician's delight because it delivers visible benefits to the protected parties while imposing the costs as a hidden tax on the public.

—*Murray L. Weidenbaum*[5]

[5]Murray L. Weidenbaum, personal correspondence with the authors. Weidenbaum is a former chairman of the President's Council of Economic Advisers and former director of the Center for the Study of American Business of Washington University.

As you can see, courting special-interest groups helps politicians solicit campaign contributions and generate votes on the one hand. On the other hand, little political gain can be derived from poorly organized and largely uninformed consumers. Given this incentive structure, the adoption of trade restrictions is not surprising.

The U.S. tariff code itself is a reflection of the politics of trade restrictions. It is both lengthy (the schedule fills 3,151 pages) and highly complex. This makes it difficult for even a well-educated citizen to figure out how it works. High tariffs are imposed on some products (for example, apparel, tobacco, and footwear), whereas low tariffs are imposed on others. Highly restrictive quotas limit the import of a few commodities, most notably agricultural products. Even though this complex system of targeted trade restrictions is costly to administer, it is no accident. It reflects the rent seeking of special-interest groups and the political contributions and other side payments the system generates for politicians.

TRADE BARRIERS AND POPULAR TRADE FALLACIES

Fallacies abound in the area of international trade. Why? Failure to consider the secondary effects of international trade is part of the answer. Key elements of international trade are closely linked; you cannot change one element without changing the other. For example, you cannot reduce imports without simultaneously reducing the demand for exports. The political incentive structure is also a contributing factor. As business, labor, and political leaders seek to gain from trade restrictions, they will often use half-truths and wrong-headed ideas to achieve their political objectives. Two of the most popular trade fallacies involve the effects of imports on employment and the impact of trade with low-wage countries. Let's take a closer look at both.

TRADE FALLACY 1: TRADE RESTRICTIONS THAT LIMIT IMPORTS SAVE JOBS AND EXPAND EMPLOYMENT

Like most fallacies, this one has just enough truth to give it some credibility. When tariffs, quotas, and other trade barriers limit imports, they are likely to foster employment in the industries shielded from competition. But this is only half of the story: Simultaneously, jobs in other domestic sectors will be destroyed. Here's how: When trade barriers reduce the amount of goods Americans buy from foreigners, sales to foreigners will also fall. This is because our imports provide foreigners with the dollars they need to buy our exports. Because foreigners cut back on the items they would normally buy from us, other U.S. sectors will suffer job losses because they're selling less.

Furthermore, when trade restrictions are imposed on a resource domestic producers use as an input, they will have to pay a higher price for it than their foreign rivals. This will increase their costs and make it more difficult for them to compete internationally. As a result, they will have to lay off some of their employees. The import quotas imposed on steel during 2002–2003 vividly illustrate this point. The quotas helped the domestic steel industry, but they virtually wiped out the domestic industry producing steel barrels, a product the United States had exported prior to the quota being imposed. The quota also increased costs and reduced the competitiveness of industries that were major users of steel, like the automobile- and appliance-manufacturing industries. Employment in those industries fell as well. The same phenomenon occurred after the United States imposed sugar quotas. The import quotas pushed domestic sugar prices to two or three times the world price. As a result, several large candy makers relocated abroad so that they could buy sugar at the lower world price. Again, the jobs lost in U.S. industries using sugar were offset by any increase in employment by U.S. sugar producers.

On balance, there is no reason to expect that trade restrictions will either create or destroy jobs. Instead, they will reshuffle them. The restrictions artificially direct workers and other resources toward the production of things that we do poorly, as shown by our inability to compete effectively in the world market. Simultaneously, employment will decline in areas where American firms would be able to compete successfully in the world market if it were not for the side effects of the restrictions. In other words, more Americans will be employed producing things we do poorly and fewer will be employed producing things we do well. As a result, our overall income level will be lower than it would have been otherwise.

Unfortunately, the jobs "saved" by the import quotas are more visible than those destroyed in other sectors. This increases the political popularity of trade restraints and perpetuates the fallacy that the restraints increase employment. But it does not change the reality of the situation. As Exhibit 1 shows, imports increased from 6 percent of GDP in 1980 to 16 percent in 2010. If the growth of imports destroys jobs, as the proponents of trade restrictions argue, this huge increase in imports should have retarded U.S. employment. But this was not the case. On the contrary, civilian employment in the United States rose from 99 million in 1980 to 119 million in 1990 and 139 million in 2010. Far from retarding employment, the unprecedented growth of imports during the last three decades was associated with a substantial expansion in employment.

TRADE FALLACY 2: FREE TRADE WITH LOW-WAGE COUNTRIES LIKE MEXICO AND CHINA WILL REDUCE THE WAGES OF AMERICANS

Many Americans believe that without trade restrictions, their wages will fall to the wage levels of workers in poor countries. How can Americans compete with workers in countries like Mexico and China who are willing to work for $1 or less per hour? This fallacy stems from a misunderstanding of both the source of high wages and the law of comparative advantage. Workers in the United States generally are well educated, possess high skill levels, and work with large amounts of capital equipment. These factors contribute to their high productivity, which is the source of their high wages. Similarly, in countries like Mexico and China, wages are low precisely because productivity is low. Workers are generally less skilled in these countries, and there is less capital equipment to make them more productive.

The key thing to remember, though, is that gains from trade emanate from comparative advantage, not absolute advantage (see Exhibits 3, 4, and 5). The United States cannot produce *everything* more cheaply than Mexico or China merely because U.S. employees are more productive and work with more capital. Neither can Mexico and China produce *everything* more cheaply merely because their wage rates are low compared with the United Sates.

As long as there are differences between countries when it comes to their comparative advantages, gains from trade will be possible, no matter what the wages of the employees in the two countries are. Trade reflects relative advantage, not wage levels. We can illustrate this point using trade between individuals. No one argues that trade between doctors and lawn service workers, for example, will cause the wages of doctors to fall. Because of their different skills and costs of providing alternative goods, both high-wage doctors and low-wage lawn-care workers can gain from trade. The same is also true for trade between rich and poor nations.

If foreigners have a comparative advantage and can sell us a product for less than we ourselves can produce it, we can gain by buying it. This will give us more resources to invest in and produce other things. Perhaps an extreme example will illustrate this point. Suppose a foreign producer is willing to supply us automobiles free of charge (perhaps because its employees were willing to work for nothing). Would it make sense to impose tariffs or quotas to keep the automobiles from coming into the country? Of course not. Resources that were previously used to produce automobiles would then be freed up to produce other goods, and the real income and availability of goods would expand. It makes no more sense to erect trade barriers to keep out cheap foreign goods than it would to keep out the free autos.

THE CHANGING NATURE OF GLOBAL TRADE

Since World War II, there has been a gradual reduction in tariff rates and other trade barriers. Liberalized trade policies and lower transportation and communication costs have propelled the growth of international trade. The growth of trade has also resulted in a changing institutional environment. This section will focus on the institutions of international trade and the prospects for future trade liberalization.

GATT AND THE WTO

Following World War II, the major industrial nations of the world established the **General Agreement on Tariffs and Trade (GATT)**. For almost five decades, GATT played a

General Agreement on Tariffs and Trade (GATT)
An organization formed after World War II to set the rules for the conduct of international trade and reduce trade barriers among nations.

World Trade Organization (WTO)
The new name given to GATT in 1994; the WTO is currently responsible for monitoring and enforcing multilateral trade agreements among its 153 member countries.

central role in reducing tariffs and relaxing quotas. The average tariff rates of GATT members fell from approximately 40 percent in 1947 to about 3.0 percent in 2010, for example.

Following 1993, GATT was given a new name: the **World Trade Organization (WTO)**. This organization of 153 countries is now responsible for monitoring and enforcing the trade agreements developed through GATT. The WTO gives member nations a forum for development of trade rules and the settlement of disputes among members.

NAFTA AND OTHER REGIONAL TRADE AGREEMENTS

North American Free Trade Agreement (NAFTA)
A comprehensive trade agreement between the United States, Mexico, and Canada that went into effect in 1994.

Canada has been a major trading partner of the United States for many decades. In contrast, U.S. trade with Mexico was small prior to the 1990s. Historically, Mexico has been a relatively closed economy. This began to change in the mid-1980s, when Mexico began cutting its tariff rates and unilaterally removing other trade barriers. In 1988, the United States and Canada negotiated a trade agreement designed to reduce barriers limiting both trade and the flow of capital between the two countries. A few years later, the United States, Canada, and Mexico finalized the **North American Free Trade Agreement (NAFTA)**, which took effect in 1994. As the result of NAFTA, the tariffs of most goods moving among the three countries have now been eliminated. In addition to its participation in NAFTA, Mexico has also adopted a free-trade agreement with the European Union. During the last two decades, Mexico has moved from one of the world's more protectionist countries to one of its more open economies.

As **Exhibit 12** shows, U.S. trade with both Mexico and Canada grew rapidly. Measured as a share of GDP, trade with Mexico jumped from 1.4 percent in 1990 to 3.0 percent in 2010. During the same period, trade with Canada rose from 3.5 percent of GDP to 4.2 percent. This growth of trade, particularly with Mexico, however, has not been without controversy. Business and labor groups often blame employment contractions and plant closings on competition with Mexican firms. The news media generally give such stories ample exposure. However, there is no evidence that increased trade with Mexico has adversely affected the U.S. economy. The growth rate of the United States was strong and the unemployment rate relatively low during the period following the passage of NAFTA. Clearly, the dire predictions about the "jobs going to Mexico" were not realized.

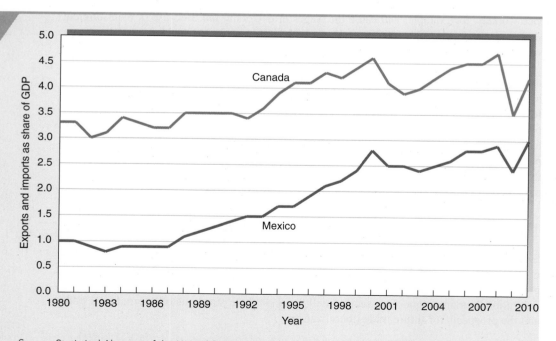

Exhibit 12

U.S. Trade with Canada and Mexico, 1980–2010

Measured as a share of GDP, U.S. trade with both Canada and Mexico has increased sharply as a result of NAFTA during the last 20 years.

Source: Statistical Abstract of the United States (various years) and http://www.bea.gov.

THE FUTURE OF FREE TRADE

For several decades following World War II, the United States and most other high-income countries were leaders among those pursuing and promoting more liberal trade policies. In contrast, India, China, and most of the less-developed economies of Africa and Latin America imposed sizable trade restraints, and they were reluctant to relax them.

Since 1980, the situation has changed dramatically. Observing the success of open economies like Hong Kong and Singapore, many less-developed countries (LDCs) unilaterally reduced many of their trade restrictions. On average, the tariff rates of LDCs are now less than half their levels in the early 1980s. Exchange rate controls are becoming increasingly rare, and capital market controls are much less restrictive than they were. Today, many leaders in LDCs recognize that free trade is the surest route to higher income levels and improved living standards. These countries are often the fiercest advocates of trade liberalization.

By contrast, the United States, Japan, and the European Union nations have agricultural price support programs contrary to free trade. It will take considerable effort to reduce, let alone remove, the price supports and subsidies to agriculture interests. To date, these countries have been unwilling to do so, and their resistance has become a major stumbling block on the road to trade liberalization. Furthermore, protectionist proponents—particularly those in high-income countries like the United States—have successfully lobbied to impose labor and environmental regulations that block trade liberalization. Meanwhile, the Internet and other technological changes continue to reduce transport and communications costs and thereby encourage the movement of goods, ideas, and people across national boundaries. All of this promises to enliven trade issues in the years ahead.

Looking Ahead

There are many similarities between domestic trade and trade across national boundaries, but there is also a major difference: International trade generally involves the exchange of one currency for another in the foreign exchange market. For students studying macroeconomics, we will now turn to this issue.

KEY POINTS

- The volume of international trade has grown rapidly in recent decades. In the United States, international trade (imports plus exports) summed to almost 29 percent of GDP in 2010, compared with 12 percent in 1980 and 6 percent in 1960.

- Comparative advantage rather than absolute advantage is the source of gains from trade. As long as relative production costs of goods differ, trading partners will be able to gain from trade. Specialization and trade make it possible for trading partners to produce a larger joint output and expand their consumption possibilities.

- Imports increase the domestic supply and lead to lower prices for consumers. Exports reduce the domestic supply and push prices upward, but this means the exporters can sell their products at higher prices. The net effect of international trade is an expansion in total output and higher income levels for both trading partners.

- Import restrictions, such as tariffs and quotas, reduce the supply of foreign goods to domestic markets. This results in higher prices. Essentially, the restrictions are a subsidy to producers (and workers) in protected industries at the expense of (1) consumers and (2) producers (and workers) in export industries. Jobs protected by import restrictions are offset by jobs destroyed in export-related industries.

- Trade restrictions generally provide concentrated benefits to the producers in industries they're designed to protect. The costs are spread thinly among consumers in the form of higher prices. Even though the impact of trade restrictions on the economy as a whole is harmful, they generate benefits for interest groups that politicians can then tap for campaign contributions and other side payments.

- Persistently open economies have grown more rapidly and have achieved higher per capita income levels than economies more closed to international trade.

CRITICAL ANALYSIS QUESTIONS

1. Why do American households and businesses buy things from foreigners? What are the characteristics of the items we buy from foreigners? What are the characteristics of the things we sell to foreigners?

2. *"Trade restrictions limiting the sale of cheap foreign goods in the United States are necessary to protect the prosperity of Americans." Evaluate this statement made by an American political leader.

3. Suppose as the result of the Civil War that the United States had been divided into two countries and that, through the years, high trade barriers had grown up between the two. How might the standard of living in the "divided" United States have been affected? Explain.

4. *Can both of the following statements be true? Why or why not?
   a. "Tariffs and import quotas promote economic inefficiency and reduce the real income of a nation. Economic analysis suggests that nations can gain by eliminating trade restrictions."
   b. "Economic analysis suggests that there is good reason to expect that trade restrictions will exist in the real world."

5. "Imports destroy jobs; exports create them. The average American is hurt by imports and helped by exports." Do you agree or disagree with this statement? Explain.

6. *"An increased scarcity of a product benefits producers and harms consumers. In effect, tariffs and other trade restrictions increase the domestic scarcity of products by reducing the supply from abroad. Such policies benefit domestic producers of the restricted product at the expense of domestic consumers." Evaluate this statement.

7. Suppose that a very high tariff was placed on steel imported into the United States. How would that affect employment in the U.S. auto industry? (*Hint:* Think about how higher steel prices will impact the cost of producing automobiles.)

8. *"Getting more Americans to realize that it pays to make things in the United States is the heart of the competitiveness issue." (This is a quote from an American business magazine.)
   a. Would Americans be better off if more of them paid higher prices in order to "buy American" rather than purchase from foreigners? Would U.S. employment be higher? Explain.
   b. Would Californians be better off if they bought goods produced only in California? Would the employment in California be higher? Explain.

9. How do tariffs and quotas differ? Can you think of any reason why foreign producers might prefer a quota rather than a tariff? Explain your answer.

10. *It is often alleged that Japanese producers receive subsidies from their government permitting them to sell their products at a low price in the U.S. market. Do you think we should erect trade barriers to keep out cheap Japanese goods if the source of their low price is a government subsidy? Why or why not?

11. The European Union has virtually eliminated trade restrictions among its members, and most members now use a common currency. What impact have these changes had on European economies?

12. *Does international trade cost Americans jobs? Does interstate trade cost your state jobs? What is the major effect of international and interstate trade?

13. "The United States is suffering from an excess of imports. Cheap foreign products are driving American firms out of business and leaving the U.S. economy in shambles." Evaluate this view.

14. *The United States uses an import quota to maintain the domestic price of sugar well above the world price. Analyze the impact of the quota. Use supply and demand analysis to illustrate your answer. To whom do the gains and losses of this policy accrue? How does the quota affect the efficiency of resource allocation in the United States? Why do you think Congress is supportive of this policy?

15. As U.S. trade with low-wage countries like Mexico increases, will wages in the United States be pushed down? Why or why not? Are low-wage workers in the United States hurt when there is more trade with Mexico? Discuss.

16. *"Tariffs not only reduce the volume of imports, they also reduce the volume of exports." Is this statement true or false? Explain your answer.

17. "Physical obstacles like bad roads and stormy weather increase transaction costs and thereby reduce the volume of trade. Tariffs, quotas, exchange rate controls, and other human-made trade restrictions have similar effects." Evaluate this statement. Is it true? Why or why not?

*Asterisk denotes questions for which answers are given in Appendix B.

Applying the Basics: Special Topics in Economics

Economics has a lot to say about current issues and real-world events. How are government spending, taxes, and borrowing affecting the future prosperity of Americans? Does the current Social Security system face problems, and what might be done to minimize them? Are stocks a good investment for a young person? What caused the economic crisis of 2008, and what are the important lessons we need to learn from it? What might be done to improve the quality of health care and education? How can we best protect the environment? This section focuses on these topics and several other current issues.

Economics is about how the real world works.

1

Government Spending and Taxation

FOCUS

- How has government spending per person changed historically in the United States?
- How has the composition of government spending changed in recent decades?
- Do taxes measure the cost of government?
- Do the rich pay their fair share of taxes? Do they pay less now than they did a couple of decades ago?
- How does the size of government in the United States compare with other countries?
- How has the share of the population paying taxes and receiving various types of transfer benefits changed in recent years? How is this likely to influence the fiscal future of the United States?

iStockphoto.com/ssrendls

[A] wise and frugal government, which shall restrain men from injuring one another, shall leave them otherwise free to regulate their own pursuits of industry and improvement, and shall not take from the mouth of labor the bread it has earned. This is the sum of good government....

—*Thomas Jefferson*[1]

I'm proud to be paying taxes in the United States. The only thing is—I could be just as proud for half the money.

—*Comedian Arthur Godfrey*

---

[1]Thomas Jefferson, First Inaugural Address (March 4, 1801).

In Chapters 5 and 6, we analyzed the economic role of government and the operation of the political process. We learned that whereas the political process and markets are alternative ways of organizing the economy, a sound legal system, secure property rights, and stable monetary regime are vitally important for the efficient operation of markets. We also noted that there may be advantages of using government to provide certain classes of goods that are difficult to supply efficiently through markets. However, as public-choice analysis indicates, the political process is not a corrective device. Even democratic representative government will often lead to the adoption of counterproductive programs. This feature will take a closer look at government in the United States and will provide additional details with regard to its spending, taxing, and borrowing.

iStockphoto.com/nicoolay

GOVERNMENT EXPENDITURES

As we noted in Chapter 6, total government spending (federal, state, and local) sums to almost 40 percent of the U.S. economy. The size of government has grown substantially over the past 80 years. Measured as a share of GDP, total government spending rose from less than 10 percent in 1930 to a little more than 30 percent in 1980 and nearly 40 percent in 2010. Approximately three-fifths of the spending by government now takes place at the federal level. Federal expenditures on just four things—(1) income transfers (including Social Security and other income-security programs), (2) health care, (3) national defense, and (4) net interest on the national debt—accounted for 88 percent of federal spending in 2010. (See Chapter 6, Exhibit 2.) This means that expenditures on everything else—the federal courts, national parks, highways, education, job training, agriculture, energy, natural resources, federal law enforcement, and numerous other programs—were less than 12 percent of the federal budget. Major spending categories at the state and local level include education, public welfare and health, transportation and highways, utilities, and law enforcement.

FEDERAL SPENDING PER PERSON, 1792–2010

Article 1, Section 8, of the U.S. Constitution outlined a limited set of functions that the federal government was authorized to perform. These included the authority to raise up an army and navy, establish a system of weights and measures, issue patents and copyrights, operate the post office, and regulate the value of money that it issued. Beyond this, the federal government was not authorized to do much else. The founders of the United States were skeptical of governmental powers, and they sought to limit those powers, particularly those at the federal level. (See the quotation by Thomas Jefferson at the beginning of this feature.)

During the United States' first 125 years, the constitutional limitations worked pretty much as planned; the economic role of the federal government was quite limited, and its expenditures were modest. In the nineteenth century, except during times of war, most government expenditures were undertaken at the state and local level. The federal government spent funds on national defense and transportation (roads and canals) but not much else.

Exhibit 1 presents data on real federal spending per person (measured in terms of the purchasing power of the dollar in 2010). Just before the Civil War, real federal expenditures were $60 per person, not much different than the $50 figure of 1800. Federal spending per person rose sharply during the Civil War, but it soon receded and remained in a range between $125 and $200 throughout the 1870–1916 period. Thus, before World War I, federal expenditures per person were low and the growth of government was modest.

Exhibit 1	**Real Federal Expenditure per Capita: 1792–2010**

Real federal spending per person (measured in 2010 dollars) was generally less than $50 before the Civil War, and it ranged from $125 to $200 throughout the 1870–1916 period. However, beginning with the spending buildup for World War I in 1917, real federal spending per person soared, reaching $11,194 in 2010—almost 80 times the level of 1916.

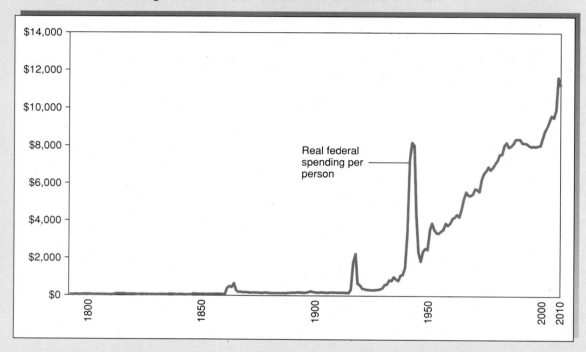

Source: U.S. Census Bureau, *Historical Statistics of the United States* (Washington, DC: U.S. Dept. of Commerce, U.S. Bureau of the Census, 1975); and *Economic Report of the President* (Washington, DC: U.S. Government Printing Office, 2011).

Beginning with the World War I spending of 1917, however, the situation changed dramatically. Federal spending remained well above the prewar levels during the 1920s and rose rapidly during the 1930s. It soared during World War II, and after receding at the end of the war, federal spending continued to grow rapidly throughout the 1950–1990 period. After a brief reduction during the 1990s, per capita real federal spending is once again on the upswing. Whereas per capita federal spending fell by 4.6 percent during the 1990s, it increased by 40 percent during 2000–2010. In 2010, it amounted to $11,194, roughly 80 times the $142 figure of 1916. The additional government expenditures came with a cost. On average, Americans paid more federal taxes in one week during 2010 than during the entire year in 1916. Based on current budget projections, the federal tax burden will continue to grow.

Not only has federal spending grown rapidly, but also there has been a dramatic shift in the composition of that spending. Since 1960, spending on defense has fallen as both a share of the budget and as a share of the economy, whereas expenditures on health care, transfer payments, and subsidies have soared.

As Exhibit 2 illustrates, defense expenditures constituted more than half (52.2 percent) of federal spending in 1960. By 2000, defense spending was only 16.5 percent of the federal budget. Largely because of the wars in Iraq and Afghanistan, defense spending has expanded during the past decade, reaching 20.1 percent of the federal budget in 2010. Government expenditures on income transfers (including Social Security and other transfer

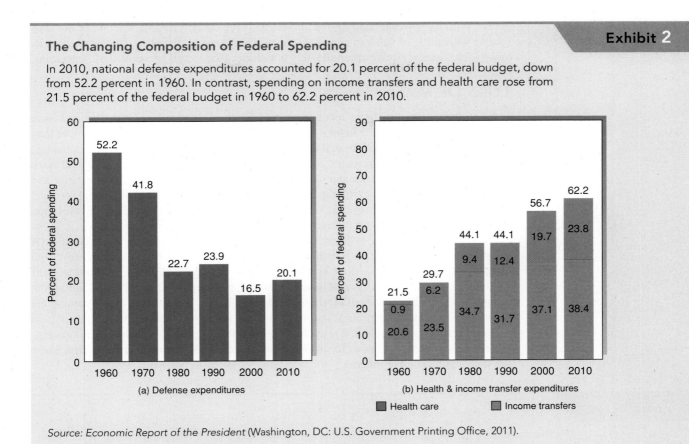

Exhibit 2

The Changing Composition of Federal Spending

In 2010, national defense expenditures accounted for 20.1 percent of the federal budget, down from 52.2 percent in 1960. In contrast, spending on income transfers and health care rose from 21.5 percent of the federal budget in 1960 to 62.2 percent in 2010.

(a) Defense expenditures

(b) Health & income transfer expenditures

■ Health care   ■ Income transfers

Source: Economic Report of the President (Washington, DC: U.S. Government Printing Office, 2011).

programs) and health care (primarily Medicare and Medicaid) have soared during the past half century. As Exhibit 2 shows, income transfers and health care expenditures rose from 21.5 percent of the federal budget in 1960 to 62.2 percent in 2010.

Thus, there has been a dramatic change in the composition of federal spending during the last five decades. In contrast with earlier times, national defense is no longer the primary focus of the federal government. In essence, the federal government has become an entity that taxes working-age Americans in order to provide income transfers and health care benefits primarily for senior citizens. Furthermore, spending on the elderly is almost certain to increase as the baby-boomers move into the retirement phase of life during the next two decades.

TAXES AND THE FINANCE OF GOVERNMENT

Government expenditures must be financed through taxes, user charges, or borrowing.[2] Borrowing is simply another name for future taxes that will have to be levied to pay the interest on the borrowed funds. Thus, it affects the timing but not the level of taxes. In the United States, taxes are by far the largest source of government revenue. The power to tax sets governments apart from private businesses. Of course, a private business can put whatever price tag it wishes on its products, but no private business can force you to buy its

---

[2]In addition to user charges, taxes, and borrowing, the operations of government might be financed by printing money. But this is also a type of tax (it is sometimes called an "inflation tax") on those who hold money balances.

goods. With its power to tax, a government can force citizens to pay, whether or not they receive something of value in return. As government expenditures have increased, so, too, have taxes. Taxes now take approximately one-third of the income generated by Americans.

TYPES OF TAXES

Exhibit 3 indicates the major revenue sources for the (1) federal and (2) state and local levels of government. At the federal level, the personal income tax accounts for more than 40 percent of all revenue. Although income from all sources is covered by the income tax, only earnings derived from wages and salaries are subject to the payroll tax. Payroll taxes on the earnings of employees and self-employed workers finance the Social Security and Medicare programs. The payroll tax also accounts for about 40 percent of federal revenue. The remaining sources of revenue, including the corporate income tax, excise taxes, and customs duties, account for a little less than 20 percent of federal revenue.

Both sales and income taxes are important sources of revenue for state governments. A sales tax is levied by 45 of the 50 states (Alaska, Delaware, Montana, New Hampshire, and Oregon are the exceptions). State and local governments derive about 17 percent of their revenue from this source. Personal income taxes are imposed by 41 states (Alaska, Florida, Nevada, New Hampshire, South Dakota, Tennessee, Texas, Washington, and Wyoming are the exceptions), and they provide approximately 12 percent of state and local government revenue.[3] Property taxes (levied mostly at the local level), grants from the federal government, and user charges (prices for government services) also provide substantial revenues for state and local governments.

Exhibit 3

Sources of Government Revenue

The major sources of government revenue are shown here. More than 40 percent of federal revenues are derived from the personal income tax. The share of federal revenue derived from the payroll tax is only slightly less. The major revenue sources of state and local governments are sales and excise taxes, personal income taxes, user charges, grants from the federal government, and property taxes.

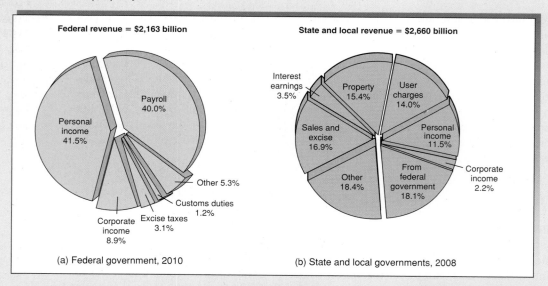

(a) Federal government, 2010

(b) State and local governments, 2008

Source: Economic Report of the President (Washington, DC: Government Printing Office, 2011) and State and Local Government Finances (2008), www.census.gov.

[3]New Hampshire and Tennessee have limited income taxes that only tax income derived from dividend and interest (so wage income is not subject to the personal income tax).

TAXES AND THE COST OF GOVERNMENT

There are no free lunches. Regardless of how they are financed, activities undertaken by the government are costly. When governments purchase resources and other goods and services to provide missiles, education, highways, health care, and other goods, the resources used by the government will be unavailable to produce goods and services in the private sector. As a result, private-sector output will be lower. This reduction in private-sector output is an opportunity cost of government. Furthermore, this cost will be present whether government activities are financed by taxes or borrowing.

Moreover, a tax dollar extracted from an individual or a business ends up costing the private economy much more than just one dollar. There are two main reasons why this is the case. *First, the collection of taxes is costly*. The administration, enforcement, and compliance of tax legislation require a sizable volume of resources, including the labor services of many highly skilled experts. The IRS itself employs more than 100,000 people. In addition, an army of bookkeepers, tax accountants, and lawyers is involved in the collection process. According to the Office of Management and Budget, each year individuals and businesses spend more than 6.6 billion hours (the equivalent of 3.3 million full-time year-round workers) keeping records, filling out forms, and learning the tax rules and other elements of the tax-compliance process.[4] More than half of U.S. families now retain tax-preparation firms like H&R Block and Jackson Hewitt to help them file the required forms and comply with the complex rules. Businesses spend roughly $5 billion each year in tax-consulting fees to the four largest accounting firms, to say nothing of the fees paid to other accounting, law, and consulting firms. In total, the resources involved amount to between 3 percent and 4 percent of national income (or 12 to 15 percent of the revenues collected). If these resources were not tied up with the tax-collection process, they could be employed producing goods and services for consumption.

Second, taxes impose an additional burden on the economy because they eliminate some productive exchanges (and cause people to undertake some counterproductive activities). As we noted in Chapter 4, economists refer to this as an *excess burden* (or *deadweight loss*) because it imposes a burden over and above the tax revenue transferred to the government. It results because taxes distort incentives. When buyers pay more and sellers receive less due to the payment of a tax, trade and the production of output become less attractive and decline. Individuals will spend less time on productive (but taxed) market activities and more time on tax avoidance and untaxed activities such as leisure. Research indicates that these deadweight losses add between 9 percent and 16 percent to the cost of taxation.[5] This means that $1 in taxes paid to the government imposes a cost of somewhere between $1.20 and $1.30 on the economy. Thus, the cost of a $100-million government program financed with taxes is really somewhere between $120 million and $130 million. As a result, the government's supply of goods and services generally costs the economy a good bit more than either the size of the tax bill or the level of government spending implies.

When considering the cost of taxation, it is also important to recognize that all taxes are paid by people. Politicians often speak of imposing taxes on "business" as if part of the tax burden could be transferred from individuals to a nonperson (business). This is not the case. Business taxes, like all other taxes, are paid by individuals. A corporation or business firm might write the check to the government, but it merely collects the money from someone else—from its customers in the form of higher prices, its employees in the form of lower wages, or its stockholders in the form of lower dividends—and transfers the money to the government.

---

[4]Office of Management and Budget, *Information Collection Budget of the United States Government,* and Tax Foundation *Special Brief,* by Arthur Hall (March 1996).
[5]The classic article on this topic is Edgar K. Browning, "The Marginal Cost of Public Funds," *Journal of Political Economy* 84, no. 2 (April 1976): 283–98.

HOW HAS THE STRUCTURE OF
THE PERSONAL INCOME TAX CHANGED?

The personal income tax is the largest single source of revenue for the federal government. The rate structure of the income tax is progressive; taxpayers with larger incomes face higher tax rates. During the past half century, the structure of the rates has been modified several times. In the early 1960s, there were 24 marginal tax brackets ranging from a low of 20 percent to a high of 91 percent. The Kennedy–Johnson tax cut reduced the lowest marginal rate to 14 percent and the top rate to 70 percent. The rate reductions during the Reagan years cut the top marginal rate initially to 50 percent in 1981 and later to approximately 30 percent during the period 1986–1988. During the 1990s, the top rate was increased to 39.6 percent, but the tax reductions during the administration of George W. Bush rolled back the top rate to 35 percent. These cuts were scheduled to expire at the end of 2010 but were extended for two more years.

Thus, since the late 1980s, Americans with the highest incomes have paid sharply lower top marginal tax rates—rates in the 30- to 40-percent range, compared to top rates of 91 percent in the early 1960s and 70 percent before 1981. These reductions in the top rate make it tempting to jump to the conclusion that high-income Americans are now getting a free ride—that they now shoulder a smaller share of the personal income tax burden than in the past. But such a conclusion would be fallacious.

Exhibit 4 presents the Internal Revenue Service data on the share of the personal income tax paid by various classes of high-income taxpayers, as well as those in the bottom half of the income distribution, for the years 1963, 1980, 1990, and 2008. These data show that the share of the personal income tax paid by high-income Americans has increased substantially since 1963, and the increase has been particularly sharp since 1980. For example, the top 1 percent of earners paid 38.0 percent of the personal income tax in 2008, up from 19.1 percent in 1980 and 18.3 percent in 1963. The top 10 percent of income recipients paid 69.9 percent of the personal income tax in 2008, compared to 49.3 percent in 1980 and 47 percent in 1963. At the same time,

---

Exhibit 4

Share of Federal Income Taxes Paid by Various Groups, 1963–2008

Even though marginal tax rates have been reduced substantially during the past three decades, upper-income Americans pay a much larger share of the federal income tax today than was previously the case. In 2008, the richest 1 percent of Americans paid 38.0 percent of the federal income tax, up from 18.3 percent in 1963 and 19.1 percent in 1980. The 5 percent of Americans with the highest incomes paid more than half of the personal income tax, whereas the entire bottom half of the income distribution (the bottom 50 percent) paid only 2.7 percent of the total.

INCOME GROUP	SHARE OF TOTAL FEDERAL PERSONAL INCOME TAX PAID			
	1963	1980	1990	2008
Top 1%	18.3%	19.1%	25.1%	38.0%
Top 5%	35.6%	36.8%	43.6%	58.7%
Top 10%	47.0%	49.3%	55.4%	69.9%
Top 25%	68.8%	73.0%	77.0%	86.3%
Top 50%	89.6%	93.0%	94.2%	97.3%
Bottom 50%	10.4%	7.1%	5.8%	2.7%

Source: Internal Revenue Service (also available online at the Tax Foundation's Web site: www.taxfoundation.org/).

the share of the personal income tax paid by the bottom half of the income recipients has steadily fallen from 10.4 percent of the total in 1963 to 7.1 percent in 1980 and 2.7 percent in 2008.

What is going on here? How can one explain the fact that high-income Americans are now paying more of the personal income tax even though their rates are now sharply lower than those in effect before 1981? Two major factors provide the answer. First, when marginal rates are cut by a similar percentage, the "incentive effects" are much greater in the top tax brackets. For example, when the top rate was cut from 91 percent to 70 percent during the Kennedy–Johnson years, high-income taxpayers in this bracket got to keep $30 out of every $100 of additional earnings after the tax cut, compared to only $9 before the rates were reduced. Thus, their incentive to earn additional income increased by a whopping 233 percent (30 minus 9 divided by 9)! Conversely, the rate reduction in the lowest tax bracket from 20 percent to 14 percent meant that the low-income taxpayers in this bracket now got to keep $86 of each additional hundred dollars that they earned compared to $80 before the tax cut. Their incentive to earn increased by a modest 7.5 percent (86 minus 80 divided by 80). Because the rate reductions increased the incentive to earn by much larger amounts in the top tax (and therefore highest-income) brackets, the income base on which high-income Americans were taxed expanded substantially as their rates were reduced. As a result, the tax revenues collected from them declined only modestly. In the very highest brackets, the rate reductions actually increased the revenues collected from high-income Americans. (See Laffer curve analysis of Chapter 4.) In contrast, the incentive effects were much weaker in the lower tax brackets and, as a result, rate reductions led to approximately proportional reductions in revenues collected from low- and middle-income taxpayers. This combination of incentive effects shifts the share of taxes paid toward those with higher incomes, the pattern observed in Exhibit 4.

Second, both the standard deduction and personal exemption have been increased substantially during the last couple of decades. This means that Americans are now able to earn more income before they face any tax liability. In 2008, for example, 36.3 percent (approximately 52 million returns) of those filing an income tax return either had zero tax liability or actually received funds from the IRS as the result of the **Earned Income Tax Credit**. This change in the structure of the personal income tax explains why people in the bottom half of income now pay such a small percentage of the personal income tax: 2.7 percent in 2008 compared to 10.4 percent in 1963.[6]

Earned Income Tax Credit A provision of the tax code that provides a credit or rebate to people with low earnings (income from work activities). The credit is eventually phased out if the recipient's earnings increase.

INCOME LEVELS AND OVERALL TAX PAYMENTS

In addition to the personal income tax, the federal government also derives sizable revenues from payroll, corporate income, and excise taxes. How is the overall burden of federal taxes allocated among the various income groups? **Exhibit 5** presents Congressional Budget Office estimates for the average amount of federal taxes paid in 2007 according to income. On average, the top quintile (20 percent) of earners are estimated to pay 25.1 percent of their income in federal taxes. The average federal tax rate for the quintile with the next-highest level of income falls to 17.4 percent, and the average tax rate continues to fall as income declines. The average tax rate of the bottom quintile is 4.0 percent, about one-sixth of the average rate for the top quintile of earners. Clearly, the federal tax system is highly progressive, meaning that it takes a larger share of the income of those with higher incomes than from those with lower income levels.

---

[6]The data of Exhibit 4 consider only the tax liability of taxpayers. They do not reflect the payments from IRS to taxpayers as the result of the Earned Income Tax Credit, which was established in the mid-1980s. If these payments to taxpayers were taken into consideration, the net taxes paid by the bottom half of income recipients would have been less than 1 percent. Thus, the data of Exhibit 4 actually understate the reduction in the net share of taxes paid by the bottom half of income recipients during the last two decades.

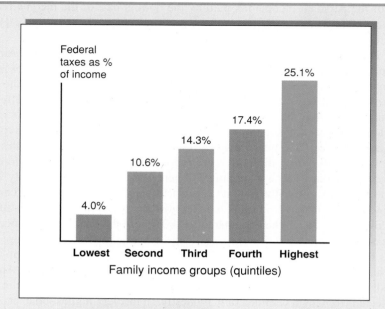

Exhibit 5

Total Federal Taxes as a Share of Income, 2007

Federal taxes are highly progressive. In 2007, federal taxes took 25.1 percent of the income generated by the top quintile (20 percent) of earners, compared to 14.3 percent from the middle-income quintile and 4.0 percent from the lowest quintile of earners.

Source: Congressional Budget Office, Average Federal Tax Rates in 2007, June 2010. Total federal taxes include income, payroll, and excise taxes.

SIZE OF GOVERNMENT: A CROSS-COUNTRY COMPARISON

There is substantial variation in the size of government across countries. As **Exhibit 6** illustrates, the relative size of government in most other high-income industrial countries is greater than that of the United States. In 2009, government spending summed to more than 50 percent of the economies of Denmark, France, Sweden, Belgium, Greece, Austria, Italy, United Kingdom, and Netherlands. Government spending as a share of the economy in Japan and Canada was similar to that of the United States, about 42 percent. Interestingly, the size of government was substantially smaller in South Korea, Singapore, Thailand, and Hong Kong—four Asian nations that have achieved rapid growth and substantial increases in living standards during the last four decades.

HOW DOES THE SIZE OF GOVERNMENT AFFECT ECONOMIC GROWTH?

Throughout this text, we have analyzed how governments influence the efficiency of resource use and the growth of income. It is clear that a legal environment that protects people and their property and provides for the impartial enforcement of contracts is vitally important. So, too, is a monetary and regulatory environment that provides the foundation for the smooth operation of markets. As we discussed in Chapter 5, there are also a few goods—economists call them *public goods*—that may be difficult to provide through markets. National defense, roads, and flood-control projects provide examples. Because they generate joint benefits and it is difficult to limit their availability to paying customers, sometimes they can be provided more efficiently through government. But public goods are rare, and the market can often devise reasonably efficient methods of dealing with them. If resources are going to be allocated efficiently, government spending on provision of public goods will generally be only a small share of the economy.

As governments expand beyond these core functions, however, the beneficial effects wane and eventually become negative as government moves into areas ill suited for political

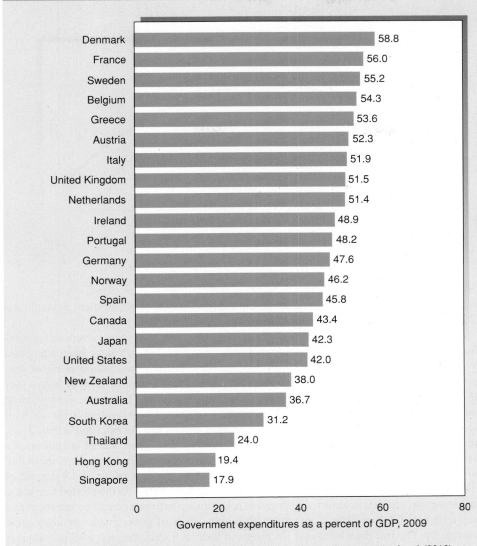

Exhibit 6

The Size of Governments— An International Comparison

The size of governments varies substantially across countries. In Sweden, government spending sums to more than 50 percent of the economy, compared to 42.0 percent in the United States and 20 percent or less in Hong Kong and Singapore.

Country	Value
Denmark	58.8
France	56.0
Sweden	55.2
Belgium	54.3
Greece	53.6
Austria	52.3
Italy	51.9
United Kingdom	51.5
Netherlands	51.4
Ireland	48.9
Portugal	48.2
Germany	47.6
Norway	46.2
Spain	45.8
Canada	43.4
Japan	42.3
United States	42.0
New Zealand	38.0
Australia	36.7
South Korea	31.2
Thailand	24.0
Hong Kong	19.4
Singapore	17.9

Government expenditures as a percent of GDP, 2009

Source: International Monetary Fund, *Government Finance Statistics Yearbook* (2010). (The data for New Zealand are for 2007.)

action and in which the political process works poorly. Thus, expansion of government activities beyond a certain point will eventually exert a negative impact on the economy. **Exhibit 7** illustrates the implications with regard to the expected relationship between the size of government and economic growth, *assuming that governments undertake activities based on their rate of return.* As the size of government, measured on the horizontal axis, expands from zero (complete anarchy), initially the growth rate of the economy—measured on the vertical axis—increases. The *A* to *B* range of the curve illustrates this situation. As government continues to grow as a share of the economy, expenditures are channeled into less-productive (and later counterproductive) activities, causing the rate of economic growth to diminish and eventually to decline. The range of the curve beyond *B* illustrates this point.[7] Thus, our analysis indicates that there is a set of activities and size of

[7]In the real world, governments may not undertake activities based on their rate of return and comparative advantage. Many governments that are small relative to the size of the economy fail to focus on the core activities that are likely to enhance economic growth. Thus, one would expect that the relationship between size of government and economic growth will be a loose one.

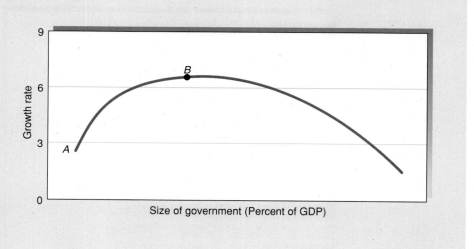

Exhibit 7

Economic Growth Curve and Government Size

If a government undertakes activities in the order of their productivity, its expenditures will promote economic growth (the growth rate will move from *A* to *B*). Additional expenditures, however, will eventually retard growth (the growth rate will move along the curve to the right of *B*).

government that will maximize economic growth. Expansion of government beyond (and outside of) these functions will retard growth.

How large is the growth-maximizing size of government? Do large governments actually retard economic growth? These are complex questions, but they have been addressed by several researchers. Exhibit 8 sheds light on these issues. This exhibit presents data on the relationship between size of government (*x*-axis) and economic growth (*y*-axis) for the twenty-three long-standing members of the Organisation for Economic Co-operation and Development (OECD). The exhibit contains four dots (observations) for each of the 23 countries—one for each of the four decades during the period 1960–1999. Thus, there are 92 total dots. Each dot represents a country's total government spending as a share of GDP *at the beginning of the decade* and its accompanying growth of real GDP *during that decade*. Government expenditures ranged from a low of about 15 percent of GDP in some countries to a high of more than 60 percent in others. As the plotted line in the exhibit shows, there is an observable negative relationship between size of government and long-term real GDP growth. Countries with higher levels of government spending grew less rapidly. The line drawn through the points of Exhibit 9 indicates that a 10-percentage-point increase in government expenditures as a share of GDP leads to approximately a 1-percentage-point reduction in economic growth.[8]

Time series data for specific countries have also been used to investigate the link between size of government and growth. Edgar Peden estimates that for the United States, the "maximum productivity growth occurs when government expenditures represent about 20% of GDP." Gerald Scully estimates that the growth-maximizing size of government (combined federal, state, and local) is between 21.5 percent and 22.9 percent of the economy. Although the methodology of these studies differs, they do have one thing in common: They indicate that in the ranges observed, high levels of government spending tend to retard economic growth.[9] They also indicate that the size and scope of most governments around the world are larger than the size that would maximize the income growth of their citizens. Moreover, the estimates imply that the recent expansion in the size of the government sector in the United States is likely to reduce the growth of income in the years immediately ahead.

[8]For additional information on the relationship between size of government and growth, see James Gwartney, Robert Lawson, and Randall Holcombe, "The Scope of Government and the Wealth of Nations," *The Cato Journal* (Fall 1998): 163–90.

[9]See Edgar Peden, "Productivity in the United States and Its Relationship to Government Activity: An Analysis of 57 Years, 1929–1986," *Public Choice* 69 (1991): 153–73; and Gerald Scully, *What Is the Optimal Size of Government in the United States?* (Dallas, TX: National Center for Policy Analysis, 1994).

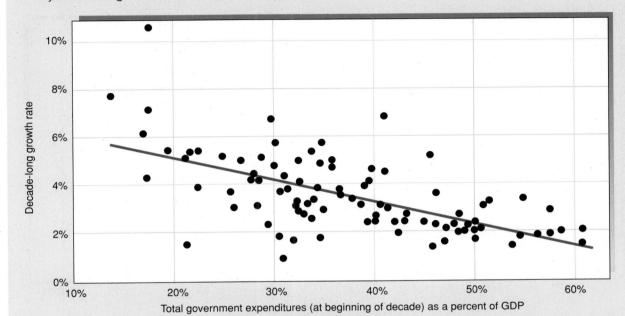

Government Spending and Economic Growth Among the Twenty-Three OECD Countries: 1960–1999

Here we show the relationship between size of government and the growth of real GDP for the 23 longtime OECD members during each decade since 1960. The data indicate that a 10-percent increase in government expenditures as a share of GDP reduces the annual rate of growth by approximately 1 percent. The data also imply that the size of government in these countries is beyond the range that maximizes economic growth.

Exhibit **8**

Source: OECD, *OECD Economic Outlook* (various issues), and the World Bank, *World Development Indicators*, CD-ROM, 2001.

EXPENDITURES, TAXES, DEBT FINANCE, AND DEMOCRACY

Exhibit 9 presents data on the percent of persons age 18 and older with and without a personal income tax liability. During the quarter of a century before 2000, the share of Americans paying income taxes fluctuated within a narrow range between 66 percent and 71 percent. However, the share paying income taxes has declined sharply during the past decade. Since 2003, 60 percent or less has had an income tax liability. In 2009, only 51 percent of Americans paid any federal income tax.

On the other hand, the percent of the population paying no income tax has risen sharply. Throughout 1975–2000, approximately one-third of Americans had no income tax liability. But the legislation passed under the administration of George W. Bush increased the "no tax" income threshold and doubled the child tax credit. These changes eliminated the income tax liability of many Americans. By 2009, nearly half of the population (49 percent) paid no income taxes. While many without an income tax liability are responsible for payroll taxes, the payroll tax is directed toward only two programs: Social Security and Medicare. Thus, payroll taxes do not contribute to the finance of government in other areas.

While the share of people paying taxes has declined in recent years, the share benefiting from transfers has been relatively constant. However, a little more than half of American families derive income from transfer programs. As Exhibit 10 shows, the percent of families receiving transfers from at least one program fell from 54.1 in 1991 to 49.5 percent in 2000,

Exhibit 9

Share of Population 18 and Older with and without a Personal Income Tax Liability

The percent of the population age 18 and older with and without a personal income tax liability is shown here. Note how the share paying income taxes fluctuated between 66 percent and 71 percent throughout 1975–2000. Since 2003, however, 60 percent or less have had an income tax liability, and the share plunged to 51 percent in 2009. Over the same period, the share with no income tax liability rose from one-third of the adult population during 1975–2000 to nearly one-half in 2009.

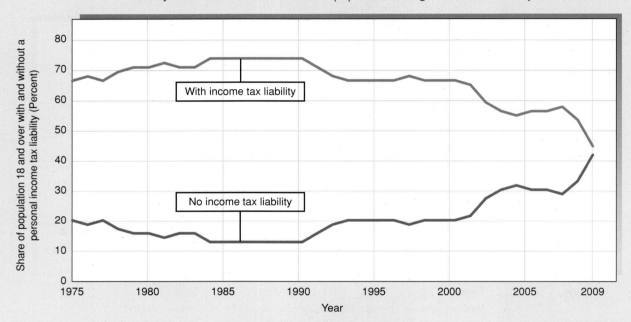

Source: Internal Revenue Service and *Economic Report of the President* (various issues). The number of persons with an income tax liability was derived by summing (1) the joint returns with a tax liability times two and (2) the number of individual returns with a tax liability. This figure was then divided by the population age 18 and older to derive the percentage of the 18 and older population with a tax liability.

but the figure has risen during the past decade, reaching 52.9 percent in 2009. When income from government employment is included, approximately three-fifths of all families benefit from government spending. In 2009, 62.3 percent of families derived income from either transfer programs or government employment. If the people employed by businesses with government contracts and those receiving subsidies (for example, the producers of ethanol, sugar and several other agricultural products, and wind and solar energy) were also included, the share of Americans heavily dependent on government would be even larger.

What are the implications of these patterns of tax payments and government spending? People who are not paying taxes have little reason to resist increases in government spending because they are not paying for them. In fact, they have every incentive to pressure politicians for more government services and transfers because someone else will be covering their cost. Similarly, people who are dependent on government spending for a sizable share of their income will be more supportive of government spending than those who derive their income from private-sector activities.

Debt financing is also related to the observed pattern of taxing and spending. Borrowing makes it possible for politicians to provide voters with current benefits without having to impose a parallel visible cost in the form of higher taxes. This enables elected officials to increase the number of people dependent on government spending without having to increase current taxes.

To a large degree, the modern democratic political process has become a game in which politicians seek to use the fiscal powers of government to assemble a political

Exhibit 10

Share of Families Deriving Income from Government, 1991–2009

More than half of American families derive income from transfer programs. The percent of families receiving transfers from at least one program fell from 54.1 in 1991 to 49.5 percent in 2000, but the figure has risen during the past decade, reaching 52.9 percent in 2009. When income from government employment is also included, more than three-fifths (62.3 percent) of American families now derive income from the government.

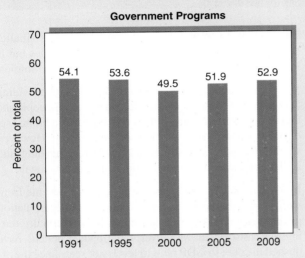

Government Programs

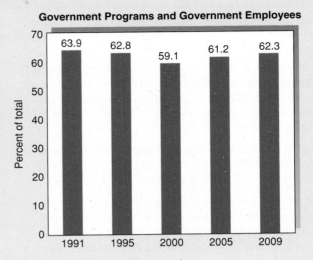

Government Programs and Government Employees

Source: These figures were derived from the Current Population Survey data. The following income transfers were included: Medicare, Medicaid, food stamps, unemployment compensation, school lunch program, housing subsidies, Social Security, and welfare.

majority. Is this a dangerous trend that may undermine democracy and lead to fiscal collapse? Eighteenth-century Scottish philosopher Alexander Tytler warned of this possibility:

A democracy cannot exist as a permanent form of government. It can only exist until the voters discover that they can vote themselves largesse from the public treasury. From that moment on, the majority always votes for the candidates promising the most benefits from the public treasury with the result that a democracy always collapses over loose fiscal policy.[10]

Is Tytler correct? Are the spending, taxing, and debt financing policies of the United States taking the country down a dangerous path? We do not know the answer to this question, but there are some troubling signs.

Measured as a share of GDP, total government expenditures are now about 7 percentage points higher than during the 1990s. During 2009 and 2010, the federal government financed approximately 40 percent of its expenditures by borrowing. The huge deficits of recent years have pushed the federal debt to nearly 100 percent of GDP, a level not seen since the aftermath of World War II. Moreover, the unfunded future benefits promised to senior citizens under the Social Security and Medicare programs are another form of debt, and these liabilities are three times the size of the official national debt. As the baby-boomers move into the retirement phase of life during the next decade, if Social Security and Medicare are not reformed, then spending on these programs will far outstrip the revenues for their finance.

Several members of the European Union (EU), including Greece, Portugal, Italy, and Spain, now confront exceedingly high debt levels and prior commitments to voters that make it difficult for them to reduce government spending. To date, other EU countries with marginally stronger government finances have been willing to provide emergency loans and other assistance. But this is not a long-run solution. The United States appears to be

---

[10]Some attribute this statement to Lord Thomas Macaulay. The author cannot be verified with certainty. For additional information on this topic, see Loren Collins, "The Truth About Tytler" at www.lorencollins.net/tytler.html.

headed down the same path. There are steps that could be taken, but special interest politics and the myopic nature of the political process may make them untenable. We are in the midst of an interesting, though unattractive, experiment in political economy as Western democracies face troubled fiscal waters in the years immediately ahead.

KEY POINTS

- During the first 125 years of U.S. history, federal expenditures per person were small and grew at a relatively slow rate. But the size and nature of government has changed dramatically during the past 100 years. Today, the real (adjusted for inflation) spending per person of the federal government is roughly 80 times the level of 1916.

- During the last five decades, the composition of federal spending has shifted away from national defense and toward spending on income transfers and health care.

- As the size of government has grown, taxes have increased. Taxes impose a burden on the economy over and above the revenue transferred to the government because of (1) the administration and compliance costs and (2) the deadweight losses that accompany taxation.

- Overall, the federal tax system of the United States is highly progressive. Taxes as a percentage of income are approximately six times greater for the top quintile (20 percent) of families than for the bottom quintile.

- The size of government of the United States is smaller than that of the major Western European countries but is larger than for a number of high-growth Asian economies.

- When governments focus on the core activities of providing (1) a legal and enforcement structure that protects people and their property from aggression by others and (2) a limited set of public goods, they promote economic growth. However, when governments grow beyond this size, expanding into activities for which they are ill suited, they deter growth.

- More than half of American families derive benefits from various transfer programs, while the share of the population paying federal income tax has declined substantially during the past decade. Moreover, large budget deficits have pushed the debt to GDP ratio to levels not seen since the aftermath of World War II. These factors, along with upward pressure on expenditures for Social Security and Medicare as the baby-boomers retire, will make it very difficult to control federal finances. Thus, the United States confronts a troublesome fiscal future in the years immediately ahead.

CRITICAL ANALYSIS QUESTIONS

1. *How do taxes influence the efficiency of resource use? How much does it cost for the government to raise an additional dollar (or $1 billion) of tax revenue?

2. During the past five decades, there has been a shift in the composition of the federal budget toward more spending on income transfers and health care and a smaller share for national defense. Does economics indicate that this change will help Americans achieve higher living standards? Discuss.

3. Because the structure of the personal income tax is progressive, a larger share of income is taxed at higher rates as real income increases. Therefore, economic growth automatically results in higher taxes unless offsetting legislative action is taken. Do you think this is an attractive feature of the current tax system? Why or why not?

4. Compared with the situation before 1981, the marginal tax rates imposed on individuals and families with high incomes are now lower. What was the top marginal personal income tax rate in 1980? What is the top

rate now? Are you in favor of or opposed to the lower marginal rates? Why?

5. *As the result of changes during the last two decades, the bottom half of income recipients now pay little or no personal income tax. Rather than paying taxes, many of them now receive payments back from the IRS as the result of the Earned Income Tax Credit and Child Tax Credit programs. Do you think the increase in the number of people who pay no taxes will affect the efficiency of the political process? Why or why not?

6. How have the size and functions of government changed during the last two centuries? Did the framers of the U.S. Constitution seek to limit the size of the federal government? If so, how?

7. Can democracy survive if a majority of the citizenry pay little or nothing in taxes while benefiting directly from a higher level of government spending? Why or why not? Discuss.

*Asterisk denotes questions for which answers are given in Appendix B.

The Economics of Social Security

FOCUS

- Why will the Social Security program confront problems in the near future?
- Will the Social Security Trust Fund make it easier to pay the promised benefits to future retirees?
- Does Social Security transfer income from the rich to the poor? How does it impact the economic status of blacks, Hispanics, and those with fewer years of life expectancy?
- How will Social Security work in the twenty-first century?

Over the next 30 years, the retirement of the baby-boom generation will pose new challenges for the Social Security program, the federal government, and the U.S. economy.

—*Dan Crippen*[1]

---

[1]Dan Crippen, Statement of Congressional Budget Office Director, before the Special Committee on Aging, United States Senate, December 10, 2001.

The Social Security program in the United States is officially known as Old Age and Survivors Insurance (OASI). It is designed to provide the elderly with a flow of income during retirement. In spite of its official title, Social Security is not based on principles of insurance. Private insurance and pension programs invest the current payments of customers in buildings, farms, or other real assets. Alternatively, they buy stocks and bonds that finance the development of real assets. These real assets generate income that allows the pension fund (or insurance company) to fulfill its future obligations to its customers.

Social Security does not follow this savings-and-investment model. Instead, it taxes current workers and uses the revenues to finance benefits for existing retirees. There is no buildup of productive assets that the federal government can use to fund the future benefits promised today's workers. When current workers retire, their promised Social Security benefits will have to come from taxes levied on future generations. *In essence, Social Security is an intergenerational income-transfer program*. The system is based on "pay as you go" rather than on the savings-and-investment principle.

The Social Security retirement program is financed by a flat-rate payroll tax of 10.6 percent applicable to employee earnings up to a cutoff level. In 2012, the earnings cutoff was $110,100. Thus, employees earning $110,100 or more paid $11,671 in Social Security taxes to finance the OASI retirement program.[2] The income cutoff is adjusted upward each year by the growth rate of nominal wages. Whereas the payroll tax is divided equally between employee and employer, it is clearly part of the employees' compensation package, and most economists believe that the burden of this tax falls primarily on the employee. The formula used to determine retirement benefits favors those with lower earnings during their working years. However, as we will discuss later, the redistributive effects toward those with lower incomes are more apparent than real.

When the program began in 1935, not many people lived past age 65, and the nation had lots of workers and few eligible retirees. As **Exhibit 1** illustrates, there were 16.5 workers for every Social Security beneficiary in 1950. That ratio has declined sharply through the years. As a result, higher and higher taxes per worker have been required just to maintain a constant level of benefits. There are currently 2.9 workers per Social Security retiree. By 2030, however, that figure will decline to only 2.1.

Exhibit 1

Workers per Social Security Beneficiary

In 1950, there were 16.5 workers per Social Security beneficiary. By 2010, the figure had fallen to just 2.9. By 2030, there will be only 2.1 workers per retiree. As the worker–beneficiary ratio falls under a pay-as-you-go system, either taxes must be increased or benefits must be reduced (or both).

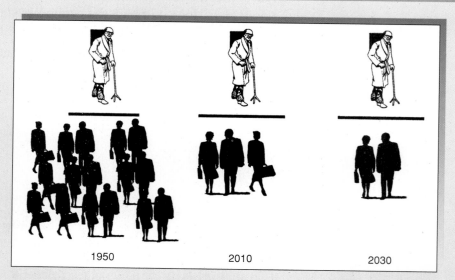

Source: 2011 Annual Report of the Board of Trustees of the Federal Old Age and Survivors Insurance and Disability Insurance Trust Funds (Washington, DC: Government Printing Office, 2011), 53.

[2]Additional payroll taxes are levied for the finance of disability programs (1.8 percent) and Medicare (2.9 percent). Thus, the total payroll tax sums to 15.3 percent, but only revenues from the 10.6 percent rate are used for the finance of benefits to retirees and surviving dependents. (*Note:* The earnings cutoff does not apply to the Medicare portion of the payroll tax.)

When there were many workers per beneficiary, it was possible to provide retirees with generous benefits while maintaining a relatively low rate of taxation. Many of those who retired in the 1960s and 1970s received real benefits of three or four times the amount they paid into the system, far better than they could have done had they invested the funds privately. The era of high returns, however, is now over. The program has matured, and the number of workers per beneficiary has declined. Payroll taxes have risen greatly over the decades, and still higher taxes will be necessary merely to fund currently promised benefits.

Studies indicate that those now age 40 and younger can expect to earn a real rate of return of about 2 percent on their Social Security tax dollars, substantially less than what they could earn from personal investments. Thus, Social Security has been a good deal for current and past retirees. It is not, however, a very good deal for today's middle-aged and younger workers.

WHY IS SOCIAL SECURITY HEADED FOR PROBLEMS?

The flow of funds into and out of a pay-as-you-go retirement system is sensitive to demographic conditions. The Social Security system enjoyed a period of highly favorable demographics between 1990 and 2010. The U.S. birthrate was low during the Great Depression and World War II. As this relatively small generation moved into the retirement phase of life during 1990–2010, the number of Social Security beneficiaries grew slowly. At the same time, the large baby-boom generation born following World War II was working and pushing the revenues flowing into the system upward. Thus, the payments to Social Security recipients increased at a modest rate, while the tax revenues grew rapidly during the two decades following 1990.

However, as Exhibit 2 shows, the situation is going to change dramatically in the years immediately ahead. The retirement of the large baby-boom generation, along with rising life expectancies, will lead to a rapid increase in senior citizens during the next two decades. The number of people age 65 years and older will soar from 40 million in 2010 to 71 million in 2030. As a result, the number of workers per Social Security retiree will fall from today's 2.9 to only 2.1 in 2030.

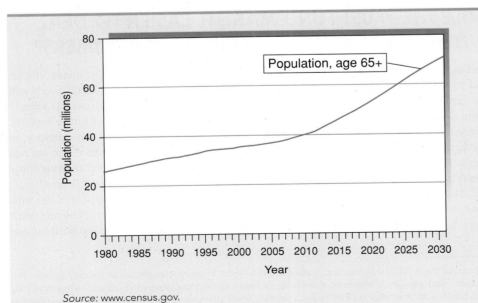

Exhibit 2

U.S. Population Age Sixty-Five and Older, 1980–2010, and Projections to 2030

As shown here, the growth rate of the elderly population will continue to accelerate rapidly as the baby-boomers move into the retirement phase of life as they have since 2010. This will place strong pressure on both the Social Security and Medicare programs.

Source: www.census.gov.

Exhibit 3

The Forthcoming Deficit between Payroll Tax Revenues and Benefit Expenditures

Given current payroll taxes and retirement benefit levels, the system will run larger and larger deficits during the 2010–2030 period and beyond.

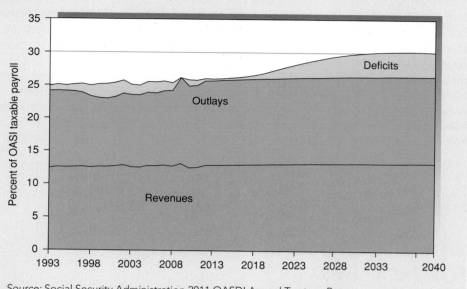

Source: Social Security Administration 2011 OASDI Annual Trustees Report, www.ssa.gov.

Exhibit 3 illustrates the impact of these demographic changes on the pay-as-you-go Social Security system. Between 1984 and 2009, the funds flowing into the system (pushed up by the large baby-boom generation) exceeded the expenditures on benefits to retirees (pulled down by the small Great Depression/World War II generation). But the retirement of the baby-boomers that began in 2010 will push the future expenditures of the system upward at a rapid rate. The deficit of revenues from the payroll tax relative to retirement benefits will grow larger and larger as the number of beneficiaries relative to workers continues to grow in the decades ahead.

What happened to the 1984–2009 surpluses of Social Security receipts relative to expenditures? Congress spent the surpluses, and the U.S. Treasury issued a special type of IOU, nonmarketable bonds, into the Social Security Trust Fund (SSTF). The future deficits of the system will draw down these bonds and are projected to deplete them by 2036.

WILL THE TRUST FUND MAKE IT EASIER TO DEAL WITH THE RETIREMENT OF THE BABY-BOOMERS?

Perhaps surprising to some, the answer to this question is "No." Unlike the bonds, stocks, and physical assets of a private pension fund or insurance company, the SSTF bonds will not generate a stream of future income for the federal government. Congress has already spent the funds, so there is no "pot of money" set aside for the payment of future benefits. Instead, the trust fund bonds are an IOU from one government agency, the Treasury, to another, the Social Security Administration. The federal government is both the payee and recipient of the interest and principal represented by the SSTF bonds. *No matter how many bonds are in the trust fund, their net asset value to the federal government is zero!*

Thus, the number of IOUs in the trust fund is largely irrelevant.[3] The size of the trust fund could be doubled or tripled, but that would not give the federal government any additional funds for the payment of benefits. Correspondingly, the trust fund could be abolished

---

[3]Of course, the SSTF bonds represent funds borrowed by the Treasury from the Social Security system. This increases the legitimacy of claims on these funds by future Social Security recipients. It also indicates that the trust fund is similar to what is called *budget authority*, which provides the legal permission for the government to spend funds on an item.

and the government would not be relieved of any of its existing obligations or commitments. In order to redeem the bonds and thereby provide the Social Security system with funds to cover future deficits, the federal government will have to raise taxes, cut other expenditures, or borrow from the public. Neither the presence nor the absence of the trust fund will alter these options.

As we indicated in Chapter 6, politicians have an incentive both to spend on programs providing highly visible benefits and conceal the burden of taxes. The Social Security Trust Fund has helped them do this. During the last two decades, the government has spent the entire surplus and even borrowed beyond these amounts. Moreover, as Congress and several presidents were spending the surpluses on current programs, most political leaders projected the view that funds were being set aside for the future retirement of the baby-boomers. Given the structure of political incentives, this art of deception should not be surprising.

THE REAL PROBLEM CREATED BY THE CURRENT SYSTEM

In the years immediately ahead, the revenues from the payroll tax will fall short of the benefits promised to retirees. These deficits will become larger and larger throughout the 2020s and 2030s. Under current law, revenues will be sufficient to pay only about three-quarters of promised benefits by 2030, and less in later years. If benefits are reduced, then current beneficiaries and people near retirement will—quite understandably—feel that a commitment made to them has been broken.

There are only four ways to cover future shortfalls: (1) cut benefits, (2) increase taxes, (3) cut spending in other areas, or (4) borrow. None of these options is attractive, and, regardless of how the gap is filled, there is likely to be an adverse impact on the economy. Moreover, not even robust economic growth will eliminate the future shortfall. Retirement benefits are indexed to average growth in nominal wages. If higher productivity enables *real* (inflation-adjusted) wages to rise quickly, so will future Social Security benefits. For example, if inflation is zero and real wages start growing at 2 percent a year instead of their previous level of 1 percent, then the formula used to calculate Social Security benefits will also begin to push those benefits up more rapidly. Higher economic growth may temporarily improve Social Security's finances, but under current law the improvement will not last.[4]

DOES SOCIAL SECURITY HELP THE POOR?

Social Security has gained many supporters because of the belief that it redistributes wealth from the rich to the poor. The system is financed with a flat tax rate up to the cutoff limit, but the formula used to calculate benefits disproportionately favors workers with low lifetime earnings.[5] However, other aspects of the system tend to favor those with higher incomes. First, workers with more education and high earnings tend to live longer than those with less education and lower earnings. As **Exhibit 4** shows, the age-adjusted mortality rate of people with less than a high school education is 8 to 10 percent higher than the average for all Americans. As years of schooling increase, mortality rates fall. The age-adjusted mortality rate of college graduates is 21 percent below the average for all Americans, whereas

[4]See Garth Davis, "Faster Economic Growth Will Not Solve the Social Security Crisis," Heritage Center for Data Analysis (February 3, 2000).
[5]Retirement benefits are based on the best 35 years of earnings from a worker's career. Benefits are calculated by taking 90 percent of the first $8,928 a year of earnings, 32 percent of earnings between $8,928 and $53,796, and just 15 percent of earnings above $53,796 up to the earnings cutoff of $106,800. Therefore, as base earnings rise, benefits fall as a percentage of average earnings (and payroll taxes paid) during one's lifetime. For example, the retirement benefits of people with base annual earnings of $10,000 sum to 84 percent of their average working year earnings. In contrast, the retirement benefits of those with base earnings of $60,000 are only 39 percent of their average pre-retirement earnings. These figures are based on the formula for 2011. The figures are adjusted each year for the growth of nominal wages.

Exhibit 4

Mortality Rates by Level of Education

As shown here, the age-adjusted mortality rates are lower for those with more education. Because of the close link between education and income, people with higher incomes tend to live longer and, therefore, draw Social Security benefits for a lengthier time period than those with less education and income.

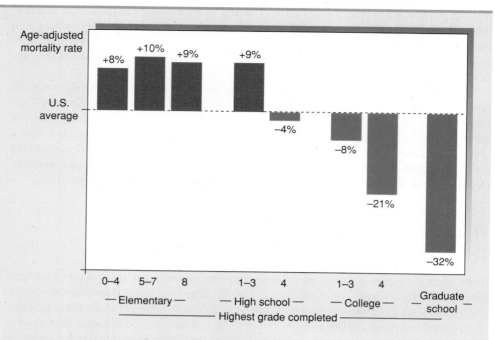

Source: Center for Data Analysis, Heritage Foundation.

the rate for people with advanced degrees is 32 percent below the average. Given the strong correlation between education and earnings, the age-adjusted mortality figures indicate that, on average, Americans with higher earnings live longer than their counterparts with less education and lower earnings. As a result, high-wage workers will, on average, draw Social Security benefits for a longer period of time than will low-wage workers. Correspondingly, low-wage workers are far more likely to pay thousands of dollars in Social Security taxes and then die before, or soon after, becoming eligible for retirement benefits.

Second, low-wage workers generally begin full-time work at a younger age. Many work full time and pay Social Security taxes for years, while future high-wage workers are still in college and graduate school. Low-wage workers generally pay more into the system earlier and therefore forgo more interest than do high-wage workers.

Third, labor participation tends to fall as spousal earnings increase. As a result, couples with a high-wage worker are more likely to gain from Social Security's spousal benefit provision, which provides the nonworking spouse with benefits equal to 50 percent of those the working spouse receives.

Two recent studies taking these and other related factors into consideration suggest that Social Security may actually transfer wealth from low-wage to high-wage workers. A research project using data from the Social Security Administration and the Health and Retirement Study found that when Social Security benefits are assessed for family units rather than for individuals, the progressivity of the system disappears. Another study adjusted for differences in mortality rates, patterns of lifetime income, and other factors. It found that if a 2 percent real interest rate (discount rate) is used to evaluate the pattern of taxes paid and benefits received, the redistributive effects of Social Security are essentially neutral. However, at a more realistic 4 percent real interest rate, Social Security actually favors higher-income households.[6]

---

[6]See Alan Gustman and Thomas Steinmeier, "How Effective Is Redistribution under the Social Security Benefit Formula?" *Journal of Public Economics* 82 (October 2001): 1–28; and Julia Lynn Coronado, Don Fullerton, and Thomas Glass, "Long Run Effects of Social Security Reform Proposals on Lifetime Progressivity," in Martin Feldstein and Jeffrey B. Liebman, eds., *The Distributional Aspects of Social Security and Social Security Reform* (Chicago: University of Chicago Press, 2002).

SOCIAL SECURITY AND THE TREATMENT OF BLACKS AND WORKING MARRIED WOMEN

When Social Security was established in 1935, the population was growing rapidly, only a few Americans lived to age 65, and the labor-force participation rate of married women was very low. Social Security was designed for this world. But today's world is dramatically different. Several aspects of the system now seem outdated, arbitrary, and in some cases, unfair. Let's consider a couple of these factors.

SOCIAL SECURITY ADVERSELY AFFECTS BLACKS AND OTHER GROUPS WITH BELOW-AVERAGE LIFE EXPECTANCY

Currently, the average retiree reaching age 65 can expect to spend 18 years receiving Social Security benefits, after more than 40 years of paying into the system. But what about those who do not make it into their eighties or even to the normal retirement age of 65? Unlike private financial assets, Social Security benefits cannot be passed on to heirs. Thus, those who die before age 65 or soon thereafter receive little or nothing from their payroll tax payments.

Social Security was not set up to transfer income from some ethnic groups to others, but under its current structure it nonetheless does so. Because of the shorter life expectancy of blacks, the Social Security system adversely affects their economic welfare. Compared with whites and Hispanics, blacks are far more likely to pay a lifetime of payroll taxes and then die without receiving much in the way of benefits. Thus, the system works to their disadvantage. In contrast, Social Security is particularly favorable to Hispanics because of their above-average life expectancy and the progressive nature of the benefit formula. As a result, Hispanics derive a higher return than whites and substantially higher than blacks.[7]

Exhibit 5 presents the expected real returns for those born in 1975, according to gender, marital status, and ethnicity.[8] Single black males born in 1975 can expect to derive a real annual return of negative 1.3 percent on their Social Security tax payments, compared with returns of 0.2 percent for single white males and 1.6 percent for single Hispanic males. Similarly, a two-earner black couple born in 1975 can expect a real return of 0.5 percent, compared with returns of 1.2 percent and 2.3 percent for white and Hispanic couples born during the same year. A similar pattern exists when comparisons are made for those born in other years.

The Social Security retirement system also works to the disadvantage of those with life-shortening diseases. People with diabetes, heart disease, AIDS, and other diseases often spend decades paying 10.6 percent of their earnings into the system only to die with loved ones unable to receive benefits from the Social Security taxes they have paid. (People with life-shortening diseases may receive disability insurance, but if they die before retirement they collect nothing from their payments into the retirement system.)

---

[7]For additional details on the redistributive effects of Social Security across ethnic groups, see William W. Beach and Gareth Davis, "More for Your Money: Improving Social Security's Rate of Return," in David C. John, ed., *Improving Retirement Security: A Handbook for Reformers* (Washington, DC: Heritage Foundation, 2000), 25–64; and Martin Feldstein and Jeffrey Liebman, "The Distributional Effects of an Investment-Based Social Security System," in Martin Feldstein and Jeffrey B. Liebman, eds., *The Distributional Aspects of Social Security and Social Security Reform* (Chicago: University of Chicago Press, 2002).

[8]It is common to calculate a rate of return on financial investments by comparing initial investments with the stream of projected future income (or benefits). Social Security is not like a regular financial investment because there is no accumulation of assets and no legal right to benefits. Nonetheless, a rate of return can be calculated by comparing the payroll taxes a worker pays with the future benefits he or she is promised. The rate-of-return figures of Exhibit 5 were derived in this manner. They assume that the current tax level and promised future benefits will be maintained. However, as we noted, projections indicate that current tax rates will cover only about three-fourths of promised benefits by 2030. Thus, higher taxes will be required to maintain the promised benefit levels. In turn, the higher taxes will lower rates of return. Therefore, the figures of Exhibit 5 probably overstate the rates of return for the various groups.

Exhibit 5

Rates of Return by Gender, Marital Status, and Ethnicity

The earnings of blacks are lower than whites, but blacks have a shorter life expectancy. The latter effect dominates, and therefore blacks derive a lower rate of return from Social Security than whites. In contrast, Hispanics have both lower earnings and a little longer life expectancy than whites. Thus, their returns from Social Security are higher than whites and substantially higher than blacks.

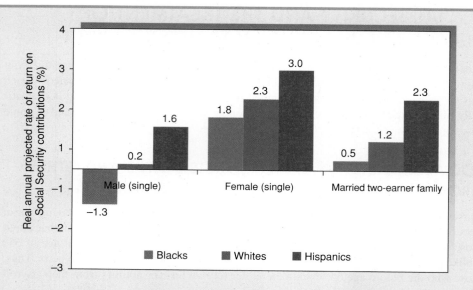

Source: Center for Data Analysis, Heritage Foundation.

DISCRIMINATION AGAINST MARRIED WOMEN IN THE WORKFORCE

When Social Security was established, relatively few married women worked outside the home. Therefore, individuals were permitted to receive benefits based on either their own earnings or 50 percent of the benefits earned by their spouse, whichever is greater. This provision imposes a heavy penalty on married women in the workforce. In the case of many working married women, the benefits based on the earnings of their spouses are approximately equal to, or in some cases greater than, benefits based on their own earnings. Thus, the payroll tax takes a big chunk of their earnings without providing them with any significant additional benefits.

IS THE STRUCTURE OF SOCIAL SECURITY SUITABLE FOR THE TWENTY-FIRST CENTURY?

When the number of retirees grows more rapidly than the number of workers, pay-as-you-go financing does not work well. The return retirees can expect from their tax payments into the system will be low. As we mentioned, today's typical worker can expect a return of only 2.0 percent from the taxes paid into the Social Security system. By way of comparison, stock market investments have averaged a real return of approximately 7 percent annually for more than a century. Furthermore, when regular investments are made into a diverse holding of stocks, the variation in the return has been relatively low.[9] Mutual funds now make it feasible for even a small novice investor to invest in a diverse stock portfolio while still keeping administrative costs low. (See Special Topic 3, a feature on the stock market.)

As a result of the changing demographics, the Social Security and Medicare programs now confront huge **unfunded liabilities**, shortfalls between promised future benefits and the revenues that can be expected at current tax rates. The trustees of these two

Unfunded liability
A shortfall of tax revenues at current rates relative to promised benefits for a program. Without an increase in tax rates, the promised benefits cannot be funded fully.

[9]See Liqun Liu, Andrew J. Rettenmaier, and Zijun Wang, "Social Security and Stock Market Risk" (NCPA Policy Report No. 244, National Center for Policy Analysis, July 23, 2001).

THE WIZARD OF ID

programs project that the unfunded liability of Social Security is $9 trillion, whereas that of Medicare is estimated to be $25 trillion.[10] The sum of these figures is more than three times the current size of the U.S. economy. Predictably, deteriorating financial conditions will lead politicians to look for ways of dealing with this situation. Thus, a combination of factors—low returns from Social Security, a structure that seems outdated, and deteriorating financial conditions—may virtually force Congress to seriously consider modifications in the future.

From an economic viewpoint, the most viable option would be some form of **personal retirement accounts (PRAs)** that would incorporate savings and investment into the financing of retirement. In varying degrees, several countries have already moved in this direction. Beginning in the early 1980s, Chile shifted to a retirement system based on saving and investing through PRAs rather than pay as you go. The Chilean plan was so successful that other Latin American countries, including Mexico, Bolivia, Columbia, and Peru, adopted similar plans in the 1990s. High-income countries have also moved in this direction. In 1986, the United Kingdom began allowing workers to channel 4.6 percentage points of their payroll tax into PRAs in exchange for acceptance of a lower level of benefits from the pay-as-you-go system. The PRA option is currently chosen by nearly three-fourths of British workers. Other countries that now permit at least some substitution of PRAs for payroll taxes and pay-as-you-go benefits include Netherlands, Australia, Sweden, and Germany.

Ownership rights exert a powerful impact on incentives. Personal retirement accounts would provide workers with a property right to the funds contributed into their accounts. The funds paid into a PRA could be passed along to heirs. In contrast with higher taxes, payments into a personally owned investment account that would enhance one's retirement income would not exert a harmful impact on the incentive to work and earn. Furthermore, PRAs would encourage saving and investment, which would help to promote economic growth. They would also reduce the dependency of senior citizens on political officials. There are numerous ways to structure personal retirement accounts. Several plans have already been put forth, and others are sure to arise in the future.

Political debate about the structure of Social Security and how to plan for retirement will continue in the years ahead. This debate is particularly important for younger people because the way it is handled will exert a major impact on their future tax liability and the quality of their life during retirement.

Personal retirement account (PRAs)
An account that is owned personally by an individual in his or her name. The funds in the account could be passed along to heirs.

---

[10]See *2011 Annual Report of the Boards of Trustees of the Federal Hospital Insurance and Federal Supplementary Medical Insurance Trust Fund*, www.cms.hhs.gov/ReportsTrustFunds/.

KEY POINTS

- Social Security does not follow the saving-and-investment model. Most of the taxes paid into the system are used to finance the benefits of current retirees.

- As the baby-boomers began moving into the retirement phase of life in 2010, the Social Security system shifted from a surplus to a deficit. The deficits will persist and become larger and larger in the decades immediately ahead.

- The previous surpluses of the Social Security system were used to cover current expenditures, and the U.S. Treasury provided the Social Security Administration with nonmarketable bonds. Because the federal government is the payee and the recipient of these bonds, their net asset value to the federal government is zero. They will not reduce the level of future taxes needed to cover the Social Security deficits.

- The major problem resulting from the current pay-as-you-go system is that large tax increases, spending cuts, or additional borrowing will be required to cover the Social Security deficits following the retirement of the baby-boom generation.

- Whereas the Social Security benefit formula favors those with lower lifetime earnings, low-wage workers have a lower life expectancy, begin work at a younger age, and gain less from the spousal benefit provisions of the current system. These latter factors largely, if not entirely, offset the egalitarian effects of the benefit formula.

- Because of their shorter life expectancy, blacks derive a lower rate of return from Social Security than whites and a substantially lower return than Hispanics.

- The demographics of the twenty-first century reduce the attractiveness of pay-as-you-go Social Security. Various plans that would place more emphasis on saving and investment are likely to be considered in the future.

CRITICAL ANALYSIS QUESTIONS

1. Is the Social Security system based on the same principles as private insurance? Why or why not?

2. *Why does the Social Security system face a crisis? Are there real assets in the Social Security Trust Fund that can be used to pay future benefits? Will the trust fund help to avert higher future taxes or benefit reductions or both when the baby-boomers retire? Why or why not?

3. Do you think workers should be permitted to invest all or part of their Social Security taxes into a personal retirement account? Why or why not?

4. How does Social Security affect the economic well-being of blacks relative to whites and Hispanics? Explain.

5. Does the current Social Security system promote income equality? Why or why not?

6. The Social Security payroll tax is split equally between the employee and the employer. Would it make any difference if the entire tax were imposed on employees? Would employees be helped if all the tax were imposed on employers? (*Hint:* You may want to consult the section on tax incidence in Chapter 4.)

*Asterisk denotes questions for which answers are given in Appendix B.

The Stock Market: Its Function, Performance, and Potential as an Investment Opportunity

FOCUS

- What is the economic function of the stock market?
- What determines the price of a stock? Can experts forecast the future direction of stock prices?
- Can an ordinary investor profit from stock market investments? If so, how and under what circumstances?
- How has the stock market been affected by the recent financial crisis? Is now a good time to invest in the stock market?

istockphoto.com/sorendls

Though the stock market functions as a voting machine in the short run, it acts as a weighing machine in the long run.

—*Ben Graham*[1]

---

[1]As quoted by Warren Buffett in Carol Loomis, "Warren Buffett on the Stock Market," *Fortune* (December 10, 2001), 80–87.

The market for corporate shares is called the *stock market*. The stock market makes it possible for investors, including small investors, to share in the profits (and the risks) of large businesses. About one-half of all households now own stock, either directly or indirectly through shares in an equity mutual fund. In recent years, changes in stock prices have often been front-page news. This feature will focus on the economic functions of the stock market and analyze its potential as an investment tool through which people can build their wealth.

THE ECONOMIC FUNCTIONS OF THE STOCK MARKET

The stock market performs several important functions in a modern economy. Let's consider three of the most important.

1. The stock market provides investors, including those who are not interested in participating directly in the operation of the firm, with an opportunity to own a fractional share of the firm's future profits. As a firm earns profits, its shareholders may gain as the result of both dividend payments and increases in the market value of the stock. Ownership of stock is risky. There is no guarantee that any firm will be profitable in the future. But the shareholders' potential losses are limited to the amount of their initial investment. Beyond this point, shareholders are not responsible for the debts of the corporations that they own.

2. New stock issues are often an excellent way for firms to obtain funds for growth and product development. Essentially, there are three ways for a firm to obtain additional financing. It can use retained earnings (profits earned but not paid out to stockholders), it can borrow money, or it can sell stock. When borrowing, the firm promises to repay the lender a specific amount, including principal and interest. Conversely, new stock issues provide the firm with additional financing, and the owner of the stock acquires an ownership right to a fraction of the future revenues generated by the firm.

Newly issued stocks are sold to the public through specialized firms. A firm that issues new stock sells it in the **primary market**. When news reports tell us about how stock prices are changing, they are referring to **secondary markets**, in which previously issued stocks are traded. Secondary markets make it easy to buy and sell listed stock. This is important to the primary market. The initial buyers want to know that their stock will be easy to sell later. Entry is more attractive when exit will be easy. This will help the corporation issuing new stock to sell it for a higher price.

A stock exchange is a secondary market. It is a place where stockbrokers come to arrange trades for buyers and sellers. The largest and best-known stock market is the New York Stock Exchange, in which more than 2,800 stocks are traded. There are other such markets in the United States, as well as in London, Tokyo, Hong Kong, and other trading centers around the world.

3. Stock prices provide information about the quality of business decisions. Changing stock prices reward good decisions and penalize bad ones. It pays for a stockholder, especially a large one, to be alert to whether the firm's decisions are good or bad. Those who spot a corporation's problems early can sell part or all of their stock in that firm before others notice and lower the price by selling their own stock. Similarly, those who first notice decisions that will be profitable can gain by increasing their holdings of the stock. Stockholder alertness benefits the corporation, too. The firm's board of directors can utilize the price changes resulting from investor vigilance to reward good management decisions.

Primary market
The market in which financial institutions aid in the sale of new securities.

Secondary market
The market in which financial institutions aid in the buying and selling of existing securities.

They often do so by tying the compensation of the top corporate officers to stock perfor-mance. How? Rather than paying these officers entirely in the form of salaries, a board of directors can integrate **stock options** into the compensation package of top executives. On the one hand, when good decisions drive the stock price up, the executives' options will be very valuable. On the other hand, if bad decisions cause the stock price to fall, then the options will have little or no value.

STOCK MARKET PERFORMANCE: THE HISTORICAL RECORD

Even after considering the sharp reductions in stock prices during the 2008–2009 reces-sion, on the whole, investors in American stocks have done exceedingly well. Furthermore, this has been true over a lengthy period of time. During the last two centuries, after adjust-ment for inflation, corporate stocks have yielded an average real return of approximately 7 percent per year, compared with a real return of about 3 percent for bonds. The historic returns derived from savings accounts and money market mutual funds are even lower. A 7 percent real return may not sound particularly good, but when it is compounded, it means that the real value of your investment will double every ten years. In contrast, it will take 23 years to double your money at a 3 percent interest return.[2]

The Standard and Poor's 500 Index (S&P 500) is one measure of the performance of the broad stock market. This index factors in the value of dividends as if they were rein-vested in the market. Thus, it provides a measure of the rate of return received by investors in the form of both dividends and changes in share prices. **Exhibit 1** presents data on the

Stock options
The option to buy a specified number of shares of the firm's stock at a designated price. The designated price is gener-ally set so that the options will be quite valuable if the firm's shares increase in price but of little value if their price falls. Thus, when used to compen-sate top managers, stock op-tions provide a strong incentive to follow policies that will in-crease the value of the firm.

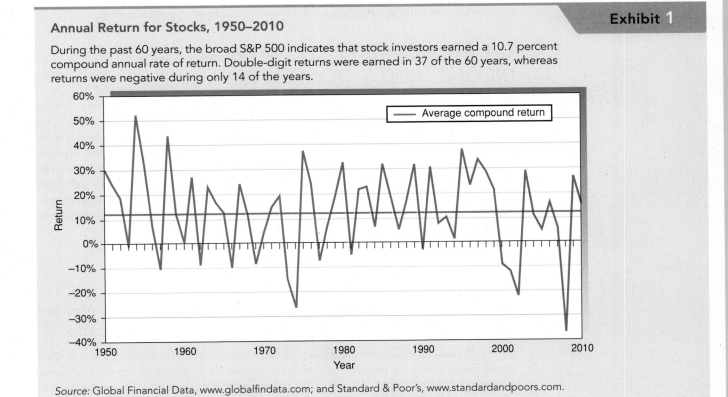

Exhibit 1

Annual Return for Stocks, 1950–2010

During the past 60 years, the broad S&P 500 indicates that stock investors earned a 10.7 percent compound annual rate of return. Double-digit returns were earned in 37 of the 60 years, whereas returns were negative during only 14 of the years.

Source: Global Financial Data, www.globalfindata.com; and Standard & Poor's, www.standardandpoors.com.

---

[2]You can approximate the number of years it will take to double your funds at alternative interest rates by simply dividing the yield into 70. This is sometimes referred to as the *rule of 70.*

real rate of return earned by stockholders each year since 1950 as measured by the changes in the S&P 500 during the year. The compound annual nominal rate of return of the S&P 500 was 10.5 percent during the 60-year period. Even after adjustment for inflation, the real compound annual return was 6.9 percent over this lengthy time period. The returns during the 1980s and 1990s were even higher. Since 2000, however, the returns have not been as high, and during 2008 alone investors experienced a negative 37 percent return.

Exhibit 1 highlights one of the risks that accompanies the ownership of stock: The returns and therefore the value of the stock can be quite volatile. The broad stock market, as measured by the S&P 500, provided double-digit returns during 37 of the 60 years between 1950 and 2010, but the returns were negative during 14 of those years. Stock market investors can never be sure what return they will earn or what the value of their stock holdings will be at a specified time in the future.

But this volatility is a big reason that stocks yield a significantly higher return than savings accounts, money market certificates, and corporate or government bonds, all of which guarantee you a given nominal return in the future. Because most people value the additional certainty in the yields that bonds and savings accounts provide over stocks, the average return on stocks has to be higher to attract investors away from financial assets with more predictable returns.

Given the rather large decline in the stock market in 2008, some might think that the stock market is no longer a good investment. However, even if one would have started a regular monthly investment program at just about the worst possible time in the history of the U.S. stock market—just before the crash of 1929 and the Great Depression of the 1930s in which the value of stocks declined by almost 90 percent—one would still have earned a better return within four years than a person who had invested in U.S. Treasury bills and would have ended up with a 13 percent nominal return (or an 11 percent real return) over the next 30 years. In fact, with stock prices now lower than they were a few years ago, this may prove to be a highly attractive time to begin investing in the stock market.

THE INTEREST RATE, THE VALUE OF FUTURE INCOME, AND STOCK PRICES

The present value of the firm's expected future net earnings (profit) underlies today's price of a firm's stock. What those future profits are worth to an investor today depends on three things: (1) the expected size of future net earnings, (2) when these earnings will be achieved, and (3) how much the investor discounts the future income. The last depends on the interest rate. As we noted in an earlier chapter, the present-value procedure can be used to determine the current value of any future income (or cost) stream. If D represents dividends (and gains from a higher stock price) earned in various years in the future (indicated by the subscripts) and i represents the discount or interest rate, the present value of the future income stream is:

$$PV = \frac{D_1}{(1 + i)} + \frac{D_2}{(1 + i)^2} + \cdots + \frac{D_3}{(1 + i)^3}$$

As this formula shows, a higher interest rate will reduce the present value of future revenues (returns), including those derived from stocks. This is true even if the size of the future returns is not affected by changes in the interest rate.

Stock analysts often stress that lower interest rates are good for the stock market. This should not be surprising because the lower rates of interest will increase the value of future income (and capital gains). For a specific annual income stream in perpetuity, the present value is equal simply to R/i, where R is the annual revenue stream and i is the interest rate. Thus, for example, when the interest rate is 12.5 percent, the discounted value of $10 of future income to be received each year in perpetuity is $80 ($10 divided by 0.125), eight times the stream of earnings. But when the interest rate is 5 percent, the discounted value of this same income stream is $200 ($10 divided by 0.05), or 20 times the stream of earnings.

Therefore, if the $10 represented the expected future income stream from a share of stock, the present value of the income stream would be higher when the interest rate was lower. Other things being constant, lower interest rates will increase the value of future income and thereby increase the market value of stocks.

How can one tell whether stock prices are high or low? The answer to that question depends on both the interest rate and expectations about the future income generated by the stock (or bundle of stocks). The price/earnings (P/E) ratio provides information on the price of a stock relative to its current earnings. It is interesting to look at the historical path of the P/E ratio and observe how it has responded to changes in interest rates and business-cycle conditions. Of course, the latter is likely to influence the future earnings prospects of business firms.

Exhibit 2 presents data on the P/E ratio over the 1950–2010 period for the stocks included in the S&P 500. The P/E ratio average during this lengthy period was 18. From the early 1950s through the mid-1990s, the P/E ratio ranged from a low of 8 to a high of 24. During the 1960s, the economy grew rapidly and both the inflation and interest rates were relatively low. Throughout most of that period, the P/E ratio was near 20. The decade of the 1970s was a period of both high inflation and high interest rates. As we just indicated, high interest rates will reduce the value of future income. Reflecting this factor, the P/E ratio during the 1970s was near 10 throughout the decade, considerably lower than during the 1960s.

Price/Earnings Ratio, 1950–2010

Exhibit 2

Since 1950, the average price/earnings ratio of the S&P 500 has been around 18. This ratio was between 8 and 24 throughout the 1951–1997 period. It was persistently near the lower end of this range (between 8 and 10) during the 1970s. It rose during the period 1985–1997 and eventually soared above 30 during the period 1998–2002. A combination of stock price declines and higher earnings as the economy recovered from the 2001 recession caused the price/earnings ratio to recede, but it briefly soared to more than 80 in 2009, primarily because of a sharp decline in earnings during the 2008–2009 recession.

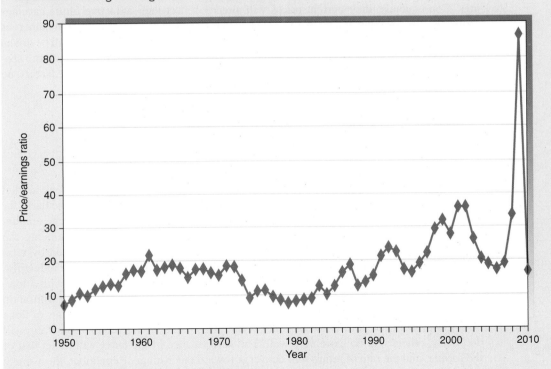

Source: Standard & Poor's, www.standardandpoor's.com.

As the economy grew rapidly, and both the inflation rate and interest rates declined and remained at a low level during the 1984–1997 period, the P/E ratio rose sharply. By the mid-1990s, it had risen to the 20 to 25 range, quite high by historical standards. But the stock market continued to boom, and by 1999 the P/E ratio had risen to an extremely high level, 31.7. By the late 1990s, there was considerable talk of a "stock market bubble," high stock prices that could not be maintained because they were out of line with the future earning prospects of business firms. The bubble burst and stock prices fell sharply. As a result, the S&P 500 lost nearly 50 percent of its value during 2000–2002 (see Exhibit 1). As the economy recovered from the recession of 2001, corporate earnings picked up and the P/E ratio receded. By 2005–2006, the P/E ratio had returned closer to its historical average, but briefly soared to more than 80 in 2009. This increase was primarily the result of sharp reductions in earnings and the marking down of bad assets during the 2008–2009 recession.

THE RANDOM WALK THEORY OF THE STOCK MARKET

Random walk theory
The theory that current stock prices already reflect known information about the future. Therefore, the future movement of stock prices will be determined by surprise occurrences. This will cause them to change in a random fashion.

Most economists adhere to the random walk theory of stock prices. According to this theory, current stock prices already reflect all available information that is known or can be predicted with any degree of accuracy, including information about the future state of corporate earnings, interest rates, the health of the economy, and other factors that influence stock prices. In other words, current stock prices will already reflect the best information currently available. In the future, the direction of stock prices will be driven by surprise occurrences—things that differ from what people are currently anticipating. By their very nature, these factors are unpredictable. If they were predictable, they would already be reflected in current stock prices.

The random walk theory applies to the price of a specific stock as well as to the market as a whole. The prices of specific stocks will reflect their future earnings prospects. The stock prices of firms with attractive future profit potential will be high relative to their current earnings. Consequently, their current prices will already reflect their attractive future earnings prospects. The opposite will be true for firms with poor future prospects. Although numerous factors affect the future price of any specific stock, changes in the current price will be driven by changes that differ from current expectations. Thus, because the future prices of both specific stocks and the market as a whole are driven by unexpected and unpredictable factors, no one can consistently forecast their future path with any degree of accuracy.

HOW THE ORDINARY INVESTOR CAN BEAT THE EXPERTS

Portfolio
All the stocks, bonds, or other securities held by an individual or corporation for investment purposes.

Equity mutual fund
A corporation that pools the funds of investors, including small investors, and uses them to purchase a bundle of stocks.

Historically, ordinary Americans have often refrained from investing in the stock market because of the risks involved. But there are ways this risk can be reduced, particularly for long-term investments. The value of any specific stock can rise or fall by a huge amount within a relatively short time period. But the risk accompanying these movements can be reduced by holding a diverse portfolio, a collection of stocks characterized by relatively small holdings of a large number of companies in different markets and industries. Equity mutual funds make this possible. They provide the ordinary investor with a low-cost method of owning a diverse bundle of stocks. An equity mutual fund is a corporation that buys and holds shares of stock in many firms. This diversification puts the law of large numbers to work for you. Whereas some of the investments in a diversified portfolio will do poorly, others will do extremely well. The performance of the latter will offset that of the former, and the rate of return will converge toward the average. Remember, the average real return of equities has been substantially higher than for bonds, savings accounts, and other readily accessible methods of saving.

As **Exhibit 3** shows, there was a huge increase in the quantity of funds flowing into mutual funds during the 1990s. The value of mutual fund investments increased from $246 billion in 1990 to approximately $4 trillion in 1999–2000. Although equity mutual fund investments declined as stock prices fell during 2000–2002, they rebounded and had soared to $6.5 trillion by 2007 before falling more than 43 percent to a value of $3.7 trillion in 2008. Their value rebounded afterward, reaching $5.7 trillion in 2010. They now account for about 30 percent of all publicly traded U.S. stocks.

A second source of risk facing the stock market investor is the possibility that nearly all stocks in the market can rise or fall together when expectations about the entire economy

Value of Equity Mutual Funds

Exhibit 3

The amount of money that people put into U.S. equity mutual funds, in order to hold shares in the ownership of stocks, rose dramatically in the 1990s. Purchasing shares in a mutual fund is a simple way for an individual to buy and hold an interest in a large variety of stocks with one purchase. Due to the recent financial crisis, the value of equity mutual funds fell by 43 percent from 2007 to 2008, before rebounding in 2009 and 2010.

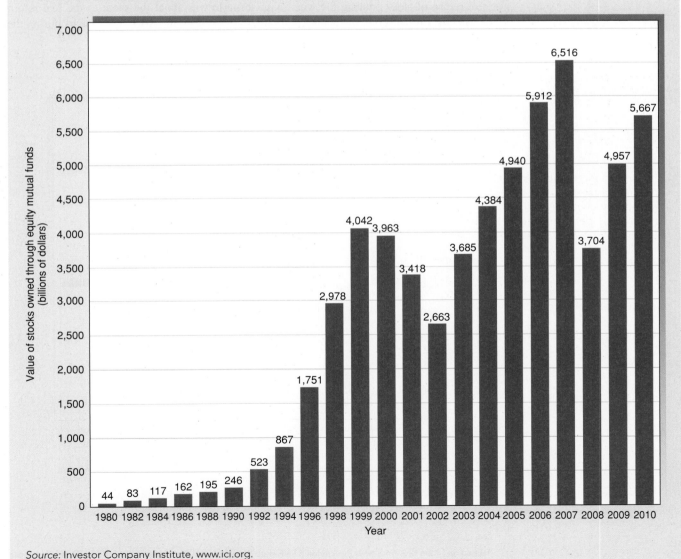

Source: Investor Company Institute, www.ici.org.

change. This has happened on several occasions. For example, on October 19, 1987, the stocks listed in the Dow Jones Industrial Average lost more than 22 percent of their value in just one trading day. The high-tech stocks listed on the NASDAQ exchange lost about 70 percent of their value during 2000 and 2001; and most recently the S&P 500 lost about 57 percent of its value between October 2007 and March 2009. However, the risks accompanying such short-term movements can be substantially reduced if an investor either continually adds to or holds a diverse portfolio of stocks over a lengthy period of time, say, 30 or 35 years.

Exhibit 4 illustrates this point. This exhibit shows the highest and lowest real returns (the returns adjusted for inflation) earned from stock market investments for periods of varying lengths between the years 1871 and 2010. The exhibit assumes that the investor paid a fixed amount annually into a mutual fund that mirrored the S&P 500, a basket of stocks thought to represent the market as a whole. Clearly, huge swings are possible when stocks are held for only a short time period. During the 1871–2008 period, the single-year returns of the S&P 500 ranged from 47.2 percent to −40.8 percent. Even over a five-year period, the compound annual returns ranged from 29.8 percent to −16.7 percent. Note that the "best returns" and "worst returns" converged as the length of the investment period increased. When a 35-year period was considered, the compound annual return for the best 35 years between 1871 and 2010 was 9.5 percent, compared with 2.7 percent for the worst 35 years.[3] Thus, the annual real return of stocks during the worst-case scenario was about the same as the real return for bonds. Furthermore, the annual real rate of return from the stock investments during the period was 7 percent—more than twice the comparable rate for bonds.

Exhibit 4

Stocks Are Less Risky When Held for a Lengthy Time Period

This exhibit shows the best and the worst annualized real performance for each investment period from 1871 to 2010. It shows that there is less risk of a low or negative return when an investment in a portfolio of stocks (S&P 500) is held for a longer period of time.

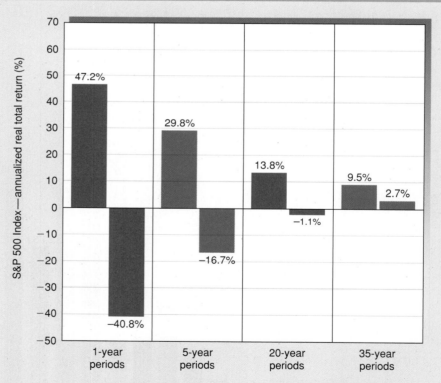

Source: Liqun Liu, Andrew J. Rettenmaier, and Zijun Wang, "Social Security and Market Risk," National Center for Policy Analysis Working Paper Number 244 (July 2001). The returns are based on the assumption that an individual invests a fixed amount for each year in the investment period. Data updated through 2010.

---

[3]Based on Liqun Liu, Andrew J. Rettenmaier, and Zijun Wang, "Social Security and Market Risk" (working paper number 244, National Center for Policy Analysis, Washington, DC, July 2001). Data updated through 2010.

Are stocks riskier than bonds? If held for only a short time—five years, for example—stocks are riskier. However, when held over lengthy periods, such as 20 or 30 years, historically the rate of return on stocks has been both higher and less variable than that of bonds. What does this imply for people in their twenties and thirties who are saving for their retirement? Where should they put their funds?

The bottom line is this: When held over a lengthy period, a diverse portfolio of stocks has yielded a high rate of return, and the variation in that return has been low. Thus, for the long-term investor, such as a person saving for his or her retirement years, a diverse portfolio of stocks is not particularly risky.

THE ADVANTAGES OF INDEXED MUTUAL FUNDS

When purchasing a mutual fund, the investor can choose either a managed or an indexed fund. A **managed equity mutual fund** is one in which an "expert," generally supported by a research staff, tries to pick and choose the stock holdings of the fund in a manner that will maximize its rate of return. In contrast, an **indexed equity mutual fund** merely holds stocks in the same proportion as they exist in a broad stock market index like the S&P 500 or the Dow Jones Industrials.

In the case of indexed funds, neither comprehensive research nor extensive stock trading is needed because the fund merely seeks to mirror the index and earn the rate of return of the broad market that it represents. Thus, because they do not spend much on either research or stock trading, the operating costs of indexed funds are substantially lower than they are for managed funds. Therefore, they are able to charge lower fees, which means that a larger share of the investor's money flows directly into the purchase of stock.

As a result, the average rate of return yielded by a broad indexed fund beats the return of almost all managed mutual funds when comparisons are made over periods of time such as a decade. This is not surprising because, as the random walk theory indicates, not even the experts will be able to forecast consistently the future direction of stock prices with any degree of accuracy. Over the typical ten-year period, the S&P 500 has yielded a higher return than 85 percent of actively managed funds. And over 20-year periods, mutual funds indexed to the S&P 500 have generally outperformed about 98 percent of actively managed funds.[4] Thus, the odds are very low, about 1 in 50, that you or anyone else will be able to select an actively managed fund that will do better than the market average *over the long run*.

Managed equity mutual fund
An equity mutual fund that has a portfolio manager who decides what stocks will be held in the fund and when they will be bought or sold. A research staff generally provides support for the fund manager.

Indexed equity mutual fund
An equity mutual fund that holds a portfolio of stocks that matches their share (or weight) in a broad stock market index such as the S&P 500. The overhead of these funds is usually quite low because their expenses on stock trading and research are low.

[4]See Jeremy J. Siegel, *Stocks for the Long Run*, 3rd ed. (New York: McGraw-Hill, 2002), 342–43.

SHOULD YOU INVEST IN A FUND BECAUSE OF ITS PAST PERFORMANCE?

People marketing mutual funds often encourage customers to invest in mutual funds that have yielded high rates of return in the past. This sounds like a good strategy, but history indicates that it is not. Mutual funds with outstanding records over a 5- or 10-year period often perform poorly in the future. The top 20 managed equity funds of the 1990s outperformed the S&P 500 by 3.9 percent per year over the course of the decade. But if investors entering the market in 2000 thought they would beat the market by choosing the "hot" funds of the 1990s, they would have been disappointed. The top 20 funds of the 1990s underperformed the S&P 500 by 1.3 percent per year during the 2000s.

Even funds that have persistently been successful in the recent past may do poorly in the future. For example, only 14 out of the more than 1,000 mutual funds were able to beat the S&P 500 for nine consecutive years during 1999–2007. Surely, these were the best managed funds. Nonetheless, only one of the 14 was able to beat the S&P index in 2008.[5]

Why is past performance such an unreliable indicator? Two factors provide insight on the answer to this question. First, some of the mutual funds with above-average returns during a period were merely lucky. After all, if you flip a coin 100 times, you will not always get 50 heads and 50 tails. Sometimes, the coin will come up heads maybe 60 times out of 100. But this does not mean you can expect 60 heads during the next sequence of 100. So it is with stock market mutual funds. Given that there are a large number of funds, some of them will have above-average performance for a time period. But this does not mean that the above-average performance can be expected in the future.

Second, a strategy that works well in one environment, inflationary conditions, for example, is often disastrous when conditions change. For example, mutual funds with substantial holdings of gold-mining companies did exceedingly well during the inflationary 1970s. But their performance was disastrous during the 1980s and 1990s as the inflation was brought under control. Similarly, some mutual funds that performed well during the bull market of the 1990s were among the worst performers during the bear market that began in 2000.

Virtually none of the experts are able to "beat the market average" consistently over lengthy time periods and changing market conditions. Thus, broad market indexes outperform the stock pickers in the long run. This is something you will not often hear from brokerage firms and other experts trying to sell their services to you. But knowing this will make you a smarter investor.

KEY POINTS

- The stock market makes it possible for investors without either specialized business skills or the time to become involved in the operation of a business firm to share in the risks and opportunities that accompany the ownership of corporate businesses.

- During the last two centuries, after adjustment for inflation, corporate stocks have yielded a real return of approximately 7 percent per year, compared with a real return of about 3 percent for bonds and even lower yields for savings accounts and money market mutual funds.

- Most economists adhere to the random walk theory of stock prices. According to this theory, current stock prices already reflect all information about factors influencing stock prices that is known or can be forecast with any degree of accuracy. Thus, the future direction of stock prices will be driven by surprise occurrences and, as a result, no one will be able to forecast future stock prices with any degree of accuracy.

- Buying and selling individual stocks without specialized knowledge for a quick profit is very risky. But holding a

---

[5]Burton G. Malkiel, *A Random Walk Down Wall Street: The Time Tested Strategy for Successful Investing* (New York: W. W. Norton & Company, 2011), 180–83.

diverse portfolio of unrelated stocks and holding them for long periods of time greatly reduces the risk of investing in the stock market.

- An equity mutual fund that is tied to a broad stock market index like the S&P 500 provides an attractive method for long-term investors to obtain relatively high yields with minimal risk. Indexed mutual funds have substantially lower operating costs than managed funds because they engage in less trading

and have no need for either a market expert or research staff.

- Stock prices declined substantially during the recent financial crisis. The S&P 500 lost about 57 percent of its value between October 2007 and March 2009. While stock prices rose as the economy recovered, they were still well below their earlier highs as of mid-year 2011. However, based on historical evidence, this does not necessarily imply that now is a bad time to invest in the stock market.

CRITICAL ANALYSIS QUESTIONS

1. *A friend just inherited $50,000. She informs you of her investment plans and asks for your advice. "I want to put it into the stock market and use it for my retirement in 30 years. What do you think is the best plan that will provide high returns at a relatively low risk?" What answer would you give? Explain.

2. Suppose that more expansionary monetary policy leads to inflation and higher nominal interest rates. How is this likely to affect the value of stocks? Explain.

3. *Microsoft stock rose from less than $10 in 1995 to more than $100 per share in 2000. Microsoft has made sizable profits but never paid a dividend. Why were people willing to pay such a high price knowing that they might not get dividends for many years?

4. If an investment adviser gives you some hot new stock tip, is it likely to be a "sure thing"? Why or why not? If you have a stockbroker and purchase the stocks promoted by the broker, are you likely to earn a high return on your stock investments? Why or why not?

5. *The stocks of some corporations that have never made a profit, especially those in high-technology industries, have risen in price. What causes investors to be willing to buy these stocks?

6. What is an indexed equity mutual fund? What is a managed equity mutual fund? How will the administrative costs of the two differ?

7. What is the random walk theory of stock prices? What does it indicate about the ability of "experts" to forecast accurately the future direction of stock prices?

8. Congress is currently considering legislation that would increase both the tax on dividends and the tax on capital gains derived from the appreciation of assets. How would an increase in the tax rate applied to dividends and capital gains income affect stock prices? Why?

9. Are stocks a risky investment? How can one reduce the risk accompanying stock market investments ?

*Asterisk denotes questions for which answers are given in Appendix B.

SPECIAL TOPIC 4

Great Debates in Economics: Keynes versus Hayek[1]

FOCUS

- Why are the views of John Maynard Keynes and Friedrich Hayek often compared and contrasted?
- What is the source of economic booms and busts?
- What might be done to reduce the impact of recessions?
- Should the government try to centrally plan the economy?
- Can the political process be counted on to promote economic stability and the efficient allocation of resources?

We've been going back and forth for a century

[Keynes] I want to steer markets,

[Hayek] I want them set free

Chorus from Keynes–Hayek video

[1] Note to instructors: This feature is developed around the Keynes–Hayek video raps (see links in the third paragraph of the following page). It is designed to be a fun exercise that highlights several key points of continuing debate among economists.

John Maynard Keynes and Friedrich August Hayek are two of the most important economists of the twentieth century. Moreover, their scholarly work represents alternative theories and ideas about the central issues of our day, including economic instability, central planning, and the operation of the political process.

Can serious economics be fun? Russell Roberts, a professor of economics at George Mason University, and filmmaker John Papola think it can be. They recently developed an eight-minute rap video with actors posing as a dueling Hayek and Keynes. The lyrics highlight the contrasting views of Keynes and Hayek on the business cycle, fiscal and monetary policy, and the role of government.

The Roberts–Papola video titled "Fear the Boom and Bust: Keynes versus Hayek" has attracted almost 3 million views. It is available at www.youtube.com/watch?v=d0nERTFo-Sk. Roberts and Papola have also done a follow-up rap, "Fight of the Century: Keynes vs. Hayek Round Two," which is available at www.youtube.com/watch?v=GTQnarzmTOc. Take a break from your studying and have a little fun watching these videos.

The views of Keynes and Hayek provide a vivid contrast on key issues in economics. Nonetheless, both command respect among professional economists. Keynes is widely regarded as the most influential economist of the twentieth century. Hayek was the recipient of the 1974 Nobel Prize in Economics.

Interestingly, Keynes and Hayek were contemporaries at Cambridge University and the London School of Economics in the early 1940s. During World War II, they even spent a night together on the roof of the chapel of King's College, Cambridge looking out for German bombers.

Keynes's *General Theory* provided a reasonable explanation of what went wrong during the Great Depression and what could be done to prevent such an event from occurring in the future. His ideas inspired a generation of economists that transformed macroeconomic analysis. Hayek was born in Vienna in 1899, and he was a rising star in the 1930s. The London School of Economics lured him from Austria, at least partly to counter the influence of Keynes and the reputation he brought to rival Cambridge University. In his 1944 book, the *Road to Serfdom*, Hayek argued that the growth of government was endangering freedom and leading to tyranny in the Western democracies, just as it had done in both Nazi Germany and the Soviet Union.

Keynes and Hayek were polar opposites not only in their economic views but also in their personality characteristics. Keynes was outgoing and dominant. Some charged that he was arrogant, but all recognized that his skills as a persuader were supreme. In contrast, Hayek was quiet and unassuming. While Keynes reveled in policy-making, Hayek was content to remain outside of policy circles. Keynes was optimistic, and his message was well suited for the "We're fixing it" mentality of politicians. On the other hand, Hayek's message was not one political officials like to hear: Policy-makers have messed things up and it will take time for the market to correct their errors.

A popular PBS video series, *Commanding Heights* (Episode One: "The Battle of Ideas"), also used the contrasting views of these two economists to illustrate how major trends in economic thinking impacted global economic events during the twentieth century.[2] Following in this tradition, this special topic will use the ideas of Keynes and Hayek, including lyrics from the videos, to explain and contrast their viewpoints and the alternative theories they represent.

Courtesy of EconStories.tv

iStockphoto.com/nicoolay

---

[2]The PBS series was based on the book by Daniel Yergin and Joseph Stanislaw, *The Commanding Heights: The Battle Between Government and the Marketplace That Is Remaking the Modern World* (New York: Simon and Schuster, 1998).

KEYNES, HAYEK, AND GREAT DEBATES IN ECONOMICS

The lyrics of the Keynes–Hayek videos present alternative views with regard to three of the most important debates in economics. Let's consider these debates and the references to them in the rap lyrics.

1. WHAT IS THE CAUSE AND CURE FOR THE BUSINESS CYCLE?

The underlying causes of the business cycle and potential effectiveness of policy responses have been a focal point of debate among economists for at least a century. The perspectives of Keynes and Hayek represent alternative viewpoints on this issue.

The Keynesian viewpoint argues that capitalism-based, market economies are inherently unstable. Private investment in particular is fickle and prone to extreme fluctuations driven by changes in business optimism, or what Keynes referred to as "animal spirits." Moreover, the booms and busts will tend to feed on themselves, and therefore a market economy will swing back and forth between a boom that will lead to inflation and a bust that will generate high rates of unemployment. But there is good news in the Keynesian theory. Government can use fiscal and monetary policy to control aggregate demand and thereby promote economic stability. During a recession, government spending should be increased to offset the weak private investment, taxes should be reduced to stimulate consumption, budget deficits should be used to finance these activities, and finally monetary policy should keep interest rates low.

The Hayekian viewpoint argues that booms and busts are caused by perverse government policy and that the economy would be considerably more stable if political decision-makers followed stable policies and refrained from activist interventions. In his research on monetary theory, Hayek argued that economic booms are the result of excessive credit expansion that pushes interest rates to artificially low levels. At the abnormally low interest rates, businesses are induced to undertake investments that will later prove to be both unprofitable and unsustainable.

Hayekians refer to these inefficient investments as malinvestment. In this view, recessions are a "hangover" or adjustment caused by improper government policy during the preceding boom. Once the government has caused the malinvestment, the proper course is to allow market prices to adjust and allow the malinvestment to be cleansed from the system. Government stimulus spending will merely slow the adjustment process and prolong the recession.

Here are some excerpted lyrics from the Keynes versus Hayek rap videos that illustrate their contrasting views on the business cycle.

[Both] There's a boom and bust cycle and good reason to fear it.

[Hayek] Blame low interest rates.

[Keynes] No…it's the animal spirits.
[Keynes] I had a real plan any fool can understand.
The advice, real simple—boost aggregate demand!
C, I, G, all together gets to Y.
Make sure the total's growing, watch the economy fly.
So if that flow is getting low, doesn't matter the reason.
We need more government spending, now it's stimulus season.
The monetary and the fiscal, they're equally correct.
Public works, digging ditches, war has the same effect.
Even a broken window helps the glass man have some wealth.
The multiplier driving higher the economy's health.

[Hayek] The place you should study isn't the bust.
It's the boom that should make you feel leery, that's the thrust

Of my theory, the capital structure is key.
Malinvestments wreck the economy.
The boom gets started with an expansion of credit.
The Fed sets rates low, are you starting to get it?
That new money is confused for real loanable funds
But it's just inflation that's driving the ones
Who invest in new projects like housing construction.
The boom plants the seeds for its future destruction.
So the boom turns to bust as the interest rates rise
With the costs of production, price signals were lies.
The boom was a binge that's a matter of fact.
Now its devalued capital that makes up the slack.
You must save to invest, don't use the printing press
Or a bust will surely follow, an economy depressed.
Your so-called "stimulus" will make things even worse.
It's just more of the same, more incentives perversed.

[Keynes] So what would YOU do to help those unemployed?
This is the question you seem to avoid.
When we're in a mess, would you have us just wait,
Doing nothing until markets equilibrate?

[Hayek] I don't wanna do nothing, there's plenty to do.
The question I ponder is who plans for whom?
Do I plan for myself or I leave it to you?
I want plans by the many, not by the few.
Let's not repeat what created our troubles.
I want real growth not a series of bubbles.
Stop bailing out losers, let prices work.
If we don't try to steer them they won't go berserk.

2. SHOULD AN ECONOMY BE DIRECTED BY GOVERNMENT CENTRAL PLANNING OR DECENTRALIZED INDIVIDUAL PLANNING AND THE INVISIBLE HAND OF MARKET PRICES?

Clearly, the main chorus of the rap lyrics stresses their differing views, as Keynes says, "I want to steer markets," and Hayek replies, "I want them set free."

The Keynesian viewpoint holds that central planning by wise government officials is needed not only to keep the macroeconomy on track but also to correct market failures and assure an equitable distribution of income. Relying on information derived from economists and other experts, Keynesians believe that policy-makers will be able to selectively intervene into markets (or sometimes outright control them entirely) in ways that will improve on market outcomes.

In contrast, Hayekians argue that central planners do not have sufficient information to direct the economy and their efforts to do so will do more damage than good. Decentralized decision-making, directed by market prices, will be a more reliable method of directing resources into productive projects and away from ones that are counterproductive. Instead of centralized planning, individuals should be left free to make their own plans relying on information and incentives communicated by market prices, competitive forces, and the profit and loss system. According to the Hayekian view, a spontaneous order will emerge from the market process that will coordinate the desires of consumers and producers, and of borrowers and lenders. Hayekians believe this will result in both more economic freedom and more rapid economic progress. Hayek highlights this point in his lyrics: "The question I ponder is who plans for whom? Do I plan for myself or I leave it to you? I want plans by the many, not by the few."

Moreover, dynamic competition provides decision-makers with a strong incentive to discover better ways of doing things, improve technologies, and institute practical innovations that will improve our lives. In this view the information necessary to guide the economy is not known to anyone in total, but is instead generated through the process of decentralized market interaction. According to Hayekians, the proper role of government is simply to provide the rule of law, enforce contracts, and protect property rights, leaving the rest to market forces.

Courtesy of EconStories.tv

Here are some excerpted lyrics from the Keynes versus Hayek rap videos that illustrate these points:

> [Hayek] His theory conceals the mechanics of change,
> That simple equation, too much aggregation
> Ignores human action and motivation.
> The economy's not a car. There's no engine to stall.
> No experts can fix it. There's no "it" at all.
> The economy is us. Put away your wrenches, the economy is organic.
>
> [Keynes] Come on are you kidding?
> Don't Wall Street gyrations challenge the world-view of self-regulation?
> Even you must admit that lesson we've learned
> Is more oversight is needed or else we'll get burned.
>
> [Hayek] Oversight? The government's long been in bed
> With those Wall Street execs and the firms that they've bled.
> Capitalism is about profit and loss.
> You bail out the losers; there is no end to the cost.
> The lesson I've learned is how little we know.
> The world is complex, not some circular flow.
> The economy is not a class you master in college,
> To think otherwise is the pretense of knowledge.

3. CAN DEMOCRATIC DECISION-MAKING BE COUNTED ON TO ALLOCATE RESOURCES EFFICIENTLY?

As we discussed in Chapter 6, public-choice analysis provides insights on the operation of the political process. It indicates that the incentives confronted by voters, interest groups, politicians, and bureaucrats will sometimes conflict with sound policy and the efficient allocation of resources. Even when decisions are made democratically, the political process will often favor well-organized interest groups and shortsighted policies that generate highly visible gains at the expense of costs that are less visible. Predictably, some inefficient use of resources will arise from these forces. Put another way, there is "government failure" as well as "market failure."

The Keynesian perspective seldom directly addresses this issue. Instead, it is assumed that the job of the economists is to figure out the ideal or optimal solutions, and once these are developed, political decision-makers can be expected to adopt them. Moreover, many Keynesians charge that analysis of how the political process works is outside of the scope of economics and therefore those who address this issue are not really addressing economic issues. Keynes himself had great confidence in his ability to convince policy-makers to adopt his advice. Within the Keynesian framework, it is essentially assumed that political decision-makers will implement policies in a proper manner.

The Hayekian perspective argues that the structure of incentives and institutions exert a major impact on how government works. The government failure described within public-choice theory will be a major problem or barrier to implementing good policy. Thus, it is vitally important to adopt institutions and constitutional rules that bring personal self-interest of policy-makers into harmony with growth and prosperity.

The father of economics, Adam Smith, held a similar view. Smith stated,

> *The man of system is apt to be very wise in his own conceit. He seems to imagine that he can arrange the different members of a great society with as much ease as the hand arranges the different pieces upon a chess-board; he does not consider that the pieces upon the chess-board have not another principle of motion besides that which the hand impresses upon them; but that, in the great chess-board of human society, every single piece has a principle of motion of its own, although different from that which the legislature might choose to impress upon it. If those two principles coincide and act in the same direction, the game of human society will go on easily and harmoniously, and is very likely to be happy and successful. If they are opposite or different, the game will go on miserably, and the society must be at all times in the highest degree of disorder.*[3]

Interestingly, Hayek makes a reference to this view of Adam Smith in the rap video.

[Keynes] You've been on your high horse and you are off to the races.
I look at the world on a case-by-case basis.
When people are suffering I roll up my sleeves
And do what I can to cure our disease.
The future's uncertain, our outlooks are frail.
That's why markets are so prone to fail.
In a volatile world we need more discretion
So state intervention can counter depression.

[Hayek] People aren't chessmen you move on a board
At your whim, their dreams and desires ignored.
With political incentives, discretion's a joke.
Those dials are twisting – just mirrors and smoke.
We need stable rules and real market prices
So prosperity emerges and cuts short the crisis.

---

[3]Adam Smith, *The Theory of Moral Sentiments*, Glasgow Edition of Oxford University Press (Indianapolis: Liberty Fund, Inc., [1790] 1976): 233–34. Also available at www.econlib.org/library/Smith.smMS6.html#VI.II.42).

Keynes and Hayek represent two of the most important strands of economic thinking. You will see their views represented in several of the special topics that follow, including the ones on the recent financial crisis, the Great Depression, lessons from Japan and Canada, government deficits and debt, the health care debate, and improving the quality of education.

KEY POINTS

- John Maynard Keynes and Friedrich Hayek are giants in the economics profession. Their theories and ideas represent contrasting alternative views on several of the central issues of economics.

- Keynes believed that market economies were inherently unstable and government intervention in the form of fiscal and monetary stimulus could be used effectively to promote economic stability. Hayek believed that economic instability was primarily the result of malinvestment generated by monetary and credit expansion and that government stimulus would slow market adjustments and the recovery process.

- Keynes believed that government central planning could improve on market outcomes. Hayek believed that policy-makers simply do not have the information or incentives to plan the economy effectively and that their efforts to do so would be far less efficient than allocation through markets.

- Keynesians believe that the job of the economist is to develop policies that will reduce economic instability and correct market failures. Keynesian analysis largely ignores how economic incentives influence the operation of the political process. Hayekians recognize that the political incentive structure often caters to well-organized interest groups and results in the adoption of shortsighted policies. Thus, they stress the importance of legal and political institutions that will provide both market participants and political decision-makers with incentives to engage in productive rather than counterproductive actions.

CRITICAL ANALYSIS QUESTIONS

1. *What* is the underlying message of the following lyrics from Keynes?

   [Keynes] Public works, digging ditches, war has
      the same effect.
   Even a broken window helps the glass man have
      some wealth.
   The multiplier driving higher the economy's health.

2. Use the following lyrics to describe the difference between Keynes and Hayek on the role of savings in the economy.

   [Keynes] So forget about saving, get it straight
   out of your head.
   Like I said, in the long run—we're all dead.
   Savings is destruction, that's the paradox of thrift.
   Don't keep money in your pocket, or that growth
      will never lift.

   [Hayek] Real savings come first if you want to invest.
   The market coordinates time with interest.
   Your focus on spending is pushing on thread.
   In the long run, my friend, it's your theory that's dead.

   Whether it's the late twenties or two thousand and five
   Booming bad investments, seems like they'd thrive.
   You must save to invest, don't use the printing
      press
   Or a bust will surely follow, an economy depressed.

3. The following lyrics discuss whether the government stimulus efforts in response to the recent financial crisis worked and also argue points about government policy during the Great Depression and the subsequent recovery. What are the major areas of disagreement on these issues as illustrated in the lyrics?

   [Keynes] Are you kidding? My cure works
      perfectly fine.
   Have a look. The recession ended in '09.
   I deserve credit. Things would have been worse.
   All the estimates prove it. I'll go chapter and verse.
   We could have done better if we'd only spent more.
   Too bad that only happens when there's a world war.
   You can carp all you want about stats and
      regression.

Do you deny that world war cut short the Depression?

[Hayek] Wow. One data point and you're jumping for joy.
The last time I checked wars only destroy.
There was no multiplier. Consumption just shrank
As we used scarce resources for every new tank.
Pretty perverse to call that prosperity.
Ration meat. Ration butter. A life of austerity.
When that war spending ended, your friends cried disaster.
Yet the economy thrived and grew faster.
Creating employment is a straightforward craft
When the nation's at war and there's a draft.
If every worker were staffed in the army and fleet
We'd have full employment and nothing to eat.
Jobs are a means, not the end in themselves.
People work to live better, to put food on the shelves.
Real growth means production of what people demand.
That's entrepreneurship, not your central plan.

4. The following lyrics discuss the appropriateness of the government bailouts in response to the recent financial crisis. Explain why Keynesians generally support these policies while Hayekians do not.

[Hayek] And yet it continues as a justification
For bailouts and payoffs by pols with machinations.
You provide them with cover to sell us a free lunch,
Then all that we're left with is debt, and a bunch.
If you're living high on that cheap credit hog
Don't look for cure from the hair of the dog.
Let's not repeat what created our troubles.
I want real growth not a series of bubbles.
Stop bailing out losers, let prices work.
If we don't try to steer them they won't go berserk.

The Crisis of 2008: Causes and Lessons for the Future

FOCUS

- How has government spending per person changed historically in the United States?
- Why did housing prices rise rapidly during 2001–2005 and then fall in the years immediately following? Did regulation play a role? Did monetary policy contribute to the housing boom and bust?
- What caused the economic Crisis of 2008?
- What lessons should we learn from the Crisis of 2008?

iStockphoto.com/sorendis

U.S. housing policies are the root cause of the current financial crisis. Other players—"greedy" investment bankers; foolish investors; imprudent bankers; incompetent rating agencies;irresponsible housing speculators; shortsighted homeowners; and predatory mortgage brokers, lenders, and borrowers—all played a part, but they were only following the economic incentives that government policy laid out for them.

—*Peter J. Wallison*[1]

[1]Peter J. Wallison, "Cause and Effect: Government Policies and the Financial Crisis," AEI Financial Services Outlook, www.aei.org/publication29015.

The headlines of 2008 were dominated by falling housing prices, rising default and foreclosure rates, failure of large investment banks, and huge bailouts arranged by both the Federal Reserve and the U.S. Treasury. The Crisis of 2008 substantially reduced the wealth of most Americans and generated widespread concern about the future of the U.S. economy. This crisis and the response to it may well be the most important macroeconomic event of our lives. Thus, it is vitally important for each of us to understand what happened, why things went wrong, and the lessons that need to be learned from the experience.

Let's take a closer look at the key events leading up to the crisis and the underlying factors that generated the collapse.

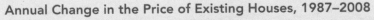

iStockphoto.com/nicoolay

KEY EVENTS LEADING UP TO THE CRISIS

The housing boom and bust during the first seven years of this century are central to understanding the economic events of 2008. As **Exhibit 1** shows, housing prices were relatively stable during the 1990s, but they began to increase rapidly toward the end of the decade. By 2002, housing prices were booming. Between January 2002 and mid-year 2006, housing prices increased by a whopping 87 percent. This translates to an annual growth rate of approximately 13 percent. But the housing boom began to wane in 2006. Housing prices leveled off, and by the end of 2006, they were falling. The boom had turned to a bust, and the housing price decline continued throughout 2007 and 2008. By year-end 2008, housing prices were approximately 30 percent below their 2006 peak.

Exhibit 1

Annual Change in the Price of Existing Houses, 1987–2008

Housing prices increased slowly during the 1990s, but they began rising more rapidly toward the end of the decade. Between January 2002 and mid-year 2006, housing prices increased by a whopping 87 percent. But the boom turned to a bust during the second half of 2006, and the housing price decline continued throughout 2007–2008.

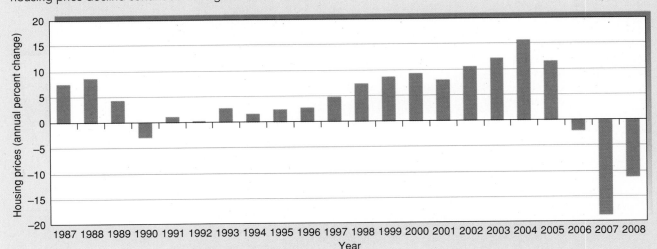

Source: www.standardpoors.com, S&P Case-Schiller Housing Price Index.

Mortgage default rate
The percentage of home mortgages on which the borrower is late by ninety days or more with the payments on the loan or it is in the foreclosure process. This rate is sometimes referred to as the serious delinquency rate.

Foreclosure rate
The percentage of home mortgages on which the lender has started the process of taking ownership of the property because the borrower has failed to make the monthly payments.

Exhibit 2 part (a) presents data on the **mortgage default rate** from 1979 through 2008. (*Note:* The default rate is also known as the serious delinquency rate.) As these figures illustrate, the default rate fluctuated, within a narrow range, around 2 percent prior to 2006. It increased only slightly during the recessions of 1982, 1990, and 2001.

However, even though the economy was relatively strong and unemployment low, the default rate began to increase sharply during the second half of 2006. By the fourth quarter of 2007, it had already risen to 3.6 percent, up from 2.0 percent in the second quarter of 2006. The increase continued and the default rate reached 5.2 percent in 2008.

As Exhibit 2 part (b) illustrates, the pattern of the housing **foreclosure rate** was similar. It fluctuated between 0.2 and 0.5 during 1978–2005. The recessions of 1982–1983, 1990, and 2001 exerted little impact on the foreclosure rate. However, like the mortgage default rate, the foreclosure rate started to increase during the second half of 2006, and it tripled over the next two years.

During 2008, housing prices were falling, default rates were increasing, and the confidence of both consumers and investors was deteriorating. These conditions were reinforced by sharply rising prices of crude oil, which pushed gasoline prices to more than $4 per gallon during the first half of the year. Against this background, the stock market took a huge tumble. As **Exhibit 3** shows, the S&P 500 index of stock prices fell by 55 percent between October 2007 and March 2009. This collapse eroded the wealth and endangered the retirement savings of many Americans.

Exhibit 2

Mortgage Default and Housing Foreclosure Rates, 1979–2008

As part (a) shows, the mortgage default rate fluctuated within a narrow range around 2 percent for more than two decades before 2006. It increased only slightly during the recessions of 1982, 1990, and 2001 but started to increase in the second half of 2006 and soared to more than 5 percent in 2008. As part (b) shows, the foreclosure rate followed a similar pattern. It ranged between 0.2 and 0.5 percent before 2006, before soaring to 1.2 percent in 2008.

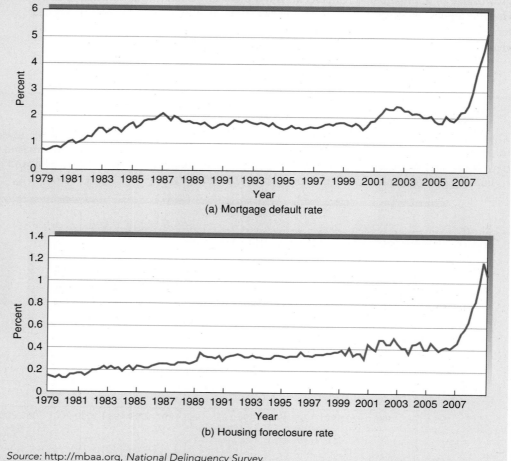

(a) Mortgage default rate

(b) Housing foreclosure rate

Source: http://mbaa.org, National Delinquency Survey.

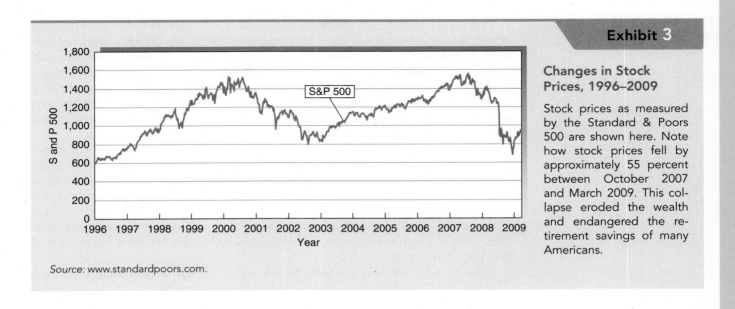

Exhibit 3

Changes in Stock Prices, 1996–2009

Stock prices as measured by the Standard & Poors 500 are shown here. Note how stock prices fell by approximately 55 percent between October 2007 and March 2009. This collapse eroded the wealth and endangered the retirement savings of many Americans.

Source: www.standardpoors.com.

WHAT CAUSED THE CRISIS OF 2008?

Why did housing prices rise rapidly, then level off, and eventually collapse? Why did the mortgage default and housing foreclosure rates increase rapidly well before the start of the recession, which did not begin until December 2007? Why are the recent default and foreclosure rates so much higher than the rates of earlier years, including those of prior recessions? Why did large, and seemingly strong, investment banks like Bear Stearns and Lehman Brothers run into financial troubles so quickly? Four factors combine to provide the answers to all of these questions.[2]

FACTOR 1: CHANGE IN MORTGAGE LENDING STANDARDS

The lending standards for home mortgage loans changed substantially beginning in the mid-1990s. The looser lending standards did not just happen. They were the result of federal policy designed to promote home ownership among households with incomes below the median. Home ownership is a worthy goal, but it was not pursued directly through transparent budget allocations and subsidies to homebuyers. Instead, the federal government imposed a complex set of regulations and regulatory mandates that forced various lending institutions to extend more loans to low- and moderate-income households. To meet these mandates, lenders had to lower their standards. By the early years of the twenty-first century, it was possible to borrow more (relative to your income) and purchase a house or condo with a lower down payment than was the case a decade earlier.

The Federal National Mortgage Association and Federal Home Loan Mortgage Corporation, commonly known as Fannie Mae and Freddie Mac, played a central role in this relaxation of mortgage lending standards. These two entities were created by Congress to help provide liquidity in secondary mortgage markets. Fannie Mae, established by the federal government in 1938, was spun off as a *government-sponsored enterprise* (GSE) in 1968. Freddie Mac was created in 1970 as another GSE to provide competition for Fannie Mae.

---

[2]For additional details on the Crisis of 2008, see Thomas Sowell, *The Housing Boom and Bust* (New York: Basic Books, 2009); Stan J. Liebowitz, "Anatomy of a Train Wreck: Causes of the Mortgage Meltdown," Ch. 13 in Randall G. Holcombe and Benjamin Powell, eds, *Housing America: Building Out of a Crisis* (New Brunswick, NJ: Transaction Publishers, 2009); Peter J. Wallison, "Cause and Effect: Government Policies and the Financial Crisis," *AEI Financial Services Outlook*, www.aei.org/publication29015; and Lawrence H. White, "How Did We Get Into This Financial Mess?" (Briefing Paper 110, Cato Institute, Washington, DC, November 18, 2008), available at www.cato.org/pub_display.php?pub_id=9788.

Basis points
One one-hundredth of a percentage point. Thus, 100 basis points are equivalent to one percentage point.

Fannie Mae and Freddie Mac were privately owned (for-profit) businesses, but because of their federal sponsorship, it was widely perceived that the government would back their bonds if they ever ran into financial trouble. As a result, Fannie and Freddie were able to borrow funds at 50 to 75 basis points cheaper than private lenders. This gave them a competitive advantage, and they were highly profitable for many years. However, the GSE structure also meant that they were asked to serve two masters: their stockholders, who were interested in profitability, and Congress and federal regulators, who predictably were more interested in political objectives.

As a result of their GSE structure, Fannie Mae and Freddie Mac were highly political. The top management of Fannie and Freddie provided key congressional leaders with large political contributions and often hired away congressional staffers into high-paying jobs lobbying their former bosses. Between the 2000 and 2008 election cycles, high-level managers and other employees of Fannie Mae and Freddie Mac contributed more than $14.6 million to the campaign funds of dozens of senators and representatives, most of whom were on congressional committees important for the protection of their privileged status.

The lobbying activities of Fannie Mae and Freddie Mac were legendary. Between 1998 and 2008, Fannie spent $79.5 million and Freddie spent $94.9 million on congressional lobbying, placing them among the biggest spenders on these activities. They also set up "partnership offices" in the districts and states of important legislators, often hiring the relatives of these lawmakers to staff these local offices.[3] The politicians, for their part, and the regulators who answered to them fashioned rules that made very high profits possible for the GSEs, at least in the short run. Although it was a relationship that reflected political favoritism (some would say corruption), members of Congress, particularly those involved in banking regulation, were highly supportive of the arrangement.

Fannie Mae and Freddie Mac did not originate mortgages. Instead, they purchased the mortgages originated by banks, mortgage brokers, and other lenders. Propelled by their cheaper access to funds, Fannie Mae and Freddie Mac grew rapidly during the 1990s. As **Exhibit 4** shows, the share of all mortgages held by Fannie Mae and Freddie Mac jumped from 25 percent in 1990 to 45 percent in 2001. Their share fluctuated around 40 percent during 2001–2008. Their dominance of the secondary mortgage market was even greater. During the decade prior to their insolvency and takeover by the federal government during the summer of 2008, Fannie Mae and Freddie Mac purchased about 90 percent of the mortgages sold in the secondary market. Because of this dominance, their lending practices exerted a huge impact on the standards accepted by mortgage originators.

Secondary mortgage market
A market in which mortgages originated by a lender are sold to another financial institution. In recent years, the major buyers in this market have been Fannie Mae, Freddie Mac, and large investment banks.

Responding to earlier congressional legislation, the Department of Housing and Urban Development (HUD) imposed regulations designed to make housing more affordable. The HUD mandates, adopted in 1995, required Fannie Mae and Freddie Mac to extend a larger share of their loans to low- and moderate-income households. For example, under the HUD mandates, 40 percent of new loans financed by Fannie Mae and Freddie Mac in 1996 had to go to borrowers with incomes below the median. This mandated share was steadily increased to 50 percent in 2000 and 56 percent in 2008. Similar increases were mandated for borrowers with incomes of less than 60 percent of the median. Moreover, in 1999, HUD guidelines required Fannie Mae and Freddie Mac to accept smaller down payments and extend larger loans relative to income.

The policies of Fannie Mae and Freddie Mac exerted an enormous impact on the actions of banks and other mortgage lenders. Recognizing that riskier loans could be passed on to Fannie and Freddie, mortgage originators had less incentive to scrutinize the creditworthiness of borrowers and more incentive to reduce the required down payment, in order to sell more mortgages. After all, when the mortgages were soon sold to Fannie or Freddie,

---

[3]For additional details, see Peter J. Wallison and Charles W. Calomiris, "The Destruction of Fannie Mae and Freddie Mac," American Enterprise Institute, online (posted Tuesday, September 30, 2008). Also see Common Cause, "Ask Yourself Why...They Didn't See This Coming" (September 24, 2008), available at www .commoncause.org/site/pp.asp?c=dkLNK1MQIwG&b=4542875; and Center for Responsive Politics, "Lobbying: Top Spenders" (2008), available at www.opensecrets.org/lobby/top.php?indexType=s.

The Share of Total Outstanding Mortgages Held by Fannie Mae and Freddie Mac, 1990–2008

Exhibit 4

Fannie Mae and Freddie Mac dominated the mortgage market for many years. Because of their government sponsorship, they were able to obtain funds cheaper than private firms. They held 45 percent of all mortgages in 2001, up from 25 percent in 1990. During 2001–2008, their share fluctuated around 40 percent. Their dominance of the secondary market, where loans are purchased from originators, is even greater. In July 2008, they were declared insolvent and taken over by the U.S. Treasury.

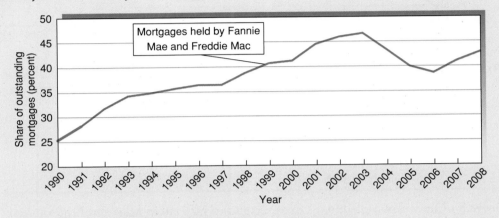

Source: Office of Federal Housing Enterprise Oversight, www.ofheo.gov.

the risk was transferred to them also. The bottom line: Required down payments were reduced and the accepted credit standards lowered.

Modifications to the Community Reinvestment Act (CRA) in 1995 also loosened mortgage-lending standards. These changes required banks to meet numeric goals based on the low-income and minority population of their service areas when extending mortgage loans. In order to meet these requirements, many banks, especially those in urban areas, were forced to reduce their lending standards and extend more loans to borrowers who did not meet the conventional credit criteria.

The lower standards resulting from the GSE and CRA regulations reduced lending standards across the board. Lenders could hardly offer low-down-payment loans and larger mortgages relative to housing value on **subprime loans**, without offering similar terms to prime borrowers. As the regulations tightened, the share of loans extended to subprime borrowers steadily increased. **Exhibit 5** illustrates this point. Measured as a share of mortgages originated during the year, subprime mortgages rose from 4.5 percent in 1994 to 13.2 percent in 2000 and 20 percent in 2005 and 2006. (*Note:* Bank examiners consider a loan to be subprime if the borrower's **FICO score** is less than 660.) When the **Alt-A loans**, those extended without full documentation, were added to the subprime, a third of the mortgages extended in 2005–2006 were to borrowers with either poor or highly questionable credit records.

As the mortgages extended to those with weak credit soared, so too did the number with little or no down payment. **Exhibit 6** shows both the number of loans issued by Fannie Mae and Freddie Mac and the share extended to borrowers with 5 percent or less down payment. Note how the number of new loans financed by the government sponsored corporations increased from less than one hundred thousand in the late 1990s to more than six hundred thousand in 2007. At the same time, the share of mortgages to borrowers making a down payment of 5 percent or less rose from 4 percent in 1998 to 12 percent in 2003 and 23 percent in 2007. Thus, Fannie Mae and Freddie Mac were flooding the market with low-down-payment loans extended to borrowers with weak credit. Meanwhile,

Subprime loan
A loan made to a borrower with blemished credit or one who provides only limited documentation of income, employment history, and other indicators of creditworthiness.

FICO score
A credit score measuring a borrower's likely ability to repay a loan. A person's FICO score will range between 300 and 850. A score of 700 or more indicates that the borrower's credit standing is good. FICO is an acronym for the Fair Isaac Corporation, the creators of the FICO score.

Alt-A loans
Loans extended with little documentation or verification of the borrowers' income, employment, and other indicators of their ability to repay. Because of this poor documentation, these loans are risky.

Exhibit 5

Subprime and Alt-A Mortgages as a Share of the Total, 1994–2007

Both subprime and Alt-A mortgages reflect loans to borrowers with a weak credit history. Note how the share of loans to borrowers in these two categories jumped from roughly 10 percent in 2001–2003 to 33 percent in 2005–2006.

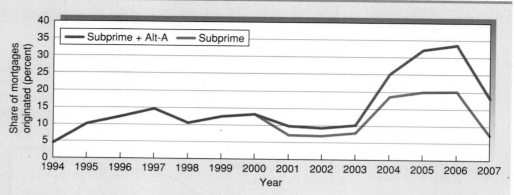

Source: The data for 1994–2000 are from Edward M. Gramlich, Financial Services Roundtable Annual Housing Policy Meeting, Chicago, Illinois (21 May 2004), www.federalreserve.gov/boarddocs/speeches/2004/20040521/default.htm. The data for 2001–2007 are from the Joint Center for Housing Studies of Harvard University, The State of the Nation's Housing 2008, www.jchs.harvard.edu/son/index.htm.

Exhibit 6

Growth of Low-down-payment Loans Extended by Fannie Mae and Freddie Mac

Following the 1999 HUD guidelines encouraging Fannie Mae and Freddie Mac to extend more low-down payment loans, the GSEs both increased the number of their mortgages (left frame) and the share extended with a down payment of 5 percent or less. As right frame shows, the share of these low down payment mortgages extended by Fannie Mae and Freddie Mac increased from 4 percent in 1998 to 12 percent in 2003 and 23 percent in 2007.

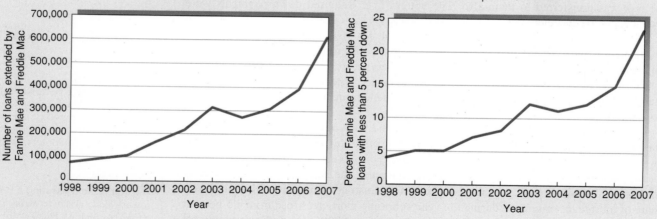

Sources: Russell Robert's, *Gambling With Other Peoples Money*, mercatus Center, http://mercatus.org/publications/gambling-other-peoples-money.

conventional loans for which borrowers were required to make at least a 20 percent down payment fell from two-thirds of the total in the early 1990s to only one-third in 2005–2006.

The shift from conventional loans to "creative finance" and "flexible standards," as the regulators called the new criteria, is highly important because the default and foreclosure rates for subprime loans ranges from seven to ten times the rate for conventional loans to prime borrowers. This differential is even greater in the case of mortgages with little or no down payment. Initially, this easy credit policy increased demand and pushed housing prices upward. But, the policy was not sustainable and it was predictable where it would lead. Eventually, the growing share of low-down-payment loans extended to those with weak credit would result in substantially higher default and foreclosure rates. This is precisely what happened.

FACTOR 2: PROLONGED LOW-INTEREST RATE POLICY OF THE FED DURING 2002–2004

Following the high and variable inflation rates of the 1970s, Federal Reserve policy focused on keeping the inflation rate low and stable. By the mid-1980s, the inflation rate had been reduced to 3 percent. Throughout 1985–1999, the Fed kept the inflation rate low and avoided abrupt year-to-year changes. In turn, the relative price stability reduced uncertainty and created an environment for both strong growth and economic stability. During this era, it was widely believed that price stability was the only objective that could be achieved with monetary policy, and if this objective was achieved, the monetary policy makers had done their job well.

However, as the lessons of this period began to dissipate, Fed policy makers, including chairman Alan Greenspan, began to focus more on control of real variables such as employment and real GDP. Since 1999, the Fed has followed a stop-and-go policy. Monetary policy was expansionary just before Y2K, restrictive prior to the recession of 2001, and then highly expansionary during the recovery from that recession. As Exhibit 7 shows, the Fed kept short-term interest rates at historic lows throughout 2002–2004. These extremely low short-term rates increased the demand for interest-sensitive goods like automobiles and housing.

The Fed's artificially low short-term rates substantially increased the attractiveness of **adjustable rate mortgages (ARMs)** to both borrowers and lenders. As Exhibit 8 shows, adjustable rate mortgages jumped from 10 percent of the total outstanding mortgages in 2000 to 21 percent in 2005. The low initial interest rates on adjustable rate mortgages made it possible for homebuyers to afford the monthly payments for larger, more expensive homes. This easy credit provided fuel for the housing boom. But the low rates and ARM loans also meant that as short-term interest rates increased from their historic low levels, home buyers would face a higher monthly payment two or three years in the future. Unsurprisingly, this is precisely what happened.

Adjustable rate mortgage (ARM)
A home loan in which the interest rate, and thus the monthly payment, is tied to a short-term rate like the one-year Treasury bill rate. Typically, the mortgage interest rate will be two or three percentage points above the related short-term rate. It will be reset at various time intervals (e.g., annually), and thus the interest rate and monthly payment will vary over the life of the loan.

Exhibit 7

Fed Policy and Short-Term Interest Rates, 1995–2009

Here we show the federal funds and one-year Treasury bill interest rates. These short-term rates are reflective of monetary policy. Note how the Fed pushed these rates to historic lows (less than 2 percent) throughout 2002–2004 but then increased them substantially during 2005–2006. The low rates provided fuel for the housing price boom, but the rising rates led to higher interest rates and monthly payments on adjustable rate mortgage (ARM) loans, which helped push the mortgage default and foreclosure rates upward beginning in the second half of 2006.

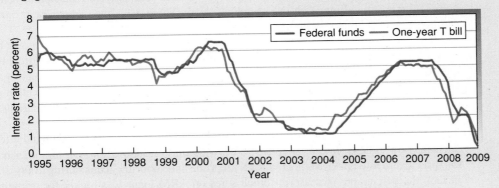

Sources: www.federalreserve.gov and www.economagic.com.

| **Exhibit 8** | **Adjustable Rate Mortgages (ARMs) as a Share of Total Outstanding Mortgages, 1990–2008** |

The interest rate and monthly payment on ARMs are tied to a short-term interest rate (e.g., the one-year Treasury bill rate). The Fed's low-interest rate policy of 2002–2004 increased the attractiveness of ARMs. Note how ARM loans increased as a share of total mortgages from 10 percent in 2000 to 21 percent in 2005.

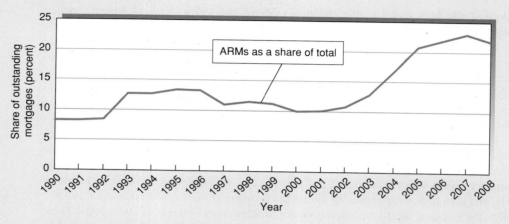

Source: Office of Federal Housing Enterprise Oversight, www.ofheo.gov.

By 2005, the expansionary monetary policy of 2002–2004 was clearly placing upward pressure on the general level of prices. The Fed responded with a shift to a more restrictive monetary policy, which pushed interest rates upward (see Exhibit 7). Many who purchased houses with little or no down payment and adjustable rate loans when interest rates were low during 2002–2004 faced substantially higher monthly payments as interest rates rose and the monthly payments on their ARM loans were reset during 2006 and 2007. These owners had virtually no equity in their homes. Therefore, when housing prices leveled off and began to decline during the second half of 2006, the default and foreclosure rates on these loans began to rise almost immediately (see Exhibits 1 and 2). Some owners with little or no initial equity simply walked away as their outstanding loan exceeded the value of their house.

Essentially, the small down payment and ARMs combination made it possible for homebuyers to gamble with someone else's money. If housing prices rose, buyers could reap a sizable capital gain without risking much of their own investment capital. Based on the rising housing prices of 2000–2005, many of these homebuyers expected to sell the house for a profit and move on in a couple of years. There were even television programs and investment seminars pushing this strategy as the route to riches.

Exhibit 9 shows the foreclosure rates for fixed interest rate and ARM loans for both subprime and prime loans. Compared to their prime borrower counterparts, the foreclosure rate for subprime borrowers was approximately ten times higher for fixed rate mortgages and seven times higher for adjustable rate mortgages. These huge differentials explain why the increasing share of loans to subprime borrowers substantially increased the default and foreclosure rates.

As Exhibit 9 shows, there was no upward trend in the foreclosure rate on fixed interest rate loans for either prime or subprime borrowers during 2000–2008. On the other hand, the foreclosure rate on ARMs soared for both prime and subprime loans during 2006–2008. In fact, the percentage increase in foreclosures on ARM loans was higher for prime than subprime borrowers. This is highly revealing. It illustrates that both prime and subprime borrowers played the low-down-payment, mortgage casino game.

Exhibit 9

The Foreclosure Rate of Fixed and Adjustable Rate Mortgages for Subprime and Prime Borrowers, 1998–2007

The foreclosure rates on fixed and adjustable interest rate mortgages are shown here for both subprime (part a) and prime (part b) borrowers. Note how the foreclosure rate was generally seven to ten times higher for subprime loans than for those to prime borrowers. As housing prices leveled off and declined in 2006–2008, the foreclosure rate on fixed interest rate mortgages did not change much. In contrast, the foreclosure rate for ARM loans soared beginning in the second half of 2006, and this was true for ARM loans to both subprime and prime borrowers. Clearly, the increasing share of both subprime and ARM loans during 2000–2005 contributed to the boom and bust of the housing market.

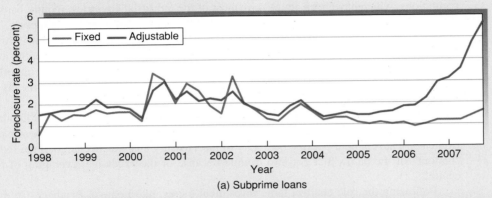

(a) Subprime loans

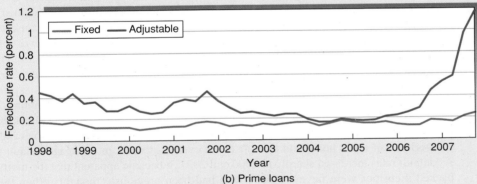

(b) Prime loans

Source: Stan J. Liebowitz, "Anatomy of a Train Wreck: Causes of the Mortgage Meltdown," Ch. 13 in Randall G. Holcombe and Benjamin Powell, eds, *Housing America: Building Out of a Crisis* (New Brunswick, NJ: Transaction Publishers, 2009). We would like to thank Professor Liebowitz for making this data available to us.

The crisis is often referred to as the *subprime mortgage crisis*. This is true, but it is only part of the story. It was also an ARM loan crisis. Fed policy encouraging ARM loans, the increasing proportion of these loans as a share of the total, and their higher default and foreclosure rates also contributed substantially, first to the housing boom and then to the bust. The combination of the mortgage lending regulations and the Fed's artificially low interest rate policies encouraged decision-makers to borrow more money and make additional investments in everything from housing to factories. Unfortunately, from an economic standpoint, these are investments that should have never been undertaken, something economists call **malinvestment**. To get the U.S. economy back on track, these malinvestments must be cleansed from the system. As the severe contraction of the construction industry illustrates, this is a costly and painful process.

Malinvestment
Malinvestment is misguided (or excess) investment caused when the Fed holds interest rates artificially low, encouraging too much borrowing. The new bank credit is invested in capital projects that cost more than the value they create. At some point, a correction must occur to cleanse these uneconomical investments from the system.

FACTOR 3: THE INCREASED DEBT-TO-CAPITAL RATIO OF INVESTMENT BANKS

Investment bank
An institution that acts as an underwriter for securities issued by other corporations or lenders. Unlike traditional banks, investment banks do not accept deposits from, or provide loans to, individuals.

Leverage ratios
The ratio of loans and other investments to the firm's capital assets.

A rule change adopted by the Securities and Exchange Commission (SEC) in April 2004 made it possible for **investment banks** to increase the leverage of their investment capital, which eventually led to their collapse. A firm's **leverage ratio** is simply the ratio of its investment holdings (including loans) relative to its capital. Thus, if a firm had investment funds that were twelve times the size of its equity capital, its leverage ratio would be 12 to 1. Prior to the SEC rule change, this was approximately the leverage ratio of both investment and commercial banks.

Essentially, the SEC applied regulations known as Basel I to investment banking. These regulations, which have been adopted by most of the industrial countries, require banks to maintain at least 8 percent capital against assets like loans to commercial businesses. This implies a leverage ratio of approximately 12 to 1. However, the Basil regulations provide more favorable treatment of residential loans. The capital requirement for residential mortgage loans is only 4 percent, which implies a 25 to 1 leverage ratio. Even more important, the capital requirement for low-risk securities is still lower at 1.6 percent. This means that the permissible leverage ratio for low-risk securities could be as high as 60 to 1.

Key investment banking leaders, including Henry Paulson who was CEO of Goldman Sachs at the time, urged the SEC to apply the higher leverage ratio to investment banks. Ironically, Paulson later became Secretary of the Treasury and was in charge of the federal "bailout" of the banks that got into trouble because of the excessive leveraging of their capital.

Following the rule change, large investment banks, like Lehman Brothers, Goldman Sachs, and Bear Stearns, expanded their mortgage financing activities. They bundled large holdings of mortgages together and issued securities for their finance. Because of the diversity of the mortgage portfolio, investment in the underlying securities was thought to involve minimal risk. **Security-rating** firms provided the **mortgage-backed securities** with a AAA rating, which made it possible for the investment banks to leverage them up to 60 to 1 against their capital.

Security rating
A rating indicating the risk of default of the security. A rating of AAA indicates that the risk of default is low.

Mortgage-backed securities
Securities issued for the financing of large pools of mortgages. The promised returns to the security holders are derived from the mortgage interest payments.

The mortgage-backed securities, financed with short-term leveraged lending, were highly lucrative. The large number of mortgages packaged together provided lenders with diversity and protection against abnormally high default rates in specific regions and loan categories. But it did not shield them from an overall increase in mortgage default rates. As default rates increased sharply in 2006 and 2007, it became apparent that the mortgage-backed securities were far more risky than had been previously thought. When the risk of these mortgages became more apparent, the value of the mortgage-backed securities plummeted because it was difficult to know their true value. As the value of the mortgage-backed securities collapsed, the highly leveraged investment banks faced massive short-term debt obligations with little reserves on which to draw. This is why the investment banks collapsed so quickly. In fact, when the Fed financed the acquisition of Bear Stearns by JP Morgan Chase, the leverage ratio of Bear Stearns was an astounding 33 to 1, about two and a half times the historical level associated with prudent banking practices.

Why didn't key Wall Street decision makers see the looming danger? No doubt, they were influenced by the low and relatively stable default rates over the past several decades (see Exhibit 2). Even during serious recessions like those of 1974–1975 and 1982–1983, the mortgage default rates were only a little more than 2 percent, less than half the rates of 2008. But one would still have thought that analysts at investment companies and security-rating firms would have warned that the low historical rates were for periods when down payments were larger, borrowing was more restricted relative to income, and fewer loans were made to subprime borrowers. A few analysts did provide warnings, but their views were ignored by high-level superiors.

However, the incentive structure also helps explain why highly intelligent people failed to see the oncoming danger. The bonuses of most Wall Street executives are closely tied to short-term profitability, and the mortgage-backed securities were highly profitable when housing prices were rising and interest rates were low. If a personal bonus of a million dollars or more is at stake this year, one is likely to be far less sensitive to the long-term dangers.

The incentive structure accompanying the regulation and rating of securities also played an important role. Only three firms—Moody's, Standard & Poors, and Fitch—are legally authorized to rate securities. These rating agencies are paid by the firm requesting the rating. A Triple-A rating was exceedingly important. It made higher leveraging possible, but, even more important, the Triple-A rating made it possible to sell the mortgage-backed securities to institutional investors, retirement plans, and investors around the world looking for relatively safe investments. The rating agencies were paid attractive fees for their ratings, and Triple-A approval would mean more business for the rating agencies as well as the investment banks. Clearly, this incentive structure is not one that encourages careful scrutiny and hard-nosed evaluation of the quality of the underlying mortgage bundle. Paradoxically, the shortsighted and counterproductive incentive structures that characterize some of Wall Street's best-known firms contributed to their collapse.

FACTOR 4: HIGH DEBT/INCOME RATIO OF HOUSEHOLDS

During 1985–2007, household debt grew to unprecedented levels. As Exhibit 10 shows, household debt as a share of disposable (after-tax) income ranged from 40 percent to 65 percent during 1953–1984. However, since the mid-1980s, the debt-to-income ratio of households climbed at an alarming rate. It reached 135 percent in 2007, more than twice the level of the mid-1980s. Unsurprisingly, more debt means that a larger share of household income is required just to meet the interest payments.

Interest payments on home mortgages and home equity loans are tax deductible, but household interest on other forms of debt is not. This incentive structure encourages households to concentrate their debt into loans against their housing. But a large debt against one's housing will mean that housing will be the hardest hit by unexpected events that force major adjustments. This is precisely what occurred in 2006–2008. The rising interest rates and mere leveling off of housing prices soon led to an increase in mortgage defaults and

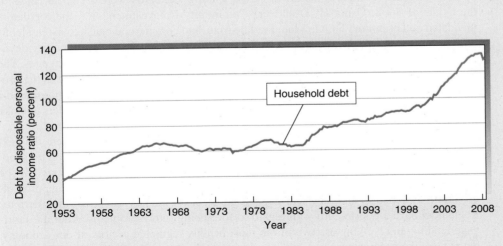

Exhibit 10

Household Debt to Disposable Personal Income Ratio, 1953–2008

Between 1953 and 1984, household debt as a share of disposable (after-tax) income ranged from 40 percent to 65 percent. However, since the mid-1980s, this debt-to-income ratio has increased dramatically. By 2007, it soared to 135 percent, more than twice the level of the mid-1980s.

Source: http://www.economagic.com.

foreclosures, because households were heavily indebted and a huge share of that indebtedness was in the form of mortgages against their housing. As the economy weakened, of course, this situation quickly worsened. Thus, the high level of household indebtedness also contributed to the Crisis of 2008.

HOUSING, MORTGAGE DEFAULTS, AND THE CRISIS OF 2008

The combination of the HUD regulations, low-down-payment requirements, and the Fed's low interest policy of 2002–2004 resulted in the rapid growth of both subprime and ARM loans during the first five years of this century. As is often the case with policy changes, the initial effects were positive—strong demand for housing, rising housing prices, and a construction boom. But the long-term effects were disastrous. The increasing share of subprime loans began to push default rates upward. Similarly, the low short-term interest rates that made adjustable rate mortgages attractive during 2004 soon reversed and led to higher monthly payments as the interest rates on ARM loans were reset in the years immediately ahead. As these two factors converged in the latter half of 2006, they generated falling housing prices and soaring mortgage default and foreclosure rates. The housing and lending crisis soon spread to other sectors and economies around the world. Moreover, the Triple-A rated mortgage-backed securities were marketed throughout the world, and, as their value plunged with rising default rates, turmoil was created in global financial markets.

It is important to note that both the mortgage default and foreclosure rates soared well before the recession began in December 2007. This illustrates that the housing crisis was not caused by the recession. Instead, it was the other way around.

LESSONS FROM THE CRISIS

What are the key lessons to be learned from the 2008 crisis? Reflection on this question requires that we think seriously about incentives, accountability, and the unintended side effects of policy. In this regard, the following three factors are important.

1. Regulation is a two-edged sword: It can have adverse as well as positive results. Regulations that undermined sound lending standards were a central cause of the Crisis of 2008. Using HUD and the Community Reinvestment Act, the regulators mandated and pressured Fannie Mae, Freddie Mac, and commercial banks to extend loans with little or no down payment, make large loans relative to income, accept poorly documented loan applications, and make more "interest only" and variable rate mortgages. The stated objective of the regulators, and the politicians who empowered them, was the promotion of home ownership, particularly among low- and moderate-income households. Nonetheless, their actions undermined sound lending practices and forced lenders to make imprudent loans.

In the aftermath of the Crisis of 2008, new regulations designed to prevent the next crisis were adopted. Will these regulations be effective? There is certainly reason for skepticism. History illustrates that regulation is not a cure all. Regulatory agencies will be characterized by "tunnel vision." They will focus on their narrow objectives (e.g., promoting home ownership), and they will largely ignore the secondary effects of their actions. Regulators have a poor record with regard to foreseeing future problems. After all, mortgage lending and banking are two of the most heavily regulated sectors of our economy, but none of their regulators foresaw the problems leading up to the 2008 crisis. With time, a sweetheart relationship will nearly always develop between the regulators and those whom they regulate. All of these factors should cause one to pause before believing that a new regulatory apparatus will head off the next crisis.

2. Monetary policy needs to focus on monetary and price stability. This is what the Fed did during the 1985–1999 era. But during the past decade, it has followed a stop–go path. When monetary policy-makers attempt to manipulate real output and employment through persistent shifts in monetary policy, their actions will generate instability rather than stability.

During the crisis, it appeared that the Fed was an extension of the Treasury. It was heavily involved in subsidizing merger deals, providing aid to nonbanking institutions, and engaging in actions that favored some business firms relative to others. Recent legislation has expanded the regulatory powers of the Fed. The experience of other countries indicates this is unlikely to be helpful. Central banks more dependent on political officials are more prone to financing government programs with money creation and inflation. Moreover, loading the Fed down with other regulatory functions will detract from its primary mission: achievement of price stability.

3. Institutional reforms that restore sound lending practices, strengthen the property rights of shareholders, and provide corporate managers with a stronger incentive to pursue long-term success would help promote recovery and future prosperity. To a large degree, the Crisis of 2008 reflects what happens when policies confront people with perverse incentives. Constructive reforms need to focus on getting the incentives right. Consider the following questions. Would the mortgage market work better if loan originators were held responsible for defaults on loans they originated, even if they sold them to another party? Does it really make sense to encourage households to concentrate all of their debt against their house, as current tax policy does? Should shareholders have more control over the salaries and bonuses of high-level corporate executives? Should high-level corporate managers be provided with a stronger incentive to pursue the long-term success of their company? Should compensation in the form of stock options require that the options must be held at least five years (rather than the current one year) in order to qualify for the lower capital gains tax rate? Incentives related to all of these questions played a role in the Crisis of 2008. Although the precise response is not obvious, the crisis suggests that review of current policies in these and other areas would be wise.

Will we address the right issues and eventually adopt constructive changes as a result of the crisis? It is too early to provide a definitive response to this question. But it is already clear that there is a major stumbling block: Politicians in both major parties are reluctant to face up to their own involvement in creating the crisis. Instead, the political incentives will encourage them to blame others and deny the adverse consequences of their policies.[4]

---

[4]Congress established the Financial Crisis Inquiry Commission to investigate the causes of the 2008 financial crisis and the commission issued its report in January 2011. Even though almost everyone recognized that deterioration in lending standards and vast expansion in loans to subprime borrowers was central to the financial crisis, the Commission failed to pursue why this occurred. The contributions of the GSEs, HUD mandates, Community Reinvestment Act, and other aspects of federal housing policy to the deterioration in lending standards were virtually ignored. Instead, the majority report of the Commission pointed to greedy lenders who victimized poorly informed borrowers, insufficient regulatory oversight, and shoddy banking practices. The Commission, dominated by politicians, left the impression that it was more interested in protecting housing policies and the Congressional leaders who crafted them than in determining why so many substandard mortgage loans were created during the decade prior to the crisis. See Financial Crisis Inquiry Commission, Final Report of the National Commission on the Causes of the Financial and Economic Crisis in the United States (Washington, DC, January 2011), http://c0182732.cdn1.cloudfiles.rackspacecloud.com/fcic_final_report_full.pdf (accessed February 4, 2011). Also see Peter J. Wallison, Financial Crisis Inquiry Commission Dissenting Statement (Washington, DC, January 2011), http://c0182732.cdn1.cloudfiles.rackspacecloud.com/fcic_final_report_wallison_dissent.pdf

KEY POINTS

- After soaring during the previous five years, housing prices began to decline during the second half of 2006, and mortgage defaults and housing foreclosures started to increase. As the housing bust spread to other sectors, stock prices plunged, major investment banks experienced financial troubles, unemployment increased sharply, and by 2008 the economy was in a severe recession.

- Fannie Mae and Freddie Mac grew rapidly during the 1990s. Their government sponsorship made it possible for them to obtain funds cheaper than private rivals. Because of their dominance of the secondary market, in which mortgages are purchased from originators, their lending standards exerted a huge impact on the mortgage market.

- Beginning in the mid-1990s, mandates imposed on Fannie Mae and Freddie Mac, along with regulations imposed on banks, forced lenders to reduce their lending standards, extend more mortgages to subprime borrowers, and reduce down payment requirements. The share of mortgages extended to subprime borrowers (including Alt-A loans) rose from 10 percent in 2001–2003 to 33 percent in 2005–2006. Correspondingly, the share of low-down-payment loans extended by Fannie Mae and Freddie Mac soared from 4 percent in 1998 to 23 percent in 2007. These changes were highly important because the default and foreclosure rates on subprime and low-down-payment loans are several times higher than for conventional loans to prime borrowers.

- The historically low interest rate policies of the Fed during 2002–2004 increased the demand for housing and the attractiveness of adjustable rate mortgages. This provided fuel for the soaring housing prices. ARM loans increased from 10 percent of total mortgages in 2000 to 21 percent in 2005. Fed policy pushed interest rates up in 2005–2006 and ARM loans were reset, pushing monthly payments higher. As a result, the default and foreclosure rates on these loans soared for prime as well as subprime borrowers.

- As a result of regulations adopted in April 2004, investment banks were allowed to leverage their capital by as much as 60 to 1 when financing mortgages with Triple-A rated securities. The rating agencies provided the Triple-A ratings, and the mortgage-backed securities were sold around the world. As the mortgage default rates rose in 2007–2008, Fannie Mae, Freddie Mac, and the major investment banks holding large quantities of these securities quickly fell into financial troubles, and several collapsed.

- The ratio of household debt to personal income increased steadily during 1985–2007, reaching a historic high at the end of that period.

- Low-down-payment requirements, the growth of subprime and ARM loans, the Fed's easy credit policy, highly leveraged mortgage-backed securities, and heavy borrowing by households fueled the run-up in housing prices. With time, however, this was a disastrous combination that provided the ingredients for the recession and Crisis of 2008.

- The Crisis of 2008 reflects the unintended consequences of regulatory and monetary policy and what happens when the incentive structure is polluted by unsound institutions and policies.

CRITICAL ANALYSIS QUESTIONS

1. Why did housing prices rise rapidly during 2002–2005? Why did the mortgage default rate increase so sharply during 2006 and 2007 even before the 2008–2009 recession began?
2. What happened to the credit standards (e.g., minimum down payment, mortgage loan relative to the value of the house, and creditworthiness of the borrower) between 1995 and 2005? Why did the credit standards change? How did this influence the housing price bubble and later the default and foreclosure rates?
3. *If owners have little or no equity in their houses, how will this influence the likelihood that they will default on their mortgage? Why?
4. When did mortgage default and housing foreclosure rates begin to rise rapidly? When did the economy go into recession? Was there a causal relationship between the two? Discuss.
5. *When mortgage originators sell mortgages to Fannie Mae, Freddie Mac, and investment banks the originators have no additional liability for possible default by the borrower. How will this arrangement influence the incentive of the originators to scrutinize the creditworthiness of the borrower? Would the incentive structure be different if the originator planned to hold the mortgage until it was paid off? Why or why not?
6. Some charge that the Crisis of 2008 was caused by the "greed" of Wall Street firms and other bankers. Do you agree with this view? Do you think there was more greed on Wall Street in the first five years of this century than during the 1980s and 1990s? Why or why not?

*Asterisk denotes questions for which answers are given in Appendix B.

6

Lessons from the Great Depression

FOCUS

- What caused the Great Depression? Was it the stock market crash of 1929?
- Why was the Great Depression so long and severe?
- Did the New Deal policies end the Great Depression?
- Did monetary and fiscal policy help promote recovery from the Great Depression?
- Does the Great Depression reflect a failure of markets or a failure of government?

We now know, as a few knew then, that the depression was not produced by a failure of private enterprise, but rather by a failure of government in an area in which the government had from the first been assigned responsibility.

—*Milton and Rose Friedman*[1]

---

[1]Milton and Rose Friedman, *Free to Choose* (New York: Harcourt Brace Jovanovich, 1980), 71.

The Great Depression is perhaps the most catastrophic economic event in American history. It is also one of the most misunderstood. Misconceptions abound with regard to what actually happened. The Great Depression is a tragic story about economic illiteracy and the adverse impact of unsound policies. People who do not learn from the lessons of history are prone to repeat them. If we want to avoid similar experiences in the future, understanding of this experience and the forces underlying it is vitally important.

iStockphoto.com/nicoolay

THE ECONOMIC RECORD OF THE GREAT DEPRESSION

Exhibit 1 presents data on the change in real GDP and the rate of unemployment during 1929–1940. As part (a) illustrates, real GDP fell by 8.6 percent in 1930, 6.5 percent in 1931, and a whopping 13.1 percent in 1932. By 1933, real GDP was nearly a third less than that in 1929. There was a temporary rebound during 1934–1936, but growth slowed in 1937 and real GDP fell once again in 1938. In 1939, a full decade after the disastrous downturn started, the real GDP of the United States was virtually the same as it had been in 1929.

While output was declining during the depression era, unemployment was soaring. As Exhibit 1, part (b), shows, the rate of unemployment rose from 3.2 percent in 1929 to 8.7 percent in 1930 and 15.9 percent in 1931. During 1932 and 1933, the unemployment rate soared to nearly one-quarter of the labor force. Even though real GDP grew substantially during 1934 and 1935, the unemployment rate remained above 20 percent during both of those years. After declining to 14.3 percent in 1937, the rate of unemployment rose to 19.0 percent during the downturn of 1938, and it was still 17.2 percent in 1939, a full decade after the catastrophic era began. The unemployment rate was 14 percent or more throughout the ten years from 1931 through 1940. By way of comparison, the unemployment rate has averaged less than 6 percent during the past quarter of a century, and it has never reached 11 percent since the Great Depression. Moreover, the statistics conceal the hardship and suffering accompanying the economic disaster. It was an era of farm foreclosures, bank failures, soup kitchens, unemployment lines, and even a sharply declining birthrate. America would never quite be the same after the 1930s.

The Great Depression was a prolonged period of falling incomes, high unemployment, and difficult living conditions. The decline in output and high unemployment were the most severe in American history. Why was the economy so weak for so long?

© Bettmann/Corbis

WAS THE GREAT DEPRESSION CAUSED BY THE 1929 STOCK MARKET CRASH?

The prices of stock shares rose sharply during the 1920s. But this is not surprising because the 1920s were a remarkable decade of innovation, technological advancement, and economic growth. The production of automobiles increased more than tenfold during the 1920s. Households with electricity, telephones, and indoor plumbing spread rapidly throughout the economy. The first regularly scheduled radio programs were broadcast in the early 1920s, providing an amazing new vehicle for mass communication. Air

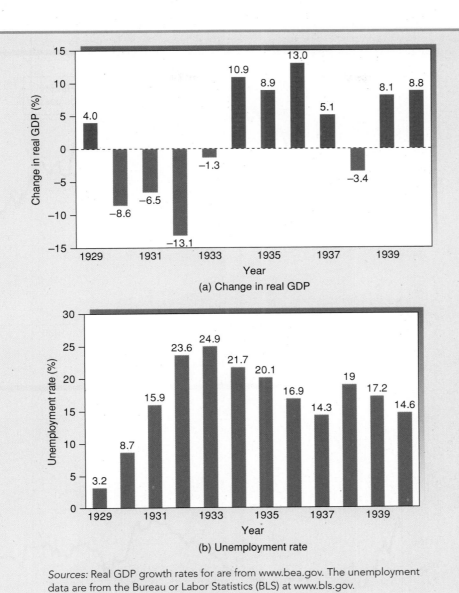

Exhibit 1

Real GDP and the Rate of Unemployment, 1929–1940

The change in real GDP (part a) and rate of unemployment (part b) figures during the Great Depression are shown here. These data illustrate both the severity and length of the economic contraction. For four successive years (1930–1933), real output fell. Unemployment soared to nearly one-quarter of the workforce in 1932 and 1933. Although real output expanded and the rate of unemployment declined during 1934–1937, the economy again fell into the depths of a depression in 1938. In 1939, a decade after the economic plunge started, 17.2 percent of the labor force was still unemployed and real GDP was virtually unchanged from the level of 1929.

(a) Change in real GDP

(b) Unemployment rate

Sources: Real GDP growth rates for are from www.bea.gov. The unemployment data are from the Bureau or Labor Statistics (BLS) at www.bls.gov.

conditioning received a boost from its use in "movie houses," as theaters were called at the time. There is good reason why the decade was known as the "Roaring Twenties." Perhaps more than any other era, the lives of ordinary Americans were transformed during the 1920s. To a large degree, the stock market was merely registering the remarkable growth and development of the decade.[2]

Generations of students have been told that the Great Depression was caused by the stock market crash of October 1929. Is this really true? Let's take a look at the figures. As **Exhibit 2**, part (a), shows, the Dow Jones Industrial Average opened in 1929 at 300, rose to a high of 381 on September 3, 1929, but gradually receded to 327 on Tuesday, October 22.

---

[2]Popular writers often argue that speculators drove the stock market to unsustainable highs in the late 1920s, but this view is an exaggeration. The price/earnings ratio for the Dow was 19 just before the crash. This places it at the upper range of normal but not at an unprecedented high. On October 9, 1929, *The Wall Street Journal* reported that railroad stocks were selling at 11.9 times earnings, which would place their P/E ratio toward the lower range of normal. RCA was the hot "high-tech" company of the era, and it earned $6.15 per share in 1927 and $15.98 per share in 1928. It traded at a high in 1928 of $420. This would imply a P/E ratio of 26, not unreasonable for a growth stock with outstanding future earning prospects.

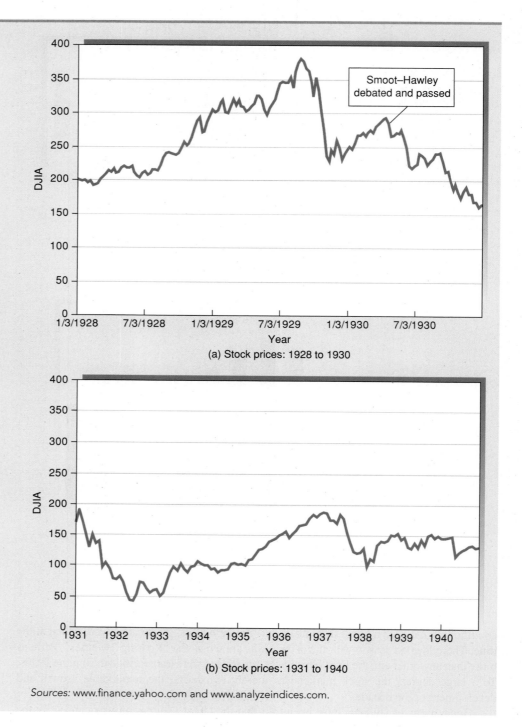

Exhibit 2

The Stock Market (Dow Jones Industrial Average), 1928–1940

The figures for the Dow Jones Industrial Average (DJIA) are shown here. Clearly, stock prices plunged in September–October 1929, but note how they recovered during the five months from mid-November 1929 through mid-April of 1930. However, this recovery reversed as the Smoot–Hawley tariff bill was debated, passed, and eventually signed into law on June 17, 1930. As part (b) shows, the Dow continued to fall throughout 1931 and 1932 and never reached 200 throughout the remainder of the decade.

(a) Stock prices: 1928 to 1930

Smoot–Hawley debated and passed

(b) Stock prices: 1931 to 1940

Sources: www.finance.yahoo.com and www.analyzeindices.com.

A major sell-off started the following day, and the Dow began to plunge. By October 29, which is known as Black Tuesday, the Dow closed at 230. Thus, in exactly one week, the stock market lost nearly one-third of its value. A couple of weeks later on November 13, the Dow fell to an even lower level, closing at 199.

However, it is interesting to see what happened during the next five months. From mid-November 1929 through mid-April 1930, the Dow Jones Industrial Average increased every month, and by mid-April the index had risen to 294, regaining virtually all of the losses experienced during the late October crash. This raises an interesting question: If the October crash caused the Great Depression, how can one explain that the stock market had regained most of those losses by April 1930?

But from mid-April throughout the rest of 1930, stock prices moved steadily downward and closed the year at 165. Apparently something happened during May–June 1930, which caused the stock market to head downward. We will return to this issue in a moment. Exhibit 2 part (b) presents data for the Dow Jones Industrials for 1931–1940. The index continued to fall in 1931–1932 and rebounded strongly in 1933 but then fluctuated between 100 and 200 for the remainder of the decade. Note the Dow stood at 131 at year-end 1940, even lower than the closing figure for 1930.

There have been several downturns in stock prices of the magnitude experienced during 1929, both before and after the Great Depression, and none of them resulted in anything like the prolonged unemployment and lengthy contraction of the 1930s. For example, the stock market price declines immediately before and during the recessions of 1973–1975 and 1982–1983 were as large as those of the 1929 crash, approximately 50 percent. But both of these recessions were over in about 18 months. Moreover, in 1987, the Dow Industrials fell from 2640 on October 2 to 1740 on October 19, a decline of 34 percent. Whereas the collapse of stock prices in 1987 was similar to the October 1929 crash, that is where the similarity ends. The 1987 crash did not lead to economic disaster. In fact, it was not even followed by a recession.

Of course, the 1929 decline in stock prices reduced wealth and thereby contributed to the reduction in aggregate demand and real output. But stock prices have fallen by 50 percent or more during other recessions, and the economy nonetheless moved toward a recovery within a year or two at the most. Thus, although the decline in stock prices may well have triggered the initial economic decline, the length and severity of the Great Depression were the result of other factors. We will now consider this issue in more detail.

WHY WAS THE GREAT DEPRESSION SO LENGTHY AND SEVERE?

The length and severity of the Great Depression were the result of bad policies. There were four major policy mistakes that caused the initial downturn to worsen and the depressed conditions to continue on and on. Let's take a closer look at each of them.

1. A sharp reduction in the supply of money during 1930–1933 and again in 1937–1938 reduced aggregate demand and real output. The supply of money expanded slowly but steadily throughout the 1920s. From 1921 through 1929, the money stock increased at an annual rate of 2.7 percent, approximately the economy's long-term real rate of growth. There was even a slight downward trend in the general level of prices during the decade.

In spite of this price stability, the Fed increased the discount rate, the rate it charges banks for short-term loans, four times between January 1928 and August 1929. During this 20-month period, the discount rate was pushed from 3.5 percent to 6 percent. After the October stock market crash, the Fed aggressively sold government bonds, which drained reserves from the banking system and reduced the money supply. As Exhibit 3 part (a) shows, the money supply fell by 3.9 percent during 1930, by 15.3 percent in 1931, and by 8.9 percent in 1932. As banks failed and the money supply collapsed, the Fed did not inject new reserves into the system. Neither did it act as a lender of last resort. The quantity of money at year-end 1933 was 33 percent less than that in 1929.

Predictably, this huge monetary contraction placed downward pressure on prices. As Exhibit 3 part (b) illustrates, the general level of prices fell by 2.3 percent in 1930, 9.0 percent in 1931, and 9.9 percent in 1932.

Economic activity takes place over time. The deflation during 1929–1933 meant that many people who bought businesses and farms in the late 1920s were unable to pay for them as the prices of their output fell during the 1930s. In essence, the monetary contraction caused unexpected changes in economic conditions. As a result, many people who undertook investments and borrowed funds suffered losses and were unable to fulfill their

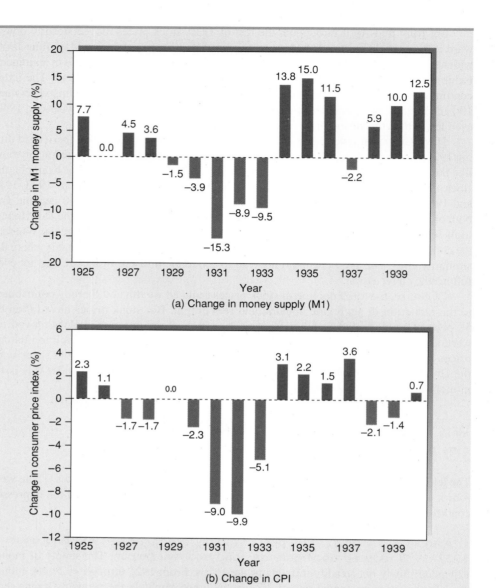

Exhibit 3

The M1 Money Supply and the Change in the General Level of Prices, 1925–1940

Note how the M1 money supply fell sharply during 1930–1933, rose during 1934–1937 but dipped again in 1938 (part a). The general level of prices followed the same pattern (part b). The sharp reduction in the supply of money and deflation during 1930–1933 changed the terms of loans, investments, and other economic activities that take place across time periods. This was a major factor underlying the initial plunge into the Great Depression. Further, the monetary contraction of 1938 stifled the recovery and contributed to still another downturn.

(a) Change in money supply (M1)

(b) Change in CPI

Sources: Change in the money supply is from December to December. The data are from Milton Friedman, and Anna J. Schwartz, *A Monetary History of the United States, 1867–1960* (Princeton, NJ: Princeton University Press, 1963); for CPI data: www.bls.gov.

contracts. As the gains from trade dissipated and aggregate demand plunged, so, too, did output and employment. By 1933, real GDP was 29 percent lower than the 1929 level, and the unemployment rate had soared to nearly 25 percent.

During 1934–1937, the Fed reversed itself and expanded the supply of money. The monetary expansion halted the deflation, and the general level of prices increased. So, too, did the level of economic activity. Real GDP expanded and the unemployment rate fell during 1934–1937. But the Fed doubled the reserve requirements between August 1936 to May 1937, leading to another decline in the money supply and the general level of prices. This caused the economy to falter again and pushed the unemployment rate to almost 20 percent in 1938.

Sound monetary policy is about price stability—following a monetary policy that keeps the inflation rate low and steady. The Federal Reserve totally failed the American people during the 1930s. The severe monetary contraction led to near double-digit deflation. This was followed by a shift to monetary expansion, which generated inflation, but the

Fed soon shifted again toward contraction, which caused still more deflation. Essentially, the monetary instability of the 1930s generated uncertainty and undermined the exchange process.[3]

2. The Smoot–Hawley trade bill of 1930 increased tariffs and led to a huge reduction in the volume of international trade. Signed into law on June 17, 1930, the Smoot–Hawley trade bill increased tariffs by more than 50 percent on approximately 3,200 imported products. Many of these tariff increases were in dollars per unit, so the subsequent deflation pushed them still higher relative to the price of the product.

Like their protectionist counterparts today, President Herbert Hoover, Senator Reed Smoot, and Congressman Willis Hawley argued that the trade restrictions would "save jobs." As Congressman Hawley put it, "I want to see American workers employed producing American goods for American consumption."[4] The proponents of the Smoot–Hawley legislation also believed the higher tariffs would bring in additional revenue for the federal government.

Senator Reed Smoot and Congressman Willis Hawley (shown here) spearheaded legislation passed in June 1930 that increased tariff rates by an average of more than 50 percent. They thought their bill would "save jobs" and promote prosperity. Instead, it did the opposite, as other nations retaliated with higher tariffs on American products and world trade fell substantially.

More than 100 years before the Great Depression, Adam Smith and David Ricardo explained how nations gained when they specialized in the production of goods they could supply at a low cost while trading for those they could produce only at a high cost. Trade makes it possible for both trading partners to generate a larger output and achieve a higher living standard. Moreover, a nation cannot reduce its imports without simultaneously reducing its exports. If foreigners sell less to Americans, then they will earn fewer of the dollars needed to buy from Americans. Thus, a reduction in imports will also lead to a reduction in exports. Jobs created in import competing industries will be offset by jobs lost in exporting industries. There will be no net expansion in employment. The view that import restrictions will generate a net creation of jobs is fallacious.

Having read both Smith and Ricardo, the economists of 1930 were well aware of the benefits derived from international trade and the harm generated by trade restrictions. More than a thousand of them signed an open letter to President Hoover warning of the harmful effects of Smoot–Hawley and pleading with him not to sign the legislation. He rejected their pleas, but history confirmed the validity of their warnings.

The higher tariffs did not generate additional revenue, and they certainly did not save jobs. The import restrictions harmed foreign suppliers, and predictably they retaliated. Sixty countries responded with higher tariffs on American products. By 1932, the volume of U.S. trade had fallen to less than half its earlier level. As a result, the federal government actually derived less revenue at the higher tariff rates. Tariff revenues fell from $602 million in 1929 to $328 million in 1932. Similarly, output and employment declined and the unemployment rate soared. The unemployment rate was 7.8 percent when Smoot–Hawley was passed, but it ballooned to 23.6 percent of the labor force just two years later. Moreover, the "trade war" helped spread the recessionary conditions throughout the world.

There was substantial opposition to the Smoot–Hawley bill, and the Senate vote was close (44–42). Last minute changes in the rate schedules were made in order to gain the final votes needed for passage. Some businesses, seeking to gain advantage at the expense of consumers and foreign rivals, lobbied hard for the legislation. But, like the economists, other business leaders recognized that trade restrictions would harm rather than help the economy.

---

[3]For a comprehensive analysis of monetary policy during the Great Depression, see the chapter on the Great Contraction in Milton Friedman and Anna Schwartz, *A Monetary History of the United States, 1867–1960* (New York: National Bureau of Economic Research, 1963; ninth paperback printing by Princeton University Press, 1993): 411–15.

[4]Frank Whitson Fetter, "Congressional Tariff Theory," *American Economic Review* 23, no. 3 (September 1933): 413–27.

As we previously discussed, stock prices had increased for five straight months following the November 1929 lows, and by mid-April of 1930, the Dow Jones Industrials had returned to the level just before the October 1929 crash (see Exhibit 2). But as the Smoot–Hawley bill moved through Congress and its prospects for passage improved, stock prices moved steadily downward. In fact, the reduction in stock prices following the debate and passage of Smoot–Hawley was even greater than that of the 1929 October crash. By year-end 1930, recovery was nowhere in sight, and the Dow Jones Industrial index had fallen to 165, down from 294 in mid-April.

The combination of highly restrictive monetary policy and the Smoot–Hawley trade restrictions were enough to push the economy over the cliff, but Congress and the president were not through.

3. A large tax increase in the midst of a severe recession made a bad situation worse. Before the Keynesian revolution, the dominant view was that the federal budget should be balanced. Reflecting the ongoing economic downturn, the federal budget ran a deficit in 1931, and an even larger deficit was shaping up for 1932. Assisted by the newly elected Democratic majority in the House of Representatives, the Republican Hoover Administration passed the largest peacetime tax rate increase in the history of the United States. As Exhibit 4 indicates, the lowest marginal tax rate on personal income was raised from 1.5 percent to 4 percent in 1932. At the top of the income scale, the highest marginal tax rate was raised from 25 percent to 63 percent. Essentially, personal income tax rates were increased at all levels by approximately 150 percent in one year! This huge tax increase reduced both the after-tax income of households and the incentive to earn and invest.

Fiscal policy analysis indicates that a tax increase of this magnitude in the midst of a severe downturn will be disastrous. Review of Exhibit 1 shows that this was indeed the case. In 1932, real output fell by 13 percent, the largest single-year decline during the Great Depression era. Unemployment rose from 15.9 percent in 1931 to 23.6 percent in 1932.

In 1936, the Roosevelt Administration increased taxes again, pushing the top marginal rate to 79 percent. Thus, during the latter half of the 1930s, high earners were permitted to keep only 21 cents of each additional dollar they earned. Moreover, the 1936 tax legislation also imposed a special tax on the retained earnings of corporations, a major source of funds

Exhibit 4

Marginal Income Tax Rates, 1925–1940

The lowest and highest marginal tax rates imposed on personal income are shown here for the period before, and during, the Great Depression. Note how the top marginal rate was increased from 25 percent in 1931 to 63 percent in 1932. Real GDP fell by 13.3 percent in 1932, and the unemployment rate soared to nearly a quarter of the labor force (see Exhibit 1). In 1935, the top rate was pushed still higher to 79 percent.

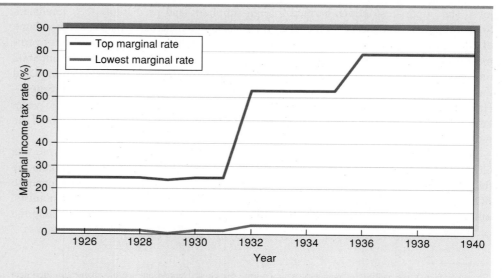

Sources: The Tax Foundation, www.taxfoundation.org; and the IRS at www.irs.gov.

for business investment. These 1936 tax increases further reduced both income levels and the incentive to earn and invest, prolonging the Great Depression and increasing its severity.

4. Price controls, anticompetitive policies, and constant structural changes during the Roosevelt administration generated uncertainty and undermined the normal recovery process. President Roosevelt was elected in 1932, and many history books still credit his New Deal policies with bringing the Great Depression to an end. Numerous policy changes were instituted during the Roosevelt years, and some of them were helpful. In 1933, President Roosevelt revalued the price of gold from $20 per ounce to $35 per ounce, and this contributed to the expansion in the money supply during the years immediately following. The Roosevelt administration also passed the Federal Deposit Insurance program, which provided depositors with protection against bank failures and reduced the occurrence of "bank runs."

The Agricultural Adjustment Act of 1933 sought to increase the prices of farm products by reducing their supply. Under this act, 6 million baby pigs were slaughtered in 1933. Did this help bring the Great Depression to an end?

However, it is equally clear that many of the major initiatives of the Roosevelt administration were counterproductive and prolonged the Great Depression. Roosevelt perceived that falling prices were a problem, but he failed to recognize that this was because of the monetary contraction. Instead, he tried to keep product prices high by reducing their supply. Under the Agricultural Adjustment Act (AAA) passed in 1933, farmers were paid to plow under portions of their cotton, corn, wheat, and other crops. Potato farmers were paid to spray their potatoes with dye so that they would be unfit for human consumption. Healthy cattle, sheep, and pigs were slaughtered and buried in mass graves in order to keep them off the market. In 1933 alone, 6 million baby pigs were killed under the Roosevelt agricultural policy. The Supreme Court declared the AAA unconstitutional in 1936, but not before it had kept millions of dollars of agricultural products from American consumers.

The National Industrial Recovery Act (NIRA) was another New Deal effort to keep prices high. Under this legislation passed in June 1933, more than 500 industries ranging from automobiles and steel to dog food and dry cleaners were organized into **cartels**. Business representatives from each industry were invited to Washington to work with NIRA officials to set production quotas, prices, wages, working hours, distribution methods, and other mandates for their industry. Once approved by a majority of the firms, the regulations were legally binding, and they applied to all businesses in the industry, regardless of whether they approved or participated in regulations' development. Firms that did not comply were fined and, in some cases, owners were even thrown in jail. A tax was levied on all firms in these industries in order to cover the administrative cost of the act. Before the NIRA, collusive behavior of this type would have been prosecuted as a violation of antitrust laws, but with the NIRA, the government itself provided the organizational structure for the cartels and prosecuted firms that dared to reduce prices or failed to comply with other regulations. Clearly, the NIRA reduced competition, promoted monopoly pricing, and undermined the market process.

Cartel
An organization of sellers designed to coordinate supply and price decisions so that the joint profits of the members will be maximized. A cartel will seek to create a monopoly in the market for its product.

Exhibit 5 tracks industrial output before, and during, the NIRA's existence. Interestingly, a recovery had started during the first half of 1933. Industrial output increased sharply and factory employment expanded by 25 percent during the four months before the NIRA took affect. But as the act was implemented in July 1933, industrial output began to decline precipitously. By the end of 1933, output had fallen by more than 25 percent from its mid-summer high. There were some ups and downs during the next year, but industrial output never returned to its pre-NIRA level until after the Supreme Court in a 9–0 vote declared the act unconstitutional in May 1935.[5]

The AAA and NIRA were just part of the persistent policy change during the Roosevelt years. The Wagner Act took labor law out of the courts and assigned it to a new

---

[5]For additional details on the impact of the NRA, see Chapter 4 of the recent book by historian Burton Folsom, *New Deal or Raw Deal* (New York: Simon & Schuster, 2008).

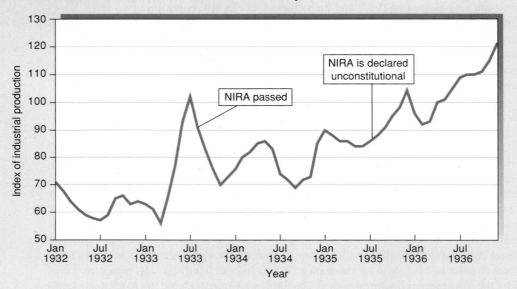

Exhibit 5

The NIRA and Industrial Production, 1932–1936

The change in industrial production before and following the passage of the National Industrial Recovery Act (NIRA) is shown here. Note how industrial output increased sharply during April–July 1933. However, when the implementation of the NIRA began in July, industrial output fell by more than 25 percent over the next six months. It never reached the June 1933 level again until after the Act was declared unconstitutional in May 1935.

Source: Historical Statistics of the United States. The base period (equal to 100) was the average of the monthly figures during 1923–1925.

regulatory commission, the National Labor Relations Board. Pro-union appointments to this new board dramatically changed collective bargaining and led to a sharp increase in unionization. The Works Progress Administration (WPA) and Civilian Conservation Corps (CCC) vastly expanded government employment. The Davis–Bacon Act required government contractors to employ higher wage union workers, which, in effect, reduced the employment opportunities of minorities and those with fewer skills. Unprecedented high marginal tax rates, establishment of a minimum wage, pay-as-you-go Social Security, and several other programs changed the structure of the U.S. economy.

This persistent introduction of massive new programs and regulations created what Robert Higgs calls "regime uncertainty," the situation in which people are reluctant to undertake business ventures and investments because the government is constantly changing the "rules."[6] Against this background, business planning was undermined and private investment came to a virtual standstill. Roosevelt's close friend and Treasury Secretary Henry Morgenthau tried to get the president to make a public statement to reassure investors and the business community. He was unsuccessful. Lammont duPont highlighted the uncertainty generated by the constant whirlwind of New Deal policy changes when he stated,

> *Uncertainty rules the tax situation, the labor situation, the monetary situation, and practically every legal condition under which industry must operate. Are taxes to go higher, lower or stay where they are? We don't know. Is labor to be*

---

[6]Robert Higgs, "Regime Uncertainty: Why the Great Depression Lasted So Long and Why Prosperity Resumed After the War," *The Independent Review* 1, no. 4 (Spring 1997).

union or non-union? Are we to have inflation or deflation, more government spending or less? Are new restrictions to be placed on capital, new limits on profits? It is impossible to even guess at the answers.[7]

Did the New Deal policies bring the Great Depression to an end?[8] Through the years, many students have been taught that this was the case. It is difficult to see how anyone could objectively review the data and accept this proposition. Before the Great Depression, recessions lasted only one or two years, three years at the most, and recovery pushed income to new highs. The Great Depression was different. In 1933, the monetary contraction was reversed, and there was evidence of a private-sector recovery. But the NIRA, AAA, and 1936 tax increases dampened productive activity, and the second monetary contraction pushed the economy into another recession within the depression. In 1938, per capita real GDP of the United States was still below the level of 1929, and the rate of unemployment was 19 percent. In 1939, seven years after the beginning of the New Deal, 17 percent of the labor force was still unemployed. The Great Depression was eventually diminished by the increase in demand for military goods of the English and Russians and our own military buildup before World War II.[9]

FISCAL POLICY DURING THE GREAT DEPRESSION

What happened to fiscal policy during the Great Depression? This was, of course, before the Keynesian revolution, and the view that the government should balance its budget, except perhaps during wartime, was widely accepted. Exhibit 6 part (a) presents the data for government spending as a share of GDP. The size of the government was much smaller as a share of the economy during this era. Total government spending (federal, state, and local) increased from 8 percent of GDP in 1929 to 16 percent in 1933. To a large degree, however, this increase reflected the maintenance of nominal government expenditures during a period of deflation and declining GDP. After 1933, total government spending as a share of GDP remained in the 15 percent to 16 percent range for the rest of the decade, except during 1937, when the ratio fell to 13 percent.

Exhibit 6 part (b) provides the figures for the federal deficit. The budget was in surplus during both 1929 and 1930. After that, the deficit was generally around 2 percent of GDP, except during 1934 and 1936, and in 1937 when a small surplus was present. Measured as a share of the economy, the increases in government spending and federal deficits during the 1930s were relatively small. Thus, there is little reason to believe that fiscal policy exerted much impact on the economy. Certainly, there is no reason to believe that spending increases and budget deficits were a significant source of fiscal stimulus during the era.

---

[7]Quoted in Herman E. Krooss, *Executive Opinion: What Business Leaders Said and Thought on Economic Issues, 1920s–1960s* (Garden City, NY: Doubleday and Co., 1970), 200.

[8]For additional details on the Great Depression, see Gene Smiley, *Rethinking the Great Depression* (Ivan R. Dee, Chicago, IL 2002); Robert J. Samuelson, "Great Depression," in *The Fortune Encyclopedia of Economics*, ed., David R. Henderson (New York: Warner Books, 1993), available online at www.econlib.org; Burton Folsom, *New Deal or Raw Deal?* (New York: Simon & Schuster, 2008); and Amity Shlaes, *The Forgotten Man: A New History of the Great Depression* (New York: HarperCollins Publishers, 2007).

[9]Many argue that the spending increases and large budget deficits of World War II provided sufficient demand stimulus to direct the economy back to full employment and solid growth. Robert Higgs challenges this view. Higgs notes that with 12 million young Americans drafted during the war, this would obviously reduce the unemployment rate to a low level. However, the growth of real GDP is more debatable because almost half of measured output was government spending, and it was added to GDP at cost. Moreover, the income of households was overstated because many goods they would have purchased were unavailable as a result of the price controls. The sharp decline in GDP following the war and the lifting of price controls also imply that the growth of GDP during the war was overstated. Thus, Higgs does not believe that real recovery from the Great Depression occurred until 1946. See Robert Higgs, *Depression, War, and Cold War: Studies in Political Economy* (New York: Oxford University Press, 2006).

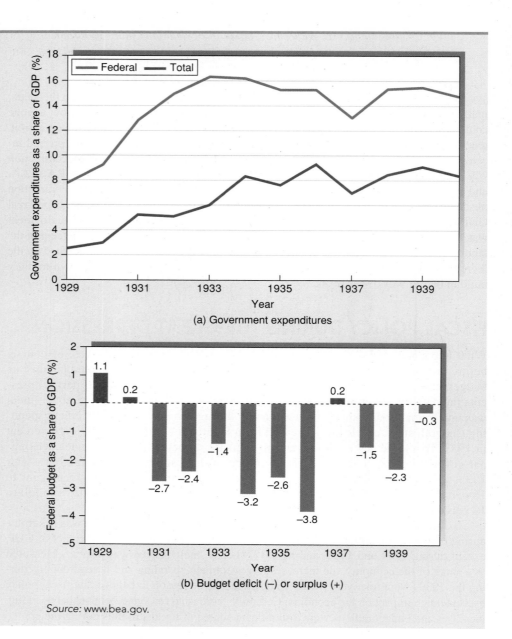

Exhibit 6

Government Expenditures and Federal Budget Deficits as a Share of GDP, 1929–1940

Measured as a share of the economy, government spending increased during the 1930s, and the federal government generally ran a budget deficit. However, given the depth of the economic decline, the deficits were too small to provide much fiscal stimulus during this era.

(a) Government expenditures

(b) Budget deficit (−) or surplus (+)

Source: www.bea.gov.

LESSONS FROM THE GREAT DEPRESSION

The Great Depression provides several lessons that can help us avoid severe downturns in the future. First, the Great Depression clearly indicates that a prolonged period of monetary contraction will undermine time-dimension economic activity and exert disastrous effects on the economy. We seemed to have learned this lesson well. As the severity of the 2008 downturn increased, the Fed injected abundant reserves into the banking system and shifted to a highly expansionary monetary policy. However, it is also true that Fed policy during 2002–2006 contributed to the housing boom and bust and, thereby, the Crisis of 2008. Monetary and price stability is crucially important for the smooth operation of markets. The Great Depression, along with experience since that era, vividly illustrates this point.

Second, the Great Depression illustrates the fallacy of the "trade restrictions will promote domestic industry" argument. Policies that reduce imports will simultaneously reduce exports. Foreigners will not have the dollars to purchase as much from us if they sell less to us. Trade restrictions will not save jobs. Instead, they will shift employment from sectors in which we are a low-cost producer to those in which we are a high-cost producer. The results are fewer gains from trade, a smaller output, and lower income levels. Both economic theory and the experience of the Smoot–Hawley trade restrictions are consistent with this view.

Third, raising taxes in the midst of a severe recession is a bad idea. Pushing taxes to exceedingly high rates is a recipe for disaster. All of the major macroeconomic theories—Keynesian, new classical, and supply side—indicate that tax increases will be counterproductive during a severe downturn. The experience with the tax increases during the Great Depression reinforces these views.

Fourth, the political incentive structure during a severe downturn is likely to encourage politicians to "do something." Even bad policies are likely to be popular, at least for a while. A better strategy would be the oath of the medical profession, "do no harm." The constant policy changes under both Hoover and Roosevelt created uncertainty and froze private-sector investment and business activity. Everyone waited to see what the next new policy regime would be; and, as they did so, the depressed conditions were prolonged.

The experience of the 1930s highlights the importance of economic literacy. The decade-long catastrophic decline did not have to happen. It was the result of wrong-headed policies based on the economic illiteracy of both voters and policy-makers.

Finally, as we noted in Chapter 1, good intentions are no substitute for sound policy. The Great Depression vividly illustrates this point. There is every reason to believe that Presidents Hoover and Roosevelt, Senator Smoot, Congressman Hawley, other members of Congress, and the monetary policy-makers of the 1930s had good intentions. But, it is equally clear that their actions tragically turned what would have been a normal business cycle downturn into a decade of hardship and suffering. The good intentions of political decision makers do not protect the general citizenry from the adverse consequences of unsound policies. This was true during the Great Depression, and it is still true today. If we do not learn from the adverse experiences of history, we are likely to repeat them.

KEY POINTS

- The Great Depression was a severe economic plunge that resulted in unemployment rates of nearly 25 percent during 1932–1933 and rates of more than 14 percent for an entire decade. It was the longest, most severe period of depressed economic conditions in American history.

- Contrary to a popular view, the Great Depression was not caused by the 1929 stock market crash. We have had similar reductions in stock prices to those of 1929, both before and after the Great Depression, without experiencing prolonged depressed conditions like those of the 1930s.

- There were four major reasons why the Great Depression was long and severe:
    1. Monetary instability: The money supply contracted by 33 percent between 1929 and 1933, and it took another tumble during 1937–1938.
    2. Smoot–Hawley trade bill: This 1930 legislation increased tariffs by more than 50 percent and led to a sharp reduction in world trade.
    3. 1932 tax increase: This huge tax increase reduced demand and undermined the incentive to invest and produce.
    4. Structural policy changes: Persistent major changes, particularly during the Roosevelt years, generated uncertainty and undermined investment and business planning.

- The budget deficits and increases in government spending failed to exert much impact on total demand and the level of economic activity during the 1930s.

- The Great Depression highlights the importance of monetary stability; free trade; avoidance of high tax rates; and avoidance of price controls, entry restraints, and persistent policy changes that generate uncertainty and undermine the security of property rights. Perhaps most important, the Great Depression vividly illustrates that good intentions are not a substitute for sound economic policy.

CRITICAL ANALYSIS QUESTIONS

1. "The Great Depression was caused by the 1929 stock market crash. The 1929 collapse of stock prices was the most severe in U.S. history, and therefore it is not surprising that it caused a prolonged period of economic hardship." Evaluate this statement.

2. Do the length and severity of the Great Depression reflect a defect in the operation of markets? Do they reflect a failure of government policy? Discuss.

3. "Franklin Roosevelt is recognized as one of our greatest presidents because his New Deal policies brought the Great Depression to an end." Evaluate this statement.

4. Could the United States ever experience another Great Depression? Why or why not?

5. *"I'm for international trade, but not when it takes jobs from Americans. If the American worker can produce the product, Americans should not buy it from foreigners." Do you agree with this statement? Why or why not?

6. What are the most important lessons Americans should learn from the Great Depression? Do you think we have learned them? Why or why not?

*Asterisk denotes questions for which answers are given in Appendix B.

7

The Economics of Health Care

FOCUS
- How much do Americans spend on health care?
- Why have the prices of health care services risen so rapidly in recent decades?
- What is likely to happen to health care prices and expenditures in the future?
- What can be done to improve the delivery of health care services?

Americans increasingly have been driven to pay for their health care through third party insurers and to purchase that insurance, when possible, from their employers. This, in turn, has led to rising health care costs while making it harder for Americans without employer-provided insurance to obtain coverage.

—*Michael Tanner*[1]

[1]Michael Tanner, "What's Wrong with the Current System," in *Empowering Health Care Consumers through Tax Reform*, Grace-Marie Arnett, ed. (Ann Arbor: University of Michigan Press, 1999).

There is considerable dissatisfaction with the operation of the health care industry in the United States. This is certainly understandable. Both the expenditures on and prices of health care have soared in recent decades. Exhibit 1 presents the expenditure figures as a share of GDP. Health care spending, including both private and government, jumped from 5.2 percent of GDP in 1960 to 9.2 percent in 1980 and 17.6 percent in 2009. Why has health care spending increased so rapidly? Will the health care legislation passed in 2010 slow the growth of this spending? Is the health care industry in need of fundamental reform? This special topic investigates these questions and related issues.

Some categories of health care spending have substantial public good components. For example, this is true for expenditures on pure research and activities that retard, and in some cases eliminate, the incidence of communicable diseases. In these cases, health care spending can generate spillover benefits for the general populace, and it would be difficult, if not impossible, to exclude nonpaying consumers from the receipt of these benefits. As we discussed in Chapter 5, under these conditions, government action might lead to an improvement in the allocation of resources. The National Institutes of Health and the Centers for Disease Control and Prevention provide examples of government organizations that justify their funding primarily on the basis of the public-good nature of their services. However, the vast majority of health care spending, including that of the government, involves private goods, goods for which the benefits accrue primarily to the consumer. This feature will focus on the provision of these personal consumption health care services.

Exhibit 1

Health care Expenditures as a Share of GDP, 1960–2009

Total expenditures (including both private- and government-financed) on health care as a share of GDP have persistently increased during the last four decades. In 2009, the United States spent 17.6 percent of its GDP on health care, up from 9.2 percent in 1980 and 5.2 percent in 1960.

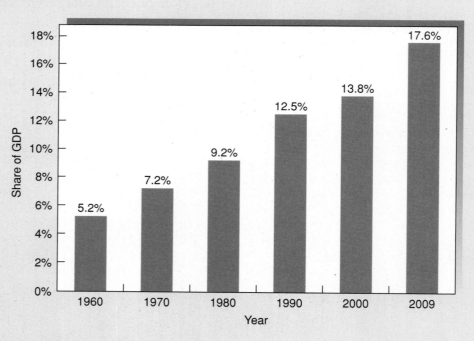

Source: www.cms.hhs.gov.

THE STRUCTURE OF THE HEALTH CARE INDUSTRY

Goods and services may be produced by either private- or government-operated firms. Correspondingly, they may be paid for by the consumer directly or by the taxpayer or some other third party.

Health care in many countries, including Canada and most of the high-income countries of Europe, is a socialized industry.[2] In these countries, hospitals are operated by the government, and their services are financed through taxes. Physicians, nurses, and other health care workers are government employees. Of course, socialization does not eliminate scarcity, costs, and the need to ration the available supply. Resources must be attracted to the health care industry, and this will involve a cost. No country is able to provide as much health care, free of charge, as its citizens would like. Therefore, when price plays a secondary role, nonprice factors will have to be used to ration health care services. Thus, in these countries, political rules, waiting lists for various treatments, and the absence (or highly restricted availability) of services such as MRIs that involve expensive equipment are used to allocate health care resources.

In the United States, there is widespread use of both private- and government-operated enterprises in the health care industry. Whereas the services of doctors are generally supplied privately, hospitals are often operated by the government, particularly local governments. Many communities, however, also have privately operated hospitals. Some of the privately operated hospitals are for-profit businesses, whereas others are operated by charitable institutions. In contrast with other industries, most health care spending (86 percent) is paid for by a third party, either the taxpayer or a private insurance company.

The Medicare and Medicaid programs have covered the bulk of the health care cost of the elderly and the poor since their establishment in the mid-1960s. Medicare's hospitalization program (Part A) uses a 2.9-percent tax on the wages and salaries of current workers to finance virtually all of the cost of hospitalization incurred by persons aged 65 and older. Medicare's Part B Supplementary Medical Insurance covers outpatient medical services, and the recently enacted Part D subsidizes the purchase of prescription drug insurance. The latter two programs are financed 75 percent by general revenues and 25 percent by beneficiary premiums. The Medicaid program provides low-income families with access to health care either free or at a nominal cost. It is a combination federal–state program financed from general revenues. The federal government covers 60 percent of the Medicaid costs, whereas states cover the other 40 percent and have some discretion regarding the structure and coverage of the program.

Exhibit 2 presents data for real expenditures (measured in 2009 dollars) on the Medicare and Medicaid programs. From the very beginning, spending on the programs rose rapidly. By 1970, combined spending on the two summed to $58 billion. Real expenditures on the Medicare program doubled between 1970 and 1980 and doubled again between 1980 and 1990. Since 1990, they have increased by another 200 percent. In 2009, the total expenditures on Medicare summed to $502 billion. Whereas it started from a lower base, spending on Medicaid has increased even more rapidly than Medicare. In 2009, government spending on Medicaid ($374 billion) was more than three times the level of 1990 and 15 times the figure for 1970. As Exhibit 2 shows, spending on Medicaid is now three-fourths that of Medicare.

DISCRIMINATION AGAINST THE DIRECT PURCHASE OF HEALTH INSURANCE

Health insurance is also an integral part of the health care industry in the United States. About two-thirds of nonelderly adults have health insurance through group plans offered by their employers. Employee compensation in the form of health insurance is not subject

---

[2]For a cross-national comparison of spending on health care, see Uwe E. Reinhardt, "Health Care for Aging Baby Boom: Lessons from Abroad," *Journal of Economic Perspectives* (Spring 2000): 71–83.

Exhibit 2

Real Expenditures on Medicare and Medicaid (Measured in 2009 Dollars)

Expenditures on both Medicare and Medicaid have soared in recent decades. Adjusted for inflation, the 2009 expenditures on Medicare are three times the level of 1990 and 14 times the figure for 1970. The real Medicaid expenditures have increased even more rapidly.

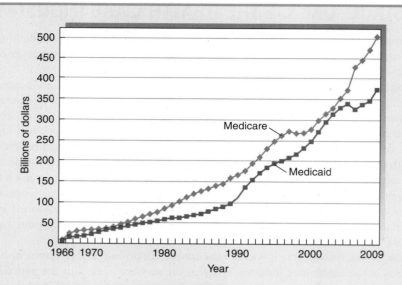

Sources: www.cms.hhs.gov and www.bea.gov.

to taxation. This makes group health insurance programs provided through one's employer particularly attractive.[3] Interestingly, this favorable tax treatment of employer-provided health insurance is a historical relic dating back to the wage and price controls of World War II. Because health insurance benefits were not counted as wages, employers were able to use them as a means to increase compensation and attract additional workers, while still complying with the wage controls imposed during the war.

In contrast with health insurance purchased through one's employer, both personal medical bills and the direct purchase of insurance by an individual or family must be paid for with after-tax dollars. When employees are provided with additional income rather than health insurance benefits, the income is subject to both payroll and personal income taxes. This makes the direct purchase of health insurance far more costly than purchase through an employer. For example, a lower-middle-income family confronting a 15 percent federal income tax and the 15.3 percent payroll tax would have to earn approximately $12,000 of additional income in order to purchase an $8,400 health insurance policy. A family in the 28 percent federal tax bracket would have to earn approximately $14,000 more in order to purchase the policy. When state and local income and payroll taxes are present, these figures are still higher.

This discriminatory tax treatment encourages employees to demand and employers to provide low deductible, small copayment health insurance policies. In essence, health care expenses covered in this manner are tax deductible, whereas those paid for out of pocket or through the direct purchase of health insurance are not.[4] As a result of this distortion, more health care bills are paid for by third-party insurers and fewer are covered directly by the health care consumer or through high-deductible insurance plans. As we will see in a moment, this affects the efficiency of health care delivery.

The linking of health insurance to employment also reduces employee mobility and increases the number of people without any health insurance coverage. When employees lose their job, they also lose their health insurance. Because purchase of a policy with after-tax dollars is so expensive, many unemployed workers remain uncovered until they are able

---

[3]In addition to the favorable tax treatment, economies resulting from the group purchase of health insurance may also make employer-provided plans more attractive.

[4]Out-of-pocket health care expenses can only be deducted if the taxpayer files an itemized return. Even in this case, only health care expenses in excess of 7.5 percent of the taxpayer's adjusted gross income are deductible.

to find a new job. Furthermore, the discriminatory tax treatment of direct purchase policies reduces the competitiveness of the health insurance industry. Unsurprisingly, the industry is dominated by a relatively small number of companies offering primarily "one size fits all" group plans.

THIRD-PARTY PAYMENTS AND HEALTH CARE INFLATION

Following the establishment of the Medicare and Medicaid programs in the mid-1960s, third-party payment of health care expenditures grew rapidly, whereas the share of medical bills paid directly by the consumer declined. As Exhibit 3 shows, 55.2 percent of the 1960 medical expenditures were paid directly by consumers. Third parties financed only 44.8 percent of the 1960 total. Through the years, the share paid out of pocket has declined, whereas that financed by third parties has risen. By 2009, third-party payments accounted for 86 percent of the medical care purchases, 47.4 percent by the government, and 38.3 percent by private insurers. Only 14 percent of the medical bills in 2009 were paid for directly by consumers.

Economic theory indicates that the growth of subsidies to health care consumers and accompanying expansion in third-party payments will push prices upward. There are two reasons why this will be the case. First, subsidies like those provided by Medicare and Medicaid will increase the demand for medical care. In turn, the stronger demand will lead to higher prices. As we discussed in Chapter 4, when the supply of a good or service is highly inelastic, suppliers will be the primary beneficiaries even if the subsidies are directed toward consumers. This is the case in the health care industry: The supply of most medical service is highly inelastic. As a result, the primary impact of the subsidies will be higher prices and increased returns for health care providers.

Second, the growth of third-party payments weakens the incentive of consumers to economize and shop for low-cost services and for producers to provide the goods at a

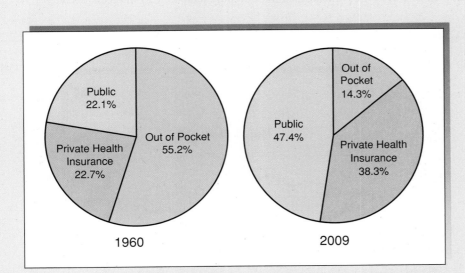

Exhibit 3

Out-of-Pocket and Third-Party Payments for Medical Care, 1960 and 2009

In 1960, out-of-pocket medical care expenditures of consumers accounted for 55 percent of the total, whereas private insurance and government programs paid 45 percent of the medical bills. By 2009, the out-of-pocket payments had fallen to only 14 percent of expenditures, whereas those covered by a third party had risen to 86 percent of the total. Economic theory indicates that growth of third-party payments will reduce the incentive to economize and lead to both higher prices and expenditure levels.

Source: www.cms.hhs.gov. Here, medical care payments are defined as personal health care expenditures.

low price. In a normal market, consumers will shop around and patronize those suppliers that provide the most value per dollar of expenditure. In turn, this shopping by consumers provides suppliers with a strong incentive to control their costs and offer their services at attractive prices. But when someone else is paying all or most of the bill, the incentive to economize is eroded. Rather than search for value relative to cost, consumers will attempt to purchase from the "best available" supplier, pretty much regardless of price.

Perhaps the following example will help explain why the substitution of third-party payments for out-of-pocket spending will lead to higher prices. Suppose that the government, insurance companies, or some other third party was willing to pay 90 percent of the bill of customers purchasing hair-styling services. Think how the behavior of both potential consumers and suppliers in the hair-styling business would be altered. Because someone else is paying most of the bill, many consumers will now get their hair styled more often, search for the very best stylists even if they are quite expensive, and patronize those providing extra services (for example, shoulder massages, pleasant surroundings, and valet parking). The strong demand will make it possible for hair stylists to raise their prices, and many will begin providing the "extras" designed to convince consumers that their services are the best. All of these adjustments will drive the price of hair-styling services upward and cause the third-party expenditures to soar.

Summarizing, economic theory indicates that higher subsidies and increased third-party payments will increase demand for the service, reduce the incentive to economize, and lead to both rising prices and expenditures. Moreover, when the supply of the service is highly inelastic, the producers will be the primary beneficiaries of the subsidies.

The evidence is supportive of this view. **Exhibit 4** shows the ratio of the medical care price index to the overall consumer price index. If the prices of medical services increase more than the prices of other consumer purchases, this ratio will rise. Note that this has been the case year after year. Since the passage of the Medicare and Medicaid programs in 1965, the prices of medical services have more than doubled relative to the general consumer price index. Thus, during this lengthy time span, on average, the prices of health care services rose at more than twice the rate of other consumer items. Furthermore, there is no evidence that the health care inflation is about to subside. In fact, the increase in medical prices relative to the general index of consumer prices has accelerated since 1980. Moreover, the prices of prescription drugs, which rose less than the consumer price index during the 1960s and 1970s, have increased more rapidly than the CPI in recent decades.

Exhibit 4

Ratio of Health care Price Indexes Relative to the Consumer Price Index

The ratio of medical care prices to the general level of consumer prices more than doubled between 1965 and 2010. After declining relative to the Consumer Price Index during 1960–1980, prescription drug prices have increased far more rapidly than the CPI since 1980.

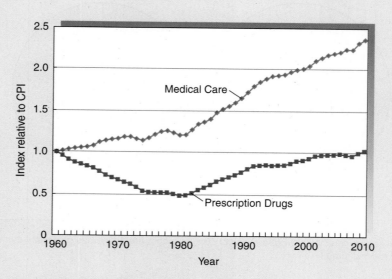

Source: htpp://www.bls.gov.

As prices and expenditures soar, third-party payees, including both insurance companies and the government, will try to control the growth of their expenditures. They may limit the amount paid for various services, require consumers to patronize only certain providers, make it more difficult to obtain permission for costly procedures, impose delays, and the like. This is essentially the route taken by the "managed-care movement" of the 1990s. Regulatory controls of this type, however, are difficult to implement successfully because they often conflict with the interest of both consumers and health care providers. As the experience with managed care illustrates, this path will tend to result in unhappy consumers and decisions that, with the benefit of hindsight, were clearly inappropriate and in some cases life-threatening. Controlling costs through rules and regulations imposed by a third party is an imperfect substitute for competition and the choices of consumers spending their own money.

THE GROWTH OF THE ELDERLY POPULATION AND HEALTH CARE

What will happen to the future demand for health care? **Exhibit 5** provides insight on this question. Between 2000 and 2010, the number of Americans age 70 and older expanded by 2.4 million. But the growth of the population in this age category will soar as the baby boomers (the generation born after World War II) reach age 70 in large numbers. This is now happening. During the two decades following 2010, the age 70 and older population of the United States will expand by 23.7 million, a whopping increase of 80 percent.

This huge increase in elderly Americans has enormous implications for the health care industry. Because health care expenses are much higher for people in their seventies than in their sixties and younger, this growth of Americans age 70 and older will increase the demand for both medical services and the share of those services financed by third parties. This will push both health care prices and expenditures upward. It will also cause spending on Medicare and other health care programs to soar and necessitate higher taxes for their

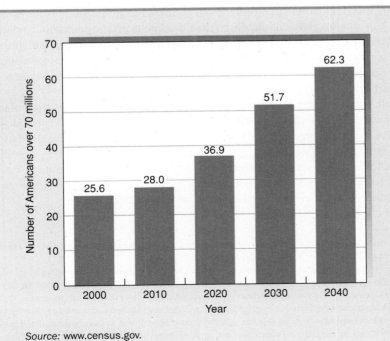

Source: www.census.gov.

Exhibit 5

Growth of the U.S. Population Age 70 and Older, 2000–2040

Between 2000 and 2010, the number of people over age 70 increased by 2.4 million. But, during the two decades that follow, the aging of the baby boom generation will push this group upward by 23.7 million. This rapid growth will place enormous pressure on the Medicare program because the medical expenses of people over age 70 are exceedingly high.

finance. Unless reform is undertaken, the health care inflation and spending growth of recent decades will not only continue but also accelerate.

The Medicare Trustees estimate that Medicare's unfunded promises—projected spending beyond revenues anticipated at current tax rates—are $24 trillion.[5] That figure is 50 percent more than the official national debt and nearly three times the unfunded liability of the Social Security system. Even more important, it is one and a half times the size of the U.S. economy.

PERVERSE INCENTIVES AND THE PROVISION OF HEALTH CARE

Some charge that market forces have failed in health care and therefore government must intervene. The truth is more nearly the opposite: Government interventions over more than six decades have generated perverse incentives that encourage people to engage in actions that impose costs on others and use resources inefficiently. These incentives clarify the forces underlying both the poor performance of the industry and the rising health care costs. They also provide insight with regard to effective action that would improve outcomes.

There are four major reasons for the poor performance of the health care industry. We will consider each of them.

First, the structure of government programs relies on third-party payments that erode the incentive to economize. Very little health care is purchased directly by consumers. Most is paid for indirectly through taxes or insurance premiums. When someone else is paying the bill, the patient has little reason to conserve on the use of the resource and the provider has little incentive to keep costs low.

Second, the huge tax advantage provided for the purchase of health insurance through one's employer undermines competition and makes it very costly for individuals or families to purchase a health insurance policy that fits their preferences. Rather than allowing consumers to choose, government subsidies and regulations push them into standardized and controlled group plans provided through employers. Moreover, under this system, if you lose your job, you also lose your health insurance. People do not generally buy auto, life, or homeowner insurance through their employer. Why do so many buy health insurance this way? Answer: The tax system subsidizes them to do so and punishes them with higher personal costs if they do not.

Third, state regulations that force insurers operating in the state to cover numerous items such as in vitro fertilization, drug rehabilitation, marriage counseling, acupuncture, and massage therapy also drive up costs and make it still more difficult for consumers to purchase a policy that fits their preferences.[6] Interestingly, the political pressure for this coverage does not come from consumers but rather from special interest producer associations wanting taxpayers to subsidize the purchase of their services.

Fourth, regulations prevent consumers from purchasing a health insurance plan offered in another state. Thus, if you would like to purchase insurance that would provide you with inexpensive basic coverage at a low cost, but you happen to live in a state that has adopted many of the expensive mandates, you are out of luck. Essentially, the government has organized the health insurance business into separate cartels that operate in each of the 50 states. You can buy most everything ranging from groceries and automobiles to life and auto insurance from providers in other states, but not health insurance.

---

[5]See *2011 Annual Report of the Boards of Trustees of the Federal Hospital Insurance and Federal Supplementary Medical Insurance Trust Fund*, www.cms.hhs.gov/ReportsTrustFunds/.

[6]Health care insurance premiums are far more economical in states with few mandates than in those that force insurers to cover marginal medical services and to accept persons with known medical problems. For example, the cost of health insurance in states with few mandates like Idaho and Iowa is about half the cost of the premiums in states like Massachusetts, New York, and Rhode Island that mandate broader coverage. The broader set of mandates prevent consumers from buying less expensive coverage tailored to their individual and family needs. Moreover, they also increase the number uninsured because more people will choose to go without insurance when the premiums are higher.

AMERICAN HEALTH CARE AT A CROSSROADS

As we have shown, health care prices have risen rapidly and spending is growing faster than GDP. In recent decades, health care expenditures have consumed approximately one additional percentage point of GDP every four years. Moreover, the movement of the baby boomers into their senior years is sure to make matters worse.

The Obama administration recognized the dangers accompanying the growth of health care spending and the need to do something about it. As a result, the Administration pushed hard for the Patient Protection and Affordable Care Act, which was passed in 2010. When this legislation is fully implemented, it will bring sweeping changes to the health care industry. The Act will require all Americans to purchase health care insurance from either a private or public-sector provider. Approximately 30 million people, not currently covered by health insurance, will be required to obtain a policy. This will be achieved through a combination of expanding the eligibility for Medicaid and subsidies to middle and lower income households for the purchase of health insurance. The law also eliminates annual and lifetime caps on coverage by health insurance companies and eliminates or reduces copayments for preventive care services.

The new health care legislation is controversial and its constitutionality is being challenged in the courts. This issue is unlikely to be resolved until the Supreme Court eventually hands down a decision. That may not occur until 2013 or later.

While the objectives of the new health care legislation are noble, there is little reason to believe that it will be effective. The more than 2,000-page bill reflects the central planning approach and the political clout of special interest. The federal government will set more than 7,000 reimbursement rates for various medical procedures. All doctors will be required to keep patient records in electronic form. In addition to the increase in number of people insured, the breadth of mandated coverage will increase. The share of medical bills covered by third-party payments will expand. The legislation focuses on the demand side of the market and does nothing to promote additional supply. In fact, the increased paperwork and regulation will cause many older doctors to hasten their retirement, and thereby reduce the supply of physician services. The health care industry is large, dynamic, and diverse. It is far too complex for government regulations and agency planners to direct, and efforts to do so will slow innovation and reduce efficiency.

Here, as in many other areas, good intentions do not assure desirable results. The Affordable Care Act fails to address the underlying causes of the soaring cost and poor performance of the health care industry.

HOW TO IMPROVE THE PERFORMANCE OF THE HEALTH CARE INDUSTRY

If the provision of health care is to become more efficient and cost-effective, greater reliance must be placed on consumer choice and direct payment of medical expenses. How can this be achieved? Several policy changes would be helpful, but the following six alternatives are particularly important.

1. Equalize the tax treatment of out-of-pocket medical expenses and the direct purchase of health insurance with that of health insurance purchased through an employer. This could be achieved by either making the health care benefits provided through one's employer taxable or by making the payment of out-of-pocket health care expenditures and the purchase of personal health insurance fully tax deductible. This deductibility would not be of much value to taxpayers with low incomes or those filing the short tax forms. These taxpayers could be provided with a 30 percent tax credit, a tax saving similar to that of employer-provided plans, for expenditures on the direct purchase of medical insurance and out-of-pocket payment of medical bills. This would also make it cheaper for people without access to employer-provided insurance to purchase coverage and pay medical bills directly.

2. Allow the residents of each state to purchase health care from out-of-state providers. This would break up the government-protected cartels now operating in each state and make the health insurance industry more competitive. It would also expand the options available to consumers and make it easier for them to purchase a plan more consistent with their personal preferences.

Health savings accounts
Special savings accounts that individuals and families can use for the payment of medical bills and the purchase of a catastrophic (high deductible) health insurance plan.

3. Encourage health savings accounts (HSAS) and the direct payment of medical bills from the accounts. Beginning in 2004, health savings accounts were made more attractive, but they are still treated less favorably than insurance purchased through one's employer. In 2009, HSAS allowed individuals with a high-deductible insurance plan ($1,150 or more) to make tax-deductible contributions of up to $3,000 per year for a single person (or $5,950 for a married couple) into a savings account to cover future medical bills. Employers making contributions into their employees' accounts may take the contributions as a business expense. Individuals have a property right to the account, and their ownership is not dependent upon their employment. Funds can be drawn from these accounts for the direct payment of medical bills not covered by the high-deductible policies. Balances in the accounts can earn interest tax-free and be rolled over from year to year. Accumulated balances can either be used in retirement or passed on to heirs. HSAS reduce the incidence of third-party payments, and with time, as more health care consumers shop for value, medical suppliers will become more cost-sensitive. These accounts have grown substantially in recent years. In 2009, HSAS covered 8 million individuals.

4. Encourage the purchase of catastrophic health insurance and discourage the purchase of policies with first-dollar coverage and small copayments. HSAS are designed to be used with a high-deductible, modest copayment insurance plan that can be purchased at an economical price. Insurance works well when it compensates people for losses resulting from unpredictable events outside of their control that seldom occur, but when they do, large losses are imposed on the unfortunate parties. Under these circumstances, the premiums of those experiencing little or no damage can be used to compensate those experiencing large losses. Large medical expenses such as those resulting from a severe injury or a catastrophic illness like diabetes or cancer generally fall into this category. It makes sense to promote the purchase of health insurance providing protection against large medical bills from sources like these. High-deductible policies—for example, one that covers most medical expenses in excess of $3,000 per year—are relatively cheap. In 2009, such a policy could be purchased for an annual premium of approximately $1,900. A system of tax credits could be utilized to encourage all (or at least most) citizens to purchase policies of this type.

In contrast, insurance works poorly when the "losses" are widespread among the insurees and when the actions of those insured influence the size of the benefits they derive. Under these circumstances, many insurees will do less to avoid actions that increase the likelihood that events triggering compensation will occur; and, as a result, insurance premiums will be costly relative to the benefits. Many health care costs, including those resulting from routine illnesses (for example, colds and flu), common childhood diseases, minor injuries, and the like, fall into this category. In varying degrees, most everyone can expect to experience such medical problems, and there are several alternative ways of dealing with them, some of which are far less costly than others. Predictably, insurance will work poorly for medical costs of this type. Furthermore, policies requiring only a small copayment for routine medical expenses promote the third-party payment system that retards economizing behavior. Thus, it makes no sense for public policy to promote such schemes.

5. Shift Medicare at least partly from a reimbursement service to a defined-benefit plan. Under this approach, Medicare recipients would receive a specific amount each year for paying medical bills directly and purchasing private insurance. All Medicare recipients would be required to purchase at least a catastrophic insurance plan. The funds not used in one year could be rolled over for use in subsequent years. This approach would increase the freedom of Medicare recipients to choose the combination of medical services and method of payment that best fits their personal situation.

6. Place more emphasis on the supply side of the health care market. Each year, the government spends several hundred billion dollars subsidizing demand and helping people purchase medical services. Very little is spent encouraging additional supply. However, without additional supply, demand subsidies merely lead to higher prices and a reallocation of health care services among consumers. The subsidy recipients, primarily the elderly and those with low incomes, obtain more medical care, and others receive less. Furthermore, the primary beneficiaries of the demand-side subsidies are the health care suppliers, who receive the higher prices for their services. Supply-side programs would focus more on the training of health care providers. For example, they might provide more aid for the growth and development of medical schools—only two new medical schools have been established in the United States during the past quarter of a century. Aid to low-income students qualified to attend medical and nursing schools might also be expanded. In contrast with demand subsidies, programs that expand the supply of medical personnel would make it easier to control future costs.

CONCLUDING THOUGHTS

Health care currently costs so much because consumers directly pay for so little of it. When consumers spend their own money, they will choose wisely and their choices will provide suppliers with a strong incentive to control costs and offer quality service. The six proposals outlined here will lead to (1) more direct payment (and less third-party payment) of health care expenses, (2) more competition in the health insurance industry, (3) lower cost of catastrophic insurance protection (but higher cost for low deductible, high copayment coverage), and (4) greater reliance on expanding supply of medical services rather than stimulation of demand. These reforms will not solve all of our health care problems, but economic analysis suggests they are a major move in the right direction.

The health care legislation of 2010 generated a "great debate" on the structure and future of health care in the United States. As this legislation is implemented and the results observed, it is almost certain that this debate will continue.

KEY POINTS

- Spending on health care has soared in recent decades. Measured as a share of the economy, total health care spending has risen from 5.2 percent in 1960 to 9.2 percent in 1980 and 17.6 percent in 2009.

- Following the enactment of Medicare and Medicaid in the mid-1960s, the direct expenditures of health care consumers gradually declined and those of third-party payees expanded. The out-of-pocket spending of consumers accounted for only 14 percent of health care spending in 2007, down from 55 percent in 1960.

- The growth of subsidies to health care consumers and greater reliance on third-party payments of recent decades (1) increased the demand for medical services and (2) reduced the incentive of both health care consumers and providers to economize. Both of these factors have contributed to the health care inflation and soaring expenditures of recent decades.

- As the baby-boom generation grows older, the number of people aged 70 and older will increase sharply between 2010 and 2030. Under the current Medicare program, this will increase the demand for health care services and the share of medical payments financed by a third party. Unless reform is undertaken, this will mean both more health care inflation and substantially higher taxes for the finance of Medicare.

- Reforms that (1) place more emphasis on direct (rather than third-party) payment of medical bills, (2) increase competition in the health insurance industry, (3) encourage catastrophic insurance protection (but not low deductible, low copayment plans), and (4) expand the supply of health care will help control rising health care expenditures.

CRITICAL ANALYSIS QUESTIONS

1. How does the substitution of third-party payments by insurance companies and the government for the out-of-pocket purchase of health care by consumers influence the demand and price of medical services? Explain.

2. *When an employer provides health insurance benefits as part of the compensation package, does this represent a gift by employers to their employees? Do employees earn these benefits? Why or why not? Justify your response.

3. Do individuals have a right to free health care? Do they have a right to force others to provide them with free health care? Discuss.

4. *How did the Medicare and Medicaid programs influence the cost of medical services purchased by Americans who were neither poor nor elderly? Explain.

5. Consider the six reform proposals suggested by the authors at the end of this feature. Indicate why you believe each is either a good or a bad idea. Explain your answers.

6. *Do personal choices influence health care expenditures? If health care is paid for by others or if everyone is charged the same premium for health care, how will this influence the incentive to make healthy lifestyle choices?

7. Suppose the government established a new program that would use revenues from a payroll tax to finance 85 percent of the maintenance and repair cost of automobiles incurred by those who are employed. How would this legislation influence (a) the prices of auto repair and maintenance services, (b) total spending on these services, and (c) the cost of this program in the years immediately ahead? Do you think this program should be adopted? Why or why not?

8. *If the government either provides (or forces insurers to provide) insurance to persons with preexisting adverse health conditions, how will this influence the incentive to purchase insurance when you are healthy?

*Asterisk denotes questions for which answers are given in Appendix B.

8

Education: Problems and Performance

FOCUS

- How do student achievement scores today compare with those of the past? How does student performance in the United States compare with other countries?

- How has spending on education changed in recent decades? How does the educational spending of the United States compare with that of other countries?

- What does economics have to say about the structure of education?

- How can the quality of education be improved?

iStockphoto.com/sorendls

Formal schooling is today largely paid for and almost entirely administered by government bodies or non-profit institutions.

—*Milton Friedman*[1]

Poor teachers are grossly overpaid and good teachers grossly underpaid. Salary schedules tend to be uniform and determined far more by seniority, degrees received, and teaching certificates acquired than by merit.

—*Milton Friedman*[2]

[1,2]Milton Friedman, *Capitalism and Freedom* (Chicago: University of Chicago Press, 1962), 85.

The structure of education differs in several important respects from most other markets. The opening quotes, both from Milton Friedman, capture important components of the problem in the United States. At the elementary and secondary levels (K–12), schools supported by the local government have nearly monopoly power because they are funded by taxpayers and thus "free" to parents with children. Teacher contracts, negotiated by local school boards with strong teacher unions that are organized nationally and send in professional negotiators at contract time, are written to minimize the ability of school principals to reward the best teachers at higher levels than those who perform less effectively.

In higher education (college and other postsecondary schools), there is more diversity and competition, but most universities and colleges are either government-owned (75 percent of all students go to public universities) or nonprofit. These characteristics affect the ability of schools to provide education effectively at reasonable cost.

There is widespread concern about the quality of elementary and high school education in the United States and increasing uncertainty about whether a college education, long considered the golden ticket to the American middle class, is worth its rising costs. This special topic investigate the sources of the deficiencies in the current educational system and report on efforts to reform it.

iStockphoto.com/nicoolay

STUDENT PERFORMANCE, EXPENDITURES, AND THE STRUCTURE OF EDUCATION

Let us begin with elementary and secondary schools. Low student performance is a major source of the dissatisfaction with the system. As **Exhibit 1** demonstrates, achievement scores fell in the 1970s and changed little during the 1980s. Since 1990, scores have generally risen, but the average achievement scores of high school graduates today are still well below those of students 40 years ago.

Exhibit 1

Average Combined SAT Score, 1967–2008

The achievement scores of American students dropped in the 1970s, changed little in the 1980s, and rose modestly during the 1990s and 2000s.

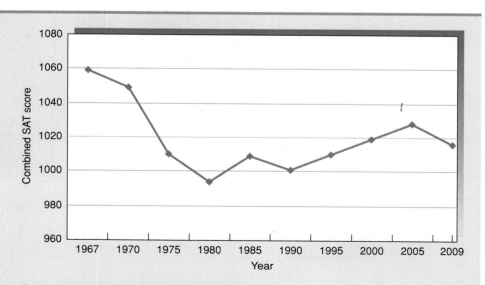

Source: Statistical Abstract of the United States, 2011.

Cross-country comparisons of achievement scores also indicate weak student performance in the United States. **Exhibit 2** shows the top 20 nations' science achievement scores from the 2009 Program of International Student Assessment, which compared achievement in more than 60 countries. Fifteen-year-olds in the United States scored about 50 points below those in Finland, Singapore, and Japan, the top scoring nations. The achievement scores for mathematics also show that U.S. students lag well behind those of most developed countries.

Average Science Achievement Scores of 15-Year-Olds: A Cross-Country Comparison, 2009

Exhibit 2

The science achievement scores of 15-year-old American students lag behind those of other countries.

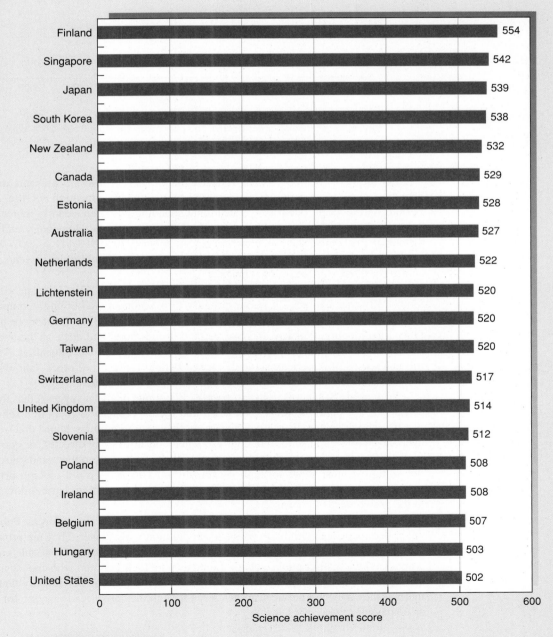

Country	Science achievement score
Finland	554
Singapore	542
Japan	539
South Korea	538
New Zealand	532
Canada	529
Estonia	528
Australia	527
Netherlands	522
Lichtenstein	520
Germany	520
Taiwan	520
Switzerland	517
United Kingdom	514
Slovenia	512
Poland	508
Ireland	508
Belgium	507
Hungary	503
United States	502

Source: OECD, *PISA* (2009).

Exhibit 3

Real Spending per Elementary and Secondary Pupil, 1970–2008

Real spending per pupil on public elementary and secondary schools more than doubled during the 1970–2008 period.

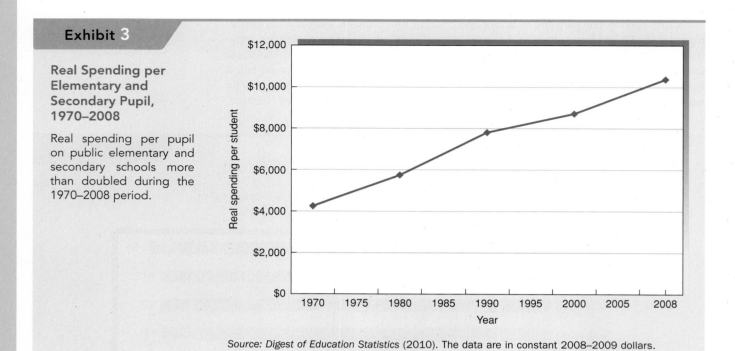

Source: *Digest of Education Statistics* (2010). The data are in constant 2008–2009 dollars.

Do the performance patterns reflect expenditures? **Exhibit 3** presents data on real spending per pupil on public elementary and secondary education for the 1970–2008 period. As the graph illustrates, educational spending has been steadily increasing. *Measured in 2008–2009 dollars*, expenditures per pupil in public elementary and secondary schools in the United States increased from $4,269 in 1970 to $10,441 in 2007–2008. Thus, per-student real spending in the United States more than doubled in 37 years, while test scores for those students fell, on balance.

How do other nations compare, in spending and in results? The U.S. spends more than almost all other nations, on public primary plus secondary schooling. Compared to the average of industrialized (OECD) nations, the U.S. spends 37 percent more per student. Only Luxembourg, Norway and Switzerland spend more, and each of them supports an additional year (actually half a year extra for Switzerland) of that education. Nonetheless, the test scores of American students ranked behind those of 20 other nations in OECD-administered science exams and behind 27 others in math exams.[3]

Why are U.S. schools doing so poorly? Economic analysis suggests that the structure of funding for public schools is an important factor. Property owners in a school district pay for schools in that district whether or not they choose public schools, and whether they even have children in school. In contrast, when consumers pay directly for goods and services, rather than through their taxes, they will shop among suppliers and patronize those providing the most value per unit of expenditure. This gives profit-seeking firms in open markets a strong incentive to operate efficiently, keep their costs and prices down, and cater to the preferences of consumers.

The structure of the U.S. market for schooling undermines these forces. Public schools are government-operated firms with substantial monopoly power. They are protected from the competition of rivals because in most places, "free" education is available only to those who attend the district public school. Students (and their parents) who choose a nonpublic school must pay for their own education and lose the government subsidy that would be theirs if they attended public schools—even though they are already paying for the school as taxpayers.

---

[3]Programme for International Student Assessment (2009), OECD at www.oecd.org/document/61/0,3746,en_32252351_32235731_46567613_1_1_1_1,00.html

This makes it very costly to switch to rival suppliers. A public school has to be very bad before it loses many customers. In the United States, according to government figures, only about 11 percent of all students attend private schools. An increasing number of students, however, are being taught at home—1.5 million students in 2007, according to a Department of Education estimate.[4] While homeschooling parents still pay taxes, they can minimize the out-of-pocket costs of education by doing much of the teaching themselves.

Because the schooling is "free" to district residents with children, school administrators have something approximating a captive market for their services. (Laws that make attendance compulsory, usually till age 16, also help local school districts maintain the attendance numbers that strongly affect the tax dollars they receive.) Thus, compared to a privately run school or business, public schools have less need to cater to the needs of their consumers, the students and parents. They do have to respond to political pressures, however, because their funding comes from taxpayers.

One effect is that they, like the managers of other government-operated firms, have a strong incentive to build the case for more government funding. When problems arise, it is convenient for them to argue that they don't have enough money. Parents often support these requests because they want the best for their children and don't have information telling them otherwise—they lack the incentive that strong competition would provide, to seek the knowledge of alternatives that might cut costs or produce better education.

A thought experiment may illuminate some of the problems with the structure of our public schools. Suppose the restaurant industry in the United States were set up in the same way as the public schools. A system of local "restaurant districts" would be established. Taxes would be levied to finance the cost of the government-operated restaurants in each district. Citizens would not be allowed to patronize public restaurants outside their local district. Customers patronizing private restaurants would have to pay for meals twice—once as a taxpayer and again as a consumer.

Clearly, there would be major problems with this organizational structure. Because the managers of the government-operated restaurants would derive their funds from the government, predictably they would spend more time satisfying those with political clout (including worker unions) and less time catering to the needs and preferences of customers. There would be little incentive to keep costs low. Similarly, there would be little reason for restaurant operators to innovate, find better ways to do things, or search for ways to provide their "customers" with better service. Poor food at the government-operated restaurants would be used as an argument for an increase in their funding. Because consumers could not take their funding and go elsewhere, they would be in a weak position to discipline the district restaurants that were not doing a good job. Predictably, restaurant food costs would rise and quality would deteriorate.

The problems posed by public K–12 schools are similar. The performance of U.S. education at the college and university level is also instructive. At those higher education levels, students have a much greater opportunity to choose among a variety of colleges and universities. Financial aid that can be used at either private or government-operated schools is available to many students. Thus, competition between private and government-operated schools (and among public schools) is much stronger at the college level. In contrast with the international standing of elementary and secondary schools, U.S. higher education leads the world in the variety of programs offered, the eminence of researchers, quality of facilities, and percentage of high school graduates attending college.

Yet here, too, structural problems are beginning to affect the quality of higher education. Increases in tuition have put many private colleges out of the reach of the majority of families, while even public universities, designed to be accessible to a state's qualified students, are also experiencing rapid price increases. For example, college tuition increased by 286 percent between 1990 and 2010, corrected for inflation. That is faster even than medical costs rose for Americans.

---

[4]U.S. Department of Education, National Center for Educational Statistics, *The Condition of Education 2011*, http://nces.ed.gov/programs/coe/indicator_hsc.asp.

So, while U.S. colleges and universities have been called the "envy of the world," it is not clear that they will remain that way far into the future. In fact, the possible decline in the value of a college degree has led to what some observers call a "bubble," similar to the housing bubble that burst in 2008, sending the U.S. economy into the worst tailspin since the Great Depression.

Political analyst Michael Barone writes in the *Washington Examiner*, "My sense is that once again, well-intentioned public policy and greedy providers have produced a bubble that is about to burst."[5] That is, if students and their parents perceive that the cost of a college education is greater than its value, there will be major pressure on colleges and universities to lower their prices, because students won't be willing to pay tuition. If that happens suddenly, the bubble will burst.

WAYS TO EXPAND THE OPTIONS OF CONSUMERS

While the problems of universities have become visible in recent years, they are not as severe—and certainly not as long-running—as those of elementary and high schools. To address the failings of the public school system, many states have adopted programs that offer options to the traditional public school system. The following section briefly considers two of the most common alternatives: school vouchers and charter schools. Keep in mind, however, that other alternatives have emerged as well. A number of states— Arizona, Florida, Georgia, Illinois, Indiana, Iowa, Louisiana, Minnesota, Pennsylvania, and Rhode Island—now allow taxpayers a tax deduction or tax credit for donations to organizations that provide scholarships to students or for parents who spend personal funds on private school expenses. And homeschooling, perhaps the most clear-cut "choice" program, continues to grow.

SCHOOL VOUCHERS

The late economist Milton Friedman and his wife Rose Friedman decided that one of their most important legacies would be to encourage choice in education. They created a foundation, still active, that promotes school choice programs, especially vouchers. The foundation reported in 2011 that 16 states have authorized 26 school choice programs.[6]

Under a pure voucher plan, rather than financing schools directly the government gives parents a certificate equal to the government's per-pupil educational expenditures. The parents can then use the voucher to finance their child's education at the public or private school they think is best for their child.

Such a plan puts competition to work to improve the schools. Because their revenues depend upon their ability to attract students, schools have to compete for students, and parents are free to choose among schools. The competition among schools encourages innovative ideas and the discovery of more effective teaching techniques. The demand for outstanding teachers rises, increasing their salaries and helping to attract quality people to the teaching profession. And the demand for poor teachers declines, encouraging them to improve or to shift to other careers.

A voucher system also encourages diversity in education. Some parents choose a highly structured school; others prefer one that is less structured. Some select a school that stresses religious values; others opt for secular education. Some choose a school with a traditional college prep program; others support schools that provide technical and vocational training. Vouchers, and the parental choice they provide, make it possible for a broader range of consumers to obtain education more consistent with their preferences.

---

[5]Michael Barone, "Will College Burst from Public Subsidies?" *Washington Examiner*, July 19, 2011, http://washingtonexaminer.com/politics/2011/07/will-college-bubble-burst-public-subisidies.
[6]Greg Forster, "A Win-Win Solution: The Empirical Evidence on School Vouchers" (Indianapolis, IN: Foundation for Educational Choice, 2011).

Voucher programs have faced strong opposition, however. Some people argue that vouchers will drain funds away from the public schools and thereby cause their quality to deteriorate. Others fear that the primary beneficiaries will be high-income Americans who already send their children to private schools. And some contend that a voucher plan will increase the racial imbalance among schools.

Such concerns led to the creation of modified vouchers specifically targeted toward families that could not otherwise utilize private schools. For example, the D.C. School Opportunity program, adopted by Congress in 2004, is a voucher program for low-income families in Washington, D.C. (The families' average income in the 2007–2008 school year was $22,736.) About 1,900 students participate in the program at any one time, each of whom can transfer up to $7,500 in public funds to a private school. Studies show that students have progressed as a result of the program, and parents are pleased at being able to keep their children from schools with high crime and poor records of performance.[7]

Even though the Washington, D.C., voucher program is limited to low-income children, the positive effects of the program cast the performance of public schools in a bad light. Opposition grew quickly after it began and Congress voted to phase it out in 2010—abruptly stopping aid to a group of children who had already been told they had received scholarships. In 2011, however, a new Congress voted to reinstate the program.

CHARTER SCHOOLS

Partly because voucher programs have been slow to take off, another approach to providing choice has emerged: charter schools. Charter schools are publicly funded but independent of the traditional public school system. They operate under a contract ("charter") with a government agency. The supervising agency usually requires the charter schools to meet a variety of standards, including financial, safety, and educational outcomes. However, because they are largely independent, they provide unique characteristics that offer parents and children a choice. For example, some schools focus on mathematics and science, others on the arts; some are directed at African American students; and still others focus on the development of leadership skills among girls.

During the 2009–2010 school year, more than 1.6 million students attended more than 4,900 charter schools in 40 states and the District of Columbia. Thirty states permit public school choice in some or all school districts(for a discussion of one public school choice program, see boxed feature "Applications in Economics: School Choice in New York City").[8]

THE EFFECT OF STRUCTURAL CHANGE

It is too early for a full evaluation of voucher programs and charter schools, but some interesting results have emerged from early research in this area.

First, there is no evidence to support the idea that charter schools skim off the highest achieving students from traditional public schools, nor that they create shifts in the racial or ethnic composition of schools. Evidence does suggest that the presence of charter schools has no discernible impact on student achievement in nearby traditional public schools.

Second, the impact of charter schools on student achievement varies substantially. One study finds significantly higher learning gains for students moving to charter schools in some states (Arkansas, Colorado, Illinois, Louisiana, and Missouri) but not in others (Arizona, Florida, Minnesota, New Mexico, Ohio, and Texas showing worse outcomes, and California, the District of Columbia, Georgia, and North Carolina showing similar

---

[7]Margaret Spellings, "Save D.C.'s Vouchers," *Washington Post*, July 8, 2008, http://www.washingtonpost.com/wp-dyn/content/article/2008/07/07/AR2008070702216.html.

[8]The facts in these paragraphs are drawn primarily from http://nces.ed.gov/pubs2011/pesschools09/tables/table_03.asp, http://nces.ed.gov/pubs2011/pesschools09/tables/table_02.asp, and http://nces.ed.gov/fastfacts/display.asp?id=30.

outcomes when compared to traditional public schools). Another study finds achievement gains in reading and math not significantly different from traditional public schools in some areas (San Diego, Philadelphia, Denver, Milwaukee, and the state of Ohio) and worse than public schools in other areas (Chicago and the state of Texas).

The impact of charter schools on achievement also differs depending on how long these schools have been in operation, and whether there are limits on the number of charter schools allowed to operate. First-year charter schools typically perform worse than traditional public schools, but performance improves as charter schools age. States with caps limiting the number of charter schools tend to see less improvement than states without these restrictions.

Studies looking beyond achievement scores find that students attending charter high schools in Chicago and the state of Florida experience substantial increases in both the probability of graduating from high school and of enrolling in college. Furthermore, parents with children in charter schools and voucher programs show a higher degree of satisfaction with their children's schools than parents with children in traditional public schools in the same community.

The federal government had previously attempted to respond to evidence of failing public schools with its own "choice" program. Congress passed the No Child Left Behind Act, signed into law in 2002. One of its provisions allows parents whose children are in failing schools the opportunity to transfer them to better-performing schools; it also authorized grants for supplemental services such as tutoring or summer school programs. Despite billions of dollars distributed under this program, however, many school districts have balked at the act's requirements. And in 2011, several school districts—including Atlanta and a few in the state of Pennsylvania—were rocked by the discovery that teachers and principals had engaged in massive cheating. Teachers erased and then replaced scores on state tests to make it look as though their students were achieving higher scores—so they would not become failing schools under the No Child Left Behind Act.[9]

APPLICATIONS IN ECONOMICS

School Choice in New York City

In 2009, a study by Stanford economist Caroline Hoxby showed that charter school students in New York City gained more than 5 points each year in both state math and state English exams than did similarly situated students who had applied for charter schools but were rejected. Student admissions and rejections were determined by lottery from the group of qualified applicants. This approach controlled for the possibility that applying for the charter school marked students as having more motivation or a different home environment than others, factors that could enhance future performance.

Hoxby's methodology approximated the conditions of a controlled experiment. But the critics were not convinced.

They argued that the self-selected set of applicants differed from the city's public school students, who, among other characteristics, experienced a much greater incidence of poverty, which might adversely affect the performance of their fellow students. As a result, the critics say, even though the students "lotteried out" of the charter school experience may have been similar to those "lotteried in," nonetheless their performance may have suffered because they had fewer other motivated students with whom to interact than those attending the charter schools. As this case highlights, it is difficult to resolve disputes about the quality of schooling with empirical research.

iStockphoto.com/sorendls

[9]Eizabeth Flock, "APS (Atlanta Public Schools) Embroiled in Cheating Scandal," *Washington Post*, July 11, 2011, www.washingtonpost.com/blogs/blogpost/post/aps-atlanta-public-schools-embroiled-in-cheating-scandal/2011/07/11/gIQAJl9m8H_blog.html; and Michael Winerip, "Pa. Joins States Facing a Cheating Scandal," *New York Times*, July 31, 2011, www.nytimes.com/2011/08/01/education/01winerip.html.

CONCLUSION

During the past four decades, educational expenditures have increased substantially, but the performance of schools, as measured by the achievement level of students, has declined. Given the structure of the schooling system, this is not surprising. There is little incentive for government firms operating in a protected market to provide high-quality service at a low cost. In most markets, competition among rival suppliers works well, and that appears to be the case in those education markets where there is substantial competition—higher education and those limited areas of K–12 education with vouchers, charter schools, or similar programs.

KEY POINTS

- Real spending per student has risen over the past several decades, but student performance on basic skill exams is now well below the levels of the late 1960s. The United States spends more on primary and secondary education than most countries, but its students performed below international averages on measures of student achievement.

- Economic analysis indicates that the structure of the educational system is a contributing factor to the poor educational performance. Education is provided by government-operated firms with substantial monopoly power. Because competition is largely absent and educational consumers have limited choices, the incentive to produce efficiently, innovate, and cater to the needs of parents and students is weak.

- Vouchers and charter schools are two possible reforms of the educational system. If they are working properly, they expand the choices of consumers and increase competition among schools. Rather than wait for a restructuring of public K–12 education, a growing number of families are teaching their children at home.

- Higher education is a varied marketplace, with a great deal of choice. However, the nonprofit and public nature of higher education reduces the incentive to control cost. This incentive structure has been a contributing factor to the substantial increase in the cost of going to college observed in the past couple of decades.

- Charter schools and voucher programs appear on balance to have had modest beneficial effects on student achievement. Parents with children in charter schools and voucher programs indicate a higher level of satisfaction with their children's schools than do parents with children in traditional public schools.

CRITICAL ANALYSIS QUESTIONS

1. "The best solution to reverse the decline in student performance in recent decades is to increase spending on education." Evaluate this statement.
2. *How does the lack of competition in the provision of education affect the quality and cost of education? Explain.
3. Should parents have the right to choose which schools their children attend? Why or why not? Discuss.
4. Consider the two reform proposals discussed in this special topic. Indicate why you believe each is either a good or a bad idea. Explain your answers.
5. Currently, students attending state colleges and universities are heavily subsidized, but those attending private higher educational institutions are less so. Do you think this is fair? Would you like to see a voucher system applied to higher education? Why or why not?

*Asterisk denotes questions for which answers are given in Appendix B.

9

Earnings Differences Between Men and Women

FOCUS
- Why are the earnings of women substantially lower than those of men? Is it because of employment discrimination?
- How has the economic status of women changed in recent decades?
- How have the educational choices and career goals of women changed? Will this affect their future earnings?

Over the past 25 years, the gender pay gap has narrowed dramatically and women have increasingly entered traditionally male occupations.

—*Francine D. Blau and Lawrence M. Kahn*[1]

[1]Francine D. Blau and Lawrence M. Kahn, "Gender Differences in Pay," *Journal of Economic Perspectives* (Fall 2000): 75.

A half century ago, the typical American woman spent most of her time at home caring for her children, preparing food, and doing laundry, cleaning, and other chores for her family. Fewer than one in four married women worked outside the household in 1950. Today, the situation is dramatically different. Most women, including those who are married, work outside the home. This special topic analyzes earnings differences of men and women and the changing economic role of women.

iStockphoto.com/nicoolay

EMPLOYMENT DISCRIMINATION AND THE EARNINGS OF WOMEN

During the last several decades, there has been a huge shift in the household versus market work choices of women. As **Exhibit 1** shows, the labor force participation rate of women rose from 37.6 percent in 1960 to 60.8 percent in 2009. Married women accounted for most of the increase.

Exhibit 1 also shows that the female–male (F–M) earnings ratio for full-time, year-round workers was approximately 60 percent from 1960 to 1980. In other words, women

Exhibit 1

Labor Force Experience of Women, 1960–2009

Between 1960 and 2009, the labor force participation of women rose from 37.6 to 60.8 percent. However, the female–male earnings ratio for full-time workers fluctuated around 60 percent during the period 1960–1980, before climbing throughout the 1980s and 1990s. By 2009, this ratio had risen to 76 percent. The hourly earnings of women working full-time were a little more than 80 percent those of men in 2009.

F/M annual earnings ratio (full-time workers)

Female/male annual earnings, full-time workers (left scale)

Percent of women age 20 and over in the labor force (right scale)

Percent in labor force

75.7

60.8

© Cengage Learning 2013

1960   1965   1970   1975   1980   1985   1990   1995   2000   2005   2009

earned only 60 percent of what men did. Since the early 1980s, though, the earnings of women have steadily increased relative to men. Nevertheless, in 2009, women working full-time, year-round still earned only 75.7 percent as much as their male counterparts. However, among those employed full time, women worked about 7 percent fewer hours than men. Thus, the hourly earnings of women working full time were a little more than 80 percent of those of full-time male workers in 2009.

Why are the earnings of women so low compared with those of men? Most people blame employment discrimination. Evidence appears to support this view. Key worker characteristics such as age, years of schooling, marital status, location, and language are similar between men and women. So these factors are not the source of the earnings difference according to gender. Women are also crowded into a few low-paying jobs, occupational data show. Until recently, more than half of all women were employed in just four occupations—as clerical workers, teachers, nurses, and food service workers.

Still, attributing all or most of the pay differences between men and women to employment discrimination is an argument that's less than airtight. The very size of the difference makes the argument suspect. If an employer could really hire women who were willing and able to do the same work as men for 15 or 20 percent less, the profit motive would give them a strong incentive to do so. Surely employers (both men and women) who don't consider themselves to be "sexist" would jump at the chance to cut their wage cost so dramatically. Of course, as more and more employers substituted women for men workers, the F–M earnings gap would close.

MARITAL STATUS AND THE EARNINGS OF WOMEN

It might be helpful to think about the problem in a historical light. Before 1980, married men typically pursued paid employment aggressively because they were expected to be the family's primary breadwinners. Because they shouldered most of the responsibility for "bringing home the bacon," they were more likely to (1) participate continuously in the labor force; (2) relocate if necessary to get a higher paying job; and (3) accept jobs with long working hours, uncertain schedules, and out-of-town travel.

In contrast, married women, who were traditionally more responsible for running the households and rearing children, sought part-time work and jobs with more flexible hours.[2] Further, they expected to drop out of the labor force or switch jobs from time to time in order to care for young children, to follow their husband to a new job location, or when their families' financial needs became less burdensome. Because of expected changes in their work status, job skills valued by a large number of employers at most any time and location were particularly valuable to women. Viewed from this perspective, the historical concentration of women in occupations like nursing, teaching, and clerical positions is not surprising.

How important are gender differences when it comes to specialization within the family and pay differences today? **Exhibit 2** shows the median annual earnings of women relative to men in 2008–2009, according to their marital status. Clearly, married women earn substantially less than do married men. Even when working full time, year-round, married women earn only 73 percent as much as men. However, the earnings gap between men and women is substantially less among those who have never married. In 2008–2009, the female–male annual earnings ratio for full-time, year-round workers was 91 percent for those never married. In other words, the earnings gap between men and women was much smaller for those who were never married than for those married or previously married. This implies that although employment discrimination may well contribute to the wage differences between men and women, factors related to marital status, perhaps differences in preferences and past educational choices based on career objectives, are also highly important.

---

[2]For an analysis of how family specialization influences the employment and earnings of women, see James P. Smith and Michael P. Ward, "Women in the Labor Market and in the Family," *Journal of Economic Perspectives* (Winter 1989): 9–23.

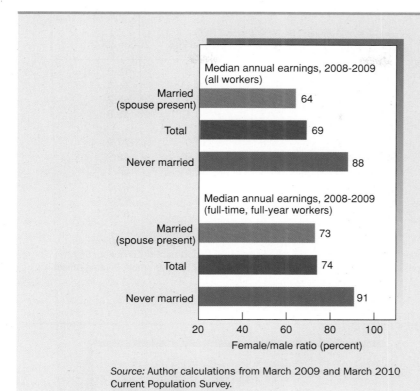

Median annual earnings, 2008-2009
(all workers)

Married
(spouse present)   64

Total   69

Never married   88

Median annual earnings, 2008-2009
(full-time, full-year workers)

Married
(spouse present)   73

Total   74

Never married   91

Female/male ratio (percent)

Source: Author calculations from March 2009 and March 2010
Current Population Survey.

Exhibit 2

Female–Male Earnings According to Marital Status, 2008–2009

The earnings of women relative to men vary substantially with marital status and time worked. For those working full-time, year-round, the female–male earnings ratio was only 73 percent for married women with spouse present, but it was 91 percent for those never married. This suggests that differences in specialization within the traditional husband–wife family contribute substantially to earnings differentials according to gender.

THE CHANGING CAREER OBJECTIVES OF WOMEN

Although the career objectives of men and women have differed substantially in the past, those differences have narrowed in recent years. In 1968, a national survey of women 14 to 24 years of age found that only 27 percent expected to be working at age 35. In contrast, a similar survey of young women in 1979 found that 72 percent expected to be working at that age.[3] These figures show that there was a dramatic increase during the 1970s in the number of young women preparing for a career and lifetime of labor force participation. Although this upward trend may have slowed, it has almost certainly continued during the last three decades.

As the percentage of women planning for a career rose, their educational choices also changed dramatically. In the early 1970s, women were much less likely than men to study and prepare for engineering, medicine, law, and similar high-paying fields traditionally dominated by men. But, as Exhibit 3 shows, the percentage of women earning degrees in these fields and others, such as accounting, veterinary medicine, dentistry, medicine, law, architecture, pharmacy, and economics, increased dramatically in the 1970s and 1980s. By the 1990s, parity was achieved in several of these areas. Increasingly, women, like men, are planning for careers in diverse areas, including high-paying professions.

The gender composition of new college graduates also suggests that women are increasingly planning for a career in the marketplace. During the last four decades, the percentage of women as a share of new college graduates has increased dramatically. As Exhibit 4 shows, only 39 percent of those completing an undergraduate degree in 1961 were women. By 1980, that figure had risen to 49 percent, and by 2010 it had jumped to 57 percent. Today, nearly three out of every five graduating seniors are women, compared with less than two out of five four decades ago.

---

[3]See Chapter 7 of the *Economic Report of the President* (1987). The numbers presented here are from tables 7–3 of the report.

Exhibit 3

Women as a Percent of People Earning Selected Professional Degrees, 1970–1971, 1987–1988, and 2008–2009

FIELD OF STUDY	1970–1971	1987–1988	2008–2009
Engineering	0.8	15.3	18.0
Dentistry	1.2	26.1	46.4
Optometry	2.4	34.3	65.2
Law	7.3	40.4	45.8
Veterinary Medicine	7.8	50.0	77.9
Medicine	9.2	33.0	48.9
Accounting	10.1	52.6	54.1
Economics	11.2	32.8	29.5
Architecture	12.0	38.7	49.3
Pharmacy	25.2	59.7	64.5

Sources: Commission of Professionals in Science and Technology, *Professional Women and Minorities* (Washington, DC: CPST, 1987); and U.S. Department of Education, *Digest of Education Statistics*, 1990 and 2010 (Washington, DC: U.S. Government Printing Office).

Exhibit 4

Women as a Percent of People Graduating from College, 1961–2010

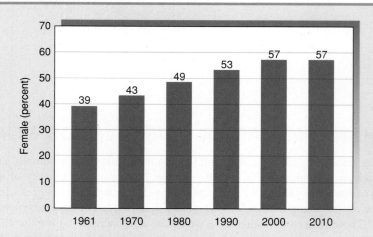

Source: Source: U.S. Department of Education, *Digest of Education Statistics*, 2010 (Washington, DC: U.S. Government Printing Office, 2011), table 279. The data are for people graduating with a four-year degree.

The fact that men are now a minority among those currently graduating from college is not particularly surprising. Jobs in fields like construction and heavy manufacturing offer attractive earnings opportunities, but they are also generally physically demanding and require employees to work either outdoors or in a less than ideal environment. Given their greater physical strength and perhaps a stronger preference for outdoor working conditions, men are more likely than women to find these physically demanding jobs attractive. As a result, the opportunity cost of going to college is higher for young men than for young women. Thus, fewer men pursue a college degree.

It is interesting to think about women's career choices in light of societal changes in the United States during the past five decades. In 1962, equal-pay legislation was passed requiring employers to pay equal wage rates to men and women doing the same jobs. In 1964, civil rights legislation was passed prohibiting employers from discriminating on the basis of both gender and race. Nonetheless, in the 1960s and 1970s, there was little change in the earnings of women relative to men. However, as the career objectives of women—perhaps pushed along by earlier legislative actions—began to change during

Charles Gupton/Getty Images

During the 1970s, an increasing proportion of women began to plan for full time, long term labor force participation. Reflecting this commitment, the career and educational choices of women shifted toward higher paying professions (see Exhibit 3). As this happened, the earnings of women began to increase steadily relative to men (see Exhibit 1).

the 1970s, the educational choices of men and women started to become more similar (see Exhibit 3).[4] Soon thereafter, the earnings of women began to rise relative to men (see Exhibit 1).

IMPLICATIONS FOR THE FUTURE

Clearly, the increased representation of women during the past several decades among both college graduates and those preparing themselves for careers indicates that women are increasingly committed to working in the marketplace. As the current generation of highly trained, well-educated young women acquires experience and moves into the prime earning years of life, the upward trend in the F–M earnings ratio can be expected to continue in the years ahead.

KEY POINTS

- The annual earnings of women working full time are approximately 76 percent of those of men. Among full-time workers, the F–M earnings ratio is 73 percent for those married with spouse present but 91 percent for people who never married.

- In addition to employment discrimination, differences in specialization within the family, educational choices, and career goals contribute to the earnings differences between men and women.

- As the educational and career choices of women have become more like those of men during the last two decades, the earnings of women have risen relative to those of men. This trend is likely to continue in the future as more and more women prepare for and acquire experience in high-paying business and professional fields that have traditionally been dominated by men.

---

[4]For additional details on recent changes in the male/female earnings gap, see Francine D. Blau and Lawrence M. Kahn, "Gender Differences in Pay," *Journal of Economic Perspectives* (Fall 2000): 75–99; June O'Neill, "The Gender Gap in Wages, circa 2000," *American Economic Review* (May 2003): 309–14; and Francine D. Blau and Lawrence M. Kahn, "The U.S. Gender Pay Gap: Slowing Convergence," *Industrial and Labor Relations Review* (October 2006): 45–66.

CRITICAL ANALYSIS QUESTIONS

1. Is employment discrimination the major cause of earnings differences between men and women? Carefully justify your answer.

2. *Between 1960 and 1990, the labor force participation rate of married women approximately doubled. What impact did this influx of married workers into the labor force have on (a) the average years of work experience of women relative to men, (b) the mean hours of work time of women relative to men, and (c) the female–male earnings ratio?

3. Physical strength is important in some jobs. Do you think differences in physical strength between men and women contribute to earnings differences according to gender? Why or why not? Do they also influence the share of men relative to women who will pursue a college education? Explain.

4. *In 2009, the median earnings of single men working full-time, year-round were only 67 percent of their married counterparts. Does this indicate that employment discrimination existed against single men and in favor of married men?

5. Compared to women, men are overrepresented in occupations like coal mining and construction, in which working conditions are more dangerous. For example, 4,216 American men were killed on the job in 2009, compared to 335 women. How will the more dangerous working conditions of men influence their earnings relative to women? Explain.

*Asterisk denotes questions for which answers are given in Appendix B.

Do Labor Unions Increase the Wages of Workers?

FOCUS

- How much of the U.S. workforce is unionized?
- Can unions increase the wages of their members? What makes a union strong? What factors limit the power of a union?
- Can unions increase the wages of all workers?

The rise and decline of private sector unionization were among the more important features of the U.S. labor market during the twentieth century.

—Barry T. Hirsch and Edward J. Schumacher[1]

[1]Barry T. Hirsch and Edward J. Schumacher, "Private Sector Union Density and the Wage Premium: Past, Present, and Future," *Journal of Labor Research* (Summer 2001): 487.

A labor union is an organization of employees, usually working in either the same occupation or same industry, who have consented to joint bargaining with employers about their wages, working conditions, grievance procedures, and other elements of employment. The primary objective of a labor union is to improve the welfare of its members. Unions have historically been controversial. Some see them as a necessary shield protecting workers from employer greed. Others charge that unions are monopolies seeking to provide their members with benefits at the expense of other workers, consumers, and economic efficiency. Still others argue that the economic influence of unions—both for good and for bad—is vastly overrated. This feature will consider the impact of unions on the wages of their members and those of other workers.

iStockphoto.com/nicoolay

UNION MEMBERSHIP AS A SHARE OF THE WORKFORCE

Labor union
A collective organization of employees who bargain as a unit with employers.

Historically, the proportion of the U.S. labor force belonging to a labor union has fluctuated substantially. In 1910, approximately 10 percent of nonfarm employees belonged to a union. As **Exhibit 1** shows, this figure rose to 18 percent in 1920. In the aftermath of World War I, union membership declined, falling to 12 percent of nonfarm workers by 1929. Pushed along by favorable legislation adopted during the Great Depression, union membership rose from 13.5 percent of nonfarm employees in 1935 to 30.4 percent in 1945. By 1954, nearly a third of nonfarm workers in the United States were unionized.

Exhibit 1	**Union Membership as a Share of Nonagricultural Employment, 1910–2010**

Between 1910 and 1935, union membership fluctuated between 12 percent and 18 percent of nonagricultural employment. During the 1935–1945 period, union membership increased sharply to approximately one-third of the nonfarm workforce. Since the mid-1950s, union membership has declined as a percent of nonfarm employment, and the decline has been particularly sharp since 1979.

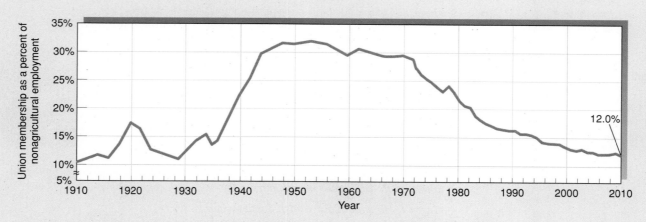

Source: Leo Troy and Neil Sheflin, *Union Source Book: Membership, Structure, Finance, Directory* (West Orange, NJ: Industrial Relations and Information Services, 1985); and Barry T. Hirsch, David A. Macpherson, and Wayne G. Vroman, "Estimates of Union Density by State," *Monthly Labor Review,* July 2001.

Since the mid-1950s, however, union membership has waned. As Exhibit 1 illustrates, it declined slowly as a share of the workforce during the period 1955–1970, and then more rapidly since 1980. By 2010, union members constituted only 12.0 percent of nonfarm employees, down from 24 percent in 1979 (and 32 percent in 1954).

Several factors have contributed to this decline. First, much of the recent employment growth has been in sectors in which unions have been traditionally weak. Such sectors include relatively small firms (fewer than a hundred employees) in service and high-tech industries. Small firms are costly for unions to organize and thus tend to be nonunion. Also, in recent decades, employment has grown rapidly in the less-organized Sunbelt while stagnating in the more heavily unionized Northeast and upper Midwest. This regional growth pattern has retarded the growth of union membership. Second, competition has eroded union strength in several important industries. Foreign producers have increased their market share in steel, mining, automobiles, and other heavy manufacturing industries. Employment has therefore been shrinking in these areas of traditional union strength. Deregulation in the transportation and communication industries has further reduced the membership of unions. As these industries have become more competitive, unionized firms have faced increased competition from nonunion producers. Finally, union membership has declined, in part, because workers have reduced their demand for unions over time. Consistent with a falling desire for union representation, opinion surveys reveal that workers believe that unions are less effective in improving their lot now than they were in the past.[2]

To some extent, several of these trends reflect the impact of unions on the wages of their members. Business investment and employment will tend to move away from geographic areas, industries, and classes of firms in which wages are high *relative to productivity*. Therefore, when unions increase the wages of their members *relative to nonunion workers of similar productivity*, they will also retard the growth of employment in unionized sectors.

As Exhibit 2 shows, there is substantial variation in the incidence of union membership across gender, racial, and occupational groups. Men are more likely than women to belong to a union. In 2010, 12.6 percent of employed men were union members, compared with only 11.1 percent of employed women. The incidence of unionization among blacks (13.4 percent) was higher than for whites (11.7 percent) or Hispanics (10.0 percent). There is substantial variation in unionization according to occupation. Less than 10 percent of the workers in sales, clerical, and service occupations were unionized in 2010. In contrast, more than 16 percent of the workers in construction, extraction, production, transportation, and material-moving occupations belonged to a union.

The biggest difference in unionization is found when the private and public sectors are compared. Although only 6.9 percent of the private wage and salary workers are unionized, 36.2 percent of the government employees belong to a union. And whereas the share of the private workforce belonging to a union has been shrinking, unionization has been increasing in the public sector. In fact, the proportion of government employees belonging to a union has more than tripled since 1960. However, there has been a recent legislative trend against public-sector unionism. For example, legislation reducing the bargaining power of public-sector unions was adopted in New Jersey, Ohio, and Wisconsin in 2011.

There is also substantial variation in the rate of unionization among states. Exhibit 3 indicates the share of wage and salary employees who are unionized for the ten states with the lowest and highest unionization rates. Southern states constitute most of the group of ten with the lowest incidence of union membership. Fewer than 5 percent of employees are unionized in North Carolina, Arkansas, Georgia, Louisiana, Mississippi, Virginia, South Carolina, and Tennessee. Heading the list of states with the highest rate of unionization are New York, Hawaii, Alaska, Washington, and California. The rate of unionization tends to

---

[2]For several recent studies examining the decline in unionism, see "Symposium on the Future of Private Sector Unions in the United States: Part I," *Journal of Labor Research* (Spring 2001); and "Symposium on the Future of Private Sector Unions in the United States: Part II," *Journal of Labor Research* (Summer 2001). Also see Barry T. Hirsch, "Sluggish Institutions in a Dynamic World: Can Unions and Industrial Competition Coexist?" *Journal of Economic Perspectives* (Fall 2007).

Exhibit 2   **The 2010 Incidence of Union Membership by Sex, Race, Occupation, and Sector**

The incidence of unionism is higher among (a) men than women and (b) blacks than whites or Hispanics. Technical, sales, clerical, and service workers are far less likely to be unionized than are craft, operator, and repair workers. As a share of the workforce, unionization among government employees is more than four times that of private-sector workers.

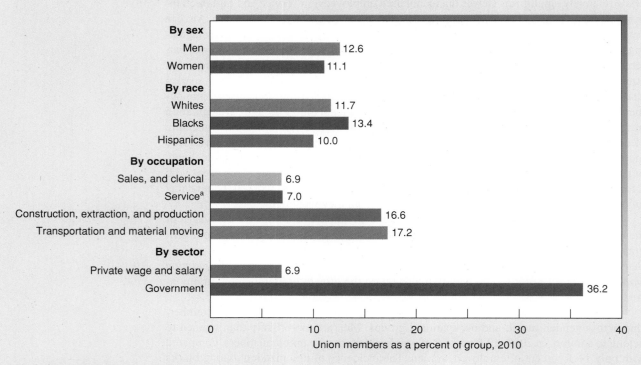

ªExcluding protective service workers.

Source: Barry T. Hirsch and David A. Macpherson, *Union Membership and Earnings Data Book: Compilations from the Current Population Survey,* 2011 Edition (Washington, DC: The Bureau of National Affairs, 2011).

Right-to-work laws
Laws that prohibit union shops, the requirement that employees must join a union as a condition of employment. Each state has the option to adopt (or reject) right-to-work legislation.

be high in the industrial states of the Northeast and upper Midwest. All ten states with the lowest incidence of unionization have **right-to-work laws,** legislation that prohibits collective bargaining agreements requiring a worker to join a union as a condition of employment. In contrast, only one of the ten states with the highest rate of union membership has right-to-work legislation.[3]

HOW DO UNIONS INFLUENCE WAGES?

The union–management bargaining process often leaves people with the impression that wages are established primarily by the talents of those sitting at the bargaining table. It might appear that market forces play a relatively minor role. However, as both union and management are well aware, market forces provide the setting in which the bargaining is conducted. They often tip the balance of power one way or the other.

High wages increase the firm's costs. When union employers face stiff competition from nonunion producers or foreign competitors, they will be less able to pass along higher wage costs to their customers. Competition in the product market thus limits the bargaining

---

[3]In 1947, Congress passed the Taft–Hartley Act; Section 14-B allows states to adopt right-to-work laws. Currently, 22 states, mostly in the Sunbelt, have such legislation.

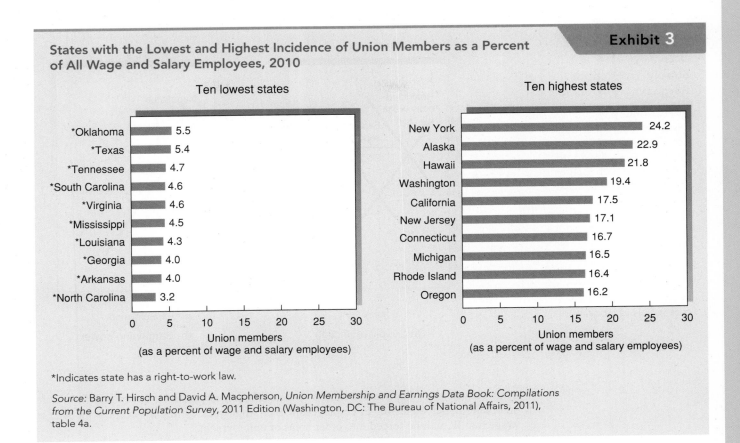

Exhibit 3

States with the Lowest and Highest Incidence of Union Members as a Percent of All Wage and Salary Employees, 2010

Ten lowest states

State	Union members (percent)
*Oklahoma	5.5
*Texas	5.4
*Tennessee	4.7
*South Carolina	4.6
*Virginia	4.6
*Mississippi	4.5
*Louisiana	4.3
*Georgia	4.0
*Arkansas	4.0
*North Carolina	3.2

Union members
(as a percent of wage and salary employees)

Ten highest states

State	Union members (percent)
New York	24.2
Alaska	22.9
Hawaii	21.8
Washington	19.4
California	17.5
New Jersey	17.1
Connecticut	16.7
Michigan	16.5
Rhode Island	16.4
Oregon	16.2

Union members
(as a percent of wage and salary employees)

*Indicates state has a right-to-work law.

Source: Barry T. Hirsch and David A. Macpherson, *Union Membership and Earnings Data Book: Compilations from the Current Population Survey,* 2011 Edition (Washington, DC: The Bureau of National Affairs, 2011), table 4a.

power of a union. Changing market conditions also affect the balance of power between unions and management. When the demand for a product is strong, the demand for labor will be high, and the firm will be much more willing to consent to a significant wage increase. When demand is weak, however, the product inventory level of the firm (or industry) is more likely to be high. Under these circumstances, wage increases will be more difficult to obtain because the firm will be much less vulnerable to a **strike** on the part of the union. (*Note:* When we speak of wage rates, we are referring to the total compensation package, including both fringe benefits and money wages.)

A union can use three basic strategies to increase the wages of its members: supply restrictions, bargaining power, and increased demand for union labor. We will examine each of these in turn.

Strike
An action of unionized employees in which they (1) discontinue working for the employer and (2) take steps to prevent other potential workers from offering their services to the employer.

SUPPLY RESTRICTIONS

If a union can successfully reduce the supply of competitive labor, higher wage rates will automatically result. Licensing requirements, long apprenticeship programs, immigration barriers, high initiation fees, refusal to admit new members to the union, and prohibition of nonunion workers from holding jobs are all practices that unions have used to limit the supply of labor to various occupations and jobs. Craft unions, in particular, have been able to restrict the supply of workers in various occupations and boost the wages of their members.

Part (a) of **Exhibit 4** illustrates the effect of supply restrictions on wage rates. Successful exclusionary tactics will reduce the supply, shifting the supply curve from S_0 to S_1. Facing the supply curve S_1, employers will consent to the wage rate W_1. Compared to a free-entry market equilibrium, the wage rate has increased from W_0 to W_1, but employment has declined from E_0 to E_1. At the higher wage rate, W_1, an excess supply of labor, AB, will result. The restrictive practices will prevent this excess supply from undercutting the

Exhibit 4

Supply Restrictions, Bargaining Power, and Wage Rates

The impact of higher wages obtained by restricting supply is very similar to that obtained through bargaining power. As illustrated in part (a), when union policies reduce the supply of one type of labor, higher wages result. Similarly, when bargaining power is used in order to obtain higher wages (1) (part b), employment declines and an excess supply of labor results.

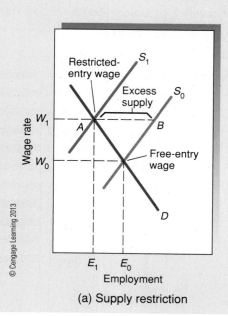

(a) Supply restriction

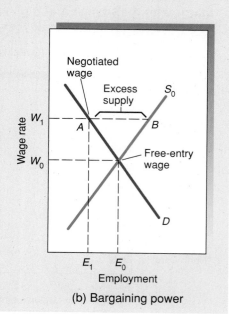

(b) Bargaining power

above-equilibrium wage rate. Because of the exclusionary practices, the union will be able to obtain higher wages for E_1 employees. Other employees willing to accept work even at wage rate W_0 will be forced into other areas of employment.

BARGAINING POWER

Must unions restrict entry? Why can't they simply use their bargaining power, enhanced by the threat of a strike, to raise wages? If they have enough economic power, this will be possible. A strike by even a small percentage of vital employees can sometimes halt the flow of production. For example, a work stoppage by airline pilots can force major airlines to cancel their flights. Because the pilots perform an essential function, an airline cannot operate without their services, even though they constitute only 10 percent of all airline employees.

If the union is able to obtain an above-free-entry wage rate, the effect on employment will be similar to a reduction in supply. As part (b) of Exhibit 4 illustrates, employers will hire fewer workers at the higher wage rate obtained through bargaining power. Employment will decline below the free-entry level (from E_0 to E_1) as a result of the rise in wages. An excess supply of labor, AB, will exist, at least temporarily. More employees will seek the high-wage union jobs than employers will choose to hire. Nonwage methods of rationing jobs will become more important.

INCREASED DEMAND

Unions can attempt to increase the demand for union labor by appealing to consumers to buy only union-produced goods. Union-sponsored promotional campaigns instructing consumers to "look for the union label" or "buy American" are generally designed to increase the demand for union-made products.

Most people, however, are primarily interested in getting the most for their consumer dollar. Thus, the demand for union labor is usually determined primarily by factors outside the union's direct control, such as the availability of substitute inputs and the demand for the product. Unions, though, can sometimes use their political power to increase the demand for their services. They may be able to induce legislators to pass laws that reduce competition from nonunion and/or foreign workers. In some areas, required inspections on construction projects will be undertaken only if the electrical or plumbing services have been performed by "licensed" (mostly union) craft workers. Unions are often supportive of import restrictions designed to increase the demand for products that they produce. In 2009, the steelworkers union, which represents rubber workers, successfully lobbied for higher tariffs restricting the entry of foreign-produced tires. Garment workers have used their political muscle to raise tariffs and reduce import quotas for clothing produced abroad. Practices that increase the demand for goods and services produced by union labor will increase product prices as well as the wages of unionized workers. Thus, it is not surprising that both management and labor of unionized firms often join together to support various restrictions designed to reduce the competitiveness of goods produced by nonunion employees and foreigners.

WHAT GIVES A UNION STRENGTH?

Not all unions are able to raise the wages of their workers. What are the factors that make a union strong? *Simply stated, if a union is to be strong, the demand for its labor must be inelastic. This will enable the union to command large wage increases while suffering only modest reductions in employment.* In contrast, when the demand for union labor is elastic, a substantial rise in wages will mean a large loss in jobs.

There are four major determinants of the demand elasticity for a factor of production: (1) the availability of substitutes, (2) the elasticity of product demand, (3) the share of the input as a proportion of total cost, and (4) the supply elasticity of substitute inputs.[4] We now turn to the importance of each of these conditions as a determinant of union strength.

AVAILABILITY OF GOOD SUBSTITUTE INPUTS

When it is difficult to substitute other inputs for unionized labor in the production of a good, the union is strengthened. The demand for union labor is then more inelastic, and employment cuts tend to be small if the union is able to use its bargaining power and the threat of a strike to push wages up. In contrast, when there are good substitutes for union labor, employers will turn to the substitutes and cut back on their use of union labor as it becomes more expensive. Under these circumstances, higher union wages will price the union workers out of the market and lead to a sharp reduction in their employment.

Some employers may be able to automate various production operations—in effect, substituting machines for union workers if their wages increase. When machines are a good substitute for union labor, the demand for union labor will be elastic, which will reduce the union's ability to push wages above the market level.

The best substitute for union labor is generally nonunion labor. Thus, the power of unions to gain more for their members will be directly related to their ability to insulate themselves from competition with nonunion labor. *When employers are in a position to substitute nonunion labor for unionized workers, the market power of the union will be substantially reduced.*

Within a given plant, a union will negotiate the wages and employment conditions for all workers, both union and nonunion. However, as union wages rise, it may be economical for unionized firms to contract with nonunion firms to handle specific operations or to supply various components used in production. Thus, contracting out often permits employers to substitute nonunion for union workers indirectly. In addition, many large firms in automobile, textile, and other manufacturing industries operate both union and nonunion plants. They may be able to substitute nonunion for union labor by shifting more and more of their production to their nonunion plants, including those located overseas or in right-to-work states, in which unions are generally weaker.

---

[4]Alfred Marshall, *Principles of Economics,* 8th ed. (New York: Macmillan, 1920).

THE ELASTICITY OF DEMAND FOR PRODUCTS PRODUCED BY UNIONIZED FIRMS

Wages are a component of costs. An increase in the wages of union members will almost surely lead to higher prices for goods produced with union labor. Unless the demand for the good produced by union labor is inelastic, the output and employment of unionized firms will decline if the union pushes up wages (and costs). If a union is going to have a significant effect on wages (without undermining employment opportunities), its workers must produce a good for which the demand is inelastic.

Our analysis implies that a union will be unable to increase wages significantly above the free-market rate when producing a good that competes with similar (or identical) goods produced by nonunion labor or foreign producers. The demand for the good produced by union labor will almost surely be highly elastic when the same product is available from nonunion and foreign producers. Thus, if higher union wages push up costs, the market share of unionized firms will shrink and their employment will fall substantially.

For example, the strength of the Teamsters union was substantially eroded when deregulation subjected the unionized segment of the trucking industry to much more intense competition from nonunion firms in the early 1980s. With deregulation, nonunion firms with lower labor costs entered the industry. Given their labor-cost advantage, many of the new entrants cut their prices and were able to gain a larger market share. In contrast, the output and employment of unionized trucking firms declined. More than 100,000 Teamsters lost their jobs. Given the sharp fall in the employment of their members, the Teamsters eventually agreed to wage concessions and a lower fringe benefit package.[5]

UNIONIZED LABOR AS A SHARE OF THE COST OF PRODUCTION

If the unionized labor input constitutes only a small share of the total production cost of a product, demand for that labor typically will be relatively inelastic. For example, because the wages of plumbers and airline pilots constitute only a small share of the total cost of production in the housing and air travel industries, respectively, a doubling or even tripling of their wages would result in only a 1 percent or 2 percent increase in the cost of housing or air travel. A large increase in the price of these inputs would have little impact on the product price, output, and employment. This factor has sometimes been called "the importance of being unimportant" because when the expenditures on a unionized resource are small relative to total cost, the position of the union is strengthened.

THE SUPPLY ELASTICITY OF SUBSTITUTE INPUTS

We have just explained that if wage rates in the unionized sector are pushed upward, firms will look for substitute inputs, and the demand for these substitutes will increase. If the supply of these substitutes (like nonunion labor) is inelastic, however, their price will rise sharply in response to an increase in demand. In turn, the higher price will reduce the attractiveness of the substitutes. An inelastic supply of substitutes will thus strengthen the union by making the demand for union labor more inelastic.

---

[5]A study of the deregulation of the trucking industry found that the wage premium of unionized truckers fell by approximately 30 percent in the regulated sector of the industry. More drivers were employed, but the percentage of drivers who were union members fell from 60 percent before deregulation to 25 percent afterward. See Barry T. Hirsch and David A. Macpherson, "Earnings and Employment in Trucking: Deregulating a Naturally Competitive Industry," in *Regulatory Reform and Labor Markets,* James Peoples, ed. (Dordrecht, Netherlands: Kluwer Publishers, 1998).

Deregulation of the trucking industry opened the market to nonunion trucking firms. This led to a sharp reduction in the employment of unionized truck drivers (Teamsters) in the early 1980s. Can you explain why?

THE WAGES OF UNION AND NONUNION EMPLOYEES

The precise effect of unions on the wages of their members is not easy to determine. To isolate the union effect, one must eliminate differences in other factors. Comparisons must be made between union and nonunion workers who have similar productivity (skills) and who are working in similar jobs.

Exhibit 5 provides estimates of the union–nonunion wage differential for private-sector workers adjusted for productivity characteristics.[6] The private union–nonunion wage differential widened during the 1970s and early 1980s. Private-sector union workers received a 28 percent premium compared with similar nonunion workers during the 1983–1984 period, up from a 19 percent premium during 1973–1974. Since the mid-1980s, the private-sector union premium has been shrinking. By 2009-2010, the premium had fallen to 20 percent.

Our theory indicates that some unions will be much stronger than others—that is, better able to achieve higher wages for their members. In some occupations, the size of the union–nonunion differential will be well above the average, whereas in other occupations, unions will have little effect on wages. Strong unions, such as those of electricians, plumbers, tool and die makers, metal craft workers, truckers (before deregulation), and commercial airline pilots, are able to raise the wages of their members substantially more than the average for all unions. Economists have found that the earnings of unionized merchant seamen; postal workers; and rail, auto, and steelworkers, for example, exceed the wages of similarly skilled nonunion workers by 30 percent or more.

Unionization appears to have had the least effect on the earnings of cotton/textile, footwear, furniture, hosiery, clothing, and retail sales workers. In these areas, the power of the union has been considerably limited by the existence of a substantial number of nonunion firms. The demands of union workers in these industries are moderated by the fear that unionized employers will be at a competitive disadvantage relative to nonunion employers in the industry.

---

[6]Barry T. Hirsch and David A. Macpherson, *Union Membership and Earnings Data Book: Compilations from the Current Population Survey, 2011 Edition* (Washington, DC: The Bureau of National Affairs, 2011). The union wage premium for all wage and salary workers is slightly smaller than for private-sector workers only. The premium for all workers (private sector and public sector) was the following: 1973–1974 (18 percent), 1977–1978 (22 percent), 1983–1984 (22 percent), 1996–1997 (21 percent), and 2009–2010 (16 percent).

Exhibit 5

The Wage Premium of Private-Sector Union Workers, 1973–2010

The wages of union workers in the private sector rose relative to similar nonunion workers during the 1970s and early 1980s, but the differential has receded during the last two decades. In 2009–2010, the estimated union–nonunion differential was 20 percent for private sector workers, down from 28 percent during 1983–1984.

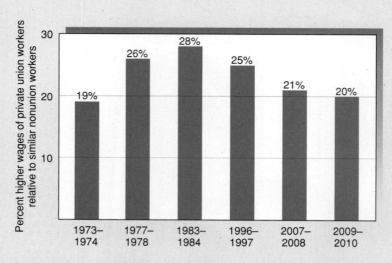

Source: Barry T. Hirsch and David A. Macpherson, *Union Membership and Earnings Data Book: Compilations from the Current Population Survey,* 2011 Edition (Washington, DC: The Bureau of National Affairs, 2011).

UNIONS, PROFITABILITY, AND EMPLOYMENT IN THE UNIONIZED SECTOR

If unions increase the wages of unionized firms above the competitive market level, the costs of those firms will rise unless (as seems unlikely) there is a corresponding increase in productivity. In the short run, the higher costs will reduce the profitability of the unionized firm. Research consistently indicates that unions do lower firm profits.[7]

If unions are able to transfer profits from unionized firms to union workers, clearly this is a two-edged sword. For a time, workers enjoy higher wages. In the long run, however, investment will move away from areas of low profitability. Like other mobile resources, capital can be exploited in the short run, but this will not be the case in the long run. Therefore, to the extent that the profits of unionized firms are lower, investment expenditures on fixed structures, research, and development will flow into the nonunion sector and away from unionized firms. As a result, the growth of both productivity and employment will tend to lag in the unionized sector. Investment, production, and employment will all shift away from unionized operations and toward nonunion firms. The larger the wage premium of unionized firms, the greater the incentive will be to shift production toward nonunion operations.

The experience of the United Auto Workers (UAW) vividly illustrates the operation of these forces. The Big Three Detroit-based automakers—General Motors, Ford, and Chrysler—were heavily unionized. For several decades, the UAW was able to increase the wages of workers employed by the Big Three substantially above those of other workers with similar skills. But the higher wages and costs of the Big Three made them more vulnerable to competition from nonunion automakers, primarily foreign-based transplants with manufacturing facilities in southern states. With time, the lower wage transplants gained a larger and larger market share, and the profitability of the Big Three shrank. By 2008–2009, all of the Big Three were in financial trouble and were only saved, at least temporarily, by financial assistance from the federal government.

---

[7]Barry T. Hirsch, "What Do Unions Do for Economic Performance?" *Journal of Labor Research* (Summer 2004): 415–55.

THE IMPACT OF UNIONS ON THE WAGES OF ALL WORKERS

Although unions have increased the average wages of their members, there is no reason to believe that they have increased the overall average wages for both union and nonunion workers. At first glance, this may seem paradoxical. However, the economic way of thinking enhances our understanding of this issue. As unions push wages up in the unionized sector, employers in this sector will hire fewer workers. Unable to find jobs in the high-wage union sector, some workers will shift to the nonunion sector. This increase in labor supply will depress the wages of nonunion workers. As a result, higher wages for union members do not necessarily mean higher overall average wages for workers.

If labor unions increased the wages of all workers, we would expect labor's share of income to be directly related to union membership. This has not been the case. Even though union membership rose sharply during the 1940s, reached a peak in the 1950s, and has been declining ever since, there was virtually no change in the share of income received by labor (human capital) during this entire period. Similarly, if unions were the primary source of high wages, the real wages of workers would be higher in highly unionized countries, such as Australia, France, and Italy, than they are in the United States. But this is not what we observe.

The real source of high wages is high productivity, not labor unions. Increases in the general level of wages are dependent upon increases in productivity per hour. Of course, improvements in (1) technology, (2) the machines and tools available to workers (physical capital), (3) worker skills (human capital), and (4) the efficiency of economic organization provide the essential ingredients for higher levels of productivity. ***Higher real wages can be achieved only if the production of goods and services is expanded. Although unions can increase the wages of union workers, they cannot increase the wages of all workers unless their activities increase the total productivity of labor.***

KEY POINTS

- Union membership as a share of nonfarm employees fluctuated substantially during the last century. During the 1910–1935 period, union workers constituted between 12 and 18 percent of nonfarm employees. Unionization increased rapidly during the two decades following 1935, however, soaring to one-third of the workforce in the mid-1950s. Since then, union membership has waned, falling to only 12.0 percent of employees in 2010.

- A union can use three basic methods to increase the wages of its members: (1) restrict the supply of competitive inputs, including nonunion workers; (2) apply bargaining power enforced by a strike or threat of one; and (3) increase the demand for the labor service of union members.

- If a union is going to increase the wages of its members without experiencing a significant reduction in employment, the demand for union labor must be inelastic. The strength of a union is enhanced if (1) there is an absence of good substitutes for the services of union employees, (2) the demand for the product produced by the union labor is highly inelastic, (3) the union labor input is a small share of the total cost of production, and (4) the supply of available substitutes is highly inelastic. An absence of these conditions weakens the power of the union.

- Studies suggest that the wage premium of private-sector union members relative to similar nonunion workers rose during the 1970s and early 1980s, but it has fallen during the last two decades. In the period 2009–2010, private-sector union workers earned about 20 percent more, on average, than similar nonunion workers.

- Even though unions have increased the average wage of their members, there is no indication that they have increased either the average wage of all workers or the share of national income going to labor (human capital rather than physical capital).

- The real wages of workers are a reflection of their productivity rather than the share of the workforce that is unionized.

CRITICAL ANALYSIS QUESTIONS

1. *Suppose that Florida's migrant workers are effectively unionized. What will be the effect of the unionization on (a) the price of Florida oranges? (b) the profits of Florida fruit growers in the short run and in the long run? (c) the mechanization of the fruit-picking industry? (d) the employment of migrant farm workers?

2. Assume that the primary objective of a union is to raise the wages of its members.
   a. Discuss the conditions that will help the union achieve this objective.
   b. Why might a union be unable to meet its goal?

3. *"If a union is unable to organize all the major firms in an industry, it is unlikely to exert a major effect on the wages of union members." Indicate why you either agree or disagree.

4. Evaluate the following statements.
   a. "An increase in the price of steel will be passed along to consumers in the form of higher prices for automobiles, homes, appliances, and other products made with steel." Do you agree or disagree?
   b. "An increase in the price of craft union labor will be passed along to consumers in the form of higher prices of homes, repair and installation services, appliances, and other products that require craft union labor." Do you agree or disagree?
   c. Are the interests of labor unions in conflict primarily with the interests of union employers? Explain.

5. *"Unions provide the only protection available to working men and women. Without unions, employers would be able to pay workers whatever they wanted." True or false?

6. *A survey of firms in your local labor market reveals that the average hourly wage rate of unionized production workers is $1.50 higher than the average wage rate of nonunion production workers. Does this indicate that unionization increases the wage rates of workers in your area by $1.50? Why or why not?

7. *Even though the wage scale of union members is substantially greater than the minimum wage, unions have generally been at the forefront of those lobbying for higher minimum rates. Why do you think unions fight so hard for a higher minimum wage?

*Asterisk denotes questions for which answers are given in Appendix B.

The Question of Resource Exhaustion

FOCUS

- Why have there been repeated forecasts that the world will run out of key resources? Why have these forecasts been consistently wrong?

- Are proved reserves the same thing as the total future supply of a resource?

- What do prices indicate has happened to resource scarcity? Will that trend continue?

- Why is there a major misallocation problem for a few key resources like water?

iStockphoto.com/isarendis

People think of the Earth as having a certain amount of oil the way you might have a certain amount of money in your bank account…but in reality, the ultimate amount available to us is determined both by economics and technology.

—*Daniel Yergin*[1]

---

[1]Daniel Yergin, chairman of Cambridge Energy Research Associates, quoted in "Why We'll Never Run Out of Oil," by Curtis Rist, *Discover Magazine* (June 1999), www.discovermagazine.com/1999/jun/featoil.

For centuries, various social commentators have argued that the world is about to run out of vital minerals and various sources of energy. Economic growth and the technological advances that help to fuel it have accelerated the use of many natural resources. Population growth has added to the rate of resource use. As the initial quote from Daniel Yergin indicates, most people think that continual use of resources that are available in finite quantities will lead to their depletion. But he goes on to claim that depletion can be put off for a long—even an indefinite—period. This feature explains why this is the case.

iStockphoto.com/nicoolay

FORECASTS OF RESOURCE EXHAUSTION

In sixteenth-century England, fear arose that the supply of wood—widely used as a source of energy—would soon disappear. Higher wood prices, however, encouraged conservation and led to the development of coal. The wood crisis soon dissipated.

In the middle of the nineteenth century, fear arose that the United States was about to run out of whale oil, at that time the primary fuel for artificial lighting. As the demand for whale oil increased, many predicted that all the whales would soon be gone and that Americans would face long nights without light. Whale-oil prices rose sharply from $0.23 per gallon in 1820 to $1.42 per gallon in 1850. The higher prices motivated consumers and entrepreneurs to seek alternatives, which included distilled vegetable oils, lard oil, and coal gas. By the early 1850s, coal oil (kerosene) had won out. A little later, petroleum replaced coal as the primary resource used to produce kerosene. As for whale oil, by 1896 its price had fallen to $0.40 per gallon, and even at that price few people used it.

As people switched to petroleum, dire predictions about its future exhaustion arose almost immediately. In 1914, the Bureau of Mines reported that the total U.S. supply of oil was 6 million barrels, an amount less than the United States now produces every two years. In 1926, the Federal Oil Conservation Board announced that oil would be depleted in the United States within seven years. The Interior Department predicted in 1939 that petroleum supplies in this nation would run out within 20 years. And in 1949, the Secretary of the Interior proclaimed that the end of oil supplies was near.[2]

Perhaps the modern predictions having the most impact were those from the authors of the book *The Limits to Growth*, published in 1972. This pessimistic book was given front-page publicity in *The New York Times* and major national magazines. Projections of resource depletion were based on large computer models, and those receiving the most notice indicated that several key minerals would be depleted, running out one by one, in the 1980s and 1990s.[3] There were also some less pessimistic projections reported by the authors, based on more optimistic assumptions, but those got little notice in the press.

WHY HAVE THE FORECASTS OF RESOURCE CRISES BEEN WRONG?

The incentives generated by markets provide the means for the expansion of supply, and thus they explain why the forecasts of resource supply crisis have always been wrong, when markets are allowed to work. Think about what happens when a resource becomes scarcer. This might happen because of either a reduction in supply or an increase in demand.

[2]Predictions are cited from Wallace Kaufman, *No Turning Back* (New York: Basic Books, 1994), 24; and from Charles Maurice and Charles Smithson, *The Doomsday Myth, 10,000 Years of Economic Crises* (Stanford, CA: Hoover Institution Press, 1987), 12.
[3]Donella H. Meadows, Dennis L. Meadows, and William W. Behrens, *The Limits to Growth* (New York: Universe Books, 1972).

In either case, the price of the resource will rise. In turn, the higher price will cause (1) users of the resource to cut back on their usage, (2) suppliers to figure out how to supply more of it or perhaps to recycle, and (3) both users and potential suppliers to search for substitutes. Each of these factors will tend to increase future supply relative to demand. The larger the initial increase in the price of a resource, the greater the incentive to cut back on usage, expand the future supply, and develop substitutes.

These adjustments will keep usage rates of the resource pretty much in line with the expected future supply. With time, they can often bring relief in the form of a lower future price. The key point is this: Although the price of a resource may increase sharply during some periods, the structure of incentives accompanying the price increase makes depletion highly unlikely and provides the seeds for future reversal.

As an analysis of the resource crisis forecasts indicates, we have seen these forces work again and again. Think about the actions producers, resource users, and consumers will take when oil prices go up. The higher prices will provide petroleum producers with a stronger incentive to search for and find new fields. They will also provide them with incentive to use technology to extract a larger share of the oil from existing fields. Up to 70 percent of the oil can now be extracted from highly productive wells that in prior decades would have yielded much less. When sustained price increases are large enough, generating expectations they will be sufficient to cover the higher-cost production methods, it becomes economical to produce petroleum products from exceedingly abundant, but less-rich petroleum resources. These include oil shale and tar sands and, indeed, such production has already begun.

On the demand side, higher oil prices also provide users with a strong incentive to reduce their consumption of petroleum. Electric power–generating firms will search for and some will shift to alternatives like coal and nuclear power. Manufacturers of plastics and other products that use petroleum as a resource will face higher costs; they, too, will seek to shift to substitute resources and cut back on their future use of petroleum. For their part, consumers will use less of the oil-intensive products and adjust their behavior accordingly, purchasing more fuel-efficient cars and trucks, commuting less, and finding other ways to economize on oil-intensive products.

These adjustments and many more on both the supply and the demand sides of the crude oil market will tend to reduce demand over time, increase supply, and thus moderate price increases. This has happened for oil and other resources many times, and these constructive pressures will continue to do so whenever resource scarcities change and market forces are permitted to work.

When the price of gasoline increases substantially, many consumers will turn to more fuel-efficient cars like this Toyota Prius, a hybrid that combines a gas engine with an electric motor and a battery.

PROVED RESERVES AND RUNNING OUT OF RESOURCES

Proved reserves
Specific mineral deposits that have been shown by scientific examination and cost calculation to be extractable and deliverable to the market for use, with current technology and expected market conditions.

Geologists use the term **proved reserves** to mean the specific mineral deposits that have been shown by scientific examination and cost calculation to be extractable and deliverable to the market for use at a cost that users can pay, using known technologies under expected market conditions. Proved reserves have often been used by doomsday forecasters to calculate the future time when we will run out of a resource. But this is a misapplication of the concept. Proved reserves are quite different than the total quantity of a resource in the ground. Put simply, proved reserves are the verified quantity that can be extracted, given investors' expectations of developing technologies and expected prices.

We have seen how improvements in technology and higher future prices can increase proved reserves. Exhibit 1 shows the proved reserves for several minerals. It indicates that existing reserves are constantly being used up, but they have been amply replaced with the "proving" of new reserves in the ground. For example, in 1950, there were 6 million tons of reserves of tin ore in the world. Over the next 50 years, 11 million tons were produced and used. Yet, in 2000, the reserves stood at 10 million tons. Additional reserves had been discovered, and technology had advanced sufficiently that the existing known reserves were larger in 2000 than 50 years earlier, even after 50 years of steady depletion. The other minerals listed show similar trends, as do most minerals over the same long period of time.

It is important to note that in shorter time periods, it is not uncommon for world reserves of a natural resource to fall. World tin reserves fell from 10 million tons in 2000, to 5 million tons in 2010, while reserves of the other four minerals in exhibit 1 all rose. The forces described earlier do not guarantee that resource prices must fall, but as we will see in the following in more detail, when those forces have been allowed to operate, the results have tended to make natural resources more available to us, even as their physical abundance in nature declines.

For producers, proved reserves are like an inventory of cars to an auto dealer. They are the quantity that can be available quickly for sale. Just as it is costly for an auto dealer to hold more inventory, it is costly for a firm to discover and sufficiently research a mineral deposit to qualify it as proved reserves. Producers who buy or develop proved reserves do not want to pay for them farther in advance than needed, just as an auto dealer wants to have cars available in stock but not too far ahead of the time they can be sold.

As with inventories, it is costly to develop and hold proved reserves for lengthy time periods. If it takes an auto dealer five weeks from the time of a new car order to receive the cars, the dealer may want something close to a ten-week supply of cars, relative to

---

Exhibit 1

World Reserves and Cumulative Production of Selected Minerals, 1950 to 2000 (Millions of Metric Tons)

For most mineral resources, existing proved reserves are constantly being used up but are being amply replaced by the "proving" of new reserves from existing resources in the ground.

Mineral	Reserves 1950	Production 1950–2000	Reserves 2000
Tin	6	11	10
Copper	100	339	340
Iron Ore	19,000	37,583	140,000
Lead	40	150	64
Zinc	70	266	190

Source: Sue Anne Batey Blackman and William J. Baumol, "Natural Resources," in *The Concise Encyclopedia of Economics*, 2nd ed., ed. David R. Henderson (Indianapolis, IN: Liberty Fund), available online at http://econlib.org/library/Enc/NaturalResources.html.

expected sales, on the car lot and available for customers to see and buy. Similarly, if it takes two years, say, for a user of iron ore to replace iron ore reserves that they have used, then a four-year supply of those reserves might be a desired amount to have available. Just as inventories are a poor indicator of the total future supply of a good like cars, proved reserves are a poor indicator of the total future supply of a mineral resource. Proved reserves will always be a small fraction of what they could be simply because proving and holding them are costly.

ARE RESOURCES BECOMING SCARCER?

If the scarcity of a resource increases relative to demand, its price will rise. If a resource is increasing in supply relative to demand and is becoming less costly to supply, its price will fall. Therefore, resource price trends provide information about how the scarcity of various resources is changing.

What have resource prices been telling us? During the past century and more, ending in 2000, the real price of most mineral resources fell. A classic study by Harold Barnett and Chandler Morse illustrates this point.[4] Using data from 1870 to 1963, Barnett and Morse found that the real price of resources declined during that long period. A later study by William Baumol and Sue Anne Batey Blackman buttresses this view. They cite a composite mineral price index, corrected for inflation and published by the U.S. Geological Survey, showing a decline in the price index from 185 in 1905 to 100 in 2000. Thus, the real price of minerals fell, on average, by 46 percent in 95 years, even as the use of those minerals had greatly expanded.[5]

What about the real price of crude oil? **Exhibit 2** shows that in constant year 2005 dollars, average annual prices fell gradually to a 1972 low near $13 per barrel, then began a rapid rise to a peak near $61 in 1981. Since then, however, the real price of crude oil fell back to near $13 in 1998, and then rose sharply again to a high of about $87 in 2008. It fell again to $51 in 2009, rising to $70 in 2010 and $91 in June of 2011, all in year 2005 dollars.

Natural gas prices have risen much more slowly than crude oil prices in recent years, as producers have developed gas resources using so-called fracking. A decades-old technology, hydraulic fracturing or *fracking* as it is commonly called, is being combined with new technologies and drilling methods, and it promises to keep energy prices lower than they otherwise would be, for many decades. In the United States, which is increasingly using fracking of deep oil shale (5,000 to 10,000 feet below the surface), the domestic price (Producer Price Index proxy) rose 157 percent for crude oil, but only 20 percent for natural gas, between 2000 and 2010. Some environmentalists are concerned about possible pollution from this new combination of techniques, but to date EPA has found no evidence of pollution problems stemming from its use. Fracking typically occurs 5,000 to 10,000 feet below the surface. Normally, multiple layers of impermeable earth contain the chemicals used or produced in fracking. Those layers keep the pollutants well away from groundwater drinking sources, which are almost always near the surface. Resource prices fluctuate from month to month and year to year, but the trends have been mainly downward, often with the assistance of technical changes like the highly productive use of fracking. For the bigger picture, see the box feature, "Is It Smart to Bet on Rising Resource Prices?"

---

[4]Harold Barnett and Chandler Morse, *Scarcity of Growth: The Economics of Natural Resource Availability* (Baltimore: The Johns Hopkins University Press for Resources for the Future, 1963). See also Julian L. Simon, *The State of Humanity* (Cambridge, MA: Blackwell Publishers, 1995), Part III, Natural Resources.
[5]Quoted by Sue Anne Batey Blackman and William J. Baumol, "Natural Resources," in *The Concise Encyclopedia of Economics*, 2nd ed., ed. David R. Henderson (Indianapolis, IN: Liberty Fund, Inc., 2007), available online at http://econlib.com/library/Enc/NaturalResources.html

Exhibit 2

Real Crude Oil Prices, 1949 to 2011 (Real Year 2005 Dollars)

Measured in constant 2005 dollars, the real price of crude oil to U.S. refiners fell gradually to a low near $13 in 1972, then rose rapidly to a high above $61 in 1981, then fell below $19 in 1988. But it rose again to a new high near $87 in 2008, only to fall by about one-third in 2009. It rose again in 2010 and 2011, reaching a high of $91 in the first half of 2011.

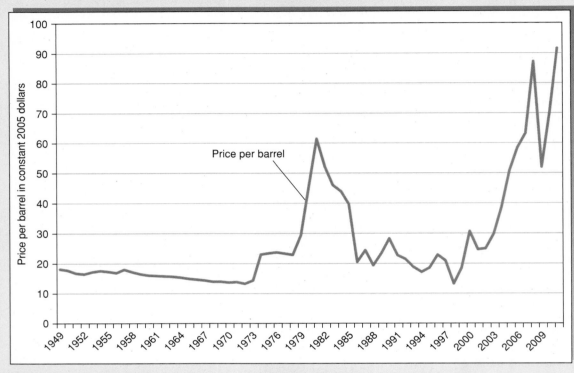

Price per barrel

Source: Energy Information Administration, *Annual Energy Review* (U.S. Department of Energy, 2010).

APPLICATIONS IN ECONOMICS

Is It Smart to Bet on Higher Resource Prices?

Rapid rises in prices of oil and other commodities in the 1970s led to widespread anxiety that the world was running out of major resources. In 1980, economist Julian Simon argued that this run-up was temporary and that, over time, prices were likely to fall. Simon offered a $1,000 bet that any raw materials selected in 1980 would be lower ten years later after adjustment was made for inflation. Environmentalist Paul Ehrlich took up the bet. He and his associates chose five metals (chrome, copper, nickel, tin, and tungsten), put $200 on each, and bet that the inflation-adjusted prices in 1990 would be higher.

Simon easily won the bet. During the decade, the real prices declined not only for the bundle but also for each of the five minerals chosen by Ehrlich. In 1990, Ehrlich wrote a check to Simon to pay off the bet. (The wager became famous after an article about it appeared in *The New York Times*.)

In 2005, a student and a professor at Michigan State University analyzed whether Simon would have won the bet had it extended over the entire twentieth century. Using U.S. Geological Survey price data for basic metals, they examined the change in prices from 1900 to 1999. "The person who took Simon's position would have won over the entire century," wrote David McClintick and Ross B. Emmett. "If someone invested $200 at 1900 metals' prices in each of these five metals, the inflation-adjusted value of the same bundle of metals in 1999 would have been 53-percent lower."[1] Of course, resource prices did not go down during every decade of the twentieth century, but they went down during most decades and for the century as a whole. Thus, history suggests that it is not too smart to bet on rising resource prices.

[1]David McClintick and Ross B. Emmett, "Betting on the Wealth of Nature," *PERC Reports* (September 2005), www.perc.org/perc .php?subsection=5&id=588.

RENEWABLE RESOURCES

To this point, we have focused on the scarcity of nonrenewable resources—those that are not created or renewed at a significant rate, and therefore they could potentially be used up over time. Our analysis, however, indicates that this is unlikely to be the case in a market setting. What about renewable resources, like timber, that can be continually replanted and replenished? Those resources, too, can become scarcer and more expensive in a market depending on (1) the ability of users to find substitutes and reduce the quantity demanded and, over time, the demand and (2) producers' ability to produce more output at the higher price and to find substitute products to bring to market for buyers.

Forests are an example of a renewable resource for which there has been concern about future availability. Deforestation can lead to a loss of timber, wildlife habitat, watershed regulation, and recreational services. Are concerns about serious deforestation justified? Rivers, lakes, and other sources of freshwater are other important renewable resources for which depletion is a serious concern. What can economic thinking and a careful look at history tell us about these two concerns?

Nonrenewable resources
Those that are not created or renewed naturally at a significant rate.

Renewable resources
Those that are renewed in nature, like water flows, or grown, like timber.

ARE FORESTS DISAPPEARING?

Use of land has changed dramatically over the centuries. When colonists arrived in what is now the United States, about half the land was forested. In parts of the world today, significant areas of woodlands, including tropical areas of Brazil and Southeast Asia, are being turned into farmland or logged for wood products. How serious are the loss of timber and the loss of wildlife habitat?

Not all the world's forests are in well-functioning market economies (that is, economies with property rights, the rule of law, and minimal corruption). Where strong market economies do exist, however, the forces of supply and demand are protecting forests from significant decline.

The United States has about the same amount of land devoted to forest as it did in 1920—and far more timber is growing on it. A study by two natural resource economists (Roger Sedjo and Marion Clawson) found that timber volume in the temperate climates, including countries such as the United States, the former Soviet Union, and Canada, is growing rapidly.[6] Indeed, in the United States, the regrowth of some forests has been dramatic. Bill McKibben, writing for the *Atlantic Monthly*, said that the "mostly unnoticed renewal of the rural and mountainous East" is "the great environmental story of the United States."[7] This has come about through market forces, as New England farms revert to forest and former cotton plantations in the South become more attractive as woodlands.

Even Latin America, Sedjo and Clawson reported, is undergoing a major transition, with an increase in tree plantations, in which trees are being grown as crops. These changes reflect the response to demand for wood and put less pressure on the existing tropical rainforest.

TECHNOLOGY AND LAND MANAGEMENT

Technology is helping to preserve land in its wooded state as well. Chemical fertilizers, pesticides, and other technologies—"high-tech" farming—do have some negative environmental impacts, but they have also freed a great deal of land from use for farming. By raising productivity per acre, technology reduces the amount of land required to produce food and fiber.

---

[6]See Roger A. Sedjo and Marion Clawson, "Global Forests Revisited," in *The State of Humanity*, ed. Julian Simon (Cambridge, MA: Blackwell Publishers, 1995).
[7]Bill McKibben, "An Explosion of Green," *The Atlantic Monthly* (April 1995), 61–83.

Indur M. Goklany has estimated that if agricultural technology had been frozen at 1961 levels, the 1998 level of food production would have required more than double the amount of land used today for farming.[8] That means that 76 percent of the world's land would be used for agriculture, compared with only 38 percent in 1998! Not only would farmland have taken up space, much of it now available as wildlife habitat, but the added land would probably have been less productive. Farmers are already cultivating the best acres among those acres not committed to other, more valuable uses. Greater land productivity enabled by new technologies has kept down the cost and price of food in world markets.

When resource users and suppliers are free to innovate and respond to changes in prices and in technologies as market participants, and when property rights hold them accountable for the cost of what they use while allowing them personally to reap benefits from fruitful innovations, the result has been economic progress in increasing prosperity from one generation to the next. Each generation has less in the way of physical natural resources in Earth, but that resource base delivers more services for a smaller sacrifice because it is better used and with less waste.

NATURAL RESOURCES WHEN MARKETS ARE NOT ALLOWED TO FUNCTION FULLY

When natural resources are not traded, or when markets are not allowed to function as well as the previously described markets, problems of waste and scarcity are common.

WATER MARKETS

"As we enter a new decade, water is the new oil: the scarce resource worth fighting over. In arid parts of the world, the fight for water has always been a fight for survival. One-third of the world's population lives where their water supply is either a stress or a crisis." Thus began an MSNBC online story in 2010.[9] The article predicted that developing nations would experience "water shortages, crop failures, and conflict over shrinking lakes and rivers." News stories like this and the more formal studies they often cite are more frequent as demands for water increase.

The world is not going to run out of water in a literal sense—the world has the same amount of moisture that it always did. And, in the words of economist Terry L. Anderson, Earth "has more than enough water to meet human demands." But, he says, "Water is often found in the wrong place at the wrong time."[10] Water supply problems reflect the fact that in most situations, water markets are missing or are incomplete. Therefore, the smoothly functioning market that might bring more effective cooperation among users and suppliers, or buyers and sellers, seldom exists.

Throughout the world, the sources of water—lakes, rivers, and streams—are often kept under tight control by governments, preventing transferable ownership that would allow supply and demand to operate. This approach is defended on the grounds that water, which is necessary for life, needs to be treated differently. To establish a system of transferable property rights is complicated by the fact that changing a water use in one place on a stream can influence everyone downstream also. But it is also true that the difficulty of

---

[8]This fact and others used in this section are from Indur M. Goklany, "The Pros and Cons of Modern Farming," in *PERC Reports* (March 2001), available online at www.perc.org/perc.php?id5307.

[9]Mark Strassmann, "Preview: America's Water Crisis," January 8, 2010, accessed Sept. 1, 2011, from www.cbsnews.com/8301-500803_162-6071729-500803.html.

[10]Terry L. Anderson, "Water Options for the Blue Planet," in *The True State of the Planet*, ed. Ronald Bailey (New York: Free Press, 1995), 275.

obtaining a property right to water provides a less certain water supply than market trades could make available. Progress is possible, and in some places where water is extremely valuable, some progress toward more trading is being made. The net benefits are being reaped by participants, in particular, and by the economy more generally.

In some places, people do own a right to water or at least the right to use some water from a lake or stream. In the arid western United States, for example, a person may own a right to divert a specific amount of water from a stream in order to irrigate crops. But state and federal laws may prevent that person from selling the right for use elsewhere or even changing its use in its current location. Other uses of the water may be far more valuable, but the owner cannot sell the water or the right to use it. The market mechanism that allocates copper and tin efficiently and prevents waste, shortages, or total depletion is very often missing in the case of water. Government subsidies to current water uses and users may also distort the allocation of this key resource.

Consider, for example, the federally funded Central Utah Project (CUP), which delivers water to farms from dams built on rivers. It illustrates the lack of complete and tradable property rights in water as well as the distortions caused by subsidies. The completed project provides water costing about $300 to deliver, per acre-foot (326,000 gallons) of CUP water, not counting the cost of building and maintaining the dam.[11] That acre-foot of water will add $30 to the value of the farm's crops, but the farmer will pay only $8. Taxpayers foot the rest of the bill. The farmers have the politically awarded right to the water and the subsidy, but they cannot sell the right and other potential users cannot bid the water away from the farmers. Meanwhile, cities and other water users in the region face shortages and are making plans to increase their own water supplies by costly means. Water trading could help buyers and sellers to reap large mutual gains from trade, but the trades are not allowed.

Some water-short cities near the ocean or other saltwater bodies are considering desalination, which uses massive amounts of energy and special equipment to make saltwater into freshwater at a cost of up to $2,000 per acre-foot. Others are seeking permission (and federal subsidies) to build more dams dedicated to storing water for their own use. The economic and environmental costs of building more dams are very high, but water is quite valuable once a shortage develops. Political interference has greatly slowed the movement of water. A farmer who is willing to pay at most $30 per unit to keep irrigation water could share gains of many hundreds of dollars per unit with buyers who are already seeking water and willing to pay ten, 20, or 50 times as much as the farmer's $30 to get the water for themselves. As more is learned from the small but increasing water trades that are allowed, economists and thoughtful environmentalists are working to introduce more market trading to displace high-cost, environmentally destructive alternatives when water shortages develop. Market trades and the signals and incentives they provide are a key to preventing resource waste and expanding effective resource supplies.

---

[11]Terry L. Anderson, "What Shortage? Water Markets Increase Market Supply," in *EcoWorld* (October 25, 2002), available online at www.ecoworld.com/home/articles2.cfm?tid = 327. The examples following are discussed in this article.

KEY POINTS

- Forecasts that the world will soon run out of various key resources have been made for centuries. These forecasts have consistently been wrong.

- Resource prices fluctuate from month to month and year to year, but for long periods, the trends have been

mainly downward. See box feature, "Is It Smart to Bet on Rising Resource Prices?"

- When resources are allocated by markets, increased scarcity leads to higher prices. The higher prices will strengthen the incentive for (1) users to reduce their consumption, (2) suppliers to search for ways to expand future supply, and (3) both producers and users to search for substitutes. All of these adjustments will increase future supply relative to demand and make it highly unlikely that the resource will be depleted.

- Proved reserves are the verifiable quantity of a resource available at current prices and technology. They are not the total supply of the resource that will be available in the future. Proved reserves can be expanded with improvements in technology and increases in prices.

- The trend in the price of resources has been downward for at least a century, indicating that the relative scarcity of most resources has been declining.

- When property rights are poorly defined or when regulations make a resource nontradable, waste will result because the resource will often be directed toward less valuable uses.

CRITICAL ANALYSIS QUESTIONS

1. If the world were about to run out of a highly valued resource, what would happen to its price? How would this affect the future supply of the resource relative to demand?

2. *"If China and India continue their economic expansion, the world cannot provide enough raw materials without terrible shortages worldwide." Evaluate this statement.

3. In the industrial nations, have succeeding generations, each with a higher income than before, left the world resource-poor, with only low-grade mineral ores left, for example? Have they been "consuming the birthright" of future generations? Explain your answer.

4. Why have cotton fields retreated and forests returned in many areas of the southeastern United States? With fewer acres farmed, will the nation continue to be able to provide food and fiber for itself? Explain.

5. *"Water is a necessity of life. It should not be bought and sold, or traded in markets!" Use the economic way of thinking to evaluate this statement.

*Asterisk denotes questions for which answers are given in Appendix B.

12

Difficult Environmental Cases and the Role of Government

FOCUS

- Why do people seek governmental regulation to improve the environment in a market economy?

- What can economics tell us about an effective policy on global warming and climate change? Will economic growth help with this problem or make matters worse?

- How can the government utilize marketlike policies to reduce the cost of environmental policy?

- Why does federal ownership of our national parks pose problems for park managers serving the public? Are there ways to lessen those problems?

iStockphoto.com/sorendls

A little richer is a lot safer.
—*Aaron Wildavsky*[1]

[1]Aaron Wildavsky and Adam Wildavsky, "Risk and Safety," in *The Concise Encyclopedia of Economics*, 2nd ed., ed. David R. Henderson (Indianapolis, IN: Liberty Fund, Inc., 2007), available online at http://econlib.com/library/Enc/RiskandSafety.html.

Private property rights can promote prosperity and cooperation and at the same time protect the environment, but do they protect the environment sufficiently? In recent years, especially since the late 1960s in the United States, people have increasingly turned to the government to achieve additional environmental improvements. Sometimes people turned to government because property rights failed to hold polluters accountable for the costs they were imposing on others. In these "external cost" cases, government may be able to improve accountability and protect rights more efficiently by regulation. In other instances, people with strong desires for various environmental amenities (for example, green spaces, hiking trails, and wilderness lands) want the government to force others to help pay for them. In this special topic, we look more closely at the possibilities for achieving environmental goals through governmental control of pollution and of natural resources, as well as the problems that arise from government action in these areas.

iStockphoto.com/nicoolay

GOVERNMENT REGULATION: GOOD FOR THE ENVIRONMENT?

As we noted in Chapter 2, courts help owners protect their property against invasions by others, including polluters. In some cases, however, it is difficult—if not impossible—to define, establish, and fully protect property rights. This is particularly true when there is either a large number of polluters or a large number of people harmed by the emissions, or both. In these large-number cases, high transaction costs undermine the effectiveness of the property rights–market exchange approach. For example, consider the air quality in a large city such as Los Angeles or Denver. Millions of people are harmed when pollutants are put into the air. But millions of people also contribute to the pollution as they drive their cars. Property rights alone will be unable to handle large-number cases like this efficiently. More direct regulations may generate a better outcome.

Although government regulation is an alternative method of protecting the environment, the regulatory approach also has a number of deficiencies. First, government regulation is often sought precisely because the harms are uncertain and the source of the problem cannot be demonstrated in a court of law, so relief from the courts is difficult to obtain. But when the harms are uncertain and thus speculative, so too are the benefits of reducing them. The costs of reducing them, however, are real and often large.

Second, by its very nature, regulation overrides or ignores the information and incentives provided by market signals. Accountability of regulators for the costs they impose is lacking, just as accountability for polluters is missing in the market sector when secure and tradable property rights are not in place. The tunnel vision of regulators, each assigned to oversee a small part of the economy, is not properly constrained by readily observable costs.

Third, regulation allows special interests to use political power to achieve objectives that may be quite different from the environmental goals originally announced. The global warming issue illustrates all of these problems and the uncertainties that they generate. Let's take a closer look at this high-profile issue.

THE ECONOMICS OF GLOBAL WARMING

The highly publicized problem of global warming generates a legitimate reason for considering governmental intervention. But the global nature of the problem and the scientific uncertainties associated with it also illustrate the problems that come with regulation.

Coal-fired power generators put large amounts of visible steam and invisible carbon dioxide into the air. Carbon dioxide is a greenhouse gas that may be warming the earth significantly.

Burning fuels such as coal, oil, and natural gas emits carbon dioxide. These emissions cause no direct harm, unlike traditional harmful pollutants such as particulates and sulfur dioxide. Carbon dioxide is not a pollutant in the normal sense, although concerns about its long-term effects on the atmosphere have led the U.S. Environmental Protection Agency to attempt to regulate it as a pollutant. Rather, carbon dioxide is a gas that is an essential food for plants, and thus is necessary to life on this planet. More of it allows plants to grow, and to use less water, and thus to be more resistant to drought.

As the world has become warmer and more industrialized, more carbon dioxide has been building up in the atmosphere. Although carbon dioxide represents a tiny part of the atmosphere, it is a "greenhouse" gas (GHG). It contributes to the formation of an invisible blanket that traps some heat on Earth that would otherwise be radiated into space. Interestingly, carbon dioxide is a "greenhouse gas" in another sense as well. It is purchased in compressed gas form by owners of greenhouses as a fertilizer for their plants because it spurs their growth.

Higher levels of carbon dioxide may be contributing to the 1.4 degrees Fahrenheit of warming Earth has experienced over the past century. Further increases might cause Earth to warm more dramatically, changing weather patterns and perhaps leading to rising sea levels around the globe. If the "worst-case scenarios" suggested by some scientists were to materialize, certain communities would face flooding of their lands and serious ecological disruption. Reports of extreme weather and melting glaciers add to the alarm surrounding this issue.

To address this potential problem, representatives of numerous nations signed an international treaty known as the Kyoto Protocol in 1997. The treaty requires industrial nations to control the total amount of emissions of carbon dioxide within their borders to no more than they produced in 1990. The U.S. government signed the 1997 treaty but did not ratify it, and the U.S. Senate rejected ratification by 95–0 in 1999. The chief reason was that the treaty would not limit emissions in some large developing nations, such as India and China. Even though its GDP is substantially less than the United States, China is now the world's largest emitter of carbon dioxide. In 2009, China emitted 7.7 trillion tons of carbon dioxide, while the United States was the second largest emitter at 5.4 trillion tons.[2]

---

[2]U.S. Energy Information Administration, "International Energy Statistics," www.eia.gov/cfapps/ipdbproject/IEDIndex3.cfm?tid=90&pid=44&aid=8.

The issue of global warming (now often called *climate change*) continues to be a topic of international concern. In recent years, however, much of the discussion has centered on the science. Are the predictions of severe increases in global temperatures due to human emissions of GHG realistic? And therefore, are the projections of impacts, such as damages from rising sea levels, scientifically valid? In spite of much study—and much rhetoric—a lot of critical information is still missing. Scientists have not quantified some of the factors causing major changes in Earth's temperature. Long before the Industrial Revolution began to pump up fossil-fuel consumption, with resulting additions to carbon dioxide in the air, global temperatures changed significantly. Two periods in the past 2,000 years stand out: the Medieval Optimum (a warm period from about 700 A.D. to 1200) and the Little Ice Age (a period of temperatures significantly colder, on average, than today, from about 1560 to 1850). Thus, Earth has experienced both warming and cooling trends in the past, and the current warm period may well be largely unrelated to human emissions of carbon dioxide and other greenhouse gases into the atmosphere.

Most predictions of significant temperature increases are based on giant computer models of Earth's atmosphere, but these models are full of information gaps. The effects of clouds and water vapor in warming or cooling Earth and the role of oceans in absorbing carbon dioxide are especially important in the models, because the projected warming effect depends heavily on water vapor and clouds. The models assume that water vapor and clouds will increase the warming effect. Indeed, in the models, they are assumed to be 10 to 20 times as important in raising future temperatures as is carbon dioxide itself. But it is quite possible that the water vapor won't increase with carbon dioxide in the way that the models assume and that changes in clouds, on balance, will do little to add to warming or might even be, on balance, a force for cooling. Scientists do agree that, by reflecting sunlight back into space clouds tend to cool Earth, while clouds also trap heat from below them, thus warming Earth.

Is a world that is warmer by one or two degrees better on the whole or worse? Climate researcher Indur Goklany points out that since 1920, as industrialization accelerated (and human-caused carbon dioxide emissions did the same) and Earth's temperature rose, deaths per million people from all extreme weather events (droughts, floods, temperature extremes, etc.) fell globally by 98 percent.[3] Burning fossil fuel may have played a part in raising Earth's temperature, but it also fueled enormous increases in people's well-being. In the same chapter, Goklany details the many roles fossil fuels have played in helping people globally to prosper mightily and be healthier as a result. His work adds hard evidence to the simple observation that when people retire from their jobs and have more freedom to live where they wish, large numbers of them move south—to Florida, for example, seeking more warmth and less rigorous winters.

Cost also matters. The opportunity cost of attempting to slow the warming by reducing greenhouse gas emissions (the "carbon footprint") would be extremely high—much economic growth would be reduced—and the expected effect on world temperatures extremely small. Economist William Nordhaus estimated that accepting the Kyoto Protocol would have cost the United States alone about $125 billion each year for the next century.[4] Yet these expenditures would have almost no effect, partly because developing countries would be allowed to increase their carbon emissions without limit. Richard Lindzen, a prominent climatologist at Massachusetts Institute of Technology, says, "Kyoto, itself, will have no discernible impact on global warming regardless of what one believes about climate change."[5]

Government regulation tends to encourage special interests, and regulation of GHGs is no exception. The public fear of the impacts of global warming has led to government support of global warming research in the billions of dollars. Inevitably, that gives scientists an

[3]Indur M. Goklany, "Economic Development in Developing Countries: Advancing Human Well-Being and the Capacity to Adapt to Global Warming," in *Climate Coup* (Washington, DC: Cato Institute, 2011).
[4]William D. Nordhaus, "Global Warming Economics," *Science* 294 (November 9, 2001): 1283–84.
[5]Richard S. Lindzen, "Climate Alarm—Where Does It Come From?" (Speech to the Houston Forum, September 9, 2004). (Verified by Richard S. Lindzen in personal correspondence with Richard Stroup on November 26, 2004.)

incentive to maintain climate change as a public issue. As Lindzen puts it, "Alarm is felt to be essential to the maintenance of funding."

MITIGATION VERSUS ADAPTATION STRATEGY

The estimated costs, the special-interest involvement, and the scientific uncertainties leave many economists unwilling to recommend strong regulations to reduce emissions of carbon dioxide. But given the possibility of serious harm from global warming, what should be done? The Kyoto Protocol attempted *mitigation*—reducing carbon emissions in order to keep global temperatures from rising as much as they otherwise would. In contrast, *adaptation* means making changes when and if actual problems begin to occur.

Climate change researcher Indur M. Goklany suggests that adaptation is the superior strategy. He examines four risk factors—hunger, malaria, water shortages, and coastal flooding—that might worsen if global temperatures increase significantly. He concludes that taking action now to address these already serious problems, independent of global warming, would cost far less than trying to reduce temperature increases, and the payoff in improved human lives would be achieved long before any significant benefits were derived from greenhouse gas reductions.[6] Economic logic suggests that a larger payoff obtained sooner for a smaller cost is the better bet.

Instead of forcing a smaller carbon footprint, which would greatly reduce national income, nations might be better off dealing with the uncertainties of global warming through growth and development. As Aaron Wildavsky implied in the quotation at the opening of this special topic, wealthier people can better handle all sorts of risks. They purchase better healthcare, make available more emergency transport and care facilities, drive safer cars, and pay for routine safety measures of all sorts. A more prosperous country is more resilient when faced with major threats, whether from a new disease, an earthquake, an asteroid striking Earth, or global warming.

A strong economy allows its citizens to help not only themselves but also others. For example, when an earthquake and tsunami hit northern Japan and killed thousands of people in March of 2011, it took Americans less than two weeks to give more than $161 million in private donations to assist the victims in Japan. The U.S. Department of Defense had a naval presence in the area, and those ships quickly began delivering food and other emergency supplies. The U.S. Agency for International Development also participated, and within nine days, USAID and the U.S. military had put more than $23 million into those supply efforts. A poor society has fewer options and less resilience. Also, richer people are far more willing and able to make sacrifices to gain greater environmental quality of all sorts. Economic development accomplishes all these goals on behalf of health and environmental safety. In contrast, reducing one risk at a large cost to economic growth makes us more vulnerable to other risks, including those that were not anticipated.

MARKETLIKE SCHEMES: REDUCING
THE COST OF SPECIFIC REGULATIONS

Policy-makers who want to take action now on global warming recognize that meaningful actions will be costly. Some emitters of carbon dioxide, however, can cut back on their emissions at much lower costs than others. To take advantage of this fact, some have proposed marketlike incentive schemes, such as a "cap-and-trade bill," which the U.S. House of Representatives passed in 2009 but it died in the Senate. They have been influenced by the apparent success of some "market-based mechanisms" in reducing

---

[6]Indur M. Goklany, "Relative Contributions of Global Warming to Various Climate Sensitive Risks, and Their Implications for Adaptation and Mitigation," *Energy & Environment* 14 (2003): 797–822.

traditional pollutants at relatively low cost. Such mechanisms have some of the incentive effects of markets, but they also have severe limits.

There are two major marketlike approaches to controlling pollution.

1. Pollution charges or taxes.   Under this approach, the government levies fees on polluters. Ideally—in order to achieve efficiency—these charges would just equal the costs of pollution borne by others downwind or downstream. Facing a pollution tax, a polluter has an incentive to reduce the contaminants it is putting into the air or water or soil. As emissions decrease, the payment of the pollution tax by the company will also decrease. The incentive to reduce emissions continues only to the point at which the cost of cutting back further would exceed the cost savings from the reduced emission charges. At that point, the company will pay tax on the remaining emissions.

This process will result in efficient emission controls only if the emission charges properly represent the marginal cost of the pollutant to those harmed. But it is difficult or impossible for the regulator to know this cost without market trades to provide information. In a true property-rights situation, would-be polluters could negotiate with those who would be harmed by the pollution and decide whether to stop the pollution or compensate those harmed. In the nineteenth century, for example, Wisconsin paper mills bought land for miles downstream from their mills so that the effluent from their manufacturing would not violate the property rights of others.

Only a few pollution charges have been adopted in the United States. Companies oppose these fees because they are an added cost of doing business. Governments are not happy with them, either. If the emission charge does reduce pollution, the government will get less revenue over time. Reluctance on the part of governments to impose them has held back their implementation.

2. Emission standards and tradable permits.   Under this approach, a pollution-control authority (such as the Environmental Protection Agency) sets the total amount of emissions (that is, it "caps" emissions). Then it assigns (or perhaps sells) permits allowing emission of that amount of pollution. These permits are then tradable.

Such a program, sometimes called "cap and trade," gives each emitter an incentive to reduce or even eliminate emissions. If a company can cheaply reduce emissions below its allowed level, it can sell emissions permits ("credits") to other companies that face higher costs and thus can save money by buying permits from low-cost reducers. The total reduction in pollution will not change, but the overall costs of meeting the standard may be much lower. The result is efficiency in attaining specified emission levels.

The best-known example of a "cap-and-trade" program in the United States was established in the Clean Air Act Amendments of 1990. This Act authorized the Environmental Protection Agency (EPA) to establish a nationwide system for trading sulfur dioxide emission reductions among power plants. The utilities that face the highest cost of emission control can purchase permits from those who can more easily control emissions. This program is lowering the long-run costs to electric utilities of meeting the legislated targets.

Such schemes can play a useful role, but they have drawbacks. For one thing, deciding on the appropriate amount of pollution reduction is difficult. How clean is clean? Cleaner is costlier, reducing net incomes. And when incomes fall, the willingness to pay for environmental quality falls, so environmentalists themselves face this trade-off. To set the allowable emissions at an efficient level, the EPA or other authority needs accurate information about both the cost of controlling emissions and the benefit (harms avoided) of doing so. But the cost to those affected is subjective, depending in part on their ability to avoid damage by moving or changing what they are doing. Subjective costs thus are difficult to estimate, other than by observation of voluntary trades of property rights.

Offers and trades to accept more pollution in exchange for compensation, are not allowed in "cap-and-trade" programs. Instead, the regulator chooses a level of pollution that must not be exceeded. But without trades, it is difficult to know the appropriate level, especially in the case of nationwide standards. The willingness and ability of citizens to pay for environmental quality are strongly dependent upon their income and the cost of environmental quality. Citizens who are poorer, will be less willing to endure the higher cost that regulation impose, to gain a specific environmental benefit. So it is difficult to know how pollution-free an area should be, taking into account both environmental goals and the benefits to all concerned from the polluting activity.

As we noted in Chapter 5, even things that are worth doing, such as reducing levels of pollution, are seldom worth doing perfectly. At some point, the benefits of achieving still lower levels of pollution will not be worth the cost. Indeed, policy analysts familiar with the formation of the 1990 Clean Air Act negotiations say that the standard chosen, a reduction of 10 million tons of sulfur dioxide per year around the country, was arbitrary. So even though the trades reduced the costs of meeting the standard, the standard may have been unreasonably strict—or too lax, for that matter. In fact, because the major problem the program addressed—acid rain—turned out to be smaller than many people expected, the overall program was probably unnecessarily costly in spite of the trades.[7]

Regulation has an additional limitation that property rights enforced in courts do not. After a court orders a reduction in pollution, the polluter and the receptor (the person affected) can then trade property rights if they wish. For example, a court may order a factory owner to halve the factory's pollution to protect the rights of a downwind farmer. However, the farmer might be willing to accept all the pollution in exchange for a payment. In the property-rights system, the freedom exists to make such a trade.

PROPERTY RIGHTS AS A TOOL FOR GOVERNMENT POLICY

Not all marketlike schemes have such flaws. When the government recognizes the power of private property rights, there is potential for successful government policy. Ocean fisheries are one example in which progress is being made.

OCEAN FISHERIES: A LACK OF PROPERTY RIGHTS CAUSES OVERFISHING[8]

Overfishing in the oceans is a classic example of overexploitation of a resource that is not privately owned. This is typically called the "tragedy of the commons."[9] Without owner-ship of the fish or of fishing rights, each fisher has little to gain from holding back, because others will get most of the fish left in the water. To cope with this tragedy of the commons, governments try to institute regulations that protect the fish. Since the 1970s, the U.S. government has regulated fishing in coastal waters. Even so, at least a third of U.S. fisheries are known to be overfished.

One reason is that the regulations encouraged a wasteful and dangerous "race to fish." To preserve the stock of fish, governments reduced the length of the fishing seasons (often to just a few days) and set limits on the kinds of gear that could be used. This meant that boats went out to sea in dangerous weather, took all the fish they could, even immature fish, and faced accidents and capsizing as their gear became entangled with other fishers' gear.

Property-rights strategies are increasingly used around the world instead of limits on season length. A prominent example is the adoption of individual transferable quotas (ITQs), which give fishers ownership of a portion of the annual allowable catch. For example, as economist Don Leal puts it in one case, "an individual who holds a 0.1-percent share in the South Atlantic wreckfish fishery is entitled to 7,400 pounds of wreckfish for the season if

---

[7]Robert W. Crandall, "Is There Progress in Environmental Policy?" *Contemporary Economic Policy* 12, no. 1 (1994): 80–83.

[8]This section is based in large part on information found in Donald R. Leal, *Homesteading the Oceans: The Case for Property Rights in U.S. Fisheries*, found at www.perc.org/perc.php?subsection=6&id=188, and from personal communications with Leal.

[9]Garrett Hardin, "The Tragedy of the Commons," *The Concise Encyclopedia of Economics*, Library of Economics and Liberty, www.econlib.org/library/Enc/TragedyoftheCommons.html.

the total allowable catch is 7,400,000 pounds."[10] Regulators could be mistaken in setting the quota, of course. However, unlike the case of air pollution, the fishery itself will give them rapid feedback. If the stock of fish falls, regulators can drop the total allowable catch to let the fishery recover. When they own ITQs, fishers support such limits to maintain the value of their fishing rights over time. Leal reports that in the United States, the number of federal fisheries adopting rights-based approaches has grown from 4 in 1995 to 15 in 2010, with more in the planning stage. At the global level however, less than 2 percent of the world's fisheries have adopted rights-based strategies.

GOVERNMENT OWNERSHIP OF RESOURCES AND PROVISION OF SERVICES

Much government intervention in environmental matters has to do with establishing regulations to control pollution. But the government also owns many natural resources and seeks to protect environmental quality through parks, refuges, and other lands it owns. When resources are not privately owned and traded in open markets, however, the vital flow of information and incentives that prices bring is missing. That is the case with our national parks.[11] Government ownership stops the flow of information and incentives provided by dynamic market data. In complex ecosystems and in a world in which incomes, scientific understanding, and resource values all are constantly changing, the absence of up-to-date knowledge, including the desires of the tax-paying public, can lead to mismanagement. That is true even with management provided by highly qualified, well-intended professionals.

Most of the funds for the national parks are tax dollars appropriated by Congress. Park visitors pay only a small fraction of the cost of the services they receive, although fees have increased since the adoption of a fee demonstration program in the late 1990s, which became law in 2004. In 1995, for example, proceeds from national park recreation fees covered only 7.5 percent of the cost of park operations. Thus, park managers had little information about how much the various services were worth to visitors. Without good information about what visitors wanted, park managers didn't know whether to improve the roads, buildings and sewers, hire more rangers for interpretive programs, or keep campgrounds open longer and add new ones. And even today, because the National Park Service's funding is dependent upon decisions in Congress, it spends more time figuring out what the relevant congressional representatives want than what park visitors want.

Even when park managers have good information, the proper incentive to use it may not be present. This was the case in 1996 when the superintendent of Yellowstone Park closed a campground. The park was short on cash, and the superintendent was trying to reduce his spending. In fact, the campground in question was profitable—that is, it earned more than it cost to operate. The problem was that although his budget paid the cost of keeping the campground open, the revenues went to the U.S. Treasury, not to Yellowstone. So the superintendent closed the campground to save money, even though doing so deprived visitors of a campground that was providing net earnings for the Treasury.

In contrast, for owners of private forests, campgrounds, amusement parks, museums, and other attractions that also draw visitors, information is always flowing, and managers always have an incentive to respond to that information. These owners must pay for the resources they use, and they collect the needed revenue from customers. If people don't come to a private museum, its revenues fall. In response, its owners must do something to attract customers who are willing to pay the full cost (or, alternatively, philanthropists who will cover the costs for them), or they will have to close their doors.

---

[10]Donald R. Leal, "Fencing the Fishery—A Primer on Ending the Race for Fish," found online at www.perc.org/perc.php?subsection=3&id=120. The data for ITQ numbers are found at www.perc.org/articles/article1271.php.
[11]Many of the facts and much of the data for this section come from Donald R. Leal and Holly L. Fretwell, "Back to the Future to Save Our Parks," *PERC Policy Series*, Issue Number PS-10 (June 1997), at www.perc.org/perc.php? subsection=6&id=654.

The National Park Service may be starting to realize that it needs better information and better incentives. The law that raised fees in 2004 also required that 80 percent of the fees be kept in the specific parks where they were collected and that they be used for projects in those parks—rather than flowing into the U.S. Treasury to be spent according to congressional mandate. "With greater accountability to those most impacted by the parks, the program is funding projects that otherwise might sit on a shelf," wrote one commentator about the fee program.[12]

CONCLUSION

People turn to government to get what they can't get in markets. In many cases, they are seeking to get what they want with a subsidy from others. Government can provide protection from harms, as in regulation that reduces pollution, or production of goods and services, as in the provision of national parks. Government can indeed shift the cost of services from some citizens to others, and can do the same with benefits from its programs. There is little reason, however, to expect a net increase in efficiency when government steps in. That is true in environmental matters, as well as in many other areas of citizen concern.

KEY POINTS

- When it is difficult to assign and enforce private property rights, markets often result in outcomes that are inefficient. This is often the case when large numbers of people engage in actions that impose harm on others. Government regulation has some promise but also poses some problems of its own.

- Global warming could exert a sizable adverse impact on human welfare, but there is considerable uncertainty about both its cause and the potential gains that might be derived from regulations that require reductions in emissions of carbon dioxide. Global temperature changes have been observed previously; we do not know for certain if the current warming stems primarily from human activity. We do not even know whether, on balance, a warming would exert an adverse impact. These uncertainties increase the attractiveness of adaptation as an option to regulation.

- Marketlike schemes can reduce the costs of reaching a chosen environmental goal, but the programs provide little help in choosing the right goal.

- Federal ownership of national parks, as with other lands, has brought troublesome results along with benefits, but there seems to be progress in moving closer to market solutions that provide better information and incentives for federal managers.

CRITICAL ANALYSIS QUESTIONS

1. *The movie *The Perfect Storm* was set in a situation in which a very short fishing season forces the fishers to go to sea despite the dangerous conditions. Explain how a move to ITQs could solve that problem.
2. "The national parks belong to us all. No one should be charged money to enter." Evaluate, using the economic way of thinking.
3. *"The buildup of carbon dioxide and other gases in the air threatens to warm the planet and cause enormous damage worldwide. We must immediately stop this buildup for the sake of future generations." Why do many economists disagree with this statement? Are they not concerned about the future? Explain.
4. *"Unlike a marketplace in which pollution is profitable, government control of resources and pollution can take into account the desires of all the people." Evaluate, using economic thinking.

*Asterisk denotes questions for which answers are given in Appendix B.

---

[12]Brian Yablonski, "The National Parks: America's Best Idea," *PERC Reports* (Vol. 27, No. 3), Property and Environment Research Center, Bozeman, MT, Fall 2009, www.perc.org/articles/article1191.php.

General Business and Economics Indicators for the United States

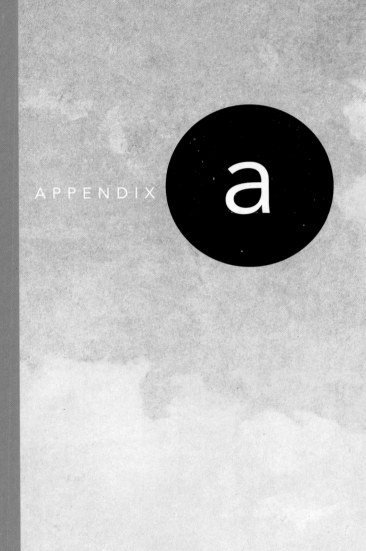

Section 1

Gross Domestic Product and its Components

Year	Personal Consumption Expenditures (Billions)	Gross Private Domestic Investment (Billions)	Govt Consumption and Gross Investment (Billions)	Net Exports (Billions)	Gross Domestic Product (Billions)	Real GDP 2005 Prices	Real GDP Annual Real Rate (Percent)	Real GDP Per Capita
1960	$331.8	$78.9	$111.5	$4.2	$526.4	$2,828.5	2.5	$15,648
1961	342.2	78.2	119.5	4.9	544.8	2,894.4	2.3	15,753
1962	363.3	88.1	130.1	4.1	585.7	3,069.8	6.1	16,452
1963	382.7	93.8	136.4	4.9	617.8	3,204.0	4.4	16,925
1964	411.5	102.1	143.2	6.9	663.6	3,389.4	5.8	17,660
1965	443.8	118.2	151.4	5.6	719.1	3,607.0	6.4	18,560
1966	480.9	131.3	171.6	3.9	787.7	3,842.1	6.5	19,543
1967	507.8	128.6	192.5	3.6	832.4	3,939.2	2.5	19,819
1968	558.0	141.2	209.3	1.4	909.8	4,129.9	4.8	20,573
1969	605.1	156.4	221.4	1.4	984.4	4,258.2	3.1	21,003
1970	648.3	152.4	233.7	4.0	1,038.3	4,266.3	0.2	20,802
1971	701.6	178.2	246.4	0.6	1,126.8	4,409.5	3.4	21,231
1972	770.2	207.6	263.4	−3.4	1,237.9	4,643.8	5.3	22,121
1973	852.0	244.5	281.7	4.1	1,382.3	4,912.8	5.8	23,180
1974	932.9	249.4	317.9	−0.8	1,499.5	4,885.7	−0.6	22,841
1975	1,033.8	230.2	357.7	16.0	1,637.7	4,875.4	−0.2	22,573
1976	1,151.3	292.0	383.0	−1.6	1,824.6	5,136.9	5.4	23,555
1977	1,277.8	361.3	414.1	−23.1	2,030.1	5,373.1	4.6	24,391
1978	1,427.6	438.0	453.6	−25.4	2,293.8	5,672.8	5.6	25,481
1979	1,591.2	492.9	500.7	−22.5	2,562.2	5,850.1	3.1	25,988
1980	1,755.8	479.3	566.1	−13.1	2,788.1	5,834.0	−0.3	25,618
1981	1,939.5	572.4	627.5	−12.5	3,126.8	5,982.1	2.5	26,008
1982	2,075.5	517.2	680.4	−20.0	3,253.2	5,865.9	−1.9	25,260
1983	2,288.6	564.3	733.4	−51.7	3,534.6	6,130.9	4.5	26,163
1984	2,501.1	735.6	796.9	−102.7	3,930.9	6,571.5	7.2	27,799
1985	2,717.6	736.2	878.9	−115.2	4,217.5	6,843.4	4.1	28,693
1986	2,896.7	746.5	949.3	−132.5	4,460.1	7,080.5	3.5	29,418
1987	3,097.0	785.0	999.4	−145.0	4,736.4	7,307.0	3.2	30,090
1988	3,350.1	821.6	1,038.9	−110.1	5,100.4	7,607.4	4.1	31,043
1989	3,594.5	874.9	1,100.6	−87.9	5,482.1	7,879.2	3.6	31,850
1990	3,835.5	861.0	1,181.7	−77.6	5,800.5	8,027.1	1.9	32,085
1991	3,980.1	802.9	1,236.1	−27.0	5,992.1	8,008.3	−0.2	31,587
1992	4,236.9	864.8	1,273.5	−32.8	6,342.3	8,280.0	3.4	32,228
1993	4,483.6	953.3	1,294.8	−64.4	6,667.4	8,516.2	2.9	32,719
1994	4,750.8	1,097.3	1,329.8	−92.7	7,085.2	8,863.1	4.1	33,642
1995	4,987.3	1,144.0	1,374.0	−90.7	7,414.7	9,086.0	2.5	34,082
1996	5,273.6	1,240.2	1,421.0	−96.3	7,838.5	9,425.8	3.7	34,948
1997	5,570.6	1,388.7	1,474.4	−101.4	8,332.4	9,845.9	4.5	36,071
1998	5,918.5	1,510.8	1,526.1	−161.8	8,793.5	10,274.7	4.4	37,207
1999	6,342.8	1,641.5	1,631.3	−262.1	9,353.5	10,770.7	4.8	38,559
2000	6,830.4	1,772.2	1,731.0	−382.1	9,951.5	11,216.4	4.1	39,716
2001	7,148.8	1,661.9	1,846.4	−371.0	10,286.2	11,337.5	1.1	39,734
2002	7,439.2	1,647.0	1,983.3	−427.2	10,642.3	11,543.1	1.8	40,062
2003	7,804.1	1,729.7	2,112.6	−504.1	11,142.2	11,836.4	2.5	40,697
2004	8,270.6	1,968.6	2,232.8	−618.7	11,853.3	12,246.9	3.5	41,727
2005	8,803.5	2,172.3	2,369.9	−722.7	12,623.0	12,623.0	3.1	42,612
2006	9,301.0	2,327.1	2,518.4	−769.3	13,377.2	12,958.5	2.7	43,332
2007	9,772.3	2,295.2	2,674.2	−713.1	14,028.7	13,206.4	1.9	43,726
2008	10,035.5	2,087.6	2,878.1	−709.7	14,291.5	13,161.9	−0.3	43,178
2009	9,866.1	1,546.8	2,917.5	−391.5	13,939.0	12,703.1	−3.5	41,313
2010	10,245.5	1,795.1	3,002.8	−516.9	14,526.5	13,088.0	3.0	42,205

Source: http://www.bea.gov.

Section 2

Prices and Inflation

Year	GDP Deflator		Consumer Price Index	
	Index (2005 = 100)	Annual Percent Change	Index	Percent Change
1960	18.6	1.4	29.6	1.0
1961	18.8	1.1	29.9	1.1
1962	19.1	1.4	30.3	1.2
1963	19.3	1.1	30.6	1.2
1964	19.6	1.6	31.0	1.3
1965	19.9	1.8	31.5	1.6
1966	20.5	2.8	32.5	3.0
1967	21.1	3.1	33.4	2.8
1968	22.0	4.2	34.8	4.3
1969	23.1	4.9	36.7	5.5
1970	24.3	5.3	38.8	5.8
1971	25.6	5.0	40.5	4.3
1972	26.7	4.3	41.8	3.3
1973	28.1	5.5	44.4	6.2
1974	30.7	9.1	49.3	11.1
1975	33.6	9.5	53.8	9.1
1976	35.5	5.7	56.9	5.7
1977	37.8	6.4	60.6	6.5
1978	40.4	7.0	65.2	7.6
1979	43.8	8.3	72.6	11.3
1980	47.8	9.1	82.4	13.5
1981	52.3	9.4	90.9	10.3
1982	55.5	6.1	96.5	6.1
1983	57.7	4.0	99.6	3.2
1984	59.8	3.8	103.9	4.3
1985	61.6	3.0	107.6	3.5
1986	63.0	2.2	109.6	1.9
1987	64.8	2.9	113.6	3.7
1988	67.0	3.4	118.3	4.1
1989	69.6	3.8	124.0	4.8
1990	72.3	3.9	130.7	5.4
1991	74.8	3.5	136.2	4.2
1992	76.6	2.4	140.3	3.0
1993	78.3	2.2	144.5	3.0
1994	79.9	2.1	148.2	2.6
1995	81.6	2.1	152.4	2.8
1996	83.2	1.9	156.9	2.9
1997	84.6	1.8	160.5	2.3
1998	85.6	1.1	163.0	1.6
1999	86.8	1.5	166.6	2.2
2000	88.7	2.2	172.2	3.4
2001	90.7	2.3	177.1	2.8
2002	92.2	1.6	179.9	1.6
2003	94.1	2.1	184.0	2.3
2004	96.8	2.8	188.9	2.7
2005	100.0	3.3	195.3	3.4
2006	103.2	3.2	201.6	3.2
2007	106.2	2.9	207.3	2.8
2008	108.6	2.2	215.3	3.8
2009	109.7	1.1	214.5	−0.4
2010	111.0	1.2	218.1	1.6

Source: http://www.bea.gov and http://www.bls.gov.

Section 3

Population and Employment

					UNEMPLOYMENT RATES			
YEAR	CIVILIAN NONINSTITUTIONAL POPULATION AGE 16+ (MILLIONS)	CIVILIAN LABOR FORCE (MILLIONS)	CIVILIAN LABOR FORCE PARTICIPATION RATE (PERCENT)	CIVILIAN EMPLOYMENT/ POPULATION RATIO (PERCENT)	ALL WORKERS	BOTH SEXES, AGE 16 TO 19	MEN AGE 20+	WOMEN AGE 20+
1960	117.2	69.6	59.4	56.1	5.5	14.7	4.7	5.1
1961	118.8	70.5	59.3	55.4	6.7	16.8	5.7	6.3
1962	120.2	70.6	58.8	55.5	5.5	14.7	4.6	5.4
1963	122.4	71.8	58.7	55.4	5.7	17.2	4.5	5.4
1964	124.5	73.1	58.7	55.7	5.2	16.2	3.9	5.2
1965	126.5	74.5	58.9	56.2	4.5	14.8	3.2	4.5
1966	128.1	75.8	59.2	56.9	3.8	12.8	2.5	3.8
1967	129.9	77.3	59.6	57.3	3.8	12.9	2.3	4.2
1968	132.0	78.7	59.6	57.5	3.6	12.7	2.2	3.8
1969	134.3	80.7	60.1	58.0	3.5	12.2	2.1	3.7
1970	137.1	82.8	60.4	57.4	4.9	15.3	3.5	4.8
1971	140.2	84.4	60.2	56.6	5.9	16.9	4.4	5.7
1972	144.1	87.0	60.4	57.0	5.6	16.2	4.0	5.4
1973	147.1	89.4	60.8	57.8	4.9	14.5	3.3	4.9
1974	150.1	91.9	61.3	57.8	5.6	16.0	3.8	5.5
1975	153.2	93.8	61.2	56.1	8.5	19.9	6.8	8.0
1976	156.2	96.2	61.6	56.8	7.7	19.0	5.9	7.4
1977	159.0	99.0	62.3	57.9	7.1	17.8	5.2	7.0
1978	161.9	102.3	63.2	59.3	6.1	16.4	4.3	6.0
1979	164.9	105.0	63.7	59.9	5.8	16.1	4.2	5.7
1980	167.7	106.9	63.8	59.2	7.1	17.8	5.9	6.4
1981	170.1	108.7	63.9	59.0	7.6	19.6	6.3	6.8
1982	172.3	110.2	64.0	57.8	9.7	23.2	8.8	8.3
1983	174.2	111.6	64.0	57.9	9.6	22.4	8.9	8.1
1984	176.4	113.5	64.4	59.5	7.5	18.9	6.6	6.8
1985	178.2	115.5	64.8	60.1	7.2	18.6	6.2	6.6
1986	180.6	117.8	65.3	60.7	7.0	18.3	6.1	6.2
1987	182.8	119.9	65.6	61.5	6.2	16.9	5.4	5.4
1988	184.6	121.7	65.9	62.3	5.5	15.3	4.8	4.9
1989	186.4	123.9	66.5	63.0	5.3	15.0	4.5	4.7
1990	189.2	125.8	66.5	62.8	5.6	15.5	5.0	4.9
1991	190.9	126.3	66.2	61.7	6.8	18.7	6.4	5.7
1992	192.8	128.1	66.4	61.5	7.5	20.1	7.1	6.3
1993	194.8	129.2	66.3	61.7	6.9	19.0	6.4	5.9
1994	196.8	131.1	66.6	62.5	6.1	17.6	5.4	5.4
1995	198.6	132.3	66.6	62.9	5.6	17.3	4.8	4.9
1996	200.6	133.9	66.8	63.2	5.4	16.7	4.6	4.8
1997	203.1	136.3	67.1	63.8	4.9	16.0	4.2	4.4
1998	205.2	137.7	67.1	64.1	4.5	14.6	3.7	4.1
1999	207.8	139.4	67.1	64.3	4.2	13.9	3.5	3.8
2000	212.6	142.6	67.1	64.4	4.0	13.1	3.4	3.6
2001	215.1	143.7	66.8	63.7	4.7	14.7	4.2	4.1
2002	217.6	144.9	66.6	62.7	5.8	16.5	5.2	5.1
2003	221.2	146.5	66.2	62.3	6.0	17.5	5.4	5.1
2004	223.4	147.4	66.0	62.3	5.5	17.0	4.9	4.9
2005	226.1	149.3	66.0	62.7	5.1	16.6	4.5	4.6
2006	228.8	151.4	66.2	63.1	4.6	15.4	4.1	4.1
2007	231.9	153.1	66.0	63.0	4.6	15.7	4.1	4.0
2008	233.8	154.287	66.0	62.2	5.8	18.7	5.4	4.9
2009	235.8	154.142	65.4	59.3	9.3	24.8	9.6	7.5
2010	237.8	153.889	64.7	58.5	9.6	25.9	9.8	8.0

Source: http://www.bls.gov.

Section 4

Federal Budget and National Debt

Year	M1 (Billions)	Annual Change (Percent)	M2 (Billions)	Annual Change (Percent)	Aaa Bonds (Percent)	Federal Budget Fiscal Year Outlays (Billions)	Federal Budget Fiscal Year Receipts (Billions)	Federal Budget Surplus/ Deficit (Billions)	National Debt[1] Billions of Dollars	National Debt[1] Percent of GDP
1960	$140.3	−0.1	$340.3	3.8	4.4	$92.2	$92.5	$0.3	$210.3	40.5%
1961	143.1	2.0	324.8	6.7	4.4	97.7	94.4	(3.3)	211.1	39.8%
1962	146.5	2.4	350.1	7.8	4.3	106.8	99.7	(7.1)	218.3	38.5%
1963	151.0	3.0	379.6	8.4	4.3	111.3	106.6	(4.8)	222.0	37.0%
1964	156.8	3.8	409.3	7.8	4.4	118.5	112.6	(5.9)	222.1	34.6%
1965	163.4	4.3	442.5	8.1	4.5	118.2	116.8	(1.4)	221.7	32.2%
1966	171.0	4.6	471.4	6.5	5.1	134.5	130.8	(3.7)	221.5	29.3%
1967	177.7	3.9	503.6	6.8	5.5	157.5	148.8	(8.6)	219.9	27.1%
1968	190.1	7.0	545.3	8.3	6.2	178.1	153.0	(25.2)	237.3	27.3%
1969	201.4	6.0	578.7	6.1	7.0	183.6	186.9	3.2	224.0	23.6%
1970	209.1	3.8	601.5	3.9	8.0	195.6	192.8	(2.8)	225.5	22.3%
1971	223.1	6.7	674.4	12.1	7.4	210.2	187.1	(23.0)	237.5	22.0%
1972	239.0	7.1	758.2	12.4	7.2	230.7	207.3	(23.4)	251.0	21.3%
1973	256.3	7.2	831.8	9.7	7.4	245.7	230.8	(14.9)	265.7	20.3%
1974	269.1	5.0	880.6	5.9	8.6	269.4	263.2	(6.1)	263.1	18.3%
1975	281.3	4.5	963.5	9.4	8.8	332.3	279.1	(53.2)	309.7	19.8%
1976	297.2	5.6	1,086.5	12.8	8.4	371.8	298.1	(73.7)	382.7	22.0%
1977	319.9	7.6	1,221.2	12.4	8.0	409.2	355.6	(53.7)	444.1	22.5%
1978	346.2	8.2	1,322.2	8.3	8.7	458.7	399.6	(59.2)	491.6	22.2%
1979	372.6	7.6	1,425.7	7.8	9.6	504.0	463.3	(40.7)	524.7	21.0%
1980	395.7	6.2	1,540.2	8.0	11.9	590.9	517.1	(73.8)	591.1	21.7%
1981	425.0	7.4	1,679.3	9.0	14.2	678.2	599.3	(79.0)	664.9	21.8%
1982	453.0	6.6	1,832.6	9.1	13.8	745.7	617.8	(128.0)	790.1	24.5%
1983	503.2	11.1	2,056.9	12.2	12.0	808.4	600.6	(207.8)	981.7	28.5%
1984	538.6	7.1	2,221.2	8.0	12.7	851.8	666.4	(185.4)	1,151.9	30.0%
1985	587.0	9.0	2,419.0	8.9	11.4	946.3	734.0	(212.3)	1,337.5	32.3%
1986	666.3	13.5	2,615.8	8.1	9.0	990.4	769.2	(221.2)	1,549.8	35.2%
1987	743.6	11.6	2,786.0	6.5	9.4	1,004.0	854.3	(149.7)	1,677.7	36.1%
1988	774.8	4.2	2,936.2	5.4	9.7	1,064.4	909.2	(155.2)	1,822.4	36.4%
1989	782.2	1.0	3,059.7	4.2	9.3	1,143.7	991.1	(152.6)	1,970.6	36.5%
1990	810.6	3.6	3,227.4	5.5	9.3	1,253.0	1,032.0	(221.0)	2,177.1	38.0%
1991	859.0	6.0	3,347.1	3.7	8.8	1,324.2	1,055.0	(269.2)	2,430.4	41.0%
1992	965.9	12.4	3,409.0	1.8	8.1	1,381.5	1,091.2	(290.3)	2,703.3	43.3%
1993	1,078.4	11.7	3,444.7	1.0	7.2	1,409.4	1,154.3	(255.1)	2,922.7	44.4%
1994	1,145.2	6.2	3,490.6	1.3	8.0	1,461.8	1,258.6	(203.2)	3,077.9	44.1%
1995	1,143.0	−0.2	3,562.9	2.1	7.6	1,515.7	1,351.8	(164.0)	3,230.3	44.0%
1996	1,106.8	−3.2	3,735.7	4.8	7.4	1,560.5	1,453.1	(107.4)	3,343.1	43.3%
1997	1,070.2	−3.3	3,924.2	5.0	7.3	1,601.1	1,579.2	(21.9)	3,347.8	40.8%
1998	1,080.7	1.0	4,203.7	7.1	6.5	1,652.5	1,721.7	69.3	3,262.9	37.7%
1999	1,102.3	2.0	4,514.0	7.4	7.0	1,701.8	1,827.5	125.6	3,135.7	34.1%
2000	1,103.7	0.1	4,784.2	6.0	7.6	1,789.0	2,025.2	236.2	2,898.4	29.5%
2001	1,140.3	3.3	5,201.9	8.7	7.1	1,862.8	1,991.1	128.2	2,785.5	27.2%
2002	1,196.3	4.9	5,594.3	7.5	6.5	2,010.9	1,853.1	(157.8)	2,936.2	27.8%
2003	1,273.5	6.5	5,978.7	6.9	5.7	2,159.9	1,782.3	(377.6)	3,257.3	29.7%
2004	1,344.2	5.5	6,257.9	4.7	5.6	2,292.8	1,880.1	(412.7)	3,595.2	30.8%
2005	1,371.6	2.0	6,523.9	4.3	5.2	2,472.0	2,153.6	(318.3)	3,855.9	31.0%
2006	1,374.2	0.2	6,866.6	5.3	5.6	2,655.1	2,406.9	(248.2)	4,060.0	30.7%
2007	1,372.2	−0.1	7,299.2	6.3	5.6	2,728.7	2,568.0	(160.7)	4,255.5	30.6%
2008	1,433.1	4.4	7,818.3	7.1	5.6	2,982.5	2,524.0	(458.6)	5,311.6	36.9%
2009	1,636.9	14.2	8,434.3	7.9	5.3	3,517.7	2,105.0	(1,412.7)	6,775.5	48.1%
2010	1,740.8	6.4	8,624.9	2.3	5.0	3,456.213	2,162.724	(1,293.5)	8,207.3	56.6%

Source: http://www.economagic.com and www.whitehouse.gov/omb/.

[1]National debt is debt held by private investors.

Section 5

Size of Government as a Share of GDP

	Size of Government as a Percent of GDP[1]				
Year	Expenditures (% of GDP)	Revenues (% of GDP)	Purchases of Goods and Services (% of GDP)	Non-Defense Purchases of Goods and Services (% of GDP)	Transfer Payments to Persons (% of GDP)
1960	23.3%	25.5%	21.2%	11.1%	5.3%
1961	24.3%	25.5%	21.9%	11.6%	5.8%
1962	24.4%	25.7%	22.2%	11.8%	5.6%
1963	24.5%	26.3%	22.1%	12.2%	5.5%
1964	24.0%	25.1%	21.6%	12.5%	5.3%
1965	23.7%	25.1%	21.1%	12.6%	5.3%
1966	24.5%	25.7%	21.8%	12.7%	5.3%
1967	26.4%	26.1%	23.1%	13.1%	6.0%
1968	27.1%	27.7%	23.0%	13.2%	6.4%
1969	27.1%	28.8%	22.5%	13.4%	6.5%
1970	28.4%	27.6%	22.5%	14.1%	7.4%
1971	28.9%	26.9%	21.9%	14.4%	8.1%
1972	28.7%	28.0%	21.3%	14.3%	8.3%
1973	27.9%	28.2%	20.4%	14.0%	8.3%
1974	29.1%	28.8%	21.2%	14.8%	9.0%
1975	31.0%	27.0%	21.8%	15.5%	10.3%
1976	30.1%	27.7%	21.0%	14.9%	10.0%
1977	29.4%	27.9%	20.4%	14.4%	9.5%
1978	28.5%	28.1%	19.8%	14.1%	9.1%
1979	28.3%	28.4%	19.5%	13.9%	9.1%
1980	30.2%	28.6%	20.3%	14.3%	10.0%
1981	30.8%	29.3%	20.1%	13.8%	10.0%
1982	33.0%	28.8%	20.9%	14.0%	10.8%
1983	33.0%	28.3%	20.7%	13.7%	10.7%
1984	31.9%	28.3%	20.3%	13.1%	9.9%
1985	32.4%	28.8%	20.8%	13.5%	9.9%
1986	32.7%	28.9%	21.3%	13.9%	9.9%
1987	32.4%	29.6%	21.1%	13.7%	9.7%
1988	31.7%	29.4%	20.4%	13.4%	9.6%
1989	31.6%	29.7%	20.0%	13.4%	9.7%
1990	32.3%	29.4%	20.3%	13.9%	10.1%
1991	33.0%	29.3%	20.6%	14.2%	10.4%
1992	33.8%	29.1%	20.1%	14.1%	11.8%
1993	33.3%	29.2%	19.4%	13.9%	12.0%
1994	32.4%	29.5%	18.7%	13.7%	11.8%
1995	32.5%	29.9%	18.5%	13.8%	11.9%
1996	32.0%	30.4%	18.1%	13.6%	11.9%
1997	31.0%	30.7%	17.7%	13.5%	11.5%
1998	30.1%	31.0%	17.4%	13.4%	11.1%
1999	29.5%	31.0%	17.4%	13.6%	10.9%
2000	29.2%	31.5%	17.4%	13.7%	10.8%
2001	30.1%	30.3%	18.0%	14.1%	11.4%
2002	30.8%	27.9%	18.6%	14.5%	12.0%
2003	31.0%	27.3%	19.0%	14.5%	12.2%
2004	30.8%	27.6%	18.8%	14.2%	12.1%
2005	31.0%	29.0%	18.8%	14.1%	12.2%
2006	31.0%	29.9%	18.8%	14.2%	12.2%
2007	31.6%	29.9%	19.1%	14.3%	12.4%
2008	33.1%	28.3%	20.1%	15.0%	13.3%
2009	35.9%	26.6%	20.9%	15.4%	15.6%
2010	36.2%	27.3%	20.7%	15.0%	15.9%

Source: http://www.bea.gov.

[1]There are some differences across reporting agencies with regard to accounting procedures and the treatment of government enterprises. This results in some differences in statistical measures of the size of government.

Section 6

Share (Percent) of Federal Income Taxes Paid by Income Groupings

Year	Top 1%	Top 5%	Top 10%	Next 40%	Bottom 50%
1980	19.1	36.8	49.3	43.7	7.0
1981	17.6	35.1	48.0	44.6	7.5
1982	19.0	36.1	48.6	44.1	7.3
1983	20.3	37.3	49.7	43.1	7.2
1984	21.1	38.0	50.6	42.1	7.4
1985	21.8	38.8	51.5	41.4	7.2
1986	25.7	42.6	54.7	38.9	6.5
1987	24.8	43.3	55.6	38.3	6.1
1988	27.6	45.6	57.3	37.0	5.7
1989	25.2	43.9	55.8	38.4	5.8
1990	25.1	43.6	55.4	38.8	5.8
1991	24.8	43.4	55.8	38.7	5.5
1992	27.5	45.9	58.0	36.9	5.1
1993	29.0	47.4	59.2	36.0	4.8
1994	28.9	47.5	59.4	35.8	4.8
1995	30.3	48.9	60.7	34.6	4.6
1996	32.3	51.0	62.5	33.2	4.3
1997	33.2	51.9	63.2	32.5	4.3
1998	34.8	53.8	65.0	30.8	4.2
1999	36.2	55.5	66.5	29.5	4.0
2000	37.4	56.5	67.3	28.8	3.9
2001	33.9	53.3	64.9	31.1	4.0
2002	33.7	53.8	65.7	30.8	3.5
2003	34.3	54.4	65.8	30.7	3.5
2004	36.9	57.1	68.2	28.5	3.3
2005	39.4	59.7	70.3	26.6	3.1
2006	39.9	60.1	70.8	26.2	3.0
2007	40.4	60.6	71.2	25.9	2.9
2008	38.0	58.7	70.0	27.3	2.7

Source: Internal Revenue Service.

Answers to Selected Critical Analysis Questions

CHAPTER 1: THE ECONOMIC APPROACH

2. Production of scarce goods always involves a cost; there are no free lunches. When the government provides goods without charge to consumers, other citizens (taxpayers) will bear the cost of their provision. Thus, provision by the government affects how the costs will be covered, not whether they are incurred.

4. For most taxpayers, the change will reduce the after-tax cost of raising children. Other things being constant, one would predict an increase in the birthrate.

5. False. Intentions do not change the effect of the policy. If the policy runs counter to sound economics, it will lead to a counterproductive outcome even if that was not the intention of the policy. Bad policies are often advocated by people with good intentions.

8. Money has nothing to do with whether an individual is economizing. Any time a person chooses, in an attempt to achieve a goal, he or she is economizing.

9. Positive economics can help one better understand the likely effects of alternative policies. This will help one choose alternatives that are less likely to lead to disappointing results.

10. Association is not causation. It is likely that a large lead, near the end of the game, caused the third team to play more, rather than the third team causing the lead.

14. This is a question that highlights the importance of marginal analysis. In responding to the question, think about the following. After pollution has already been reduced substantially, how much will it cost to reduce it still more? If the quality of air and water were already high, how much gain would result from still less pollution?

CHAPTER 2: SOME TOOLS OF THE ECONOMIST

2. This is an opportunity cost question. Even though the productivity of brush painters has changed only slightly, rising productivity in other areas has led to higher wages in other occupations, thereby increasing the opportunity cost of being a house painter. Because people would not supply house painting services unless they were able to meet their opportunity costs, higher wages are necessary to attract house painters from competitive (alternative) lines of work.

4. The statement reflects the view that "exchange is a zero-sum game." This view is false. No private business can force customers to buy. Consumers purchase various goods and services from businesses because they gain by doing so. If they did not gain, they would not continue to purchase items from a business. Similarly, the business firms also gain from their production and sale activities. Mutual gain provides the foundation for voluntary exchange, including that between business firms and their customers.

8. Yes. This question highlights the incentive of individuals to conserve for the future when they have private ownership rights. The market value of the land will increase in anticipation of the future harvest as the trees grow and the expected day of harvest grows closer. Thus, with transferable private property, the tree farmer will be able to capture the value added by his planting and holding the trees for a few years, even if the actual harvest does not take place until well after his death.

9. In general, it sanctions all forms of competition except for the use of violence (or the threat of violence), theft, or fraud.

11. If consumer demand for beef fell, the profitability of cattle herding would fall as well. Many cattle farmers would let their cattle herds dwindle and would quit keeping cattle altogether. The result would be a smaller population of cattle, not a larger one. Because cattle are privately owned, an increase in their value in human consumption results in more cattle being kept, whereas a decrease would result in fewer cattle. To "save the cows," you should eat more beef!

12. Those who get tickets at the lower price gain, whereas those who are prevented from offering a higher price to ticket holders may not get a ticket even though both the prospective buyer and some ticket holders would have gained from the exchange at the higher price. Ticket holders may simply break the law or may sell at the regulated

price only to buyers willing to provide them with other favors. Price controls, if they are effective, always reduce the gains from trade.

17. The opportunity cost of those individuals will rise, and they will likely consume less leisure.

CHAPTER 3: SUPPLY, DEMAND, AND THE MARKET PROCESS

1. Choices (a) and (b) would increase the demand for beef; (c) and (d) would affect primarily the supply of beef, rather than the demand; (e) leads to a change in quantity demanded, not a change in demand.

4. Prices reflect marginal value, not total value. The marginal value of a good is the maximum amount a consumer would be willing to pay for a specific unit. The height of the demand curve reflects the value that consumers place on each unit. The total value is the total benefit consumers derive from all units consumed. The area under the demand curve for the number of units consumed reflects the total value. Water provides an example of a good with high total value but low marginal value. With regard to the last question, are there more nurses or professional wrestlers?

8. Neither markets nor the political process leaves the determination of winners and losers to chance. Under market organization, business winners and losers are determined by the decentralized choices of millions of consumers who use their dollar votes to reward firms that provide preferred goods at a low cost and penalize others who fail to do so. Under political decision-making, the winners and losers are determined by political officials who use taxes, subsidies, regulations, and mandates to favor some businesses and penalize others.

10. **a.** Profitable production increases the value of resources owned by people and leads to mutual gain for resource suppliers, consumers, and entrepreneurs. **b.** Losses reduce the value of resources, which reduces the well-being of at least some people. There is no conflict.

12. The supply curve is constructed under the assumption that other things are held constant. A reduction in the supply of oranges such as would occur under adverse weather conditions would lead to both a higher price and smaller total quantity supplied. This is perfectly consistent with economic theory.

14. Questions for thought: What happened to the cost of producing calculators during the period? How would this affect the supply curve and price of the calculators?

16. Business firms do have a strong incentive to serve the interest of consumers, but this is not what motivates them. Instead, they are motivated by self-interest and the pursuit of income, but they must provide consumers with a quality product if they are going to be successful. Good intentions are not required for people to engage in actions that are helpful to others.

CHAPTER 4: SUPPLY AND DEMAND: APPLICATIONS AND EXTENSIONS

1. An increase in demand for housing will also increase the demand for the resources required for its production, including the services of carpenters, plumbers, and electricians. This will lead to higher wages and an increase in employment for people in these groups.

4. Agreement of both buyer and seller is required for an exchange. Price ceilings push prices below equilibrium and thereby reduce the quantity sellers are willing to offer. Price floors push prices above equilibrium and thereby reduce the quantity consumers wish to buy. Both decrease the actual quantity traded in the market.

6. **a.** Decreases; **b.** Increases; **c.** Decreases; **d.** Increases

11. The deadweight loss is the loss of the potential gains of buyers and sellers emanating from trades that are squeezed out by the tax. It is an excess burden because even though the exchanges that are squeezed out by the tax impose a cost on buyers and sellers, they do not generate tax revenue (because the trades do not take place).

12. The employment level of low-skilled workers with large families would decline. Some would attempt to conceal the presence of their large family in order to get a job.

14. No. As the tax rate approaches the revenue maximum point, the higher rates substantially reduce the number of trades that take place. This is why the higher rates do not raise much additional revenue. As rates increase toward the revenue maximum point, the lost gains from trade are large and the additions to revenue are small. Thus, rates in this range are highly inefficient.

CHAPTER 5: DIFFICULT CASES FOR THE MARKET, AND THE ROLE OF GOVERNMENT

1. When payment is not demanded for services, potential customers have a strong incentive to attempt a "free ride." However, when the number of nonpaying customers becomes such that the sales revenues of sellers are diminished (and in some cases eliminated), the sellers' incentive to supply the good is thereby reduced (or eliminated).

4. The antimissile system is a public good for the residents of Washington, D.C. Strictly speaking, none of the other items is a public good because each could be provided to some consumers (paying customers, for example) without being provided to others.

9. By reducing output below the efficient level, sellers of toasters would no longer produce or exchange some units of the good, despite the fact that the consumers value the marginal units more than it costs to produce them.

11. A public good reflects the characteristics of the good, not the sector in which it is provided. Elementary education is not a public good because it is relatively easy to exclude nonpaying customers and establish a one-to-one link between payment for and receipt of the good.

14. A government intervention would be efficient if the benefits from the intervention exceeded the cost of the intervention. All opportunity costs (such as tax money required, resources utilized, and deadweight losses) would need to be considered in the comparison. A government intervention would be considered inefficient if the costs exceeded the benefits.

CHAPTER 6: THE ECONOMICS OF COLLECTIVE DECISION-MAKING

2. Corporate officers, although they surely care about the next few months and the profits during that time, also care about the value of the firm and its stock price. If the stock price rises sufficiently in the next few months—as it will if investors believe that current investments in future-oriented projects (planting new trees, for example) are sound—then the officers will find their jobs secure even if current profits do not look good. Rights to the profits from those (future) trees are salable now in the form of the corporation's stock. There is no such mechanism to make the distant fruits of today's investments available to the political entrepreneurs who might otherwise fight for the future-oriented project. Only if the project appeals to today's voters, and only if they are willing to pay today for tomorrow's benefits, will the program be a political success. In any case, the wealth of the political official is not directly enhanced by his or her successful fight for the project.

4. The problem is not so much that the "wrong guys" won the last election as it is the incentive structure confronted by political decision makers. Even if the "right people" were elected, they would be unlikely to improve the efficiency of government, at least not very much, given the strong incentive to support special interest and shortsighted policies and the weak incentives for operational efficiency when decisions are made by the political process.

6. True. Because each individual computer customer both decides the issue (what computer, if any, will be purchased) and bears the consequences of a mistaken choice, each has a strong incentive to acquire information needed to make a wise choice. In

contrast, each voter recognizes that one vote, even if mistaken, will not decide the congressional election. Thus, a voter has little incentive to search for information to make a better-informed choice.

8. It is difficult for the voter to know what a candidate will do once elected, and the rationally ignorant voter is usually unwilling to spend the time and effort required to understand issues because the probability that any single vote will decide the issue is exceedingly small. Special-interest voters, in contrast, will know which candidate has promised them the most on their issue. Also, the candidate who is both competent and prepared to ignore special interests will have a hard time getting these facts to voters without financial support from special-interest groups. Each voter has an incentive to be a "free rider" on the "good government" issue. Interestingly, controlling government on behalf of society as a whole is a public good. As in the case of other public goods, there is a tendency for too little of it to be supplied.

10. No. The government is merely an alternative form of organization. Government organization does not permit us to escape either scarcity or competition. It merely affects the nature of the competition. Political competition (for example, voting, lobbying, political contributions, and politically determined budgets) replaces market competition. Neither is there any reason to believe that government organization modifies the importance of personal self-interest.

12. When the welfare of a special-interest group conflicts with that of a widely dispersed, unorganized majority, the legislative political process can reasonably be expected to work to the benefit of the special interest.

15. The presence of the sugar price supports and highly restrictive import quotas reflect the special-interest nature of the issue. Even though there are far more sugar consumers than growers, politicians apparently gain more by supporting the sugar growers and soliciting their political contributions than by representing the interests of consumers. Government action in this area has almost certainly reduced the income levels and living standards of Americans.

CHAPTER 7: CONSUMER CHOICE AND ELASTICITY

1. Revenue will rise (fall) if students who enroll pay more (less) extra revenue than is lost due to lower enrollment. Revenue will remain the same if those who enroll pay just enough more to offset the loss from reduced enrollment. A price elasticity of –1.2 implies that raising tuition rates would reduce tuition revenue.

2. If your opportunity cost of time is more than $10, it will make sense to take the plane. Thus, Mary will take the plane and Michele the bus.

3. It is likely that the income effect of cigarette price changes is much larger for low-income smokers than for high-income smokers, perhaps because expenditures on cigarettes are a larger proportion of the household budget for those with lower incomes. Thus, the income effect will be larger for this group.

6. Both income and time constrain our ability to consume. Because, in a wealthier society, time becomes more binding and income less binding, time-saving actions will be more common in a wealthier society. As we engage in time-saving actions (fast food, automatic appliances, air travel, and so on) in order to shift the time restraint outward, our lives become more hectic.

9. All three statements are true.

10. The answer to the first question is "No." Even for things we like, we will experience diminishing returns. Eventually, the cost of additional units of pizza will exceed their benefits. And, in answer to the second question, perfection in any activity is generally not worth the cost. For example, reading every page of this text three, four, or five times may improve your grade, but it may not be worth it. One function of a text is to structure the material (highlighted points, layout of graphs, and so on) so that the reader will be able to learn quickly (at a lower cost).

11. Carole

12. **a.** –1.59; elastic **b.** –1.54; elastic

CHAPTER 8: COSTS AND THE SUPPLY OF GOODS

2. **a.** The amount paid for the course is a sunk cost. It is not directly relevant to whether one should attend the lectures. **b.** There is an opportunity cost of one's house even if it is paid for. **c.** The decline in the price of the stock is a sunk cost and therefore it is not directly relevant to whether or not to sell at this time. **d.** There is an opportunity cost of public education even if it is provided free to the consumer.

5. True. If it could produce the output at a lower cost, its profit would be greater.

7. At low output, the firm's plant (a fixed cost) is underutilized, implying a high average cost. As output rises toward the designed output level, average cost falls, but then rises as the designed or optimal output for that size plant is surpassed and diminishing returns set in.

11. Because owners receive profits, clearly profit maximization is in their interest. Managers, if they are not owners, have no property right to profit and therefore no direct interest in profit maximization. Because a solid record of profitability tends to increase the market value (salary) of corporate managers, they do have an indirect incentive to pursue profits. However, corporate managers may also be interested in gaining power, having nice offices, hiring friends, expanding sales, and other activities, which may conflict with profitability. Thus, owners need to provide incentives for managers to seek profits and to monitor the results.

12. **a.** The interest payments; **b.** The interest income forgone. The tax structure encourages debt rather than equity financing because the firm's tax liability is inversely related to its debt/equity ratio.

14. Check list. Did your marginal cost curve cross the *ATC* and *AVC* curves at their low points? Does the vertical distance between the *ATC* and *AVC* curves get smaller and smaller as output increases? If not, redraw the three curves correctly. See Exhibit 6b.

17. $2,500: the $2,000 decline in market value during the year plus $500 of potential interest on funds that could be obtained if the machine were sold new. Costs associated with the decline in the value of the machine last year are sunk costs.

18. Because they believe they will be able to restructure the firm and provide better management so that the firm will have positive net earnings in the future. If the firm is purchased at a low enough price, this will allow the new owners to cover the opportunity cost of their investment and still earn an economic profit. Alternatively, they may expect to sell off the firm's assets, receiving more net revenue than the cost of purchasing the firm.

CHAPTER 9: PRICE TAKERS AND THE COMPETITIVE PROCESS

1. In a highly competitive industry such as agriculture, lower resource prices might improve the rate of profit in the short run, but in the long run, competition will drive prices down until economic profit is eliminated. Thus, lower resource prices will do little to improve the long-run profitability in such industries.

2. The market price will decline because the profits will attract new firms (and capital investment) into the market and supply will increase, driving down the price until the profits are eliminated.

5. **a.** Increase; **b.** Increase; **c.** Increase: firms will earn economic profit; **d.** Rise (compared with its initial level) if coffee is an increasing-cost industry, but return to initial price if it is a constant-cost industry; **e.** Increase even more than it did in the short run; **f.** Economic profit will return to zero.

6. **a.** Decline; **b.** Increase; **c.** Decline; **d.** Decline

9. Competition virtually forces firms to operate efficiently and produce goods and services that consumers value highly relative to cost. Firms that fail to do so will find it difficult to compete and eventually losses will drive them from the market.

11. **a.** The reduction in supply led to higher prices. **b.** Because demand is inelastic, the total revenue from sales increased. **c.** Overall, the profitability of farming increased,

although some of the producers that were hardest hit by the drought experienced losses because of their sharp reduction in output.

15. **b.** Six or seven tons—$250 profit; **c.** seven or eight tons—$600 profit; **d.** five or six tons—$50 loss. Because the firm can cover its variable cost, it should stay in business if it believes that the low ($450) price is temporary.

CHAPTER 10: PRICE-SEARCHER MARKETS WITH LOW ENTRY BARRIERS

3. The amount of variety is determined by the willingness of consumers to pay for variety relative to the cost of providing it. If consumers value variety highly and the added costs of producing different styles, designs, and sizes is low, there will be a lot of variety. Alternatively, if consumers desire similar products, or if variation can be produced only at a high cost, little variety will be present. Apparently, consumers place a substantial value (relative to cost) on variety in napkins but not in toothpicks.

7. No. A firm that maximizes *total* revenue would expand output as long as marginal revenue is positive. When marginal costs are positive, the revenue-maximizing price would be lower (and the output greater) than the price that would maximize the firm's profits.

8. In any of these cases, the answer is competition. To survive, a given type and size of firm must be able to produce at a low cost. Those firms with high per-unit cost will be driven from the market.

10. Building the new resort is more risky (and less attractive) because if the market analysis is incorrect, and demand is insufficient, it probably will be difficult to find other uses for the newly built resort. If the airline proves unprofitable, however, the capital (airplanes) should be extremely mobile. However, the resort would have one offsetting advantage: If demand were stronger than expected, and profits larger, it would take competitors longer to enter the market (build a new resort), and they would be more reluctant to make the more permanent investment.

12. In a competitive setting, only the big firms will survive if economies of scale are important. When economies of scale are unimportant, small firms will be able to compete effectively.

14. Competition provides the answer. If McDonald's fails to provide an attractively priced, tasty sandwich with a smile, people will turn to Burger King, Wendy's, Dairy Queen, and other rivals. If Walmart does not provide convenience and value, people will turn to Kmart, Target, and other retailers. Similarly, as recent experience has shown, even a firm as large as General Motors will lose customers to Ford, Honda, Toyota, Chrysler, Volkswagen, and other automobile manufacturers if it fails to please the customer as much as rival suppliers do.

17. **a.** Total revenue: $0; $8,000; $14,000; $18,000; $20,000; $20,000; Total cost: $0; $5,000; $10,000; $15,000; $20,000; $25,000; Economic profit: $0; $3,000; $4,000; $3,000; $0; $5,000 (loss).

   b. Marginal revenue: $8,000; $6,000; $4,000; $2,000; $0; Marginal cost: $5,000; $5,000; $5,000; $5,000; $5,000.

   c. Profit-maximizing price: $7,000.

   d. Rod will sell two boats at the profit-maximizing price of $7,000.

   e. Rod's economic profits will be $4,000 per week. Sales volume will be 2.

   f. Yes, boats 1 and 2 are the only boats for which marginal revenue is higher than marginal cost.

   g. Because of the existence of economic profit, more boat dealers will open up in the area. This will result in more competition and lower prices. The entry will continue until boat dealers' economic profits fall to zero.

   h. When demand is elastic, lowering price increases total revenue; thus, Rod's demand is elastic between the prices of $9,000 and $5,000. When demand is unitary elastic, lowering price leaves revenue unchanged; thus, Rod's demand is unitary elastic between the prices of $5,000 and $4,000. One could also assume that Rod's demand would eventually become inelastic below a price of $4,000 because the elasticity of demand keeps falling as one moves down along a demand curve. When this happens, Rod's total revenue will begin to fall as he continues to lower price. For example, at a price of $3,000, Rod may sell six boats per week, resulting in only $18,000 in revenue, which is less than the revenue Rod receives at a price of $4,000.

CHAPTER 11: PRICE-SEARCHER MARKETS WITH HIGH ENTRY BARRIERS

1. The statement is true. Profits cannot exist in the long run without barriers to entry because without barriers new entrants seeking the profits would increase supply, drive down price, and eliminate the profits. But barriers to entry are no guarantee of profits. Sufficient demand is also a necessary condition.
3. No; No; No.
8. Because use of product variation and quality improvements to obtain a larger share of the market will be more difficult to monitor and control than a simple price reduction.
11. Reductions in the cost of transportation generally increase competition because they force firms to compete with distant rivals and permit consumers to choose among a wider range of suppliers. As a result, the U.S. economy today is generally more competitive, in the rivalry sense, than it was hundred years ago.
12. The stock price, when the uncle bought the stock, no doubt reflected the well-known profits. The previous owners of the stock surely would not have sold it at a price that failed to reflect its high expected rate of future profit. Thus, there is no reason to believe that the stock purchase will earn a high rate of return for the uncle.
13. **a.** $15, profit = $110,000; **b.** $10.

CHAPTER 12: THE SUPPLY OF AND DEMAND FOR PRODUCTIVE RESOURCES

3. **a.** Five; **b.** $350; **c.** Four. The firm will operate in the short run, but it will go out of business in the long run unless the market prices rise.
4. Yes. General increases in the productivity of the labor force will cause a general increase in wages. The higher general wage rates will increase the opportunity cost of barbering and cause the supply of barbers to decline. The reduction in the supply of barbers will place upward pressure on the wages of barbers, even if technological change and worker productivity have changed little in barbering.
6. The job opportunities outside of teaching are more attractive for people with math and science training than for those with English and history degrees. Therefore, the same salary that attracts a substantial number of English and history teachers will be insufficient to attract the required number of math and science teachers.
8. No. The dressmaker needs to employ more capital and less labor because the marginal dollar expenditures on the former are currently increasing output by a larger amount than the latter.
10. Other things being constant, a lengthy training requirement to perform in an occupation reduces supply and places upward pressure on the earnings level. However, resource prices, including those for labor services, are determined by both demand and supply. When demand is weak, earnings will be low, even though a considerable amount of education may be necessary to perform in the occupation. For example, the earnings of people with degrees in English literature and world history are generally low, even though most people in these fields have a great deal of education.
12. **a.** MP 14; 12; 11; 9; 7; 5; 4. TR 70; 130; 185; 230; 265; 290; 310. MRP 70; 60; 55; 45; 35; 25; 20. **b.** 4; c. Employment would decline to 3.

CHAPTER 13: EARNINGS, PRODUCTIVITY, AND THE JOB MARKET

2. U.S. workers are more productive. By investing in human capital, the laborers are somewhat responsible, but the superior tools and physical capital that are available to U.S. workers also contribute to their higher wages.

6. Although this statement, often made by politicians, sounds true, in fact, it is false. Output of goods and services valued by consumers, not jobs, is the key to economic progress and a high standard of living. Real income cannot be high unless real output is high. If job creation were the key to economic progress, it would be easy to create millions of jobs. For example, we could prohibit the use of farm machinery. Such a prohibition would create millions of jobs in agriculture. However, it would also reduce output and our standard of living.

8. The opportunity cost of leisure (nonwork) for higher wage workers is greater than it is for lower wage workers.

9. False. Several additional factors, including differences in preferences (which would influence time worked, the trade-off between money wage and working conditions, and evaluation of alternative jobs), differences in jobs, and imperfect labor mobility, would result in variations in earnings.

10. Scenarios (a), (b), (e), and (f) will generally increase hourly earnings; (c) and (d) will generally reduce hourly earnings.

11. Hourly wages will be highest in B because the higher wages will be necessary to compensate workers in B for the uncertainty and loss of income during layoffs. Annual earnings will be higher in A in order to compensate workers in A for the additional hours they will work during the year.

CHAPTER 14: INVESTMENT, THE CAPITAL MARKET, AND THE WEALTH OF NATIONS

1. All the changes would increase interest rates in the United States.

4. No. The average outstanding balance during the year is only about half of $1,000. Therefore, the $200 interest charge translates to almost a 40 percent annual rate of interest.

6. *Hints:* Which has been considered to be more risky—purchasing a bond or a stock? How does risk influence the expected rate of return?

8. 6 percent.

10. **a.** Mike; **b.** Yes, people who save a lot are able to get a higher interest rate on their savings as the result of people with a high rate of time preference; **c.** Yes, people who want to borrow money will be able to do so at a lower rate when there are more people (like Alicia) who want to save a lot.

11. They are helped. This question is a lot like prior questions involving Alicia and Mike. Potential gains from trade are present. If obstacles do not restrain trade, the low-income countries will be able to attract savings (from countries with a high saving rate) at a lower interest rate than would exist in the absence of trade. Similarly, people in the high-income countries will be able to earn a higher return than would otherwise be possible. Each can gain because of the existence of the other.

12. **a.** Approximately $1.277 million; **b.** Yes; **c.** The lottery earnings are less liquid. Because there is not a well-organized market transforming lottery earnings into present income, the transaction costs of finding a "buyer" (at a price equal to the present value of the earnings) for the lottery earnings "rights" may be higher than for the bond, if one wants to sell in the future.

14. No. The present value of the $500 annual additions to earnings during the next ten years is less than the cost of the schooling.

16. Consider the following when answering this question: Whose money is being invested by each of the two entities? If a private investment project goes bad, who is hurt? If a

private project is successful, who reaps the gain? Answer the same two questions for political officials.

CHAPTER 15: INCOME INEQUALITY AND POVERTY

2. Differences in family size, age of potential workers, nonmoney "income," taxes, and cost-of-living among areas reduce the effectiveness of annual money income as a measure of economic status. In general, high-income families are larger, are more likely to be headed by a prime-age worker, have less nonmoney income (including leisure), pay more taxes, and reside in higher-cost-of-living areas (particularly large cities). Thus, money income comparison between high- and low-income groups often overstates the economic status of the former relative to the latter.

4. If there were no intergenerational mobility, the diagonal numbers would all be 100 percent. If there were complete equality of opportunity and outcomes, the numbers in each column and row would be 20 percent.

6. No. The increase in marginal tax rates will reduce the incentive of the poor to earn income. Therefore, their income will rise by $1,000 minus the reduction in their personal earnings due to the disincentive effects of the higher marginal tax rates.

7. 67 percent

CHAPTER 16: GAINING FROM INTERNATIONAL TRADE

2. Availability of goods and services, not jobs, is the source of economic prosperity. When a good can be purchased cheaper abroad than it can be produced at home, a nation can expand the quantity of goods and services available for consumption by specializing in the production of those goods for which it is a low-cost producer and trading them for the cheap (relative to domestic costs) foreign goods. Trade restrictions limiting the ability of Americans to purchase low-cost goods from foreigners stifle this process and thereby reduce the living standard of Americans.

4. Statements (a) and (b) are not in conflict. Because trade restrictions are typically a special-interest issue, political entrepreneurs can often gain by supporting them even when they promote economic inefficiency.

6. True. The primary effect of trade restrictions is an increase in domestic scarcity. This has distributional consequences, but it is clear that, as a whole, a nation will be harmed by the increased domestic scarcity that accompanies the trade restraints.

8. **a.** No. Americans would be poorer if we used more of our resources to produce things for which we are a high-opportunity-cost producer and less of our resources to produce things for which we are a low-opportunity-cost producer. Employment might either increase or decrease, but the key point is that it is the value of goods produced, not employment, that generates income and provides for the wealth of a nation. The answer to (b) is the same as (a).

10. In thinking about this issue, consider the following points. Suppose that the Japanese were willing to give products such as automobiles, electronic goods, and clothing to us free of charge. Would we be worse off if we accepted the gifts? Should we try to keep the free goods out? What is the source of real income—jobs or goods and services? If the gifts make us better off, doesn't it follow that partial gifts would also make us better off?

12. Although trade reduces employment in import-competing industries, it expands employment in export industries. On balance, there is no reason to believe that trade either promotes or destroys jobs. The major effect of trade is to permit individuals, states, regions, and nations to generate a larger output by specializing in the things they do well and trading for those things that they would produce only at a high cost. A higher real income is the result.

14. The quota reduces the supply of sugar to the domestic market and drives up the domestic price of sugar. Domestic producers benefit from the higher prices at the expense of domestic consumers (see Exhibit 9). Studies indicate that the quota expanded the gross income of the 11,000 domestic sugar farmers by approximately $130,000 per farm in the mid-1980s, at the expense (in the form of higher prices of sugar and sugar products) of approximately $6 per year to the average domestic consumer. Because the program channels resources away from products for which the United States has a comparative advantage, it reduces the productive capacity of the United States. Both the special-interest nature of the issue and rent-seeking theory explain the political attractiveness of the program.

16. True. If country A imposes a tariff, other countries will sell less to A and therefore acquire less purchasing power in terms of A's currency. Thus, they will have to reduce their purchases of A's export goods.

SPECIAL TOPIC 1: GOVERNMENT SPENDING AND TAXATION

1. Taxes reduce economic efficiency because they eliminate some exchanges and thereby reduce the gains from these transactions. Because of (a) the deadweight losses accompanying the elimination of exchanges and (b) the cost of collecting taxes, the costs of additional tax revenue will be greater than the revenue transferred to the government. Studies indicate that it costs between $1.20 and $1.30 for each dollar of tax revenue raised by the government.

5. As we discussed in Chapter 6, the political process works better when there is a close relationship between who pays for and who benefits from government programs. An increase in the number of people who pay no income taxes is likely to weaken this relationship. Whereas those with low incomes pay payroll taxes, the revenues from this tax are earmarked for the finance of the Social Security and Medicare programs. Thus, expansions in government are financed primarily by the personal income tax. In the future, exemption of large numbers of people from this tax is likely to make it more difficult to control the growth of government. If you do not have to help pay for more government spending, why would you oppose it?

SPECIAL TOPIC 2: THE ECONOMICS OF SOCIAL SECURITY

2. The pay-as-you-go Social Security system is facing a crisis because the inflow of tax revenue is insufficient to cover the promised benefits. Although the Social Security Trust Fund has bonds, they are merely an IOU from the Treasury to the Social Security Administration. To redeem these bonds and provide additional funds to finance Social Security benefits, the federal government will have to raise taxes (or pay the interest on additional Treasury bonds it sells), or cut other expenditures, or both. Thus, the presence of the SSTF bonds does not do much to alleviate the crisis.

SPECIAL TOPIC 3: THE STOCK MARKET: ITS FUNCTION, PERFORMANCE, AND POTENTIAL AS AN INVESTMENT OPPORTUNITY

1. History shows that in the U.S. stock market, fairly high returns can be gained at a relatively low risk by people who hold a diverse portfolio of stocks in unrelated industries for a period of twenty years or more. An indexed equity mutual fund is an option that would allow a person to purchase a diverse portfolio while keeping commission costs low.

3. The expectation of high profits in the future drove up the price of the stock, despite the lack of a dividend payment in the first years of the firm. Investors are equally happy with high dividends or the equivalent in rising stock value due to the firm's retaining its profits for further investment.

5. Investors are buying such a stock for its rising value (price), which reflects expected future earnings and dividends.

SPECIAL TOPIC 4: GREAT DEBATES IN ECONOMICS: KEYNES VERSUS HAYEK

1. Keynes is arguing that it does not matter much how the government spends stimulus funds. According to the Keynesian view, the key consideration is to spend the funds so they will generate income for those undertaking the project, and as those funds are spent, a multiple expansion in income and aggregate demand will result.

SPECIAL TOPIC 5: THE CRISIS OF 2008: CAUSES AND LESSONS FOR THE FUTURE

3. The less equity the owner has in his or her house, the more likely he or she will default. This is particularly true in the United States because most home mortgages here are nonrecourse loans: The owner is not responsible for the debt beyond turning the property over to the lender in case of default. The lender has no legal claim on assets of the borrower beyond the asset that was mortgaged. Thus, when the value of a house falls below the outstanding loan, the borrower will often gain by simply abandoning the property. This is precisely what many have done in recent years.
5. The incentive to evaluate the borrower's creditworthiness carefully is reduced. If the mortgage originator had to keep the loan until it was repaid, there would be greater incentive for the lender to evaluate the creditworthiness of the borrower more diligently.

SPECIAL TOPIC 6: LESSONS FROM THE GREAT DEPRESSION

5. The statement reflects a failure to recognize the secondary effects of limiting imports. If we buy less from foreigners, they will have fewer dollars that are required for the purchase of our exports. Therefore, a reduction in imports will also reduce exports and there is no reason to expect any net increase in employment. Instead, trade restraints lead to less output and lower incomes.

SPECIAL TOPIC 7: THE ECONOMICS OF HEALTH CARE

2. Health insurance benefits are a component of the employee's compensation package. Unless the employer values the services of the employee by an amount greater than or equal to the total cost of the employee's compensation, the worker will not be hired. Thus, like other components of the compensation package, health insurance benefits are earned by employees.
4. Medicare and Medicaid increased both total health care spending and the share of that spending paid by a third party. Both of these factors increased the demand for and prices of medical services, thereby making them more expensive for people who do not qualify for these programs.
6. Personal choices exert a major impact on health care expenditures. Individuals who smoke, consume alcohol, and eat excessively; fail to exercise and control their weight; use recreational drugs; and engage in other risky behavior will have higher health care cost. Under systems in which all are charged the same premium, the incentive to adopt a healthy lifestyle is reduced. Persons who make choices that promote good health are forced to subsidize those who do not. This perverse incentive structure also pushes health care costs upward.
8. The incentive to purchase insurance when you are healthy will be reduced.

SPECIAL TOPIC 8: EDUCATION: PROBLEMS AND PERFORMANCE

2. The incentive is weak to keep costs low because the suppliers (public schools) don't face competition from rivals. Because consumers cannot take their funding and go elsewhere, they are in a weak position to discipline the district schools that are not doing a good job. Furthermore, a lower quality of service can often be used as an argument for more government funding. Economics indicates that an absence of competitive forces will lead to higher costs and lower quality of the product or service supplied. There is no reason to expect that education will be an exception.

SPECIAL TOPIC 9: EARNINGS DIFFERENCES BETWEEN MEN AND WOMEN

2. **a.** The average years of work experience of women relative to men would decline because many of the women entering the labor force would have little prior work experience.

   b. The average hours of work of women would also decline because many of the married women would be looking for part-time employment and hours that were complementary with their historic household responsibilities.

   c. The increased labor force participation of married women would cause the female/male earnings ratio to fall.

4. Not necessarily. Compared with married men, single men tend to be younger, have fewer dependents, be more likely to drop out of the labor force, and be less likely to receive earnings-enhancing assistance from another person. All these factors will reduce their earnings relative to married men.

SPECIAL TOPIC 10: DO LABOR UNIONS INCREASE THE WAGES OF WORKERS?

1. If the union is able to raise the wages of the farm workers: (a) The cost of Florida oranges will rise, causing supply to decline and price to rise in the long run; (b) profits of the Florida orange growers will decline in the short run, but in the long run they will return to the normal rate; (c) mechanization will be encouraged; and (d) the employment of fruit pickers will decline—particularly in the long run.

3. If only part of an industry is unionized, if the union pushes up the wages of the unionized firms, this will increase their cost and make it difficult for them to compete effectively with their nonunion rivals. Thus, the union will be unable to increase wages much without experiencing a substantial reduction in the employment of its members.

5. False. Competition constrains both employers and employees. Employers must compete with other employers for labor services. To gain the labor services of an employee, an employer must offer a compensation package superior to one that the employee can get elsewhere. If the employer does not offer a superior package, the employee will work for a rival employer or choose self-employment. Similarly, employees must compete with other employees. Therefore, their ability to demand whatever wage they would like is also restrained. Thus, competition prevents both the payment of low (below-market) wages by employers and the imposition of high (above-market) wages by employees.

6. Not necessarily. Adjustment must be made for differences in (a) the productivity characteristics of the union and nonunion workers and (b) the types of jobs they occupy (for example, work environment, job security, likelihood of layoff, and so on). Adjustment for these factors may either increase or reduce the $1.50 differential.

7. Remember, union members compete with other workers, including less-skilled workers. An increase in the minimum wage makes unskilled, low-wage workers more expensive. A higher minimum wage increases the demand for high-skilled employees who are good substitutes for the low-skilled workers. Union members are overrepresented among the high-skilled group helped by an increase in the minimum wage. Therefore, although union leaders will generally pitch their support for a higher minimum wage in terms of a desire that all workers be paid a "decent wage," the effect of the legislation on union members suggests that self-interest rather than altruism underlies their support for the legislation.

SPECIAL TOPIC 11: THE QUESTION OF RESOURCE EXHAUSTION

2. When demand expands in resource markets, prices send signals and provide the incentives that will reduce future demand relative to supply. These forces will avoid lasting shortages.

5. If any resource, including water, is bought and sold, then market signals will automatically be provided to signal the desires of users to have, and the abilities of suppliers to supply, more. A market provides productive incentive to all concerned. Users conserve more when a market price rises, suppliers provide more, and there is greater incentive to develop and use substitutes for the higher priced resource. If markets are not used to allocate a resource, these benefits will be lost.

SPECIAL TOPIC 12: DIFFICULT ENVIRONMENTAL CASES AND THE ROLE OF GOVERNMENT

1. The ITQ would allow fishers to fish at their own speed without fear of losing their quota to others.

3. The cost of stopping the buildup would be very large. Avoiding the buildup would be very costly. That large opportunity cost could accomplish instead much else that would help future generations. The forecasted risks are only speculatively the result of the buildup and would occur mostly far in the future. And a warmer world has advantages as well as disadvantages.

4. In a market with strong property rights in place, a polluter would have to be concerned about harming others and being sued by them for damages. Without strong property rights in place, regulation might help. Or it might not. In any case, regulators need information available only in a market to judge how tightly to regulate if the regulator is seeking efficiency.

Glossary

A

Absolute advantage A situation in which a nation, as the result of its previous experience and/or natural endowments, can produce more of a good (with the same amount of resources) than another nation.

Accounting profits The sales revenues minus the expenses of a firm over a designated time period, usually one year. Accounting profits typically make allowances for changes in the firm's inventories and depreciation of its assets. No allowance is made, however, for the opportunity cost of the equity capital of the firm's owners, or other implicit costs.

Activists Economists who believe that discretionary changes in monetary and fiscal policy can reduce the degree of instability in output and employment.

Adaptive-expectations hypothesis The hypothesis that economic decision-makers base their future expectations on actual outcomes observed during recent periods. For example, according to this view, the rate of inflation actually experienced during the past two or three years would be the major determinant of the rate of inflation expected for the next year.

Adjustable rate mortgage (ARM) A home loan in which the interest rate, and thus the monthly payment, is tied to a short-term rate like the one-year Treasury bill rate. Typically, the mortgage interest rate will be two or three percentage points above the related short-term rate. It will be reset at various time intervals (e.g., annually), and thus the interest rate and monthly payment will vary over the life of the loan.

Administrative lag The time period after the need for a policy change is recognized but before the policy is actually implemented.

Aggregate demand curve A downward-sloping curve showing the relationship between the price level and the quantity of domestically produced goods and services all households, business firms, governments, and foreigners (net exports) are willing to purchase.

Aggregate supply curve The curve showing the relationship between a nation's price level and the quantity of goods supplied by its producers. In the short run, it is an upward-sloping curve, but in the long run the aggregate supply curve is vertical.

Alt-A loans Loans extended with little documentation and/or verification of the borrowers' income, employment, and other indicators of their ability to repay. Because of this poor documentation, these loans are risky.

Anticipated change A change that is foreseen by decision-makers in time for them to make adjustments.

Anticipated inflation An increase in the general level of prices that was expected by most decision-makers.

Appreciation An increase in the value of the domestic currency relative to foreign currencies. An appreciation increases the purchasing power of the currency over foreign goods.

Automatic stabilizers Built-in features that tend automatically to promote a budget deficit during a recession and a budget surplus during an inflationary boom, even without a change in policy.

Automation A production technique that reduces the amount of labor required to produce a good or service. It is beneficial to adopt the new labor-saving technology only if it reduces the cost of production.

Autonomous expenditures Expenditures that do not vary with the level of income. They are determined by factors such as business expectations and economic policy.

Average fixed cost Total fixed cost divided by the number of units produced. It always declines as output increases.

Average product The total product (output) divided by the number of units of the variable input required to produce that output level.

Average tax rate (ATR) Tax liability divided by taxable income. It is the percentage of income paid in taxes.

Average total cost Total cost divided by the number of units produced. It is sometimes called per-unit cost.

Average variable cost The total variable cost divided by the number of units produced.

B

Balance of merchandise trade The difference between the value of merchandise exports and the value of merchandise imports for a nation. It is also called simply the *balance of trade* or *net exports*. The balance of merchandise trade is only one component of a nation's total balance of payments and its current account.

Balance of payments A summary of all economic transactions between a country and all other countries for a specific time period, usually a year. The balance-of-payments account reflects all payments and liabilities to foreigners (debits) and all payments and obligations received from foreigners (credits).

Balance on current account The import–export balance of goods and services, plus net investment income earned abroad, plus net private and government transfers. If the value of the nation's export-type items exceeds (is less than) the value of the nation's import-type items plus net unilateral transfers to foreigners, a current-account surplus (deficit) is present.

Balance on goods and services The exports of goods (merchandise) and services of a nation minus its imports of goods and services.

Balanced budget A situation in which current government revenue from taxes, fees, and other sources is just equal to current government expenditures.

Bank reserves Vault cash plus deposits of banks with Federal Reserve banks.

Barriers to entry Obstacles that limit the freedom of potential rivals to enter and compete in an industry or market.

Basis points One one-hundredth of a percentage point. Thus, 100 basis points are equivalent to one percentage point.

Black market A market that operates outside the legal system in which either illegal goods are sold or legal goods are sold at illegal prices or terms.

Budget constraint   The constraint that separates the bundles of goods that the consumer can purchase from those that cannot be purchased, given a limited income and the prices of the products.

Budget deficit   A situation in which total government spending exceeds total government revenue during a specific time period, usually one year.

Budget surplus   A situation in which total government spending is less than total government revenue during a time period, usually a year.

Business cycle   Fluctuations in the general level of economic activity as measured by variables such as the rate of unemployment and changes in real GDP.

C

Capital   Human-made resources (such as tools, equipment, and structures) used to produce other goods and services. They enhance our ability to produce in the future.

Capital account   The record of transactions with foreigners that involve either (1) the exchange of ownership rights to real or financial assets or (2) the extension of loans.

Capitalism   An economic system in which productive resources are owned privately and goods and resources are allocated through market prices.

Cartel   An organization of sellers designed to coordinate supply and price decisions so that the joint profits of the members will be maximized. A cartel will seek to create a monopoly in the market for its product.

Central bank   An institution that regulates the banking system and controls the supply of a country's money.

Ceteris paribus   A Latin term meaning "other things constant" that is used when the effect of one change is being described, recognizing that if other things changed, they also could affect the result. Economists often describe the effects of one change, knowing that in the real world, other things might change and also exert an effect.

Choice   The act of selecting among alternatives.

Civilian labor force   The number of people 16 of age and over who are either employed or unemployed. To be classified as unemployed, a person must be looking for a job.

Collective decision-making   The method of organization that relies on public-sector decision making (voting, political bargaining, lobbying, and so on) to resolve basic economic questions.

Collusion   Agreement among firms to avoid various competitive practices, particularly price reductions. It may involve either formal agreements or merely tacit recognition that competitive practices will be self-defeating in the long run. Tacit collusion is difficult to detect. In the United States, antitrust laws prohibit collusion and conspiracies to restrain trade.

Commercial banks   Financial institutions that offer a wide range of services (for example, checking accounts, savings accounts, and loans) to their customers. Commercial banks are owned by stockholders and seek to operate at a profit.

Comparative advantage   The ability to produce a good at a lower opportunity cost than others can produce it. Relative costs determine comparative advantage.

Compensating wage differentials   Wage differences that compensate workers for risk, unpleasant working conditions, and other undesirable nonpecuniary aspects of a job.

Competition as a dynamic process   Rivalry or competitiveness between or among parties (for example, producers or input suppliers) to deliver a better deal to buyers in terms of quality, price, and product information.

Competitive price-searcher market   A market in which the firms have a downward-sloping demand curve, and entry into and exit from the market are relatively easy.

Complements   Products that are usually consumed jointly (for example, bread and butter, hot dogs and hot dog buns). A decrease in the price of one will cause an increase in demand for the other.

Constant returns to scale   Unit costs that are constant as the scale of the firm is altered. Neither economics nor diseconomies of scale are present.

Constant-cost industry   An industry for which factor prices and costs of production remain constant as market output is expanded. The long-run market supply curve is therefore horizontal in these industries.

Consumer price index (CPI)   An indicator of the general level of prices. It attempts to compare the cost of purchasing the market basket bought by a typical consumer during a specific period with the cost of purchasing the same market basket during an earlier period.

Consumer sentiment index   A measure of the optimism of consumers based on their responses to a set of questions about their current and expected future personal economic situation. Conducted by the University of Michigan, it is based on a representative sample of U.S. households.

Consumer surplus   The difference between the maximum price consumers are willing to pay and the price they actually pay. It is the net gain derived by the buyers of the good.

Consumption function   The relationship between disposable income and consumption. When disposable income increases, current consumption expenditures rise, but by less than the increase in income.

Consumption opportunity constraint   The constraint that separates consumption bundles that are attainable from those that are unattainable. In a money–income economy, this is usually a budget constraint.

Contestable market   A market in which the costs of entry and exit are low, so a firm risks little by entering. Efficient production and zero economic profits should prevail in a contestable market.

Corporation   A business firm owned by shareholders who possess ownership rights to the firm's profits, but whose liability is limited to the amount of their investment in the firm.

Countercyclical policy   A policy that tends to move the economy in an opposite direction from the forces of the business cycle. Such a policy would stimulate demand during the contraction phase of the business cycle and restrain demand during the expansion phase.

Creative destruction   The replacement of old products and production methods by innovative new ones that consumers judge to be superior. The process generates economic growth and higher living standards.

Credit   Funds acquired by borrowing.

Credit unions   Financial cooperative organizations of individuals with a common affiliation (such as an employer or a labor union). They accept deposits, including checkable deposits, pay interest (or dividends) on them out of earnings, and lend funds primarily to members.

Crowding-out effect   A reduction in private spending as a result of higher interest rates generated by budget deficits that are financed by borrowing in the private loanable funds market.

Currency   Medium of exchange made of metal or paper.

Currency board   An entity that (1) issues a currency with a fixed designated value relative to a widely accepted currency (for example, the U.S. dollar), (2) promises to continue to redeem the issued currency at the fixed rate, and (3) maintains bonds and other liquid assets denominated in the other currency that provide 100 percent backing for all currency issued.

Current account   The record of all transactions with foreign nations that involve the exchange of merchandise goods and services, current income derived from investments, and unilateral gifts.

Cyclical unemployment   Unemployment due to recessionary business conditions and inadequate labor demand.

D

Deadweight loss   The loss of gains from trade to buyers and sellers that occurs when a tax is imposed. The deadweight loss imposes a burden on both buyers and sellers over and above the actual payment of the tax.

Decreasing-cost industry   An industry for which costs of production decline as the industry expands. The market supply is therefore inversely related to price. Such industries are atypical.

Demand deposits   Non–interest-earning checking deposits that can be either withdrawn or made payable on demand to a third party. Like currency, these deposits are widely used as a means of payment.

Demand for money   A curve that indicates the relationship between the interest rate and the quantity of money people want to hold. Because higher interest rates increase the opportunity cost of holding money, the quantity of money demanded will be inversely related to the interest rate.

Democracy   A form of political organization in which adult citizens are free to participate in the political process (vote, lobby, and choose among candidates), elections are free and open, and majority voting, either directly or by elected representatives, decides outcomes.

Deposit expansion multiplier   The multiple by which an increase in reserves will increase the money supply. It is inversely related to the required reserve ratio.

Depository institutions   Businesses that accept checking and savings deposits and use a portion of them to extend loans and make investments. Banks, savings and loan associations, and credit unions are examples.

Depreciation (of assets)   The estimated amount of physical capital (for example, machines and buildings) that is worn out or used up producing goods during a period.

Depreciation (of currency)   A reduction in the value of a currency relative to foreign currencies. A depreciation reduces the purchasing power of the currency over foreign goods.

Depression   A prolonged and very severe recession.

Derived demand   The demand for a resource; it stems from the demand for the final good the resource helps produce.

Differentiated products   Products distinguished from similar products by characteristics like quality, design, location, and method of promotion.

Discount rate   The interest rate the Federal Reserve charges banking institutions for short-term loans.

Discounting   The procedure used to calculate the present value of future income, which is inversely related to both the interest rate and the amount of time that passes before the funds are received.

Discretionary fiscal policy   A change, in laws or appropriation levels, that alters government revenues and/or expenditures.

Division of labor   A method that breaks down the production of a product into a series of specific tasks, each performed by a different worker.

Dumping   Selling a good in a foreign country at a lower price than it's sold for in the domestic market.

E

Earmarking   The direction of budgeted funds to specific projects, programs, and locations. The technique is costly but provides major benefits to business firms and other concentrated constituent groups, and to the districts where the spending takes place. The benefits are often targeted to those willing to make substantial campaign contributions.

Earned Income Tax Credit   A provision of the tax code that provides a credit or rebate to people with low earnings (income from work activities). The credit is eventually phased out if the recipient's earnings increase.

Economic efficiency   A situation that occurs when (1) all activities generating more benefit than cost are undertaken, and (2) no activities are undertaken for which the cost exceeds the benefit.

Economic freedom   Method of organizing economic activity characterized by (1) personal choice, (2) voluntary exchange coordinated by markets, (3) freedom to enter and compete in markets, and (4) protection of people and their property from aggression by others.

Economic profit   The difference between the firm's total revenues and its total costs, including both the explicit and implicit cost components.

Economic theory   A set of definitions, postulates, and principles assembled in a manner that makes clear the "cause-and-effect" relationships.

Economies of sale   Reductions in the firm's per-unit costs associated with the use of large plants to produce a large volume of output.

Economizing behavior   Choosing the option that offers the greatest benefit at the least possible cost.

Employment discrimination   Unequal treatment of people on the basis of their race, gender, or religion, restricting their employment and earnings opportunities compared with others of similar productivity. Employment discrimination may stem from the prejudices of employers, customers, fellow employees, or all three.

Employment/population ratio   The number of people 16 years of age and over employed as civilians divided by the total civilian population 16 years of age and over. The ratio is expressed as a percentage.

Entrepreneur   A person who introduces new products or improved technologies and decides which projects to undertake. A successful entrepreneur's actions will increase the value of resources and expand the size of the economic pie.

Equation of exchange $MV = PY$, where M is the money supply, V is the velocity of money, P is the price level, and Y is the output of goods and services produced in an economy.

Equilibrium   A state in which the conflicting forces of supply and demand are in balance. When a market is in equilibrium, the decisions of consumers and producers are brought into harmony with one another, and the quantity supplied will equal the quantity demanded.

Equity mutual fund   A corporation that pools the funds of investors, including small investors, and uses them to purchase a bundle of stocks.

Excess burden of taxation   Another term for deadweight loss. It reflects losses that occur when beneficial activities are forgone because they are taxed.

Excess reserves   Actual reserves that exceed the legal requirement.

Exchange rate   The price of one unit of foreign currency in terms of the domestic currency. For example, if it takes \$1.50 to purchase an English pound, the dollar–pound exchange rate is 1.50.

Expansionary fiscal policy   An increase in government expenditures and/or a reduction in tax rates, such that the expected size of the budget deficit expands.

Expansionary monetary policy   A shift in monetary policy designed to stimulate aggregate demand. Injection of additional bank reserves, lower short-term interest rates, and acceleration in the growth rate of the money supply are indicators of a more expansionary monetary policy.

Expenditure multiplier   The ratio of the change in equilibrium output to the independent change in investment, consumption, or government spending that brings about the change. Numerically, the multiplier is equal to 1 *divided by* $(1 - MPC)$ when the price level is constant.

Explicit costs   Payments by a firm to purchase the services of productive resources.

Exports   Goods and services produced domestically but sold to foreigners.

External benefits   Spillover effects that generate benefits for nonconsenting third parties.

External costs   Spillover effects that reduce the well-being of nonconsenting third parties.

Externalities   Spillover effects of an activity that influence the well-being of nonconsenting third parties.

External debt   The portion of the national debt owed to foreign investors.

F

Fallacy of composition   Erroneous view that what is true for the individual (or the part) will also be true for the group (or the whole).

Federal Deposit Insurance Corporation (FDIC)   A federally chartered corporation that insures the deposits held by commercial banks, savings and loans, and credit unions.

Federal funds market   A loanable funds market in which banks seeking additional reserves borrow short-term funds (generally for seven days or less) from banks with excess reserves. The interest rate in this market is called the federal funds rate.

Federal Open Market Committee (FOMC)   A committee of the Federal Reserve System that establishes Fed policy with regard to the buying and selling of government securities—the primary mechanism used to control the money supply. It is composed of the seven members of the Board of Governors and the twelve district bank presidents of the Fed.

Federal Reserve System   The central bank of the United States; it carries out banking regulatory policies and is responsible for the conduct of monetary policy.

Fiat money   Money that has neither intrinsic value nor the backing of a commodity with intrinsic value; paper currency is an example.

FICO score   A mathematically determined score measuring a borrower's likely ability to repay a loan, similar to a credit score. The FICO score takes into account a borrower's payment history, current level of indebtedness, types of credit used and length of credit history, and new credit. A person's FICO score will range between 300 and 850. A score of 700 or more indicates that the borrower's credit standing is good, and therefore the risk of providing them with credit would be low. FICO is an acronym for the Fair Isaac Corporation, the creators of the FICO score.

Final market goods and services   Goods and services purchased by their ultimate user.

Fiscal policy   The use of government taxation and expenditure policies for the purpose of achieving macroeconomic goals.

Fixed exchange rate   An exchange rate that is set at a determined amount by government policy.

Flexible exchange rates   Exchange rates that are determined by the market forces of supply and demand. They are sometimes called floating exchange rates.

Foreclosure rate   The percentage of home mortgages on which the lender has started the process of taking ownership of the property because the borrower has failed to make the monthly payments.

Foreign exchange market   The market in which the currencies of different countries are bought and sold.

Fractional reserve banking   A system that permits banks to hold reserves of less than 100 percent against their deposits.

Franchise   A right or license granted to an individual to market a company's goods or services or use its brand name. The individual firms are independently owned but must meet certain conditions to continue to use the name.

Free rider   A person who receives the benefit of a good without paying for it. Because it is often virtually impossible to restrict the consumption of public goods to those who pay, these goods are subject to free-rider problems.

Frictional unemployment   Unemployment due to constant changes in the economy that prevent qualified unemployed workers from being immediately matched up with existing job openings. It results from imperfect information and search activities related to suitably matching employees with employers.

Fringe benefits   Benefits other than normal money wages that are supplied to employees in exchange for their labor services. Higher fringe benefits come at the expense of lower money wages.

Full employment   The level of employment that results from the efficient use of the labor force taking into account the normal (natural) rate of unemployment due to information costs, dynamic changes, and the structural conditions of the economy. For the United States, full employment is thought to exist when approximately 95 percent of the labor force is employed.

G

Game theory A tool used to analyze the strategic choices made by competitors in a conflict situation like the decisions made by firms in an oligopoly.

GDP deflator A price index that reveals the cost during the current period of purchasing the items included in GDP relative to the cost during a base year (currently 2005). Unlike the consumer price index (CPI), the GDP deflator also measures the prices of capital goods and other goods and services purchased by businesses and governments. Because of this, it is thought to be a more accurate measure of changes in the general level of prices than the CPI.

General Agreement on Tariffs and Trade (GATT) An organization formed after World War II to set the rules for the conduct of international trade and reduce trade barriers among nations.

Going out of business The sale of a firm's assets and its permanent exit from the market. By going out of business, a firm is able to avoid its fixed costs, which would continue during a shutdown.

Goods and services market A highly aggregated market encompassing the flow of all final-user goods and services. The market counts all items that enter into GDP. Thus, real output in this market is equal to real GDP.

Government failure A situation in which the structure of incentives is such that the political process, including democratic political decision-making, will encourage individuals to undertake actions that conflict with economic efficiency.

Gross domestic product (GDP) The market value of all final goods and services produced within a country during a specific period.

Gross national product (GNP) The total market value of all final goods and services produced by the citizens of a country. It is equal to GDP minus the net income of foreigners.

H

Human resources The abilities, skills, and health of human beings that contribute to the production of both current and future output. Investment in training and education can increase the supply of human resources.

Health savings accounts Special savings accounts that individuals and families can use for the payment of medical bills and the purchase of a catastrophic (high deductible) health insurance plan.

I

Impact lag The time period after a policy change is implemented but before the change begins to exert its primary effects.

Implicit costs The opportunity costs associated with a firm's use of resources that it owns. These costs do not involve a direct money payment. Examples include wage income and interest forgone by the owner of a firm who also provides labor services and equity capital to the firm.

Implicit marginal tax rate The amount of additional (marginal) earnings that must be paid explicitly in taxes or implicitly in the form of lower income supplements. The marginal tax rate establishes the fraction of an additional dollar earned that an individual is permitted to keep, so it is an important determinant of the incentive to work and earn.

Import quota A specific limit or maximum quantity (or value) of a good permitted to be imported into a country during a given period.

Imports Goods and services produced by foreigners but purchased by domestic consumers, businesses, and governments.

Income effect That part of an increase (decrease) in amount consumed that is the result of the consumer's real income being expanded (contracted) by a reduction (rise) in the price of a good.

Income elasticity The percentage change in the quantity of a product demanded divided by the percentage change in consumer income that caused the change in quantity demanded. It measures the responsiveness of the demand for a good to a consumer's change in income.

Income mobility Movement of individuals and families either up or down income distribution rankings when comparisons are made at two different points in time. When substantial income mobility is present, a person's current position in the rankings will not be a very good indicator of what his or her position will be a few years in the future.

Increasing-cost industry An industry for which costs of production rise as output is expanded. In these industries, even in the long run, higher market prices will be needed to induce firms to expand total output. As a result, the long-run market supply curve in these industries will slope upward to the right.

Index of leading indicators An index of economic variables that historically has tended to turn down prior to the beginning of a recession and turn up prior to the beginning of a business expansion.

Indexed equity mutual fund An equity mutual fund that holds a portfolio of stocks that matches their share (or weight) in a broad stock market index such as the S&P 500. The overhead of these funds is usually quite low because their expenses on stock trading and research are low.

Indifference curve A curve, convex from below, that separates the consumption bundles that are more preferred by an individual from those that are less preferred. The points on the curve represent combinations of goods that are equally preferred by the individual.

Indirect business taxes Taxes that increase a business firm's costs of production and, therefore, the prices charged to consumers. Examples are sales, excise, and property taxes.

Inferior good A good that has a negative income elasticity, so that, as consumer income rises, the demand for the good falls.

Inflation An increase in the general level of prices of goods and services. The purchasing power of the monetary unit, such as the dollar, declines when inflation is present.

Inflationary premium A component of the money interest rate that reflects compensation to the lender for the expected decrease, due to inflation, in the purchasing power of the principal and interest during the course of the loan. It is determined by the expected rate of future inflation.

Innovation The successful introduction and adoption of a new product or process; the economic application of inventions and marketing techniques.

Institutions   The legal, regulatory, and social constraints that affect the security of property rights and enforcement of contracts. They exert a major impact on transaction costs between parties, particularly when the trading partners do not know each other.

Intermediate goods   Goods purchased for resale or for use in producing another good or service.

International Monetary Fund (IMF)   An international banking organization, currently with more than 180 member nations, designed to oversee the operation of the international monetary system. Although it does not control the world supply of money, it does hold currency reserves for member nations and makes currency loans to national central banks.

Invention   The creation of a new product or process, often facilitated by the knowledge of engineering and science.

Inventory investment   Changes in the stock of unsold goods and raw materials held during a period.

Investment   The purchase, construction, or development of capital resources, including both nonhuman capital and human capital. Investments increase the supply of capital.

Investment bank   An institution that acts as an underwriter for securities issued by other corporations or lenders. Unlike traditional banks, investment banks do not accept deposits from, or provide loans to, individuals.

Investment in human capital   Expenditures on training, education, skill development, and health designed to increase human capital and people's productivity.

Invisible hand principle   The tendency of market prices to direct individuals pursuing their own interests to engage in activities promoting the economic well-being of society.

L

Labor force participation rate   The number of people in the civilian labor force 16 years of age or over who are either employed or actively seeking employment as a percentage of the total civilian population 16 years of age and over.

Labor union   A collective organization of employees who bargain as a unit with employers.

Laffer curve   A curve illustrating the relationship between the tax rate and tax revenues. Tax revenues will be low at both very high and very low tax rates. When tax rates are quite high, lowering them can increase tax revenue.

Law of comparative advantage   A principle that states that individuals, firms, regions, or nations can gain by specializing in the production of goods that they produce cheaply (at a low opportunity cost) and exchanging them for goods they cannot produce cheaply (at a high opportunity cost).

Law of demand   A principle that states there is an inverse relationship between the price of a good and the quantity of it buyers are willing to purchase. As the price of a good increases, consumers will wish to purchase less of it. As the price decreases, consumers will wish to purchase more of it.

Law of diminishing marginal utility   The basic economic principle that as the consumption of a product increases, the marginal utility derived from consuming more of it (per unit of time) will eventually decline.

Law of diminishing returns   The postulate that as more and more units of a variable resource are combined with a fixed amount of other resources, using additional units of the variable resource will eventually increase output only at a decreasing rate. Once diminishing returns are reached, it will take successively larger amounts of the variable factor to expand output by one unit.

Law of supply   A principle that states there is a direct relationship between the price of a good and the quantity of it producers are willing to supply. As the price of a good increases, producers will wish to supply more of it. As the price decreases, producers will wish to supply less.

Less-developed countries   Countries with low per capita incomes, low levels of education, widespread illiteracy, and widespread use of production methods that are largely obsolete in high-income countries. They are sometimes referred to as developing countries.

Leverage ratios   The ratio of loans and other investments to the firm's capital assets.

Licensing   A requirement that one obtain permission from the government in order to perform certain business activities or work in various occupations.

Liquid asset   An asset that can be easily and quickly converted to money without loss of value.

Loanable funds market   A general term used to describe the market that coordinates the borrowing and lending decisions of business firms and households. Commercial banks, savings and loan associations, the stock and bond markets, and insurance companies are important financial institutions in this market.

Logrolling   The exchange between politicians of political support on one issue for political support on another.

Long run (in production)   A time period long enough to allow the firm to vary all of its factors of production.

Loss   A deficit of sales revenue relative to the opportunity cost of production. Losses are a penalty imposed on those who produce goods even though they are valued less than the resources required for their production.

M

M1 (money supply)   The sum of (1) currency in circulation (including coins), (2) checkable deposits maintained in depository institutions, and (3) traveler's checks.

M2 (money supply)   Equal to M1 plus (1) savings deposits, (2) time-deposits (accounts of less than $100,000) held in depository institutions, and (3) money market mutual fund shares.

Macroeconomics   The branch of economics that focuses on how human behavior affects outcomes in highly aggregated markets, such as the markets for labor or consumer products.

Malinvestment   Malinvestment is misguided (or excess) investment caused when the Fed holds interest rates artificially low, encouraging too much borrowing. The new bank credit is invested in capital projects that cost more than the value they create. At some point, a correction must occur to cleanse these uneconomical investments from the system.

Managed equity mutual fund   An equity mutual fund that has a portfolio manager who decides what stocks will be held in the fund and when they will be bought or sold. A research staff generally provides support for the fund manager.

Marginal   Term used to describe the effects of a change in the current situation. For example, a producer's marginal cost is the cost of producing an additional unit of a product, given the producer's current facility and production rate.

Marginal benefit   The maximum price a consumer will be willing to pay for an additional unit of a product. It is the dollar value of the consumer's marginal utility from the additional unit, and therefore it falls as consumption increases.

Marginal cost   The change in total cost required to produce an additional unit of output.

Marginal product (MP)   The increase in the total product resulting from a unit increase in the employment of a variable input. Mathematically, it is the ratio of the change in total product to the change in the quantity of the variable input.

Marginal propensity to consume (MPC)   Additional current consumption divided by additional current disposable income.

Marginal rate of substitution   The change in the consumption level of one good that is just sufficient to offset a unit change in the consumption of another good without causing a shift to another indifference curve. At any point on an indifference curve, it will be equal to the slope of the curve at that point.

Marginal revenue (MR)   The change in a firm's total revenue that results from the production and sale of one additional unit of output.

Marginal revenue product (MRP)   The change in the total revenue of a firm that results from the employment of one additional unit of a resource. The marginal revenue product of an input is equal to its marginal product multiplied by the marginal revenue of the good or service produced.

Marginal tax rate (MTR)   The additional tax liability a person faces divided by his or her additional taxable income. It is the percentage of an extra dollar of income earned that must be paid in taxes. It is the marginal tax rate that is relevant in personal decision-making.

Marginal utility   The additional utility, or satisfaction, derived from consuming an additional unit of a good.

Market   An abstract concept encompassing the forces of supply and demand and the interaction of buyers and sellers with the potential for exchange to occur.

Market failure   A situation in which the structure of incentives is such that markets will encourage individuals to undertake activities that are inconsistent with economic efficiency.

Market organization   A method of organization in which private parties make their own plans and decisions with the guidance of unregulated market prices. The basic economic questions of consumption, production, and distribution are answered through these decentralized decisions.

Market power   The ability of a firm that is not a pure monopolist to earn persistently large profits, indicating that it has some monopoly power. Because the firm has few (or weak) competitors, it has a degree of freedom from vigorous competition.

Means-tested income transfers   Transfers that are limited to people or families with an income below a certain cutoff point. Eligibility is thus dependent upon low-income status.

Medium of exchange   An asset that is used to buy and sell goods or services.

Microeconomics   The branch of economics that focuses on how human behavior affects the conduct of affairs within narrowly defined units, such as individual households or business firms.

Middleman   A person who buys and sells goods or services or arranges trades. A middleman reduces transaction costs.

Minimum wage   Legislation requiring that workers be paid at least the stated minimum hourly rate of pay.

Monetarists   A group of economists who believe that (1) monetary instability is the major cause of fluctuations in real GDP and (2) rapid growth of the money supply is the major cause of inflation.

Monetary base   The sum of currency in circulation plus bank reserves (vault cash and reserves with the Fed). It reflects the purchases of financial assets and extension of loans by the Fed.

Monetary policy   The deliberate control of the money supply, and, in some cases, credit conditions, for the purpose of achieving macroeconomic goals.

Money interest rate   The percentage of the amount borrowed that must be paid to the lender in addition to the repayment of the principal. The money interest rate overstates the real cost of borrowing during an inflationary period. When inflation is anticipated, an inflationary premium will be incorporated into this rate. The money interest rate is often called the nominal interest rate.

Money market mutual funds   Interest-earning accounts that pool depositors' funds and invest them in highly liquid short-term securities. Because these securities can be quickly converted to cash, depositors are permitted to write checks (which reduce their share holdings) against their accounts.

Money rate of interest   The rate of interest in monetary terms that borrowers pay for borrowed funds. During periods when borrowers and lenders expect inflation, the money rate of interest exceeds the real rate of interest.

Money supply   The supply of currency, checking account funds, and traveler's checks. These items are counted as money because they are used as the means of payment for purchases.

Monopolistic competition   A term often used by economists to describe markets characterized by a large number of sellers that supply differentiated products to a market with low barriers to entry. Essentially, it is an alternative term for a competitive price-searcher market.

Monopoly   A market structure characterized by (1) a single seller of a well-defined product for which there are no good substitutes and (2) high barriers to the entry of any other firms into the market for that product.

Mortgage default rate   The percentage of home mortgages on which the borrower is late by ninety days or more with the payments on the loan or it is in the foreclosure process. This rate is sometimes referred to as the serious delinquency rate.

Mortgage-backed securities   Securities issued for the financing of large pools of mortgages. The promised returns to the security holders are derived from the mortgage interest payments.

Multiplier principle   The concept that an increase in spending on a project will generate income for the resource suppliers, who will then increase their consumption spending. In turn, their additional consumption will generate income for others and lead to still more consumption. As this process goes through successive rounds, total income will expand by a multiple of the initial increase in spending.

N

National debt The sum of the indebtedness of the federal government in the form of outstanding interest-earning bonds. It reflects the cumulative impact of budget deficits and surpluses.

National income The total income earned by a country's nationals (citizens) during a period. It is the sum of employee compensation, self-employment income, rents, interest, and corporate profits.

Natural monopoly A market situation in which the average costs of production continually decline with increased output. In a natural monopoly, the average costs of production will be lowest when a single, large firm produces the entire output demanded by the marketplace.

Natural rate of unemployment The "normal" unemployment rate due to frictional and structural conditions in labor markets. It is the unemployment rate that occurs when the economy is operating at a sustainable rate of output. The current natural rate of unemployment in the United States is thought to be approximately 5 percent.

Net exports Exports minus imports.

Net income of foreigners The income that foreigners earn by contributing labor and capital resources to the production of goods within the borders of a country minus the income the nationals of the country earn abroad.

New classical economists Economists who believe that there are strong forces pushing a market economy toward full-employment equilibrium and that macroeconomic policy is an ineffective tool with which to reduce economic instability.

Nominal GDP GDP expressed at current prices. It is often called money GDP.

Nominal values Values expressed in current dollars.

Nonactivists Economists who believe that discretionary macro policy adjustments in response to cyclical conditions are likely to increase, rather than reduce, instability. Nonactivists favor steady and predictable policies regardless of business conditions.

Nonhuman resources The durable, nonhuman inputs used to produce both current and future output. Machines, buildings, land, and raw materials are examples. Investment can increase the supply of nonhuman resources. Economists often use the term *physical capital* when referring to nonhuman resources.

Nonpecuniary job characteristics Working conditions, prestige, variety, location, employee freedom and responsibilities, and other nonwage characteristics of a job that influence how employees evaluate the job.

Nonrenewable resources Those that are not created or renewed naturally at a significant rate.

Normal good A good that has a positive income elasticity, so that, as consumer income rises, demand for the good rises, too.

Normal profit rate Zero economic profit, providing just the competitive rate of return on the capital (and labor) of owners. An above-normal profit will draw more entry into the market, whereas a below-normal profit will lead to an exit of investors and capital.

Normative economics Judgments about "what ought to be" in economic matters. Normative economic views cannot be proved false because they are based on value judgments.

North American Free Trade Agreement (NAFTA) A comprehensive trade agreement between the United States, Mexico, and Canada that went into effect in 1994.

O

Objective A fact based on observable phenomena that is not influenced by differences in personal opinion.

Official reserve account The record of transactions among central banks.

Oligopoly A market situation in which a small number of sellers constitutes the entire industry. It is competition among the few.

Open market operations The buying and selling of U.S. government securities and other financial assets in the open market by the Federal Reserve.

Opportunity cost The highest valued alternative that must be sacrificed as a result of choosing an option.

Opportunity cost of production The total economic cost of producing a good or service. The cost component includes the opportunity cost of all resources, including those owned by the firm. The opportunity cost is equal to the value of the production of other goods sacrificed as the result of producing the good.

Opportunity cost of equity capital The rate of return that must be earned by investors to induce them to supply financial capital to the firm.

Other checkable deposits Interest-earning deposits that are also available for checking.

P

Paradox of thrift The idea that when many households simultaneously try to increase their saving, actual saving may fail to increase because the reduction in consumption and aggregate demand will reduce income and employment.

Partnership A business firm owned by two or more individuals who possess ownership rights to the firm's profits and are personally liable for the debts of the firm.

Pegged exchange rate system A commitment to use monetary and fiscal policy to maintain the exchange rate value of the domestic currency at a fixed rate or within a narrow band relative to another currency (or bundle of currencies).

Per capita GDP Income per person. Increases in income per person are vital for the achievement of higher living standards.

Personal consumption Household spending on consumer goods and services during the current period. Consumption is a flow concept.

Personal retirement account (PRA) An account that is owned personally by an individual in his or her name. The funds in the account could be passed along to heirs.

Phillips curve A curve that illustrates the relationship between the rate of inflation and the rate of unemployment.

Pork-barrel legislation A package of spending projects benefiting local areas financed through the federal government. The costs of the projects typically exceed the benefits in total, but the projects are intensely desired by the residents of a particular district who get the benefits without having to pay much of the costs.

Portfolio   All the stocks, bonds, or other securities held by an individual or corporation for investment purposes.

Positive economics   The scientific study of "what is" among economic relationships.

Positive rate of time preference   The desire of consumers for goods now rather than in the future.

Potential deposit expansion multiplier   The maximum potential increase in the money supply as a ratio of the new reserves injected into the banking system. It is equal to the inverse of the required reserve ratio.

Potential output   The level of output that can be achieved and sustained in the future, given the size of the labor force, its expected productivity, and the natural rate of unemployment consistent with the efficient operation of the labor market. Actual output can differ from the economy's potential output.

Poverty threshold income level   The level of money income below which a family is considered to be poor. It differs according to family characteristics (e.g., number of family members) and is adjusted when consumer prices change.

Present value (PV)   The current worth of future income after it is discounted to reflect the fact that revenues in the future are valued less highly than revenues now.

Price ceiling   A legally established maximum price sellers can charge for a good or resource.

Price controls   Government-mandated prices that are generally imposed in the form of maximum or minimum legal prices.

Price discrimination   A practice whereby a seller charges different consumers different prices for the same product or service.

Price elasticity of demand   The percentage change in the quantity of a product demanded divided by the percentage change in the price that caused the change in quantity. The price elasticity of demand indicates how responsive consumers are to a change in a product's price.

Price elasticity of supply   The percentage change in quantity supplied, divided by the percentage change in the price that caused the change in quantity supplied.

Price floor   A legally established minimum price buyers must pay for a good or resource.

Price searchers   Firms that face a downward-sloping demand curve for their product. The amount the firm is able to sell is inversely related to the price it charges.

Price takers   Sellers who must take the market price in order to sell their product. Because each price taker's output is small relative to the total market, price takers can sell all their output at the market price, but they are unable to sell any of their output at a price higher than the market price.

Primary market   The market in which financial institutions aid in the sale of new securities.

Principal–agent problem   The incentive problem that occurs when the purchaser of services (the principal) lacks full information about the circumstances faced by the seller (the agent) and cannot know how well the agent performs the purchased services. The agent may to some extent work toward objectives other than those sought by the principal paying for the service.

Private investment   The flow of private-sector expenditures on durable assets (fixed investment) plus the addition to inventories (inventory investment) during a period. These expenditures enhance our ability to provide consumer benefits in the future.

Privately held government debt   The portion of the national debt owed to domestic and foreign investors. It does not include bonds held by agencies of the federal government or the Federal Reserve.

Private-property rights   Property rights that are exclusively held by an owner and protected against invasion by others. Private property can be transferred, sold, or mortgaged at the owner's discretion.

Producer surplus   The difference between the price that suppliers actually receive and the minimum price they would be willing to accept. It measures the net gains to producers and resource suppliers from market exchange. It is not the same as profit.

Production possibilities curve   A curve that outlines all possible combinations of total output that could be produced, assuming (1) a fixed amount of productive resources, (2) a given amount of technical knowledge, and (3) full and efficient use of those resources. The slope of the curve indicates the amount of one product that must be given up to produce more of the other.

Productivity   The average output produced per worker during a specific time period. It is usually measured in terms of output per hour worked.

Profit   An excess of sales revenue relative to the opportunity cost of production. The cost component includes the opportunity cost of all resources, including those owned by the firm. Therefore, profit accrues only when the value of the good produced is greater than the value of the resources used for its production.

Progressive tax   A tax in which the average tax rate rises with income. People with higher incomes will pay a higher percentage of their income in taxes.

Property rights   The rights to use, control, and obtain the benefits from a good or resource.

Proportional tax   A tax in which the average tax rate is the same at all income levels. Everyone pays the same percentage of income in taxes.

Proprietorship   A business firm owned by an individual who possesses the ownership right to the firm's profits and is personally liable for the firm's debts.

Proved reserves   Specific mineral deposits that have been shown by scientific examination and cost calculation to be extractable and deliverable to the market for use, with current technology and expected market conditions.

Public goods   Goods for which rivalry among consumers is absent and exclusion of nonpaying customers is difficult.

Public-choice analysis   The study of decision-making as it affects the formation and operation of collective organizations, like governments. In general, the principles and methodology of economics are applied to political science topics.

Purchasing power parity method (PPP)   Method in which the relative purchasing power of each currency is determined by comparing the amount of each currency required to purchase a common bundle of goods and services in the domestic market. This information is then used to convert the GDP of each nation to a common monetary unit like the U.S. dollar.

Pure competition   A market structure characterized by a large number of small firms producing an identical product in an industry (market area) that permits complete freedom of entry and exit. Also called price-taker markets.

Q

Quantity theory of money   A theory that hypothesizes that a change in the money supply will cause a proportional change in the price level because velocity and real output are unaffected by the quantity of money.

Quartile   A quarter (25 percent) of a group. The quartiles are often arrayed on the basis of an indicator like income or degree of economic freedom.

R

Random walk theory   The theory that current stock prices already reflect known information about the future. Therefore, the future movement of stock prices will be determined by surprise occurrences. This will cause them to change in a random fashion.

Rational ignorance effect   Because it is highly unlikely that an individual vote will decide the outcome of an election, a rational individual has little or no incentive to search for and acquire the information needed to cast an informed vote.

Rational-expectations hypothesis   The hypothesis that economic decision-makers weigh all available evidence, including information concerning the probable effects of current and future economic policy, when they form their expectations about future economic events (like the probable future inflation rate).

Rationing   Allocating a limited supply of a good or resource among people who would like to have more of it. When price performs the rationing function, the good or resource is allocated to those willing to give up the most "other things" in order to get it.

Real earnings   Earnings adjusted for differences in the general level of prices across time periods or geographic areas. When real earnings are equal, the same bundle of goods and services can be purchased with the earnings.

Real GDP   GDP adjusted for changes in the price level.

Real interest rate   The interest rate adjusted for expected inflation: It indicates the real cost to the borrower (and yield to the lender) in terms of goods and services.

Real rate of interest   The money rate of interest minus the expected rate of inflation. The real rate of interest indicates the interest premium in terms of real goods and services that one must pay for earlier availability.

Real values   Values that have been adjusted for the effects of inflation.

Recession   A downturn in economic activity characterized by declining real GDP and rising unemployment. In an effort to be more precise, many economists define a recession as two consecutive quarters in which there is a decline in real GDP.

Recognition lag   The time period after a policy change is needed from a stabilization standpoint but before the need is recognized by policy-makers.

Regressive tax   A tax in which the average tax rate falls with income. People with higher incomes will pay a lower percentage of their income in taxes.

Renewable resources   Those that are renewed in nature, like water flows, or grown, like timber.

Rent-seeking   Actions by individuals and groups designed to restructure public policy in a manner that will either directly or indirectly redistribute more income to themselves or the projects they promote.

Repeat-purchase item   An item purchased often by the same buyer.

Required reserve ratio   The ratio of reserves relative to a specified liability category (for example, checkable deposits) that banks are required to maintain.

Required reserves   The minimum amount of reserves that a bank is required by law to keep on hand to back up its deposits. If reserve requirements were 15 percent, banks would be required to keep $150,000 in reserves against each $1 million of deposits.

Residual claimants   Individuals who personally receive the excess, if any, of revenues over costs. Residual claimants gain if the firm's costs are reduced or revenues increase.

Resource   An input used to produce economic goods. Land, labor, skills, natural resources, and human-made tools and equipment provide examples. Throughout history, people have struggled to transform available, but limited, resources into things they would like to have—economic goods.

Resource market   A highly aggregated market encompassing all resources (labor, physical capital, land, and entrepreneurship) contributing to the production of current output. The labor market is the largest component of this market.

Resource markets   Markets in which business firms demand factors of production (for example, labor, capital, and natural resources) from household suppliers. The resources are then used to produce goods and services. These markets are sometimes called factor markets or input markets.

Resource mobility   The ease with which factors of production are able to move among alternative uses. Resources that can easily be transferred to a different use or location are said to be highly mobile. Resources with few alternative uses are immobile.

Restrictive fiscal policy   A reduction in government expenditures and/or an increase in tax rates such that the expected size of the budget deficit declines (or the budget surplus increases).

Restrictive monetary policy   A shift in monetary policy designed to reduce aggregate demand and put downward pressure on the general level of prices (or the rate of inflation). A reduction in bank reserves, higher short-term interest rates, and a reduction in the growth rate of the money supply are indicators of a more restrictive monetary policy.

Ricardian equivalence   The view that a tax reduction financed with government debt will exert no effect on current consumption and aggregate demand because people will fully recognize the higher future taxes implied by the additional debt.

Right-to-work laws   Laws that prohibit union shops, the requirement that employees must join a union as a condition of employment. Each state has the option to adopt (or reject) right-to-work legislation.

Rule of 70   If a variable grows at a rate of x percent per year, $70/x$ will approximate the number of years required for the variable to double.

S

Samaritan's dilemma   The dilemma that occurs when assisting low-income citizens with transfers reduces the opportunity cost of choices that lead to poverty. Providing income transfers to the poor and discouraging behavior that leads to poverty are conflicting goals.

Saving   The portion of after-tax income that is not spent on consumption. Saving is a "flow" concept.

Savings and loan associations   Financial institutions that accept deposits in exchange for shares that pay dividends. Historically, these funds were channeled into residential mortgage loans, but today they offer essentially the same services as a commercial bank.

Scarcity   Fundamental concept of economics that indicates that there is less of a good freely available from nature than people would like.

Scientific thinking   Developing a theory from basic principles and testing it against events in the real world. Good theories are consistent with and help explain real-world events. Theories that are inconsistent with the real world are invalid and must be rejected.

Secondary effects   The indirect impact of an event or policy that may not be easily and immediately observable. In the area of policy, these effects are often both unintended and overlooked.

Secondary market   The market in which financial institutions aid in the buying and selling of existing securities.

Secondary mortgage market   A market in which mortgages originated by a lender are sold to another financial institution. In recent years, the major buyers in this market have been Fannie Mae, Freddie Mac, and large investment banks.

Security rating   A rating indicating the risk of default of the security. A rating of AAA indicates that the risk of default by the borrower is low.

Shirking   Working at less than the expected rate of productivity, which reduces output. Shirking is more likely when workers are not monitored, so that the cost of lower output falls on others.

Short run (in production)   A time period so short that a firm is unable to vary some of its factors of production. The firm's plant size typically cannot be altered in the short run.

Shortage   A condition in which the amount of a good offered for sale by producers is less than the amount demanded by buyers at the existing price. An increase in price would eliminate the shortage.

Shortsightedness effect   The misallocation of resources that results because public-sector action is biased (1) in favor of proposals yielding clearly defined current benefits in exchange for difficult-to-identify future costs and (2) against proposals with clearly identifiable current costs that yield less concrete and less obvious future benefits.

Shutdown   A temporary halt in the operation of a firm. Because the firm anticipates operating in the future, it does not sell its assets and go out of business. The firm's variable cost is eliminated by the shutdown, but its fixed costs continue.

Socialism   A system of economic organization in which (1) the ownership and control of the basic means of production rest with the state, and (2) resource allocation is determined by centralized planning rather than market forces.

Special-interest issue   An issue that generates substantial individual benefits to a small minority while imposing a small individual cost on many other citizens. In total, the net cost to the majority might either exceed or fall short of the net benefits to the special-interest group.

Stock options   The option to buy a specified number of shares of the firm's stock at a designated price. The designated price is generally set so that the options will be quite valuable if the firm's shares increase in price but of little value if their price falls. Thus, when used to compensate top managers, stock options provide a strong incentive to follow policies that will increase the value of the firm.

Store of value   An asset that will allow people to transfer purchasing power from one period to the next.

Strike   An action of unionized employees in which they (1) discontinue working for the employer and (2) take steps to prevent other potential workers from offering their services to the employer.

Structural unemployment   Unemployment due to the structural characteristics of the economy that make it difficult for job seekers to find employment and for employers to hire workers. Although job openings are available, they generally require skills many unemployed workers do not have.

Subjective   An opinion based on personal preferences and value judgments.

Subprime loan   A loan made to a borrower with blemished credit or one who provides only limited documentation of income, employment history, and other indicators of creditworthiness.

Subsidy   A payment the government makes to either the buyer or seller, usually on a per-unit basis, when a good or a service is purchased or sold.

Substitutes   Products that serve similar purposes. An increase in the price of one will cause an increase in demand for the other (examples are hamburgers and tacos, butter and margarine, Microsoft Xbox and Sony PlayStation, Chevrolets and Fords).

Substitution effect   That part of an increase (decrease) in amount consumed that is the result of a good being cheaper (more expensive) in relation to other goods because of a reduction (increase) in price.

Sunk costs   Costs that have already been incurred as a result of past decisions. They are sometimes referred to as historical costs.

Supply shock   An unexpected event that temporarily increases or decreases aggregate supply.

Supply-side economists   Economists who believe that changes in marginal tax rates exert important effects on aggregate supply.

Surplus   A condition in which the amount of a good offered for sale by producers is greater than the amount that buyers will purchase at the existing price. A decline in price would eliminate the surplus.

T

Tariff   A tax levied on goods imported into a country.

Tax base   The level or quantity of an economic activity that is taxed. Higher tax rates reduce the level of the tax base because they make the activity less attractive.

Tax incidence   The way the burden of a tax is distributed among economic units (consumers, producers, employees, employers, and so on). The actual tax burden does not always fall on those who are statutorily assigned to pay the tax.

Tax rate   The per-unit amount of the tax or the percentage rate at which the economic activity is taxed.

Team production   A production process in which employees work together under the supervision of the owner or the owner's representative.

Technological advancement   The introduction of new techniques or methods that increase output per unit of input.

Technology   The technological knowledge available in an economy at any given time. The level of technology determines the amount of output we can generate with our limited resources.

Total cost   The costs, both explicit and implicit, of all the resources used by the firm. Total cost includes a normal rate of return for the firm's equity capital.

Total fixed cost   The sum of the costs that do not vary with output. They will be incurred as long as a firm continues in business and the assets have alternative uses.

Total product   The total output of a good that is associated with each alternative utilization rate of a variable input.

Total variable cost   The sum of those costs that rise as output increases. Examples of variable costs are wages paid to workers and payments for raw materials.

Tournament pay   A form of compensation in which the top performer (or performers) receives much higher rewards than other competitors, even if the others perform at only a slightly lower level.

Trade deficit   The situation when a country's imports of goods and services are greater than its exports.

Trade surplus   The situation when a country's exports of goods and services are greater than its imports.

Transaction costs   The time, effort, and other resources needed to search out, negotiate, and complete an exchange.

Transfer payments   Payments to individuals or institutions that are not linked to the current supply of a good or service by the recipient.

U

Unanticipated change   A change that decision-makers could not reasonably foresee. The choices they made prior to the change did not take it into account.

Unanticipated inflation   An increase in the general level of prices that was not expected by most decision-makers.

Underground economy   Unreported barter and cash transactions that take place outside recorded market channels. Some are otherwise legal activities undertaken to evade taxes. Others involve illegal activities, such as trafficking drugs and prostitution.

Unemployed   The term used to describe a person not currently employed who is either (1) actively seeking employment or (2) waiting to begin or return to a job.

Unemployment rate   The percentage of unemployed people in the labor force. Mathematically, it is equal to the number of people unemployed divided by the number of people in the labor force.

Unfunded liability   A shortfall of tax revenues at current rates relative to promised benefits for a program. Without an increase in tax rates, the promised benefits cannot be funded fully.

Unit of account   A unit of measurement used by people to post prices and keep track of revenues and costs.

User charges   Payments users (consumers) are required to make if they want to receive certain services provided by the government.

Utility   The subjective benefit or satisfaction a person expects from a choice or course of action.

V

Value marginal product (VMP)   The marginal product of a resource multiplied by the selling price of the product it helps produce. For a price-taker firm, marginal revenue product (MRP) will be equal to the value marginal product (VMP).

Velocity of money   The average number of times a dollar is used to purchase final goods and services during a year. It is equal to GDP divided by the stock of money.

W

World Trade Organization (WTO)   The new name given to GATT in 1994; the WTO is currently responsible for monitoring and enforcing multilateral trade agreements among its 153 member countries.

Note: "n" after a page number indicates information in a footnote on that page.

Environmental Protection Agency, 450
equilibrium, 58–61
    consumer, 134–135
    in resource market, 243
equity capital, opportunity cost of, 153
equity mutual funds, 352–354
    indexed, 355
ethanol subsidies, 90, 125–126, 278
ethnicity, Social Security and, 343, 344
European Union
    debt levels in, 335
    price supports in, 319
excess burden of taxation, 81
exchange, 21–23
exchange rate controls, 312–313
expansionary monetary policy, Crisis of
    2008 and, 373–375, 392
expectations, changes in, 50
experimental economics, 180–181
explicit costs, 153
exports
    producer benefits from, 307–309
    see also international trade
externalities, 98–102
    external benefits, 98, 99–102
    external costs, 98–99

F

Facebook, 204
Fair Labor Standards Act, 76
fallacy of composition, 15
family/families, 286, 290
Fannie Mae, 125, 278
    Crisis of 2008 and, 369–371, 378
    declared insolvent, 371 fig.
    as government-sponsored enterprise,
        369–371
    politicalness of, 370
    share of mortgages held by, 371
favoritism, 122, 123–126, 221
    see also special interests
Fed. See Federal Reserve System
federal budget, deficit, 335
federal debt. See national debt
federal deficit, 335
    Great Depression and, 391–392
Federal Home Loan Mortgage
    Corporation. See Freddie Mac
Federal National Mortgage Association.
    See Fannie Mae
Federal Reserve System
    Crisis of 2008, interest rate policy and,
        373–375
    Crisis of 2008, response to, 379, 392
    Great Depression and, 385–387
Federal Trade Commission Act, 222
FedEx, 202, 203
Feldstein, Martin, 342n, 343n
Ferguson, Adam, 69, 70
Fetter, Frank Whitson, 387n
FICO score, 371, 372

financial crisis of 2008. See Crisis of 2008
fiscal policy
    in Great Depression, 391–392
    Keynesian view, 360
fisheries, 451–452
Five Guys, 192
fixed costs, 155–156
Flock, Elizabeth, 414n
flower auctions, 172
Folsom, Burton, 389n, 391n
Food and Drug Administration, 104
food stamps, 89, 283, 294, 295
Ford, Henry, 31
foreclosure rates, 368, 374, 378
foreclosures, 368, 374–375, 378
    ARMs as share of, 374
    see also Crisis of 2008
forests, 441
Forster, Greg, 412n
Fortune Encyclopedia of Economics,
    3n, 391n
franchises, 104
Frank, Robert, 252n
Frankel, Jeffrey A., 314n
Freddie Mac, 125, 278
    Crisis of 2008 and, 369–371, 378
    declared insolvent, 371 fig.
    politicalness of, 370
    share of mortgages held by, 371
Freeman, Richard B., 242, 242n
free riders, 102–103
free trade, 307–309
    fallacies about, 317
    future of, 319
    see also international trade; open
        markets
Fretwell, Holly L., 452n
Friedberg, Leora, 261n
Friedman, Milton, 18, 21, 381, 386, 387n
    on education, 407, 408, 412
Friedman, Rose, 18, 21, 381
fringe benefits, 249
Fullerton, Don, 342n
future expected earnings and assets, 272
future income and costs, present value
    of, 269–271
future value of income, stock prices and,
    350–352

G

gains from trade, 32–34, 38–39, 302–307
game theory, 219–220
gasoline
    price of, 50
    tax on, 82, 83
Gates, Bill, 31, 35, 103
GATT (General Agreement on Tariffs and
    Trade), 317–318
Gaynor, Martin, 141
GDP (Gross Domestic Product)
    federal debt and, 335

Great Depression and, 382, 383, 391, 392
    trade openness and, 315
gender
    earnings differentials and, 258, 416–422
    employment discrimination and,
        252–253, 258
    labor union membership and, 425, 426
    leisure time and, 285
    new college graduates, 419–420
    Social Security and, 344
    see also women
General Agreement on Tariffs and Trade
    (GATT), 317–318
General Electric, 124–125
General Motors, 163, 278, 432
*General Theory of Employment, Interest,
    and Money* (Keynes), 359
generational mobility, 289
George, Henry, 313, 313n
gerrymandering, 115
Gillen, Andrew, 89n
Glass, Thomas, 342n
Gleason, Jackie, 248
global markets, see also international
    trade; open markets
global warming, 446–451
    "cap-and-trade," 449, 450–451
    economics of, 446–449
    marketlike action schemes, 449–451
    mitigation vs. adaptation strategy, 449
Godfrey, Arthur, 322
going out of business, 176–178
Goklany, Indur, 448, 448n, 449, 449n
Goldman Sachs, 125, 376
good(s)
    inferior, 145
    normal, 144
    public, 102–103, 330
Google, 204
Gospodinov, Nikolay, 141
government, 95–96, 109–111
    allocation of resources, 41, 102, 106,
        111, 118, 123, 278, 362–364
    central planning by, 361–362
    compared with markets, 111–112
    debt financing by, 121–122, 278,
        333–336
    economic role of, 95–96
    efficiency in, 116
    favoritism and, 123–126
    finance of, 325–326
    growth of, 109–111
    inefficiency in, 118–123
    majority rule and, 112, 121
    market regulation and, 97
    ownership of resources and provision of
        services, 452–453
    political process and, 115–123
    productive function of, 96
    protective function of, 95–96, 126
    public goods and, 102
    size of, 109–111, 330–333

government (*cont.*)
  special-interests and, 118–121, 278
  subsidy programs, 87–90
  tax levies/revenue, 84–85
  see also federal budget; political process
government bureaucrat incentives, 115
government debt. *See* national debt
government failure, 106, 126
government licensing, 209–210
government-operated firms, 225
government regulation, 223–224
  antitrust laws, 97, 218, 222
government revenues. *See* taxes
government spending, 109–110, 322–336
  changes in, 324–325
  on defense, 324, 325
  on healthcare, 324–325
  per person (1792–2010), 323–325
  taxes and, 325–329
government-sponsored enterprise (GSE), 369–371
government transfer payments. *See* transfer payments
Graham, Ben, 347
Gramlich, Edward M., 372
Great Depression, 381–394, 391n
  economic record of, 382, 383
  fiscal policy during, 391–392
  length and severity of, reasons for, 385–391
  lessons from, 392–393
  money supply and, 385–387
  New Deal policies and, 389–391
  Smoot–Hawley trade bill and, 309, 384, 387–388
  stock market crash of 1929 and, 383–385
  tax increase and, 388–389, 391
greenhouse gases, 447
Greenspan, Alan, 300, 373
Gregory, Anthony C., 293n
Gross Domestic Product. *See* GDP
Grossman, David C., 14n
growth. *See* economic growth
Gustman, Alan, 342n
Gwartney, James, 116n, 332n

H

Hamilton, Alexander, 313
Hardin, Garrett, 451n
Hawley, Willis, 387, 393
Hayek, Friedrich A., 26, 42, 43, 70n, 171, 187
  Keynes vs. Hayek debate, 358–365
healthcare, 395–406
  costs, controlling, 401, 402, 403–405
  direct purchase insurance, 397–399, 403
  elderly population and, 397, 401–402
  expenditures on, 396, 397–400
  government interventions in, 402

government spending on, 324–325, 397, 398
health savings accounts (HSAs), 404
incentives, perverse, 402
industry, improving performance of, 403–405
industry, structure of, 397–399
inflation of prices, 399–401
legislation, new (2010), 403, 405
out-of-pocket expenditures, 398, 399, 403
out-of-state providers, 404
price indexes, 400
reform of, 403–405
regulation of, 402, 403
socialized, 397
subsidies, 296, 397–398, 399–400, 402
supply side emphasis, 405
tax incentives/disincentives, 397–399, 402, 403
third-party payments, 399–401
U.S. crossroads of, 403
health insurance, 397–399, 403–404
  catastrophic, 404
  competitiveness in, 399
  direct purchase of, 397–399, 403
  employer/group programs, 397–399, 402, 403
  first-dollar coverage, 404
  incentives and regulations and, 402, 403
  reforming, 403–405
  taxes and, 397–398, 402, 403
Henderson, David R., 3n, 75n, 130, 131, 201n, 220, 391n, 438n, 439n, 445n
Higgs, Robert, 390, 390n, 391n
higher education. *See* college; education
high-income earners, taxes on, 86–87
hiring decisions, 236–240
Hirsch, Barry T., 257n, 423, 424, 425n, 426, 427, 430n, 431n, 432, 432n
Hobbes, Thomas, 5
Holcombe, Lora P., 104
Holcombe, Randall G., 104, 332n, 369n, 374
Holland, John H., 42, 43
homeschooling, 412
Homestead Act of 1862, 296
Ho, Mun S., 261n
Hong Kong, 319
Hoover, Herbert, 387, 393
households, debt/income ratio of, 377–378
housing
  black markets in, 74
  Crisis of 2008 and, 367–369, 378
  foreclosures, 368, 374, 378
  HUD affordability regulations, 370–371, 378
  prices, boom and bust cycle in, 278, 367–369
  prices, decrease in, 367, 378

prices, increase in, 367
rent control, 74–75
subsidies, 295
see also foreclosures; mortgage defaults; mortgage loans
Housing and Urban Development, Department of (HUD), 370, 378
Houthakker, Hendrik S., 141, 144n
Hoxby, Caroline, 414
Human Capital (Becker), 232
human capital, investment in, 232, 251, 273–274
human ingenuity, 34–35
human resources, 4, 232
hurricanes
  price ceilings after, 73–74
  subsidized insurance programs, 296
Hurst, Erik, 265, 265n
hybrid vehicles, 437

I

Immelt, Jeffrey, 124–125
implicit costs, 153
implicit marginal tax rate, 292–294
import quotas, 311–312
imports
  consumer benefits from, 309
  tax on (tariff), 309–311
  see also international trade
incentives, 9, 363, 376–377
  business organization and, 149–150
  corporate management, 151–152
  to earn, 292–294
  government bureaucrat, 115
  politician, 114–115
  private ownership as, 23–26
  public vs. private sector, 123
  voter, 113–114
income
  debt/income ratio, 377–378
  future income, 269–271, 350–352
  international trade and, 306, 315
  poverty threshold income level, 289–290
  progressive income tax, 295
  taxes and, 329, 330
  see also income inequality
income effect, 135
income elasticity, 144–145
income inequality, 281–298
  factors affecting, 283–286
  high- and low-income families, 284
  income mobility and, 287–289
  increase in, reasons for, 286–287
  pervasiveness of, 282
  poverty, 289–294
  tax rates and, 287
  in U.S., 282–287
  worldwide, 287
  see also poverty
income mobility, 287–289

income taxes, 326, 328–329
    percentage of U.S. not paying, 333–334
indexed equity mutual fund, 355
indexes
    consumer price, 400
    healthcare price, 400
    S&P 500, 349–350, 355, 369
individual transferable quotas (ITQs),
    451–452
inefficiency
    economic, 93, 96–106
    in government, 118–123
inelastic demand curves, 47–48
inelastic supply curves, 55–56
infant-industry argument, 313
inferior good, 145
inflation
    of healthcare costs, 399–401
    interest rates and, 268
inflationary premium, 268
information
    choice and, 131–132, 201
    cost of, 10
    problems of, 103–104
    as profit opportunity, 104–106
    voters and, 113–114
innovation, 30–31, 34, 201–204
    capital market and, 277–278
    competitiveness and, 226
    economic prosperity and, 277–278
    incentives for, 201–203
insurance subsidies, after disasters, 296
Intel, 277
intentions, outcomes and, 14, 393, 403
interest, 268, 269
    components of, 269
interest rates, 266–269
    Crisis of 2008 and, 372, 373–375
    determination of, 266–268
    equilibrium, 268
    Fed and, 373–375
    inflation and, 268
    inflationary premium, 268
    money interest rate, 268–269
    real interest rate, 268
    risk and, 268–269
    stock prices and, 350–352
international trade, 300–320
    changing nature of, 317–319
    comparative advantage and, 302–303,
        306, 317
    fallacies about, 316–317
    gains from, 302–307, 387
    Great Depression and, 387–388
    income levels and, 306
    supply and demand and, 307–309
    trade restrictions, 309–313
International Trade Commission, 314
Internet, transactions costs and, 22
invention, 30
inventions, patents for, 210

investment, 30, 264–280
    capital (physical and human), 265,
        276–278
    corporate, 272–273
    defined, 265
    discounting and, 269–285
    entrepreneurship and, 274–276
    future expected earnings and assets, 272
    government allocation of capital, 278
    in human capital, 232, 251, 273–274
    income returns to, 276
    innovation and, 277–278
    malinvestment, 360, 375
    mistakes in, 277
    profitability of, 271–276
    reasons for, 265–266
    uncertainty and, 274–276
investment banks, 376–377
investment in human capital, 232, 251,
    273–274
investors, 277
    corporate investments and, 272–273
    ordinary vs. expert, 352–355
    in stock market, 348
invisible hand principle, 64–66
iPad, 203
iPhone, 202
iPod, 202
Irvine, Ian, 141

J

Jackman, Michael, 130n
James, LeBron, 20, 251
Japan
    earthquake and tsunami (2011), 449
    inflation in, 268
    interest rates in, 268
    price supports in, 319
    science achievement scores in, 409
    trade examples, 303–306
Jefferson, Thomas, 322
job(s)
    nonidentical jobs, earnings and, 253–
        254
    nonpecuniary job characteristics, 253
    trade barriers and, 316–317, 387,
        392–393
    worker productivity and skills,
        249–253
job market, earnings and productivity and,
    248–263
job opportunities, minimum wage and,
    76–78
Jobs, Steven, 31
John, David C., 343n
Johnson, Lyndon, 291
Johnson, William, 257n, 294n
Johnston, Brian D., 14n
Jorgenson, Dale W., 261n
JP Morgan Chase, 376

K

Kahn, Lawrence M., 257n, 416, 421n
Katz, Jane, 288
Kaufman, Wallace, 436
Kennedy-Johnson tax cut, 328–329
Keynes, John Maynard, 7, 7n
    Keynes vs. Hayek debate, 358–365
Keynesian economics
    business cycle, 360
    central planning, 361
    fiscal policy, 360
    political process and, 363
King, Stephen, 35
Knowledge and Decisions (Sowell), 3n, 21
Kocieniewski, David, 125n
Kroc, Ray, 31
Krooss, Herman E., 391n
Krueger, Alan, 274
Kyoto Protocol, 447, 449

L

labor force participation, 417
labor law, 389–390
labor market, 71
    differences across countries, 302–303
    earnings and productivity and, 248–263
    mobility of labor, 254
    see also unemployment
labor unions, 423–434
    bargaining power, 426, 428
    competitive markets and, 426, 427
    cost of production and, 430
    defined, 424
    demand elasticity and, 430
    demand increases and, 428–429
    membership, 424–426, 427
    objectives of, 424
    profitability and employment and, 432
    right-to-work laws, 426
    strategies of, 427–429
    strength of, factors determining,
        429–430
    substitutes, availability of, 429, 430
    supply restrictions and, 427–428
    wages and, 254, 426–429, 430
    wages and, by sector, 431–432
    wages of all workers and, 433
Laffer, Arthur, 85
Laffer curve, 85–87
    mountain-climbing deaths and, 87
LaFranchi, Howard, 183
land management, 441–442
Landsburg, Steven, 264
land use change, 441
"large-number" cases, 99
large-scale production, gains from,
    306–307
law, rule of. See legal system
law of comparative advantage, 33, 302
law of demand, 44, 131, 135

The Evolution of

Adam Smith (1723–1790)

Smith's book *An Inquiry into the Nature and Causes of the Wealth of Nations* provided the first comprehensive analysis of wealth and prosperity and introduced "the invisible hand" principle. It also explained that the wealth of a nation was determined by its production of goods and services, not by its gold and silver.

David Ricardo (1772–1823)

In his book *On the Principles of Political Economy and Taxation*, Ricardo developed the law of comparative advantage and used it to explain why trade leads to mutual gains.

William Stanley Jevons (1835–1882)

Along with Carl Menger and Leon Walras, Jevons (in *The Theory of Political Economy*) introduced (1) the idea that the value of goods is determined subjectively rather than by the labor required for production, and (2) the law of diminishing marginal utility. Independently, the same concepts were developed by Menger in *Grundsätze* (1871) and Walras in *Elements of Pure Economics* (1874). These two concepts are still an integral part of modern analysis.

Alfred Marshall (1842–1924)

In his book *The Principles of Economics*, Marshall introduced and developed many of the key concepts of modern microeconomics, including concepts like supply and demand, equilibrium, short run and long run, elasticity, and consumer and producer surplus. The book went through eight editions between 1890 and 1920.